A CENTENNIAL BOOK

One hundred books
published between 1990 and 1995
bear this special imprint of
the University of California Press.
We have chosen each Centennial Book
as an example of the Press's finest
publishing and bookmaking traditions
as we celebrate the beginning of
our second century.

UNIVERSITY OF CALIFORNIA PRESS
Founded in 1893

EMERSON

EMERSON

The Mind on Fire

A BIOGRAPHY BY
Robert D. Richardson Jr.

WITH A FRONTISPIECE BY BARRY MOSER

University of California Press
Berkeley   Los Angeles   London

The publisher wishes to acknowledge with gratitude the generous support of the National Endowment of the Humanities.

University of California Press
Berkeley and Los Angeles, California

University of California Press, Ltd.
London, England

Library of Congress Cataloging-in-Publication Data

Richardson, Robert D., 1934–
    Emerson : the mind on fire / Robert D. Richardson, Jr. ; with a
frontispiece by Barry Moser.
        p.   cm.
    Includes bibliographical references and index.
    ISBN 0-520-08808-5 (cloth: alk. paper)
    ISBN 0-520-20689-4 (pbk.: alk. paper)
    1. Emerson, Ralph Waldo, 1803–1882—Biography.   2. Emerson, Ralph
Waldo, 1803–1882—Knowledge and learning.   3. Authors,
American—19th century—Biography.   I. Title.
PS1631.R53   1995
814'.3—dc20   94-36008
                                                              CIP

Printed in the United States of America

3 4 5 6 7 8 9

The paper used in this publication meets the minimum requirements of American National Standard for Information Sciences—Permanence of Paper for Printed Library Materials, ANSI Z39.48-1984 ∞

FOR ANNIE,

who also knows the days to be gods

Contents

Illustrations following page 336

Preface

᭶

THIS BOOK WAS ORIGINALLY PLANNED AS AN INTELLECTUAL
biography, a companion piece to *Henry Thoreau: A Life of the Mind* (1986).
My approach to both Thoreau and Emerson has been to read what they read
and then to relate their reading to their writing. The story, however—and
it is a story—of Emerson's intellectual odyssey turned out to be incom-
prehensible apart from his personal and social life. The result is an intellectual
biography as well as a portrait of the whole man. A great deal of newly
available material (the letters of Emerson's brothers, of his aunt Mary Moody
Emerson, and of his friend Caroline Sturgis, for example) has brought to
light an Emerson strikingly more lively than the plaster sage of Concord.

Emerson lived for ideas, but he did so with the reckless, headlong ardor
of a lover. He associated the human mind and its capacity for thought with
activity and energy. He hated the passive notion of the mind as a blank slate.
He concentrated instead on the individual's sources of power, on access to
the central fires that ignite the mind. His main image of the creative mind
is of a volcano. "We must have not only hydrogen in balloons and steel
springs under coaches," he wrote, "but we must have fire under the Andes
at the core of the world."

Freed of his vast, unfortunate, and self-perpetuating reputation, Emerson
steps forth as a complicated, energetic, and emotionally intense man who
habitually spoke against the status quo and in favor of whatever was wild
and free. The great spokesman for individualism and self-reliance turns out
to have been a good neighbor, an activist citizen, a fond father, a loyal
brother, and a man whose many friendships framed his life. Emerson's main
project, never realized to his satisfaction, was to write a natural history of
intellect; I have tried to honor this aim by reconstructing the natural history
of his enthusiasms.

Biographies of Emerson appear at regular intervals because his life and
work—like Jefferson's and Lincoln's—continue to shape American self-

perception. Emerson never wrote for groups or classes or institutions; his intended audience was always the single hearer or reader. Where this biography parts company with its many worthy predecessors is in its lack of interest in institutional Emersonianism—in Emerson's influence—and in its concentration instead on the man. What kind of individual was this prophet of individualism?

I have had a great deal of help with this project. Many scholarly and critical debts are recorded in the notes. I wish also to thank, for their various services, the Ralph Waldo Emerson Association, Chris Steele of the Massachusetts Historical Society Library, the Society for the Preservation of New England Antiquities, David Wood of the Concord Museum, Marcia Moss of the Concord Free Public Library, the Thoreau Lyceum, the Boston Athenaeum, the Houghton Library at Harvard, the Boston Museum of Fine Arts, Liz Gwillam and Paul O'Pecko of Mystic Seaport, Elizabeth Swaim, curator of Special Collections, and Joan Jurale, reference librarian at Wesleyan University, Tina Furtado and the New Bedford Free Public Library, and Michael Preston, who is continuing work on Eugene Irey's mammoth computerized concordance to Emerson. Zhou Guangyuan, Beth Marsh, Gayle Smith, and Ida Walters taught me as students. For various kinds of aid and support, cheerfully given, I am also grateful to Susan Bardens, W. J. Bate, Delores Bird Carpenter, Victor Castellani, Gary Collison, Rebecca Frazier, Greg Gatenby, Joan Goodwin, Victor Gourevitch, Robert Gross, Philip Gura, Justin Kaplan, Phyllis Rose, David Schorr, and Paul Schwaber. Eleanor M. Tilton let me see typescripts of her new volumes of Emerson letters. Bob Burkholder shared his incomparable knowledge of Emerson bibliography. Al von Frank let me see typescripts of the new edition of Emerson's sermons. George Goodspeed let me read his collection of unpublished Emerson family letters. For help with identifying and reproducing photographs I am deeply indebted to the advice and expertise of Harry Orth and Daniel Jones.

No one can mention, let alone repay, all the intellectual debts one accumulates during an eight-year project. Roscoe Hill helped me with Plato, Phyllis Cole with the difficult and fascinating Mary Moody Emerson, Megan Marshall with Elizabeth Peabody. To Jere Surber I owe whatever grasp of German idealist thought I have. Burton Feldman and Allen Mandelbaum have kindly attended to my continuing education in too many areas to list; so have my daughters, Anne and Lissa. Stanley Holwitz has been a steady source of encouragement. The John Simon Guggenheim Foundation gave me a year's support, a very great boon, which came at just the right time.

Joel Myerson, the dean of American transcendentalist scholars, made an extraordinary contribution. With the generosity for which he is famous, he turned over to me several thousand pages of transcripts he had made of the letters and other writings of Emerson's brothers Charles, Edward, and William. This material has made possible a new level of understanding of the Emerson family. Joel also gave my entire manuscript a searching and profoundly helpful reading. Larry Buell, Annie Dillard, Amanda Clark Frost, and David Robinson also read the book in manuscript. I have profited from the incomparable knowledge of each; remaining lapses and gaffes are, of course, exclusively mine. The dedication inadequately records my greatest debt of all.

We measure ourselves by many standards. Our strength and our intelligence, our wealth and even our good luck, are things which warm our heart and make us feel ourselves a match for life. But deeper than all such things and able to suffice unto itself without them, is the sense of the amount of effort we can put forth . . . He who can make none is but a shadow; he who can make much is a hero.

William James

The Student

1. Prologue

ON MARCH 29, 1832, THE TWENTY-EIGHT-YEAR-OLD EMERSON visited the tomb of his young wife, Ellen, who had been buried a year and two months earlier. He was in the habit of walking from Boston out to her grave in Roxbury every day, but on this particular day he did more than commune with the spirit of the departed Ellen: he opened the coffin. Ellen had been young and pretty. She was seventeen when they were engaged, eighteen when married, and barely twenty when she died of advanced tuberculosis. They had made frantic efforts at a cure, including long open-air carriage rides and massive doses of country air. Their life together had been stained almost from the start by the bright blood of Ellen's coughing.

Opening the coffin was not a grisly gothic gesture, not just the wild aberration of an unhinged lover. What Emerson was doing was not unheard of. At least two of Emerson's contemporaries did the same thing. A Unitarian minister and good friend of Margaret Fuller's, James Freeman Clarke, once opened the coffin of the woman he had been in love with when he was an undergraduate. Edgar Allan Poe's literary executor, the anthologist Rufus Griswold, opened the coffin of his dead wife forty days after the funeral.[1]

Emerson opened not only the tomb or family vault but the coffin itself. The act was essential Emerson. He had to see for himself. Some part of him was not able to believe she was dead. He was still writing to her in his journals as though she was alive. Perhaps the very deadness of the body would help a belief in the life of the spirit. A modern writer has said that "beside the corpse of the beloved were generated not only the idea of the soul, the belief in immortality, and a great part of man's deep-rooted sense of guilt, but also the earliest inkling of ethical law." We do not know exactly what moved Emerson on this occasion, but we do know that he had a powerful craving for direct, personal, unmediated experience. That is what he meant when he insisted that one should strive for an original relation to the universe. Not a novel relation, just one's own. Emerson is the great American champion of self-reliance, of the adequacy of the individual, and of the importance of

3

the active soul or spirit. Never content with mere assertion, he looked always for the sources of strength. Emerson's lifelong search, what he called his heart's inquiry, was "Whence is your power?" His reply was always the same: "From my nonconformity. I never listened to your people's law, or to what they call their gospel, and wasted my time. I was content with the simple rural poverty of my own. Hence this sweetness."[2]

Emerson's direct facing of death owed something to his aunt Mary Moody Emerson, the brilliant and original sister of Emerson's father, who deliberately lived with death every day of her life and drew much of her own power from that grim helpmeet. Her jagged, combative prose uses death and pain as probes for faith. "Did I not assure good Lincoln Ripley, long since," she wrote, "that I should be willing to have limbs rot, and senses dug out, if I could perceive more of God?"[3]

Emerson had also by now learned to think of ideas not as abstractions but as perceptions, laws, templates, patterns, and plans. Ideas were not less real than the phenomenal world. If anything, ideas were more important than phenomena because they lay behind them, creating and explaining the visible world. Ideas for Emerson were tangible and had force. "Believe in magnetism, not in needles," he wrote. Ideas, even the idea of death, could not be separated from sense experience.

Emerson's own journal entry for this March day was terse: "I visited Ellen's tomb and opened the coffin." They had been utterly in love, and for a moment, on September 30, 1829, their wedding day, the future had seemed clear. Notes and letters flew back and forth. They traveled and wrote verses together and laughed at the Shakers who tried to woo them to celibacy. She intended to be a poet, he a preacher. He had accepted a pulpit in Boston, and they had set up a home that became at once the center of the Emerson family, as both Waldo's mother and his younger brother Charles came to live with them. Now, a little more than a year after Ellen's death, Emerson's life was unraveling fast. He was so desolate and lonely that his mother tried to persuade his invalid brother Edward to come back from the West Indies to look after him. His professional life was also going badly. Though he was a much-loved minister in an important Boston church, he was having trouble believing in personal immortality, trouble believing in the sacrament of Communion, and trouble accepting the authority and historical accuracy of the Bible. The truth was that Emerson was in a fast-deepening crisis of vocation. He could not accept his ministerial role, he was unsure of his faith, and he felt bereft and empty. He was directionless.

His brother Charles wrote to Aunt Mary that "Waldo is sick . . . I never saw him so disheartened . . . things seem flying to pieces."[4]

At Ellen's grave that day in Roxbury in 1832 Emerson was standing amidst the ruins of his own life. More than ten years had passed since he had left college. Love had died and his career was falling apart. He was not sure what he really believed, who he really was, or what he should be doing. He felt the "vanishing volatile froth of the present" turning into the fixed adamantine past. "We walk on molten lava," he wrote.

In the months immediately ahead he continued to walk to Ellen's grave every day, but now his concentration on death was broken and he wrote a sermon called "The God of the Living" and another on astronomy. He reached a major watershed in his long struggle with religion. "Astronomy irresistibly modifies all religion," he wrote. "The irresistible effect of Copernican astronomy has been to make the great scheme of the salvation of man absolutely incredible." He would live no longer with the dead. "Let us express our astonishment," he wrote in his journal in May, "before we are swallowed up in the yeast of the abyss. I will lift up my hands and say Kosmos."[5]

Before the year was out, Emerson had resigned his pulpit, moved his mother, sold his household furniture, and taken ship for Europe. He set out on Christmas Day, 1832. A northeast storm was on its way as the ship sailed from Boston, plunging into the grey expanse of the North Atlantic.

2. Emerson at Harvard

ELEVEN YEARS EARLIER, IN THE SPRING OF 1821, RALPH Emerson was in the last semester of his senior year at Harvard. He had just turned eighteen and had decided he wanted to be called Waldo. Graduation was set for August and he was to be class poet. The honor was less than meets the eye, for six other members of his class had already declined the post. And though he took poetry seriously enough, he was not otherwise a distinguished student. He ranked in the middle of his class; he was not elected to Phi Beta Kappa. He was tall and thin and had reached his height of nearly six feet awkwardly early, at fourteen. He had long arms and legs, a pale complexion, light sandy hair, a large roman nose, and blue eyes. He was full of high spirits and boyish silliness, but there was also an odd self-possession about him. No one ever saw him run and no one ever tried to slap him on the back. Josiah Quincy, a classmate of Emerson's and later president of Harvard, said that Emerson was only a fair scholar. Like many another young person, Emerson did not shine in the things Harvard then knew how to measure. His extracurricular reading was at least three times as extensive as his reading for courses, and he was already in the habit of getting up at 4:30 or 5 in the morning to tend his correspondence and write in his journals.

Emerson's Harvard was a small, nondescript place, half boys school, half center for advanced study. It had fewer than two hundred fifty students. Emerson's class had sixty, with most of the boys coming from Massachusetts and New England, and with 27 percent of the students coming from elsewhere. There was a marked southern presence. Eleven of Emerson's classmates, 18 percent of the class, were from South Carolina alone. In Emerson's day, a student commonly entered college at thirteen or fourteen, graduating at seventeen or eighteen. As a result, college life had at times a certain rowdiness. In Emerson's sophomore year an epic food fight broke out on the first floor of University Hall. The fight quickly got beyond the throwing of food and almost all the school's crockery was smashed. But it would be a mistake to assume this was the dominant tone of college life.

Young people grew up faster then. Emerson could read before he was three; he taught his first class at fourteen. Girls were little women, boys little men. The curriculum shows that Harvard was not like either the high school or the college of today; it offered a combination of basic and advanced studies, functioning as a sort of early college.

Emerson took the same set of required courses everyone else did. He learned enough Greek to read both the *Iliad* and the New Testament. In Latin he read Livy, Horace, Cicero, Juvenal, and Persius as well as Hugo Grotius's *De veritate religionis Christianae*. He studied algebra, plane geometry, analytic geometry, and spherical geometry. He took Roman history in his freshman year and during his senior year he studied the principles of American constitutional government, reading the *Federalist Papers*. In science he did physics (matter, motion or mechanics, hydrostatics, pneumatics, electricity, and optics) and astronomy as a junior, chemistry as a senior. He studied political economy. In philosophy he took courses in formal logic as well as the broadly conceived and attractively written moral philosophy of Dugald Stewart and William Paley. He read Locke's *Essays*.

Harvard gave Emerson a solid education, liberal, not hidebound, and practical in a number of ways. Along with the expected heavy emphasis on Greek and Latin, there was also an interesting emphasis on English. As a freshman Emerson studied Robert Lowth's workaday *English Grammar* and also read John Walker's *Rhetorical Grammar,* a book devoted almost entirely to elocution, to reading aloud, and to public speaking. Walker is concerned with "correct" speaking. Emerson learned not to say "uppinion" for opinion, "sensubble" for sensible, or "terrubble" for terrible. As a sophomore Emerson studied Blair's classic *Lectures on Rhetoric* and wrote frequent compositions. Blair provided a lucid, reasonable, widely accepted approach to English style. Blair treated figurative language not as "the invention of schools" but as the natural clothing of the energetic and passionate speech of ordinary people.[1]

Much can be said against the prescribed course of study Emerson followed. Emerson himself said later that even though you knew the university was hostile to genius, you sent your children there and hoped for the best. But in some areas, and practical English is one, the college offered thorough, concrete, and useful training.

Religious education was another matter. Emerson read the great liberal defenses of Christianity by Paley and Butler, monuments of rational sober thought, postdeist defenses of revealed religion as not inconsistent with eighteenth-century scientific thought. Paley's most interesting proof of the existence of God is his detailed argument for design centering on the human eye. Butler's *Analogy* (1736) has been called the most famous volume of English theology, as important in its sphere as Bacon in the sciences. In Emerson's day the *Analogy* was as old, as widely accepted, and as outdated as Weber's *The Protestant Ethic and the Spirit of Capitalism* (1904) is in ours. Its argument is that the deist accepts his impersonal Creator or First Principle on essentially the same grounds and in the face of the same difficulties that make him reject revelation. Both Paley and Butler thus argue that revealed Christianity is at bottom perfectly compatible with natural religion and with the findings of modern science. In his defense of revelation, of the Bible, Butler already is subtly shifting the standard defensive grounds. There is more than a hint in the *Analogy* that the authenticating proofs of religion are to be sought in man's mind, not in books or institutions. "The proper motives of religion," Butler says, "are the proper proofs of it from our moral nature, from the presages of conscience." Paley's and Butler's books are not Calvinist, not jeremiads, not emotional or reactionary appeals. Like required religious texts everywhere, they stirred resentment. At the same time these books contained the seeds of a new approach to religion.[2]

The college text Emerson used for the study of the New Testament also contained the first stirrings of a theological revolution. Griesbach's edition of the Greek New Testament is the port of entry through which the new German biblical scholarship first reached a wide range of educated Americans. Griesbach bases his edition, with its copious notes, on the hypothesis that the Gospel of Matthew preceded the other gospels, which themselves were not eyewitness accounts but versions of Matthew. This suggestion was disturbing to many. If one or more of the gospels should be found not to be a reliable eyewitness account, if Luke's or Mark's gospel should turn out not to represent the writer's original relation of the events but something secondhand, then the absolute authority of the Bible becomes an open question.[3]

Emerson's college writings show him for the most part to have been a surprisingly conventional young man. He hated mathematics and did poorly in the subject. He preferred his literary soliloquies to chemistry and to the "accursed Enfield lessons" in physics. His own ideas were commonplace. He thought of history as the fall of successive empires; his standpoint is that of a moralized Gibbon. His undergraduate poem on India, "Indian Superstition," is a jejune, xenophobic, condescending, even racist overview of

Indic mythology from the vantage of European Christianity. He expressed a vigorous puritan disapproval of theater and drama, and his religious remarks contain conventional references to the degradation of human nature and the coming Day of Judgment.[4]

Emerson was very poor while he was at Harvard. He felt his poverty keenly and later remarked that his life would have been quite different had he had money. His mother's rent, his younger brothers' schooling, and his own college tuition all depended now on the money his older brother William made teaching school in Maine. Other boys spent six hundred dollars a year at college; Emerson spent less than three hundred dollars during his four years. He held a work-study position as the "President's Freshman" his first year, running errands for the college president in return for tuition. Later he won a scholarship for poor boys which had been left to the college in the form of a rental home. As holder of the scholarship, Emerson was obliged to go and collect the rent from the tenant.

College life became more attractive to Emerson after his first year. Emerson joined a number of clubs, one of which he helped found. Along with classes, studying, outside reading, and club activities, he made time for daily walks to the rural area of Cambridge called, after the town in Goldsmith's poem *The Deserted Village,* "Sweet Auburn." His feeling for nature was already intense. He was exhilarated—his word—when the persistent spring clouds gave way to the blue skies of June. "I love the picturesque glitter of a summer's morning landscape," he wrote. "It kindles this burning admiration of nature and enthusiasm of mind."[5]

Back in the college yard, there was class football every day at noon. And there were new friendships. Emerson found himself strangely and powerfully attracted by a new freshman named Martin Gay. With an unembarrassed frankness he wrote in his journal about the disturbing power of the glances he and Gay exchanged. He would remain susceptible to such crushes, expressed at first through glances, all his life; most of them would involve women. Later he wrote about the quickness with which a glance could arouse a depth of interest. He had a sort of theory of "the glance." And while he heavily crossed out the Martin Gay journal notes at some later time, his initial recording of them indicates his essential emotional openness. He may have been quiet, he certainly did not cut a commanding figure, but he did not shrink from direct experience.

Since the Emerson boys were only a few years apart, they overlapped one another at Harvard. Since they were poor, they looked for ways to make a little extra money. Sometimes they wrote papers for others. His brother Edward once wrote a paper for another student, carefully adjusting the level of the writing to the skill of the buyer. The boy came down to the steps of his dorm and called a group over to read them the paper to see if it was really worth the fifty cents he had paid for it.[6]

Outside the college the country and the world were changing. On August 10, 1821, two weeks before Emerson's graduation, Missouri joined the Union. After a divisive, acrimonious debate, Missouri had been granted statehood despite its deliberately unconstitutional and insulting legislative exclusion of free blacks from other states. Far from being put to rest by the Missouri Compromise, the slavery issue in America would never sleep again. In South America revolt against Spain was afoot. Bolívar had become president of Greater Colombia (including Venezuela, Ecuador, and Panama) in 1819. In 1820 revolution broke out in Naples, in the Piedmont, in Spain, and in Portugal. As Emerson's class graduated in 1821, Europe's autocrats were collaborating to crush the revolt in Naples. To the east the Greek war for independence broke out.[7]

3. The March of Mind

EMERSON REACHED A MAJOR TURNING POINT MIDWAY THROUGH his junior year. In December of 1819 he began to keep a list of books he had read. In early January of 1820 he began to keep a notebook for quotations, comments on his reading, and original verses. He decided to write an essay for the Bowdoin Prize competition. Later in the month he began the first of what was to be a series of notebooks he called "Wide World." By February he was giving up the name Ralph and signing himself Waldo.

Emerson's sense of himself had changed during the past three months. He was now more organized and more ambitious, newly interested in imagination and newly committed to the business of writing. The new journals also marked a new originality. For example, in his reading of Abraham Tucker's *The Light of Nature Pursued*, an aptly named work that toiled after its subject through eight substantial volumes, Emerson found a point of interest far from the work's main focus. Tucker was out to explore "whether Reason alone be sufficient to direct us in all parts of our conduct, or whether Revelation and Supernatural aids be necessary." (The answer is the former.) From a few words Tucker drops by the way, Emerson constructs an elaborate paragraph about the parts of the world uninhabited by man being perhaps "the abodes of other orders of sentient beings invisible or unexperienced." In the strongest possible contrast to the rationalist curriculum, Emerson's journal shows a marked and steady interest in imagination, in fairyland, in legend, folktale, fiction, and poetry.[1]

Emerson was now feverishly active. He spent the end of his junior year "reading and writing and talking and walking." In addition to schoolwork and letters from his family, he read, between December 1819 and February 1820, Byron's *Don Juan*, Archibald Alison's *Essay on Taste*, Edward Channing's inaugural discourse, Ben Jonson's *Life*, *Every Man in His Humour*, and *Every Man Out of His Humour*, a volume of Joanna Baillie's plays, Samuel Rogers's poem "Human Life," Thomas Campbell's *Essay on English Poetry*, the new *North American Review*, Thomas Blackwell's *Life and Writ-*

ings of Homer, Robert Lowth's *Lectures on the Sacred Poetry of the Hebrews,* Washington Irving's *Sketch Book,* Bacon's *Essays,* the first volume of Dacier's *Dialogues of Plato,* Scott's *Bridal of Triermain,* a volume of Crabbe, and H. H. Milman's *Samor, Lord of the Bright City.* The list is weighted toward imaginative literature, from the satires of Jonson and Byron to the Tolkien-like fantasy of Milman's *Samor.* Threaded through the purely literary reading list this winter of 1819–1820 are books and ideas that were to become perennial with Emerson. Here is his interest in Plato and his interest in Bacon not as a father of modern experimental science but as stylist and essayist.

The unusual books here are Blackwell on Homer and Lowth on Hebrew poetry. These two works are among the most important foundations for modern criticism of Homer and the Bible and for the modern conception of the poet as prophet. Blackwell and Lowth wrote in England in the mid-eighteenth century. The founders of the so-called "higher criticism" in Germany built on the foundations provided by Blackwell and Lowth. In its German dress this new method of reading the Bible then returned to England, to be received to the United States in the early nineteenth century.[2]

Thomas Blackwell launches the historical critique of Homer. He tries to dislodge the notion that Greek myths are just fairy tales with the argument that Greek myth is Greek religion and that the Homeric poet is, like Orpheus, a true teacher-founder of philosophy, history, and politics. And just as Blackwell sees Greek myth and literature and religion in its historical context, so Lowth (in *The Sacred Poetry of the Hebrews,* 1747) argues that the Bible can fruitfully be approached as Hebrew poetry. He points out that the words for poet and prophet are the same in Hebrew; he treats the Old Testament prophets as the poets of their era—and thus made it possible for modern poets to claim the role of prophet for their era. The concept of the modern poet-prophet runs from Lowth to Blake, to Herder, and to Whitman. If we can approach Homeric poetry as Greek religion and Hebrew religion as Jewish poetry, the result is, on one side, skepticism about the historical reliability of either text, but on the other side, the elevation of the poet as the prophet of the present age, the truth teller, the gospel maker, the primary witness for his time and place. If Homer is now seen as essentially Greek and the Bible as properly Hebrew, then the modern English or American or German poet-prophet may legitimately ask, "Where is our scripture? Where are our witnesses?" The young Emerson formed his idea of the role of the poet partly from the challenge implicit in the writings of Blackwell and Lowth.[3]

Emerson did not come upon these books by accident this winter of 1819–1820. Lowth and Blackwell were important books for Edward Everett, the popular young Harvard teacher whose arrival was the great event in Cambridge in late 1819. Everett influenced Emerson more than any of his other Harvard teachers. He was more than Emerson's first intellectual hero; he was, for a time, his personal idol.[4]

Edward Everett was twenty-five when he returned to the United States from Göttingen to take up his professorship of Greek literature at Harvard. He was young, vital, forceful and eloquent, the very antithesis of Dr. Popkin, "Old Pop," the dull drillmaster who had been serving as Greek teacher. Emerson later recalled with warmth Everett's "radiant beauty of person," his large eyes, marble lids, and his rich and compelling voice. Everett knew the most up-to-date and disturbing scholarship. He was also interested in modern affairs and modern literature and he made the study of Greece seem like the high road to wisdom, power, and eloquence. As Emerson noted, Everett made his students "for the first time acquainted with Wolf's theory of the Homeric writings." (Careful analysis of the text convinced Wolf that the *Iliad* and the *Odyssey* were not the work of one poet but of several, perhaps many, over a long period of time.) Everett also brought the critical ideas of Christian Gottlob Heyne to Cambridge. Heyne taught that all religion, including Judaism and Christianity, begins in philosophy expressed mythologically.[5]

In introducing Heyne, Everett was bringing to New England the modern history-of-religions view that mythology precedes theology. In introducing Wolf, Everett brought to America the original deconstruction of Homer into oral folk epic. Everett also introduced American students to the work of J. G. Eichhorn, the founder of modern biblical scholarship, the so-called higher criticism that inaugurated modern disintegrative studies of the Bible, breaking the one book down into multiple narratives written at different times by different people. This was heady stuff, and Emerson was deeply impressed with the new professor and his messages. "The novelty of the learning lost nothing in the skill and genius of his relation," wrote Emerson, "and the rudest undergraduate found a new morning opened to him in the lecture room of Harvard Hall." Here was a minister-scholar-orator-editor-author, a leader of his generation. Emerson vowed in his journal: "I here make a resolution to make myself acquainted with the Greek language and antiquities and history with long and serious attention and study." His ambition had been touched and stirred. He wrote a poem for the Pythologian Club in April 1820 in which he recalled a great past "Made vocal once, alas no more / And why? ask not! the Muses blush to tell / Since gowned monks with censer crass and bell / Clogged the free step and mighty march of Mind." Fired with new ideas from Everett, Emerson's poem was about the liberation of poetry from rhyme, which, he said, had been invented by "monks in their cloisters in the Dark Ages" in order "to shackle poetry or the soarings of the mind."[6]

Emerson also decided at this point to enter the Bowdoin competition with an essay on the character of Socrates. Although Emerson here combined two of his great subjects, ethical thought and Plato, this earliest of his essays is disappointingly flat, and its flatness can only be partly explained by noting that philosophy at Harvard at this time was the rather flat utilitarianism of Paley, Butler, and Tucker. Emerson's prose shows promise when he writes of Socrates' studying nature "with a chastised enthusiasm." At the center of the essay, which did not win the prize, Emerson made an important point, one that characterizes his later thought. Socrates was more interested in mind than in knowledge. Socrates aimed, he said, "not to impart literary knowledge or information or science or Art, but to lay open to his own view the human mind." In the rest of the essay Emerson was able neither to speak his own mind forcefully nor to give a cogent or memorable account of Socrates' mind. Emerson's own mind was unfocused, his aim unclear. He was not uninterested in philosophy but he was also interested in eloqence, in oratory, in religion, in writing gothic fiction, and in being a poet.[7]

Emerson's religious notes during his last year and a half at Harvard range from conventional views of the awful immanence of the Day of Judgment to efforts to apprehend "the immediate presence of God," which he thought "a fine topic of sublimity." What these thoughts had in common was an interest not in dogma or theology but in the immediate personal experience of religion. More often, however, it was religious eloquence that Emerson hungered for. Everett was eloquent and talked about eloquence. The textbooks of Walker and Blair emphasized public speaking, and the new professor of oratory and rhetoric, the English teacher of Emerson—and later of Thoreau and Richard Henry Dana, Jr.—was also much interested in oratory. His name was Edward Channing.

Edward Channing was twenty-eight. He was a younger brother of the famous Boston minister William Ellery Channing and had just joined the Harvard faculty in 1819. His inaugural talk on December 8, 1819, which Emerson read later, had for a theme the power and importance of the orator. Channing, like Everett, was involved in current literature, serving before Everett as editor of the *North American Review*. Channing was also young enough to be a sort of model for Emerson. Channing was quiet, far from being the blaze of energy Everett was. But Channing had interesting ideas about writing and fresh advice for writers. He encouraged students to write rapidly and impetuously. He was aware of the dangers involved in "constant association with great writers," and he was vehement about the folly of always comparing ourselves to others, which, Channing said, is the beginning not of wisdom but of weakness: "We gradually lose the power of discerning what is good and beautiful in the very writers who have gained this fatal possession of our admiration. They disown us, and we perceive it not." Channing's interest in oratory helped feed Emerson's sustained interest in eloquence. Channing also spoke to the condition of the young writer.[8]

In writing, as in other endeavors, Emerson did not find his characteristic voice while at college, although some traits begin to emerge. In prose he was working on wildly diverse projects. One was a lurid gothic tale about a Norse prophetess and sibyl and her magician son. The fantasy is overheated and overwritten—more dream than anything else, a sort of Norse *Vathek*. The heroine Uilsa speaks:

> Did I not wake the mountains with my denouncing scream—calling vengeance from the north? Odin knew me and thundered. A thousand wolves ran down by the mountain scared by the hideous lightning and baring the tooth to kill; they rushed after the cumbrous host. I saw when the pale faces glared back in terror as the black wolf pounced on his victim.[9]

Offsetting this Nordic riot is Emerson's second try at the Bowdoin Prize, his essay on "The Present State of Ethical Philosophy." After first praising the ancient Stoics for their "rational and correct views of ethics," he surveys the work of Hobbes, Cudworth, Clark, Price, Butler, Reid, Paley, Smith, and Stewart, concluding that the moderns are more practical than the ancients. He notes how paternal authority was extended in ancient Rome, how the father, empowered, becomes a tyrant, and he noted that such a thing "could not be tolerated at the present." Emerson's prose, even in this sober academic exercise, has become florid and purple in emulation of Everett:

> The commissioned apostles of peace and religion were seen arming the nations of Europe to a more obstinate and pernicious contest than had ever been known; and pursued with fatal hostility, with seven successions of bloodshed and horror, till its dye was doubled on the crimson cross.

In most respects these early writings serve mainly to take the temperature of Emerson's youthful fervor. The Uilsa story reveals his strong, almost violent emotional side and his ability to tap the Dionysian spirit; the ethics essay reflects his lifelong interest not in epistemology but in ethics. Already his question is not "What can I know?" but "How should I live?"[10]

During his last year and a half in college, Emerson thought of himself more as a poet than anything else. The idea of the poet, now and later, had for Emerson the larger sense of writer as well as the more limited sense of maker of verses. But none of his college poetry was good enough for him to want to print it later. There are passable lines ("Thy loud-voiced bards are murmuring tones of woe") and isolated images ("the silver fetters of old Rhyme"). He admired Milton and Shakespeare. Among modern poets he idolized Byron and made fun of Wordsworth, tastes he would later reverse. His college writings, like his college life, were full of contradictions. His long poem "Indian Superstition" was a Southey-inspired tirade against the Hindu religious tradition he would later come to admire. He wrote a rhymed attack on rhyme, and he wrote endless poems and sketches full of the schoolboy sublime, while he confessed in his journal to feeling sick, scared, and worried about his talent, not at all eager for college to be over.[11]

In August of 1821, during the same month that saw Missouri admitted as a state and revolution in Europe and just a few days before Emerson graduated, a young master's candidate named Sampson Reed delivered his "Oration on Genius" at Harvard. Reed was three years older than Emerson. His oration was better written by far than anything of which Emerson was capable. Reed made a strong impression on Emerson that August day. Years later in a letter to Margaret Fuller he still remembered the speech as his first—and still standing—benchmark for true genius or original force.

Reed's oration was not a critique, an exercise, an endorsement, or an argument. It was no mere commentary. It was a primary statement, a personal affirmation of what the speaker himself believed. It was alight with passion and had the solidity and self-possession of conviction. "The human heart has always had love of some kind," Reed began. "There has always been fire on the earth." Reed takes for granted the importance of the individual. "Every man has a form of mind peculiar to himself." But what he had come to say was not that genius is the apotheosis of individual talent but the opposite, that geniuses are the means by which general truths are revealed to the rest of us. "The intellectual eye of man is formed to see the light, not to make it," Reed says. "When the power of divine truth begins to dispel the darkness," he goes on, "the first things we see are the geniuses, so-called, the people of strong understanding and deep learning." Completing his wonderful cosmological metaphor, Reed says that when truth begins to get through to us is when "Luther, Shakespeare, Milton, Newton, stand with their bright side toward us."[12]

Reed's vision is religious, but it is not narrow or sectarian. "Know, then," he says, "that genius is divine, not when the man thinks that he is God, but when he acknowledges that his powers are from God." He then looks to science and scientists, to the study of nature, for new truth. He shows no interest at all in the church. "It needs no uncommon eye to see," he observes, "that the finger of death has rested on the church."

Reed's advice to his hearers has an edge. They were not to take comfort in existing forms of college or church but must "take care that the life which is received be genuine." He looked, he said, for a "unison of spirit and nature"; he knew that for the present generation as for any other, "thought falls to the earth with power, and makes a language out of nature." And as he looked ahead Reed predicted that "science will be full of life, as nature is full of God." The time was now. The night was over; the morning was at hand.[13]

4. Home and Family

THE BOSTON TO WHICH EMERSON RETURNED AFTER COLLEGE
in 1821 was a prosperous, growing, commercial seaport of just over 40,000
people. It was organized as a town and run by town meeting. After remaining
stable at around 20,000 for most of the eighteenth century, the town's
population had grown by 30 percent in each of the first two decades of the
nineteenth century. By 1820 the pace of growth had quickened further.
Boston was to grow by 40 percent to 61,000 persons by 1830. The din and
clutter of construction was universal. The tidal flats surrounding the original
pear-shaped peninsula were filled in, beginning in 1804. In the mid-twenties
six hundred Boston house carpenters went on strike (unsuccessfully) for a
ten-hour workday. In 1822, having grown too large to function as a town,
Boston reorganized itself as a city.[1]

Emerson had been born, on May 25, 1803, in a house at the corner of
Summer and Chauncy streets. Nearby were sheds, woodhouses, barns, and
a pond; as late as 1815 there was a two-acre pasture near Summer street.
But the town had already essentially replaced the countryside. Emerson
remembered that as a child he had felt "imprisoned in streets and hindered
from the fields and woods."[2]

Emerson's father was a minister; his salary, after 1809, was twenty-five
dollars a week, thirty cords of wood a year, and the use of a house. The family
was too poor for dancing and horseback riding. Emerson never had a sled
and would have been afraid to use one on account of neighborhood toughs.
He later recalled how he had once lost the money he had been given to buy
new shoes and his "being sent to look among the fallen leaves under the
poplar trees opposite the house for the lost bank note." The Emersons were
bookish. They prized education, and Emerson had warm memories of the
studious family circle, "the eager blushing boys discharging as they can their
little chares [chores], and hastening into the parlor to the study of tomorrow's merciless lesson yet stealing time to read a novel hardly smuggled in
to the tolerance of father and mother and atoning for the same by some pages
of Plutarch or Goldsmith." He recalled too "the warm affectionate delight

with which they behold and greet the return of each after the early separation of school, or business." Three days a week they had chocolate for breakfast, with toasted bread, but no butter. On Saturdays it was "salt-fish dinner, with all its belongings of vegetables, melted butter, pork scraps etc."[3]

Ralph was the third of six sons. Like some other middle children, he was the silly one. His father called attention to his levity, a trait that marks his letters well into college. He wrote cheerful verse letters to Aunt Sarah Alden Bradford, a rebus letter to older brother William which starts out "[deer] Brother: [eye] [hoop] [yew] [last *will* and testament scroll] [knot] [bee] offend [head] if [eye] attempt . . ." He wrote verses about doing dishes ("melodious knife! and thou harmonious sand / Tuned by the Poet-scourer's rugged hand"), and he loved Byron's "They grieved for those who perished in the cutter, / And likewise for the biscuit tubs and butter." In general, however, Ralph was thought by his relatives to be the least promising of the Emerson children. There are many fond anecdotes, written down after he became famous, about his early poems and recitation pieces, but in one of the few surviving documents from his childhood, the boy's father is seen complaining, some time before his son was three, that "Ralph does not read very well yet." Looking back later, Emerson said, "The advantage in education is always with those children who slip up into life without being objects of notice."[4]

If the boy was unobserved, he was not unobserving. He remembered wartime Boston, when, during the War of 1812, he and the other nine-year-olds were ferried out to Noddle's Island in Boston Harbor to help dig fortifications. What he chiefly remembered was how intolerably thirsty he got that day.

He also remembered going up on the roofs with the rest of Boston to watch the *Chesapeake* sail out of the harbor to do battle with the British frigate *Shannon*. June 1, 1813, was a beautiful summer day. There was little or no swell; a light breeze rippled the water. The *Shannon*, with thirty-eight guns, had sailed into the outer harbor hoping to provoke a fight and Captain Lawrence of the American frigate *Chesapeake* obliged. Lawrence set out after the *Shannon* and both ships silently drew away from the shore, looking for fighting room accompanied by an enthusiastic spectator fleet of small boats. At four P.M. the *Chesapeake* opened fire. Fifteen minutes later the fight was over. The *Shannon* had boarded and captured the *Chesapeake*. Lawrence was mortally hurt. Both ships looked like floating hospitals. There were twenty-four dead and fifty wounded on the *Shannon*, forty-seven dead and ninety-nine wounded on the *Chesapeake,* which was sailed off as a prize to Halifax. It was a black day in Boston.[5]

Emerson's father, the Reverend William Emerson, is an indistinct and minor figure in his son's life. He was minister of the First Church in Boston, where he played an active role in public affairs. Emerson remembered him as a "somewhat social gentleman" who was severe with the children. Emerson recalled how his father tried to teach him to swim: he "put me in mortal terror by forcing me into the salt water off some wharf or bathing house." The experience was so strong that after more than forty years Emerson could "still recall the fright with which, after some of this salt experience, I heard his voice one day (as Adam that of the Lord God in the garden) summoning us to a new bath, and I vainly endeavoring to hide myself."[6]

William Emerson died in 1811, when Ralph was eight. He had been a Federalist, that is to say, a conservative in politics, and a Unitarian, or liberal, in religion. He was interested in science, had read Priestley and Paine, and his characteristic writing has a bland, correct, rational tone. He was much interested in literature, helped pick out selections for *The Polyanthos,* a magazine for young people, and he was active in founding *The Christian Monitor* and *The Monthly Anthology,* the latter of which was a forerunner of the *North American Review.* William Emerson also edited *A Selection of Psalms and Hymns* (1808), the first American hymnbook to give the name of a tune and a suggested key for singing each psalm. He also wrote a *Historical Sketch of the First Church in Boston,* a minor *Magnalia* that includes the entire history of the Massachusetts Bay colony. His characteristic tone is a calm deism, modern but uninsistent: "Yes, my brethren, the vast creation is the dwelling place of the most High. Every ray of light is a proof of His presence. The awful womb of night is the pavillion of his rest. You feel his breath in every wind that blows." When he died at age 42 of a "consuming marasmus," a large scirrhous tumor of the lower intestine, his sister Mary Moody Emerson found it impossible to grieve for him, so deeply did she disapprove of his religious views. Later, however, she regretted the response. It is typical of Emerson's lack of interest in his father that in later years he paid more attention to his aunt's response than to his father's death.[7]

Emerson's mother, born Ruth Haskins, kept the family together after her husband's death. She took in boarders and found ways to get her sons educated. Later she lived in her middle son's house in Concord until her death in 1853. She had been born a British subject, Emerson liked to recall, and she was the middle child of thirteen. A strongly religious woman, she married William Emerson before his move to Boston. For years she kept a diary to "write down minutely the dealings of God toward me." She was a calm undisturbed woman, never impatient, never heard to express dissatisfaction. She was undemonstrative but not unfeeling. Emerson recalled a time when he and his older brother William were late getting home. Their mother exclaimed, "My sons, I have been in agony for you." "I went to bed in bliss," Emerson remembered, "at the interest she showed."[8]

One event that hit Ruth Emerson very hard was the death in 1807—when Ralph was four—of her eldest child, John Clarke, then aged eight. She was devastated, writing to her sister three months later, "I feel daily the agonizing pain arising from his loss but little diminished by the length of time elapsed since his death." She struggled to reconcile her grief with the knowledge that all things come from God. It would be a mistake to think that Ruth Emerson turned to religion only in times of trial. She led a deeply religious life. Every day after breakfast she retired to her room for reading and contemplation, and she was not to be disturbed.[9]

The religious strain in Emerson can be traced to his mother. Emerson's father showed "a studied reserve on the subject of the nature and offices of Jesus." Emerson thought later that his father had not been able to make up his mind about religion, but his mother had no such reservation. She was a strong believer and a practicing, observing Christian. She expected her children to be kind "to all animals and insects." She read Fénelon, William Wogan's *An Essay on the Proper Lessons of the Church of England*, John Flavel's *On Keeping the Heart*, and John Mason's *Self-Knowledge*. These books are not academic, polemical, or controversial. They are not about theology or church history or church government. Nor are they books of formal prayer and structured devotion, though she kept and read all her life the Church of England prayerbook with which she was raised. These books are works of consolation and comfort; they teach spiritual self-help. They are intended to be useful and practical guides to living a spiritual life in a material world. Ruth Emerson's books are not Unitarian, nor are they Puritan, or even exclusively Protestant. Her great favorite, Fénelon, is Catholic. Wogan is Church of England, Flavel is Presbyterian, and Mason was an early Methodist.[10]

What these books have in common is an intense interest in religious thought and feeling, in personal, immediate religious experience. They emphasize religious self-knowledge and religious self-cultivation. Fénelon insists that we must conquer self-love. Flavel says the main business of Christian life is "keeping the heart" in the face of prosperity, adversity, danger and public distraction, outward want, injury, injustice, and death. His entire book is on how to keep whole the inner person or soul, how to face life by working up one's inner resources of heart. Mason teaches a religious tending of one's own self. "Self-knowledge," he says, "is that acquaintance with ourselves, which shows us what we are, and do, and ought to be, and do, in order to live comfortably and usefully here, and happily hereafter." The means urged is self-examination, the purpose self-government and "self-fruition." These books share a consuming interest in the daily quality of the personal religious life, in the possibility of everyday spirituality, and in the authenticating feelings of individual religious experience. This introduction to the life of the spirit was not something Emerson could have got from his father, even had his father lived longer.[11]

Emerson was raised, as was Nietzsche, by and among women of notable intellectual and spiritual accomplishments. First of all, there was his thoughtful mother. There were frequent visitors such as Hannah Adams, author of the first American *Dictionary of Religion* and of the first history of Judaism by an American. There was Sarah Alden Bradford Ripley, in whose husband's school Emerson first began teaching. She knew Latin, Greek, French, Italian, and German. She knew the literatures as well as the languages, and she tutored boys for entrance to Harvard. She read Homer, Plato, mathematics, natural philosophy, psychology, and theology, including the modern and revolutionary developments in German criticism and German theology. She was, said Emerson, "absolutely without pedantry." Above all, more brilliant and original than all, was Emerson's aunt, his father's sister, Mary Moody Emerson.[12]

5. The Angel of Death

THE SINGLE MOST IMPORTANT PART OF EMERSON'S EDUCATION
was that provided by his aunt Mary Moody Emerson. It was she and not
the Boston ministers or Harvard professors who set the real intellectual
standards for the young Emerson and his brothers. Her correspondence with
him is the single best indicator of his inner growth and development until
he was well over thirty. Emerson said that in her prime his aunt was "the
best writer in Massachusetts." He noted that she set an "immeasurably high
standard" and that she fulfilled a function "which nothing else in his
education could supply." She was widely read and formidably articulate. She
could be damagingly candid. She possessed enormous force of character and
limitless energy, and she had a gift for attracting young people. She was a
tireless controversialist; she was a vigorous theologian. Above all, she was an
original religious thinker, almost a prophet. Her writing, which has been
shamefully ignored, is personal and testamentary; her strange style has great
energy, beauty, and intensity. She is "no statute book or orderly digest," said
Emerson, "but a Bible." Mary Moody Emerson was an American Jakob
Boehme. Her everyday life was spent wrestling with angels.[1]

Mary Emerson's oddities have made her a Dickensian figure for us. She
was four feet three inches tall. She had her bed made in the shape of a coffin.
She wore her burial shroud when she traveled, and she traveled so much she
wore out several shrouds. Her energy was phenomenal. "She could keep step
with no human being," her nephew recalled. "She would tear into the chaise
or out of it, into the house or out of it." She was amazingly outspoken. The
obituary writer for the *Boston Commonwealth* said "she was thought to have
the power of saying more disagreeable things in half an hour than any person
living." Emerson commented, "I see he was well acquainted with Aunt
Mary." She left a trail of anecdotes behind her, all vivid enough, but mostly
serving to replace her original genius with an eccentric caricature. She was
at bottom not an amusing maiden aunt but a visionary.[2]

Mary Emerson came frequently to visit Ruth and her sons, and when she
was away she directed a stream of high-energy correspondence at each one,

catechizing, informing, probing, tearing apart ideas and texts, and recommending reading. She expressed herself on every conceivable topic and obliged the boys to do the same. She took the most serious interest in young people. "When she met a young person who interested her, she made herself acquainted and intimate with him or her at once, by sympathy, by flattery, by raillery, by anecdote, by wit, by rebuke, and stormed the castle." "She gave herself full swing in these sudden intimacies," as Emerson wrote, "for she knew she should disgust them soon, and resolved to have their best hours." In Waldo's case, she eventually came to disapprove of his new ideas and she withdrew from her position of unofficial spiritual adviser, but her effect on him was permanent.[3]

Mary Emerson was brought up outside her own family, as was common then, and she lived her entire life in calamitous poverty. Destitution was her muse, said Emerson. She never married, though she was asked. Sometimes she lived alone, sometimes with others. Much of her life she lived in Maine, at a farm called Vale, near Waterford. She was, she said, "surrounded in every instant of my journey by little means, less virtues, and less vices." Her daily life involved both books and housework. Looking back over a typical week, she wrote when she was thirty,

> Rose before light every morn; visited from necessity once, and again for books; read Butler's *Analogy;* commented on the Scriptures; read in a little book,—Cicero's letters,—a few; touched Shakespeare,— washed, carded, cleaned house, and baked.[4]

She was self-educated. One of her earliest enthusiasms was a book-length poem her copy of which lacked both cover and title page. When she later looked up the works of famous poets, she found that the anonymous poem she had so admired was called *Paradise Lost.* Her early reading also included the English poets Young and Akenside. She read Samuel Clarke and Jonathan Edwards. Later, as her nephew noted, she read Plato, Plotinus, Marcus Aurelius, Stewart, Coleridge, Cousin, Herder, Locke, Mme. de Staël, Channing, Mackintosh, and Byron. Every one of these writers was also to be important to Emerson. Mary Emerson was more learned than most of the New England ministers she talked with. She had read Spinoza, Wollstonecraft, Rousseau, Eichhorn, Boehme, William Law, and Goethe. As she said of herself, she read zigzag through fields, authors, and even single books. The cardinal points of her intellectual compass were New

England's old Puritan religion, Samuel Clarke's reconciliation of revelation with the discoveries and world view of Newton, Richard Price's *Review of Morals,* with its Kantian assertion—made independently of Kant—of the objective content of moral consciousness, and the work of Germaine de Staël. Mary Emerson particularly admired *Corinne,* with its sympathetic portrait of the gifted, doomed heroine of intellect, imagination, and feeling, and her *Germany,* with its powerful defense of enthusiasm.[5]

When her brother was editing *The Monthly Anthology* in 1804 and 1805, Mary Emerson contributed a piece on the importance of imagination in religious life and one on natural history and its connection with natural theology. Her work is as good as anything in the magazine, but her genius did not flourish in the polite epistolic and dialogic forms favored by the Federalist literary mind. She also disagreed with her brother in religious matters. His religion was a nonreligious Unitarianism, a rational, science-oriented but churchy deism that was more social cement than inspiration. Mary Emerson, like the best of the Puritans before her, and like Melville and Emily Dickinson later, could neither believe completely nor be comfortable in her unbelief. She vastly preferred Calvinism to Unitarianism, though, as Emerson later observed, she "was not a Calvinist, but wished everybody else to be one, like Dr. Johnson's minister to the Hebrides, who wished Dr. Johnson to believe in Ossian, but did not himself." She describes herself as a "deistic pietist"; it is a good label. She embraced Christ as a mediator but looked forward to the time when she could do without him. She could imagine, she said, a higher being, a greater prophet, than Christ.[6]

Mary Emerson's unpublished writings became one of Emerson's most important books. Over a period of time, beginning probably in his early thirties, he carefully copied out the best of her letters, her conversation, and her table-talk into four substantial notebooks, totaling some 870 manuscript pages, all carefully paginated and indexed. He returned at regular intervals to the study of her work. Its effect on him was always the same. "Aunt Mary, whose letters I read all yesterday," he wrote in 1841, "is a Genius always new, subtle, frolicsome, judicial, unpredictable. All your learning of all literatures and states of society of Platonistic, Calvinistic, English or Chinese, would never enable you to anticipate one thought or expression." Everything about her was bold, vigorous, extravagant. She advised the Emerson boys: "Always do what you are afraid to do." Her active mind and strong imagination served a personality that was emotionally open. "I never expected matrimony," she wrote to her favorite nephew, Charles, youngest of the Emerson brothers. "My taste was formed in romance, and I knew I was not destined to please."[7]

Emerson copied out a number of his aunt's letters to Charles which record her growing uncertainty about the development of Waldo's thought. He could watch himself being discussed and dismissed. "As to Waldo's letter," she told Charles in January, 1832, "say nothing to him. It is time he should leave me. His sublime negations, his non-informations I have no right in the world to complain of. His letters are always elegantly spiced with flattery, which I love. What he thinks . . . or intends, time and report may unfold."[8]

Mary Emerson also had a deep current of feeling for the natural world and for its connection with crucial moments of human experience. In 1828, looking back on the death of her brother, Emerson's father, she wrote:

> This day, seventeen years since, was the last day of the man I first loved and admired. Different words, education and faith led us to view each other with indifference, but the remembrance of that death, of that day in which I erred, will not cease to pain in this life. While he lay dead, I fasted and prayed, but not with fervor. This morning I have been playing with the goslings,—how astonishing is nature! They have no parent—yet discover a strange instinct for each other's society, though there is no protection from it.

Her life was one of destitution, pain, and anticipation of death, but there is a seventeenth-century vigor to her morbidity. Pain was for her the epitome of strong feeling, and feelings were her principal index to life itself. She once wrote: "Give me, my God, to know that it is thy immediate agency touches each nerve with pain, or digs the eye, or severs the bone. I can then, *with thee,* joy and praise for all the heights to which men and angels climb." She uses the imagery of the body with unnerving force. Of gossip she said, "Society is like a corpse that purges at the mouth." On great subjects she could write greatly. The following passage on immortality may be contrasted with the cool reasonableness of Paley, Butler, Tucker, or Price. To the twenty-four-year-old Emerson, she writes:

> Would I could die today. That this aching sense of immortality might be satisfied or cease to ache. The difficulty remains the same when I

struggle with the extension of never, never, never, just as I repeated the exercize in childhood,—can't form an idea, can't stretch myself to that which has no ending. . . . Is it because of these lumps of matter which move with us and above us, of their perpetual changes and influences, that we cannot form an idea of the identical immortal substance which is to remain essentially and absolutely the same without end? Had it a beginning? or was it always an idea of God like Plato's notion,—after ages of individuality will it be reabsorbed? New Orders rise. In those orders will transmigrate this immortal (but what is immortal?) this identical essence, principle, within this coffined case,—these excrements of the inhabitant. I'll go to the woods—but there I shall see a sort of immortal matter,—a reproduction of seeds. Well but I shall not think, don't think, only feel pleasantly abroad, rather don't try,—can never think, there's this crazy yeast-like matter which makes the task unwholesome.[9]

No one, not even Carlyle, ever wrote Emerson letters that better combined philosophical acuity and passionate personal statement. Her letters give her essential style, a style that, Emerson said, "admits of all the force of colloquial domestic words, and breaks, and parenthesis, and petulance—has the kick and inspiration of that,—has humor, affection, and a range from the rapture of prayer down to the details of farm and barn and *help*. All her language in writing was happy but inimitable as if caught from some dream." Although she never achieved formal control of her language, she used strong physical imagery. She was, for Emerson, the Angel of Death, death being for her, as for Dickinson, the ultimate experience of life. Above all, her hunger for personal experience of the strongest, most direct kind must have pushed Waldo to settle for nothing less authentic, less direct, or less original in his own life.[10]

Mary Moody Emerson taught the dangers of prosperity, the uses of poverty, the necessity of doing what you are afraid to do, and the defiant right of the individual reader to bring all texts to judgment. Nothing Mary Moody Emerson felt or communicated was secondhand. Her example explains why Emerson later was so open to Alcott, to Margaret Fuller, to Sampson Reed, to Jones Very, to Jakob Boehme, and to Swedenborg. Because of his aunt's failures, Emerson knew there was "an innavigable sea of silent waves between us and the things we aim at." Because of her presence and example, he was pushed onward by her undrownable spirit, which was perpetually reaching farther up the beach than the last wave of language had taken it. Principally through the vivid example of the seer Tnamurya, as he always anagrammed "Aunt Mary" in his journals, Emerson was from early on at home with that very select company of the always failing and never defeated creators of the world's half-born gospels.[11]

6. Scottish Common Sense

AFTER GRADUATION FROM HARVARD, EMERSON RETURNED TO his mother's home on Federal Street in Boston and went to work as a teacher in the school for girls his brother William ran out of their home. He was eighteen. In his spare time he wrote drafts of essays on a wide variety of topics. By January 1822 he was again filling commonplace books, as he had in college, with scraps and sketches at the rate of almost a notebook a month. He was reading Sismondi's huge works *The Literature of Southern Europe* and *The History of the Italian Republics.* He loyally read a book on Europe by Edward Everett's brother Alexander and praised it to friends. He read a good deal of fiction. And for the next two years he read more or less continuously the writings of the Scottish philosophers of common sense, Adam Smith, Thomas Brown, James Mackintosh, Thomas Reid, and especially Dugald Stewart. One of Emerson's students later remembered that the way to please the young schoolmaster was to praise Dugald Stewart.

Scottish Common Sense philosophy was the prevailing mode of thought at Emerson's Harvard. It was, in Stewart's hands, a broad and generous way of thinking, centered in moral issues and problems. Stewart's thought was unusually coherent, both in itself and in relation to other schools of thought, because Stewart himself wrote a full-length history of modern thought, which, like Hegel's account of German idealism, explained prior philosophy as a sort of background and preparation for his own work. Stewart also wrote a graceful, lucid English prose that made his views widely accessible. What William Gass says of Thomas Reid is also true of Stewart, that he not only wrote about common sense, he used it. Stewart was, above all, current. The second half of his history of modern thought, called—formidably—*Dissertation: Progress of Metaphysical, Ethical, and Political Philosophy,* appeared in 1821. What Emerson got from this book was a kind of roadmap of modern ideas, a framework within which to think or from which to depart. The intellectual universe of Dugald Stewart provided Emerson with a set of working ideas and assumptions, some of which he retained all his life.[1]

Stewart's *Dissertation* traces the modern era in thought to Francis Bacon. Stewart explains, at the beginning of this five-hundred-page piece written for the *Encyclopedia Britannica,* that he set out at first simply to complete Bacon's own sketchy but grand outline of modern knowledge. But Stewart found he had to reject Bacon's breakdown of knowledge into history (based on memory), philosophy (based on reason), and poetry (based on imagination). Stewart also rejected Locke's taxonomy, which divided knowledge into physics (or natural philosophy), ethics (or moral philosophy), and logic, including rhetoric. In place of these tripartite schemes, Stewart proposed two main divisions, matter and mind, as the "two most general heads which ought to form the groundwork of an Encyclopedical classification of the arts and sciences." This is Stewart's starting point, and it shows how close Scottish Common Sense and German idealism are in their fundamentals.[2]

For Stewart much of the history of modern thought is the history of the arguments over whether the human mind possesses innate ideas and whether the mind is essentially active or passive. Stewart's clear and now somewhat neglected argument gives a surprisingly sophisticated version of all this, starting with Descartes, whom Stewart regards as the real "Father of the Experimental Philosophy of the Human Mind." More important, Stewart shows how Locke was misunderstood and simplified, even by his followers and disciples. Stewart shows that the blunt belief that "all our knowledge appears plainly to derive its origin from the senses" reflects the position of Locke's followers Gassendi, Condillac, and Diderot, but not Locke. Locke himself, says Stewart, believed that our knowledge arises from both sensation *and* reflection, and he carefully cites Locke's description of the latter power:

> The other function, from which experience furnishes the understanding with ideas, is the perception of the operations of our own mind within us, as it is employed about the ideas it has got: which operations, when the soul comes to reflect on and consider, do furnish the understanding with another set of ideas, which could not be had from things without.

If this is not quite a pure insistence on a noumenal self, existing apart from experience, space, and time, it is a far more complex and qualified view of the mind than the often cited image Locke once offered of the mind as a blank slate on which sense experience writes.[3]

The real enemy for Stewart is not Locke but David Hume. Stewart understood Hume to have claimed that "all the objects of our knowledge are divided into two classes, impressions and ideas." Impressions are sense impressions; ideas are "copies of impressions." Hume thus directly doubts the existence of such a thing as mind. He doubts what Descartes said could not be doubted, "the existence of a thinking percipient I." Not only did Hume consider mind an imaginary substance, he also thought matter to be "an imaginary and exploded substance." Further yet, and most dramatically, Hume denied the existence of cause and effect, maintaining that "physical causes and effects are known to us merely as antecedents and consequents." In other words, there is no cause and effect; there is only sequence. The result of this rupture between cause and effect is radical skepticism. "As we can have no idea of anything which never appeared to our outward senses or inward sentiment, the necessary conclusion seems to be, that we have no idea of connexion or power at all." In Stewart's view Hume aimed "to establish a universal skepticism, and to produce in the reader a complete distrust of his own faculties."[4]

Taking his lead from Stewart, Emerson was to struggle against Hume for years. To a great extent Emerson's life and work—indeed, transcendentalism itself—constitutes a refutation of Hume. It is therefore important to recognize how fully Emerson and his contemporaries confronted and recognized the potential for nihilism in Hume. As a writer in the *Edinburgh Review* put it in a long article on Stewart that Emerson read,

> the doctrine of Mr Hume . . . is not that we have not reached the truth, but that we can never reach it. It is an absolute and universal system of scepticism, professing to be derived from the very structure of the understanding, which, if any man could seriously believe it, would render it impossible for him to form any opinion upon any subject—to give the faintest assent to any proposition—to ascribe any meaning to the words Truth and Falsehood,—to believe, to inquire, or to reason: and, on the very same ground, to disbelieve, to dissent or to doubt—to adhere to his own principle of universal doubt; and, lastly, if he be consistent with himself, even to think.[5]

Scottish Common Sense philosophy is itself a series of answers to Hume. The ground shared by Reid, Mackintosh, Smith, Brown, and Stewart is the belief, as Stewart puts it, in the "universality of moral perceptions as an essential part of the human constitution." Frances Hutcheson, an early figure in the movement, asserted that "moral distinctions are apprehended directly by means of, or as the consequence of, a special capacity of the soul, designated as the moral sense." The idea is that moral distinctions do not depend on reason or intellection but on our feelings or emotions. Adam Smith goes furthest with this link between morality and feeling in a book Emerson read in July 1824, *The Theory of Moral Sentiments*. Smith argues that "as we have no immediate experience of what other men feel, we can form no idea of the manner in which they are affected but by conceiving what we ourselves should feel in the like situation." Through our imagination we can place ourselves in the situations of others. By our fellow feeling for the misery of others, we can imagine how we would feel in similar circumstances and can act accordingly. In other words, the moral sentiment arises from sympathy and from sympathetic identification.[6]

The first teaching of Scottish Common Sense then is that we all possess something called the moral sense or the moral sentiment, which is anchored in the emotional, feeling, sympathetic part of human nature. This ability to prefer good actions to bad, to prefer some values (as they are now called) to others, is shared by all people in all times. The second great teaching of these thinkers is what Reid calls common sense and what Stewart calls the fundamental laws of human belief, or the primary elements of human reason. These primary elements arise from a belief in our own identity and the evidence of memory. What comes first, for Stewart, is consciousness, which assures us we exist. Then comes memory. The fundamental laws of human belief follow. First, I exist. Second, I am the same person today I was yesterday. Third, the material world has an existence independent of my mind. Fourth, the general laws of nature will continue in future to operate uniformly, as in time past.[7]

Scottish Common Sense philosophy avoids both the pure materialism of Gassendi, Diderot, Holbach, and la Mettrie and the pure idealism of Leibniz and Berkeley. Affirmative rather than skeptical, it insists on the reality of morality; it asks, "How should I live my life?" It also affirms the reality and importance of consciousness. "As all our knowledge of the material world rests ultimately on facts ascertained by observation," says Stewart, "so all our knowledge of the human mind rests ultimately on facts for which we have the evidence of our own consciousness." Stewart goes further, claiming that "the capacities of the human mind have been in all ages the same, and that the diversity of phenomena exhibited by our species is the result merely of the different circumstances in which men are placed." If mind or consciousness has been essentially the same in all ages and places, so has the moral sense. "The universality of moral perceptions are an essential part of the human constitution." What makes consciousness and morality universal is our "susceptibility of education, which is acknowledged to belong universally to the race." In respect to these three qualities, then, morality, consciousness, and educability, not only all times and places but all persons are essentially the same, that is to say, essentially equal.[8]

Scottish Common Sense had limitations for Emerson. As a system it left little place for imagination, art, or literature. It was too exclusively moral. It left room for, but put no great emphasis on, original force or insight, and it vastly underrated the rival philosophy of Kant and his followers. Kant is dismissed by Stewart as being no real advance on Cudworth. Emerson would have to fight to appreciate Kant. Nevertheless, the body of ideas and the historical approach taken by the Scottish thinkers gave Emerson a world view that emphasized ethical—rather than epistemological or metaphysical—thought, an outlook that was predisposed to affirmation, that was remarkably comprehensive (Stewart had read Sir William Jones and was able to compare Hindu thought and Berkeleian idealism), and that was open both to science and to religion.[9]

Outside Emerson's books and beyond his schoolroom, the world at the end of 1821 and the beginning of 1822 seemed headed for increasing turmoil. Napoleon died on far-off St. Helena. The independence movement in Naples was utterly crushed by a coalition of European monarchies. In Milan Silvio Pellico wrote against the Austrians and was confined in the jails he would write about in *My Prisons*. A movement to repatriate American blacks created Liberia. Bolívar and San Martin, the liberator of Peru, met at Guayaquil in Ecuador to determine, they hoped, the future of South America. The movement for Greek independence widened into a major war, calling up a wave of popular sympathy all over Europe. Byron, at the height of his fame, celebrated and ennobled the Greeks in his lyrics.

Emerson was feeling other stirrings besides intellectual ones. At the end of February 1822 he noted that he had been unable to achieve the "cold, frigid tone" necessary for oracular writing. He was experiencing, he thought, the beginnings of love. He recorded, in Latin, a wave of feeling for two friends, one male, one female, neither named. He hoped, with an ardor known only to himself, that they both would become "a part of life, a part of me."[10]

7. The Brothers Emerson

THE YOUNG MAN WAS PROBABLY MARTIN GAY FROM COLLEGE days. As the year 1822 progressed, Emerson—who was nineteen—noted how the ardor of his friendship with Gay declined and then became very nearly extinct. Living in the pre-Freudian era, Emerson was rather innocent and essentially unembarrassed by his feelings for Gay. He easily acknowledged his "ardor" to himself and put only some of his journal comments into Latin, a common device to keep sexual matters secret, but only from children. There is no hint who the young woman was. Emerson tutored Elizabeth Peabody in Greek for a while in 1821, when she was eighteen and he nineteen; the two of them were so shy "they never lifted their eyes from their books." For one day he tutored Elizabeth Hoar, also in Greek, but she was only eleven.[1]

What we do know about Emerson's emotional life during the years just after college is that he was deeply involved in his immediate family, especially with his accomplished, ambitious brothers. They supported, encouraged, and criticized one another; they were extremely close and open with one another and with Aunt Mary. There are several contexts or backgrounds against which we can see young Emerson's emergence. There is Boston in the 1820s, the world of Harvard and Unitarianism; there is the intellectual background of Scottish Common Sense and its account of the preceding two centuries; and there is his astonishing aunt. But it is impossible to understand Emerson's motives and feelings during this period without knowing something about the brothers. Just as Simone de Beauvoir's life really began when her friend Zaza died and just as John Thoreau's death somehow set Henry Thoreau free to write, so Emerson's growth—and the difficult ups and downs of his early years—are very tightly interwoven with the tragic failures of his gifted and ambitious brothers.

Eight children were born to Ruth and the Reverend William Emerson. Phebe, born in 1798, lived two years. Second was John Clarke, born in 1799. It was his death in 1807 at age eight that so shattered his mother. The last born, Mary Caroline, lived only three years, from 1811 to 1814.

In between John Clarke and Mary Caroline came five boys, all of whom lived to grow up. William was the oldest, born in 1801. Ralph came next, in 1803, followed by Edward in 1805, Robert Bulkeley in 1807, and Charles in 1808. There was only a seven-year spread among them. They went to school together, roomed together at college, taught together, shared books, wrote letters, sent money to each other, and they all put forth their best efforts for Aunt Mary. They were a close family group, holding frequent meetings to decide whose turn it was to work and whose to study or travel. Their future lives and careers were a matter of constant mutual concern. All through college and for quite a few years afterward, Ralph was the least interesting, the least enterprising, the least promising, and the most fortunate.[2]

William had the usual advantages and burdens of being the eldest. He started college at Harvard when he was thirteen and graduated in 1818, by which time Ralph had finished his freshman year. William went at once to Kennebunk, Maine, to teach high school. He taught steadily for the next five and a half years, seeing Ralph and Edward through college and Charles into his second year. The "heroic burdens assumed and sacrifices made by him in youth and early manhood" became part of family legend. William had a good deal of dignity. His brothers called him "his Deaconship" and "the Mogul" and "our Sultan." Emerson said William had "personal ascendency" and "the temperamental eye of a soldier or a schoolmaster." Emerson's son later recalled that the early burden of cares and responsibilities "left its stamp on [William] through all his days."[3]

William's great chance came in December 1823 when he was released from his labors to go to Germany to study theology at Göttingen to prepare for the ministry. What he learned there impressed and amazed him at first. But the coldly analytical and dispassionately historical world of German religious studies soon undermined William's faith in Christianity and derailed his ambition to become a minister. After all his sacrifices, delays, hopes, and planning, he returned home demoralized. For sixty dollars more he could have had a German doctorate, but it was no longer worth it to him. He decided without much enthusiasm to move to New York and go into law. There he struggled to get established, teaching school and writing and translating for the *Journal of Commerce* in addition to reading law. Over the years he succeeded in the law and eventually he became a judge. But his intellectual interests and ambitions had been permanently numbed by his experience in Germany.[4]

William Emerson married, had children, and lived to be sixty-seven, remaining on close, warm terms with his New England relatives. He was always the honored older brother. It was never said—but always felt—that the respectable, established figure William cut represented a defeat, a taking refuge in the standing order of things after his personal faith and force had failed. Certainly the law was not what Aunt Mary wanted for any of the boys. She wanted them all to go into the ministry, not for respectability or position or fame but from the kind of heroic faith and the personal sense of mission she herself felt.

Waldo was two years younger than William; Edward was two years younger than Waldo. Edward was handsome and graceful. He was five feet ten inches tall with light hair, blue eyes, and a sharp nose. He carried himself like a soldier and was in fact an officer in the college militia. He had confidence, executive ability, and eloquence. Waldo had a "romantic admiration" for Edward, who seemed to have all the qualities he lacked. Waldo was embarrassed by his own sluggish life, passive actions, and flippant speech when he compared himself to Edward, who "lived, acted, and spoke with preternatural energy." Edward had great ambitions and was propelled by an unsleeping, goading conscience. He was at the head of his class, not only first, but first by a wide margin. His graduation from Harvard in 1824 was his moment of glory. The aged Lafayette, hero of the Revolution, sat on the platform while Edward Emerson gave the oration and addressed the hero.[5]

Some hint of Edward's enormous drive can be picked up from a letter he wrote during January of his triumphant senior year to Charles, then a freshman and also at or near the head of his class. Edward warned Charles that he had to be first, that being second meant nothing, for after graduation, in the real world,

> those who had taken first place in a *thousand* little classes, in the academies and colleges, come forward, and upon entering the great School of the world, take their places in the first rank, and the poor number two who flattered himself, with the idea of having but *one* above him, now finds a *thousand* to whom he must "give the wall."[6]

After his brilliant commencement oration, Edward was offered a tutorship in the college, but he had now chosen the law over teaching or the ministry and so entered the law office of the already famous Daniel Webster, who had taken a personal interest in him. Edward drove himself hard, as

William had, teaching on the side for the money. He had never enjoyed really good health. As a boy of fourteen, teaching in his uncle Ripley's school in Waltham, he had complained of persistent coughing and headache. There was no heat in his part of the house, even when it got down to 26 degrees above zero, and he told his mother he had violent fits of uncontrollable perspiration for an hour every night. He was sent to Alexandria, Virginia, for half a year to get strong enough for college. One year out of college his health broke again and he spent a year traveling in Europe. He returned in October 1826 more exhausted than when he left. He continued to push himself. He began to have premonitions that he was nearing the end of his strength, grimly noting that he was going to become a lawyer, "if I live." He wrote William that he felt tired, adding, "I think however it will require a few more years to exhaust the vital bowl, albeit the shallow liquor betrays the near bottom." His brother Charles also saw trouble coming for Edward, and he wrote William that "Edward hardly seems to have the strength necessary for the race he ought to run." Charles added, "It would be a dark dispensation to us if he should be cut off . . ." In the spring of 1828, when he was twenty-three, Edward finally let up on himself, writing to William, "I read no law, almost no letters. I have ceased to resist God and Nature." He confided that "from the moment of surrender, I am wiser, healthier, happier."[7]

Ten days later Edward suffered a complete mental collapse. He behaved crazily. He came downstairs and derided kindly old Dr. Ripley. He became violent. "Edward is very sick," Charles wrote. After a lucid interval, Edward's mind collapsed again in late June and he was taken to McLean's Asylum. His mother was so devastated and appalled that she thought he would be better off dead.[8]

Edward recovered his sanity but not his energy or decisiveness. He vacillated about continuing in the law, cautiously seeking advice and approval from all sides. "His main spring seemed broken," his nephew and namesake Edward Waldo Emerson wrote years later. His physical health was still poor as well. The tuberculosis that had probably been there since boyhood worsened. He took ship for Puerto Rico, took a job as a clerk, and in 1834, at age twenty-nine, he died.[9]

Robert Bulkeley—or Bulkeley, as he was always called—was the next youngest. Born in 1807, he was retarded, and though he lived to be fifty-two, he came to have a child's mind in a man's body. As a boy his voice was too loud, his manners embarrassing. Later he became irritable and garrulous. He had periodic breakdowns that required him to be institutionalized. He was cared for all his life, often at home, sometimes in Maine, sometimes at McLean's. For a while he lived with a family in Roxbury, for a long time with a farm family in Chelmsford. Family correspondence refers to him often. He is usually reported as well, and once in a while we get a glimpse of a sort of god's fool, leading a simple life, and far from unhappy. He even played at his version of the family business. He got away one time, for fourteen days, Emerson wrote William, and made his way from Chelmsford to Mount Vernon, New Hampshire, where "he carried about a paper proposing to teach a singing school and succeeded in getting fifteen or sixteen subscribers, ere the wise men of Gotham found him out."[10]

Charles, born in 1808, was the youngest. He was of medium height, had a full head of hair and less of the large Emerson nose than his brothers. He was very bright and a general favorite—especially with Aunt Mary. He won the Latin prize in high school, found the college admission examination much less formidable than expected, and won the Bowdoin Prize his sophomore year at Harvard. Things came easily to him—too easily, his brothers thought. His letters speak casually of expected future honors. At bottom Charles was not in the least sure of himself. But he felt, as he told his aunt, that it was his duty to strive to be first. One part of him, the Cinderella part, thought he was as good as any, if only the truth were known. "I see none whom my vanity acknowledges as more intelligent than myself," he confided to her, while in a later letter he acknowledged how difficult it was to be humble and how hard it was "to draw away my thoughts from being absorbed in those petty honors I receive or anticipate." But underneath he felt differently: "At home where they surely ought to know best, why they think but little of me." Aunt Mary had Charles writing to her every week, and to her he told both sides. Defending his preference for law over the ministry, he explained to her, "I greatly distrust my fitness for the sacred office . . . my mind is of a very secondary order."[11]

However precarious Charles's expressed self-esteem may have been, it irritated both Edward and Waldo. Edward sternly pushed Charles to greater exertions when he was an easy-going freshman, and throughout college Charles continued, Waldo thought, to be the "same honey catcher of pleasure, favor, and honor that he hath been and without paying for it like Edward with life and limb." Edward's horrifying mental collapse occurred just before Charles's graduation. Charles was valedictorian; he was to deliver one of the commencement orations. With Edward confined at McLean's, Waldo listened to Charles and wrote him a long, blunt letter, cast in the form of a negative review, and referring to Charles in the third person. The speaker's great error, said Waldo, was in taking his audience for granted, in assuming the listeners were interested in him, instead of assuming that it was his job to interest them. The speech was beautiful, conceded Waldo, but never eloquent. It did not reach out to people, did not try to act on them, did not address them: "Instead, therefore of feeling that the audience was an object of attention from him, he [Charles] felt that he was an object of attention from the audience." Emerson's lengthy, detailed critique says a good deal about what he had himself learned about public speaking by 1828. Its effect on Charles can be imagined. In the letdown after his oration and after Waldo's letter, Charles wrote his aunt, "I need a long Sabbath, and yet my silly and volatile spirit derives no growth or lasting spring from Sabbaths, and new moon or spiritual festivals. I almost despair."[12]

Charles's life changed after graduation. He read law in the office of Charles Upham. Later he enrolled in the new Harvard Law School. Although Daniel Webster thought him good enough to attract clients even if he practiced in the backwoods of Maine, Charles found the law hard going. His cockiness disappeared. His literary interests deepened. Waldo not only let up on him but became an ever closer and more admiring friend and companion. In 1832, just as he was graduating from law school, Charles became seriously interested in Elizabeth Hoar, the young, intelligent, and extraordinarily beautiful daughter of Rockwood Hoar of Concord. Charles's interest was returned. They fell deeply in love. It was the great event of Charles's life; by far the largest part of his literary remains are his letters to Elizabeth. They became engaged and eventually planned a wedding for September 1836.

There had always been a dark side to Charles. Beneath the ambition, the yearning for eminence and greatness—for *notice* of some kind—was an ominous feeling of emptiness. Charles struggled for years, first with religious belief, then with the idea of a philosophy based on the self. He came to the conclusion that the latter was nothing but confusion: "When we look at the world from Self as center, nothing can be more perplexed." Like his mother's beloved Fénelon, Charles yearned for the self to be swallowed up in something greater. But his path appeared to him always darker and headed downward. "Every step I advance into the crowd," he wrote Aunt Mary when he was not yet a year out of college, "the atmosphere grows thicker and fouler, the further my soul seems to have wandered from its nature and proper place."[13]

Along with this brooding, Hamlet-like despondency went genuine literary ability. Emerson kept a notebook of Charles's sayings. Charles once described his sense of alienation: "I am an American coin in a Spanish country, the metal is the same, but it doesn't pass current." He felt that "the nap is worn off the world" and noted with weary elegance that he could "see no reason why the world should not burn up. The play has been over, some time." He loved Milton. Emerson said he was Milton's reader and recalled the "diamond sharpness of his poetic recitation of *Samson Agonistes*."[14]

Charles's health worsened. He had the same underlying tuberculosis that had killed Edward in 1834. His life was lighted only by his love for his adored Lizzie, who completely reciprocated it. But he could not escape his premonitions and his mind ran more and more on death. "Life wears away," he wrote; "day follows day, night after night. Blessed emancipation from flesh, and all the ills that flesh is heir to—may I desire it unblamed?" Like Aunt Mary, he could see himself dead. He noted in his diary, "It shall be nothing then to me that the cold rains of November drench the bare fields."[15]

In the spring of 1836 Charles's health, never robust, worsened suddenly. He went to New York, to William's house, for rest. On May 9, four months before the wedding, he went for a walk in the morning, came in, lay down, and was dead by nightfall. Among his papers were a number of poems, including one called "Thekla's Song," which ends:

> For the world feels cold, and the heart gets old
> And reflects the bright aspect of nature no more.
>   Then take back the child, Holy Virgin, to thee
>   I have plucked the one Blossom that hangs on Earth's tree
> I have lived, and have loved, and die.[16]

8. The Young Writer

BETWEEN GRADUATION IN 1821—WHEN HE WAS EIGHTEEN— and the family move to Roxbury in May of 1823, Emerson taught in William's school for young women. He was at best a middling teacher. Perhaps Hannah Stevenson spoke for most when she said that "neither the parents nor the pupils considered the school a failure." For some it was better than that. As a tutor Emerson made a deep impression on both Elizabeth Peabody and Elizabeth Hoar. In another of the many schools he was to keep as a young man, he taught Richard Henry Dana, Jr., but taught him nothing useful about writing, as he realized with chagrin years later when he read and admired Dana's masterpiece *Two Years Before the Mast.* He had an occasional adoring disciple such as Peter Hunt, who drank in every word, regarded him as an oracle, and made it all seem worthwhile. But Emerson's heart was never in his schoolteaching. He took up his oar in what Charles called the old family galley and he did his share, but he was always dissatisfied. He dreamed of being a poet, an orator, a minister. What these dreams had in common was writing, and it was to the business of writing that Emerson gave all the time and energy he could salvage from teaching.[1]

Except for the presence of his brothers and his correspondence with Aunt Mary, Emerson was intellectually isolated during these early years out of college, living—in a phrase he got from Charles Lamb—in a "solitude of unshared energies." He had formed no friendships with his professors, and now he found himself composing long formal letters to some of his classmates trying to stir up some literary and intellectual correspondence. One thing he had learned in college was how to keep journals. Beginning in 1819, when he was a sophomore, Emerson began keeping a college theme notebook as well as a list of books he had read. A third notebook, begun for drafts of his college essay on Socrates, turned into a notebook for poetry. A fourth, begun in 1820 for notes in a lecture course by George Ticknor, grew into a general notebook for drafts of essays and poems. Also in 1820 he began a series of notebooks, each called "Universe," each with a number, which were commonplace books full of quotations from his reading. He began yet another series of notebooks in 1820 called "Wide World." He filled two the first year. After a lapse in 1821—graduation year—he began again in earnest in 1822, filling "Wide World" notebooks 3 through 9 with his own thoughts and observations on a wide range of subjects. He filled three more in 1823.

Emerson's organized, persistent, purposeful journal keeping is one of the most striking aspects of his early intellectual life. He wrote constantly, he wrote about everything, he covered hundreds of pages. When he had nothing to say, he wrote about having nothing to say. He read and indexed and reread what he had written. He copied letters into his journals and prose from his journals into his letters. He laughed at much of it when he read it over, inserting comments such as "dead before it reached its subject," but he kept at it. These early journals are mostly dross and largely unoriginal, but they are impressive in their fluent persistency. They are efforts, *essayings* at original composition, first reachings for the essay that became his lifelong form.[2]

Dreaming in the attic of the house on Federal Street, Emerson accumulated notes, ideas, and passages on a wide range of topics. On the question of what is evil, he wrote: "There is an answer from every corner of the globe . . . the enslaved, the sick, the disappointed, the poor, the unfortunate, the dying, the surviving cry out, it is here." He wrote on contrast as "a law of the human mind" and on power as an idea that "seems to have been every where at the bottom of the theology." He wrote of social feelings that "man was as evidently intended for society as the eye for vision," and later, "It is the social, not the solitary state under which man in fact lives." He was interested in greatness and thought that the highest kind of greatness was "that which abandons earthly consanguinity, and allies itself to immortal minds . . . which exists in obscurity and is least known among mankind." He wrote a good deal about the decline of civilization. "There is a tendency in all things to decay." Some of his worst writing came in a long and oddly impassioned diatribe against "the evil influence of dramatic exhibitions." He railed against the "poison and rottenness" and the "existing viciousness of the drama," concluding that "theatre is the sewer in which the rebellious vices exhaust themselves."[3]

He wrote about prophecy, being less interested in predictions than in the state of mind of the prophet. Of martyrdom he said it "proves the existence of a consistency and force of character which might else to common minds appear chimerical." He wrote on the populace, wondering whether it was the same in all ages. Most of this work is exercise and practice. After one entry he listed several references, then wrote, "I shall resume this subject when I have more to say," to which he added, evidently at some later date, "Spare us." But as a pump will bring up muddy water before it brings up clean, there were occasions when he brought up real insights and managed a rough but important formulation. Writing in March 1822 he observed that while "we complain of change and vicissitude," we ought rather to say "there pursues us an eternal sameness, an unchanging identity . . . the world, the universe is just the same; only each man's mind undergoes a perpetual change."[4]

During this active seedtime, Emerson was also reading in all directions. He read systematically only for a particular project. He read current books and old books. He habitually read the *North American Review,* the *Edinburgh Review,* and the *Christian Examiner.* And from almost everything he read he culled phrases, details, facts, metaphors, anecdotes, witticisms, aphorisms, and ideas. He kept this energetic reading and excerpting up for over forty years; the vast system of his personal notebooks and indexes—including indexes to indexes—eventually reached over 230 volumes, filling four shelves of a good-sized bookcase. The notebooks were in part his storehouse of original writing and in part a filing system, designed to store and give him access to the accumulating fruits of this reading on every topic that ever interested him throughout his life.

Now, during late 1821, 1822, and early 1823, he was reading the Swiss economist Sismondi's *History of the Italian Republics in the Middle Ages* and Mosheim's *Ecclesiastical History.* His aunt questioned him about Eichhorn's *Apocalypse* (a radical new "literary" interpretation of the Book of Revelation) and about Ram Mohan Roy, the great Hindu monotheist and founder of modern Hindu liberalism, then making a small stir in the pages of the *Christian Examiner.* He read Shakespeare's *Hamlet* and *Antony and Cleopatra.* He read Mme. de Staël's feminist novel *Corinne,* another cherished book and favorite author of Aunt Mary. He read Cooper's *The Spy* (1820) and *The Pioneers* (1823). He read Scott's *Waverly* (1814) and *Quentin Durward* (1823) and Catherine Sedgewick's *Redwood* (1824). Emerson was never as interested in the classics as Thoreau, though he continued to read them. He now read the Roman Stoic Seneca's *Letters,* Ovid's *Remedies of Love,* and Lucretius's *De rerum naturae.* He now first became interested in Rousseau, through Mme. de Staël's *Lettres sur les ouvrages de Rousseau.* He also read Gibbon, who left a momentary mark on Emerson's prose style. He read Bacon and Plato (the *Meno*), two thinkers to whom he returned frequently.[5]

The visible result of Emerson's first year and a half out of college is his first published essay, "Thoughts on the Religion of the Middle Ages." Emerson never included it in any collection of his writing, perhaps because it is so thoroughly unlike anything he wrote later. It is about decay and decline, that favorite topic of very young men. Emerson treats the European Middle Ages as an interval of barbarism between classical civilization and the Reformation. The essay poses the question why civilization should succumb to barbarism at all. The essay is derivative and negative; its brief, muted affirmations of the Reformation are decisively outweighed by the scornful attacks on Roman superstition. The prevailing tone of the piece is not merely skeptical, it is the scornful skepticism of the radical Enlightenment of the philosophes.[6]

Both the tone and the subject of the piece, which is finally about the "common submission [in European countries] of the freedom of opinion to the ordinances of the councils and court of Rome," are more understandable when we recognize that Emerson was at this time still struggling against—yet fascinated by—the sweeping negations of the archskeptic, David Hume. Emerson's letters to Aunt Mary during this time are full of Hume, and in October 1823 he read "Of the Idea of Necessary Causation," the coldly titled but crucial center of Hume's *Enquiry Concerning Human Understanding*. In this chapter Hume argues that our ideas of power, force, and energy are all dependent on our ideas of necessary connection. "It seems a proposition which will not admit of much doubt," Hume begins with mild convivial preemption, "that all our ideas are nothing but copies of our impressions." It is, he says, "impossible for us to *think* of anything which we have not antecedently felt." "When we look about us," he goes on, "toward external objects, and consider the operation of causes, we are never able, in a single instance, to discover any power or necessary connection, any quality which binds the effect to the cause." The key word is "binds." We do not really perceive cause and effect, Hume says. We perceive only sequence, one event following another. We are not "able to comprehend any force or power by which the cause operates, or any connection between it and its supposed effect." Emerson had known Hume's famous critique of cause and effect, but now he saw that challenging cause and effect meant challenging our knowledge of power itself. "Events seem conjoined, but never connected," Hume writes. "But as we can have no idea of anything which never appeared to our outward sense or inward sentiment, the necessary conclusion seems to be, that we have no idea of connection or power at all, and that the words are absolutely without any meaning."[7]

So there it was. Whether in science or theology, if there is no cause and effect, there is no power, no first cause, no God. Power is only power when it causes something. Hume's logic leads to a completely disconnected world, without energy to cause or create. Where does one go from there? The question was especially pressing for Emerson, the central work of whose life was to be uncovering and making available those sources of power that exist in people and in the world. To be cut off from a knowledge of basic, creating power was a state almost of nonbeing. This was not a state Emerson could accept, even if logically demonstrated. Emerson's notebooks for this period show his keen awareness that Hume would have to be answered.

The economic depression brought on by a combined cotton-boom failure and a land-boom failure in 1819 lifted in 1823, making life a little easier for the Emersons, but January 1823 found Emerson restless and dissatisfied. "I keep school," he wrote a friend. "I study neither law, medicine or divinity, and write neither poetry nor prose." He talked with George Bancroft, who was just back from his studies in Germany at Göttingen and who was excitedly planning an American secondary school along the lines of the European gymnasium. Emerson went to hear his idol, Edward Everett, lecture on the Eleusinian mysteries. Everett was not the only one he admired now. He had also heard Harrison Gray Otis speak in 1823 and was, he said, "astonished and delighted." Late in 1823 he went to hear William Ellery Channing's sermon on Revelation. He was vastly impressed, and from this time his interest in Everett slowly waned as he came more and more to admire Channing's thought and style.[8]

In May 1823 the Emerson family moved from Federal Street in Boston to a section of Roxbury called Canterbury. They lived in a little house in a rural lane that later became Walnut Avenue near Blue Hill Avenue. This part of Roxbury was at the time still countryside, "a picturesque wilderness of savin, barberry bush, catbrier, sumach, and rugged masses of pudding stone." The house was close enough to Boston for Emerson to walk there yet wild enough so that he sometimes took an old gun for hunting when he went out rambling in the fields and woods. In August he took a walking trip to the Connecticut valley, climbed Mt. Holyoke, and attended Amherst College's commencement. He took along Bacon's *Essays* for reading, and he visited a local lead mine. The miner had worked twelve years digging 975 feet. He spent all his time alone in this "damp and silent tomb." He told Emerson it was "excellent for meditation, and that he saw no goblins."[9]

Emerson's own mood this fall was gloomy. With the sad hopelessness of age twenty, he complained that "the dreams of my childhood are all fading away and giving place to some very sober and very disgusting views of a quiet mediocrity of talents and condition." With melancholy elegance he noted how "we bury in an undefined procrastination all our obligations." He was drifting and was fearful that life was passing him by. He recorded the bottom of this self-accusing mood in his journal: "You will sleep out life in this desperate reverie—the purposes for which you live unsought, unfound."[10]

William, by contrast, was going to Germany to study. Edward Everett, George Bancroft, and George Ticknor had all come back from Göttingen full of the latest German scholarship and criticism. By early October 1823 letters of recommendation were gathered together and on December 5, 1823, William departed to study theology at Göttingen.

9. The Paradise of Dictionaries and Critics

As William was preparing to leave for Germany, Waldo was becoming more and more interested in the ideas and example of William Ellery Channing. Channing, a Boston minister and the greatest of the founding figures of American Unitarianism, was at the height of his powers. In 1819 he had delivered a sermon in Baltimore called "Unitarian Christianity" which was at once recognized as the defining scripture of the new movement, institutionalized as a separate denomination in 1825. Channing's Baltimore sermon asserted a belief in one and only one God. He objected to the doctrine of the Trinity as "subverting the unity of God." According to Channing, Unitarians believed in "Jesus Christ as a being distinct from and inferior to God." They also believed in the "parental character" of God and in this world as a place not of penance and mourning but of education. Unitarians broke sharply with Calvinism, were opposed to emotional excesses in religion, and founded their faith on a belief in that moral sense that Scottish Common Sense said could be found in all persons. Unitarianism looked on itself as the true reformation come at last. Channing himself possessed both moral force and intellectual energy. He was an accomplished and effective speaker, and he ended "Unitarian Christianity" with a call for revolution: "Our earnest prayer to God is, that he will overturn, and overturn, and overturn the strong-holds of spiritual usurpation."[1]

The strength of the Unitarian movement lay partly in its intellectual emphasis on the moral teachings of Jesus, partly in its modernizing of deism to shape a religion that embraced modern science, and partly in its impassioned rejection of key elements of Calvin. In 1820, when Emerson was a junior at Harvard, Channing wrote "The Moral Argument against Calvinism," an angry, ringing call to arms against Calvinism's roots in fear and terror. Channing rehabilitated fallen natural man. "It is an important truth," Channing says, "that the ultimate reliance of a human being must be on his own mind." Our moral sense might not be as clear and as uniform as we would like, Channing argued, but if we cannot trust our own moral sense, then God can be totally malignant. Channing delivers the high point and conclusion of the argument with the offended anger of an Ivan Karamazov. "If God's justice and goodness are consistent with those operations and modes of government [eternal damnation, hellfire, vengeance] which Calvinism ascribes to him, *of what use* is our belief in these perfections?" Channing asks. "If it consist with divine rectitude to consign to everlasting misery beings who have come guilty and impotent from his hand, we beg to know what interest we have in this rectitude, what pledge of good it contains, or what evil can be imagined which may not be its natural result?"[2]

On March 14, 1821, just a few months before Emerson graduated from college, he heard Channing give the lecture "Evidences of Revealed Religion," which made a profound impression. Emerson used the talk as a sort of standard or touchstone for years. Channing was forty-one now, about twice Emerson's age. Like Everett, he represented to Emerson the best of the generation immediately before his. In this vigorous talk Channing took up Hume's argument about our being unable to prove cause and effect, and Channing helps us see why the argument was so momentous. Channing speaks for the other side, of course. "All the evidences of Christianity may be traced to this great principle—that every effect must have an adequate cause," Channing says, and, he goes on, "We claim for our religion a divine original because no adequate cause for it can be found in the powers or passions of human nature, or in the circumstances under which it appeared."[3]

Channing was quite content to say that the Bible was a book like any other, subject to interpretation like any other, but the result of his own extensive biblical studies had been to persuade him that the Bible was thoroughly trustworthy. He observed that the Gospels give a perfectly consistent and unified view of Christ's character and that the Epistles show precisely "the very state of mind which must have been generated by the peculiar conditions of the first propagation of the religion." In all crucial matters then, the Gospels and the Epistles completely fulfilled their function, which was to explain the rise, nature, and early spread of Christ's message. Channing regards the Bible as an authentic account, one that is essentially consistent and to be trusted as the exclusive source of our ideas of Christianity. In October of 1823, just as William was preparing to leave for Germany, Emerson heard Channing deliver another sermon on the reliability of biblical revelation. When the Emerson family asked his opinion on the matter, Channing counseled William against going to Germany to study theology. Germany might be well enough for the study of history, well enough for a George Bancroft, but it would not do for theology.

Channing was fearful of the effect of the vigorous new German historical criticism of the Bible because it was mostly negative and destructive. Year after year, scholar after scholar showed how this or that portion of the Bible was open to charges of myth, miracle, magic, folklore, superstition, self-contradiction and inconsistency. Channing's own beliefs had been formed before he became aware of the powerful questionings of German biblical research. As a result, Channing's faith remained intact, but it was deprived of the insights of the equally powerful counterattack, the romantic rebirth of Christianity in the early nineteenth century, which also had its sources in Germany, in the work of Kant, Herder, and Schleiermacher.

William Emerson sailed for Europe on December 5, 1823, on the brig *Ocean*. Much of what he had to report from Germany was discouraging. Pulpit eloquence of the kind Waldo found so impressive and important seemed not to exist in Germany. The university at Göttingen was huge. With fifteen hundred students, it was five times the size of Harvard. William wrote home that he had no desire to import a German university. The sheer size of the crowd of students was "an obstacle to their improvement," he thought. The students were rowdy; they drank, fought duels incessantly, and had virtually no contact with the professors. The theology students were the worst. They drank more, fought more, and had less self-respect, William reported. Despite all this, William worked up his German and in May 1824 went to hear the first of a series of lectures on the first three Evangelists by J. G. Eichhorn.[4]

Johann Gottfried Eichhorn (1752–1827), the "father of modern Old Testament criticism," was in 1824 nearing the end of his long and distinguished career. With formidable scholarly inclusiveness, including patient systematic consideration of all opposing evidence and viewpoints, Eichhorn effectively converted the central text of the Jewish and Christian tradition to a more or less unreliable set of stories, myths, and legends, mixed with historical events in a way that made the resulting narrative no more reliable than, say, Herodotus. (To be sure, it is also no less reliable than Herodotus.) With steady, good-natured intelligence, Eichhorn studied the Bible as one would study any other text, checking for sources and analogs, alert to internal inconsistencies and contradictions, borrowings, and scribal errors. He looked for changes of diction, imagery, or rhetoric that might signal changes of authorship. He and his many colleagues and students also checked the Bible against other evidence, such as that of Josephus or that of archaeology. Eichhorn and his disciples insisted that the Bible had been written by human beings, as had all other books, and they argued, in modern terms, that the Bible should not be privileged above other books but must be open to interpretation by the same scholarly and critical methods used elsewhere. Eichhorn produced the monumental *Einleitung in das Alte Testament* in 1783; the work was his central achievement and he reissued it and revised it frequently until his death in 1827.[5]

A similar movement was afoot in Homeric criticism. As F. A. Wolf (1759–1824) argued that "Homer" was in reality a collection of different texts by different hands, so Eichhorn argued that "Moses," the supposed author of the Pentateuch (the first five books of the Bible), was actually several different authors writing at different times. Furthermore, Eichhorn was a rationalist, a child of the Enlightenment. He believed in science and in the orderly Newtonian view of the world, and he interpreted all miracles as misunderstood natural phenomena. When Moses' face shone on the mountain, it was not the radiance of God but the physical exertion of the climb showing in his face.[6]

Not all of these ideas were new. What Eichhorn did was to make views that had once been the province of sneerers and atheists intellectually respectable. He gave these ideas enormous scholarly support. Professor Eichhorn had an attractive manner. He was friendly and accessible and he was widely admired. By early August 1824, three months after meeting him, William had fallen under Eichhorn's spell. "My mind seems to have undergone a revolution which surprises me," he wrote to a friend, explaining, "I cannot avoid tracing much of this to the books and lectures of Eichhorn." He still planned to be a minister and he was still urging Waldo to come to Germany. Although the destructive side of the new critical spirit was decisive for him, William was at least aware that there was a constructive side as well. He recommended that Waldo read Eichhorn's critical but not his historical books, and he told his brother in a letter of August 1824 that he should read all of Herder. By March of 1825 William was also recommending Schleiermacher to his younger brother. Waldo followed both suggestions.[7]

In December 1823, when William had just sailed for Germany, Waldo was stuck in his unrewarding teaching without any clear plans for the future. His mood all fall had been low. He complained of the "nightmare" of "hideous inactivity" made all the worse because he felt a need for action. His journals are full of preacherly dispirited comments. He fretted that "we put up with time and chance because it costs too great an effort to subdue them to our wills," and he noted the "coldness and poverty of our views of heaven . . . the meagerness and hollow declamation of all uninspired descriptions of the same."[8]

But something about William's departure stirred Waldo. Instead of continuing to complain about his lot, about feeling left at home, provincial and superfluous, Emerson responded to William's good fortune by insisting—almost paradoxically—on his own. By late December 1823 his journal has, in addition to the Hamlet-like plaintiveness and Byronic sense of isolation, a new and extraordinary note of exultation. Like Ahab standing on the deck in the storm, Emerson takes on the universe: "Who is he that shall control me? Why may not I act and speak and write and think with entire freedom? What am I to the universe, or, the universe, what is it to me? Who hath forged the chains of wrong and right, of Opinion and Custom? And must I wear them?" Accompanying his sense of detachment was a remarkable surge of power, a wonderful feeling of strength and liberation. "I am solitary in the vast society of beings," he wrote. "I see the world, human, brute, and inanimate nature,—I am in the midst of them, but not of them; I hear the song of the storm . . . I see cities and nations and witness passions . . . but I partake it not . . . I disclaim them all."[9]

The outburst is not so much isolation as defiance, a redefining of what is center and what periphery. It reminds one of Thoreau's hawk, which was not lonely but made everything lonely beneath it. It is a feeling of absolute and unquestioned self-validation, an extraordinary self-assertion, a wild romantic cogito that answers Hume not by logical argument but by felt experience. No matter what else existed, Emerson knew *he* existed: "I say to the universe, Mighty One! thou art not my mother. Return to chaos if thou wilt. I shall still exist. I live. If I owe my being, it is to a destiny greater than thine. Star by star, world by world, system by system shall be crushed,—but I shall live."[10]

10. Mme. de Staël and the Other Germany. Divinity Studies

THE IMAGE OF GERMANY THAT FILTERED BACK TO EMERSON from Göttingen was bookish and learned. In a letter to William Waldo flippantly called it the "paradise of dictionaries and critics." At the same time Emerson had another and quite different view of Germany, picked up from his reading of Mme. de Staël's celebrated book *Germany* (1813). His acquaintance with her work went back several years, for she was a favorite writer of Aunt Mary's. Anne Louise Germaine Necker, baronne de Staël Holstein, had made her way in French intellectual circles by her wit and intelligence and by her force of character, in which she was said to rival Napoleon. The author of two novels, *Corinne* and *Delphine,* books on Rousseau and the French Revolution, and the *Influence of the Passions* as well as her masterpiece, *Germany,* she was a leading intellectual in revolutionary and postrevolutionary France. Napoleon was sufficiently afraid of her to forbid her to live within forty leagues of Paris.

Mary Moody Emerson could sympathize with de Staël for a number of reasons. De Staël was a self-reliant, heroic woman of letters (as was the heroine of *Corinne*), de Staël had come from a strict Calvinist background, which she converted into a passionate interest in the power of religious feelings. She wrote the last three chapters of *Germany* in praise of enthusiasm, which she considered the indispensable foundation of all worthwhile thinking and acting.

Mme. de Staël died at the height of her fame in 1817, the year Emerson entered college. She was talked about, translated, reviewed, and reprinted. She was considered "the most powerful writer that her country has produced since the time of Voltaire and Rousseau." Emerson had taken out *Corinne* and *Germany* from the library in March 1822, but he seems not to have got around to reading them. He did read *Corinne* in October 1822. The novel is about a brilliant and gifted young woman, an improvisational artist and performer who has passionate friendships with men but who lives her own independent life. In January of 1823 Emerson read de Staël's *Considerations sur la Revolution.* In February he read her *Mémoires.* In May he made another try at *Germany,* in September he read her book on Rousseau, and in the early months of 1824 he was running down numbers of the *Edinburgh Review* that had long review articles about *Germany* and about her book on the French Revolution.[1]

Just as William was reporting back on academic Germany, Waldo was getting de Staël's wholly different—and much broader—perspective on that country. *Germany* is still one of the best books written on one country by a native of another. It had a huge effect on American intellectual life. George Ticknor went to Germany because of her praise of German learning. Edward Everett, Moses Stuart, James Marsh, George Bancroft, George Ripley, John S. Dwight, James F. Clarke, Theodore Parker, Margaret Fuller, and Henry Longfellow all were impelled by the book to the study of German language and literature. The book is attractive, lucid, and accessible. Its four parts cover Germany and the Germans, literature and the arts, philosophy, and religion. There is practically nothing in the book about biblical criticism aside from a paragraph that mentions Michaelis. But there is an excellent and still valuable introduction to Kant and his followers, and there is a great deal about the religious spirit as it flourished in Germany.

Religion for de Staël centers in "the feeling of the infinite," which she carefully separates from the infinite itself. The infinite, she explains, "consists in the absence of limits: but the feeling of the infinite, such as the imagination and the heart experience, is positive and creative." De Staël is interested, as is Mary Moody Emerson and her nephew and later William James, in religious *experience,* not in dogma, theology, history, or ritual. She valued enthusiasm because it "is excited by the sentiment of the infinite," and she gave this example:

> When we contemplate the starry heavens, where the sparks of light are universes like our own, where the brilliant dust of the milky way traces with its worlds a circle in the firmament, our thoughts are lost in the infinite, our hearts beat for the unknown, for the universe, and we feel that it is only on the other side of earthly experience that our real life will commence.[2]

Mme. de Staël also thought that religion was too important to be restricted to Sunday morning. "Religion is nothing," she says, "if it is not everything, if existence is not filled with it, if we do not incessantly maintain in the soul this belief in the invisible, this self-devotion, this elevation of desire." Her ideal was that the whole of life should be "naturally and without effort, an act of worship at every moment."[3]

She thought nothing great could be accomplished without enthusiasm. Enthusiasm is "the quality which really distinguishes the German nation," the quality responsible for its great achievements in literature, religion, and philosophy. Aunt Mary had heard this message and Emerson had already heard it when he began systematically reading Mme. de Staël. Emerson came back to de Staël over and over. She is one of his early constant reference points, one of the people he read and reread, turning the books a little each time like a kaleidoscope, so that a new pattern could emerge from the familiar elements. In time perhaps American life and literature could catch the sacred fire of enthusiasm. There was no reason it had to remain a German phenomenon. Enthusiasm was more strongly linked to its etymology than it was to any particular place. As de Staël pointed out, it means "god in us."[4]

December of 1823 and January of 1824 were rich and productive months for Emerson. In addition to de Staël, he was reading Dugald Stewart, Adam Smith's *Wealth of Nations,* Burke's *Reflections on the Revolution in France,* MacLauren's biography of Newton, and Leibniz's *Letters.* He was also reading Rousseau and Voltaire. He read Montesquieu's *Spirit of the Laws,* Neal's *History of Puritanism,* and Ellis's *Journal of the Late Embassy to China.* His notes speak of both Jonathan Edwards and Benjamin Franklin, especially Franklin, who seemed to him to have the influence of an institution all by himself. "He was a man of that singular force of mind," Emerson noted, "which seems designed to effect by individual influence what is ordinarily done by the slow and secret work of institutions and national growth." Emerson's own journals for this period show a new force of thought and a new gift for phrase. Thinking about how myth evolves, he noted (without specifying any one figure) how in Greece an "unprincipled bandit" became "a hero in the second generation, a giant in the third, and a god in the fourth." His themes now included friendship, self-trust, and history.[5]

He was spread thin and he knew it. "A man is made great by concentration of motive," he had written in March of 1823. Now, almost a year later, Emerson felt himself pulled in several directions at once. He felt overwhelmed by books. In February of 1824 he was uncharacteristically wishing he had been born in a much earlier age. "The patriarchs were never troubled with libraries of names and dates," he grumbled. "Life is wasted in the necessary preparation of finding what is the true way, and we die just as we enter it." He was torn between theology and literature, asking himself, "Shall I subdue my mind by discipline, or obey its native inclination?" Should he be a scholar, a learned parson, or should he try to write something original, out of his own personal materials? He was no longer dazzled by the lure of study. He rather liked Hobbes for saying "If I had read as much as other men I should be as ignorant."[6]

His mood in March was gloomy and petulant: "Shall I embroil my short life with a vain desire of perpetuating its memory when I am dead and gone in this dirty planet?" His reactions to some of his reading are comic in their extremes: "The Celestial Empire,—hang the Celestial Empire! I hate Pekin." But he knew where he needed to turn, and he wrote his aunt asking her—even while he apologized for the request—if she would give him her papers when she died. His twenty-first birthday was approaching. He felt compelled to do something, to take a step. By mid-April he seems to have made up his mind. "I am beginning my professional studies," he wrote solemnly, "and I deliberately dedicate my time, my talent, and my hopes to the Church." In a long, self-conscious journal entry Emerson took a Faustian survey of his talents, hopes, and ambitions. Although he decided for divinity, his choice was not altogether for religious reasons. He wanted to be first, to succeed, to thrive, to be eloquent, and to be known to be eloquent. At the same time, contradictorily, his self-assessment was that he had a weak reasoning faculty, that he was indolent and self-indulgent, that he lacked emotional warmth. He felt, as everyone who has been obliged to give up the wide world for the narrow berth of a single profession has felt, waves of weakness, shame, and humiliation. Sometimes he felt fraudulent and was afraid "they would find me out."[7]

Once Emerson made the decision to study divinity, he began to act on it and his mood lifted somewhat. He got from Channing a reading list of fourteen books, which included the Puritan Richard Baxter on the pastoral office and Henry Scougal's *Life of God in the Soul of Man* (1677). The list also included Jeremy Taylor's *Holy Living* and his *Holy Dying*, powerful seventeenth-century works by an Anglican high churchman. Also on the list were William Law's *Serious Call to a Devout and Holy Life* (1729)—the book John Wesley said sowed the seeds of Methodism—and writings by William Paley, Hannah More, James Beattie, and David Hartley. Channing's list is inspirational rather than professional. It includes many of the high points of English spirituality of the seventeenth and early eighteenth centuries, mixing Baxter's earnest Puritanism with Taylor's moving reflections occasioned by the death of his wife, who, like a rose, in Taylor's great simile, "fell into the portion of weeds and outworn faces." Scougal's book stayed with Emerson; many years later he was still recommending it to others. Religion, said Scougal, was not a matter of sect, external duties, or even "rapturous heats and ecstatic devotions." Religion was, he insisted, a "union of the soul with God, a real participation of the divine nature, the very image of God drawn upon the soul, or, in the Apostle's phrase, *it is Christ formed within us.*"[8]

Many of these works were not new to Emerson, who was not now in a very spiritual frame of mind anyway. In his eagerness to get on with his preparation and certification, he began working on other, more austere books, and he began the technical study of Scripture and scriptural commentary. In July it was Proverbs and Nathaniel Lardner's *History of the Apostles and Evangelists.* But even as he settled into the grind of textual detail, he kept alive his ambition to write one of "those books which collect and embody the wisdom of their times." As he worked over the book of Proverbs, Emerson was not content to be an annotator; he imagined himself its author. When he thought about the kind of book he himself hoped to write, he listed the Proverbs of Solomon and Montaigne's and Bacon's essays, saying, "I should like to add another volume to this valuable work."[9]

But the way ahead was far from clear and Emerson's own situation made him more frequently glum than elated. In late August Edward graduated with his incredible and discouraging preeminence. Charles seemed almost equally promising. William was in Germany, standing under the Niagara Falls of modern knowledge. Waldo, by contrast, was still teaching, living at home, doing divinity studies part-time, and longing, a trifle bitterly, for a life of literature. He wrote letter after letter to William, urging him repeatedly to say, plainly, what the advantages of German education were and whether he, Waldo, should come, no matter at what cost. There is a pleading tone and more than a touch of career panic in his letters.

But now, as indeed all through his twenties, Emerson's best advice, his greatest intellectual challenge, and the most original force bearing down on him and demanding attention was his aunt. Sometime this summer of 1824 he sent her a "letter to Plato," an epistle "on the manner in which a Greek would read the Christian books." He offers ironic condolences to Plato at his having been superseded by revelation. He attacks the church, especially the "depraved details of the theology under whose chains Calvin of Geneva bound Europe down." Christianity is, for the writer of this letter, a falling off from Plato and Socrates. His aunt's spirited and impassioned reply has never been printed. With superb scorn Mary Moody Emerson, writing as "Plato," sweeps past poor Waldo's critique, arguing in effect that his opinions of both Plato and Christianity are ludicrously low. She makes a quick, forceful defense of the *Republic*. Then, in a breathtaking passage that rivals the close of the *Republic* itself, she describes Plato's death, his enlightening in the afterlife, and his astonished perception of how close he had come to the great truths of Christianity. Aunt Mary's letter is an unacknowledged classic of Christian humanism. Her urgent, vivid, fable-making belief is irresistible. While Waldo was still measuring himself by his skeptical skill, by his capacity to doubt, his aunt, through her fable of Plato, was showing him the vastly superior power of belief.[10]

In November 1824 Emerson decided to give up teaching. He turned, with sharply increased seriousness, to the study of divinity. He saw Channing weekly and was evidently told that he might, by independent study, cut a year off the usual three-year divinity course offered at Harvard. He obtained a second reading list from Channing, this one a thirty-four-page comprehensive syllabus and book list. The character of this list is important both for Emerson's study of religion and for early Unitarianism. The entire syllabus is clearly dominated by Bible study. Channing lists editions, concordances, lexicons, historical and geographical aids, harmonies (books that undertake to show the essential congruence of all four Gospels, or of the Old and New Testaments), chronologies, and commentaries. Channing's course in divinity is devoted entirely to exhaustive study of the Bible in its original languages and with full scholarly apparatus. Since the Bible is the key document and source of Christianity, he argued, it alone should be studied by the Christian minister. Only when the Bible and its interpretation had been mastered could one look into theological controversy or church history. Faced with this mass of demanding professional reading, Emerson set up schedules for himself. He read Leland *On the Advantages and Necessity of Revelation,* he bought Thomas Newton's *Dissertation on the Prophecies,* he worked on LeClerc's *Letters Concerning Inspiration,* and he studied with minute care the text of the prophets and the Epistles with the aid of a Bible he carefully interleaved with blank pages for notes.[11]

But Emerson did not or could not give himself entirely to this sort of committed, focused, professional study, at least not yet. In December his daily work plan shows that he was simultaneously pursuing three different fields in addition to theology. He was continuing his study of Greece by reading Mitford's huge *History of Greece,* he was working on "eloquence" by reading every day in Cicero or Edward Everett, and he spent some time each day on literature, meaning Shakespeare, Milton, Johnson, Pope, and Montaigne. He still felt pinched by poverty. He was increasingly attracted to Channing, who was now replacing Everett as his ideal. Though he admired Channing's sermons and his intellectual breadth, he shrank from the years of Bible study that he now saw underpinning Channing's work. He still felt strongly about Calvinism, sounding at times like the First Blast of the Trumpet of Reason against the Demon of Geneva. He was revolted, he said, by the "double deity, gross Gothic offspring" of the Genevan school.

At the end of December 1824 Emerson took a further step toward the ministry. He closed the girls school and plunged yet deeper into preparation for divinity school. He worked along in Griesbach's Greek *New Testament* and in Rosenmüller's *Commentary.* He worked on Humphrey Prideaux's *The Old and New Testament Connected in the History of the Jews* and on MacKnight's *Harmony of the Four Gospels.* He read Buckminster's *Sermons,* works by West and Butler, and he took careful notes on Connop Thirlwall's monograph-length introduction to Schleiermacher's *A Critical Essay on the Gospel of St. Luke.* This last volume was a brand-new book, just out in 1825, and not on either of Channing's lists. Emerson's notes show that while he was pursuing divinity in New England, under Channing's approval, he also kept one eye open on the new German work.[12]

Even with all this reading for divinity, Emerson made time for literature. He projected an essay on the evils of imagination; he read Gibbon and Rousseau. The strain of all this work began to show in his writing. Images of a slumbering volcano occur and he struggled with the heavy weight of the past. Aunt Mary reminded him how his ancestors had been clergymen for four generations. Now that both William and Edward had jumped ship and gone into the law, the continuation of the tradition rested squarely on Emerson. "But the dead sleep in their moonless night," he told himself. "My business is with the living." "The present moment is in your power," he reminded himself, "but the past is inalterable, the future is inscrutable."[13]

In February 1825 Emerson left Roxbury, moved to Cambridge, registered for divinity school, and took a room—number 10 Divinity Hall. He wrote his aunt a strong letter denouncing myth in ultrarationalist terms. He spoke of "frivolous mythology," "mythological flummery," and "gross superstition." Though this is a good critical, demythologizing approach, it is also a skeptical, rational, Enlightenment approach, hardly what one would associate with a life of faith. Within a month of his taking up residence at the divinity school, Emerson's eyes failed, making further study impossible.[14]

Divinity

11. Pray without Ceasing

THE EYE DISEASE THAT STRUCK EMERSON IN EARLY 1825 WAS almost certainly uveitis, a rheumatic inflammation of the eye that gave the sufferer headaches and was often linked with rheumatism. The underlying cause was probably tuberculosis, which was pandemic at the time. Half the adults in Boston had it; one third of all deaths were from it. Over the next nine months Emerson underwent two operations in which his cornea was punctured with a cataract knife. By September 1825 he was well enough to teach school again, this time in rural Chelmsford, north of Concord. In November he could do a little reading in Plato, but he did not take up his journals again until January 1826.[1]

Stress also probably helped bring on the episode. Not only was Emerson working feverishly at his technical theological studies, he was teaching and struggling again with fundamental doubts. His eyes had failed him in the middle of an essay he was writing about the centerpiece of Unitarian theology, an essay called "The Unity of God." Emerson begins with Plato, whose "whole philosophy involves the idea of the divine unity." But he is soon wrestling with Hume again. Emerson had realized for some time now that any intellectually defensible theism would have to meet Hume's skeptical objections. He had become so steeped in the study of Hume that his aunt later told him she was afraid he had become "so imbued with his manner of thinking that you cannot shake him off."[2]

Emerson was now confronting head-on the famous objection attributed to Epicurus and central to Hume, the objection that opens the way for the Manichaean argument that there must be two first principles, not one. Assume there is a God, says Epicurus: "Is he willing to prevent evil but not able? Then is he impotent. Is he able but not willing? Then is he malevolent." Emerson's skeptical questioning was vigorous and profound. He was already troubled by Hume's denial of the link between cause and effect, a denial that opens the way to Baron Holbach's brutally indiscriminate skepticism in which there is no creator and no creation. The universe, says Holbach, consists of matter and motion, both of which have always existed.

Emerson also knew the brilliantly clever arguments of Cicero, whose *De natura deorum* underlies and informs Hume's more famous but not more cogent *Dialogues on Natural Religion*.[3]

The question, says Cicero, is not whether the gods exist. Let us concede that they do, if only for the sake of argument.

> But the crux and centre of the argument is the question whether the gods do nothing, care for nothing, and take their ease detached from all concern with the care and government of the world, or whether on the contrary all things have been created and formed by them from the dawn of time, and will be ruled by them to all eternity.

In other words, the question is not whether the gods exist but whether they intervene in our affairs. Emerson was unable to solve either this or the Manichaean proposition that unless one posits an evil deity as well as a good one, one must somehow accept the paradox "that evil may arise from the fountain of all good." With that phrase Emerson stopped writing. Skepticism could go no further. At this point his uveitis set in and he was forced to abandon his studies.[4]

In an effort to find rest and relaxation, Emerson went out to his uncle Ladd's farm in Newton to try, as he said, "the experiment of hard work for the benefit of health." He worked in the fields with the laborers, one of whom was a Methodist named Tarbox. As Emerson later recalled, Tarbox "said to me that men were always praying, and that all prayers were granted. I meditated much on this saying, and wrote my first sermon therefrom." The conclusion Emerson drew from this assertion was that "we must beware then, what we ask." This insight, delivered from the fields by the uneducated to the unenlightened, is in striking contrast to Emerson's learned and abstruse toil in the field of theology in Cambridge. It is an insight common among religious people; it is the same insight as de Staël's remark that the whole of life should be one continuous act of worship, but it is clear that Emerson first felt its force for real life from the laborer Tarbox, whose first name we no longer know but whom Emerson later placed at the head of a list of his special benefactors.[5]

In October 1825 William returned from Germany. His faith had been shaken by his studies, and he had confessed as much to Goethe when he went to meet the great poet. Goethe had encouraged him to persevere in his ministerial plans, saying his private beliefs were no business of his parishioners. But a terrible storm had come up at sea while William was on his way home and for a while it looked as if the ship would go to the bottom. On deck, in a "gale that was bending the masts," William felt himself to be a figure in a biblical drama. "I was obliged to look nearly at eternity," he wrote his aunt. He realized, he said, that he could neither live nor die content with such an insincere arrangement as Goethe had proposed. The ship weathered the storm. William arrived home and promptly told his brother he was renouncing the ministry and taking up the study of law. Edward's health was now failing, and Edward waited only long enough to see William home before he broke off his own law studies and set off for southern Europe in search of health. Aunt Mary's response to these setbacks was to advise Waldo to prepare to preach *at once,* whether he had the full use of his eyes or not, with or without his degree. In crisis after crisis, whether of events or convictions, it was Mary Moody Emerson's hand on the tiller that got Emerson through. He fought more with his aunt than did his brothers, but he trusted her, at bottom, much more than they did.[6]

As his sight returned, Emerson used it not for the dry and interminable biblical studies syllabus but for reading that could illuminate him, as though sight was too valuable to be spent on anything other than insight. In November 1825 he was reading Plato. In December, while his eyes were still recovering and while he was seriously lame from a bad attack of rheumatism in his hip, he read Plutarch's *Moralia* and wrote William about the family copy of a volume of Montaigne.[7]

Emerson's interest in Plato would become a major preoccupation. Plato was the single most important source of Emerson's lifelong conviction that ideas are real because they are the forms and laws that underlie, precede, and explain appearances. Emerson found Plato the way Schliemann found Troy. Over a period of many years, Emerson dug down through successive layers of translation, commentary, and editorial arrangement until he came to the real thing. Emerson could read Greek; he was familiar with the Platonic texts, but he preferred to work with translations. His general understanding of Plato evolved through at least seven discernible stages.

Emerson's first Plato is the early eighteenth-century Plato of André Dacier and Nicholas Souverain, who treat Plato as a proto-Christian whose works, while not exactly revelation, nevertheless teach all the important doctrines of Christianity. His second Plato was that of Ralph Cudworth, Henry More, and the Cambridge Platonists, who aimed to reconcile faith and reason. They also had a mystical streak and a strong belief in the inner light of immediate religious experience. Benjamin Whichcote, the founder of the Cambridge Platonist movement, liked to quote Proverbs 20: "The spirit of man is the candle of the Lord." Emerson's third Plato was that of Moses Mendelssohn, the great eighteenth-century spiritual leader of German Jewry whose *Phaedon* was a rewrite of Plato's *Phaedo* in the light of modern, Leibnizian thought.

Emerson's fourth Plato was that of Thomas Taylor and Floyer Sydenham, who provided the first complete Plato in English but whose Plato is essentially that of Proclus and other Neoplatonists. Taylor's Plato is a neo-Pythagorean, a pagan who offers a proud alternative conception of the divine, one that is philosophically congruent with Christianity but theologically, mythologically, and ecclesiastically quite different. The fifth version of Plato Emerson read was that of Victor Cousin, whose Plato was a great eclectic. The sixth was the Plato of Schleiermacher, who was the first of Plato's modern translators to set out in search of Plato's own philosophy. Schleiermacher worked from a strict and disciplined examination of Plato's own texts—and only his own texts. Schleiermacher is the founder of the modern tradition in Plato translation which regards Plato as primary and foundational, not a secondary carrier of Christian or neo-Pythagorean ideas. Emerson's seventh Plato is the Bohn Library edition of 1848–1854, an English translation of Stallbaum's text which led Emerson to write a supplement to his Plato essay in *Representative Men*.[8]

Emerson read volume 1 of Dacier's Plato sometime toward the end of college. In December of 1823 he was interested in the *Meno*. In May of 1834 he wrote the "Letter to Plato" to which his aunt wrote her imaginative reply. Soon after this Emerson read the *Republic*, the book Rousseau called "the finest treatise on education ever written." In March of 1825, as his eyes were failing, he was vigorously writing about Plato from Dacier's point of view. Plato's whole philosophy, he wrote, "invokes the idea of the divine unity." Emerson finds Plato's testimony consistent with the Mosaic history. One of Dacier's points was that Plato comes historically right after the last of the Hebrew prophets, as though Plato were indeed the next in succession. Emerson also noted that "what is called polytheism in Plato . . . is a polytheism perfectly consistent with a common opinion among Christians which imparts a portion of divine power to Angels."[9]

Plutarch and Montaigne were, like Plato, familiar names for Emerson in 1825. He had done at least some reading in both, and when he framed his own ambition to write something that would be primary, original, personal, and yet valuable, it was Plutarch and Montaigne (and to a lesser extent

Bacon) he was thinking of. Emerson reread books; he repeatedly went back to certain authors. He withdrew some books again and again from the library without getting around to them. It is therefore sometimes hard to tell exactly when a given book really made an impact on him.

Coleridge notes that there are four kinds of readers: the hourglass, the sponge, the jelly bag, and the Golconda. In the first everything that runs in runs right out again. The sponge gives out all it took in, only a little dirtier. The jelly bag keeps only the refuse. The Golconda runs everything through a sieve and keeps only the diamonds. Emerson was not a systematic reader, but he had a genius for skimming and a comprehensive system for taking notes. Most of the time he was the pure Golconda, what miners call a high-grader, working his way rapidly through vast mines of material and pocketing the richest bits. He read rapidly, looking for what he could use. Certain books, among them Plutarch and Montaigne, were particularly rich for him and could bear endless rereading. In Plutarch he admired the Stoic biographical approach to problems of the conduct of life in the *Lives* and the lively curiosity and the habit of making his points through example and anecdote in the *Moralia,* a multivolume, badly titled work that is an early example of the essay and deserves to be remembered as Plutarch's "Essays."[10]

Late in December of 1825 Emerson left his school in Chelmsford and moved back to Roxbury, where he reopened brother Edward's school in January 1826. He went back to his journals, writing on compensation, on history, and on the essential solitariness of each individual. In February 1826 he took up his theological studies again; a month later he gave up the Roxbury school. He was suffering from extreme lameness. The timing of Emerson's bouts of illness has suggested that his problems may have been psychosomatic, that he may have been blinded by rationalism and crippled by doubt, but it seems more likely that both his eyes and his hip were suffering tuberculosis-related attacks. The stress of study made matters worse and may even have triggered the attacks, but Emerson's inner life was now moving away from, not toward, pervasive doubt. His illness depressed him. He complained in March that "my years are passing away." This almost despairing mood of self-accusation was never to leave him entirely. Emerson was haunted for most of his life by the sense that the days were slipping past him, one by one, in an irrevocable procession. He seldom felt he had made the fullest possible use of a day. He recorded the thought over and over, sometimes in verse, sometimes in prose. His 1826 version went

"My days roll by me like a train of dreams / A host of joyless undistinguished forms."[11]

One of these spring days of 1826 was put to splendid use when Emerson discovered Montaigne. Prevented by his eyes from pursuing his austere and impersonal studies at Harvard, Emerson found in Montaigne not just another of those "studies that end in new studies and do not tend to lessen the price of bread" but a window on life itself and a pattern for a kind of writing that was sharply different from the biblical commentary that dominated divinity school. "Reader, thou hast here an honest book," Montaigne begins, and he goes on to explain. "I desire therein to be viewed as I appear in mine own genuine, simple and ordinary manner, without study or artifice; for it is myself I paint." The self that Montaigne put forward was energetic, gritty, physically immediate, and a Stoic. He cared neither for theory nor abstraction. His essays, like those he admired of Plutarch and Pliny, consist almost entirely of example and anecdote. "Cut these words and they bleed," says the admiring later Emerson about the Montaigne who wrote a good deal about the body, about eating and drinking, and about pain and blood itself. Of one of Alexander the Great's victims Montaigne wrote that Alexander "commanded his heels to be bored through causing him alive, to be dragged, mangled and dismembered at a cart's tail."[12]

Emerson's long fascination with Montaigne provided him with another way to look at one of the major problems that confronted him. Montaigne was a skeptic, but of a very different sort from Hume, Cicero, or Bolingbroke. Hume especially had come to seem more destructive than helpful. Emerson approvingly copied down Pierre Bayle's comment that philosophy is a corrosive, "proper at first to confront error, but if she be not stopped there, she attacks truth itself." Montaigne was not the kind of skeptic who believed in nothing. Indeed, his longest essay, and one Emerson was now reading, is his "Apology for Raimonde de Sebonde," a lively narrative essay that defends both Christianity and natural theology while taking pains to describe the proud human race as only one part of a vast natural order, all of which is entitled to our awe and wonder. As he would later say in his essay on Montaigne in *Representative Men*, Emerson came to see in Montaigne a position between the pure idealist and the pure sensualist. "The abstractionist and the materialist, thus mutually exasperating each other, and the scoffer expressing the worst of materialism, there arises a third party to occupy the middle ground."[13]

Montaigne claims this ground in every sentence. One hears his distinctive voice throughout his writing, and it is as different as can be imagined from the pulpit style with which Emerson was currently struggling. Montaigne can talk about ideas and about the "close, luscious, devouring, viscid, melting kisses of youthful ardor." He does not overvalue books. "If I am a man of some reading, I am a man of no retention," he says, encouragingly, adding, "I do not bite my nails about the difficulties I meet with in my reading . . . I do nothing without gaiety . . . My sight is confounded and dissipated with poring." Montaigne had an extraordinary and lasting effect on Emerson, and the impact came at a time when a number of powerful books were making claims on his attention. He read Montaigne in a state of high empathetic excitement. "It seemed to me as if I had written the book myself in some former life," he recalled later. "No book before or since was ever so much to me as that." It would be many years before Montaigne's style would have its full effect on Emerson's. But now, in early 1826, Montaigne seems to have pointed the way out of the Humean slough of nihilism and scoffing.[14]

In June Emerson wrote his first sermon, "Pray without Ceasing." In some sense, Emerson says, every secret wish and every desire of the mind is a prayer. He also knew by now—and was able to say—that the past "except as a means of wisdom is, in the nature of things, actually nothing" and that "all that can be done for you is nothing to what you can do for yourself." Emerson's mature style is not yet formed, but certain ideas and attitudes familiar in his later work are beginning to coalesce.

Sick he might be, but this summer of 1826 was a turning point, a time of affirmation, when the pendulum of doubt had swung as far as it could go and was beginning to swing back. In a letter to his aunt on June 15, 1826, Emerson recorded with Cartesian simplicity his rock-bottom belief and starting point: "I know that I exist, and that a part of me, as essential as memory or reason, is a desire that another being exist." This is a basic—a foundational—proposition, similar to those Channing and Schleiermacher posit as the basis for a modern Christianity. "The principle in human nature from which religion springs," says Channing, "is the desire to establish relations with a being more perfect than itself." Schleiermacher, in the words of his American admirer and translator George Ripley, held that "religion . . . in its primitive elements, is neither knowledge nor action, but a sense of our dependence on God, and of our need of redemption from sin."[15]

In August 1826 came the public funeral for John Adams and Thomas Jefferson. Emerson heard Webster speak and was impressed. Later that month came Charles's triumphant graduation, complete with his second Bowdoin Prize. But the event that affected Emerson most this fall, capping a half year of new ideas, new hope, and new belief, was his reading of Sampson Reed's just published *Observations on the Growth of the Mind*. Emerson had been struck by Reed's "Oration on Genius" five years earlier. Now, Reed's little ninety-one-page book came to Emerson at a decisive moment. He thought it "one of the best books I ever saw" and was so overwhelmed by it that he told William rather extravagantly that it was "the best thing since Plato of Plato's kind."[16]

Reed was like Emerson in many ways. He was the son of a minister (of Bridgewater, Massachusetts); he had gone to Harvard, then to Harvard Divinity School to prepare for the ministry. He had not finished the course and was unable to find a position as minister. He tried teaching, tried to become a physician, and finally became a pharmacist, then a pharmaceutical wholesaler. Reed's serious interest continued to be in modern religion. He had become interested in Swedenborg in college and was for years the chief spokesperson for Swedenborgianism in Boston. His 1826 *Observations on the Growth of the Mind* is a book of the same size and ambition as Emerson's 1836 *Nature*. It is Reed's personal statement of belief, and it contains an astonishing group of ideas that over the years ahead were to become crucial parts of Emerson's fundamental view of life.

Reed announces a new era in the human mind's long history of rising to full consciousness. It is a new age precisely because of the new interest in mind and the need for an adequate philosophy of mind. In what is perhaps the most original aspect of the book, Reed attacks our conventional chronological sense of time, saying that time does not itself produce change; our idea of time "is itself the effect of changes." Time, like space, is part of the permanent context of life. Time does not pass, we pass: "Time, then, is nothing real so far as it exists in our own minds." The effect of this dechronologizing of time is to put all persons and eras on the same plane, that of personal, present time. The result is a liberation from the concept of chronological history, which was and is a widely accepted convention. Chronology was also the dominant, controlling feature of the divinity school curriculum Emerson was working on at the time. Enormous effort went into the reconciliation of sacred and secular accounts of events so that all events would fit into a single, trustworthy chronology. Reed freed Emerson from

Prideaux's *Connections* and Isaac Newton's *Chronology of the Ancient Kingdoms Amended* and from the minutely detailed historical approach to both Old and New Testament study.[17]

Reed also had, for Emerson, an attractive emphasis on the active—as opposed to the passive—powers of the mind, especially memory and affection. His book actively insists that "the natural sciences are the basis of all useful knowledge." Reed calls for a religion that sees God in everything. He also argues, in what is simultaneously a theory of language, a theory of symbolism, and a metaphysic, that there is a language of things as well as a language of words. As for criticism and interpretation, Reed says there is "one law of criticism" and that is for the reader or critic "to approximate to that intellectual and moral condition in which the work originated." Emerson would maintain all his life that every piece of writing should be judged by the spirit that brought it forth. Reed believed more in process than in product. To make a child acquainted with poetry, he said, one should "call forth the power of poetry in himself."[18]

After his eye trouble this year, Emerson would never again be indifferent to eyes, sight, and vision. Metaphors of vision run all through his writing. Even here Reed was his teacher. "The understanding is the eye," Reed writes, "with simply the power of discovering the light; but reason is the eye whose powers have been enlarged by exercise and experience." The growth of a mind is for Reed an educational process, not a self-regarding self-development but growth in "active usefulness." *Observations on the Growth of the Mind* showed Emerson what could be hoped for; it was a powerful personal testament by a contemporary, a gospel of the present moment.[19]

Reed's effect on Emerson may be seen in a letter Emerson wrote to his aunt this fall in which he said that "it is wrong to regard ourselves so much in a historical light as we do, putting time between God and us." He goes on to say "that it were fitter to account every moment of the existence of the universe as a new creation, and all as a revelation proceeding each moment from the divinity to the mind of the observer." This new understanding of the relation of the present to time and history is the first of Emerson's great characteristic conceptions, and he never wholly lost sight of it from this time on. The idea informs both *Nature* in 1836 and the first of his published essays in 1841.[20]

In the fall of 1826 things were not going smoothly for the Emerson who still had to live in time. He was indeed approved—or, in the bureaucratic language of the Middlesex Minister's Association, "approbated"—to preach in October, and he did in fact preach his first sermon, "Pray without Ceasing," in his half-uncle Samuel Ripley's church in Waltham. But now to the problem with his eyes and his hip was added a painful "stricture" in the chest, almost certainly an attack of pleurisy. Emerson gave up teaching school again. "The summer is past, the harvest is ended, and we are not saved," he mourned in his journal, quoting Jeremiah. But he was able to read, and he plunged into a program not of biblical chronologies and commentaries but of the most exhilarating and bracing books he knew: de Staël on Germany, Plutarch, and Stewart, to which was now added Marcus Aurelius's *Meditations* and Coleridge's *Biographia Literaria*. He also made his first acquaintance with Taylor's Plato this November. With winter coming on and his health deteriorating, Emerson borrowed seventy dollars from Uncle Samuel Ripley and set out for a warmer climate. On November 24, 1826, he sailed from Boston in the *Clematis,* bound for Charleston, South Carolina.[21]

12. The Prince of Lipona

THE TRIP FROM BOSTON TO CHARLESTON IN THE 105-FOOT sailing ship *Clematis* took fourteen days. This was Emerson's first trip outside his native New England and it was full of wonders. He remarked on the power of the sea, and he brooded, like a young Henry Adams, on power itself. He marveled at how the "men of this age work and play between steam engines of tremendous force" and how the sailors "brave the incalculable forces of the storm." In Charleston there were a few old friends and acquaintances such as classmate Mellish Motte and Unitarian minister Samuel Gilman. Emerson was impressed by how much better southern manners were than northern. He made long journal entries on the formation of moral character and on whether there were any new discoveries in morals. He wrote William he was neither well nor sick but "luke-sick." Finding the latitude of Charleston still too cold, he headed farther south, taking ship on January 10 for St. Augustine.[1]

Florida was stranger than Charleston and made a deeper impression on Emerson. Florida had been ceded by Spain to the United States in 1819, organized as a territory in 1822, but would not become a state until 1845. Its own congressional delegate admitted in 1824 that Florida was not much more than a "tangled mass of vines and a labyrinth of undergrowth." John Randolph of Roanoke gave it as his opinion that "no man would immigrate into Florida—not even from hell itself."[2]

As his ship approached St. Augustine, Emerson said they "heard the roaring on the beach long before we saw land, and the sea was full of green twigs and feathers." Emerson had little to do in St. Augustine. He complained a good deal, but he grew fond of the place before he left. He even wrote verses praising the "little city of the deep" and its warm sun and simple hospitality. St. Augustine was the oldest continuous European settlement in North America. It had been a Spanish center for two and a half centuries when Emerson saw it with its old Spanish castle, its ancient city gates, narrow streets, walled gardens, central plaza and Catholic church, the whole town surrounded by a double row of yucca. St. Augustine was not at all like

Boston, and Emerson adapted himself to doing what the natives did. He was not writing sermons, or anything else, and since he did not play billiards, he found himself taking long walks. "I stroll on the sea beach," he wrote William, "and drive a green orange over the sand with a stick." Oranges were St. Augustine's main crop; 1.2 million were raised each year. Emerson felt, he said, like the barnacles in the harbor, which looked uncomfortable where they were but were unable to move.[3]

Emerson turned to poetry. When he returned from this trip, he began his first "Poetry Notebook" in order to record his St. Augustine poems. His tone is narrative and elegiac. He describes himself: "And I am here / On the green earth contemplating the moon." He wrote about exile: ". . . heavily / And all alone I walk the long sea shore / And find no joy." He wrote about the city itself: "I saw St. Mark's grim bastions, piles of stone / Planting their deep foundations in the sea / Which spoke to the eye of Spain." His mood was Byronic; he was Childe Harold in Florida. St. Augustine reminded him of the old Belgian city of Dort, the sunken city in the sea, where sailors "can yet descry many fathoms down below the level of the sea the broken spires, the ruins covered with sea grass." He felt his own mortality sharply. "Decay, decay is written on every leaf of the forest," he wrote. "Every wind that passes is loaded with a solemn sound. All things perish."[4]

The great event of Emerson's southern trip of 1826–1827 was his meeting with Achille Murat, a planter, nephew of Napoleon, and former crown prince of Naples. Murat and Emerson lived in the same house in St. Augustine; Emerson heard about Murat's plantation near Tallahassee, two hundred miles west of St. Augustine. Later they occupied the same cabin on a long, stormy ship passage from St. Augustine to Charleston. "I have connected myself by friendship," Emerson wrote, a little stiffly, "to a man who with as ardent a love of truth as that which animates me . . . is yet a consistent Atheist, and a disbeliever in the existence, and of course, in the immortality of the soul."[5]

Emerson was twenty-four, Murat twenty-six, when they met. Murat was five feet seven inches tall, handsome, with an oblong face, a Greek nose, and a full round forehead. His father, Marshall Joachim Murat, had been Napoleon's favorite cavalry general. His mother was Napoleon's youngest sister, Caroline. Marshall Murat had been made king of Naples, and though he had been ousted and executed after Waterloo, his son still called himself Prince Murat and called his plantation Lipona, anagram of Napoli. Murat had detested his uncle Napoleon. The great man—who had died just a few years earlier, in 1821—had pulled the boy Achille's ear one day and Achille had flared up, saying to Napoleon, "You are a villain, a wicked wicked villain." Napoleon had then cuffed the boy and stormed out of the room." Now after the execution of his father and the defeat of the Bonapartists everywhere, Achille was exiled from Europe and was fast becoming an American. He arrived in Florida in 1824 and went to work carving out a plantation. He owned slaves and had a child by one of them. He had eaten alligator steak, boiled owl, and roast crow. He showed Emerson a marble copy of a bust of his mother by Canova. His life was full of vivid contrasts. He loved physical activity; he was also an intellectual and he and Emerson spent a great deal of time talking together, especially on shipboard. Emerson thought Murat's mind surpassed his own "in the variety of its research." Emerson later included Murat on a short list of his major intellectual benefactors, and it seems likely that Murat's bold skepticism acted both to deepen Emerson's own skepticism and to stimulate him to rebuttal.[6]

When Emerson and Murat met, Achille was in the middle of writing a book about the United States. "I have travelled a good deal about the country," he wrote in his preface, "am settled in the woods, where I have seen a new nation spring up." Murat especially admired the "practical liberty of Americans" and the *principle* of American government, which is, he said, "government by the people themselves." He explained what he meant by saying, "Let it [the government] leave to each branch of power, to each opinion, to each party, and to each individual, the degree of power and moral weight which respectively belongs to them, and that will approach very nearly to liberty, if it be not the thing itself." Murat's Italian sympathies fitted in nicely with a southern point of view. Accustomed to thinking of how Rome was destroyed by barbarians from the north, Murat set down a largely unflattering picture of the North: "The Northern States are jealous of our slaves and our prosperity: we envy them nothing." Murat grimly noted that should the North ever force emancipation, then the "finest edifice raised by man, the American Confederation, would be broken up."[7]

Murat had already written his chapters on the general condition of the country, on political parties, and on new settlements before he met Emerson. His chapter on slavery was written after he had met Emerson but before he knew him really well. On this subject the two young men were far apart. Murat noted that while the general southern view was that slavery was necessary but an evil, he himself was inclined to regard it as a positive good. Slavery made it possible to employ great capital in agriculture in a new country and slavery made it possible for the planter to "cultivate his mind," making him thereby "one of the most perfect models of the human race." Before his trip south, Emerson had already entered his flat judgment against slavery, and in St. Augustine he became vividly aware of the "peculiar institution." He attended a meeting of the Bible Society one day in the government house while a slave auction was going on in the yard outside. The auction could be heard through the open windows. "One ear therefore heard the glad tidings of great joy," Emerson noted, "whilst the other was regaled with 'Going, gentlemen, going'!" "Almost without moving from one's seat," he added, "we could aid in sending the scriptures into Africa or bid for four children, without the mother, kidnapped from the same place."[8]

On March 30, 1827, Emerson began his trip back home, leaving St. Augustine aboard the sloop *William*. It was a terrible trip. At first they were becalmed. Then it stormed for many days. Then they ran out of food. At the height of the storm, Murat and Emerson lay in their bunks one above the other, talking incessantly. Shortly after this passage Emerson recorded his strong feelings of friendship for Murat. Murat acknowledged in a later letter that Emerson's ideas had affected him strongly and that he now thought his own position on religious matters stood only a fifty-fifty chance of being right. And in his chapter on religion, written four years later, Murat went out of his way to praise the "pure theists, enlightened and virtuous philosophers" of New England Unitarianism. He calls Channing "a genuine Plato" and concludes that Unitarianism "is likely to become the predominant sect among enlightened persons." It is a handsome acknowledgment.[9]

Murat in turn had a profound though quite different effect on Emerson. In the first place, Murat was as different a person from Emerson as can easily be imagined. He was a nobleman, a prince, an Italian, a relative of Napoleon, a comfortable atheist, a slave-owner, a man whose life consisted mostly of action and whose intellectual interests were almost entirely political. Literature is barely mentioned in Murat's book. Talking with Murat was an education in mostly unfamiliar territory. Emerson's own basic convictions did not change, but he was impressed that people so different could not only talk but become friends. Above all, Emerson was buoyed by a sense of his own intellectual adequacy to this occasion.

The southern trip had gone well for Emerson. His weight was up from 141 to 152 pounds; he was flirting with the possibility of being a poet, a novelist, or even a painter. He had seen a new part of the world, he had become fond of St. Augustine even while he felt exiled there, and he had confronted slavery. Murat had written how "the horrible and monstrous in theory becomes frequently perfectly tolerable in practice." Emerson had not found it so. On the return trip Emerson's ship had run into a storm, just as his brother William's had when William was returning from Germany. In contrast to William, Waldo was equal to the threat. In some obscure way the storm affirmed him. "Every moment makes me a more powerful being," he wrote to his aunt. He could hold his own, not only against Hume in the study but against Murat in real life. "There is a pleasure in the thought that the particular tone of my mind at this moment may be new in the universe," he wrote. While Murat taxed Emerson's powers of philosophical speculation, Murat's eye was dull and blind, Emerson thought, to that fundamental view of the world that sees God in everything, the view that an associate of Emerson's once said was not pantheism but hypertheism. Emerson weathered more than one storm in his lower bunk on the *William*. Confirmed and approbated now by trial in the outside world, he returned, reinvigorated, to the business of preaching and spreading the good news.[10]

As Emerson turned north again, back toward the church, he did not feel that he was returning to a world of calm, settled certainties. Murat saw the church being "carried away by the great current of opinion, literature, and modern philosophy, which nothing can resist." He foresaw that it would "certainly end by overthrowing the Christian religion." As Murat understood it, Unitarianism—which was antisuperstition—was one of the most powerful forces working to undermine traditional Christianity. Emerson also saw a crisis coming. He wrote his brother Edward on May 8 observing that whenever the average intellect of the clergy declines in the balance with the average intellect of the people, "the churches will be shut up and a new order of things begin." He was still trying to weigh his own future; he told Edward he had felt the balance beam trembling all through the past winter.[11]

13. The Balance Beam

DURING APRIL, MAY, AND EARLY JUNE 1827 EMERSON WORKED his way north, seeing friends and relations and delivering an occasional guest sermon. In Baltimore he saw Boston Unitarians Samuel Barrett and F. W. P. Greenwood. On the Baltimore steamer he met a Hicksite Quaker named Edward Stabler, a deeply impressive person who had developed a striking view of justice as compensation. Stabler gave a strong impression of apostolic self-assurance. And what Stabler said was so deeply in harmony with Emerson's already long-held ideas about compensation that Emerson never forgot his remarks and kept repeating them in later years. Stabler said: "If a man sacrificed his impurity, purity should be the price with which it would be paid; if a man gave up his hatred, he should be rewarded with love." Stabler's son said his father's "one great object was, to impress the minds of his hearers with the importance of examining things for themselves,—of attending to their own experience,—of reading over and over the leaves of their own lives."[1]

In Alexandria there were the Ladds, who were cousins on his mother's side. In Philadelphia there was much to see, including the studio of Thomas Sully and Benjamin West's painting of Christ healing the sick. There was also William Henry Furness, Emerson's boyhood friend, schoolmate, life-long friend, and comfortable old gossip. In New York he saw his brother William, who had just been giving lectures on Germany. Emerson himself was moving slowly on purpose, watching his health and strength. He certainly felt renewed and restored by his southern trip, but at the same time he was now, as almost always, haunted by a sense that time was passing. His characteristic image for this is a procession of days—individualized, personified—passing by like figures in a pageant. Eventually the image would form his best single poem, "Days," the fullest expression of his sense that he never seemed to be using his opportunities and his time as well as he might. This May he wrote in his journal:

My days run onward like the weaver's beam. They have no honour among men, they have no grandeur in the view of the invisible world.

It is as if a net of meanness were drawn round aspiring men thro'
which their eyes are kept on mighty objects but the subtle fence is
forever interposed.[2]

After arriving home in June Emerson wrote his brother William that he
was considering "total abdication of the profession on the score of ill
health." But the problem was more than bad health. There was a more
fundamental question of vocation, of whether to turn author or preacher.
Because of the example of Everett, Emerson sometimes thought he could
be both writer and minister, but as the days walked haughtily past him
the two roles seemed more and more to beckon in opposite directions.
The image that recurs in his letters and journals of this time is that of the
balance beam of an old-fashioned scale, inclining first one way, then the
other.[3]

When Emerson reached home in June and took a room in Divinity Hall
in Cambridge, the balance was tipping strongly toward the ministry. He was
asked to come and preach most of the summer at the First Church in Boston.
He set himself to writing sermons and preaching in his father's city, in his
father's church, in his father's faith. These sermons have many premonitions
of ideas and phrases in Emerson's later work, but their general tone is one
of trimming, toning down, reinterpretation, and adjustment. They mark
their author's essential acceptance of the institutions that had shaped him.
The sermons were delivered forcefully and to great admiration, but they are
distinguished by a mush of intellectual concession and plea bargaining and
in places by a simple retreat from spiritual issues. In a sermon on being a
Christian believer, Emerson said that "an immediate connexion and dependence upon God is too lofty a motive to sustain and console our virtue
in the daily warfare of the world." The rest of the sermon is on how "we
are virtuous and vicious as social beings." In the name of realism and
practicality, Emerson took on the great spiritual questions of Christianity
and gave modern, Unitarian, liberal answers. Preaching on compensation,
he claimed that in general justice is done—and on earth. On the importance
of suffering and the "house of mourning," he insisted that Christ is an
example of the sufferer, not our redeemer from suffering. He preached on
the usefulness of the Sabbath as a day of rest. He praised Christianity as
progressive because it had managed to throw off Calvinism, reject the idea
of this world as the "scaffold of divine vengeance," and abolish other
"austere macerating monkish observances." To the question "What is
man?" Emerson replied that the meaning of human life is individual

education. In a sermon asking "What is ignorance?" Emerson asserts that it is simply an appetite for knowledge that exists in order to be satisfied.[4]

In one sermon on showing piety at home, which was by far Emerson's most popular sermon—he gave it twenty-seven times—he comes closer to what will be one of his great subjects, arguing that "the main regard of religion must be to make us good at home," that Providence may have appointed our situation in life "but our virtue is in all cases determined by ourselves." Lest we think this easy, he adds, "Let anyone try to spend one hour a day without spot or blemish."[5]

Emerson's language in these sermons is on the whole profoundly conventional. He uses the long, periodic sentence of the late eighteenth century. Sentences routinely run to ten or fourteen lines of print and sometimes to as much as eighteen lines. There is very little edge to them, very little concreteness. They are full of Sunday morning objections raised only in order to be answered, earnest exhortations to long-understood thought and accepted behavior. He uses rhetorical questions with a numbing frequency; sometimes there are twenty in a half-hour sermon. His theology is modern, liberal, reminiscent of Channing—and in some cases Schleiermacher—but his stylistic model is still Edward Everett. In many instances, especially in matters of style, one cannot tell Waldo Emerson's sermons from those of his father. The reader quails before the repeated and ritualized intimacy of "And now, my friends, let me call your attention to . . ."[6]

Emerson knew in a general way what was wrong with his sermons. Like so many of his revealing statements, the explanation comes in a letter to Aunt Mary: "If men would avoid that general langauge and general manner in which they strive to hide all that is peculiar and would say only what was uppermost in their own minds after their own individual manner, every man would be interesting." Although the conventional form and accepted subjects for sermons worked against the personal tone and although the relation of shepherd to flock put him inescapably in a position of uneasy (because unearned) moral leadership, Emerson continued to work on his public speaking. During the second half of 1827 he traveled extensively in Massachusetts, preaching in Northampton, Deerfield, Greenfield, Lennox, Harvard, Waltham, Watertown, and New Bedford.[7]

Preaching and writing sermons did not occupy all his time. He continued to read in Montaigne, Plutarch, Plato, and Herder. Although at the moment he could not get much if any of the intellectual vigor and forcefulness of expression of these writers into his own productions, he kept reading them, thereby keeping great models in front of him, models that kept him from too quickly accepting his own current efforts as the best of which he might be capable.

He was also writing poetry. He had begun to admire Wordsworth and the Felicia Hemans of "The Lost Pleiade" ("And is there glory from the heavens departed? / O void unmark'd—thy sisters of the sky / Still hold their place on high"). His own verse had now outgrown its adolescent violence and hypertrophied emotion. When he returned north in 1827, he had started the first of his poetry notebooks in which he collected drafts and scraps. He was working on three different kinds of poems. One was romantic elegy, an example of which is his poem on St. Augustine: "There liest thou, little city of the deep . . . Farewell; and fair befall thee, gentle town." A second was the Wordsworthian personal narrative in blank verse, generally auto-biographical, about his feelings and growth in the midst of nature. He hoped, as he wrote, to have readers who, like himself, had

> . . . left his books, and vulgar cares
> And sallied forth across the freshened fields
> With all the heart of highborn cavalier
> In quest of forest glades hid from the sun,
> And dim enchantments that therein abide.

He wrote long poems about finding "the honored orchis—seldom seen / The low pyrola with a lilac's smell, / Or the small cinquefoil, the wild strawberry's friend." He wrote about the beach at St. Augustine and about his return to Concord ("Awed I behold once more / My old familiar haunts . . .").[8]

The third—and best—kind of poem Emerson was tinkering with was the short romantic lyric, in which, in accordance with his moods, he could express a wide range of feelings. In what are perhaps his best early lines, the feeling is of being bereft.

> Fast fast across the savage sea
> My little bark is blown
> Down in the ocean mournfully
> The stars sank one by one
> Jesu Maria pray for me
> My hope is well nigh gone.

But by the time of his return north in June hopelessness has turned into hope. The second stanza of the following would prove prophetic.

> This cup of life is not so shallow
>   That we have drained the best
> That all the wine at once we swallow
>   And lees make all the rest.
>
> Maids of as soft a bloom shall marry
>   As Hymen yet hath blessed
> And fairer forms are in the quarry
>   Than Phidias eer released.[9]

As the fall lengthened, the balance beam trembled. On one side was everything connected with the sermon: tradition, institutional approval, his father, his father's church, the urging of Aunt Mary, a steady salary, stability for himself and his family, a ready-made social position, respectability, Old Concord, Old Boston, the rhetoric of Everett, Buckminster, Channing, Sparks, and Tucker. On the other side of the scale was poetry and everything associated with poetry: originality, personal feeling, enthusiasm, his aunt's example (if not her advice), freedom to read, speculate, and write as he wished, the life-charged language of Montaigne, Plutarch, Plato, Herder, Sampson Reed, and Carlyle.

Not only did Emerson's thoughts about his profession swing back and forth, so did his moods and convictions. To Aunt Mary he wrote in June that his soul was "in a polite equilibrium" on the issue of immortality. He expected, he said, that the dissolution of the body would "have a wondrous effect on the opinion of all creedmongers." It would be "a glorious moment," he said, adding "and yet a young man does not wish it arrived." In August he wrote her that while he was very curious "to know what the scriptures do in very deed say about that exalted person who died on Calvary," he was unwilling to spend his life looking for the answer by "weighing phrases and hunting in dictionaries." In rejecting technical biblical scholarship, he articulated one of the first of the insights that never left him and that have come to seem so characteristic. "A portion of the truth," he told his aunt, "bright and sublime, lives in every moment in every mind."[10]

In November he was writing Aunt Mary about religious feeling, not about theology or churches or rhetoric. Here too one can see how the unresolved crisis of the still-balancing scales pushed him toward real inner growth. Emerson felt a powerful pull toward the enthusiasm of his aunt, of de Staël, and of the religious mystics, but this enthusiasm was firmly rejected by the reigning rationalism of Channing's Unitarianism. Many of the world's best men, he told her, were antienthusiasm, "cold and prudent Christians," such as Bacon, Locke, Butler, Johnson, Buckminster. "But the enthusiast admits or insists on the fact that the world is against him and appeals confidently to the received language of religion in every age, which has always expected the suffrage only of a minority." He knew that "the proper emotion is wonder," but he found it a continuing problem "in adjusting life betwixt reason and feeling." Out of this challenge was coming better poetry and even a more forceful prose, though not often evident in his sermons. "Facts become knowledge; events become discipline," he wrote in his journal in mid-December. The great fact of December, which came during a visit to preach in Concord, New Hampshire, was his meeting with Ellen Tucker.[11]

14. Ellen Tucker

ELLEN TUCKER WAS SIXTEEN WHEN SHE MET THE TWENTY-four-year-old Waldo Emerson on Christmas Day in 1827. Although we have only a lifeless miniature of her, we can see that she was full-figured and narrow-waisted, with a high forehead and dark plentiful hair that she wore up in a great shock of tight curls. Ellen had a long nose, full mouth, and dark, large eyes. She was by all accounts very beautiful, but it was her spirit more than her beauty that caught one's attention. She lived in the midst of a large family and her life was full of activity and gaiety. Her father, Bezaleel Tucker, the owner of a Boston rope factory, had died, and Ellen was now living in Concord, New Hampshire, with her mother, Margaret, and her stepfather, Colonel William A. Kent. She loved the outdoors. Her letters show that she paid attention to nature. She speaks of the flowering fruit trees "in the glory of full blossom—without one single leaf of green." Her family kept horses; she herself was fond of riding. She surrounded herself with animals. She had a spaniel named Byron, a lamb, a canary, white mice, and squirrels.[1]

A year after they met, Waldo and Ellen became engaged. His letters to her are lost, but hers are warm, open, utterly endearing love letters, mostly about trifles made luminous by affectionate intent. Her letters run on verve and eagerness and they have enough I-love-you-Waldo-Emersons to delight the most smitten of suitors. Ellen had had quite a number of interested young men around her already. When she settled on Emerson, she gave her heart completely. "I am yours entirely now and ever shall be," she wrote. "Dear Waldo I love you says Ellen T." "I dream about you again night and day." "Good night and be thinking of coming to see me . . . for I am still your own, your own your own." Everything suggests that Emerson loved her just as much as she him. They had pet names for each other. At first it was Ellinelli and Grandpa, then later it was Queen and King.[2]

Ellen had wit and a mind of her own. "I want to tell you that I love you very much and I would like to have you love me always," she says in one letter, adding with mock solemnity, "if consistent with your future plans."

Another time she apologized for writing "such a whip-syllabub sort of a letter." Of her sister she wrote once that "Margaret is reading the new novel and has just looked up to sigh." She made independent judgments. She didn't like the miniature she had of Emerson. Later she thought Thomas Sully had missed the likeness of Emerson's friend Mrs. Furness of Philadelphia. When Emerson set her to reading Scougal, she was cool and articulate about how Scougal dissipated his point by repetition.[3]

Ellen intended to become a poet. She felt that she had a gift; she read a good deal, and her surviving poems are nearly the equal of Emerson's own during this time. The best have a clean lyrical grace: "We've been roaming, we've been roaming / Where the river views are sweet." She could express sadness without being mawkish or lachrymose. In one poem she imagines dying because she is no longer loved:

> Sweeter the green sod for my bones
> The black earth for my head
> The wind, than thy cold altered tones
> Whence all of love had fled.

Her best poetry was, like her life, death-marked. She also had a strong sense of color: "I am the grave's, its seal is set upon me / Its chalky white and startling vermeil red." She already had tuberculosis. It was a family affliction. She jokingly suggested a drop of blood vermeil as the family crest. She joked about it because there was no avoiding it. Her brother George had died of tuberculosis in 1825. As Ellen wrote Waldo, in the last line of his journal George wrote of "the blood feeling like melted lead in his veins." After George died, Ellen took over George's journal for her own, as if to continue his life in some form. She seems to have known—perhaps at some unacknowledged level she and Waldo both knew—that the likelihood of their both living was small. In a comment that lets us see far into the fear that lay beneath Ellen's happy surface, she wrote to Waldo: "Few, let them love ever so ardently and purely, have the happiness to lie down in the earth together—the hand of death while it destroys one, merely numbs (chills) the other as warning or as *a comfort*." There is nothing artificial, nothing "literary" about her desire to overstamp death with love. "Let us love thus, oh my good Waldo. I believe we do now and we need not be united to increase our affec—— 'A sea'—surely!!—whose waters cast up pearls and gems."[4]

At the start of the new year, 1828, just as he was becoming acquainted with Ellen, Emerson was "living cautiously," as he told William, "treading on eggs to strengthen my constitution." He was reading Abraham Tucker again and his sympathy for a rational natural religion was running high. He wrote a few sermons. Sometimes he just dithered: "I lose days in determining how hours should be spent." He had been reading Rousseau's *Emile* and was repelled by Rousseau's contempt for the sick. But Rousseau's prose was as vigorous, as attention-getting as anything he had read. "The natural man lives for himself," says Rousseau. "He is the unit, the whole, dependent only on himself and on his like." Rousseau's style in *Emile*—abrupt, pithy, energetic, fluent, and extravagant—is closer to Emerson's mature style than any of his other reading thus far, including Cotton's Montaigne. The subject matter of *Emile* was also congenial. "All his life long man is imprisoned by our institutions," Rousseau says. "To be something, to be himself, and always at one with himself, a man must act as he speaks, must know what course he ought to take, and must follow that course with vigor and persistence."[5]

Emerson also kept on with Plato, becoming interested in February in Socrates' daemon ("an invisible Genius which governed his actions") as an image—or, more accurately, as a mythological figure—for the inner voice. He preached frequently in such different Massachusetts towns as Waltham, Carlisle, Dedham, Lexington, and Medford, but he avoided accepting any engagement that promised to become permanent. He was deliberately holding back from a full-time commitment, husbanding his strength.

Emerson felt no equivalent sense of caution when it came to Ellen. In May 1828 he was back in Concord, New Hampshire. Just at this moment Edward suffered his mental collapse and Waldo rushed the sixty miles back to Concord, Massachusetts, to help. When Edward seemed better, Emerson went back to New Hampshire. Then Edward's mind gave way again and again Emerson returned to look after his brother, who had now to go to McLean's. Just when Emerson's capacity for sympathy and compassion was being seriously drawn upon for the first real tragedy in the family, he and Ellen were falling in love. Emerson dealt with trouble by turning to life. Inside the family, however, he dealt with Edward's collapse by holding both himself and Charles to high standards, to Edward's standards. In July Charles took a Bowdoin Prize, after which Emerson sent him the long, critical letter that shows how little Emerson thought the public speaker is allowed to take for granted. He was now beginning to supply the pulpit, often at the Second Church in Boston. The incumbent, Henry Ware, was in poor health, and the church would soon be looking for a new minister. Now that he was in love, Emerson began to be much more interested in the possibilities for a permanent position.[6]

His natural history interests were also branching out into a spell of science reading. He read J. E. Smith's *Introduction to Physiological Botany,* Jacob Bigelow's *Florula Bostoniensis,* and Humphry Davy's *Elements of Chemical Analysis* as well as Malthus and Benjamin Rush. This reading, though not in direct response to Edward's illness, was not entirely unconnected with it. Edward's shocking mental collapse made Emerson hold on the more firmly to his rational assumptions and his basic Stoic morality. The world is out of joint because we do not rule ourselves. He insisted too on controlling the passions even as his interest in Ellen Tucker grew beyond control.

Just how his brother's calamity, his interest in Ellen, and the ever greater likelihood that the Second Church would call him to be its minister combined to force him to take stock of himself can be seen in his sermon 27, delivered in late November 1828. This was the last sermon he would deliver this year and the last—and culminating effort—of his apprenticeship. The text is from Paul's First Epistle to the Corinthians: "Let none be disturbed with a pitiful controversy about a man, an instrument, for all things are yours, whether Paul, or Apollos, or Cephas, or the world, or life, or death, or things present, or things to come." Emerson's tone, like the tone of the passage with its long line of rising promissory excitement, is triumphant. Since all things are ours, he says, "Let us rejoice in life." The point of Christ's life is that "it shows eternity to depend on time." The business of that life in time, our life, is to "Know Thyself." "We may read history, but this [ourselves] is what we learn there or we learn nothing." Whether a result of his new interest in Ellen, his self-protective reaction to Edward's illness, or his being sought after by several churches, Emerson displays a new sureness, a new sense of personal conviction in this piece. "You carry your fortunes in your own hand," he said. "You are the universe to yourself." "There is nothing really desireable to us that wisdom and perseverance cannot obtain."[7]

Early in December 1828 the search for a minister became urgent at the Second Church in Boston. Emerson was under serious consideration for the position, and he wished to get away for a while so as not to seem to be preventing other candidates from being heard. With his brother Edward, who was now convalescing, Emerson went back to Concord, New Hampshire, where, on December 17, not quite a year after they had first met, he and Ellen Tucker became engaged. She was seventeen, he twenty-five. He was, as he wrote William, "now as happy as it is safe to be." His utter good fortune, untroubled except by the contrast of his two older brothers, made him feel suddenly as vulnerable as he had felt omnipotent only a month before. He was understandably fearful of so much prosperity.

On January 11 the Second Church voted 74 to 3 to 1 to invite Emerson to be its junior minister. This was more good fortune, but his engagement to Ellen dominated his mood. The young rationalist turned and prayed. "Will God forgive me my sins and aid me to deserve this gift of his mercy," he wrote in his journal for June 17, 1829, in an entry unique for its submission. As usual, in his letter to Aunt Mary he expressed himself best. He reminded her "on what straitened lines we all walked up to manhood." William had now begun to live by the law, Edward had recovered his reason and his health, Bulkeley was never more comfortable, and Charles was "prospering in all ways." And now he, Waldo, seemed on the edge of professional success and personal happiness, of a "particular felicity which makes my own glass very much larger and fuller." "There's an apprehension of reverse always arising from success," he told Aunt Mary, and he concluded with a new humility that is uncharacteristic but not feigned. In his moment of fulfillment he refuses to take personal credit. Nor does he feel that he stands alone, either theologically or emotionally. "I cannot find in the world without, or within, any antidote, any bulwark against this fear like this, the frank acknowledgement of unbounded dependence." Part of the power of Emerson's individualism is his insistence, at crucial moments, that individualism does not mean isolation or self-sufficiency. This is not a paradox, for it is only the strong individual who can frankly concede the sometimes surprising extent of his own dependence.[8]

15. Ordination and Marriage: Love and Reason

THE SECOND CHURCH IN BOSTON WAS IN THE NORTH END. NO longer in a fashionable part of town, the church was nevertheless old and proud, dating back to 1650, to Increase and Cotton Mather. It was a solid church of about a hundred families who were accustomed to having a first-rate minister. Henry Ware, whom Emerson was succeeding, went on to a professorship at Harvard; he had already made an important contribution to Unitarianism through his insistence on the importance of effective extemporaneous preaching. Emerson responded to the church's call, as he responded to his engagement with Ellen, with a flourish of self-abnegation. "I have learned the lesson of my utter dependency," he wrote in his official letter of acceptance. It is an uncharacteristic note for a man whose name became synonymous with self-reliance, but the feeling of dependence that was now uppermost was a strong and constant element in Emerson's makeup. His repeated calls for self-reliance were not empty egotism; they represent ground won back from dependency. This feeling of dependency went hand in hand with feelings of humility and self-deprecation, which can be considered Emerson's Fénelon mood.[1]

François de Salignac de la Mothe Fénelon was Emerson's mother's favorite reading. Fénelon was an eighteenth-century Catholic archbishop of Cambrai who favored both quietism and the liberalizing of women's education. He was a saintly man whose concern for the poor once led him to go through enemy lines in order to find and bring back a cow that was the sole livelihood of an evacuated peasant. A new selection of Fénelon's writing was published in Boston in 1829 and was extensively reviewed by Channing in the *Christian Examiner* for March 1829. Fénelon teaches that the devout life is one of self-crucifixion; he calls us "to die to ourselves and live to God," "to renounce our own wills and to choose the will of God as our only rule," "to distrust ourselves and to put our whole trust in God," "to crucify self-love and to substitute for it the love of God." Self, for Fénelon, is the great barrier between the soul and God. Emerson's gradually evolving convictions would emphasize the opposite belief, that the self is one's only path to the divine. But his ultimate position gets much of its strength from having to be forcibly reclaimed from the self-abnegation urged by Fénelon, a self-abnegation that was profoundly familiar to the Emerson family. One sees it not only in Ruth Emerson but in Charles as well.[2]

Although the new job represented a major career success, it also meant the end of Emerson's freedom. He felt it keenly. His ordination was set for March; he wrote to William that his "execution day" approached. The ordination itself was a major event. Many ministers came to take part; there was a large dinner. Edward noted the repeated references to their father, "in whose stead Waldo has risen up."[3]

Emerson began his ministry with a two-part sermon on the duties of a Christian minister, which were, he said, preaching, prayer, performing the sacraments, and pastoral care. Emerson himself undertook these duties with mixed success. Preaching—and the study that went into it—was by far his greatest interest; articulating his thoughts on prayer led him closest to his own personal convictions and point of view. Disagreements with his parishioners over the sacrament of Communion would eventually lead Emerson out of the ministry. At pastoral work he was hopeless. "The mightiest engine which God has put into the hands of man to move man is eloquence," Emerson told his new congregation. He took his text from Paul's Epistle to the Romans, "I am not ashamed of the gospel of Christ," and he prepared himself for preaching by asking himself what Paul would have done in his place. Henry Ware wrote Emerson twice to complain about the paucity of reference to Scripture in his sermons. The truth was that Emerson did not often refer to Scripture (after he announced the text, which was invariably from the Bible) because the Bible was no longer for him an object of study; it was an example for emulation. He was interested in his own primary, personal religious experience and that of his parishioners, not in repeating and deferring to the reported religious experiences of long-departed historical personages. When he studied, say, the Book of Proverbs, he no longer thought of himself as a commentator but as the potential author of a similar book.[4]

Now, as Emerson turned to the active ministry, he tried empathetically to recover the original fervor of a Paul. When he later came to a parting of the ways with the church, he would see himself as a modern Luther. This personal identification with the great is for Emerson at bottom a hunger for a religion by revelation to *us*—as he would say in *Nature*—and not just the

90

history of someone else's religion. He wished to feel Christianity with feelings as strong as Paul's. He did not wish merely to report Paul's feelings as though such things were impossible in the modern world. Emerson would not publicly compare himself to St. Paul, of course, and honest old Henry Ware had no way to gauge the real depth and power of Emerson's passion for original experience.

Emerson was not daunted by Ware's criticism, though he did confess that he sometimes felt terrified at the prospect of having to write a sermon a week for the rest of his life. Pastoral calls were an even greater trial. By late March he had made fifty. In his preaching he could choose his subject. In parish work his role was strictly defined by custom and expectation. Charles laughed at him because he sometimes set off to make calls without detailed directions and therefore spent time visiting complete strangers who had the same name or lived in the same street as a parishioner. Attending the deathbed of an old revolutionary soldier named Captain Greene, Emerson could think of nothing to say. Seeing a collection of medicine bottles on the table beside the captain's bed, he began to talk about glassmaking. "Young man," said the not-yet-departed hero, "If you don't know your business, you had better go home."[5]

Emerson's salary for all this was a very handsome twelve hundred dollars a year, which was raised to the amazing sum of eighteen hundred dollars a year in July. The latter figure was more than a full professor would make at Harvard a decade later. Emerson became at once the financial center of the family, loaning money to William and supporting Charles. The position of minister of the Second Church in Boston also gave Emerson a solid institutional identity and immediately involved him in other public institutional positions. He became chaplain to the Massachusetts legislature in May 1829 and before the year was out he was a member of the Boston school committee. Emerson the private person became more or less overnight a complete institutional person. As minister of an important Boston church, Emerson became a public symbol of faith and learning before he had found out who he was or what he really believed.[6]

In June Ellen had an "episode," not her first. Emerson told Charles she was "taken sick in the old way,—very suddenly and suffered in the night great distress." She had coughed up blood, but not as much as on earlier occasions. They tried to be hopeful, though Emerson confessed, "Tis bad enough at the best." Dr. Jackson of Boston prescribed fresh air and "jolting," perhaps the worst possible advice, but no one at the time knew any better, and they followed the doctor's recommendation with pathetic faith. Ellen rode all over New England trying to shake the tuberculosis out of her system. Meantime, back in Boston, the young minister, working on his journals, would break out in the middle of a thought, "O Ellen, I do dearly love you." In July he was preaching often—and well—on death. Unwanted experience made for rapid maturity. In August he traveled with Ellen in New Hampshire. They were "soundly jounced over thirty miles of pine plain and gridiron bridge and steep and stony hill through much wind and shower," he wrote after one day's ride. After two hundred miles of jolting, Ellen seemed, incomprehensibly, much better.[7]

On September 30, 1829, Waldo Emerson and Ellen Tucker were married in Concord, New Hampshire. The festivities lasted three days. Curiously, the only member of Emerson's family to attend was Charles, who predictably felt left out and ignored. The young couple moved to a Mrs. Keating's house on Chardon Street in Boston and began life together. Controversy was building among Emerson's parishioners about who should be allowed to take Communion. Emerson wished to exclude no one. But such matters seemed minor this fall of 1829. Waldo and Ellen were blissfully happy with each other. Ellen also had her mother and sisters living with them. Ellen was welcomed into the Emerson clan by Aunt Mary, and she wrote happy latters about her "rosy hours" and "rosy life." Emerson turned often to poetry to express his feelings for Ellen, and now he tried, like the Shakespeare of the sonnets, to face down death with letters and love and to defeat time with the countertime of verse. He explored in imagination a future that time would never bring.

> Dear Ellen, many a golden year
> May ripe, then dim thy beauty's bloom.
> But never shall the hour appear
> In sunny joy, in sorrow's gloom
> When aught shall hinder me from telling
> My ardent love, all loves excelling.[8]

The period immediately following their marriage was also a time of remarkable intellectual and emotional growth for Emerson, a time when a number of books and ideas converged in a rush of excitement. A new and convincing argument about the nature of the mind came to him from Coleridge via James Marsh, and J. G. Herder showed him how one might reinstate the individual as the center and starting point of history and cosmology.

Coleridge's *Aids to Reflection* (1826) is the book that more than any other single volume catalyzed the synthesis between the new ideas Emerson was finding in Sampson Reed and the new importance of the old ideas he found in Plato, Plutarch, Montaigne, and the seventeenth century. James Marsh's long, fifty-eight-page introduction to the American edition of *Aids to Reflection* clearly and excitedly puts its finger on the central interest of Coleridge's book. Marsh begins, as Bacon, Locke, and the Scots had all begun, with the human mind. "The first principles, the ultimate grounds of [philosophy, morals, and religion] must be sought and found in the laws of our own being or they are not found at all," he says. But, Marsh maintains, in pursuing those laws, Hume and Brown had somewhat rashly concluded that "the notion of a power in the will to act freely is . . . nothing more than an inherent capacity of being acted upon, agreeably to its nature, and according to fixed law, by the motives which are present in the understanding."[9]

Here Marsh objects, as did Coleridge and Kant: "So long as we refuse to admit the existence in the will of a power capable of rising above this law, and controlling its operation by an act of absolute self-determination, so long shall we be involved in perplexities both in morals and religion." On examination, Marsh says, we find that we are indeed "possessed of some peculiar powers—of some source of ideas distinct from the Understanding." This source is called reason. What matters here is not whether Coleridge exactly follows Kant or whether Marsh or Emerson fully understood the nuances of either Coleridge or Kant. What matters is the idea of reason itself and what Emerson does with it.

In Coleridge, with indispensable clarification from Marsh, Emerson found a fully articulated, carefully defended argument for an active power in the self that is capable of self-determination. This power, called reason, is higher than the senses and higher than the understanding, which depends wholly on input from the senses. Not only did Marsh—and after him Emerson—find this power set forth in Coleridge, he found it explained in language that was itself "a living power, consubstantial with the power of thought that gave birth to it, and answering and calling into action a corresponding energy in our minds." This is Marsh at his best on Coleridge at his best, and the combination had an electric effect on Emerson. Here was a sober, modern, defensible, intellectually rigorous account of the nature of the power that resides in each individual soul. Marsh's formulation became over the next few years a conviction Emerson would hold for the rest of his life.[10]

At the same time he was reading Marsh's Coleridge, Emerson was reading again in Herder's *Outlines of a Philosophy of the History of Man*. Just as Coleridge fought against the "daring malignants who dole out discontent, innovation, and panic in political journals," so Herder protested against the "barren astonishment" of those who felt that human beings had been displaced from the center of the universe by the new science. Herder objected specifically to

> viewing the earth as a grain of sand moving in that great abyss, where the Earth fulfills her course around the Sun, this Sun with thousands more round their common center, and probably yet many other such systems of sun in separate spaces of the heavens; till at length both the understanding and the imagination are lost in this sea of immensity and eternal magnitude, and find neither exit nor end.

Herder himself understood that the great principle underlying science is that the laws of nature are the same everywhere. From this Herder concludes, in ringing affirmative prose that lost little in the English translation of 1800, that

> the power, which thinks and acts in me, is, from its nature, as eternal as that which holds together the Sun and the stars: its organs may wear out, and the sphere of its action may change, as earths wear away, and stars change their places; but the laws, through which it is where it is, and will again come in other forms, never alter. Its nature is as eternal as the mind of God; and the foundations of my being (not of my corporeal frame) are as fixed as the pillars of the universe.

Herder then concludes that "the structure of the universe confirms the eternity of the core of my being, of my intrinsic life. Wherever or whatever I may be, I shall be, as I am now, a power in the universal system of powers, a being in the inconceivable harmony of some world of God."[11]

This self-situating and self-validating point of view also became habitual with Emerson. As he wrote in his journal on November 7, 1829: "When I look at the rainbow I find myself the center of its arch. But so are you;

and so is the man that sees it a mile from both of us. So also the globe is round, and every man therefore stands on the top. King George, and the chimney sweep no less." Many years later Virginia Woolf said of Emerson that "what he did was to assert that he could not be rejected because he held the universe within him. Each man, by finding out what he feels, discovers the laws of the universe."[12]

16. We Are What We Know

LIFE WAS BUSY FOR THE YOUNG MARRIED COUPLE DURING THE
fall of 1829. Emerson had his senate chaplaincy duties, which were light,
and his Boston school committee duties, which were heavy, as well as his
church to look after. Boston was now the leading seaport in the United
States and its North End, where Emerson's church was located, was ringed
by docks and crowded with sailors and with commerce.

Edward Taylor (the colorful original of Melville's Father Mapple, the
sailor-preacher in *Moby Dick*) was just starting his work at the Seaman's
Bethel in the North End. Mary Peabody later recalled that Taylor and
Emerson had worked together in those early years and had developed a
profound respect for each other. They remained friends over the years.
Emerson learned something important about language from Taylor, and
Taylor bore witness that Emerson's ministry was more effective than most
other accounts suggest. Taylor was what was then called a shouting Methodist—which was very far indeed from Unitarianism—but Emerson loved
Taylor's heady, vigorous speech and he maintained that Taylor was one of
the two great poets of America. Taylor attended at least one meeting of the
Transcendental Club. Emerson said of him that he "lavished more wit and
imagination on his motley congregation of sailors and caulkers than you
might find in all of France."[1]

Taylor was a wiry, supple man of medium height with a face "as full of
wrinkles as the sea." Tough, indefatigable, and intense, he was one of the
original seven who founded the great Cape Cod camp meeting that began
at Wellfleet, Massachusetts, in 1819, then moved to nearby Eastham.
Taylor's meetings, said one admirer, were "conducted in a marvelous way,
by surprises, battery-shocks, hitty, witty, wise suggestions and illustrations,
flashing, burning, star-thoughts of faith, hope, and love, Jesus, holiness, and
heaven, never to be forgotten." His recorded speech really does sound like
Father Mapple's. One hearer described him preaching about the one perfectly straight, square law in the universe: "God's law, *that* was right up and
down like the windlass bitts, didn't twist any more than a pump-bolt, but

went right straight through everything—; that was the course for us to steer." Later, when Emerson was in the middle of his quarrel with his church over the significance of Communion, someone in Father Taylor's hearing suggested that Emerson was insane. Taylor did not agree with Emerson about the Lord's Supper, but he flashed to Emerson's defense. "Mr. Emerson might think this or that, but he was more like Jesus Christ than anyone he had ever known. He had seen him," said Taylor, "where his religion was tested, and it bore the test." Once, when a group of ministers were clucking about Emerson's leading the youth to hell, Taylor remarked: "It may be that Emerson is going to hell, but of one thing I am certain; he will change the climate there, and emigration will set that way."[2]

Ellen pursued her doctor's instructions to exercise as much as possible for her health. Emerson joined in companionably, buying a set of dumbbells. Ellen had a good deal of money and Emerson now had a handsome salary. The young couple kept two equipages, one for each of them. Their expenses were considerable. Emerson sometimes paid the landlady Mrs. Keating a hundred dollars a month. They were cheerful and happy together. Ellen was working on her poetry; she tried to write something every day. Emerson was in the middle of one of his periods of rapid growth, both intellectually and emotionally. Life was full and fulfilling.

But accompanying all this cheerful busyness was the unchanging fact, the ever-present groundswell of Ellen's illness. For his end-of-the-year stock-taking sermon in 1829 Emerson told his congregation that in ten years' time a "fourth part of us will have died, and in fifty or sixty years not one individual that breathes in this house shall breathe in the earth." Mortality, once a matter only for statistics, was now a daily reality. "Our own pleasant dwelling has been the house of pain," he said. "The lamp of our life is burning already in the socket."[3]

As the new year, 1830, began, Emerson was working out a new and strikingly modern theology. He started from the premise that "Christianity is validated in each person's life and experience or not at all." Following Coleridge's life-giving observation that "Christianity is not a theory or a speculation, but a life—not a philosophy of life but life itself, not knowledge but being," Emerson insists that "every man makes his own religion, his own God." To the question "What is God?" he now replies, "the most elevated conception of character that can be formed in the mind. It is the individual's own soul carried out to perfection." From this position he began to work out in his January sermons a theology of friendship. The relation of Christ to the soul of a good person is not that of redeemer but of friend. Our feeling for Christ is that of "profoundest friendship." Emerson's effort to relocate and reconstitute theology starting with human nature came about partly because Emerson was already sympathetic to the radical new religious thought of the time—this is the Schleiermacher legacy—and partly because he was rapidly becoming a deeper, warmer, more human person himself as he and Ellen struggled to live with her illness.[4]

In February 1830 he wrote Ellen a love poem of the kind meant to preempt death itself. It is a prospective elegy about their declining years together far in the future, "when the greybeard years / Have brought us to life's evening hour . . . / When all but love itself is dead." In March he went south with Ellen, traveling through Hartford and Wethersfield (where Aunt Mary was currently riding at anchor) to New Haven, New York, and Philadelphia. They kept a lighthearted rhyming journal together by turns, but Ellen's coughing spells, her "red wheezers," were ominous. They were caught in a gale on Long Island Sound and were forced back to land; Emerson fretted about the hardships of the trip for Ellen. Later, when she was only marginally better, she stayed on in Philadelphia while he returned to his duties in Boston. In April, on the anniversary of his ordination, he preached on how "our life is hurrying to an end." He was conscious, he said, of failure and of how little had been accomplished: "Man eats the bitter herbs of regret and becomes acutely sensible of the sore side of his condition." In May he preached on one of his mother's old topics, "keeping the heart," trying to draw strength from the great Christian consolatory tradition. In another sermon he tried to show why it is just as well that we don't know any more about the next world than we do. "Fifteen or sixteen people die in this parish every year," he noted grimly. "Do we really want to know who they are?"[5]

He preached again and again on the death that was now always so close by. "So live as to be ready to die," he said in a June sermon. His images reverted to the ocean as they did so often at moments of strain or crisis: "Let us walk thoughtful on the silent shore of the vast ocean we must sail so soon." In August Ellen suffered yet another attack. She and Waldo considered giving up the church; they considered moving south. He was prepared, he said, to "break all bonds" and to do whatever might help her.[6]

Marriage and Ellen's illness had deepened and matured Emerson, had brought out his capacity for sympathy. Their time together was so precious—as they were aware—that they lived extensively, perhaps exclusively, on the hope and trust of young love. Emerson's belief in immortality had never been stronger or more desperately needed. He was personally stronger as well, for Ellen had in some manner given him himself—had made it possible for him to reach for, arrive at, and articulate what can from now on be recognized as Emerson's fundamental and particular conviction in the final authority of the individual self. In September 1830, the anniversary month of their marriage, Emerson preached a splendid sermon on self-culture, or the oracle within. Here are the first full phrasings of some of the sentences that would ring through the essays "Self-Reliance" and "The Poet" still ten years and more in front of him. "We must do nothing without intention," he said. "To believe your own thought, that is genius." "The man of genius apprises us not so much of his wealth as of the common wealth." "Genius is representative." "There is in every human mind a power greater than that mind." The style has risen to match the subject. Aphoristic sureness and short, biting sentences have replaced the long rhetorical periods of only a year or so earlier. "It is only so far as you find Christianity within your own soul that I recommend it," he told his hearers. He advised each of them to "hold his own nature in a reverential awe." On another day this September Emerson preached one of his old sermons, on gentleness, at the Twelfth Church in Boston. A young woman from Plymouth named Lydia Jackson was there to hear him.[7]

Emerson's new expressions of self-trust coincided with great feats of reading. Emerson was an enormous reader all his life. He reread old favorites such as Plato, Montaigne, Plutarch, de Staël, Dugald Stewart. He kept up with new books and periodicals. He read widely in every field that interested him and he was always pushing into new fields. He read, as he wrote, rapidly. Like Montaigne, he did not pore. He read actively, as a writer does, looking for what he could use. "We read either for antagonism or confirmation," he once noted, adding that it made little difference which. He was alert to the curious way in which our reading seems always to refer to whatever project we have in hand at the moment. "For only that book can we read which relates to me something that is already in my mind." Emerson knew well enough that in saying "Trust yourself" he was laying himself open to the objection that surely one cannot recommend that every uneducated person rely stoutly and solely on his or her own meager resources without trying to increase them. Far from praising ignorance, Emerson kept repeating in his journal Coleridge's quiet incitement to study, *quantum scimus sumus*—we are what we know. The greater one's knowledge, the more justified one's self-reliance. He insists that reading be active and formative, anything but the passivity implied by the word *input*. "There is then creative reading as well as creative writing," he would say in "The American Scholar." "When the mind is braced by labor and invention, the page of whatever book we read becomes luminous with manifold allusion." He also found it easy to admit how much of his own material was in fact drawn, via reading, from the work of others. He noted with approval Goethe's saying "the greatest genius will never be worth much if he pretends to draw exclusively on his own resources." "What is genius," Goethe goes on, "but the faculty of seizing and turning to account any thing that strikes us . . . every one of my writings has been furnished to me by a thousand different persons, a thousand different things." The same was true of Emerson. He read voraciously and took notes on everything he read. His reading emptied directly into his writing, and his writing in turn gave direction and purpose to his reading. "Every word we speak is million-faced or convertible to an indefinite number of applications. If it were not so we could read no book. Your remark would only fit your case, not mine."[8]

Both Coleridge and Herder pushed Emerson toward increased reading in science this year. Herder cited the universality of physical laws in order to recenter the human being in the universe. Coleridge appealed to Huber's work on bees and to Kirby and Spence's four-volume *Introduction to Entomology*. The latter was also being discussed currently by Sampson Reed in a marathon review in the *New Jerusalem Magazine* which ran for twelve installments across three years. Emerson now read George Combe's *The Constitution of Man* (1828), a founding document of modern social science and an early effort to create a science of human behavior based on analysis of the different functions of the brain. Emerson called Combe's book "the best sermon I have read for some time." Combe locates twenty-seven specific functions of the brain, nineteen of which, he said, we share with animals. These include self-esteem, love of approbation, cautiousness, and benevolence. Of the sentiments proper to human beings alone, Combe emphasizes veneration, hope, ideality, consciousness, and firmness. Veneration is the tendency to worship; hope is a tendency to expect and look forward. Ideality is the love of the beautiful and the desire for excellence. Its related tendency is wonder. Combe traces the sentiment of justice to what he calls consciousness; firmness means firmness of character or purpose. Religion, Combe notes, is rooted in our tendencies to veneration, hope, and wonder. This scientific taxonomy of human qualities, based (prematurely) on then current knowledge of the human brain and its functions, gave Emerson hope for a science of man that would provide a more solid basis for human life than, say, revelation. Indeed, it now seemed to Emerson that science itself had a greater capacity for real wonder and a greater claim on our veneration than either the arid textual scholarship that passed for training in divinity or the barren doubt of skeptical philosophy. He delighted in Newton's having said, a little before he died,

> I don't know what I may seem to the world, but to myself I seem to have been only like a boy playing on the seashore and diverting myself in now and then finding a smoother pebble or a prettier shell than ordinary, while the great ocean of truth lay all undiscovered before me.[9]

In June of 1830 Emerson was working on local botany, reading Bigelow's *Florula Bostoniensis* and the same author's *American Medical Botany.* In December he was reading Alexander von Humboldt's *Personal Narrative of a Voyage to the Equinoctial Regions,* the fascinating and detailed account of South America that would haunt mid-nineteenth-century North Americans and would find its greatest artistic expression in the great canvases of Frederick Church. In February of 1831, as Ellen lay gravely ill, Emerson was starting to read Cuvier, the famous French zoologist, founder of modern comparative anatomy and paleontology and originator of the natural system of animal classification.

Natural history offered Emerson an ever expanding horizon of wonder. He was interested in the subject both for itself and as a sort of self-standing and self-validating natural theology. But even that venerable phrase "natural philosophy" would no longer serve. Emerson was now turning slowly but inexorably from theology to science. Pantheism is the theological term for seeing God in all things. Emerson began to wonder if pantheism could be expressed and given new force with a term of science. In Kirby and Spence he read that "to see God in all things, in the mirror of the creation to behold and adore the reflected glory of the creator is no mean attainment." In his journal he began to use the term *theoptics,* feeling now, as T. S. Eliot would a century later, that "we have a mental habit which makes it much easier for us to explain the miraculous in natural terms than to explain the natural in miraculous." Or, as Walt Whitman would soon be saying, "A mouse is miracle enough to stagger sextillions of infidels."[10]

17. Gerando and the First Philosophy

DURING THE FALL OF 1830, AS ELLEN'S CONDITION SLOWLY worsened, Emerson declared himself willing to break all his social and professional ties for Ellen's sake. At the same time he found himself breaking intellectual ties, undergoing the beginning of a fundamental philosophical realignment. Ellen concluded she would be better off by not traveling south. Her doctor agreed. It was Charles's opinion that no climate could now save her. Charles saw the dark side of everything, but in this case it was the truth. For Ellen and Waldo life was now reduced to essentials, to a matter of plain survival.

In October, perhaps because he had to work at something, Emerson began a new notebook specifically for his notes on a new book recommended by Channing, Joseph de Gerando's three-volume *Histoire comparée des systèmes de philosophie*. Emerson came to Gerando at just the right time. In Gerando's hands philosophy was the new queen of the sciences, replacing the cramped and arid study of theology. Gerando regarded philosophy as the focal point of learning; he asked basic questions and he demanded usable answers. Philosophy was, for Gerando, more than a list of names; it consisted of real principles and ideas, ideas conceived of not as intellectual counters but as perceptions, as revelations of power, as recognitions of webs of relationship, and as starting points for action. Gerando's philosophy was not a skeptical weapon against enthusiasm, it was an agent for it, able to go where the cooler Common Sense philosophy could not. Emerson read Gerando just when Ellen's life was ebbing away; Gerando gave Emerson new possibilities for belief with which to fight his despair.[1]

Gerando took as his starting point two ideas Emerson found deeply congenial. Both are articulated in Gerando's treatise *Self-Education*, which was translated and published by Elizabeth Peabody this year, 1830. "The life of man is in reality but one continued education, the end of which is, to make himself perfect." But if life is fundamentally self-cultivation and self-development, one does not live divorced from society, from politics or from social justice. Gerando's real starting point is Kant's categorical imperative: "Act only on those principles that you can will to be principles for everybody." "The state of society," says Gerando, "is a state of nature. Society is the grand vocation of nature for man. Without it he would never truly become a man. It is to the faculties of his heart what the material universe is to his senses." As the human cannot exist without the social, so individual justice is meaningless apart from justice for others.

> We cannot fully enter into the conceptions of what is just, without putting ourselves, in imagination, completely into the situation of another, so as to perceive how he would see and feel, and thus understand what should be done for him, as if it were to be done for ourselves.

Emerson was bothered this fall by the problem of freedom and by the need for a general standard of freedom for all, not just for an educated elite. "Few are free, all might be" is his laconic conclusion this November.[2]

As a historical account of the development of philosophy, Gerando's *Histoire comparée* is even more ambitious than Stewart's. Stewart intended only to sketch philosophy since Bacon. Gerando set out to find the primary questions of all philosophy, the enduring themes that inform the thought of all places and times; he envisioned a sort of key to all philosophies. In order to do so, he went back to the Greeks and to other traditions—Chinese, Hindu, Persian—and he came down to the present, giving a major and extended account of Kant and his followers. Indeed, Gerando's book is conceived as a defense of idealism against Scottish Common Sense and against Paley. Scottish Common Sense had limits for Emerson. It did not have a convincing reply to Hume. It did insist on a universal moral sense, but it lacked a satisfying concept of freedom. Paley's calculated self-interest and expediency had a similar failing in being too utilitarian. It was Paley's chapter on civil obedience that moved Thoreau to frame his famous reply. Gerando's work had fresh, exciting solutions to these and to other problems.

Gerando's enthusiasm for philosophy, his passion for what is essential or original, and his clarity of mind and prose are combined with an unusual breadth of knowledge. He cites the Mahabharata as an example of primitive idealism in which we can see how the "senses are the soul's instruments of action; no *knowledge* comes by them." He argues for concepts of nature and law so fundamental that they can be found both in the Greeks and in *The Invariable Milieu* of the Chinese. "The order established by heaven is called nature," says the latter. "What is conformed to nature is called law. This establishment of law [in the mind] is called instruction." Emerson took careful notes on these observations, coming, for the first time, to the realization that ancient Hindu, Chinese, and Persian thought was on a philosophical par with Hebrew, Greek, and Christian and that it was not only entitled to serious attention but was a probable source for fresh insight. Gerando treats all thought as primary, interesting in itself, potentially valid.

Emerson worked through the book in the original French, taking careful notes. Gerando treats the Greek pre-Socratic philosophers as especially valuable, and Emerson now recognized in them some of his own most important themes. He noted how, for Thales, "water was the beginning of all things," how "the essence of the soul is motion" and "free activity." In Anaximander he recognized what he called "transcendentalism" in the comment that "the infinite is the beginning of all things, an infinite altogether immutable and immense." He noted how Anaxagoras went a step beyond pantheism, separating world from author and suggesting that the final cause may not be power but intelligence.[3]

Emerson got much from Gerando's treatment of Pythagoras and Heraclitus. His new interest in science was stirred by Pythagoras's teaching that reality is mathematical, that the fundamental principles of things are numbers, and that beings are bound together by laws as by numbers. It was Pythagoras who gave the name cosmos—meaning order, harmony, and, by extension, beauty—to the world, who taught that moderation is the essential characteristic of virtue, and that "empire over self" is the means of obtaining it. It was Pythagoras who insisted that the soul is an emanation of the divine. Emerson would always prize knowing over knowledge, process over product, activity over object. Now he found this distinction brilliantly put in Gerando's sympathetic account of Heraclitus. Wisdom, for Heraclitus, consisted not in accumulating a great pile of knowledge but in "discovering the law which governs all things. All nature is governed by constant laws. The phenomena themselves which appear discordant concur in the harmony of the whole. Meantime all change." What Heraclitus holds out is the possibility of believing in perpetual change and in fixed laws at the same time.[4]

From Coleridge via Marsh Emerson had come to accept the idea that the highest, most trustworthy knowledge consists of intuitive graspings, moments of direct perception, free mental acts of cognition and recognition, a series of mental activities that, as he now realized, could be summed up in the word *reason*. Customarily he used visual imagery for these acts of knowing, calling them insights, perceptions, or visions. What he was now doing, with Gerando and with all of his reading henceforward, was looking for traces of the momentary outbreaks of reason—these flashings forth of the intuitive truth as Melville called them—down through history. And already he was recognizing his own ideas reflected back to him in the ideas of Confucius, Pythagoras, and Heraclitus. Instead of proving him wrong, history kept validating Emerson's own perceptions. So strong was this sense of validation while working on Gerando in November of 1830 that Emerson could write, in language he would later use for the essay "Self-Reliance," that

> when a man has got to a certain point in his career of truth he becomes conscious forevermore that he must take himself for better for worse as his portion, that what he can get out of his plot of ground by the sweat of his brow is his meat, and though the wide universe is full of good, not a particle can he add to himself but through his toil bestowed on this spot.

Gerando was his meat this fall. Gerando gave him a history of the operation and findings of reason in various eras and countries, a sort of natural history of reason.[5]

The year 1830 was one of upheaval in the great world beyond Boston. Simon Bolívar's dream of a United South America was shattered and he himself died on his way into pensioned exile. Had he not lost his beloved wife, Bolívar said, his life would have been much different; he would never have gone into politics. In Van Diemen's Land (Tasmania) Governor Arthur swept a cordon of armed whites at absurd expense across the huge island in an effort to trap and eradicate the remaining aborigines, most of whom slipped through the line leaving the operation with a net catch of two persons. The July Revolution in Paris overthrew the Bourbons and installed Louis Philippe on the French throne. In the United States the rift between North and South deepened with the nullification issue and the Hayne-Webster debate.

As the winter darkness of November crept upon him, Emerson was fighting against a demoralizing, unhinging fear of death. He noted that even powerful natures, such as Samuel Johnson's, exhibited "strong apprehension, great gloom . . . at the thought of dissolution." And far from removing the apprehension, Christianity had, he thought, "done much to increase the fear of death" by increasing moral sensitivity and by failing to prevent increasing fearfulness.[6]

In December there was more bad news. Edward was suddenly worse. Despite Emerson's efforts to lure him from New York to Boston for the winter, Edward decided to head south to the island of St. Croix. Emerson was now reading Sir Thomas Browne's *Urn Burial.* Such reading for Emerson was not consolatory but rather a sort of literary inoculation. Perhaps he felt that reading Browne's imaginative treatment of death would somehow prepare him for the looming event. He noted that Browne's famous essay "smells in every word of the sepulchre." He was especially struck by Browne's extension of his theme to the New World: "That great antiquity America lay buried for thousands of years and a large part of the earth is still in the urn to us." Browne associates death with the land, not with the landscape. It was a connection that William Cullen Bryant explored in "Thanatopsis." We bury our dead in the land and therefore, with every generation that passes, our attachment to that land grows stronger. Perhaps it is only by death and burial that any people ever comes to feel a land as their true home. Home is where your losses are. Emerson's feeling for nature had many sides; from now on, one of those would be a growing attachment to the land that held his dead.[7]

The year 1831 opened on a combative note. On January 1 William Lloyd Garrison published the first number of *The Liberator:* "I will not excuse. I will not equivocate. I will not retreat a single inch, and I will be heard." The South, henceforward with a capital S, would experience Nat Turner's rebellion this year, while out west, not yet with a capital W, the Black Hawk War broke out over the issue of relocation. On January 24 Ellen was sick again and Emerson wrote to Edward that they now prefixed "if" to all their plans. It was no longer a matter of when but if she might be better. Searching for any comfort he could find, Emerson groped back toward the dark world of Calvinism, whose "errors," he now conceded, "are exaggerations only, [which could] generally be traced to some spiritual truths from which they spring."[8]

On January 30 Charles roused himself from his drift and self-doubt to take an active role in protesting the government's policy regarding the American Indians. Despite sixteen treaties negotiated by the federal government and six by Georgia, "all admitting the right of the Indians to the soil they occupy to be perfect and exclusive," the government was trying to turn out the Indians once more. Charles was outraged. President Jackson's December 4 (1830) message to Congress said flatly, "It is therefore a duty which this government owes to the new States, to extinguish, as soon as possible, the Indian title to all lands which Congress themselves have included within their limits." On this issue Charles became an activist. He organized an indignation meeting in Cambridge. He was not taken in by the rhetoric of relocation. The government, he said, was "just now driving [the Indians], by force of intimidation and oppression and open bribery, into the desert to die."[9]

18. The Wreck of Earthly Good

ELLEN WAS "SADLY SICK" IN LATE JANUARY. THE DOCTOR CAME frequently, they hired a nurse, Charles came in from Cambridge. Ellen went out riding when she could. At home her hands were cold and the nurse rubbed them to improve the circulation. On Wednesday, February 2, she was well enough to go out riding twice. But when Charles returned three days later on Saturday, he found Ellen "sadly altered." Now, for the first time, Waldo and Ellen's mother despaired of her recovery. The nineteen-year-old Ellen faced the end with courage and self-possession; she spoke of it "with serenity and sweetness." Waldo took it harder: it was he who was "bowed down under his affliction" and it was Ellen who comforted him.[1]

By Sunday she was "on the brink of the grave." Charles wrote William, "Every breath is distress." It did not seem as if she could live through the day. Waldo was in despair. "He is," said his brother, "a man over whom the waters have gone." By Monday morning Ellen was weaker yet, though the night had been easier than the preceding one. Her mother and sisters were there. Grandfather Ripley came in the afternoon to pray with her. At four o'clock a heavy-hearted Charles went up to see Ellen and "bid her my last good-bye." Waldo's heart was with the dying, but Ellen's was still with the living. She asked Charles to try to cheer up Waldo when she was gone and "not to let him think too much of her."[2]

Shortly after two in the morning on Tuesday, February 8, she felt she was going. She prayed for herself and for the watchers, kissed them all, and then sank rapidly. Throughout her ordeal Ellen had faced forward, believing in God and in the hereafter, braced to accept her death by these beliefs and by her own strength of character. But her last words seem to look backward to this life and to their little happiness together. She rambled, said something inarticulate. Then Waldo heard her say, "I have not forgot the peace and joy." She died at nine o'clock in the morning.[3]

A little later that same morning Emerson wrote to Aunt Mary, to the one person who had always stood as an unfailing source of strength. He was in a strange frame of mind, compounded of shock, unnatural calm, and "grief sharpened into anguish by the 'complete wreck of earthly good,'" as he later called it. In part it is Ellen's own calm and faith that are reflected in Emerson's telling his aunt, "My angel is gone to heaven this morning and I am alone in the world and strangely happy." Ellen's battle was over; the pain from which she was now released is vividly evident in the next sentence: "Her lungs shall no more be torn nor her head scalded by her blood nor her whole life suffer from the warfare between the force and delicacy of her soul and the weakness of her frame." The last few days had been, he said, "the most eventful of my life." He was pathetically eager for comfort from the aunt who had lived on terms of daily intimacy with her own death and whom Emerson called the angel of death. "Say, dear aunt, if I am not rich in her memory?"[4]

Five days after Ellen's death, Emerson faced his journal, expressing himself for once in the comforting Christian language he ordinarily avoided, especially in his public utterances: "Five days are wasted since Ellen went to heaven to see, to know, to worship, to love, to intercede. God be merciful to me a sinner and repair the miserable debility in which her death has left my soul." Ellen had been associated in Emerson's mind with strong, self-effacing religious faith right from the start. Their engagement, their wedding, her death, and—from now on—her memory were always associated with private statements of faith and dependence, with feelings of humility, unearned happiness, and with an impulse toward prayer. Ellen's death caught Emerson without any personal (that is to say, earned) defenses against loss. His defenses, such as they were, were time-honored and conventionally Christian ones. As time passed, he kept her memory sacred—she became for him an ideal, as Beatrice had for Dante—but he also strove to prevent himself from ever having to endure such another loss.[5]

There is both in Ellen's writing and in Emerson's at this time a sort of romantic longing for death. In the first sermon Emerson could manage, on February 20, twelve days after Ellen's death, he spoke of the "sublime attraction of the grave": "When we have explored our desolate house for what shall never there be seen, we return with an eagerness to the tomb as the only place of healing and peace." For Emerson, as for Keats, this is not a morbidly premature preoccupation with death but an emotional facing up to the inevitable. It is a question not just of accepting but of embracing the given. It is a response that not everyone is capable of making but that Mary Moody Emerson would have fully understood.[6]

Emerson was twenty-seven when Ellen died. Her loss and the simultaneous spiritual crisis Emerson was undergoing constitute his second birth. Before this time Emerson was a rationalist who was fascinated but not wholly convinced by the truth of idealism. After this time Emerson believed completely, implicitly, and viscerally in the reality and primacy of the spirit, though he was always aware that the spirit can manifest itself only in the corporeal world. At this moment of Ellen's death, however, what Emerson felt most keenly was a sense of loss and alienation that expressed itself specifically as a consciousness of separation. The dead, said Emerson, "follow their Lord. They are gone with him into the house, and the door is shut." His world had come apart, quite literally. "Shall I ever again be able to connect the faces of outward nature, the mist of the morn, the star of eve, the flowers and all poets, with the heart and life of an enchanting friend? No. There is one birth and one baptism and one first love and the affections cannot keep their youth any more than men." Not only did he feel that his personal world was cut off from the natural world and that he was cut off from Ellen, he felt cut off from himself, as he managed to say with Donne-like force in one of the many poems he now wrote about Ellen: "Teach me I am forgotten by the dead / And that the dead is by herself forgot / And I no longer would keep terms with me."[7]

Emerson was, as he recognized, "unstrung, debilitated by grief." In the days after her death Emerson still heard her breathing, saw her dying. He called out to her, addressed her directly, prayed to her as to an intercessory saint. His life took on a tone of "unrepaired regret" and "miserable apathy." But Emerson was incapable of the kind of chronic despair Charles lived with. Even as he grieved, he was aware that the grief would abate. "I almost fear when it will," he noted in his journal. At the same time he clung to the idea of Ellen's spirit as something that survived the death of the body. He was reading Plotinus and his notes show that he now first came to take a personal interest in the Neoplatonist who was so intensely and exclusively preoccupied with the spirit that he was ashamed of and humiliated by his body. Contempt for the flesh was one way to affirm the mind and the spirit. Emerson worked this out in a poem in June:

> Why fear to die
> And let the body lie
> Under the flowers of June
> Thy dust doth good

110

The insects food
And thy grave smiled on by the visiting moon.

The death of Ellen left Emerson with a sense of loss and regret that he never entirely outlived. The following lines catch perfectly the empty equipoise of his life in June 1831.

The days pass over me
And I am still the same
The Aroma of my life is gone
Like the flower with which it came.[8]

Emerson pulled himself back to his duties. Besides his regular sermons, he was committed to give a series of lectures on the Gospels, beginning March 8 and running through early May. These are detailed, scholarly, critical performances, summarizing the most recent biblical research. They are utterly unlike the personal statements of the sermons. In these lectures Emerson undertook to show what is known of each of the Evangelists, to provide a history of the transmission of the Bible, and to review the various theories about the origin of the three synoptic Gospels (Matthew, Mark, and Luke) and their relation to one another. Just when the loss of Ellen was leaving him feeling cut off from life, he was obliged to conduct a thorough and public examination of the evidence for the genuineness of those books of the Bible that were the primary basis for Christian faith.

Emerson used respectable sources. He used Herbert Marsh's "Dissertation on the Origin and Composition of the First Three Gospels" (1802) for a summary of early views on the subject from Le Clerc to Eichhorn and Herder. He also used Connop Thirlwall's long, 150-page introduction to his translation of Schleiermacher's *Treatise on Luke* (1825) for the views of Schleiermacher and Gieseler. Emerson's first lecture reviews the evidence outside the Bible for the historical existence of Matthew, Mark, and Luke, concluding that they did indeed exist. The third lecture reviews in detail the transmission of the texts from St. Jerome (d. A.D. 420) to the present. Emerson was strongly inclined to accept the genuineness of the Gospels. In prose that seems to echo and then to answer Gibbon, Emerson concludes:

These four short narratives have outlasted the mighty monuments of the Jewish and Roman architecture under whose shadow they were written, and which now lie in ruins, have outlasted the barbarous

111

institutions of the middle ages which they civilized and have now come down safe to our eyes and our ears and our hearts across the vast tract of so many ages of war and ignorance.[9]

To make a general affirmation about the survival of the Gospels is one thing; to specify the exact steps in that survival is another. On the difficult question of the origins of St. Jerome's Vulgate, Emerson notes that all four Gospels are mentioned and quoted in the work of Justin Martyr, who was born in A.D. 98. Justin Martyr gets us back to within seventy years of the death of Jesus. The real question, which is still an issue in biblical studies, is how, where, when, and by whom the Gospels were transmitted during those seventy years between the death of Jesus and the birth of Justin Martyr.[10]

The main problem is that Matthew, Mark, and Luke share a good deal of common material, some of it word for word. It seems clear that either the Evangelists copied from one another or they copied from a common source. Eichhorn and Marsh held that there must be a lost earlier gospel from which each of the Evangelists drew. Owen argued that Matthew wrote before Luke. Büsching argued that Luke wrote before Matthew. Storr held that Mark came before either. Griesbach, in the text Emerson had used in college, argued that Mark is based on Matthew and Luke. Emerson generally agreed with Schleiermacher's rejection of most of this work as tending to regard the Evangelists as German academic textual specialists. He agreed with the proposal of Gieseler and Daniel Veysie that instead of searching for a missing gospel, we should work on the assumption that the earliest gospel was not written but oral and that it consisted of the sayings of Jesus, since Veysie had noted that agreement between different Gospels is greatest when quoting Jesus. Emerson saw no reason to doubt the genuineness of the Gospels. But he no longer thought that they—or any other external evidence—were of much help to the individual in his quest for a religious life. "If we leave the letter and explore the spirit of the apostles and their master, we shall find there is an evidence that will come from the heart to the head, an echo to every sentiment taught by Jesus."[11]

Just when Emerson might be thought to be in most need of external support, he rejects the idea that Christianity rests on old writings or institutions. He has not yet gone so far as Theodore Parker when the latter declared that he sometimes thought Christianity would survive better without the Gospels than with, nor is he so firm yet as William Law, the eighteenth-century writer who was a favorite of Aunt Mary, of Charles, and of his mother. Law began

> from a conviction of the utter futility of the external evidences of Christianity, and of the whole theological conception to which they were congenial ... We know the fact by our own direct consciousness; and need not go to Moses for it; he does not prove the fact, but only tells us the how and the when.

It was Emerson's instinct—and a major key to his strength—that in extreme situations he tended not to reach for traditional supports, not even for the Bible, but to reach for his own resources and to go it alone.[12]

19. In My Study My Faith Is Perfect

THE LECTURES ON THE GOSPELS WERE EMERSON'S VALEDICTION to biblical studies. He did not exactly reject the Gospels, but as he recognized that there were many more than four of them and that Sampson Reed was as reliable a witness to the central truths of the human condition as St. Matthew. In May 1831, after these lectures and three months after Ellen's death, Emerson found another scripture in the Bhagavad Gita, as described by the French philosopher Victor Cousin.

Cousin (1792–1867) was eleven years older than Emerson. He had begun with the ultrarationalism of Condillac but had come to admire Scottish Common Sense and, after that, the thought of Kant, Schelling, and Hegel. His edition of Proclus had appeared between 1820 and 1827, and he had begun translating Plato himself in 1825. In 1827 his *Cours de l'histoire de la philosophie* appeared; this was the work Emerson read in 1831. Cousin belongs to the Eclectic school of philosophy. Eclecticism in this sense does not mean proceeding piecemeal, by patchwork, but rather adapting the psychological method to the history of philosophy. Cousin was interested in how the mind works; his main theme is the development of idealist philosophy as a challenge to the philosophy of sensation. His *Cours* is a sort of anatomy of philosophy. He finds four primitive archetypal "systems"— sensationism, idealism, scepticism, and mysticism—which recur again in every later age and country and always in the same order. Cousin is the Polybius of the history of philosophy. Cousin found the earliest cycle in India, where he calls Vedanta the idealist phase and the Bhagavad Gita the mystical phase. Cousin called the latter "the most interesting monument of mysticism in ancient India."[1]

Until he read Cousin, Emerson's attitude toward India may be adequately summarized in the title of his college poem "Indian Superstition." From Cousin's brilliant short treatment of the argument between Arjuna and Krishna, Emerson now learned that India possessed powerful sophisticated scriptures of its own, religiously as well as ethically a match for the Christian scriptures. To Arjuna's expressed unwillingness to fight, because he has friends and family in the opposing army, Krishna replies, in Cousin's account, "Why do you speak of friends and of relations? Why of men? Relations, friends, men, beasts or stones all are one. A perpetual and eternal energy has created all which you see and renews it without cessation." This scene struck Emerson—it is the kernel of his poem "Brahma"—as it would Thoreau and later T. S. Eliot. "Therefore do battle," says Krishna. "For as all is illusion, action itself, when it is regarded as real, is illusion also. . . . It is necessary to act, undoubtedly, but to act as if one acted not."[2]

Emerson understood that here in the Bhagavad Gita was a history without chronology, a belief in the fundamental identity of all things, beyond and beneath appearances, and a profound conception of universal justice and equilibrium. This was deeply congenial to the man who was already brooding on the idea that all things have their compensations.[3]

Cousin was on a path parallel to Emerson's in several respects. Lecture 10 of the *Cours* is an extensive treatment of great men, understood by Cousin as by Emerson, not as individuals but as representative or symbolic figures. Great persons are "representations of nations, epochs, of humanity, of nature, and of universal order." Cousin was farther down this road than Emerson at the moment, but Emerson would return to this theme in the 1840s.[4]

From Emerson's excited reading of Cousin in 1831 came his first serious interest in and respect for Indic thought and expression. Gerando primed him for the encounter, but Emerson always gave the credit to Cousin. Henceforward he turned his back on the missionary scorn and Southey-esque condescension to Hindu "idolatry." From now on Emerson always thought of the Bhagavad Gita as a scripture of equal standing with the Gospels.[5]

In June Emerson took a trip with Charles to the Green Mountains of Vermont and to Lake Champlain, in the course of which they met James Marsh, the Coleridgean who was now president of the University of Vermont. In late October Emerson began reading Wordsworth with new appreciation. He read the sonnet sequence inspired by the River Duddon, the "Ode to Duty," and especially "Dion." Emerson read "Rob Roy," "The Poet's Epitaph," and "The Happy Warrior." He was moved by the inwardness of Wordsworth and he asked in his journal, "Are not things eternal exactly in the proportion in which they enter inward into nature—eternal according to their *in*-ness?" Above all, Emerson now admired Wordsworth's skill and power as a writer, how he "shuns with brave self-denial every image and word that is from the purpose," intending "to stick close to his own thought and give it in naked simplicity."[6]

Emerson's mind had been running on writing since July. "No man can write well who thinks there is any choice of words for him," he had then written. "In writing there is always a right word, and every other than that is wrong." He approved of Friedrich Schlegel's saying, "In good prose, every word should be underlined." From the irresistibly titled *Guesses at Truth* by the brothers Hare, he copied out, "When you sit down to write, the main thing is to say what you have to say." In isolated fragments all during the second half of 1831, we sense a rising tide, a building up of internal pressure as Emerson thought about what he really knew and had to say and about what it would take to write really well. At the same time his hunger for life itself, not to be satisfied with mere commentary on life, is evident in his citing with approval Schelling's comment that "some minds think about things, others think the things themselves." In late October, as he was reading Wordsworth, he also turned to Shakespeare's sonnets, which he thought more helpful than the plays in trying to fathom Shakespeare's genius and in which he admired the "assimilating power of passion that turns all things to its own nature."[7]

Emerson walked out to Ellen's grave in Roxbury every day. He wrote poems about her and to her. Sometimes his journal entries about her break off mid-sentence, even mid-word. He continued to preach, and he became enmeshed in an emotional attack on the Boston public schools instigated by an outraged parent. Then in October Charles's health abruptly collapsed. In late September Emerson had written Edward that Charles was physically very frail, looking, he said, "like a wilted apple." Then Charles caught a bad cold accompanied by a cough that left him in "a great stupor and indisposition to any exertion, even so much as to speak." His friend Arthur Lyman came every day and read to him. Charles now gave up. Earlier in the year he seems to have given up intellectually, complaining that he could make nothing of Cousin. Now he virtually stopped talking. "He desponds of himself though perfectly calm and wise," Emerson wrote William. In early December it was decided to send Charles to Puerto Rico to join Edward in the search for better health in the south. Of the brothers only Waldo now remained unbroken and undeflected from the life Aunt Mary had imagined for them all. To William he wrote part of what was on his mind: "Who would have thought that Edward and Charles on whom we put so much fond pride should be the first to fail whilst Ellen, my rose, is gone."[8]

Emerson's own way seemed dark and uncertain, especially as regarded his career. Deep inside, however, Emerson was neither crushed nor despairing. However difficult the parish and school board duties, he noted with self-conscious irony that "in my study my faith is perfect." He commented that he was just the opposite of Hume, who doubted when he was alone in his study and believed when he was out in the world. Emerson held on to his own granite conviction, his foundational insight that "my own mind is the direct revelation I have from God." December of 1831 was a cold month. All Boston shrank, braced and blued with a steady cold that deepened without a break from December 10 through Christmas. Fuel was scarce, prices rose. It was perfectly clear who would suffer. "God save the poor," Emerson wrote in letter after letter.[9]

20. Separation

ELLEN'S DEATH UNDERMINED BOTH EMERSON'S PERSONAL world and the public institutional world he had embraced while married. He reacted to being separated from Ellen by separating himself from the church, from Boston, from the prevailing thought of the time (Scottish Common Sense), from the now hollow dignities of the Boston school board and the Massachusetts senate chaplaincy, and from the cramping form of the sermon. The loss that darkened his life also freed him. Ellen's death cut Emerson loose. Excluded from conventional happiness, he abandoned conventional life. He redoubled his efforts, albeit with a touch of panic, to live his own life and think his own thoughts.

As he surveyed his life at twenty-eight, he noted with chagrin how Alexander the Great had conquered the world at thirty. For all his loss Emerson still had his ambition, and now he began seriously to project a book. "Shall I not write a book on topics such as follow?" he wrote. He sketched out nine chapters, eight of them phrased as propositions or theses. One, that the mind is its own place. Two, that exact justice is done. Three, that good motives are at the bottom of bad actions. Four, that the soul is immortal. Five, on prayers. Six, that the best is the true. Seven, that the mind discerns all things. Eight, that the mind seeks itself in all things. Nine, that truth is its own warrant.[1]

This is an early and faint blueprint for the book Emerson would publish in 1836 as *Nature*. In its 1831 form we can see how Emerson is working on the same subject as Sampson Reed, Coleridge, Gerando, and Cousin— that is, on the nature and power of the mind. From the first to the ninth chapter the outline proceeds in a circle, an extreme example of the Fichtean emphasis on the self alone. The best title for the work thus sketched would have been *Mind*. What is most clearly missing is any emphasis on—even any sense of—the world on which the mind must work, the world of nature.

Propositions one and nine indicate the direction Emerson's mind was going. A statement is not to be considered true because the Church, the Gospels, or the Fathers say so. In saying "truth is its own warrant," Emerson is signaling his own shift from theology to science. To put it another way, he now insists that theological and moral truth must stand the same tests as scientific or natural truths. Just how far his theology has evolved can be seen not so much in his sermons, which were still being tailored not to offend his parishioners, but in a conversation Emerson had with Reed and Thomas Worcester (another Swedenborgian) this January: "God, we agreed, was the communication between us and other spirits departed or present." The radicalism of this position is its unwillingness to rest content in the belief that God communicates with us and its insistence rather that God *is* communication. This sophisticated bit of theology, far in advance of his church (or, indeed, of any contemporaneous church except the Swedenborgian and the Quaker), suggests that in an important sense Emerson had already left the church.[2]

Emerson's concern with the power of communication itself (a theme in Schleiermacher's religious thought that would continue to interest New Englanders through the 1840s) may also be seen in the early months of 1832 in other ways. Emerson went to hear Father Taylor preach in Channing's church, and he noted with real satisfaction that the somewhat self-satisfied Channing had to sit and listen to someone else do what he, Channing, could not. Emerson also went to a large meeting at the Federal Street Church to hear the Cherokees Elias Boudinot and John Ridge. Emerson was deeply impressed with the latter. "He said he would speak like an Indian, plain, right on," Emerson wrote in his notebook, "and fair fine Indian eloquence it was." Emerson noted too that Ridge "fully understood the oratorical advantages of his situation—the romance—and availed himself to the full thereof" and that he completely eclipsed the other speakers, Alexander Everett, Samuel Hoar, and Dr. Beecher.[3]

Ridge's real name was Kah-nung-da-tla-geh, the Man Who Walks on the Mountain's Top (or ridge). Born around 1771, he was now a white-haired powerful-looking man of sixty-one. A contemporary portrait shows a commanding face, with a large nose, high furrowed forehead, and deep burning eyes. Dressed in tailored clothing, he had a senatorial air. He had been a warrior when young, had joined the tribal council at twenty-one, and had opposed relocation when the question first came up. He was a spokesman for his people for many years, meeting presidents Jefferson, Madison, and Monroe. He was a Christian and he sent his son to Cornwall, Connecticut, to be educated. He helped introduce the Cherokees to the plow, the spinning wheel, and the loom. He persistently opposed President Jackson's and the State of Georgia's relocation policy, and he toured the country to rouse people against relocation. When relocation became inevitable, he reluctantly endorsed it, believing it better than fighting. Examples of his speaking style have been preserved. It was unlike anything Emerson had ever heard. At the end of Jefferson's administration, when the proposal to migrate beyond the Mississippi was first raised, Ridge publicly opposed the principal chief of the tribe. Rising in council after the move had been proposed, he said:

> My friends, you have heard the talk of the principal chief. He points to the region of the setting sun as the future habitation of this people. As a man he has a right to give his opinion: but the opinion he has given as the chief of this nation is not binding; it was not formed in council, in the light of day, but was made up in a corner—to drag this people, without their consent, from their own country, to the dark land of the setting sun.[4]

What Ridge and Taylor had in common was a vivid and forceful personal style, full of fresh imagery drawn directly from their own lives; it was a style Whitman would later characterize as marked by "the concrete and its heroisms." It is a significant and overlooked fact that just as Emerson was breaking away from his Boston, Harvard, Common Sense, Unitarian world, he was turning to a Methodist spellbinder and a Cherokee chief as well as to Swedenborgians for live ideas and fresh speech. Just after his account of Walker-on-the-Mountain, he noted glumly to Charles that, as of the day before, he had now written 146 sermons: "How many, and not one!"[5]

There is an air of gathering excitement in Emerson's journals during the first half of 1832. He was reading avidly, setting his own agenda, and following hunches. New interests crystallized for him; he was interested both in the new ideas and in the process by which they became apparent. "What can we see, read, acquire, but ourselves?" he asked in February. "Cousin is a thousand books to a thousand persons. Take the book, my friend, and read your eyes out; you will never find there what I find." A little earlier he had noted how the mind covers ground, shooting now this way, now that, much as crystals form in nature. "There is a process in the mind very analogous to crystallization in the mineral kingdom," he wrote. "I think of a particular fact of singular beauty and interest. In thinking of it, I am led to many more thoughts which show themselves first partially and afterwards more fully."

He thought of both crystal formation and this mental process of thought crystallization as "God's architecture." It was what he hoped to catch and commit to paper in his projected book.[6]

Meantime Emerson was racing through books. Some were books by energetic authors, such as Cousin or David Hartley, whose *Observations on Man* he now read. More of them were books about great figures. He read Brewster's *Life of Newton,* Nitsch's book about Kant's thought, Lydia Child's biographies of Mme. de Staël and Mme. Roland, Biber's book about the great Swiss educational reformer Pestalozzi, and Teignmouth's *Life of Sir William Jones,* the English jurist and linguist who was a key figure in the new Western awareness of ancient India. Emerson was as much interested in the achievers as the achievements. He was most interested at the moment in how the great figures had done their work. This extended reading in the lives of the great took place literally in the shadow of the grave. Emerson continued his daily walks to Roxbury to visit Ellen's grave and commune with her spirit. On March 29, without any explanation, he noted in his journal that he had opened her coffin.[7]

Just as Emerson observed that it was impossible ever to guess what Aunt Mary would say or write next, so it is impossible to know what went through Emerson's mind as he looked at what remained of Ellen's body. Flaubert once said that every heart contains a royal chamber. Ellen occupied that chamber in Emerson's heart. Flaubert went on to say that he had bricked up the royal chamber in his own heart. Emerson never did. He deliberately kept Ellen's memory alive, even allowed others close to him to read her letters to him. In one way this scene at the grave—which has so disturbed some commentators that they have concluded it must have been a dream— was pure Emerson. Be it life or death, he had to see for himself. Whether the decay of the body only confirmed and made more poignant the reality of the spirit that had so obviously departed from the body or whether he was facing up to death in the seventeenth-century manner of Jeremy Taylor or Sir Thomas Browne is unclear. The effect of the visit is somewhat clearer. He was casting off old ties and embracing new ideas and new possibilities. Coming face to face with the dead forced Emerson to choose between the dead and the living. His sermons for April are insistently this-worldly. He talked on successive Sundays about "the virtues near at hand," "the pleasures near at hand," "the God of the living." He was also extending his reading beyond the Western and Christian traditions. Fired perhaps by reading Jones, he sought out and began to study the work of Anquetil-Duperron on Zoroastrianism, the first authentic and sympathetic account of ancient Persian religion to reach the West. Emerson was struck by the figures of Ahriman and Ormuzd and even more by the manner of the stories. "Do we not feel," he asked "that these primeval allegories are globes and diagrams on which the laws of living nature are explained? Do we not seem nearer to divine truth in these fictions than in less pretending prose?"[8]

May 1832 was an extraordinary month for Emerson. He was, for whatever reason or conjunction of reasons, very much open to the world. He looked at Charles's shell collection with a surprised sense of instant recognition. Of each new form and color, it seemed, he said, that he could "recognize the thing the first time I see it." Everything seemed alive, full of possibility: "Every knot of every cockle has expression." The shells fascinated him: "I suppose an entire cabinet of shells would be an expression of the whole human mind; a Flora of the whole globe would be so likewise, or a history of beasts; or a painting of all the aspects of the clouds. Every thing is significant." What is being reported here is a moment of heightened awareness. And Emerson's response to such moments and moods is to embrace and accept. Nature and its beauty move him—and it is his most characteristic response—to praise. "Is it not better," he wrote in mid-May, "to intimate our astonishment as we pass through this world if it be only for a moment ere we are swallowed up in the yeast of the abyss? I will lift up my hands and say Kosmos." If there is a single moment at which the conventional Christian parish ministry—even a liberal Unitarian one—could no longer contain and give meaning to Emerson's life, it would be this moment when he recognized that his proper response to the world must be astonishment, his proper expression celebration.[9]

What is remarkable is not so much the ideas here, or even the fact of a moment of extraordinary awareness, but the almost visionary intensity of that awareness. Emerson was fully alive in the present and fully aware of what that meant: "The vanishing volatile froth of the present which any shadow will alter, any thought blow away, any event annihilate, is every moment converted into the Adamantine Record of the past." In an extraordinary image he suggests how the ephemeral process of the present—an immediate volcanic present—is changed into a fixed, inflexible record, how life dies down into the inert forms of the historical record. "We walk," he said, "on molten lava on which the claw of a fly or the fall of a hair makes its impression, which being received, the mass hardens to flint and retains every impression forevermore." Less than ten months after this entry,

Emerson decided to leave both the Second Church in Boston and the active parish ministry.

The image of the volcano was a suggestive one for Emerson. Later he would visit Etna and Vesuvius, and he kept a print of the latter in eruption hanging in his front hall in Concord for the rest of his life. Now, in 1832, the reference to molten lava suggests the heat and urgency of new interests rising within him. He was again reading heavily in science, in books about the natural world, as if he already saw the need to balance his book about mind with a corresponding attention to nature. He read Sir Humphry Davy's *Elements of Agricultural Chemistry,* Leslie's *Elements of Natural Philosophy,* Mawe's *Linnaean System of Conchology,* Drummond's *Letters to a Young Naturalist,* Hauy's *Elementary Treatise on Natural Philosophy,* and Huber's *New Observations of Bees.* Of most importance was his reading, back in December of 1831, of J. F. W. Herschel's *Preliminary Discourse on the Study of Natural Philosophy.*

The astronomer John Herschel, born in 1772, was the famous son of a famous father. His *Preliminary Discourse* is an attractive and accessible book on the scientific mind. Though we are physically weak, says Herschel, human beings have become the lords of the universe because "man is constituted as a speculative being; he contemplates the world, and the objects around him, not with a passive, indifferent eye, but as a system disposed with order and design."[10]

Herschel is at his most interesting and most unusual when he turns from external nature to consider the nature of the mind. He is interested in the nature of human creativity in science. What he cares about, even more than new discoveries, is the power to make new discoveries. He notes that the investigator "cannot help perceiving that the insight he is enabled to obtain into this internal sphere of thought and feeling is in reality the source of all his power."[11]

Herschel's enthusiasm for science rivals and takes over the language of religious enthusiasm. "The character of the true philosopher," he says, "is to hope all things impossible, and to believe all things not unreasonable." Herschel respects fact, of course, but he respects the principles governing facts even more: "We must never forget that it is principles not phenomena,—laws, not insulated, independent facts, which are the objects of inquiry of the natural philosopher." At the same time, he was completely alive to the potential interest and significance of all phenomena. He speaks continually of the "great sources of delight" which the natural sciences impart, and he insists that "to the natural philosopher there is no natural object unimportant or trifling." Here is Herschel's conception of the scientist, the natural philosopher: "Accustomed to trace the operation of general causes, and the exemplification of general laws, in circumstances where the uninformed and unenquiring eye perceives neither novelty nor beauty, he walks in the midst of wonders."[12]

Emerson warmed to this book at once. It quickened his already lively interest in science. He read everything he could find of the younger Herschel's. He recommended him to friends and watched for new books. No single volume was more important than Herschel's *Discourse* in shaping Emerson's new interest in science and nature. For a while Emerson even preferred Herschel to Milton: "What is there in 'Paradise Lost' to elevate and astonish like Herschel or Somerville?" The result of Emerson's new interest in science and his even newer belief in its power and findings led him to say, first in his journal and then in the sermon to his congregation on May 27, 1832, "I regard it as the irresistible effect of the Copernican astronomy to have made the theological scheme of redemption absolutely incredible." The new astronomy had revealed a world and a universe that could no longer usefully be described as fallen.[13]

21. A Terrible Freedom

EMERSON'S EXPRESSED PREFERENCE FOR ASTRONOMY OVER conventional Christian theology constitutes his break with the church. It is not a break with theism, not a rejection of the religious view of the world. It is a specific rejection of the idea that the center of Christianity is the fall of humankind in Adam and Eve and the redemption of humanity through the sacrifice of Christ. This conception of Christianity as the "scheme of redemption" is what gives meaning to the sacrament of Communion, or, as some Protestants call it, the Lord's Supper. Within a week of his calling the scheme of redemption "absolutely incredible," Emerson sent his church a letter saying he had changed his views about Communion and wished now to change the administration of that sacrament. He expected that the church would balk at his request and that he would as a result resign his position as minister. The church was not eager to lose Emerson. Neither could it in good conscience do away with what it regarded as the central sacrament of Christianity. In mid-June a committee declared that Emerson was free to believe as he might but that Communion must remain. The entire church then met to ratify this decision.[1]

Emerson stuck to his position. He withdrew dramatically into the mountains of New Hampshire to think over the matter and by mid-July he had decided to resign, come what may. As he wrote to Aunt Mary, he was "not prepared to eat or drink religiously." It is not quite true, however, to say that Emerson left the church over the issue of Communion. Emerson's disagreement with his church was simply the occasion for announcing and formalizing a separation that had already occurred. It is also untrue that his break with the church marked a loss of faith. If anything, Emerson believed too much, not too little. He found the Communion ceremony meaningless because it reduced Communion to eating and drinking. Emerson's position on this issue was not lightly taken or undefended. He had recently been studying the Quaker arguments on the subject. The Quakers made a careful distinction between Jesus' remarks at Capernaum about his being the bread of life (as reported by John) and the Last Supper. They took the latter to be a special form of Passover, designed only for the disciples and not for all future times. The remarks at Capernaum authorized a new institution—not simply a modernized Passover, but one intended to be celebrated in a spiritual sense only. The Quakers held not only that the bread and wine were symbolic but that the body and blood for which they stand were also symbolic, being metaphors for the spiritual state of being at one with Christ. Physical eating and drinking, even ceremonially, were therefore seen as inappropriately material for an entirely spiritual experience.[2]

Emerson's break with formal Christianity had been coming a long time, since before Ellen's death. In December of 1829 he was already complaining to Aunt Mary about the "warfare between the heroical and the proper." In February of 1832, long before the actual break, Aunt Mary, with her customary gift for seeing things first, was pleading with Emerson to stay in the ministry. But by early June he saw clearly that "in order to be a good minister it was necessary to leave the ministry." His deepest problem was that the church relied heavily, necessarily, on forms and Emerson was increasingly unable to live within the old inherited forms. As he noted to himself in New Hampshire in July, "Religion in the mind is not credulity and in the practice is not forms. It is a life. It is the order and soundness of a man. It is not something else *to be got,* to be *added,* but is a new life of those faculties you have."[3]

Emerson's new life seemed to those around him only a new failure. His family was disappointed. Charles clucked that he had done too much "for the expression of individual opinion." Aunt Mary thought he was in dangerous waters indeed. Leaving the Second Church in Boston was a repudiation of the world of his father. Emerson was also giving up institutional affiliation and support, a guaranteed social position, and a generous and assured salary. But these same facts, from another perspective, bespeak a kind of victory, a freeing of himself from the confining forms of church and state, a chance to begin again, to live entirely—and literally—on his own terms. He once observed that if he had the making of the rules, "I should gazette every Saturday all the words they were wont to use in reporting religious experience, as 'Spiritual Life,' 'God,' 'Soul,' 'cross,' etc and if they could not find new ones next week they might remain silent." In September 1832 he formally resigned from his church. In October the resignation was accepted. He started a poem, beginning:

> I will not live out of me
> I will not see with others' eyes

My good is good, my evil ill
I would be free.

His general mood in October was anything but resigned. "Why then shall I not go to my own heart first?" he asked. "A man must teach himself, because he can only read according to his state." "The true philosophy is the only prophet."[4]

In the late fall of 1832 Emerson suffered a physical and emotional letdown after the great crisis. After a brief burst of enthusiasm in October, he found himself utterly, appallingly free. He was free to start over, to go back to where the balance beam had been tipped toward the settled salaried life of the minister, free to take the other path. He was honest enough to concede that the new freedom was in some ways frightening.

> It is awful to look into the mind of man and see how free we are—to what frightful excesses our vices may run under the whited walls of a respectable reputation. Outside, among your fellows, among strangers, you must preserve appearances,—a hundred things you cannot do: but inside,—the terrible freedom![5]

He was sick and dispirited all fall. A prolonged attack of diarrhea left him very weak. Charles wrote Aunt Mary that he had never seen Waldo so disheartened. He had many ideas for projects but no one project. He reminded himself that "the modern Plutarch is yet to be written." He flirted with the idea of founding a magazine. He read Carlyle's essays on modern German literature and he began to think about the work of Goethe. He thought he might write a lecture on God's architecture, a sketch of a winter's day as a microcosm of creation. He began to think of going south again for the climate. He took out books on the West Indies.[6]

Then, on December 10, on the spur of the moment, because a ship was about to sail in that direction, he decided to go to southern Europe instead. He gave up his house, put his furniture up for sale at auction ("that domestic crack of doom and type of all forlornness") and moved his mother, who had been living with him. His wife was dead, his career in the ministry finished. He was leaving theology and the pastoral office behind and setting out toward a goal he could not see but which he knew involved both literature and natural history. "Things seem flying to pieces," Charles wrote Aunt Mary. Late in December 1832 the brig *Jasper*, 236 tons, cleared for Malta. There was a northeaster coming as Captain Ellis headed the ship, with Emerson aboard, out into the gray Atlantic swells. It was Christmas Day.[7]

The Inner Light

22. The American Eye

EMERSON HAD BEEN SUFFICIENTLY SICK THAT CAPTAIN ELLIS
had not wanted to take him aboard lest he not survive the voyage. The first
week of the trip was rough; the storm kept the passengers confined to "the
irremediable chagrins of the stateroom, to wit, nausea, darkness, unclean-
ness, harpy appetite and harpy feeding, the ugly sound of water in mine ears,
anticipations of going to the bottom." He set himself, as he had once before
in a storm at sea, to retrieve Milton's "Lycidas" from memory, "clause by
clause, here a verse and there a word, as Isis in the fable the broken body
of Osiris."[1]

The storm eased, Emerson's health sprang back, and he began to spend
long hours on deck. Emerson was impressed by the practical competence
of the sailors and by the voyage itself. He learned to use a sextant and
lamented his ineptness at arithmetic, astronomy, and geography. The long
voyage forced his attention to turn outward, away from himself and toward
the world. He wrote continually in his journal about the eye, about what
he saw. He drew conclusions from everything. Life at sea taught Burke's
lesson, he thought, "that there is no knowledge that is not valuable." The
voyage itself came to appear to him as an image of human life; he wrote of
"the planet on which we are embarked and making our annual voyage in
the unharboured deep."[2]

What life on shipboard really taught him was the value of action and the
insufficiency of words alone—of mere language. "It occurred forcibly this
morning," he wrote, "that the thing set down in words is not [thereby]
affirmed. It must affirm itself or no form of grammar and no verisimilitude
can give it evidence." Emerson clinched his comment with unaccustomed
vehemence: "This is a maxim which holds to the core of the world." About
other things he was much less certain. He did not really know, for example,
why he was going to Europe. He got up early one morning "and under the
lee of the spencer sheet had a solitary thoughtful hour." He was particularly
struck by the clouds, which seemed to him to be lit by the same light that
shone on Europe, Africa, and the Nile: "What, they said to me, goest thou

so far to seek—painted canvas, carved marble, renowned towns?" The point, he told himself, was that these celebrated things all began with the same light; one must look to nature for "the creative efflux from whence these works spring." He was aware, as he said, that "you reach no nearer the principle in Europe. It animates man. It is the America of America."[3]

As he approached the Old World, which was associated in his mind with history, chronology, society, cities, and art, Emerson was feeling defensive. He was also trying to act from the sturdy Stoic principle—"follow nature"—when he observed "this strong winged sea gull and striped shearwater that you have watched as they skimmed the waves under our vault—they are works of art better worth your enthusiasm." Though he had not yet landed, he was already bracing himself against the prospective pressure of Europe by asserting, more strongly than he had ever done before, his sense of his own Americanness. "Peeps up old Europe yet out of his eastern main?" he wrote, with Ishmaelian good humor.

> Sleep on, old Sire, there is muscle and nerve and enterprize enow in us your poor spawn who have sucked the air and ripened in the sunshine of the cold West to steer our ships to your very ports and thrust our inquisitive American eyes into your towns and towers and keeping rooms.[4]

After five weeks at sea the *Jasper* reached Malta on February 2, 1833. There it sat, at anchor, in quarantine, for a seemingly interminable fortnight. Finally, on February 15 Emerson and his fellow passengers landed and began to wander about the old town of Valletta in a transport of enthusiasm and wonder. Having expressed his reservations and given himself attitude talks, Emerson was now free to take it all in.

> All day with my fellow travellers I perambulated this little town of stone. It is from end to end a box of curiosities. And though it is very green and juvenile to express wonder, I could not hinder my eyes from rolling continually in their sockets nor my tongue from uttering my pleasure and surprize.

He especially admired the churches. "I yielded me joyfully to the religious impression of holy texts and fine paintings and this soothfast faith." He loved the organ music and the chanting friars, and he thought the church buildings vastly superior to those he knew: "How could anybody who had been in a Catholic church devise such a deformity as a pew?" It was a good beginning. Emerson was doing his European trip from south to north, reversing the route Goethe and others had taken. He liked the idea of entering Europe "at the small end" and he felt rejuvenated by what he was seeing. "Welcome these new joys," he wrote of Malta. "Let my American eye be a child's again to these glorious picture books."[5]

After a week in Malta, Emerson sailed for Syracuse, the southeasternmost point of Sicily, in a brigantine called *Il Santissimo Ecce Homo*. Arriving at noon, after a sixteen-hour passage, Emerson found himself surrounded by places and names he had heard about since childhood. From his room in the Strada Amalfitana in Ortygia—the peninsula of ancient Syracuse—he could see Mount Etna. "I have drunk the waters of the fountain Arethusa," he wrote home to William. "I have plucked the papyrus on the banks of the Anapus; I have visited the catacombs which Cicero admired . . . For my breakfast they give me most fragrant Hyblaean honey." He picked "dozens of beautiful flowers only three or four miles from the fountain Cyane where Proserpine went down with gloomy Dis." Emerson would come to believe that each life recapitulates all life. Now he was finding that his European trip was a recapitulation of European history. In Sicily he walked as in the age of myth; as he traveled he felt he was in "the playground of the gods and goddesses." The town of Syracuse was old and small. He could see the pillars of the temple of Capitoline Jove, the tomb of Archimedes, and the Ear of Dionysius from his hotel room. The city had once held 800,000 people. The current population was less than a twentieth of that. Everything was ruins, but Emerson knew what they were ruins of. Besides being a place of myth, Sicily for Emerson was associated with the tyrants Dionysius and Hiero, with Plato who had left Athens for Sicily, and with Cicero who had been an official in Sicily and who broke his own rule against speaking for the prosecution in order to lambaste the corrupt Sicilian proconsul Verres. Above all, Sicily meant the Plutarchan heroes Timoleon and Dion. Both Timoleon, subject of a later poem by Melville, and Dion, subject of a poem by Wordsworth already admired by Emerson, were republican heroes, enemies of tyranny who were remembered in Emerson's America for not only conquering the tyrants of Sicily and restoring the Republic but for themselves refusing absolute power when they could easily have had it.[6]

After a few days in Syracuse, Emerson took the mule path through Mellili to Catania, which he found a town of lava and earthquake. He was exhilarated by the cathedral church of St. Agatha in the midst of the busy, crowded city. He went on to Messina, passing over the flank of Etna, the vast active volcano dominating the eastern end of Sicily. Etna is 180 miles in circumference; it rises to over 11,000 feet and has 115,000 people living on its gentle, lethal slopes. From Messina, which had been rebuilt after the earthquake of 1783, Emerson went by steamer to Palermo, through the Straits of Messina, past Scylla and Charybdis, seeing Stromboli and the volcanic Lipari—or Aeolian—Islands. He was impressed with views of Palermo from the sea and from Monreale, with the grisly Capuchin burial vaults, lined with hundreds of partially clothed skeletons, and with the four hundred churches and convents that currently dominated a city that had once been an Islamic bridgehead to the West and a forest of minarets. Emerson was now reading Goethe's *Italian Journey,* slowly, in German, but he saw the public gardens in Palermo before he read about Goethe's moment of vision there, the moment when Goethe suddenly grasped the concept of what he called the *Urpflanz.*[7]

Emerson went by steamer next to Naples and at last stood upon the Continent itself. He fought against being overimpressed, against having his own existence effaced by the weight of the stones of the famous old city. "And what if it is Naples?" he wrote in his journal. "I won't be imposed on by a name. . . . Here's for the plain old Adam, the simple genuine self against the whole world." He stayed twelve days in Naples, and while there were no companions for the simple genuine self to talk with, he was impressed with the riches of the place and with the utter dominance of past over present, as least in the appearance of the city. He went to the Accademia to see works by Raphael, Titian, Guido, and Correggio. He loved the "rich collection of marble and bronze and frescoes from Herculaneum, Pompeii, and the baths of Caracalla" and above all the statues and portrait heads, "Cicero, Aristides, Seneca, and Dianas, Apollos without end. Nothing is more striking," he goes on, "than these contrasts of the purity, the severity expressed in these fine old heads, with the frivolity and sensuality of the mob that exhibits and the mob that gazes at them. They are," he concluded, "the countenances of the first born, the face of man in the morning of the world." He visited Baiae, Lake Avernus, the Villa Reale, Herculaneum, and Pompeii, and "many, many, nameless ruins." He was amazed that Goethe had found Naples a happy place. "You cannot go five yards in any direction without seeing [the] saddest objects and hearing the most piteous wailings. Instead of the gayest of cities, you seem to walk in the wards of a hospital." He climbed Vesuvius, finding it a fearful place on top where "the soil was warm and smoking all around and above us" and from which one could look down into the caldera, as one can today, feeling the heat through one's shoes and watching "the hollow of salt and sulphur smoking furiously beneath us."[8]

Emerson hurried on to Rome, arriving on March 27 to spend a month. As Sicily had reminded him of the age of myth and of Greece, so Naples— Neapolis—had represented for him the linking of Greek and Roman civilization. Now Rome, for Emerson, was dominated by the Renaissance. He went on April 4 to hear the Miserere sung in St. Peter's and was utterly awed by the place, quite against all his principles: "When night was settling down upon it and a long religious procession moved through a part of the church, I got an idea of its immensity such as I had not before." A few days later he said, simply, "I love St. Peter's. It is an ornament of the earth." Though he disapproved of superstition (he was amused when a bust of San Zenobio was touched to a person's head to ward off headaches for the year ahead), and though he kept his Protestant prejudices, he warmed to Catholic Italy. He confessed himself delighted by the churches, tempted by the monasteries, soothed by the rituals. It all pleased him without claiming him, in part because he could barely speak the language.[9]

Emerson had companions in Rome. It was a city of only a few more than 138,000 people, but there was a substantial foreign community. Emerson saw sights with Lewis Stackpole and William Pratt, both classmates of his brother Edward's. He got to know the American artists John Cranch and William Wall. Through a man named Eichthal he obtained a letter of introduction to John Stuart Mill, who in turn would give him a letter to Thomas Carlyle. Also in Rome he visited the studios of the American sculptor Horatio Greenough and the great Danish sculptor Bertel Thorwaldsen. He spent some pleasant hours in the company of Anna Bridgen of Albany.[10]

Emerson's visual sense expanded and reveled in the sights of Rome. He saw everything, from the Pantheon to Tivoli. He went to the Vatican Museum as often as it was open to the public. "On we went from chamber to chamber through galleries of statues and vases and sarcophagi and bas reliefs and busts and candelabra—through all forms of beauty and richest materials—till the eye was dazzled and glutted with this triumph of the arts. Go and see it, whoever you are," he wrote in his journal. "It is the wealth of the civilized world. It is a contribution from all ages and nations of what is most rich and rare. He who has not seen it does not know what beautiful stones there are in the planet." Emerson admired many conventionally

135

admired works, the Laocoön, Michelangelo's Moses, Raphael's Transfiguration. He also admired, in the fashion of the day, Canova's sculpture and Guido Reni's painting. And at times he went his own way, admiring the "beautiful head of the Justice who sits with Prudence on the monument of Paulus III on the left of the tribuna in St. Peter's" and the "Vision of St. Remoaldo" by Andrea Sacchi. He particularly liked the hooded form of the last Carmelite in the train in Sacchi's painting, a form that may have reminded him of the man on the road to Emmaus and that reminds us of the hooded figures of the all-giving days in his poem "Days." Rome even fashioned his dreams, Emerson said: "All night I wander amidst statues and fountains."[11]

In Florence, where he spent the month of May, the great attractions for Emerson were the work of Michelangelo and the company of Walter Savage Landor, the English poet whose *Imaginary Conversations* he greatly admired. Emerson visited Landor at his villa in Fiesole. This encounter was his first with a certifiably important English poet. Landor epitomized English arrogance and self-satisfaction. He had overbearing opinions on everything and Emerson pushed him as hard as he dared. He was amazed and a little shocked to find Landor preferring Philip of Macedon to Alexander, overvaluing Lord Chesterfield, undervaluing Burke, unwilling or unable to talk about Carlyle, full of Southey ("He pestered me with Southey; what is Southey?" Emerson fussed in his journal), and ignorant even of the name of Herschel. Many years later, when Emerson's account of the actual conversation with Landor appeared in *English Traits,* Landor was nettled and published an open letter to Emerson in which he misspelled Herschel's name while blustering on that he was not so much ignorant as "culpably inattentive."[12]

In Florence at Landor's he also met Augustus Hare, who with his brother Julius had written a book with the winning title *Guesses at Truth.* It is an unconventional collection of snippets of original sentences and paragraphs on the general subject of modern morals and manners. ("The ancients dreaded death; the Christian can only fear dying." "It is curious that we express personality and unity by the same symbol.") Emerson admired the book; he also admired Manzoni's *I promessi sposi,* preferring its manners to those he saw in the street. Emerson found Italy entertaining as well as instructive. He was amused at the frequently encountered superlative: "At the trattoria, when I asked if the cream was good, the waiter answered, "Stupendo."[13]

After Florence Emerson continued north and east, traveling by carriage, stopping at Bologna, Ferrara, Padua, and Venice. He then traveled west, back through Verona and Brescia to Milan. He left Milan on June 11 for Switzerland, having spent five months in Italy. Italy stimulated his visual imagination, giving him concrete images for his already vast reading knowledge of the past. He was perhaps even more struck by Italian scenery and nature than by the art. Etna had dominated his earliest sight of Sicily. His favorite spot of all was the Villa d'Este, outside Rome, where house, grounds, gardens, and fountains all fitted together into a splendid whole. Emerson admired it all, "the piazza, with its vast prospect, the silver river, the sun that shone, and the air that blew—I would fain keep them in my memory, the fairest image of Italy."[14]

23. I Will Be a Naturalist

EMERSON CAME INTO SWITZERLAND OVER THE SIMPLON PASS road built by Napoleon. It was an all-day trip. For brakes on the way down, "the wheel of the diligence is chained and shod with a heavy log of green wood." He passed Lake Leman, the castle of Chillon, and Vevay on his way to Lausanne, where he visited Gibbon's house. Switzerland meant people, not landscape to Emerson. In Emerson's progressive recapitulation of history, Switzerland also represented the eighteenth century. The "stern old town" of Geneva reminded him, he said, of Calvin, Rousseau, Gibbon, Voltaire, de Staël, and Byron. He noted, and he commendably refrained from gloating, that the Calvinist clergy of Geneva had just recently been ousted and replaced by Unitarians. He was dragged out by his fellow passengers to see Voltaire's home at Ferney, "protesting all the way upon the unworthiness of his memory."[1]

Coming to Paris, Emerson found it a "loud modern New York of a place," completely lacking the dreamy "air of antiquity and history" that hung over Italian towns. In Paris he completed his journey through European history and reentered the nineteenth-century present. He was now a seasoned traveler. He was not the shopper Thomas Jefferson had been, but he was just as avid for experience. "I collect nothing that can be touched, smelled, or tasted," he wrote, though he also noted ruefully that he was in danger of returning to America "without saying anything in earnest except to Cranch and Landor" in the preceding six months.[2]

"I stare and stare at the thousand thousand shop windows," he wrote William. It was a city of mirrors:

> All Paris is a perpetual puzzle to the eye to know what is object and what is reflection. . . . Even on the dessert service at the dinner table they set mirrors into the fruit stands to multiply whips, cherries and sugarplums, so that when I took one, I found two were gone.

He visited the Louvre and the King's Library, he went to a July 4 dinner for Lafayette, and he heard a French Unitarian, the Abbé Chatel. He haunted the splendid Parisian reading rooms, some of which subscribed to four hundred journals. He marveled at the more than two hundred newspapers in Paris alone. His own lack of direction made him keenly aware of the same thing in others. "All young men thirst for a *real* existence," he wrote, "for an object, for something great and good which they shall do with all their heart. Meantime, they all pack gloves, or keep books, or travel, or draw indentures, or cajole old women."[3]

Above all for Emerson on this trip, Paris meant science. Science had been very much on his mind just before his departure. In Florence he was struck by Landor's ignorance of Herschel. Also in Florence he visited the telescope maker, Giovanni Amici, and he went to the natural history museum. Early in his month-long stay in Paris, Emerson went to the Sorbonne, where he heard Louis Thenard and Joseph-Louis Gay-Lussac lecture on chemistry. Then on the thirteenth of July 1833 Emerson visited the Jardin des Plantes and the Cabinet of Natural History. It was a moment of vocational epiphany, complementing and answering his experience in the Vatican Museum. It was certainly the high point of his European trip to date and very much akin to the sudden insight into the *Urpflanz* which came to Goethe in the public garden at Palermo.[4]

The Jardin des Plantes was the old King's Garden, reorganized and renamed—as was everything else in France—after the Revolution. The deep continuity of the place lay in its management by three successive generations of Jussieus, running from the middle of the eighteenth to the middle of the nineteenth century. Botanical gardens during this time were major research centers, not at all the genteel indoor gardens of today's cities. The great botanical gardens were the Dow Chemical Companies of their time, funded by the government and engaged in pioneering work in pharmacology, food development, and forestry as well as in pure science. At the time of Emerson's visit no question was more important to the scientists of the Jardin des Plantes than the issue of plant classification. Emerson's own description of the place emphasizes this subject. "They have attempted," Emerson said, "to classify all the plants *in the ground* [that is, as living organisms and not as dead and mounted specimens], to put together, that is, as nearly as may be, the conspicuous plants of each class on Jussieu's system."[5]

Modern botanical classification was essentially created by Antoine Laurent de Jussieu (1748–1836), author of the *Genera Plantarum* (1789) and for many years the guiding spirit of both the Jardin des Plantes and French botany in general. In 1826 he handed on his chair to his son, Adrian, who was conducting public botanizing expeditions when Emerson was in Paris. The garden was laid out on the elder Jussieu's natural system of classification, the significance of which was not lost on Emerson. Herschel's *Discourse on the Study of Natural History* takes up the general problem of classification. So does James Drummond's *Letters to a Young Naturalist* (1831), which Emerson had been reading just before embarking for Europe. After he returned home, he read a book called *Elements of the Philosophy of Plants* (1821), the first three parts of which are a translation of Augustin-Pyramus de Candolle's *Théorie élémentaire de la botanique* (1819).

The artificial system of Linnaeus was a major mid-eighteenth-century effort to create order among the rapidly growing number of known plants. Linnaeus proposed a classification of twenty-four classes, based primarily on the number of stamens in the flower of the plant. (De Candolle noted that Linnaeus paid a disproportionate attention to the male sexual part of the flower.) The great advantage of this system is that as soon as one can determine the number of stamens in a given specimen, one has the name of its class. Plants whose flowers have five stamens belong to the class pentandria, flowers with six, to the class hexandria, and so on. The problem with the system is that it ignores all the many other parts of plants and the relations between parts which point to other significant groupings. Linnaeus himself recognized the limitations of his famous system, and while he said he could not himself produce a true or natural system, he called for one and even provided some large fragments of a natural system that were picked up and made into a thorough classification of a hundred classes by A. L. Jussieu. The difference between artificial and natural systems is easy to discern in the post-Darwin era. Any number of artificial systems are possible, but there can be only one natural system. Darwin pointed out that the principle of "descent with modification" (the basis of his own theory of evolution) was first discovered and pursued as the natural system of botanical classification.[6]

The exhibits Emerson saw at the Jardin des Plantes were laid out on Jussieu's natural system of classification, and Emerson's excited response to the exhibits was in large part a response to their arrangement. Classification implies connection. The debate on classification was a debate not just about how species are distributed in the natural world but about how they are connected to each other. What stirred Emerson was, first, the rich abundance and stupefying range of exotic flora and fauna gathered in one place and, second, the evident connections between the various specimens in each exhibit. He was amazed, for example, by the ornithological exhibits: "I wished I had come only there." He listed many of the birds, from the New Holland parrots to the tiny hummingbirds of Brazil, birds of paradise, black swans and white peacocks, ibis, flamingos, toucans, and vultures. He was oddly moved by what he saw.

> The fancy-coloured vests of these elegant beings made me as pensive as the hues and forms of a cabinet of shells, formerly. It is a beautiful collection and makes the visitor as calm and genial as a bridegroom. The limits of the possible are enlarged.[7]

In another section of the cabinet, or museum, was a display of minerals, "grand blocks of quartz, native gold in all its forms and crystallization, threads, plate, crystals, dust and silver black as from fire." It was like gazing on a treasure in the *Arabian Nights*. The effect on Emerson was magical and provocative:

> Ah, said I, this is philanthropy, wisdom, taste,—to form a cabinet of natural history. The Universe is a more amazing puzzle than ever as you glance along this bewildering series of animated forms, the hazy butterflies, the carved shells, the birds, beasts, fishes, insects, snakes, and the upheaving principle of life everywhere incipient in the very rock aping organized forms.

Throughout the garden and the indoor exhibits Emerson noted "how much finer things are in composition than alone." Emerson was fascinated by the web of relation and analogy, the very stuff of classifications, which, said Herschel, "cross and intersect one another, as it were, in every possible way, and have for their very aim to interweave all the objects of nature together in a close and compact web of mutual relations and dependence."[8]

Herschel's description of the purpose of classification provides a key to Emerson's response to the Jardin des Plantes. He gazed at the exhibits and saw relationships everywhere. Not only were the specimens linked to each other, they were also linked to him: "Not a form so grotesque, so savage, nor so beautiful but is an expression of some property inherent in man the observer." Perhaps for the first time since Ellen's death, Emerson felt an agitated, sympathetic—almost physical—connection with the natural world. He was powerfully affected. "I feel the centipede in me—cayman, carp, eagle and fox. I am moved by strange sympathies. I say continually, I will be a naturalist."[9]

Emerson's interests now took a marked turn toward the scientific. He did not become a scientist or even a naturalist; for all his interest in the physical world his reaction to the Jardin des Plantes was not that of a scientist. But from now on he acknowledged an unbreakable tie between his own mind and the natural world, and in his investigations into that tie he never lost his interest in the methods and materials of science.

Emerson had read or would soon read a number of works on natural theology, books such as Paley's *Natural Theology*, Drummond's *Letters to a Young Naturalist*, and Charles Bell's *The Hand*. Yet his interest in science is not now primarily theological. He does not reject the argument from design; indeed he welcomes it, but that argument is not what matters most. Emerson is much more interested in the relationship between the natural world and the human mind than he is in the natural world as proof of a designing deity.

A distinguishing mark of both American and German transcendentalism is to insist on the connection between the mind and nature. In Emerson's work, as in that of Thoreau later, the interest in nature is at least partly an interest in what science can teach us about nature. Emerson's interest in science and his interest in the natural world reinforce each other. He read books of science and scientific biography. He became particularly fascinated with the working of the scientific mind, with the nature of scientific knowledge, and with the strange union of precision and wonder in scientific inquiry. Over the years, Emerson's openness to science kept his thought ballasted with fact and observation and his writing anchored solidly in the real world.

24. A White Day in My Years

EMERSON'S MOMENT OF INSIGHT INTO THE INTERCONNECTED-
ness of things in the Jardin des Plantes was a moment of almost visionary
intensity that pointed him away from theology and toward science. That
moment had the emotional quality of a new beginning. Leaving Paris for
England four days later, Emerson reflected on what his European trip had
taught him so far. He had learned, he said, that his own instincts and
judgments were solid enough to have stood the test of European experience.
He thought he could no longer be dismissed or condescended to as an
undereducated and inexperienced provincial. He came now to England and
to London by ship up the Thames estuary. He was in an impatient frame
of mind. He saw the usual sights, but without gusto, for he was now bent
on seeing people. He was glad to be back in a country where he understood
what even the children at play were saying, but hearing English again only
reminded him that he had been without real companionship, intellectual
or other, for a long time. He saw Milton's house and the Hunterian
museum. Then on August 5 he went to see Coleridge at Highgate.[1]

Coleridge was sixty-one; he had less than a year to live, but conversa-
tionally speaking he was loaded to the muzzle as always. Emerson describes
him as "a short thick old man with bright blue eyes, black suit and cane,
and anything but what I had imagined, a clear clean face with fine complexion—a great snuff taker which presently soiled his cravat and neat black
suit." His hair was gray and he had a high forehead, which Hazlitt said
seemed "light, as if built of ivory, with large projecting eyebrows and his
eyes rolling beneath them like a sea with darkened lustre."[2]

Emerson was familiar with a good deal of Coleridge's work and he came
prepared to do homage. He had read the *Biographia Literaria* (1817) in
1826, he had known the *Aids to Reflection* since October 1829. In December
1829 he read *The Friend*. It kindled him and he wrote to Aunt Mary, "What
a living soul, what a universal knowledge." To Emerson Coleridge was a
citizen of the universe, one who believed "the mind was made to be spectator
of all, inquisitor of all; taking post at the center and as from a specular mount

143

sending sovereign glances at the circumference of things." Emerson also knew Coleridge's poetry, as published in *Sibylline Leaves,* which means he knew "The Ancient Mariner" but perhaps not "Kubla Khan" or "Christabel." He had found Coleridge's writing profoundly stimulating, especially his work on philosophical and religious ideas and on the nature of the mind and imagination. Coleridge was a post-Kantian. What he had to say about reason and understanding and fancy and imagination had been forged in response to the best thought of the preceding fifty years. No more penetrating and brilliant analysis of the creative mind and imagination than Coleridge's existed, at least in English.[3]

The great man greeted his American visitor, then held him as though bound, talking for an hour without letup. It was enormously decent of Coleridge to make time for this totally unknown young man, though the young man could not help feeling a little disappointed by Coleridge's tirade, which was directed against a Unitarianism Emerson was long past wishing to defend. Coleridge was himself a lapsed Unitarian. He had been a Unitarian minister in his youth and had come close to accepting a parish. He had moved away from his youthful liberalism toward a sterner, trinitarian, Church of England orthodoxy. Coleridge talked too about Channing, whom he had met, saying what a shame it was that he had ended up Unitarian. The trouble with Channing, said Coleridge—and it was his most telling argument against Unitarianism in general—was that "he loved Christianity for what was lovely and excellent—he loved the good in it and not the true."[4]

When Coleridge stopped for a moment to draw a breath, Emerson remarked, perhaps more out of loyalty to Channing than out of personal conviction, that it was only fair to inform him that he himself was a Unitarian. "'Yes,' he said, 'I supposed so,' and continued as before." Emerson did manage, subsequently, to ask about *The Friend,* to say that many Americans read Coleridge "with pleasure and profit who did not subscribe to his theology," and to ask if he corresponded with James Marsh, his American disciple and editor. Coleridge was warm in his praise of the painter Washington Allston and wished particularly to be remembered to him. After an hour of Coleridge's talk, most of which sounded like paragraphs from Coleridge's writings—"perhaps the same, not to be easily followed"—Emerson came away. He was not the first visitor to leave Coleridge with a heightened sense of fellow feeling for the wedding guest in "The Ancient Mariner." He made careful notes, as though he recognized that the encounter might have value beyond the present moment, but he had not been swept off his feet. There had been no give and take. Coleridge was too set in his ways to bend to a new companion. But the meeting was not entirely discouraging. Coleridge had not left Emerson feeling intimidated or inadequate. If anything, the great English critic and poet seemed caught up in sectarian issues and theological technicalities that Emerson was in the process of discarding as no longer vital.

Emerson traveled north through England, visiting Kenilworth, Warwick, and Matlock. He noted how similar the botany of England was to that of America. He recognized clematis, the mints, the goldenrods, the gerardias, the wild geraniums, and the wild parsley. But the loneliness of foreign travel was becoming more and more oppressive. "It will not do," he told himself, "to visit even these fine things alone." On August 16 he got to Edinburgh and on the twenty-sixth, after much enquiry and some difficult travel "romancing from Edinburgh to the Highlands," Emerson arrived at the door of Jane and Thomas Carlyle's house in Craigenputtock, sixteen miles from Dumfries, "amid wild and desolate heathery hills."[5]

Thomas Carlyle was then thirty-seven, already a successful essayist, and planning now to become the great poet of history and of the French Revolution. He was, said Emerson,

> tall and gaunt, with a cliff-like brow, self-possessed, and holding his extraordinary powers of conversation in easy command; clinging to his northern accent with evident relish; full of lively anecdote, and with a streaming humor, which floated everything he looked upon.

He was beset by terrible dyspepsia, the scourge of his life. His biographer Richard Garnet said "it was as if a rat were always gnawing at the pit of his stomach." With him at Craigenputtock was his witty, strong, and brilliant wife, Jane Welsh Carlyle, who had as a child persuaded her parents to let her learn Latin ("I want to learn Latin; please let me be a boy"), who had tied a weight to one ankle at night so she would not sleep too much, and who was so attractive a young woman that any man who talked with her for five minutes felt impelled to make her an offer of marriage."[6]

Emerson had learned the name Thomas Carlyle only two months before setting out for Malta, but he had been enthusiastically reading the anonymously published essays of this "Germanick new-light" writer for years. Carlyle had first come to wide public notice in 1827 with a long essay in the *Edinburgh Review* on Jean-Paul Richter, an extravagant and wildly experimental German writer. Emerson read Carlyle's essay when it appeared and thought the description of Richter's style would do for Aunt Mary as well. It also describes the style soon to be famous in English as Carlylese, in which "every work, be it fiction or serious treatise, is embedded in some fantastic wrappage, some mad narrative accounting for its appearance, and connecting it with the author."[7]

Emerson was originally drawn to Carlyle's work by the wild familiar style, but his real enthusiasm is for the Carlyle of "The State of German Literature" (1827), "Signs of the Times" (1829), and "Characteristics" (1831). These are great essays, each with a clear, positive position to advocate. They are written in forceful, colorful English and are wholly different from the intemperate and intolerant tirades, the soul-wearying complaints, and fustian blusterings of the later Carlyle. In denouncing the materialist and mechanical age of utilitarianism and in calling for a new age of mind, Carlyle in 1827 was a bold new prophet.

More than any other piece, "The State of German Literature" is the call-to-arms of transcendentalism. One can see Emerson's American scholar and Whitman's American poet in Carlyle's praise of the Fichte who said, "There is a Divine Idea pervading the visible universe; which visible universe is indeed but a symbol and sensible manifestation," and who then insisted that not theologians but

> literary men are the appointed interpreters of this Divine Idea: a perpetual priesthood, we might say, standing forth, generation after generation, as the dispensers and living types of God's everlasting wisdom, to show and embody it in their writings and actions, in such particular forms as their own particular times require it in.

To the question of what exactly is this "Divine Idea," Carlyle replies with a hint of the conception of the essential unity of all things. What the "Divine idea" means, says Carlyle, is "Under what other names and in what other formulas do I already know the same thing, which thou expressest by so strange and to me so unknown a symbol." This is the germ of the philosophy of identity that Emerson later recognized in Schelling and in Hinduism. It holds that there is fundamental unity, a basic similarity in all human experience which is more important, finally, than the many obvious differences.[8]

Nor is this all. "The State of German Literature" has a second part that takes up the charge of mysticism, which Carlyle says is merely the impression created by the English inability to understand the new, strict, difficult, and far-reaching philosophy of mind of Kant and his followers. The Kantists proceed from within and work out. They reject Locke and Hume. They look for primary truth in the fundamental nature—we would now say the deep structure—of the human mind. They insist that we have more in our minds than can be accounted for by the simple accumulation of sensory experience. They "believe that both Understanding and Reason are organs, or rather, we should say, modes of operation, by which the mind discovers truth." Kantians think that "Reason discovers truth itself, the absolutely and primitively true, while Understanding discovers only relations, and cannot decide without *if*."[9]

Carlyle demolishes the intellectual pretensions of those who mock German literature as being in bad taste and German thought as mystical. Carlyle's later proclivity for attack is already evident; he is the self-appointed hammer of mediocrity. In "Signs of the Times" (1829) Carlyle denounces the present as a mechanical age in which "there is now no such thing as a science of mind, only more or less advancement in the general science . . . of matter." He calls for a new age of "dynamism" and a compensating new science of "dynamics" to "treat the primary unmodified forces and energies of man, the mysterious springs of love, and fear, and wonder, of Enthusiasm, Poetry, Religion, all which have a truly vital and infinite character." The human, he says, "is not the creature and product of mechanism, but in a far truer sense, its creator and producer." "Signs of the Times" is one of the best pieces Carlyle ever wrote. Critique is balanced by prospectus, denunciation by advocacy. "This deep paralysed subjection to physical objects comes not from nature, but from our own unwise mode of viewing nature." Nowhere in English is there a more forceful statement of the importance of the German concept of *Bildung*. "To reform a world, to reform a nation, no wise man will undertake; all but foolish men know, that the only solid, though a far slower reformation, is what each begins and perfects in himself."[10]

"Characteristics" (1831) is the third of Carlyle's great early essays. Emerson read it, as he read the others, in an already receptive mood. "Characteristics" tries to describe just what is meant by the "intuitive" as opposed to the "logical" and the "argumentative." Doubt and inquiry are both necessary but are only to be understood as an intermediate phase in human thought. What is needed is that thought should again recover its earliest character of affirmation and sacred precept. What Carlyle says he has learned from "Kantism, Fichtism, Schellingism, Cousinism" is that "a faith in religion has again become possible and inevitable for the scientific mind."[11]

Emerson had read these and other essays of Carlyle's with preconditioned interest and a disposition to believe. He also read Carlyle on Schiller, on Luther, on the Corn Law Rhymer, and on Goethe. It made a difference to Emerson that Carlyle was a contemporary while Coleridge and Wordsworth were of the earlier generation. Even before they met, Emerson knew they had a considerable range of common ground.

When Emerson showed up at Craigenputtock, they hit it off at once, walking and talking all day. The Carlyles persuaded Emerson to prolong his planned visit. He stayed the night and the flow of talk continued. They talked about magazines, about America, about Landor, Plato, Mirabeau, Gibbon, Tristram Shandy, Robinson Crusoe, Robertson's *History of America,* and Rousseau. They talked about social issues such as "English pauperism, the crowded country, the selfish abdication by public men of all that public persons should perform." They walked over the long hills, looked across and down into Wordsworth's country, and talked about all things above and below. "Christ died on the tree," said Carlyle. "That built Dunscore Kirk yonder: that brought you and me together. Time has only a relative existence."[12]

Emerson always looked back on this visit as "a white day in my years." He had been wonderfully taken with Carlyle's restless energy and powers of articulation. Here was a living, not an extinct, volcano whose "lava-torrents of fever frenzy enveloped all things." Carlyle's report of the meeting to another recent friend, John Stuart Mill, shows how far Emerson had come from the sick and discouraged condition in which he had sailed from Boston. "What I loved in the man," Carlyle told Mill, "was his health, his unity with himself; all people and all things seemed to find their quite peaceable adjustment with him." Jane Carlyle later insisted that Emerson's visit was the most memorable event in their life at Craigenputtock, like the visit of an angel. If the meeting between Carlyle and Emerson was not quite the most memorable meeting on a Scotch moor since Macbeth encountered the witches, as an early biographer of Carlyle has it, it was still a remarkable conjunction, a moment when two extraordinary natures, both still in the formative stage, met, a day like that on which Melville met Hawthorne or like the day Dorothy Wordsworth always remembered when Coleridge burst into her life and William's. She recalled how Coleridge left the high road as he approached and "leapt over a gate and bounded down the pathless field by which he cut off an angle."[13]

Two days later it was Emerson who came to see Wordsworth at Rydal Mount. The poet was then sixty-three. His major work was behind him; he was living in a generally feeble state of health and under a perpetual threat of blindness. Wordsworth had the distinguished air of a public man. Balding, with a fine forehead and flying white hair, he had large prominent eyes—much prone to inflammation—a long nose with a marked bridge, and a long upper lip. When Emerson met him, Wordsworth was much diminished by poor health, appearing plain, elderly, unprepossessing, and "disfigured by green goggles," which he wore to help his inflamed eyes. Emerson had been reading his poetry since at least his junior year in college. In 1826 he had first read "Dion" and the Immortality ode. From 1828 on he went back to Wordsworth every year. He read "Rob Roy," "The Happy Warrior," and "Tintern Abbey." He particularly admired the "Ode to Duty," the sonnets to Liberty, and the first books of *The Excursion*. A young acquaintance of Emerson's later said that Emerson knew by heart most of *The Prelude* and *The Excursion*. Privately, in his journal, Emerson both admired and kept up a running quarrel with Wordsworth, "a man of such great powers and ambition, so near to the *dii majores* to fail so meanly in every attempt." But he did not pester Wordsworth with the hypercritical fault-finding of young ambition.[14]

Wordsworth was kind and genial and he put himself out for his young American. He talked about America, referred warmly to Channing, and got off on his then favorite topic, which was his disapproval of public education on the grounds "that society is being enlightened by a superficial tuition, out of all proportion to its being restrained by moral culture." Emerson tried his new enthusiasms out. Wordsworth "abused" Goethe's *Wilhelm Meister* "with might and main" and thought that Carlyle wrote obscurely, that he was "sometimes insane." Even Coleridge, he said, wrote more clearly. Wordsworth had only heard of Cousin. He praised Lucretius as a far higher poet than Virgil because of his "power of illustration." He had just come from a visit to Staffa and was writing sonnets on Fingal's cave, some of which he recited for Emerson. When it came time to go, Emerson recalled that Wordsworth "said he would show me a better way toward the inn; and he walked a good part of a mile, talking, and ever and anon stopping short to impress the word or the verse, and finally parted from me with great kindness, and returned across the field."[15]

The following day Emerson arrived in Liverpool, ready to take ship for home. His nine-month European trip had ended on a high note. But he was ready to close out his European account. He was full of plans and energy, and he waited, fretting, in a fever of impatience for the ship to sail.

25. The Instructed Eye

Day after day passed while the winds pinned the restless Emerson in Liverpool: "If the vessel do sail they say we shall be drowned on the lee shore; if she do not sail I perish waiting." His eagerness to be home made him realize that he felt no regret in not being born English. Fresh from encounters with Coleridge, Carlyle, and Wordsworth, he could still say that the best thing about England was that it was the "most resembling country to America which the world contains." He felt he had seen the best minds of England, and he concluded grumpily and uncharitably that "not one of them is a mind of the very first class." He felt further that Europe had not given him a new scale by which to judge but had rather "confirmed me in my convictions." He hugged his impulses toward enthusiasm, saying, "I believe in my heart it is better to admire too rashly, as I do, than to be admired too rashly, as the great men of this day are." He was leery of what he called "premature canonization"; he thought those canonized missed "a great deal of necessary knowledge."[1]

While Emerson waited in his room in Liverpool, he returned in his journal to the problems he had left behind. With a new decisiveness and clarity he formulated for himself what he called the "errors of traditional Christianity as it now exists" and of "religionists." The latter, he thought, "are clinging to little, positive, verbal, formal versions of the moral law . . . while the laws of the Law, the great circling truths whose only adequate symbol is the material laws, the astronomy etc. are all unobserved, and sneered at when spoken of." He now counted both Calvinism and Unitarianism among the imperfect versions. We usually think of Emerson as an embracer, an affirmer, but frequently enough the platform for an affirmation is a four-square rejection. Here Emerson makes his explicit break with most of orthodox, formal Christianity. A three-point affirmation follows immediately. "I feel myself pledged," he wrote, "to demonstrate that all necessary truth is its own evidence: that no doctrine of God need appeal to a book; that Christianity is wrongly received by all such as take it for a system of doctrines . . . it is a rule of life not a rule of faith." Each

151

sect is a false, imperfectly crystallized form of the one moral law, the "one bottom." The underlying unity explains why "the eminent men of each church, Socrates, à Kempis, Fénelon, Butler, Penn, Swedenborg, Channing, all say the same thing." Emerson set himself to list and enumerate a few of the remarkable properties of that central, uniform teaching.[2]

The first three items in this sketch of what would become *Nature* are modern restatements of Stoic thought. They sound particularly like Marcus Aurelius: "A man contains all that is needful to his government within himself. He is made a law unto himself. All real good or evil that can befall him must be from himself." In addition to this concept of autarchy—as opposed to anarchy—Emerson lists the ideas of compensation and correspondence. "Nothing can be given to him or taken from him but always there is a compensation. There is a correspondence between the human and everything that exists in the world [and] is known to man." Rushing on— working now in bold strokes—Emerson outlines the purpose of life not in terms of the traditional catechism but in terms of Goethe's *Bildung,* or self-cultivation: "The purpose of life seems to be to acquaint a man with himself." He declares himself free not only of the conventional past but of the conventionally conceived future: "He is not to live to the future as described to him, but to live to the real future by living to the real present." He closes his sketch of main points with a simple statement of the central truth of religious—not secular—humanism, the idea that is also the foundation of democratic individualism: "The highest revelation is that God is in every man." This is not anthropomorphism but its antithesis, theomorphism.

Finally the ship sailed. "I saw the last lump of England receding without the least regret," Emerson wrote. It proved a stormy passage. Gales and headwinds locked the passengers below. They listened apprehensively to "every rope that snaps and every spar that cracks overhead." The steerage passengers sat up all night or lay in wet berths. The cow refused to get up to be milked. Emerson noted in his journal how the four dogs "shiver and totter about all day, and bark when we ship a sea." But Emerson was content. He was bound home, to "a land without nobility or wigs or debt / No castles, no cathedral and no kings / Land of the forest." And his internal direction was now fixed, even if certain external, practical considerations were not. "I like my book about nature," he wrote, "and wish I knew where and how I ought to live."[4]

Emerson plunged himself into activity as soon as his ship touched shore. He arrived in Boston on October 9, 1833; within two days he had committed himself to give the inaugural lecture of the season to the recently organized Boston Society of Natural History. He saw his mother, Aunt Mary, his brothers Charles and William. William announced that he was soon to be married. Asked to preach at his old church, Emerson used the occasion to signal his change of direction. "The teacher of the coming age must occupy himself in the study and explanation of the moral constitution of man more than in the elucidation of difficult texts," he wrote in his journal. In the sermon he expanded on the importance of the teacher: "Teaching is the perpetual end and office of all things. Teaching, instruction is the main design that shines through the sky and earth." We may smile at the young man who identifies his next career step with the final purpose of the universe, yet along with the overearnest tone is a fresh awareness of design in nature: "The end of being is to know; and if you say, the end of knowledge is action,—why, yes, but the end of that action again, is knowledge." Self-knowledge and self-cultivation he now sees not as a means to something but as the ends and goals of life itself. The insight was new to Emerson—and thus original in that sense—but it was hardly novel, as he knew. He told his hearers that this point of view revived old Stoic maxims and precepts. Emerson made a little sequence of them, beginning with "Know thyself." If it was also true, as the Stoics claimed, that the good man differs from God in nothing but in duration, then the result was to "know thyself a man and be a God." That realization leads in turn to the injunction "Revere thyself."[5]

Emerson now had neither home nor furniture, and for over a year after his return from England he moved about from place to place in Boston and Newton. In the months immediately after his return he wrote and delivered a loosely related group of four lectures on science. The Lyceum movement was just beginning, there was a demand for public lectures, and Emerson saw a possible new career as a Lyceum lecturer. With his new profession he had a new subject. Though he was no scientist, he was extremely interested in the mind of the scientist and in the meaning of science for modern life. In 1793 Thomas Paine had said, with his usual unforgivable but unforgettable bluntness, that "science is the true theology" because it is the study of the power and works of God. Emerson now recalled that Bacon had also said that "man is the minister and interpreter of nature" and that we are intended "not only to explain the sense of each passage but the scope and argument of the whole book [of nature]."[6]

Emerson was now consumingly interested in the connection between man and nature. He shares this concern with Kant, Schelling, and the

English romantic poets. "There is more beauty in the morning cloud than the prism can render account of," he wrote. "There is not a passion in the human soul, perhaps not a shade of thought but has its emblem in nature." This connection, for Emerson, was the undersong of science, the "concurrent text" running alongside the book of nature, and it was precisely his own focus of interest. The connection—the analogy—between the human mind and nature "is felt to be deeper and more universal for every law that is revealed. It almost seems as if an unknown intelligence in us expressed its recognition of each new disclosure."[7]

On November 5, 1833, less than a month after his return, Emerson delivered the first of his new science lectures, "The Uses of Natural History." He gave an excited, expanded account of his experience in Paris, dwelling on the botanical garden as a "grammar of botany where the plants rise, each in its class, its order, and its genus." "Imagine," he said, "how much more exciting and intelligible is this natural alphabet, this green and yellow and crimson dictionary, on which the sun shines, and the winds blow." As with Jussieu's garden, so with the whole earth. Contradicting the sad song of Ecclesiastes, Emerson insists that "the eye is filled with seeing." He went on to suggest the main uses of natural history. The study of natural history is first of all healthy, leading to an outdoor life. Second, it is useful, to farmers and to others; it furnishes us with our commodities. Third, and of more importance to Emerson, science delights the mind. "It needs only to have the eye informed," he said, "to make everything we see, every plant, every spider, every moss, every patch of mould upon the bark of a tree, give us the idea of fitness, as much as the order and accommodation of the most ingeniously packed dressing box."[8]

Emerson now found design everywhere, but he was no longer concerned, as Paley was, to move from design to designer. Rather he was interested in design itself and in how it is that the human mind can see and understand the complexity and the design in things. "If a man should study the economy of a spire of grass," he said, "how it sucks up sap, how it imbibes light, how it resists cold, how it repels excess of moisture, it would show him a design in the form, in the color, in the smell, in the very posture of the blade as it bends before the wind." Fourth, says Emerson, the study of nature has an educative, disciplining effect on the mind, making it exact and also generating enthusiasm, which he calls "the highest state of the character." Finally, he says, "it is the effect of science to explain man to himself," and he offers the hope that "the knowledge of all the facts of all the laws of nature will give man his true place in the system of beings." Emerson's thought, in this lecture and elsewhere, shows how the old argument from design would transmute itself, once it dropped its overriding interest in proving the existence of a designer, into the modern scientific interest in how things fit together in nature.[9]

Emerson is also interested—overwhelmingly—in nature as a language, as the main source of effective imagery in writing and in speech. Much of what he says about the correspondence between nature and the human mind becomes at once completely practical when we understand it as a concern with the writer's use of nature as a source of language, metaphor, and images of all kinds. When Emerson talks—as he does in this lecture—about the "power of expression which belongs to external nature, or that correspondence of the outward world to the inward world of thought and emotions," or when he talks about the "secret sympathy which connects men to all the animals and to all the inanimate beings around him," or when he says "the whole of nature is a metaphor of the human mind," he means that the writer draws mainly on nature for language and for symbol and that these symbols—white whales, ravens, Walden Ponds, leaves of grass—can be used as symbols because of the primary connections that already exist between nature and every mind. Some of the difficulties of Emerson's difficult assertions (such as "particular natural facts are symbols of particular spiritual facts") evaporate when understood in terms of the writer's or artist's use of nature for expression or self-expression. Emerson himself recognized and emphasized this self-expression. His lecture ends: "Nature is a language and every new fact one learns is a new word; but it is not a language taken to pieces and dead in the dictionary, but the language put together into a most significant and universal sense. I wish to learn this language," he announced, "not that I may know a new grammar, but that I may read the great book which is written in that tongue."[10]

For Emerson it is always the instructed eye, not the object seen, that gives the highest delight, that connects us with the world. Partly for that reason his favorite symbol for inquiry and knowledge and wisdom was the image of the active eye. He knew the importance of the eye. He liked Tacitus's saying that "in battle the eye is first conquered." The eye is Emerson's great symbol. "To an instructed eye the universe is transparent," he wrote in his journal this fall of 1833. The eye was always more than a metaphor. Emerson lived a good deal in his senses, observing that "the exercise of all the senses is as intense pleasure, as anyone will find, who recovers the use of one after being deprived of it." It is this felt, lived quality as well as his never-diminished interest in the process of observation that give his best images their astonishing power and vividness. "To the astronomer," said Emerson in the January lecture "The Relation of Man to the Globe," "the earth is a moveable observatory,—enabling him to change his place in the universe" and get a new angle on other planets and stars, "as if this planet were a living eye sailing through space to watch them."[11]

26. Mary Rotch: Life without Choice

On November 9, 1833, a month after his return from Europe and just a few days after his initial lecture on science, Emerson went to New Bedford, Massachusetts, for a month, preaching there in the Unitarian church in place of his cousin Orville Dewey. Between November 1833 and April 1834 Emerson spent almost three months in the old whaling town of New Bedford, where he heard all sorts of stories about the fishery. A seaman in a coach told him "the story of an old sperm whale which he called a white whale which was known for many years by the whalemen as old Tom and who rushed upon the boats which attacked him and crushed the boats to small chips in his jaws."[1]

New Bedford had been a strongly Quaker town since the seventeenth century, refusing to pay taxes for the support of ministers, formally opposing slavery as early as 1716, and becoming a city of refuge for runaway slaves. Frederick Douglass would get his new name and new start there among the Quaker abolitionists, one of whom was the Daniel Ricketson who became a good friend of Thoreau. Emerson boarded in 1833–1834 with a Quaker named Deborah Brayton, and it was the Quakers who most interested him about the town. He also met and was profoundly impressed by a Quaker named Mary Rotch, whose story interested him. He read the manuscript account of her expulsion from the local Friends council of elders in 1823. Mary Rotch and her sister Elizabeth Rodman were removed from the council because of their support of Mary Newhall, a powerful and progressive New Light Quaker whose views sharply challenged the old Quaker order. As a result of this expulsion the liberal Quakers left the meeting in a group and joined the Unitarian church, the one at which Emerson was now preaching.[2]

Emerson's interest in the Quaker way did not begin here. He had taken part in a public forum on William Penn at Harvard in 1820, and in 1827, on his way home from St. Augustine, he had been impressed by the Quaker druggist from Alexandria, Edward Stabler. Emerson compared Stabler implicitly with Jesus. Stabler spoke, said Emerson, "as one having authority."

157

In 1830 Emerson was again reading the works of William Penn, and in 1832, just as his decision to leave the Second Church was coming to a head over the issue of Communion and just as his new interest in science was rising, Emerson immersed himself in an intensive reading of Quaker writers. Besides Clarkson's *Portraiture of Quakerism* (1806), Sewel's *History of the Quakers* (1722), and more of Penn, he read Henry Tuke's *Memoir of the Life of Fox* (1815). When on September 9, 1832, he preached the sermon on the Lord's Supper in which he articulated the reasons for his break with the church, he took an important part of his argument directly from Clarkson.[3]

Quaker ideas were deeply and powerfully congenial to Emerson. When asked point blank about his religion by a relative, David Haskins, around 1839, Emerson replied carefully "with greater deliberateness and longer pauses between his words than usual" that he was "more of a Quaker than anything else. I believe in the 'still small voice' and that voice is Christ within us." Emerson's familiarity with Quaker ideas is a good example of the difficulties of talking about the influences on Emerson. With Quakerism, as with de Staël, Coleridge, Carlyle, Kant, and Hinduism and Stoicism, Emerson was not so much converted as he was confirmed. When he went to New Bedford in 1833, Emerson already believed in something resembling the Quaker's fundamental principle of absolute trust in the inner voice, the "Inner Light."[4]

The Quaker way, as understood by George Fox, the founder and apostle of the movement, and as understood by his followers and by the historians Emerson read, represented the true Reformation. "Quakerism," says Clarkson,

> may be defined to be an attempt, under the divine influence, at practical Christianity, so far as it can be carried. Those who profess it, consider themselves bound to give up such of the customs, or fashions of men, as militate, in any manner, against the letter or the spirit of the gospel.

Quakerism has an iron core. Clarkson observes that Quakers consider themselves also under an obligation to follow virtue, not ordinarily, "*but even to the death.*" Thomas Clarkson was an important eighteenth-century abolitionist who got so much support from the Quakers that he wrote a three-volume work on Quakerism as a thank-you. Clarkson lucidly and sympathetically explains how the well-known Quaker prohibitions (no music, no dancing, no novels, no theater, no destruction of animal life for pleasure), the peculiar Quaker customs (no separate salaried ministers, no officiated marriages, baptisms, or funerals, the use of singular "thee" and "thou" instead of the inaccurate plural "you"), and Quaker social activism (refusal to pay taxes for support of ministers, abolitionism, equality of women, pacifism) are all founded on simple positive religious principles. "God has given to all," says Clarkson, "besides an intellectual, a spiritual understanding. . . . This spirit may be considered as the primary and infallible guide—and scriptures but a secondary means of importance."[5]

Quakerism was thus for Emerson the ultimate Protestantism, the decisive locating of religious authority in the individual. "This spirit," Clarkson insists, "as a primary and infallible guide, has been given to men universally and sufficiently. Those who resist it, quench it." Quakerism is theologically consistent. "This spirit then besides its office of a spiritual guide, performs that of a redeemer to men." This redemption leads to a new birth, which is "as real from the spiritual seed of the kingdom as that of plants and vegetables from their seeds in the natural world."[6]

But the real strength and energy of the Quakers comes from neither prohibitions nor theology but from "the centering of life on the realities of inward intercourse with God." Quakerism is supremely committed to the individual's own experience. "No other religious community so deliberately and emphatically bases its individual and corporate life upon the supreme fact of the soul's immediate contact with God," says a modern Quaker historian. The reality of the inner light and its practical accessibility give it an emphasis on ethics and action, not on knowledge or mystery.

> It was in this focusing on moral effort that the Quakers differed from most other sects of the Commonwealth period. Their views were not novel or original. Every one of them had already been proclaimed by some individual or by some religious party. What was new was the fixing of their ideas into one living truth, which was henceforth *to be done,* was to be put into life and made to march.

Resolutely followed, Quakerism is not only a religion in which "the form has continually to be subordinated to the life" but also "a religious experience that makes all life sacred, all nature a sanctuary, all work a sacrament, and gives to every man and woman . . . fit place and service."[7]

This was the Quaker way Emerson read about in Clarkson, in William Penn, and in William Sewel's *History of the Quakers*. The latter is an early book mostly concerned with the life and labors of George Fox. Penn's comments on the marks and fruits of Quakerism were particularly pertinent. "They were changed men themselves before they went about to change others," Penn said. "They directed people to a principle in themselves though not of themselves." It was not only Quaker words but Quaker lives that Emerson found fascinating. He read several lives of Fox, who had himself insisted, "What I am in words, the same I am in life." Emerson vividly remembered Stabler, and now in New Bedford in the fall of 1833 he met and talked with Mary Rotch, who furnished Emerson with a completely believable example and a compelling explanation of the exact nature and operation of the inner light itself.[8]

Mary Rotch was born in 1777 in Nantucket. She was of the same generation as Mary Moody Emerson and Ruth Haskins Emerson. Her father was one of the most prosperous whaling merchants of the time; the Rotches had launched three generations of Quaker whalers by 1759. On her mother's side Mary Rotch was descended from the Starbucks of Nantucket. Her father favored neutrality for Nantucket during the Revolution. As a result the family was forced to live abroad in France and England when Mary was in her teens. She returned to America when she was eighteen. In 1812 she and others formed a discussion group, wrote papers, and read books by such writers as Dugald Stewart and Johann Kaspar Lavater. When the "New Light" views of Mary Newhall of Lynn began to spread to New Bedford in the early 1820s, Mary Rotch was in her mid-forties and an elder of the New Bedford Meeting. She was a formidable person, a modern Ann Hutchinson. She defended the "New Light" beliefs that "the Light Within, not the Bible, was the final authority in Religion, for the Bible was only one expression of the spirit constantly active in every human soul."

After a protracted series of debates and meetings, the "Old Lights" won; Mary Rotch was ejected as an elder. She then led a mass exodus of "New Lights" from the Quaker Meeting to the New Bedford Unitarian church, to which Emerson's cousin, the Rev. Orville Dewey, had recently come. The force of Mary Rotch's personality is everywhere evident in accounts of the time. After meeting her, Dewey said, "Wife! were ever hearts taken by storm like that?" She herself said of her position during the controversy, "As regards my own case, if the extending of my arm would alter the least point, I could not, I would not do it."[9]

Emerson was powerfully affected by this modern Luther-like rebel. He said of her, "If she had said yea and the whole world had thundered in her ear nay, she would still have said yea." He heard her story, read the manuscript account of her "trial," and talked with her about her deepest convictions, which he wrote about at some length in his journal:

> She was much disciplined she said, in the years of Quaker dissension and driven inward, driven home, to find an anchor, until she learned to have *no choice*, to acquiesce without understanding the reason when she found an obstruction to any particular course of action.

She was not willing to have the experience reduced to an easy or approximate label. "She objected to having this spiritual direction called an impression, or an intimation, or an oracle. It was none of them." Neither Hartley's language, nor Wordsworth's, nor even Reed's would do. "It was so simple it could hardly be spoken of. It was long, long before she could attain to anything satisfactory. She was in a state of great dreariness." She had a friend who told her

> to dwell patiently with her dreariness and absence, in the confidence that it was necessary to the sweeping away of all her dependence upon tradition, and that she would finally attain to something better. And when she attained a better state of mind, its beginnings were very, very small.[10]

Emerson found this account sufficiently compelling to set it as a goal for himself. "Can you believe, Waldo Emerson," he wrote, "that you may relieve yourself of this perpetual perplexity of choosing, and by putting your ear close to the soul, learn always the true way?" Miss Rotch's experience was fully convincing in itself, but Emerson noted with joy how well it agreed with the notion of Socrates' daemon and with the "grand unalterableness of Fichte's morality." Above all, Emerson was struck by the serene and perfect assurance of Miss Rotch. He copied down her best expression of it. "I found," she said, "though the sympathy of friends was most pleasant, yet the little faith I had, tho' but a grain of mustard seed, nothing could shake, and I found that nothing could confirm it."[11]

On the twenty-first of March Emerson was reading the records of the debates of 1823 in which Mary Rotch figured. On the next day he wrote in his journal: "The subject that needs most to be presented, developed, is the principle of Self Reliance, what it is, what it is not, what it requires, how it teaches us to regard our friends." Mary Rotch's effect on Emerson was profound. Not only did she confirm his direction, she showed him the next step, and she seems to have helped him clear the path to his own inmost self.[12]

Shortly after his return from New Bedford in April 1834, Emerson found himself sitting in a sunny hollow at Mt. Auburn in Cambridge.

> I opened my eyes and let what would pass through them into the soul. I saw no more my relation how near and petty to Cambridge or Boston, I heeded no more what minute or hour our Massachusetts clocks might indicate—I saw only the noble earth on which I was born, with the great star which warms and enlightens it. I saw the clouds . . . It was Day, that was all Heaven said. The pines glittered with their innumerable green needles in the light and seemed to challenge me to read their riddle. The drab oak leaves of the last year turned their little somersaults and lay still again. And the wind bustled high overhead in the forest top.[13]

Less than a year later Emerson wrote and delivered a lecture on George Fox as part of a series of lectures called "Biography." Several points in the lecture suggest how central the Quaker angle of vision had become to him. The passion of love and the sentiment of religion are, he says, "the remedial force by which the decay and degeneracy of the human race is hindered." (Fox, in this lecture, exemplifies the sentiment of religion. Other lectures treated Luther as the representative of reform, Michelangelo of art, and Milton of poetry.) Emerson gives a description of the inner light and how it operates "to bring the universe into the possession of a single soul." The inner light was "an infallible guidance . . . by which he [Fox] understood nothing that was peculiar to himself but a leading that was tendered to every man who yielded himself to it." Emerson further understood that the inner light is the irreducible source not only of personal religious experience but of modern political, indeed democratic ideals. The inner light is "the most republican principle," he says.

> All religious movements in history and perhaps all political revolutions founded on claims of Rights, are only new examples of the deep emotion that can agitate a community of unthinking men, when a

truth familiar in words, that "God is within us," is made for a time a conviction.[14]

Part of Fox's appeal was also that he was both idealist and realist—idealist because he sought to "accommodate the shows of things to the mind" and realist because he always substitutes a "thing for a hollow form." Fox's experiences and the phrasing associated with them were passing permanently into Emerson's deepest well of convictions. Fox came to see that "to be bred at Oxford or Cambridge was not enough to make a minister of Christ" and that "the scriptures cannot be understood but by the same spirit that gave them forth." The latter came to be Emerson's cardinal principle of criticism.[15]

We all read hundreds of books, but the reading does not make us great writers, nor does it very often change our lives. When we have canvased Emerson's vast reading, it will by itself have told us little or nothing about the creative process or the growth of character. Sometimes the books of a month of Emerson's life are merely an inventory of a month's distractions. Anyone can amass an impressive amount of reading. But the active filtration and the tight focus of constant intention which convert that reading into real life experience and then into adequate expression, these are the exclusive properties of the great writer.

As Fox combined the idealist and the realist, so the truth of Quakerism seemed to Emerson to illuminate the connection between the spiritual and the natural. Emerson's periods of greatest interest in Quakerism are also the periods of his greatest interest in science. Both science and the Quakers taught that all great truths are self-evident; no other authorities can or should be invoked. In notes for his Fox lecture Emerson pushed the connection: "I say natural but who shall tell me the limits of the natural? Spiritual helps are natural, they are part of the nature with which every man is endowed." In the convergence of Quakerism and science with the Platonism and the Stoicism that already form the central stream of Emerson's thought we can see a common principle: the crucial illumination that the spiritual is not a realm apart from the natural but is instead revealed—and alone revealed—through the natural.[16]

27. A Living Leaping Logos

IN A LETTER TO EDWARD IN DECEMBER 1833 EMERSON WAS full of condolence for his brother's exile in Puerto Rico. But, he added, none of them was really at home. Ruth was in Newton, Charles "sleeps in Washington Street, boards with G. B. Emerson and spends the day in Court Street," while he himself had just returned to Boston from an extended stay in New Bedford. He felt, he said, a great sense of the family's dispersal. In the month ahead the family was to draw together again. Also during this time a great deal of Emerson's intellectual and social life was to come together. He was newly serious about writing. Recognizing that his journals were his "savings bank," he approached them more systematically than he had, buying uniform-sized volumes, making more extensive indexes, and dating entries with more care. In his new situation he was familyless, free to move about, and able to accept sermon or lecture engagements as he chose, which gave him an unaccustomed and welcome sense of freedom. Just as his interests in science and in Quakerism were growing, he came across an electrifying article on Coleridge and the new German thought, written by an acquaintance named Frederic Hedge.[1]

Hedge was a Unitarian minister in West Cambridge; he was the son of the Harvard professor of logic and he was two years younger than Emerson. He had been tutored by George Bancroft and at age thirteen had gone to Germany, where he spent four years in gymnasium. Returning to Cambridge in 1822 he entered the junior class at Harvard, which included Edward Emerson, Caleb Stetson, George Ripley, and Horatio Greenough. From college he went on to Harvard Divinity School, taking a degree in 1829. He had been known as Germanicus Hedge in college. He was short and stout. Later, when he turned up on Carlyle's doorstep with a tall, thin man named Chapman, Carlyle said they looked like a circle and a tangent. He had honest kind gray eyes, Carlyle noted, and he made a forceful impression; he had a "face like a rock, a voice like a howitzer."[2]

Hedge's article on Coleridge is forceful and charged too. There is no fawning, no ritual praise. Hedge calls Coleridge an intellect of the highest order, a profound thinker and a powerful writer but not a great poet or critic. Hedge notes all the unfinished projects that littered Coleridge's life, and he remarks that the secret of his failures is that his centrifugal force is out of all proportion to his centripetal. He laments that Coleridge never gave us a thorough interpretation of Kant and his followers as he was so well suited to do. Then, without fanfare, Hedge undertakes to do—in just a few pages—what Coleridge did not. With superb confidence (and with Kant, Fichte, and Schelling under his belt in the original German), Hedge boldly maps out the "Copernican revolution" of Kant.

> As in astronomy the motions of the heavenly bodies seem confused to the geocentric observer and are intelligible only when referred to their heliocentric place, so there is only one point from which we can clearly understand and decide upon the speculations of Kant and his followers; that point is the interior consciousness, distinguished from the common consciousness, by its being an active and not a passive state.[3]

Kant and his followers were dissatisfied with the kind of philosophy "which, talking of mind, but thinking of brick and mortar," reduced all things to impressions, ideas, and sensations. But, says Hedge,

> in the transcendental system, the object is to discover in every form of finite existence, an infinite and unconditioned [quality or state] as the ground of its existence, or rather as the ground of our knowledge of its existence, to refer all phenomena to certain noumena or laws of cognition.[4]

Hedge hardheadedly emphasizes method. He shows how Kant brooded on the recent advances of science, concluding that they were the result of superior method. Kant then proposed a new method for philosophy: "Since the supposition that our intuitions depend on the nature of the world without will not answer, [let us] assume that the world without depends on the nature of our intuitions." This is the center of the argument, the "key to the whole critical philosophy, the very essence of which consists in proposing an absolute self as unconditionally existing, incapable of being determined by anything higher than itself, but determining all things through itself." Hedge notes that Fichte pushed this too far, attempting to systematize everything on this ground and becoming thereby "too subjective" in the process. Hedge himself prefers the position taken by Schelling, the position that appealed so strongly to Coleridge and that Emerson was now to take up. "In all science, therefore," says Hedge in summarizing Schelling's *Transcendentaler Idealismus,*

> there are two elements or poles, subject and object, or intelligence and nature, and corresponding to these two poles then are two funda-mental sciences, the one beginning with nature and proceeding up-ward to intelligence, the other beginning with intelligence and ending in nature. The first of these is natural philosophy, the second tran-scendental philosophy.[5]

If there is a single moment after which American transcendentalism can be said to exist, it is when Emerson read Hedge's manifesto. In a letter to his brother Edward, Emerson called the essay a "living, leaping, logos." It is high, astonishing praise, but the essay is indeed a brilliant one—com-pressed, rigorous, and clear. Germanicus Hedge's knowledge of the texts and of formal logic is unassailable, his expression of the ideas is as clear and forceful as Carlyle's in "The State of German Literature," and the essay as a whole is far superior in intellectual energy and grasp to anything Emerson himself had yet written. And when one adds to Hedge's piece Marsh's introduction to Coleridge's *Aids to Reflection* and Sampson Reed's *Obser-vations on the Growth of the Mind,* it is possible to see how Emerson now began to feel that the group of thinkers in New England in 1834 was a match for England, where Carlyle seemed to labor alone, unable even to get an English publisher to bring out *Sartor Resartus* as a book.

Emerson read and reread Coleridge during these months. The great distinction between reason and understanding—the romantic revaluation of reason—came more and more to have a practical, daily, urgent reality for Emerson in 1834. This was the year of Coleridge's death and the torch was now passing not to Carlyle, as Emerson thought, but to Emerson himself. He wrote Edward in May to say that

> reason is the highest faculty of the soul—what we mean often by the soul itself; it never *reasons,* never proves, it simply perceives; it is vision. The Understanding toils all the time, compares, contrives, adds, argues, near-sighted but strong-sighted, dwelling in the present, the expedient, the customary.[6]

What Emerson now perceived was that the "reason" of Milton, Coleridge, and the Germans was another name for what the Quakers recognized as the inner light. The same phenomenon was explained philosophically and logically by one group; it was made practically available and psychologically real by the other. Together, these conceptions of reason make up the fundamental basis, the necessary bottom rung, of Emerson's self-reliance. Coleridge and the Quakers both show why it is reasonable, indeed necessary, to trust the basic self.

In December 1833 Emerson had been again thinking of starting a magazine as a forum for the new ideas. Brother Charles gave a lecture in Concord on Socrates. During January of the new year, 1834, Emerson was still unsettled, busy with a wide range of projects. He gave a pair of lectures, "The Relation of Man to the Globe" and "Water" and he rekindled his never long dormant interest in biography, reading lives of Newton, Laplace, Cuvier, Luther, and Michelangelo. He was interested, he said, in the implied comparison between the intellectual and ethical qualities of the subject and our own. He thought that the interest of biography is not mainly objective documentation and not exclusively the announced subject. What interested Emerson in a biography was the writer's coming to grips with the subject.

In February 1834, while he was preaching in New Bedford and talking with Miss Rotch, Emerson made a side trip to preach at Plymouth. One member of the congregation was Lydia Jackson. Lydia was thirty-one, Emerson thirty, when they fell in love this year. She came from an old Plymouth family that went back to John Cotton, whose shadow hung over the present as in a Hawthorne novel. Lydia never was able to forget the "religious terrors of her childhood . . . when every lightning seemed the beginning of conflagration and every noise in the street the crack of doom." "Terror," she said, "was bred in her bones," and she told her daughter Ellen that no matter how her mind refused to believe it, "the moment she was sick or tired, she became a prey to it."[7]

Lydia was not the beauty Ellen had been, but she was attractive. She had long hair that had never been cut. Her head was very small. Her pictures, mostly from later periods, show a strong, brooding face. She had taken dancing lessons when young and always retained a beautiful walk. Her father and mother both died when she was sixteen. She remembered that she had felt no grief at the time. She also remembered that her mother had grieved for the childhood death of her son, Lydia's brother. The outward austerity of the Jackson family was such that Lydia could only recall her mother kissing her once. She loved animals. She had cats named Purry, Blacklegs, and Squaller. She had strong emotions and she took things hard. One winter night her aunt refused to take in or feed a pair of stray cats. "And there they sat," said Lydia, "*screaming* with cold and hunger on the wood-pile, with their fur blowing in the wind . . . I used to wish I had never been born."[8]

Lydia Jackson was interested in poetry. She filled several small notebooks with poems, at least some of which were copies of poems she admired. She liked "My Life Is Like the Summer Rose" by the Georgia poet Richard Henry Wilde. It is noteworthy that she turned for inspiration to American poets, some of them southern, as well as to the fashionable English poets. She loved the poetry of Young and Cowper and knew a great deal by heart. She read *Don Quixote* and took German lessons, which introduced her to German poetry. She read Goethe's *Wilhelm Meister* and was "carried away with it." While reading Scott's *Betrothed* on a visit to Woods Hole in 1825, she had a powerful, long-remembered experience that put her, she said, in a new state. That same year she experienced a religious conversion.

Lydia had heard Emerson preach before. The first time, several years earlier, she had been so enthralled that she discovered after he was done that she had been sitting absolutely rigidly, immobilized in admiration and without moving a muscle the entire time. Now, in 1834, a friend asked her after the service how she liked hearing her own ideas preached.[9]

Emerson was in Plymouth for four days in February and again for a while in March. He was now working up his Italian travels into a pair of elaborate illustrated lectures, and he was reading Mme. de Staël's *Corinne* with extravagant admiration, with "as much emotion as a book can excite in me." He found it a "true representation of the tragedy of woman," and while he thought the plot improbable and Oswald's grief for his father excessive, he thought the position and feelings of Corinne to be both possible and "more true than history." Perhaps Italy and *Corinne* prepared Emerson for Lydia, perhaps she prepared him for *Corinne*. It was not his first try at the book, which was a favorite of Aunt Mary's: he had taken it out of the library many times before now. Corinne is committed to enthusiasm and to the emotional life. Corinne's Rome is "a world quickened by feeling, without which the world itself is but a desert." Corinne is a poet, an improvisational artist and performer, able through her art to make the ruins of Rome express what the hero Oswald feels but cannot express. Corinne's effect on the sorrowing Oswald suggests something of the effect of Lydia on the Emerson still sorrowing over Ellen. "What if he could recover memories of his native land and at the same time a new life through the imagination: what if he could be reborn to the future and yet not break with the past?"[10]

Emerson was increasingly committed to lecturing and writing during the early months of 1834. He had not yet found his subjects; neither illustrated travel lectures nor science would sustain his full interest long. He was moving away from preaching and was actively imagining a new relation to his hearers, that of the teacher. He was shrewdly alive to the drawbacks of the position. "Every teacher acquires a continually increasing stationary force," he said, "a cumulative inertia in proportion to the eloquence of his innovating doctrines." As followers are attracted, their presence increases the pressure on the teacher to continue as before. But there were powerful advantages as well. "The whole secret of the teacher's force lies in the conviction that men are convertible," he wrote, adding cheerfully, "and they are." He was also newly alive to the requirements of good writing. "In good prose," he said, quoting Schlegel, "every word should be underscored." And he already knew that one needed to aim for the main gate. In preparing to write, as in everything else, "the material is so much that the spiritual is overlaid and lost." As the writer starts to think about a subject, first "a society must be collected, and books consulted and much paper blotted. . . . Alien considerations come in, personal considerations" until finally he loses the thing one meant to say in the first place. "It was no superfluous rule he gave who said, when you write do not omit the thing you meant to say."[11]

Emerson's mood was bright during April. Despite his duties and a "discontented unfed spirit," he felt an infusion of energy—not from the pulpit but "from M[ary] M[oody] E[merson], from Carlyle, from this delicious day [when] I woke to a strain of highest melody." He felt he was "on the brink of an ocean of thought into which we do not swim."[12]

28. A Theory of Animated Nature

EMERSON'S YEAR OF WONDERS WAS 1834. HE TURNED THIRTY-one. Everywhere he turned there was the fresh stimulus of new corroboration. The Quakers, Coleridge, Hedge, Lydia Jackson, Italy—each had an effect on him. He was still keenly pursuing science, and he was reading Goethe and Carlyle with new eyes. There was always time too for nature itself. Late April was very rainy. Emerson courted the "sober solitude" of the Newton woods: "I saw a hawk today wheeling up to heaven in a spiral flight and every circle becoming less and less to the eye till he vanished into the atmosphere." At his feet he saw dwarf andromeda, coerulea, running cinquefoil, triandria, green briar, laurel, and privet. Two days later he saw low blueberry, swamp pyrus, wood anemone, and wild strawberry. In early May he addressed the fourth annual meeting of the Boston Society of Natural History with his fourth science lecture, "The Naturalist," in which he talked about the place of natural history in education.[1]

Science points always to the present hour, he said: "An everlasting Now reigns in nature that produces on our bushes the selfsame rose which charmed the Roman and the Chaldean." The lecture echoed Carlyle and quotes Goethe. After listing the obvious utilitarian advantages of the study of nature, Emerson moved to consider its effect on our thinking. "Natural science sharpens the discrimination," he claimed. "There is no false logic in nature. All its properties are permanent: the acids and metals never lie; their yea is yea, their nay, nay. They are newly discovered but not new." He thought that we might also resort to nature to guard against certain possible evils of science, such as the kind of technological advances that make our senses useless to us: "The clock and compass do us harm by hindering us from astronomy."[2]

Emerson's interest in science was still considerable, though he had by now developed some misgivings about classification and taxonomy as such. He thought that "the classification of all Natural Science is arbitrary," and he had some reason to think so. In Emerson's day the Linnaean system of classification still had adherents; the study of general properties of bodies was called somatology, the study of laws of motion was phoronomics, of light photonomics, of heat pyronomics. Emerson recognized the convenience and the introductory nature of much classification, but he saw that the pursuit of taxonomy could also reduce a human being to a "mere insect hunter." But he was more enthusiastic than ever about the kind of scientific inquiry Goethe undertook in his *Metamorphosis of Plants*, and from Goethe's example Emerson now laid down a challenge for himself. "We have no theory of animated nature," he wrote. "When we have it, it will be itself the true Classification." This is a premonition of what Darwin would do. But Emerson had in mind something else. He understands the word "animated" to refer not just to movement but to the source of movement, to will, mind, or soul. He was interested in a kind of science that was not purely material or mechanical but would explain the living world. He wished to understand not only matter but the directing and organizing of matter.[3]

The person who had gone farthest down this particular road at the time was Goethe, and now, in the spring and summer of 1834, Emerson turned again to the study of Goethe. He had read him before. He had tried to read him in German in 1828, had read an anonymously translated volume called *Memoirs of Goethe* (New York, 1824) in 1828, *Faust* in 1830, and *Wilhelm Meister's Apprenticeship* in 1832. It was during 1832, when he was reading everything he could of Carlyle's, that he began, through Carlyle, to see the possibilities in Goethe. Carlyle had called Goethe "the most distinguished poet and thinker of his age" and had argued that "the history of his mind is, in fact, the history of German culture in his day." Carlyle proclaimed that Goethe had come "in these hard, unbelieving utilitarian days, [to] reveal to us glimpses of the Unseen but not unreal world, that . . . the Actual and the Ideal may again meet together."[4]

Emerson had been struck in 1832 by a review of Goethe in which Carlyle gave excerpts from *Wilhelm Meister* on reverence. Goethe here acknowledges reverence as the basis of religion. Reverence for what is above us leads to ethnic or national religion, reverence for what is around us leads to philosophic religion, reverence for what is under us is Christian: "Out of these three reverences springs the highest Reverence, Reverence for oneself, and these [others] again unfold themselves from this."[5]

During his own Italian journey Emerson read Goethe's account of his trip, including his exciting moment of sudden insight into the nature of plants in the public gardens at Palermo. Emerson later gave his own understanding of Goethe's botanical idea:

> Goethe suggested the leading idea of modern botany, that a leaf or the eye of a leaf, is the unit of botany, and that every part of the plant is only a transformed leaf to meet a new condition, and by varying the conditions, a leaf may be converted into any other organ and any other organ into a leaf.

In Goethe's view what needs to be explained in botany is the process of growing rather than the grown product. He is interested in metamorphosis rather than taxonomy. Goethe extended this way of seeing, this fundamental conception of life as process, beyond the study of plants to the understanding of humankind itself. The novel *Wilhelm Meister's Travels,* which Emerson now read in Carlyle's translation and called "a novel in every sense, the first of its kind . . . the only delineation of modern society," is also focused on education, on the unfolding process the Germans call *Bildung.* Emerson now saw that everything Goethe did was characterized by a focus on development. Of the *Roman Elegies* Emerson wrote, "The problem to be solved, is, how shall this soul called Goethe be educated?" In June he summed it up: "Self-cultivation is yet the moral of all that Goethe has written."[6]

Goethe had great talents and the even rarer ability to use them. One of the qualities that makes him such a great teacher is his willingness to talk about using talents. Emerson copied out long passages in which Goethe talks about originality and the influence of others. Far from feeling a need to do nothing except what is completely original and novel, Goethe actually defines genius as "the faculty of seizing and turning to account every thing that strikes us." He protested that he himself would have got nowhere "if this art of appropriation were considered as derogatory to genius." It was enormously helpful to Emerson to hear Goethe committing himself so clearly to the extensive and frank reuse of others' material. This method Emerson already found congenial. "Every one of my writings," said Goethe, "has been furnished to me by a thousand different persons, a thousand different things. . . . My work is that of an aggregation of beings taken from the whole of nature: it bears the name of Goethe." As important to Emerson as the concept of *Bildung* (self-cultivation) was Goethe's liberating endorsement of this literary appropriation, itself a key process in *Bildung.*[7]

Such appropriation does not mean, of course, that one adopts the ideas of others because one has no thoughts of one's own. It does mean that the individual must be free not only to have his own thoughts but to take up the thoughts of others when they coincide with, restate, or extend his own. Similarly Eliot could say the mature artist steals, the immature artist imitates; a writer of India could claim that at a certain level there can be no misappropriation since we can take only those things that already belong to us. Goethe's greatest gifts to Emerson were two. First was the master idea that education, development, self-consciousness, and self-expression are the purposes of life; second was the open, outward-facing working method of sympathetic appropriation and creative recombination of the world's materials.

There is an important corollary to the axiom of appropriate appropriation. Along with Emerson's freedom to take whatever struck him went the equally important obligation to ignore what did not. Emerson read widely and advised others to do so, but he was insistent about the dangers of being overwhelmed and overinfluenced by one's reading. "Do not attempt to be a great reader," he told a young Williams College student named Charles Woodbury. "Read for facts and not by the bookful." He thought one should "learn to divine books, to *feel* those that you want without wasting much time on them." It is only worthwhile concentrating on what is excellent and for that "often a chapter is enough." He encouraged browsing and skipping. "The glance reveals what the gaze obscures. Somewhere the author has hidden his message. Find it, and skip the paragraphs that do not talk to you."[8]

What Emerson was really recommending was a form of speed-reading and the heightened attention that goes with speed-reading. When pressed by young Woodbury, Emerson gave details:

> Learn how to tell from the beginnings of the chapters and from glimpses of the sentences whether you need to read them entirely through. So turn page after page, keeping the writer's thoughts before you, but not tarrying with him, until he has brought you the thing you are in search of. But recollect, you only read to start your own team.

The last point is crucial. Reading was not an end in itself for Emerson. He read like a hawk sliding on the wind over a marsh, alert for what he could use. He read to nourish and to stimulate his own thought, and he carried this so far as to recommend that one stop reading if one finds oneself becoming engrossed. "Reading long at one time anything, no matter how it fascinates, destroys thought," he told Woodbury. "Do not permit this. Stop if you find yourself becoming absorbed, at even the first paragraph." Not only must one have the courage to appropriate freely whatever one recognizes as one's own, one must have the much greater courage to resist and refuse everything that is not one's own material.[9]

The ethic of self-realization was coming at Emerson from yet another point of view this year, from Carlyle's *Sartor Resartus,* which Emerson was reading in installments in *Frazer's Magazine.* He was, he told Carlyle in a letter, put off by the form of the book and suggested that Carlyle "skip those excursive involved glees, and give us the simple air, without the volley of variations." But despite the "grotesque teutonic apocalyptic strain of yours," Emerson told Carlyle he relished the message. Like Teufelsdrockh, Carlyle's ebullient professor of things-in-general, Emerson was also looking for "how, at length, instead of Denial and Destruction, we were to have a science of Affirmation and Reconstruction." He liked the book's self-declared preference for the transcendental rather than the "descendental," the insistence on understanding the person, not the clothing he wears: "The thing in any way conceived as visible, what is it but a garment, a clothing of the higher, celestial invisible?" Like Emerson, Carlyle loved the imagery of vision. His book, he said, was "a mixture of insight, inspiration, with dulness, double-vision, and even utter blindness." "The man who cannot wonder," Carlyle says, "is but a pair of spectacles behind which there is no eye." "All visible things are emblems," he insists, in a language later spoken by Captain Ahab. And in a language soon to be spoken by Emerson in *Nature,* Carlyle says, "The beginning of all wisdom is to look fixedly on clothes . . . with armed eyesight, till they become transparent." The true emperor never has any clothes.[10]

Carlyle accepted, as did Emerson, the saying of gold-lipped Chrysostom that "the true Shekinah [dwelling place of the Lord] is Man." "Where else," asks Carlyle, "is the God's Presence manifested not to our eyes only, but to our hearts, as in our fellow man?" Carlyle believed in work as the proper product of education, in "harmonious self-development by cultivating the special, not the vague or general capabilities which are innate in us." Even more important for Emerson at the moment was Carlyle's conviction that nothing is separate: "The withered leaf is not dead and lost, there are forces in it and around it, though working in inverse order; else how could it rot?" This conviction of the wholeness of nature was a central theme of the poetry that during this year of years Emerson was bringing to its first full fruition.[11]

29. Each and All

In May 1834 Emerson began a correspondence with Carlyle, sending him a volume of Webster's speeches and Reed's *Observations on the Growth of the Mind.* Carlyle replied with a long, warm letter full of news, looking forward to his book on the French Revolution and insisting that "the only poetry is History, could we tell it right." Emerson also wrote encouraging letters this year to James Freeman Clarke, the Unitarian minister of Louisville, Kentucky. Clarke was seven years younger than Emerson, a distant cousin and good friend of Margaret Fuller's. Clarke had gone to Harvard College and Harvard Divinity School. He knew Elizabeth Peabody, William Henry Channing, Oliver Wendell Holmes, Christopher Cranch, John S. Dwight, and many others who were soon to be involved in the transcendental movement. Clarke, now twenty-four, had become interested in Carlyle and in Goethe and had written a piece defending Carlyle from an attack by the conservative Andrews Norton. Emerson praised the piece, urged publication, and included in his reply to Clarke some choice bits from Carlyle's recent letter. Emerson had a way of making his friends feel like insiders.[1]

In May the estate of Ellen Tucker was finally settled. There had been delays, a result of the death of one of Ellen's sisters, Margaret, and of her mother, and there had been some unpleasantness because the husband of a surviving sister apparently resented Emerson's claim to Ellen's share of the Tucker family money. The upshot was that Emerson was obliged to go to law for a settlement. The court awarded Emerson the whole of Ellen's share of the two-thirds of the Tucker estate that went to the children. He was now, he thought, assured of an annual income of about $1,200. This sum was less than Emerson had been making as a minister and he still had years to wait before getting the full amount from the Tucker estate. Yet he had many claims on his income: he helped support his mother and his brothers Charles and Bulkeley and he loaned large sums of money to the strapped William in New York. If Emerson was no longer poor, he was far from rich. He never had anything like the $10,000 a year that Henry James, Sr., had, for example. He certainly did not feel well-off. Worries about money figure prominently in his correspondence for the next decade, through the financial panic and crash of 1837 and into the mid-1840s.[2]

In July Emerson made a trip to Bangor, Maine, to preach. Bangor was a booming lumber town and deep-water port with a hundred and fifty mills turning out boards that were shipped all along the East Coast. More than a thousand ships a year, most of them lumber schooners, cleared from Bangor. Emerson reported on the brash boom-town euphoria of Bangor's plans for itself: "Whenever they shall have stripped the whole territory of timber, they will then become an agricultural and manufacturing people." Emerson went on north of Bangor on the Penobscot river, visiting Oldtown and its Indian villages and meeting an impressive man named Neptune, possibly the Louis Neptune who was later to serve as a guide for Thoreau in the Maine woods.[3]

Back in Boston Emerson had the sad duty of conducting the funeral for his old friend and supporter from his Second Church days, George Sampson. Elizabeth Peabody and Bronson Alcott were among the mourners. Peabody, an energetic and ebullient young intellectual of thirty, was already acquainted with Emerson. It was she who had passed Clarke's defense of Carlyle along to Emerson. Alcott was running a school in Boston and had not yet met Emerson.[4]

Emerson came to maturity as a poet in 1834. Several of his best, most characteristic poems were written this year. From December of 1833 through the early summer of 1834 Emerson was profoundly affected by Hedge's Coleridge piece, by the work for his lectures on science and for those on Italy, by his reading of *Corinne,* by his contact with Quakerism and Mary Rotch, by his conscious shift from preaching to teaching, and by Goethe and Carlyle. His life was no longer flying to pieces. On the contrary, it was coming together with a surprising new solidity. He was becoming ever more concerned with the expression of his new convictions and with the question of appropriate forms, both in verse and prose.

Predating Emerson's desire to be a preacher was his ambition to be a poet. This was the oldest and in some ways the most important of Emerson's private dreams for himself. As a child he had written elegies and nonsense verse. At ten he wrote an epic called "Fortus" about a hero who slew twenty thousand foemen and two dragons. At college he was class poet. He knew vast amounts of Milton and Wordsworth by heart. He wrote some touching verses for and about Ellen. His moments of New World collision with

Naples and Rome resulted in poems. He once said Thoreau's emotional life could be seen best in his poetry. The same is true for Emerson. When he began to write to explain himself to Lydia Jackson, when they were courting, he made a point of telling her, "I am born a poet, of a low class without doubt yet a poet. That is my nature and vocation."[5]

As the Harvard Phi Beta Kappa poet for 1834, Emerson was obliged to produce, on schedule, a suitable number of lines for commencement. His lines on Daniel Webster have an old-fashioned stateliness, a Miltonic sonority, and more than a touch of Pope's skill at rhymed couplets: "Not on its base Monadnoc surer stood / Than he to common sense and common good." But the lines he customarily wrote in someone's album when asked for a remembrance point in quite a different direction: "O what is heaven but the fellowship / Of minds that each can stand against the world / By its own meek but incorruptible will." In February 1835 he explained his idea of the poet to Lydia Jackson: "I am a poet in the sense of a perceiver and dear lover of the harmonies that are in the soul and in matter, and specially of the correspondences between these and those." This is the first faint outline of the expressionist concept of poetry he was later to describe in "The Poet." In that essay he says, "It is not metre but metre-making argument that makes a poem." The legitimation of criticism, Emerson says, is that the poem "is a copy of some text in nature with which it ought to be made to tally." The real poem is not the words on the page, it is the event or feeling or idea behind the words. Emerson's way of saying this in 1834 was to repeat, as a kind of reminder to himself, a phrase he found in the congenial Coleridge: "Luther was a great man, and, as Coleridge says, acted poems."[6]

Sometime during 1834 Emerson began a new notebook in which to save his live verse. The earliest of this year's poems, "The Rhodora," was written in May, just after the tonic, eventful month of April when he was back from New Bedford and when he had his moment of extraordinary vision in Mt. Auburn cemetery. It is a sixteen-line poem, a sort of extended or long sonnet, rhymed and anchored by a strong last line. It begins like most of Emerson's poems, out of doors. "In May, when sea-winds pierced our solitudes / I found the fresh Rhodora in the woods." The poem is full of color—purple petals, black water, the red bird. Its point is the same as that of his exhilarating moment at Mt. Auburn. The flower's simple existence is the answer to the restless critical seeking to know why beauty exists.

"Tell them," says the poet to the rhodora, "that if eyes were made for seeing, / Then Beauty is its own excuse for being." Beauty—meaning here

177

harmony, or *kosmos*—is not a secondary attribute or a means of praising something we really prefer for other reasons. Beauty is primary, basic, foundational, a given. As Emerson will soon put it in *Nature:* "The world thus exists to the soul to satisfy the desire of beauty. This element I call an ultimate end. No reason can be asked or given why the soul seeks beauty. Beauty, in its largest and profoundest sense, is our expression for the universe." It is what the Greeks meant by calling the world *kosmos,* or beauty. "The standard of beauty," says Emerson, "is the entire circuit of natural forms." In "The Rhodora" Emerson reaches the center of that circle: "O rival of the rose! / I never thought to ask, I never knew [why it existed] But, in my simple ignorance, suppose / The self-same power that brought me here brought you."[7]

Some ideas for poems appear in Emerson's notes this year even though they have not yet achieved their poetic shapes. The perception behind "Days," the nagging regretful sense that the days are gods, each one laden with gifts we are never quite able to take, was expressed scores of times in Emerson's notes, letters, and journals. In New Bedford in February 1834 he wrote: "The days and months and years flit by, each with his own black ribband, his own sad reminiscence. Yet I look at the almanack affectionately as a book of promise." In May he wrote down another seedling poem, this one about the relation of each thing to the rest of the world: "I remember when I was a boy going upon the beach and being charmed with the colors and forms of the shells. I picked many up and put them in my pocket. When I got home I could find nothing that I gathered, nothing but some dry ugly mussel and snail shells." This memory quickly became the poem "Each and All." The chastened poet re-creates the beach experience and then observes, "I covet truth, Beauty is unripe childhood's cheat." The expression of the loss triggers a Keatsian moment of expanding sense awareness. "As I spoke, beneath my feet / The ground-pine curled its pretty wreath / Running over the club-moss burrs." The world is wiser than the poet. "Pine cones and acorns lay on the ground: / Over me soared the eternal sky." Beauty is not something to be isolated, abstracted, taken home and pinned up. "Again I saw, again I heard / The rolling river, the morning bird; / Beauty through my senses stole; / I yielded myself to the perfect whole."[8]

A late December snowstorm moved Emerson to jot down this comparison of his voice and the storm's: "To the music of the surly storm that thickens the darkness of the night abroad and cracks the walls and fans my cheek through the chinks and cracks, I would sing my strain though hoarse and small." As in "The Rhodora" and "Each and All," the faint effort of the poet's conscious art is as nothing to the creative power of the world itself—though the latter can be *expressed* through the poet. The result this time, "The Snow-Storm," the poem that later inspired Whittier's "Snow Bound," is one of Emerson's best poems. From its opening, "Announced by all the trumpets of the sky / Arrives the snow . . ." the first part of the poem moves from the storm outside to the people inside, caught by the storm: "The housemates sit / Around the radiant fireplace, enclosed in a tumultuous privacy of storm." The storm, a "fierce artificer," goes to work curving "his white bastions with projected roof / Round every windward stake or tree or door." The "north wind's masonry" creates a white world overnight, a north-country palace of Aladdin, leaving, "when the sun appears, astonished art / To mimic in slow structures, stone by stone, / Built in an age, the mad wind's night-work / The frolic architecture of the snow."[9]

All these poems are animated by the same fundamental insight that is now a living, emotionally experienced reality for Emerson. The world itself is the great poem, the source of all the verbal approximations of itself. When the poet can hold fast to this connection, he has access—through his own poor powers—to the world's power and beauty. This is one of the central insights of Emerson's life. Not only did it never leave him, it never lost its sweet urgency, its sensuous hold on him, its ability to lift the common moments of everyday life on the updrafts of awareness that readers are always wanting to call mystical experience. At the core of Emerson's life from now on is this willed surrender, this giving oneself over to the unregarded epiphanies of every blessed day.

Explaining his vocation as a poet to Lydia, Emerson observed that his singing was very husky and "is for the most part in prose." He was already unwilling to draw a firm line between poetry and prose. He used the word *poet* sometimes to mean versemaker and sometimes to mean writer. It is significant that much of the actual phrasing and many of the best lines and images of "Each and All" and "The Snow-Storm" were first written as prose and only later arranged into metrical or near-metrical lines.[10]

In 1834 Emerson reached not only poetic maturity but prose maturity as well. Many sentences from the journals and lectures of this year found their way essentially unchanged into his later writings. In March he wrote: "It is seldom that a man is truly alone. He needs to retire as much from his solitude as he does from society. . . . While I am reading and writing in my chamber I am not alone though there is nobody there." Emerson's strong short declarative sentences strengthen their assertions by setting them against explicit alternatives or negatives. "We are always getting ready to live, but never living," he says in April. "The wave moves onward but the particles of which it is composed do not." He tethers abstractions to small concrete images with vivid language to keep them from floating off. "Give me the eye to see a navy in an acorn," Emerson writes. "What is there of the divine in a load of bricks? What of the divine in a barber's shop or a privy? Much, all." To the call to refrain from eating certain kinds of foods, he replies, "Does nemesis care for a whortleberry?" He gives the reader an image for every general statement: "It cannot be but that at intervals throughout society there are real men intermixed . . . as the carpenter puts one iron bar in his bannister for every five or six wooden ones." He now uses the imperative mode with ease and he is continually conscious of point of view, both in life and in writing. "Turn the head upside down by looking at the landscape through your legs, and how charming is the picture though of your own woodlot and barnyard."[11]

Now Emerson can advance the familiar ideas about self-reliance with a fitting language of complete, unarguable conviction. "Insist on yourself. Never imitate. For your own talent you can present every moment with all the force of a lifetime's cultivation, but of the adopted stolen talents of anybody else you have only a frigid brief extempore half-expression." Emerson once told Charles Woodbury that "definition saves a deal of debate." The definition that redraws the boundaries of its subject now becomes a hallmark of Emerson's style: "The education of the mind consists in a continual substitution of facts for words." He can put a sting in the tail of a familiar saying: "Every man's Reason is sufficient for his guidance, if used." The aphoristic style toward which Emerson is working is the perfect medium for turning personal observation into forceful generalization. Attention to rhythm and word choice helps make the surprising seem inevitable: "There is no object in nature which intense light will not make beautiful." Emerson's prose style is now moving further and further from the excursive, expository norms of his education. He no longer wishes to argue, to prove, to present evidence, to base conclusions on prepared logical grounds. He is seeking, as Nietzsche and Kierkegaard would do—and for similar reasons—an appropriate language for the direct statement of personal intuition. The declarative or imperative form of the aphorism presents a discovery in language so taut and trig that the statement is taken for its own evidence.[12]

In late August Emerson delivered his fifteen-page Phi Beta Kappa poem at Harvard. It is not very good, as Emerson recognized; he never included more than a few lines of it in later collections of his work. He told Charles it was as incomplete "as every other work that ever went from the same unlucky fingers." Charles tried to cheer him up, saying it was a giant step, a failure that was a stepping-stone, a Roman defeat, "three of which were equal to a victory." Emerson was not mollified, and he told Charles, "My entire success, such as it is, is composed wholly of particular failures—every public work of mine of the least importance, having been (probably without exception) noted at the time as a failure." No matter how much success came his way later, Emerson never quite shook off the feeling that he was not wanted by the world. "Every man is wanted," he once said, "and no man is wanted much." He also said, astonishingly, that "there was no time of his life when the offer of a professorship of rhetoric and oratory, even from the smallest country college, would not have been tempting to him." No matter how well his life went, it never quite came up to the requirements of his imagination. A comment of his this fall of 1834 catches the feeling perfectly: "I never was on a coach that went fast enough for me."[13]

30. Confluence

IN SEPTEMBER CRICKETS FILLED THE WOODS AND ROADS. "As soon as one falls by the way," Emerson noted, "the rest eat him up." In October 1834 Emerson came to Concord to board with his stepgrandfather, Ezra Ripley, at the parsonage called the Old Manse. His brother Charles and his mother came as well. The house had been built by Emerson's grandfather, William Emerson, and was located on the bank of the Concord River, just upstream from the confluence of the Concord and the Assabet rivers, adjacent to the Revolutionary War battlefield and the old North bridge. Emerson's grandfather, William Emerson of Concord, had been minister of the First Parish during the Revolution. He had been present at the fight at the bridge, had gone off with the army to Ticonderoga, and had died in 1776 from camp fever, when he was thirty-one. His son, Emerson's father, was seven, and his daughter Mary Moody Emerson was one when the young patriot-minister died.[1]

Grandfather Emerson's widow, Phebe, then married Ezra Ripley. Ripley completely supplanted Emerson's grandfather; he married his wife, inherited his land, and succeeded him as minister of the First Parish. Born in 1751, Ripley was a figure from another age. Emerson, boarding with the old man, found him cunning, vain, manipulative, and essentially uninterested in his fellow creatures, living therefore in tragic isolation: "It is as frightful a solitude as that which cold produces round the traveller who has lost his way." Emerson's study in the Old Manse was the northwest room on the second floor, overlooking the river and the battlefield. The move to Concord in 1834 was a return to his ancestral home and roots, though he made little of this. There is, for example, little family feeling in his peppery assessment of Stepgrandfather Ripley. The manse was a good place to work. The book on nature and the next set of lectures—those on biography—took shape there. But in Emerson's mind it was the writing that gave the place meaning, not the other way round. Though he now had his room and board in Concord, he had no place, no position there. In December he was thinking of locating in Waltham. As he gazed over the ancestral fields of Concord, he was writing to Carlyle that "utterance is place enough."[2]

A week after the move to Concord the news came from Puerto Rico that Edward was dead. His death was not completely unexpected. Edward had long been living from day to day, as he wrote his brother, not letting himself look ahead and glad if only he was not in pain. There were still flashes of the old Edward, as when in a letter to Waldo he objected to the new Coleridgean terminology of reason and understanding. He preferred the old word *soul* for the former and insisted that "it is only confounding and not enlightening people to tell them that they 'reason' with [their] 'understanding.'" The warm climate of Puerto Rico may have helped Edward's tuberculosis a little, but, as he himself put it, "the arrow of the angel had gone too deep." Edward died when he was twenty-nine. He was the first of the brothers to die, and though he died far away, Emerson felt that the angel's arrow had nicked him as well. He wrote in his journal: "So falls one pile more of hope for this life. I see I am bereaved of part of myself."[3]

As though to compensate for the loss of Edward, Emerson was closer than ever to Charles this year. Charles had hung out his shingle as a lawyer, but business was slow. "I sit in the office," he told William. "I see no clients. I read law." He wrote love letters full of longing to Elizabeth Hoar every day or two. He attended the trial of some pirates. He worked on a pair of lectures on the individual and society. He read New England history, preparing himself for a lecture on Governor Winthrop. He was disgusted with the Puritans' actions in the Pequot War, calling them dishonorable, cruel, and cowardly. He read Sewel's *History of the Quakers,* Coleridge's *Table Talk,* Sampson Reed, Carlyle, and Mme. de Staël's *Delphine.* Charles had come around on Coleridge, if Edward had not, and he was now deeply impressed with Waldo's Quaker-derived "doctrine, heretofore broached, of *having no choice:* of standing by and letting God decide for you." Charles told Lizzie:

> It is the simplest of principles: it is no more than acting ever from the impression which *all* the facts make on us. It is studying to live unconsciously as far as possible. We are to go forward with freedom until we feel ourselves checked. This check we are never to contend with; when it is right for us to act it will be removed.

"Act from yourself then," Charles concludes, "not because it is more dignified, but because it is a necessity."[4]

Edward died on the first of October, 1834. Shortly thereafter, Aunt Mary moved to Concord to join Waldo, Charles, and Ruth at the Old Manse. She stayed with them in Concord for the next year and a half. At every crucial turning in the first half of Emerson's life, Aunt Mary managed to be there. There are no letters between them from this period, naturally, but it seems very likely that it was this long stay of 1834–1835 that prompted Emerson to begin collecting his aunt's writings and sayings as a separate project that eventually filled four manuscript volumes.[5]

Emerson himself was conscious of a gathering and concentration of forces this fall. "As soon as I read a wise sentence anywhere, I feel at once the desire of appropriation," he wrote in his journal. He stood this fall at the threshold of his first major work, the book *Nature*. What made it possible was a process that had been going on in him since his return from Europe, a process that can best be described by what Eudora Welty calls "that wonderful word, confluence." A whole series of ideas, impressions, insights, convictions, and readings all ran together like a series of streams into a river. The process was a confluence because it was not so much a change of direction as an augmentation. There were the lessons of science that the world is governed by laws and that a true theory will be its own evidence. There was Mary Rotch's arresting conception of the inner light as a stoplight, a signal from which, once recognized, could be neither rejected nor confirmed by others. There was the insistence of Sampson Reed and Edward Taylor and Walker-on-the-Mountain on the experience of individual persons and the language of life in the streets, in the fields, on the decks, and around the council fire. There were the old books by Flavel, Law, Scougal, and à Kempis which focused on the inner life and experience of each person. To these streams were joined the modern heroic individualism of Fichte and the philosophical subjectivism of Kant, both of which came most forcibly and most recently to Emerson from Carlyle and from Hedge on Coleridge. There was also Coleridge's practical, catalytic distinction between reason and understanding. There were Asian and Persian tributaries such as Anquetil-Duperron's account of Zoroastrianism, the Confucian *Shi Ching,* and the Bhagavad Gita of India, which already suggested confirmation from non-Western cultures. Older currents included the Stoic legacy, with its progression from "Know thyself" to "Revere thyself," and the concept of *Bildung,* or self-development, which Emerson knew from Channing, Gerando, and above all Goethe. Deepest of all, the central, never-turned current, was Plato, with the only mythology Emerson ever took seriously enough to live by, that of Socrates' daemon. All these influences were given direction by Emerson's final resource, the monist's bedrock conviction that what is beyond nature is revealed to us through nature, that the miraculous is revealed through the scientific and the natural, and that the inner life is revealed through the life of the senses.

The central element of Emerson's inner life during these years is not to be found in any one or even any six of these currents. Rather it arises from the astonishing and inevitable convergence, the rising potential of this concord of waters. Its direction is to affirm the autonomy and sufficiency of the individual consciousness, an affirmation that will form henceforward the broad central current of Emerson's life and writing.

As part of the process of convergence, he reorganized his notebooks, began new ones and reindexed old ones. He clarified for himself his role as teacher and as poet. With Edward's death a part of him died too, as it had with Ellen's death. Expression of what remained was now the more imperative. This fall he was aware that his life was coming to a head. His insights now have a new aphoristic ring of utter conviction, and they are important insights that will undergird the work of the next ten years. "The root and seed of Democracy is the doctrine Judge for yourself."

> Democracy/Freedom has its root in the sacred truth that every man
> hath in him the divine Reason . . . though few men since the creation
> of the world live according to the dictates of Reason, yet all men are
> created capable of so doing. That is the equality and the only equality
> of all men.

This conviction now has the force of a credo: "I believe in the existence of the material world as an expression of the spiritual or real." In December he wrote, even more bluntly, "I believe the Christian religion to be profoundly true." His reason for believing is, he says, because Christianity "taught, it teaches, the eternal opposition of the world to the truth and introduced the absolute authority of the spiritual law."[6]

Nature itself was more to him than ever.

> What can be conceived so beautiful as actual Nature? I never see the
> dawn break or the sun set as last evening when from every grey or slate
> colored cloud over the whole dome depended a wreath of roses, or
> look down the river with its tree planted banks (from the bridge north

of the house) absolutely affecting an elegancy, without a lively curiosity as to its reality and a self-recollection that I am not in a dream.

He made a quick trip to Brooklyn, New York, to lecture and returned to Concord glad to be out of the political turmoil of the city, glad for the "quiet fields of my fathers."[7]

He was ready to work. He was fortified by reading how Coleridge had taken steps to focus his energies. "I would not lecture," said Coleridge, "on any subject for which I had to *acquire* the main knowledge . . . on no subject that had not employed my thoughts for a large portion of my life since earliest manhood, free of all outward and particular purpose." As so often happened to Emerson, the heartening example of another triggered a new and in this case vital resolve to do his own work, to write. With characteristic—if borrowed—bravado, he stepped forward in his new position, alone at a lectern, free and able at last to represent no one but himself. He wrote in his journal: "Henceforth I design not to utter any speech, poem or book that is not entirely and peculiarly my work."[8]

Nature

31. Lidian

THE SERIES OF SIX LECTURES ON BIOGRAPHY THAT EMERSON
gave before the Society for the Diffusion of Useful Knowledge beginning
on January 29, 1835, is the first fruit of his resolve to do only his own work.
He had been actively interested in biography for years and he had long
nourished the ambition to write a modern *Plutarch's Lives*. Even Emerson's
daily life was lighted by that habitual vision of greatness, apart from which,
Whitehead says, education is impossible. Within ten days of hearing the
news of the death of Edward, as though feeling the spur dig suddenly deeper
into his side, he began actively to reflect again on what biography had to
teach about what was possible in life. "Michel Angelo Buonaroti: John
Milton: Martin Luther: George Fox: Lafayette, Falkland, Hampden. Are not
these names seeds?" He was not interested in biography for its own sake,
nor as the worship of force, and certainly not to elevate the noble past at
the expense of the present. He took for granted the Plutarchan concept of
biography as educative. Moses Hadas has said that Plutarch aimed to make
of Hellenism a way of life that could survive the loss of national sovereignty.
Emerson had a similar goal. Almost from the beginning he proposed to use
the attainments of the departed great to illustrate the range of possibilities
open to nineteenth-century Americans. He was fascinated by the processes
by which we link ourselves to the great. He saw biography to be a medium,
like language. "Every man is bipolar," he wrote,

> never a circle; somewhere therefore in each one of never so many
> million you shall find the contrariety, inconsistency of his nature. And
> as language translates language, verb verb, and noun noun, so, could
> their surfaces be adjusted to each other, might we find one age
> corresponding to another age in every minute peculiarity and every
> one man to every other man.[1]

Emerson was concerned to make "the biography of Luther as practical
and pertinent today as the last paragraph from Liverpool upon the price of

cotton." He envisioned a "Portraiture of Man which should be at once history and prophecy," explaining, with a question, "Does it not seem as if a perfect parallelism existed between every great or fully developed man and every other?" No matter what figure from the past he worked on, he found it crucial to remember his own part in the process. "I have not so near access to Luther's mind through his works as through my own mind when I meditate upon his historical position." He was convinced that not only he but any reader could find the link between his own life and the great person: "Let a man work after a pattern he really sees and every man shall be able to find a correspondence between those works and his own and to turn them to some account in Rome, London, or Japan, from the first to the hundredth century."[2]

All biography then is at last autobiography. Far from narrowing us, this perception opens the gates. "I consider," Emerson wrote in his journal in December,

> that each fine genius that appears is already predicted in our con-
> stitution inasmuch as he only makes apparent shades of thought in
> us of which we hitherto knew not, (or actualizes an idea,) and when
> I consider the absolute boundlessness of our capacity—no one of us
> but has the whole untried world of geometry, fluxions [calculus],
> natural philosophy, ethics, wide open before him.

The consequences of this view are enormous. Not only are the great predicted by our own constitutions, the great in turn contain the seeds of all our institutions: "Every great man does in his nature point out and imply the existence and well being of all the institutions and orders of a state."[3]

The lectures themselves were written by a man who was in love once again. On January 24, 1835, Emerson wrote to Lydia Jackson, proposing marriage. Her acceptance letter reached him on the twenty-eighth. The next day he gave the opening lecture of the series. During most of February they wrote warm, eager letters back and forth. He visited her in Plymouth when he could snatch a few hours from the frantic rush of lecture writing. All Plymouth was on the watch for his visits. She was thirty-three, he thirty-two this year, and if their relationship did not have the lyrical, romantic quality of his with Ellen, it nevertheless had an impetuousness of its own and an intensity that was both intellectual and emotional. Emerson's immersion in biography was reminding him how rare is the "perfect sympathy that exists between like minds." "We are imprisoned in life," he wrote in mid-January, "in the company of persons powerfully unlike us." Only now and then comes a "commissioned spirit" that speaks to us. Lydia Jackson was just such a spirit to Emerson and he to her. Their meeting was marked by high moments of excitement that had the aura of portent. "It happened once," Emerson wrote in his January journal, "that a youth and a maiden beheld each other in a public assembly for the first time." He was remembering, apparently, his meeting with Lydia in February 1834: "The youth gazed with great delight upon the beautiful face until he caught the maiden's eye." The glance thus exchanged was so significant, so striking that he remarked on it at the time. He spoke of eyetraps, and even constructed a sort of theory of "the glance." "There are some occult facts in human nature that are natural magic," he wrote. "The chief of these is the glance (*oeillade*). The mysterious communication that is established across a house between two entire strangers, by this means moves all the springs of wonder."[4]

This new meeting naturally recalled the earlier one with Ellen, whose lovingly tended memory was to be stitched, by mutual consent, into the fabric of the generally happy marriage of Waldo and Lydia. With unnecessary honesty Emerson (and Charles and Elizabeth Hoar) kept the image of Ellen alive. Ellen meant delicious memories of youth, brief moments and meetings "when affection contrived to give a witchcraft surpassing even the deep attraction of its own truth to a parcel of accidental and insignificant circumstances." Lydia meant a meeting of minds. If this sounds less romantic, we should recall that mind—that is, consciousness—was everything to Emerson; no higher compliment was possible. "It is a great happiness," he noted, "when two good minds meet, both cultivated, and with such difference of learning as to excite each other's curiosity, and such similarity as to understand each other's allusions in the touch-and-go of conversation."[5]

Emerson's proposal letter shines with an intellectual ardor that matches the physical thrill of the glance. In Quakerly terms he tells her how he cannot resist his impulse to "beseech you to love me." His proposal comes, he says, from his "highest impulses." The "tender respect" she has inspired in him rejoices him "in my Reason as well as my Understanding." In the language of Coleridge, which was now for Emerson the language of real life and not an examination question, this is the highest human love there can be. He is in love, he tells her, "after a new and higher way." It is all nonsense, of course, but it is love nonsense, and there is no mistaking the smitten tone:

"I am persuaded that I address one so in love with what I love . . . that an affection founded on such a basis cannot alter." In earnest talk one day Lydia stopped nervously to ask if he found her conversation uninteresting. "Uninteresting!" he replied. "It is heaven."[6]

We do not have Lydia's reply to the proposal, but it came swiftly. She, like him, put second thoughts aside and took the plunge. Within a week he was calling her Lidian (though he continued for a while to write Lydia on the envelope) and they began planning a life together. It has been suggested that Emerson called her Lidian in order to head off the inevitable New England pronunciation of her married name as Lydiar Emerson, but all that we know for certain is that he remarked to a cousin at the time that "the philistines baptized her Lydia, but her name is Lidian." Lidian, as she soon hereafter called herself, was not only an educated, intelligent woman, she was an intellectual. Friends and family recognized the similarity of her thought to Emerson's; Frank Sanborn was surely right in saying Emerson learned from her. She took part in Margaret Fuller's colloquia, and she wrote a clever satire called "The Transcendental Bible" with advice to the radicals who gathered bearded and barefoot around Emerson in the early days. In a long letter to Elizabeth Peabody written during the summer of 1835, we see Lidian's intellectual side clearly. She says she is most struck by Swedenborg and his followers, especially by the ideas of correspondence and analogy. She does not identify herself with any particular denomination but says she finds in the sayings of Christ and his apostles the ultimate source of those rays of light that she herself sees from time to time. She believes "that each individual should consider himself as but a part of a great whole" and that "our individual being . . . is not complete in itself." At the same time she thinks that each of us has "some peculiarity of nature that fits him for his place," and she insists that "the *will* to see our calling must be attained before the power to discern it is given." She thinks that the familiar remark that people generally marry their opposites is true and that the most perfect marriage would be one in which opposite temperaments were united. She has her own version of the concept of *Bildung*, saying, "It seems to me that in the cultivation of our own nature—it is our duty to respect its peculiarities;—that we should not attempt to become like every body or anybody else."[7]

She always called Emerson Mr. Emerson, and we have to estimate the real affection and affinity between the two of them across the stone walls of traditional New England reserve. Their daughter Ellen once said, "The tremendous manner in which she loved father was always as astonishing to me as the coolness with which she treated him." During their courting days and for some ten years after they were married, Lidian's excitement whenever a letter came from him was "uncontrollable." "It was utterly impossible for Mother to open it in the presence of another person," wrote Ellen. "It must always be with locked doors, and she must read it many times, get used to it, and recover from the excitement before she could carry it into Grandmother's room." In *Woman in the Nineteenth Century* Margaret Fuller lists four kinds of marriage, the first and simplest being the mutual defense league of two persons against the world. The Emersons, at least in the early years, are an example of Fuller's highest type, what she called the "pilgrimage of two souls toward a common shrine."[8]

Lidian possessed an uncanny clairvoyant streak. Ellen recounts that one day, well before Emerson's bolt-from-the-blue proposal, Lidian "saw a clear image of herself dressed as a bride walking down those stairs [of the Winslow home in Plymouth] with Father to be married." Ellen also mentions the moment on January 26, 1835, the day before Emerson's letter arrived, when her mother "beheld Father's face, very beautiful, close to her, gazing at her, just for a moment. Then it was gone." She enjoyed the *sortes biblicae,* the blind opening to a page in the Bible at random for guidance. She believed in portents and omens. She was interested in the wave of spiritualism, mediums, and table-rapping that swept the country in the 1830s and 1840s. This interest was not superstitious, at least not in the usual sense. It was rather a passionate interest in high moments of insight, in coincidences, and in those intensities of consciousness that seem to validate a view of life as more than physical cause and effect. Lidian's intensity was famous. Emerson called her Asia sometimes because, he said, "no New Englander that he knew had ever possessed such a depth of feeling that was continually called out on such trivial occasions."[9]

Photographs of Lidian with her children on her lap show a woman of great tenderness. A later picture of her shows a woman of sorrows with a fixity reminiscent of Emerson's mother, Ruth, but with eyes of extraordinary depth and forcefulness. Lidian's health was never good after she had scarlet fever at nineteen. She was often sick, often fatigued. There was also a dark place in her spirit that was more than poor health. She was terribly over-conscientious, a condition that only got worse as time went on. It had a comic side; she could wake up in the night remembering that she had left a large book lying on top of a smaller one. But the underlying anxiety is not really funny.

Lidian was overwhelmed at the start by the idea of having to be worthy of the locally much-admired Mr. Emerson. She was also overwhelmed by the prospect of running a large establishment. Of the little difficulties and failures of any housekeeping, her daughter once said, "It was her nature to take them with a curiously exaggerated view of their importance and to expend on them an amazing amount of indignation and shame." Deep in Lidian's nature was a persistent and unmistakable tragic thread that occasionally showed on the surface in moments of hopelessness or despair. In black moods she was capable of wishing she had never been born. She was haunted by many things, by the terror of her childhood, by Emerson's first marriage, and by the feeling that he was not hers for good. They talked together about Ellen, and one night Lidian dreamed that she and Emerson were together in heaven and they met Ellen. In the dream Lidian then went away, leaving Emerson with Ellen. It may not have helped much when Emerson responded to Lidian's account of the dream with intended comfort, saying, "Only the noble dream such dreams."[10]

Lidian's second daughter, Edith, would later maintain that her older sister, in her life of Lidian, had seriously exaggerated in saying that for thirty years after 1841 "sadness was the ground-color" of their mother's life. Certainly the Emersons were happy in 1835. And for the next five years Lidian was to say that she and Mr. Emerson were getting "more married all the time."[11]

32. The New Jerusalem

Emerson was thirty-two in 1835. He was a tall man, standing six feet in his shoes, erect, with rather narrow and unusually sloping shoulders and a long neck. His hair was dark brown, his eyes very blue. He dressed in loose-fitting clothes; more than one observer said he looked like a prosperous farmer. He carried his money in an old wallet with twine wrapped around it four or five times. In his mid-thirties he got up at six, had a cup of coffee, then worked until twelve or one. (Much later, by the time of his California trip, he took up the old New England custom of pie for breakfast.) His rule was forty pages for a lecture. When he delivered one, he stood looking down at his manuscript, hands folded in front, except to turn the page. He had been told early in his career to keep his eye on a person toward the back of the audience, for by so doing "the voice naturally elevates itself to such a pitch that that person can hear." His customary gesture was to clench his right fist—knuckles upward, arm bent at the elbow—then to deliver a downward blow of the forearm, full of power bridled. He accompanied this gesture, says Hawthorne's son Julian, by "such a glance of the eye as no one ever saw except from Emerson: a glance like the reveille of a trumpet."[1]

The biography lectures reflect Emerson's new hopefulness and vigor. Examining the lives of others seems to have given him hope for his own. In Michelangelo he saw "the perfect image of the artist," one who was born to see and express the beauty of the world. He admired how Michelangelo had "lived one life, pursued one career," in marked contrast to his own meandering present and unclear future. Much as he admired Michelangelo's works, he admired "the more perfect sculpture of his life" more. He loved the disinterestedness and spirit of the deal Michelangelo offered the Pope for his work rebuilding St. Peter's in Rome: "no fee and no interference." Emerson emphasized the sculptor's interest in ideal beauty, how "he sought through the eye to reach the soul," but he knew that the test of artist and writer alike is not in intent but in execution. He quoted with approval

195

Michelangelo's saying "he alone was an artist whose hands can execute perfectly what his mind has conceived."[2]

Emerson's Luther is "a scholar leading a spiritual revolution by spiritual arms alone." He makes Luther vivid through personal detail. He describes the publishing of his theses against indulgences—the central crisis of his life in which he "nailed his attention to the ecclesiastical abuses which could not be seen by a sane eye without indignation." Emerson notes Luther's "volcanic temper" and how he had "the most terrible determination that ever lived in a human breast." Luther was for Emerson a modern Isaiah, "the prophet, the poet of his time and country." He was not a poet

> in the literary sense. He wrote no poems, but he walked in a charmed world. Everything to his eye assumed a symbolical aspect. All occurrences, all institutions, all persons seemed to him only occasions for the activity of supernatural agents . . . All objects, all events are transparent. He sees through them the love or malignity which is working behind them.

As the Michelangelo lecture prefigures much of what Emerson will say in *Nature* about beauty, so "Luther" and "Milton" are his first drafts for "The Poet." Luther is set apart from the mere versemaker. Where "other poets describe their imaginations, he believed and acted his."[3]

Milton is like Jeremiah for Emerson, having an equally undiminished power to inspire. There was for him "no one whose mind still acts on the cultivated intellect of England and America with an energy comparable to Milton." And it is from Milton himself that Emerson gets his conviction that the poet's life is the real poem. "He who would aspire to write well hereafter in laudable things ought himself to be a true poem," says Milton. Emerson admired the personal element in all Milton's writing, and most of all, his interest in liberty, whether civil, ecclesiastical, literary, or domestic.[4]

The fourth lecture was on George Fox, who stands, in Emerson's treatment, as the embodiment of the religious sentiment—the inner light—and of the operation of the latter "to bring the universe into the possession of the single soul." For the last of his series Emerson chose Burke as embodying the idea of eloquence and for bringing "principles to bear upon the public business of England." Burke stands in this series as Napoleon stands in *Representative Men* for the real world of politics and power. Emerson uses this lecture to disclaim personal and provincial standards of judgment and to reach for the high ground of a Samuel Johnson. "There is no caprice and no chance in the final award upon human merit," Emerson said. "Every newcomer takes his true place by a force which no furtherance can help and no opposition can hinder, namely by the real importance of his doing and thinking to the constant mind of man."[5]

Emerson learned a good deal from his forays into biography. "How precisely parallel are the biographies of religious enthusiasts," he wrote in January.

> Swedenborg, Guyon, Fox, Luther, and perhaps Behman [Boehme]: each owes all to the discovery that God must be sought within, not without. That is the discovery of Jesus. Each perceives the worthlessness of all institutions, and the infinity of wisdom that issues from meditation.

As both he and his friends perceived, Emerson had now moved beyond Unitarianism but not beyond religion. Both Hedge and Fuller's good friend James Freeman Clarke pressed him now to the study of Schleiermacher, whose revolutionary Christian romantic theology begins with the decisive location of the religious spirit in the human spirit.[6]

Emerson's sympathies were clearly no longer Unitarian. Nor were they ever, now or earlier, in the slightest degree Calvinist. His sympathies now are with groups and individuals most of whom were even farther out of the Christian mainstream than Unitarianism, not so much with Methodism as with the idiosyncratic and salty Father Taylor, who called on the Lord to "bless the bleached sail," not so much with Quakerism as with George Fox and Mary Rotch, not so much with the Church of the New Jerusalem as with Swedenborg and Sampson Reed.

We follow Emerson's interest in Plato, Kant, Goethe, Plutarch, or Montaigne without surprise. But his fascination with Swedenborg, Reed, and Oegger is another matter. It is easy to turn to the certified great for inspiration, but it requires originality to be able to see in the work of a minor or marginal or flawed figure what no one has seen before. Goethe's interest in the semifraudulent Ossian, Melville's in the sailor-poet Dibden, Thoreau's in the Roman agricultural writers such as Varro and Columella, and Emerson's in Swedenborg show how some minds can build a palace out of materials the rest of us have agreed to reject. Swedenborg is a good example. He is widely regarded as marginal, perhaps a crank; yet Goethe, Kant, Blake, Coleridge, and Emerson were all interested in his work. Emerson announced this year that "the teacher that I look for and await shall enunciate with more precision and universality, with piercing poetic insight, those beautiful but severe compensations that give to moral nature an aspect of mathematical science." If this describes Kant's project it also describes Swedenborg's.[7]

Emanuel Swedenborg (1688–1772), whom Czeslaw Milosz calls "the great Swedish master of the imagination," set out, like Kant, to illuminate the connection between the mind and nature, between inner nature and outer, between religion and science. His starting point was science. His early writings were on air pumps, mining and smelting, salt extraction, currency control, and navigation. He moved from mining and metallurgy to the animal kingdom (skipping over the vegetable). In several long works on anatomy, physiology, and psychology, he examined in detail and made numerous important discoveries about the brain, the nervous system, the cortex, and the endocrine glands. The overarching principles that unify all of Swedenborg's work are the avowed search for the soul and the idea that everything that exists on the physical plane—our world of space and time—has a counterpart in the immaterial world of mind. This is Swedenborg's famous doctrine of correspondences. Swedenborg is a sort of eighteenth-century Plato working out his ideas in the post-Newtonian laboratories of the Enlightenment.

Swedenborg's Latin works, *Oeconomia regni animalis* (1740–1741) and *Regnum animale* (1744–1845), were not translated until 1844 and 1845. Before that, Emerson got most of what he knew about Swedenborg from Sampson Reed or Guillaume Oegger. Reed's *Observations on the Growth of the Mind* had caught Emerson's attention in part because Reed insisted that the present age was a period of revolutionary change in the way people think. Reed emphasizes change over and over, always leading it back to the same cause: "All the changes which are taking place in the world originate in the mind." He is as sure as Kant that "the laws of the mind are in themselves as fixed and perfect as the laws of matter." Reed also believed that the human mind is active, not passive, and that "the natural sciences are the basis of all useful knowledge." He accepted Swedenborg's master idea of correspondence. Everything in the natural world has a counterpart in the world of mind. Swedenborg and Reed believe that God has designed it that way. Emerson is as interested in the correspondence of inner and outer, of mind and world, as any, but he is not dogmatic, and he is interested in how this correspondence *works*. For this reason he was greatly pleased when, this summer of 1835, he read Elizabeth Peabody's manuscript translation of the first part of Guillaume Oegger's *The True Messiah*.[8]

Oegger was a French Swedenborgian who reasoned that just as Rousseau and others could speak of a state of nature as a sort of starting point or baseline for political ideas, so we must recognize the language of nature as the key to our idea of language. Oegger begins by showing how "the visible creation then, can not, must not . . . be anything but the exterior circumference of the invisible and metaphysical world."[9]

It follows, says Oegger, that "everything we see, touch, smell; everything from the sun to a grain of sand, from our own body with its admirable organs, to that of the worm; everything has flowed forth, by a supreme reason, from that world where all is spirit and life." Language embodies our "perception of the emblems of life and intelligence, which nature contains in her bosom, and the faculty of transmitting that perception to others."[10]

This is the view that the world itself is symbolic, the view C. S. Lewis adopts when he notes that in symbolism it is we who are the allegory, the view that Robbe-Grillet rejects when he says, disapprovingly, that if you begin by believing in metaphor you will end by believing in God. Whether one reaches that latter position or not, Oegger leads us to consider nature as the original basis and source of language. Nature is the original quarry out of which language comes. This insight has metaphysical implications, but it also has immense practical consequences, making it possible for us to trace our words back to their origins in the natural world. "Supercilious" means raised eyebrow, "consider" means to study the stars, "experience" means something snatched from danger. Etymology reveals some natural phenomenon behind every word if only we can get back far enough.[11]

Emerson's reading this winter also embraced Sophocles' *Electra* and Coleridge's *The Statesman's Manual.* From the latter he copied down one of the laws he had been trying to live by since college: "Nothing great was ever achieved without enthusiasm." In March, as spring approached, Emerson went walking in the woods; the ideas and the experiences for his little book on nature began to pile up.

> As I walked in the woods I felt what I often feel, that nothing can befal me in life, no calamity, no disgrace (leaving me my eyes) to which Nature will not offer a sweet consolation. Standing on the bare ground, with my head bathed by the blithe air, and uplifted into the infinite space, I become happy in my universal relations. The name of the nearest friend sounds then foreign and accidental. I am the heir of unaccustomed beauty and power.[12]

33. The Art of Writing. Jakob Boehme

IN MARCH AND APRIL OF 1835 EMERSON WAS URGING CARLYLE to come to America to lecture. He also mentioned a new magazine, to be called *The Transcendentalist* or perhaps *The Spiritual Enquirer*. There was talk of Hedge for editor, but now he left for Bangor. Emerson suggested that Carlyle might take up the task. New magazines were springing up everywhere in America. In addition to Reed's *New Jerusalem Magazine,* founded back in 1827, there were *The Knickerbocker* (1833), the *Southern Literary Messenger* (1834), the *Southern Literary Journal* (1835), and the *Western Literary Messenger* (1835).[1]

Emerson was himself working on *Nature* and looking ahead to a volume of essays. "When will you mend Montaigne?" he asked himself in his journal. "Where are your Essays?" He took an ever greater interest in the process of writing now, whether the result was to be delivered from a lecture platform or published as a book. He began regularly to keep a new notebook for each new lecture series he undertook. His practical rules for writers were few and simple. First, he said, "Sit alone." Second, keep a journal "for the habit of rendering account to yourself of yourself in some more rigorous manner and at more certain intervals than mere conversation."[2]

Public lecturing had sharpened his sense of the importance of keeping your real audience in mind while writing. "Happy is he who looks only into his work to know if it will succeed, never into the times or the public opinion; and who writes from the love of imparting certain thoughts and not from the necessity of sale—who always writes to the unknown friend." Emerson already had a substantial amount of material banked in his journals, which he was now organizing in a new way. "When I was quite young, I fancied that by keeping a manuscript journal by me over whose pages I wrote a list of the great topics of human study, as Religion, Poetry, Politics, Love, etc., in the course of a few years I should be able to complete a sort of Encyclopedia." Emerson tried this sort of pre-indexing for a while, but discovered it did not work: "Year after year our tables get no completeness, and at last we discover that our curve is parabola, whose arcs will never meet." He tried a new method, which he later explained to Elizabeth Peabody. "He advised me," she recalled,

> to keep a manuscript book—and to write down every train of thought which arose on any interesting subject with the imagery in which it first came into my mind. This manuscript was to be perfectly informal and allow of skipping from one subject to another with only a black line between. After it was written I could run a heading of subjects over the top—and when I wanted to make up an article—there were all my thoughts ready.

Indexing was a crucial method for Emerson because it allowed him to write first and organize later and because it gave him easy access to the enormous mass of specific materials in his ever-increasing pile of notebooks.[3]

He was now trying to capture not just major conclusions and insights, but the slightest, most evanescent hints and glimmers that rose to the surface of his mind and then as quickly sank from sight: "For the best part . . . of every mind is not that which [a person] knows, but that which hovers in gleams, suggestions, tantalizing unpossessed before him." Emerson's journals show that for years he fished along the edges of consciousness, eager to note down the smallest fresh suggestion or hint of a suggestion. He made an effort to recall and write down dreams, to record first impressions, not second thoughts, to recall "what so rankled at heart and kept the eyes open all night." These were all struggles to forestall and cheat the repressive processes of the mind, to snatch and write down everything that reached the surface of consciousness. Much of Emerson's journal is not intended as finished work or public utterance, nor even as the record of private conviction. He is concerned to explore—and then to save—impulses, essays, hints, trials, spurts, exaggerations, the most fleeting and evanescent flowers of the mind.[4]

Despite self-deprecating comments about "my usual gypsy diligence," Emerson spent a good deal of time methodically copying and recopying journal material, indexing, alphabetizing indexes, and eventually making indexes of indexes. When he came to write a lecture, he would work through his indexes, making a list of possible passages. He then assembled, ordered, and reordered these into the talk or lecture. When he was doing a lecture series, he needed about twenty hours of actual writing to produce one forty-page lecture.[5]

One key to Emerson's writing then is the topic, the index heading. But the secret of his prose is the sentence. Emerson's mature essays are not mainly secular preaching in sermon form, nor are they personal essays, like Lamb's, or excursions, like Thoreau's. Emerson's essays are collections of great sentences on a single topic—just as Plutarch's or Montaigne's are collections of vivid anecdotes around a topic. His style has been described as "an army all officers" and as "a bag of duck shot held together by canvas." Emerson himself understood this aspect of his style, and he also used the language of projectile and propellant. "I am a rocket manufacturer," he said. He understood early that he "who can make a good sentence can make a good book." He knew perfectly well that his essays had very little formal structure—beyond the taut logic of the individual sentence—and that the very force and closure of each sentence set it off from all the others. "Here I sit and read and write with very little system," he wrote, "and as far as regards composition, with the most fragmentary results; paragraphs incompressible, each sentence an infinitely repellent particle."[6]

One of the most recurrent themes in Emerson's journals, one he only fitfully indexed and never wrote on, was the topic of writing itself. He had much to say about the practical process of writing that never found its way into his essays "The Poet" or "The Scholar." Although he wrote so rapidly he had trouble getting ink to dry, writing was never without its problems and never something he could take for granted. "I never seem well to do a particular work until another is due. I cannot write the poem though you give me a week, but if I promise to read a lecture day after tomorrow, at once the poem comes into my head."[7]

His journals and conversation are full of practical advice for the writer. "Drop adjectives," he told Woodbury, "let the noun do the work." "The art of writing consists in putting two things together that are unlike and that belong together like a horse and cart." He made lists of phrases that should be banned, including "after all," "kindred spirit," "yes, to a certain extent," and "as a general thing." He believed in throwing himself on his work. "An artist spends himself, like the crayon in his hand, till he is gone." Writing was like shooting: "Success depends on the aim, not the means. Look at the mark, not on your arrow." When in doubt, plunge: "The way to write is to throw your body at the mark when your arrows are spent."[8]

Emerson's best comments are on the actual process of composition. "In writing," he said, "the casting moment is of greatest importance, just as it avails not in Daguerre portraits that you have the very man before you, if the expression has escaped." Anyone can write; the trick is to get life into it. He sought "contagion, yeast, 'emptins,' anything to convey fermentation, import fermentation, induce fermentation into a quiescent mass." His habit of watching his every shade of thought carried over to observing his quick-silver moods as a writer: "Three or four stubborn necessary words are the pith and fate of the business, all the rest is expatiating and qualifying; three or four real choices, acts of will of somebody, the rest is circumstance, satellite, and flourish."[9]

Emerson read William Howitt's *The Seasons* in March of 1835. The book is a calendar of the natural year, a poetic and picturesque catalog of natural phenomena which varies in tone only from "sheep-washing is begun in many places" to "field paths are at this season particularly attractive." Emerson thought that he might one day write "a natural history of the woods around my shifting camp for every month in the year," a book of which Howitt should be "not so much the model as the parody." Although Emerson himself never came close to carrying out such a project, Henry Thoreau would spend the best energies of his last years on just such a project, a comprehensive account of a natural year.[10]

Emerson was again reading Cudworth's *True Intellectual System of the Universe* and admiring its strong Platonism. Emerson was himself after large game, aiming at setting out the principles of "the first philosophy," to which a new notebook was now dedicated. The phrase came from Bacon. Emerson uses it to mean "the original laws of the mind . . . the science of what is, in distinction from what appears."[11]

Emerson and Lidian wrote back and forth. He wished to settle in Concord, she in Plymouth. Eventually Concord won. The wedding was set for mid-September. Meanwhile, during the summer, Emerson's work on *Nature* was drawing him ever more deeply into philosophical idealism. Reading Elizabeth Peabody's manuscript for *Record of a School,* he noted how it "aims all the time to show the symbolical character of all things to the children." He fretted and fingered again the old master idea of compensation, what he called his "one conviction, that moral ideas hold," that all seeming must be replaced by being, that everything has its cost, that "when the vain speaker has sat down, and the people say 'what a good speech,' it still takes an ounce to balance an ounce."[12]

As he worked on *Nature,* Emerson became clearer about what he did not want to do. Reading John Norris's 1701 *Essay towards the Theory of the Ideal or Intelligible World,* he noted that Norris "fights the battles and affirms the facts I had proposed to myself to do." But Norris does so in a language heavy with abstraction and technical philosophical jargon. "All this polemics, syllogism, and definition is so much wastepaper," he concluded.[13]

A visit to the Harvard Divinity School led to the same conclusion. "At the Divinity School this morning I heard what was called the best performance but it was founded on nothing and led to nothing." In the afternoon another speaker spoke "with pathetic tones and gestures, and the most approved expressions, and all about nothing; and he was answered by others . . . and still it was all nothing."[14]

There were, however, other books that Emerson found substantial and to the point. There was Oegger's suggestive and detailed account of nature as the language of spirit. Above all, this summer of 1835, there was Jakob Boehme's *Aurora,* which Emerson read in early August. Boehme (1575–1624) was a Prussian shoemaker, a follower of Luther, who had two major illuminations, one in 1600, the other in 1610. As a result of these he broke with that aspect of medieval religion that insisted that man try to climb up to God. "I did not climb up into the Godhead," Boehme wrote in *Aurora.* "Neither can so mean a man as I am do it; but the Godhead climbed up in me, and revealed such to me out of his love." This idea has been called the "mystical heart of Lutheranism," the idea that came from Staupitz to Luther, that God's love is in men even before they search for him.[15]

Boehme was more a Gnostic than a mystic. His writings present a wisdom grounded in revelation and employing myth and symbol rather than concept. He believed that "the visible world is a manifestation of the interior spiritual world of eternal light and darkness . . . a reflection of eternity which allows eternity to make itself visible." Man, for Boehme, is both a microcosm and a microtheos. The spiritual and invisible world is the foundation of the material and visible world. God can be found only in the depths of one's own heart. It is vain to seek divine wisdom in academies or books.[16]

Boehme presented all this as direct personal knowledge. His *Aurora* told of his own awakening to the sunrise of an eternity situated firmly in this world. Direct and convincing personal experience was what Emerson missed in Norris and at the divinity school. He found it in Alcott and in Boehme, and he said of the latter that he was "the best helper to a theory of Isaiah and Jeremiah. You were sure he was in earnest, and, could you get into his point of view the world would be what he describes. He is all imagination."[17]

So is Emerson. He once wrote to a person who had inquired about his life:

I have no history, no fortunes that would make the smallest figure in a narrative. My course of life has been so routinary, that the keenest eye for point or picture would be at fault before such remediless commonplace. We will really say no more on a topic so sterile.

What he was absorbed in now, and for most of his life, was making sentences, "launch[ing] out into the infinity and build[ing] a road into Chaos and Old Night." The idea was to use only words that stood for things. "There is every degree of remoteness," he wrote, "from the line of things in the line of words." His mood now was upbeat; he felt capable of something. If utterance was place enough, as he had told Carlyle, it was also action enough. In a burst of enthusiasm he proposed to himself a rule of life, a sort of answer to Bartleby: "I will no longer confer, differ, refer, defer, prefer, or suffer. I renounce the whole tribe of *fero*. I embrace absolute life."[18]

34. Marriage and Concord

DURING JULY AND AUGUST OF 1835, JUST AS EMERSON WAS excitedly absorbing Oegger, Peabody, and Boehme, he was busy with two other projects as well. By late June he had agreed to give the main address at Concord's two-hundredth anniversary celebration, and by early July he had agreed to buy the Coolidge house in Concord as a home for Lidian and himself. Though he sometimes complained, busyness and variety stimulated him. For the Concord talk Emerson now plunged into historical research. This was the only time in his life when he showed any sustained interest in New England's colonial past. He read Edward Johnson's *Wonder-Working Providence,* Hubbard's *Indian Wars,* Cotton Mather's *Magnalia,* John Winthrop's *Journal,* Thomas Hutchinson's *History of Massachusetts,* Bancroft's *History of the United States,* and much more. He dug out his grandfather's account of the Battle of Concord; he interviewed survivors of the fight at the bridge. He borrowed the proofs of Lemuel Shattuck's forthcoming *History of the Town of Concord.* The result, a two-hour speech on Sepember 12, was Emerson's public introduction to his new home, his symbolic entrance on the stage of Concord.[1]

The address was not a personal statement. It was a chronological and detailed historical account of the town. Emerson described the rise of town-meeting democracy, and he juxtaposed the town's pride in its traditions of freedom and self-government with its shabby treatment of the Indians who had been there first. He carefully documented the town's development, a subject close to Shattuck's heart. Emerson used Shattuck's work, particularly for statistics, and he noted the current problem of the exodus of young people from the town. Ten veterans of the Revolution sat in front at the festivities, living links with the past.[2]

The speech was printed. It was Emerson's first real publication. He was thirty-two; he had a reputation as a minister and to some extent as a lecturer, but only in eastern Massachusetts. He had written a great deal, but he had withheld it all from publication. He had written enough sermons to fill four volumes, enough lectures for another volume, and enough letters for a large volume; his written journals by now were sufficient to fill five or six closely printed volumes of five hundred pages each. Of course, the public delivery of sermons and lectures was a major form of publication at the time, and there is no reason to think Emerson was dissatisfied with everything he had written. But in a certain sense, Emerson's writing until now, in his own mind, was preparatory. Later on, even when he was famous, Emerson never published any of the work he had done before the move to Concord. His four volumes of sermons, his early lectures, and all the notes and indexes were, so to speak, suppressed. The work represented two apprenticeships—three, if we count that of poet. The results of all this early work were plowed back in for the sake of the next crop. If we now collect and publish his early work, it can show us how he grew, it can show us his reading, and it can show us Emerson in his time. But it does not show us Emerson as he wished to be seen or as he was seen outside eastern Massachusetts in his own time. That is the function of *Nature,* the published *Essays,* the two volumes of poems, and the other books he himself published.

On the thirteenth of September, 1835, the day after the historical address, Emerson set out in a chaise for Plymouth. On the fourteenth he and Lidian were married there in her family home. She was delayed in getting dressed and the impatient bridegroom went upstairs to get her. They met on the stairs and came down together, against all convention but fulfilling her previsionary image of the preceding January. The wedding itself was a modest affair, as most weddings then were in Massachusetts. Only one friend of Emerson's was present, George Bradford. Neither his mother nor his brother Charles came. Lidian received one wedding present, a double inkstand. All day it was dark and rainy, but in the late afternoon the sky cleared and there was a golden sunset in time for the evening wedding ceremony. The next day the couple drove to Concord, to the house they were to live in for the rest of their lives.

The white house was large and L-shaped, with barn and doghouse, and sat about three hundred yards from the center of Concord, just where the road from town branched. The right-hand fork—called the Concord and Union Turnpike—was a hilly road, not much used, which led to Cambridge via what is now Route 2. The left-hand road, the Great County Road (today's Route 2A), led to Lexington, five miles off, then to Boston. The house sat on two acres of rather low ground, sloping away behind the house to the Mill Brook, on the other side of which stood the town poorhouse and asylum. The Emerson house had a white fence out front, on the lower rail of which Emerson used to deposit his half-smoked cigar when he came in. The high ground of Revolutionary Ridge, across the road to the north, was supposed to provide some protection from the worst of the winter winds. The house was large enough to accommodate, in addition to the newlyweds, Emerson's mother and a cook, Nancy Colesworthy. Charles and Aunt Mary took meals at the new house but had rooms elsewhere in Concord. The house, built in 1828 by J. J. Coolidge and known as Coolidge Castle, was renamed and deromanticized by the Emersons, who called it simply Bush. The establishment was substantial from the start. Emerson had never lived anywhere but in rented quarters. Lidian had lived her whole previous life in a house so large it was often called a mansion. At Bush there were carpets to be laid, trees and shrubs to be planted. Lidian had her own roses sent up from Plymouth, including a pink Damask rose, single and double white English tree roses, and blush roses. The young couple was hospitable, and there was often a crowd for dinner. Ellen Emerson later said all her mother's recipes began "beat two dozen eggs . . ."[3]

Concord in 1835 was a quieter place than Boston, though that is not saying much. Boston had grown an astonishing 41 percent between 1820 and 1830 and was in the middle of a second growth spurt of 34 percent between 1830 and 1840. Its sixty thousand people would be ninety thousand by 1840. The pace of development its citizens took in stride would now be considered a boom-town rush. The future still seemed to be with water. Mills were going up wherever a stream permitted. Boston was flinging out canals in all directions; its fishing fleet was so large that one might see a hundred and fifty sails at sea at once. One enterprising Boston merchant named Tudor was cutting ice on local ponds and shipping it, packed in thick beds of sawdust, to ports as far away as Calcutta.[4]

Concord was not just Emerson's refuge from "the compliances and imitations of city society." He was positively attracted by what he called the "lukewarm milky dog-days of common village life." Concord had 2,021 persons. The census of 1830 listed 28 free persons of color, down from 34 in 1820. The town was, despite its low and generally marshy situation, a healthy place. One out of five persons lived to age seventy, compared with one in thirty-one for France, one in ten for London, and one in eight for Connecticut. The average age was forty-eight. Consumption accounted for only 14 percent of all deaths; various fevers accounted for 20 percent, while about 8 percent of the population died of old age.[5]

Parish affairs and town affairs overlapped substantially. Church and state were not officially separated in Massachusetts until 1834, and as late as that date is, Concord did not comply with the new law until 1856. The church was no longer the only social force in town. When Emerson moved there, Concord had an exclusive group called the Social Circle, limited to twenty-five members, which went back to 1778 (and which still continues), and a library that had been started in 1794 and reorganized in 1821. There was a Female Charitable Society and a Society for the Suppression of Intemperance, both dating from 1814. By Emerson's time there was a strong antislavery society, in which Cynthia Thoreau, mother of David Henry, was active. The women of Concord sent frequent petitions and memorials to the government in Washington. A lyceum was begun in 1828; it incorporated an earlier debating society. A Mozart society was founded in 1832.

By 1835 Concord had sixty-six college graduates, with another four or five currently enrolled as undergraduates. The town itself had six school districts, with separate schools for boys and girls. The schoolhouses, one of which was directly across the street from the Emersons' new house, were plain and bare, without paint or equipment. Heated by a single stove each, they were always too hot or too cold, and they struggled with an absentee rate that averaged 33 percent. There was a small, precariously maintained private academy for college-bound students.

The land was much more open then. Of Concord's fifteen thousand acres, 13 percent were in woods and almost all the rest was open. Nearly a quarter of the land, 23 percent, was unimprovable marsh or swamp. Pastures, meadows, and a modest thousand acres (7 percent) planted to crops made up the main features of the landscape. There were few trees in town or around houses. One could see to the horizon from almost anywhere in Concord. When the Emersons moved in, they set to work at once to plant trees. There was already a row of nine horse chestnut trees out front along the road, and they planted four elms and two balsam firs in an oval east of the house. Charles superintended that and the planting of fifteen other balsam firs around the house.

Agriculture was the leading occupation in Concord, but manufacturing ran it a close second. There was a cotton mill, employing forty-two persons, thirty of them young women. The mill had 1,100 spindles, 20 looms, and used 50,000 pounds of cotton a year to make 180,000 yards of cloth.

Another manufacturing concern used 300,000 pounds of lead annually to make lead pipes and lead sheeting. A steam-driven smithy used 100,000 pounds of iron and 4,000 pounds of steel a year. The town manufactured chaises, harness, carriages, boots, shoes, cloaks, hats, bellows, guns, bricks, barrels, soap, and cabinetware. Pencils were made by Nehemiah Ball and also by John Thoreau, whose second son, David Henry, was a sophomore at Harvard. The little industrial village of Concord also had two sawmills, two gristmills, a bookstore and bindery, six warehouses and a busy carrying trade that kept innumerable wagons with teams of two, four, or six horses on the roads during all the daylight hours. Concord was a hard-drinking town; there were three large taverns in the center of town and all stores sold liquor by the gallon or quart. According to Horace Hosmer, "Many large estates were squandered by farmers who neglected their farms and lounged in the Tavern bar rooms week in and week out." Ministers also drank "and *got drunk*, helplessly so," Hosmer added.[6]

The slow-moving Sudbury River, called Musketaquid, or grass-ground, by the Indians, joins the Assabet at Concord to become the Concord River, which in turn flows into the Merrimack. Concord's flat, marshy situation made it a poor place for dams and therefore for waterpower. Forward-looking men such as Lemuel Shattuck hoped to run a canal through town so that it might become, if not a great mill town, at least a center for the carrying trade. A number of important roads ran through Concord. The town maintained eight bridges, which together with liberal outlays for roads, schools, and welfare—all of which were handled entirely at the local level—meant that taxes were "supposed to be higher, in proportion to its wealth, than in many towns, amounting to about $3.00 on every inhabitant."[7]

Before the coming of the railroad in 1845 the trip to Boston by cart, carriage, or horse took about two and a half hours. There was regularly scheduled stage service that passed right by the Emerson house, so that even if a visitor was not quite packed in time, Emerson could dash out of the house to flag down the passing coach so that the friend could catch the last trip back to Boston.

35. Alcott and English Literature

ONE OF THE FIRST AND MOST FREQUENT VISITORS IN THIS FALL
of 1835 was Bronson Alcott. Emerson had read the extraordinary little book
about his Temple School in June and he had heard from George Bradford
about Alcott. Alcott's first long visit to Emerson's house took place in late
October 1835. Alcott was four years older than Emerson. Born Amos B.
Alcox in Wolcott, Connecticut, he was completely self-educated. He spent
three and half years in Virginia as a peddler. He loved Virginia but had no
head for business, returning from each trip without a penny of profit but
with superb self-assured southern manners. His early reading took him from
Flavel's *Keeping the Heart* to Bunyan's *Pilgrim's Progress,* to Adam Smith's
Theory of Moral Sentiments, to Robert Owen's *A New View of Society.* This
last was an extreme rationalist work, maintaining, almost as B. F. Skinner
would later, that since we are born empty or blank we can be taught anything
at all, if given early and complete enough training. Owen claimed he could
teach a tiger if he got it early enough.[1]

From Owen Alcott moved on to Pestalozzi, the great Swiss educator who
laid the foundation for modern primary education. Fired with enthusiasm
for teaching, Alcott abandoned peddling and opened the first of a series of
schools. In 1828 he came to Boston to teach, heard Emerson, and married
Abigail May. In 1830 he went to Germantown, Pennsylvania, where over
the next three and a half years he both kept school and did his serious
reading. In 1833 he discovered and was instantly converted to Platonism.
He marked the day in red on his calendar, a distinction used otherwise only
for his marriage, the birth of his daughters, the opening of the Civil War,
and the death of Lincoln. He also read Carlyle, Coleridge's *Aids to Reflection,*
Proclus, Plotinus (in Thomas Taylor's edition), Herder, Swedenborg, a life
of Boehme, and two books on Kant.[2]

In 1834 Alcott returned to Boston to start the Temple School (so named
because it was located in the Masonic Temple on Tremont Street), to be
run on an entirely new plan of his own devising. He was a striking figure,
six feet tall, given to wearing unusual hats. His head was arched and domed,

his forehead high. Photographs show a good-looking, serene, deeply self-possessed man with a large, firm, well-chiseled mouth with two deep creases sweeping downward beyond its corners. His hair was perfectly straight, growing back above and behind his large ears, down and over his coat collar.

Alcott now and for the rest of his life believed that the world of spirit is the only real world, and like William Blake he lived almost entirely in that world. Religion was for Alcott the contemplation of spirit in its infinite being, science was for him the contemplation of spirit in external nature, while he understood the social and human sciences to start from contemplating spirit in ourselves and in our fellow human beings. "Contemplation of spirit," he wrote, "is the first principle of Human Culture," the foundation of self-education. Alcott believed—and lived as though he believed—that "God is present in his whole nature and being in every part of every particle of the universe, including the souls of each individual man." His school was designed in every detail to lead out of each pupil what Alcott knew was already there.[3]

Alcott had a thin streak of genius, but he had little talent for writing. He lacked even a hint of negative capability, that is, the ability to set aside his own personality and enter imaginatively into the lives and situations of others. He could make nothing of Shakespeare. He had no irony and no humor. His yearning earnestness and uncapped high-mindedness expressed itself most effectively in conversation (at which he was an acknowledged master) and in his schools. To see Alcott at his best, it is necessary to ignore at the outset his "Orphic Sayings" and late writings and look at the operation of his school. Elizabeth Peabody has preserved Alcott's teaching for us in *Record of a School* (1835) and *Conversations with Children on the Gospels* (1836). Alcott's recorded talk and especially the introduction to *Conversations,* which was printed separately in 1836 as *The Doctrine and Discipline of Human Culture,* suggest something of the originality, courage, and brilliance of the man Emerson consistently admired as a modern prophet.[4]

"Every man is a revelation," Alcott told Emerson this fall, "and ought to write his record." But he seemed already to know that his own would not be with a pen. "His book is his school," Emerson observed, "in which he writes all his thought." Alcott took enormous pains with the school, spending much time and money to create an atmosphere of calm and beauty. The mullioned windows and high ceilings were an unimaginable contrast to the usual schoolrooms of the period, often no more than a bare box twenty feet by eight by seven. Alcott's school had pictures and statues. Every student had a desk of his or her own with a chair that could be moved about the room. They had individual blackboards, and there was a sofa for visitors. Alcott's school included girls as well as boys, and it had, most unusually for the time, one black student. When Alcott called the students together, they brought their chairs and ranged them in front of his desk. He both gave and got absolute attention. If anyone's eyes so much as left him, he waited, silent, until they came back. The students took part in the running of things. All punishments were discussed and agreed to by the students. Alcott understood the power of vicarious atonement. Once he had a student hit him—the teacher—for every infraction committed by the student. Elizabeth Peabody's account shows how this profoundly Christian device quickly got to the obdurate boy in question and reduced him to sobbing and to better behavior. Alcott's instruction was almost exclusively by close questioning, of a gentle and persistent sort. Of course there was a schedule and lots of reading and writing and exercises, but the dialogues with the grade-school pupils were what Alcott loved best. Alcott stood in the sharpest possible contrast to the schoolmasters common at the time, one of whom admitted, "I never looked upon a child that I have not felt for the moment as tho' I wanted to fall to whipping it."[5]

Elizabeth Peabody was Alcott's assistant at the Temple School. Sometimes she sat and listened and took notes. One day, for example, Alcott asked the children to give him "some fact or appearance, in the external world, with which to picture out and typify birth." Peabody's account goes on:

> They were quite animated by this, and the following were the most striking analogies. One said, the seed sown, and springing up. What do you mean by the seed, body or soul? Both. Another said, the branches from the trunk. The soul is the trunk and the branches are the body. Another said I should think the trunk was God, and the branches were the soul. . . . Another said God is a rock, and we are pieces broken off. Violently? No, not violently. The next said, God is the water, and our souls are drops; he afterwards added, that God was the only real person, and we were pictures of him.

Alcott was not, at least in his schoolroom, a monologist. He believed in and deliberately practiced a dialogic mode. He elicited what he wished, no doubt, as did Socrates, but at least he recognized and honored each of his students as an individual and as a mind.[6]

On October 18 Alcott went to Concord for his first real visit with Emerson. They had a long talk, starting Saturday evening and continuing on Sunday. Emerson thought him "a wise man, simple, superior to display." Alcott was impressed with both Waldo and Charles. "To have a few such friends is the joy and content of life," he wrote. "In communion with such the spirit finds itself." But Alcott did not live in isolation from his era any more than Emerson did. On the day Alcott went to Concord to see Emerson, William Lloyd Garrison was holding an abolition meeting in Boston. So unpopular was the cause that a riot ensued, in which a large crowd of respectable Bostonians of all classes seized Garrison and dragged him through the streets of Boston with a rope around his neck. Garrison barely escaped with his life. The authorities put him in jail. "On returning from Concord," wrote Alcott in his journal, "I visit the gaol with my wife and see Garrison."[7]

The main work of Emerson's first fall in the new house was the series of lectures on English literature he wrote and gave from early March 1835 to mid-January 1836. There were nine lectures; the series was almost twice as ambitious as any of his previous ones. This is the work in which he was absorbed just before turning to work full-time on *Nature*. There were at the time no English departments in colleges, no surveys of English—let alone American—literature, and few histories of the subject. Wharton's *History of English Poetry* had appeared in 1824. There was just barely such a thing as a professor of English, the first one being appointed in England in 1827. The student's understanding of literature was not much helped by what Emerson called "the barren season of discipline" with college rhetoric texts.[8]

One reason the study of English literature was not yet institutionalized was that the importance of England and its literature was taken for granted by Emerson's audience. Emerson still accepted the idea that the so-called American character was "only the English character exaggerated." Perhaps he was himself exaggerating for effect as he told his audience (the lectures were sponsored by the Society for the Diffusion of Useful Knowledge) that "the Island of Great Britain is the most pleasing spectacle which history shows," that it "has reached the highest point of civilization," that it is the country of established law and the place where "religious feeling has been most universally diffused." The writers Emerson treats—including Chaucer, Shakespeare, Bacon, Jonson, Herbert, Herrick, the seventeenth-century prose writers, and the moderns from Byron to Coleridge—meant far more to Emerson and to other Americans at the time than any earlier American writers. When Emerson ends this lecture series championing an American literature, he is thinking not of the past but of American literary possibilities in the present.[9]

Emerson already had a love-hate relationship with England. In his first lecture he remarked cheerfully that the wise and refined nation of modern England had "descended out of the loins of as abominable savages as any whom history describes." His authority for this—and much else in the early lectures of the series—is Sharon Turner's *History of the Anglo-Saxons*. Turner divides the post-Babel human race into civilized and uncivilized peoples and argues at great length that the English are descended exclusively from the latter. Turner represents the original Britons as fierce, bloody, and gloomy—and the Saxons as "fearless, active, and successful pirates."[10]

Emerson turned to Turner for colorful historical anecdote; he turned to Coleridge's *On the Constitution of Church and State* for an intellectual approach to literary history. What Coleridge did for church and state, Emerson now tried to do for English literature. Not content to produce a mere chronological account, Emerson tried to get at the idea of English literature, at its essential character and aim. For this reason he begins his series of lectures with a powerful introductory lecture on the function of literature. The lecture, the best of the series, strongly prefigures the little book Emerson was working on at the time, and this lecture helps us see just how profoundly Emerson's *Nature* is rooted in essentially literary concerns.[11]

Emerson begins by emphasizing the immense power of ideas, which "tyranize over him, and dictate or modify every word out of his mouth, every act of his hand." "The ideas in every man's mind make him what he is," says Emerson. "His whole life is spent in efforts to create outside of him a state of things conformed to his inward thought." He does this mainly through language, which in turn is derived from nature. Emerson's account of English literature—or any literature—is from the point of view of the writer. It is the writer, the poet, who "converts the solid globe, the land, the sea, the sun, the animals, into symbols of thought." Literature is "the clothing of things of the mind in the things of matter." It is "to give voice to the whole of spiritual nature." Not only the chapter "Language" in *Nature* but in some respects the whole book is an enlargement of the main argument of this opening lecture. Nature is the means by which the mind expresses itself. What that statement means in practice is that writers—all of us—find material in nature, both subjects and language with which to express them.[12]

None of the other lectures in this series has the intellectual vigor of the first one. Emerson surveys traits of English genius in the second lecture, the age of fable in the third. He makes fun of the material of romance: "The nobility undertook pilgrimages to countries that were never found in a map and amused themselves with challenging unknown antagonists to mortal combat for ladies whom they never saw." He compared the gothic fables of the Middle Ages to Greek myth, much to the disadvantage of the former. The fourth lecture, on Chaucer, introduces the first writer Emerson really admires, though what Emerson emphasizes about Chaucer and medieval writing generally is its frankly derivative nature, the fact that every work is built on previous work, without apology. "The truth is," says Emerson,

> all works of literature are Janus-faced and look to the future and the past. Shakespeare, Pope and Dryden borrow from Chaucer and shine by his borrowed light. Chaucer reflects Boccaccio and Colonna and the troubadors, Boccaccio and Colonna elder Greek and Roman authors, and these in their turn others if only history would enable us to trace them.[13]

Two lectures on Shakespeare emphasize Shakespeare's enormous capacity for "subordinating nature for the purposes of expression." Shakespeare is Emerson's ideal poet. He is particularly fond of the sonnets and has some unusual favorites. He gave one lecture on Francis Bacon, whom Emerson continued to admire for his audacious effort to reshape our knowledge of the world, "to heave the whole globe of the Sciences from their rest, expose all the gulfs and continents of error, and with a creative hand remodel and reform the whole." In some ways Emerson's own ambition now was not much lower than this.[14]

He devoted one lecture to Jonson, Herbert, and Herrick, and another—Emerson's most interesting departure from the usual—to what he called "ethical writers," that class of writers "who help us by addressing not our taste but our human wants." In this tradition—in what is more or less a genealogy of Emerson's own mind—he lists Pythagoras, Xenophanes, Plato, Plutarch, Diogenes, Zeno, Socrates, Epictetus, Marcus Aurelius, Cicero (*Offices*), Seneca (*Morals*), and the "ethical passages" in the work of Homer, Juvenal, Lucretius, Horace, Euripedes, and Sophocles. He jumps then to the English Bible and the great seventeenth-century prose writers—Bacon, Spenser, Sidney, Hooker, John Smith, Henry More, Jeremy Taylor, Archbishop Leighton, Harrington, Algernon Sidney, Milton, Donne,

Sir Thomas Browne, Bunyan, and Lord Clarendon—all of whom he treats as "for the most part versed in [Plato's] works and called Platonists."[15]

The final lecture, on modern literature, touches on Byron, Scott, Stewart, Macintosh, and Coleridge; it is a short course of some of Emerson's own enthusiasms since his college days. Emerson ends by asking what English literature means to an American. He argues that literature exists to show the beauty of the world, apart from narrow nationalist concerns, whether English or American.

36. All in Each: Writing Nature

THE WINTER OF 1835–1836 WAS ALL SNOW. IT WAS ALSO ONE of the coldest on record in New England, with temperatures averaging ten degrees below normal. Beginning in early December Concord had four months of unbroken sleighing. Emerson finished his lectures on English literature in mid-January and plunged into work on *Nature*. He worked over his early journals, collecting and sifting material. In late January, to the intense delight of both Lidian and her husband, Lidian became pregnant. They had already begun to wonder if they were destined to have children. All winter Emerson helped Le Baron Russell collect subscriptions for an American edition of Carlyle's *Sartor Resartus*. Russell had come to Carlyle through Lidian. He had borrowed the English stitched-pamphlet version of *Sartor* that Emerson had given Lidian, was "carried away by it," and began to negotiate with a Boston publisher. At Russell's request Emerson wrote a preface, and in April 1836 Emerson proudly sent Carlyle a copy of the first edition of his own book, not to be published in England until 1838.[1]

The Emerson household was expanding rapidly. Hillman Sampson, the young son of Emerson's recently deceased friend George Sampson, stayed with the Emersons and went to school in Concord. Lidian's sister, Lucy Brown, came to stay, as did Emerson's brother Charles. In April, as the snows were at last starting to melt, Emerson and Lidian started a major addition to the house. "Diggers and builders" were everywhere; "the yard is cumbered with timber," Charles wrote Lizzie. Emerson went to Cambridge as a member of a committee to examine the Harvard students in logic. He was a member of Concord's school committee. He undertook to give a series of lectures in Salem starting in early April. In Salem he saw the work of a gifted young art copyist, Sophia Peabody. From mid-April Charles's health became a serious worry.[2]

Charles's company and conversation were of ever increasing importance to Emerson. His journals this winter and spring are peppered with "Charles says," "Charles thinks," "Charles wonders," "Charles doubts." Charles wondered "that I don't become sick at the stomach over my poor journal."

Charles doubted "whether all truth is not occasional." He thought "there is no Christianity and has not been for some ages." To the question of why the world exists, Charles said: "There sits the sphinx from age to age in the road and every wise man that comes by has a crack with her."[3]

Along with the busy outer life went an equally lively interior one. In his usual fashion Emerson leafed through book after book. Some were new; some were familiar but seen now in new ways. In late October of 1835 he had been reading the great twelfth chapter of Coleridge's *Biographia Literaria,* the most lucid and powerful exposition in English romanticism of the ancient injunction "Know thyself" and a central chapter for transcendentalism. What Emerson noted this time in Coleridge was a bit Coleridge quoted from Plotinus in defense of intuitive knowledge as an irreducible first principle: "It is not lawful to inquire whence it sprang as if it were a thing subject to place and motion." Emerson was also reading Johannes von Müller's *Universal History,* a book he often recommended to others, and was drawing from it a preference for Sparta over Athens—a common view both in America and Europe at the time. The Spartan spoke only what must be spoken, the Athenian made "all talk a Recitation, talking for display." He was reading Swedenborg's *Apocalypse Revealed* (for the first time) and Cudworth's *True Intellectual System* (again), seeing both of them through Carlylean eyes. Emerson noted particularly "the sublime emotion I taste in reading these lines" of Swedenborg: "The organical body with which the soul clothes itself is here compared to a garment because a garment invests the body, and the soul also puts off the body and casts it away as old clothes when it emigrates by means of death from the natural world into its own spiritual world." In March he pulled from his old notes on Gerando the comment of Xenophanes about "all things hasting back to unity, Identity."[4]

In early March Emerson found and read Joshua Marshman's 725-page volume of Confucius's *Lun-gnee.* It is a impressive large quarto book, with spacious margins, enormous Chinese characters, and an English translation set in large, handsome roman type. The volume is altogether an astonishing achievement for a tiny missionary press in Serampore in 1809. Emerson was in perpetual quest of basic books, books that bore original witness, books that met Montaigne's stern query "What do I know?"—books that were not just distilled from other books and that, as Whitman said, would probably pass away. Emerson wanted books that declared solidly, without derivation or support, without apology or disclaimer, what the author observed and knew. The Confucius was such a book; Emerson responded to the clipped aphoristic sentences in which Marshman presents Confucius, and he copied out several pages' worth: "Have no friend unlike yourself." "Grieve not that men know not you; grieve that you are ignorant of men." "First cut, then smooth; carve then polish."[5]

Emerson was a vast reader, and it sometimes seems as though no book published from 1820 until his death evaded his attention completely. But he was not an indiscriminate reader. There were whole categories of books he would not read. He would not read theological or academic controversy, for example. He disliked books intended to comment on other books. In a blunt moment he called them "books by the dead for the dead." He wanted original firsthand accounts—travel books, memoirs, testaments, statements of faith or discovery, poems. He would read your poem or your novel but not your opinion on other people's poems or novels.

Emerson took it for granted that people find different things in the same book. "In every book [one] finds passages which seem confidences or asides, hidden from all else, and unmistakeably meant for his ear. No book," he added, "has worth by itself, but by the relation to what you have from many other books, it weighs." To know Emerson is to know not only what he was reading but what he was getting out of it and what stayed with him over time. In November of 1835 Charles and Waldo were reading Sophocles' *Antigone,* in March *Electra.* They went slowly. In effect, Charles, with his superior Greek, read to Emerson. Charles reported to Lizzie that Waldo "is quite enamoured of the severe beauty of the Greek tragic muse."[6]

Right next to the extracts from Confucius this spring in Emerson's journal are his comments on Alcott's "Psyche." Alcott had quickly become a close friend, returning to Emerson's house in Concord for a visit of several days in early December and in February giving Emerson his manuscript book on childhood and his 1835 journal to read. The idea of "Psyche; or the Breath of Childhood" is that each child is an incarnation, the godhead made flesh. The child's life exhibits the growth of a soul in a body: "The Supernatural is quickened into life and asketh for its own forms of significance." This form is the child itself—the "very incarnate Word."[7]

Alcott had already written five "books" on this theme, from 60 to 340 pages each, based on meticulous, loving observation of his own daughters Anna (b. 1831), Louisa (b. 1832), and Elizabeth (b. 1835). Now, with Lidian pregnant, the already appealing theme of childhood as incarnation became irresistible for Emerson. He worked through "Psyche" and through Alcott's journal for 1835, altogether a thousand pages of handwriting for which a more discouraging word than illegible is needed. But the real problem was not the handwriting. Alcott's prose is rapt, impassioned, sincere, and completely unreadable: "She [Psyche] taketh man's spirit by the hand, and, now, flying through the Empyrean, she vivifieth the imagination." Emerson proposed severe cuts, extensive recasting, and a change of style, including dropping the "eth" verb endings throughout. Alcott wrote and rewrote, year after year, with no visible improvement. Alcott was surely "a lamb among men," wrote James Russell Lowell, "but he went to sure death when he went to his pen." One might raise similar objections to the difficult styles of Mary Moody Emerson, or Jakob Boehme, or Swedenborg, or Thomas Taylor. Alcott's work, like theirs, has the real prophetic fire at its core, and Emerson was able in the spring of 1836 to feel it. "I set out from the wide ground of Spirit," Alcott had closed his annual journal volume for 1835. "This is; all else is its manifestation. Body is Spirit at its circumference."[8]

There is an undersong of elegy in Emerson's writing, present in his journals and letters as well as his essays and poems. And this elegiac strain is rooted in his life. Reading *Antigone,* his mind wandered back to "a very different image of female loveliness . . . which a few years ago shed on me its tender and immortal light." Emerson was also reading Dante this year, and while he did not yet know *La vita nuova,* his idealizing of Ellen was already making her into a sort of American Beatrice: "She needed not a historical name nor earthly rank or wealth. She was complete in her own perfections. She took up all things into her and in her single self sufficed the soul."[9]

As Emerson worked on *Nature* his mind and his notebooks were crammed with ideas, other books, family life, friendship, public duties, and always reading and yet more reading. Across the warp of Emerson's interests, themes, and insights come the books, the cross-threads of which *Nature* was woven. His temper of mind just now was a complex mixture of elegiac mood, new interest in tragic Greek heroines, and admiring sympathy with Alcott's soaring idealism and his deeply human view of childhood. Emerson also braced himself with rereadings of Carlyle, Coleridge, Swedenborg, and Boehme. And there was always too the persistent, powerful influence of Goethe, pulling at Emerson's tides like the great full moon.

The effect of Goethe on Emerson is nearly impossible to overestimate. From 1828 on, when he began to read Goethe in German, through the mid-1840s and the drafting of his essay on Goethe, the famous German writer was virtually a daily presence in Emerson's life. In the mid-thirties Emerson worked his way through practically everything in the fifty-five-volume edition he owned of Goethe's writings. If his German was not perfect, if he occasionally got something wrong, if he liked *Faust* less than *The Italian Journey, Wilhelm Meister, The East-West Divan, Egmont, Iphigenia,* the poems, the *Farbenlehre,* the *Metamorphosis of Plants,* the *Autobiography,* or the *Conversations,* it still will not do to condescend to Emerson's grasp of Goethe. Many things in Goethe kept Emerson (who hated having to read in the original if a translation was available) laboriously working in his imperfect German year after year on the study of the vast body of Goethe's writing. Emerson skimmed and skipped in many books, but not in Goethe's. Goethe laid down fundamental lessons that over the years became part of Emerson's own bedrock. "Goethe teaches courage," he would write on the last page of the last essay in *Representative Men,* "and the equivalence of all times: that the disadvantages of any epoch exist only to the faint-hearted." Now, as he worked on *Nature,* Emerson jumped at Goethe's insistence that beauty is fundamental, separate, underived. "The nature of the Beautiful . . . lies out of the limits of the cogitative power." Not so, however, for the standard of beauty, which is apparent to all: "What is there for a standard of true beauty except the entire circuit of all harmonious relations of the great whole of Nature?" With equal enthusiasm Emerson seized on Goethe's idea that "all is in each:" "Every natural form to the smallest, a leaf, a sunbeam, a moment of time, a drop, is related to the whole, and partakes of the beauty of the whole." "A leaf is a compend of Nature, and Nature a colossal leaf."[10]

One might list a hundred kindling ideas Emerson found in Goethe, though the two just mentioned are the chief ones Emerson worked over as he set to getting *Nature* ready for the printer. But Emerson was now drawing from Goethe not only ideas, perhaps not mainly ideas. He was discernibly fascinated with the way Goethe's mind worked. Goethe's mind had a hard edge of realism, classicism, and clarity which was utterly lacking in many of the books whose *ideas* Emerson valued: the writings of Mary Moody Emerson, Swedenborg, Boehme, Alcott, Plotinus. Even Coleridge ran toward the abstract, the unbodied, the theoretical. Goethe's perpetual sanity, his realism, his language, are for Emerson the counterbalances to the lighter-than-air prose of the great Platonist visionaries. Emerson noted how for Goethe "the moment is everything," how Goethe "gives a theory of every institution, art, art-work, custom which he observes." (Goethe traces, for example, the obelisk back to a common fracture pattern in Upper Egyptian granite deposits.) Emerson admired and approved Goethe's self-knowledge. "I get very fast a notion of every region," Goethe wrote, "because, at the smallest brook, I enquire whence it comes and into what river it runs." Emerson found he could spend his time no better than in reading Goethe, "for you shall find no word that does not stand for a thing." From Goethe he learned to regard nothing as a trifle and to value gradation, discrimination, separation, and nomenclature. His own deepest ambition was to do as he saw Goethe to have done:

> It were life enough to one man merely to lift his hands and say Kosmos! Beauty. Well, this he did. . . . Here is a man who in the feeling that the thing itself was so admirable as to leave all comment behind, merely went up and down, from object to object, lifting the veil from every one and did no more.

What Goethe had said of Lavater, Emerson now turned on Goethe, and we may in turn apply it to Emerson's own ambition. "It was fearful," said Goethe, "to stand in the presence of one before whom all the boundaries within which Nature has circumscribed our being were laid flat."[11]

37. Nature: *The Laws of the World*

CHARLES EMERSON AND ELIZABETH HOAR PLANNED TO BE married in September of 1836, after a three-year engagement. They were to move into a couple of rooms being built for them in Waldo and Lidian's new house. Charles's health got slowly worse, but still they planned and hoped. One day in April, while holding a measuring string against a wall to see if her piano would fit into the space, Elizabeth suddenly burst out: "It is of no use. It never will be." Charles caught a cold, got weaker, and went south for relief from "this lake of fire I am bearing about in my breast." He stayed with William in New York. On May 9 Charles collapsed after a walk and before the hastily summoned Emerson and Elizabeth could arrive he died. Aunt Mary's boy, Milton's reader, the man his brother-in-law-to-be called "the most brilliant intellect Massachusetts ever produced," the brother who was so full of fun, who danced around the table in his velvet cloak, and who could make Emerson laugh more than anyone else was gone.[1]

Emerson was stricken. After the funeral he turned away from the grave with a strange abrupt laugh and said to the man next to him: "When one has never had but little society—and all that society is taken away—what is there worth living for?" He wrote to Lidian from New York that he had lost a piece of himself: "How much I saw through his eyes." He felt, he said, "not only unfastened and adrift but a sort of shame at living at all." Two weeks later he was still groping in the darkness and declaring that "night rests on all sides upon the facts of our being, tho' we must own, our upper nature lies always in Day."[2]

Emerson had long talks with Elizabeth. They tried to separate the best of Charles—what he stood for, the meaning of his life—from the actual physical person. For Emerson the memory of Charles became transmuted into his personal principle or archetype for friendship. With some bitterness he observed that once a friend "has revealed to you a new nature . . . expect thenceforward the hour in which he will be withdrawn from your sight." Charles's brother and his fiancée were both trying to assuage grief by constructing a version of Charles through a sort of secular immortalizing that took the place of the personal immortality Emerson could no longer believe in. Emerson also tried to pull together a volume of Charles's writings but found little in a finished state and far too much of the dark, hopeless, self-pitying streak. He gave up on the volume, though in some ways *Nature* was Emerson's open letter to the world on behalf of Charles, who is "the friend" so movingly apostrophized at the end of the chapter "Discipline."[3]

After ten days of "helpless mourning," Emerson began to find himself again and even to remember moments of mountain-top exhilaration and insight. He drew up a list of the "scattered company who have ministered to my highest wants" and listed Edward Stabler, Peter Hunt, Sampson Reed, Tarbox, Mary Rotch, Jonathan Phillips, Alcott, and Murat. That he left out Mary Moody Emerson probably means either that she was the one he was talking with when he made the list or that she was in a class by herself, a steady, long-term influence, not a sudden accession. He also left out Charles.[4]

During the rest of May and all of June Emerson worked on *Nature*. The writing went well and his mood was often exultant. He was now working by the glare and heat of ideas that form the core not only of *Nature* but of future essays. "To believe your own thought, that is Genius," he wrote. "All powerful action is by bringing the forces of nature to bear upon our objects." He walked out into the storm and he wrote in his journal, "I love the wood god. I love the mighty Pan." By the end of June he was writing passages that would go into the short chapter called "Spirit," and he wrote his brother William that his little book was almost done.[5]

Three other American books published this year, besides Emerson's *Nature*, asserted the new conception of religion as a phenomenon that manifested itself more fully through nature, especially human nature, than through old texts, religious institutions, or reported miracles. Orestes Brownson invoked Benjamin Constant and Schleiermacher in *New Views of Christianity, Society, and the Church* for his claim that "the religious sentiment is universal, permanent and indestructible; religious institutions depend on transient causes." George Ripley's *Discourses on the Philosophy of Religion Addressed to Doubters Who Wish to Believe* also invoked Schleiermacher, most obviously in the title. Ripley argued that belief in the invisible world really should be understood as belief in the inner world. The believer "is conscious of an inward nature, which is the source of more important and comprehensive ideas than any which the external senses suggest, and he follows the decision of these ideas as the inspiring voice of God." Emerson's old friend W. H. Furness brought out in Philadelphia a book called *Remarks on the Four Gospels* in which he argued for Christianity as a modern, that is to say, a self-evident truth. Furness also said that "every history is unconsciously and unavoidably a history of its author," and he wrote attractively about the miracle of the natural. "The existence of the merest atom, when we duly consider it, is an unspeakable miracle."[6]

This year also saw Lydia Child's historical novel *Philothea,* which dramatizes the inherent superiority of ethical monotheism over paganism, and Alcott's *Doctrine and Discipline of Human Culture,* which is cast as a manifesto of Christian *Bildung.* Each human being is a new incarnation; the purpose of life is personal growth and self-development. Jesus is the great model and archetype of this process.

All these books—and we might add Reed's *Observations on the Growth of the Mind*—may fairly be seen as bearing modern witness to core truths of Christianity. Emerson's *Nature* is different. It bears personal witness to core truths about the self and the world, or consciousness and nature. And if the book is at some points compatible with Christianity, it is at least as compatible with classical Stoicism. *Nature* must be compared not only with the great twelfth chapter of Coleridge's *Biographia Literaria* and with Carlyle's *Sartor Resartus* but also with the *Meditations* of Marcus Aurelius and the *Enchiridion* of Epictetus. But even those famous little books are mainly self-help guides, officers' manuals for the warfare of living the just life, so Emerson's *Nature* may even more fitly be compared to Lucretius's *De rerum natura*—which Rolfe Humphries translated *The Way Things Are.*

Nature is a wholly audacious inquiry into "the laws of the world and the frame of things." Emerson begins by clearing the table with a broad dismissive sweep: "Our age is retrospective. It builds the sepulchres of the fathers. It writes biographies, histories and criticism." His point is that earlier generations "beheld God and nature face to face" while the present sees all things through the eyes of the past. His often quoted call, "Why should not we also enjoy an original relation to the universe?" is not a call for novelty or innovation, nor is it a claim for American exceptionalism. The stress is on the word "also." He goes on: "Why should not we have a poetry and philosophy of insight and not of tradition, and a religion by revelation to us, and not the history of theirs?"[7]

The present generation is entitled to its own primary, firsthand, authentic relation to things. We need not make do with the history of other people's fundamental encounters. Just as science is more immediate and exciting than the history of science, so is insight more compelling than a history of insight. "Why should we grope among the dry bones of the past?" he asks, adding, with the simple declarative force of Ecclesiastes, "The sun shines today also."[8]

The introduction goes on to stake out the ground Emerson intends to occupy. He asks not only what nature is and how it operates but "To what end is nature?" He takes for granted that his inquiry is allied to, if not actually, science. Separating, for purposes of argument pure science from technology, he says, "All science has one aim, namely, to find a theory of nature." His conception of what constitutes proof is scientific: "Whenever a true theory appears, it will be its own evidence. Its test is that it will explain all phenomena." He was willing to have his own work judged by this standard. The book *Nature* is not designed as an appeal to earlier or other authority but as a self-evident, self-validating account, a book that, like Robert Frost's idea of a poem, rides on its own melting like a piece of ice on a hot stove. With straightforward clarity Emerson concludes his brief introduction on methods and aims with definitions of terms. "Philosophically considered, the universe is composed of Nature and the Soul," or, as we might now prefer to say, nature and consciousness, or the world and the mind. "Strictly speaking, therefore, all that is separate from us, all which Philosophy distinguishes as the *not me,* both nature and art, all other men and my own body, must be ranked under this name, nature."[9]

As the title indicates, *Nature* is heavily weighted toward the world. Most of the book was written while Emerson still envisioned writing a second, matching piece to be called "Spirit." It is hard to say exactly what rescued Emerson from starting with spirit, as most declarations of idealism do. Perhaps it was the admonishing monuments of earlier efforts, including Norris and Alcott, perhaps it was the bias toward the concrete which resulted from his commitment to living metaphor. Perhaps it was his still-growing absorption in Goethe and his never-shaken love of Shakespeare and Michelangelo and their reckless, total, untheoretical embracing of the real world of people and things. Perhaps it was nature itself.

The success of Emerson's *Nature* for most readers depends on the success of the first chapter, which aims to convey and re-create for the reader the impression made on him by nature. Emerson uses his own experience, but he frames it so the reader can stand with him and share the experience. Here and throughout the book we are constantly reminded that it is no abstract "nature of things" but the closely observed natural world that lies at the heart of the book. "In July, the blue pontederia or pickerel-weed blooms in large beds in the shallow parts of our pleasant river, and swarms with yellow butterflies in continual motion." Dawn may be a metaphor for awakening, as it is in Boehme, but it is also the light of ordinary daybreak: "I have seen the spectacle of morning from the hill-top over against my house. . . . The long slender bars of cloud float like fishes in the sea of crimson light. From the earth, as a shore, I look out into that silent sea." Similarly with sunset. Of a late January afternoon Emerson writes,

> The western clouds divided and subdivided themselves into pink flakes modulated with tints of unspeakable softness; and the air had so much life and sweetness, that it was a pain to come within doors. . . . The leafless trees become spires of flame in the sunset, with the blue east for their background, and the stars of the dead calices of flowers, and every withered stem and stubble rimed with frost, contribute something to the mute music.[10]

We cannot speak of experience except as experience of something, and that something, says Emerson, is nature. And the experience Emerson most values is the exhilaration that can arise sometimes from our presence in nature, though we cannot say quite why: "Crossing a bare common, in snow puddles, at twilight, under a clouded sky, without having in my thoughts any occurrence of special good fortune, I have enjoyed a perfect exhilaration. I am glad to the brink of fear." The famous "transparent eyeball" passage is an account of another such experience, similar to the one that had happened to him at Mt. Auburn in Cambridge. Its point is exactly the opposite of narcissistic self-absorption: "Standing on the bare ground—my head bathed by the blithe air, and uplifted into infinite space—all mean egotism vanishes. I become a transparent eyeball; I am nothing; I see all." If this is mysticism, it is mysticism of a commonly occurring and easily accepted sort. The aim of the mystic is to attain a feeling of oneness with the divine. Experiences of the kind Emerson here describes have happened to nearly everyone who has ever sat beneath a tree on a fine clear day and looked at the world with a sense of momentary peace and a feeling, however transient, of being at one with it.[11]

The words that come most readily and most frequently to Emerson as he describes his life in nature are "delight" (used four times at the end of chapter 1 alone) and "wild." He uses the language of vision and rapture. He speaks of light and delight, of wild delight, of wildness, of exhilaration, of gladness, and of the wild beauty of Shakespeare's unmatchable gift for metaphor. Not only does Emerson accept the Greek idea that the universe *is* beauty, *kosmos,* but he emphasizes the experience of that beauty as a wild delight. This inner wildness, this habit of enthusiasm, this workaday embracing of the Dionysian is quintessential Emerson. He is wild or he is nothing.

38. Nature: *The Apocalypse of the Mind*

THE MAJOR PART OF *NATURE* EXPLORES THE RELATION OF NA-
ture to human beings. The Stoics had always maintained that nature teaches
us how to live. Emerson's *Nature* describes a series of nature's gifts, benefits,
and lessons, in ascending order of importance, and specifies how each works.
First is nature as commodity, the most easily grasped and the most quickly
discussed. In an era before anyone understood the extent of the damage
humans could inflict on nature, Emerson describes the simple use of nature
as a reservoir of raw materials for our use. Not until George Perkins Marsh's
1864 book did it became clear, even to a few people, that human beings
could indeed modify nature in major, permanent, or harmful ways. But if
Emerson underestimated the dangers in this aspect of his subject, he was
not oblivious to what is now called the "commodification" of nature. He
insists that our use of nature for material is the lowest and least important
benefit we owe to nature.[1]

Of much more interest to Emerson is the way in which nature furnishes
us with our ideas and standards of beauty, whether of physical beauty, moral
beauty (virtue), or intellectual beauty (truth): "The standard of beauty is the
entire circuit of natural forms—the totality of nature." Beauty is inherent
in the world: "Such is the constitution of all things, or such the plastic power
of the human eye, that the primary forms, as the sky, the mountain, the tree,
the animal, give us a delight *in and for themselves.*" The highest beauty is
finally in relations: "Nothing is quite beautiful alone: nothing but is beautiful
in the whole." Beauty is fundamental, primary, not derived from anything
else: "The world thus exists to the soul to satisfy the desire of beauty."[2]

As our aesthetics are grounded in nature, so is our language. What we
call words are signs for natural facts. Even abstractions, says Emerson, if
traced to their origins, will be seen to be rooted in things. *Consider* comes
from the Latin *con siderare,* meaning to study the stars. *Supercilious* comes
from the Latin for raised eyebrow, *super cilia.* Experience was originally that
which was snatched *ex pericolo,* from danger. *Sierra* means saw. Abstractions
are words that have been cut away from their roots, losing their vitality
because they no longer appeal to the imagination. Long before George

Orwell, Emerson realized that ordinary language is full of dead metaphors. The job of the writer is to "pierce this rotten diction and fasten words again to visible things." Because "this immediate dependence of language upon nature, this conversion of an outward phenomenon into a type of somewhat in human life never loses its power to affect us," Emerson can say, in one of his strangely angled insights, "Hence good society and brilliant discourse are perpetual allegories."[3]

We follow Emerson to this point with relative ease. But now the full Platonist in him emerges. The reason the writer can so successfully use nature for image and trope, noun and verb, is because nature itself is a language, an expression of the laws or forms or ideas that lie behind and beneath the visible world. With the utmost simplicity, logic, and compression (which the typesetter of *Nature* misapprehended and bungled in the first edition), Emerson moves from the proposition that "words are signs of natural facts" to the further proposition that "particular natural facts are symbols of particular spiritual facts." This latter, in its deceptive simplicity, is not just a step in a demonstration. It is a metaphysic, the fundamental religious view of the world that holds that nature and we ourselves are the great allegory.[4]

Nature provides us with beauty and with language for expressing that beauty. In the fifth chapter, "Discipline," Emerson considers all the other ways in which nature schools us. The chapter might as easily be called "Education." But *Nature* is more ambitious yet. Having surveyed the ways in which nature educates, informs, and endows us, Emerson now shifts gears, going from questions of how nature serves to asking what nature is. Is there something behind nature or is visible nature our final and only reality? In the chapters "Idealism" and "Spirit" Emerson turns to the other side of the subject. With evident feeling and a sense of urgency, he begins with the claim of the radical idealist: "In my utter impotence to test the authenticity of the report of my senses, to know whether the impressions they make on me correspond with outlying objects, what difference does it make, whether Orion is up there in heaven, or some god paints the image in the firmament of the soul." And with equal fervor he moves away from the extreme, Fichtean, solipsistic conclusion. "Any distrust of the permanence of laws [e.g., gravity] would paralyse the faculties of man." He goes on to what is the pivotal claim of the book:

> It is the uniform effect of culture [i.e., education] on the human mind, not to shake our faith in the stability of particular phenomena, as of heat, water, azote [nitrogen]; but to lead us to regard nature as a

phenomenon, not a substance; to attribute necessary existence to spirit; to esteem nature as an accident and effect.

Difficult as this idea sounds, it is of particular and practical usefulness to the writer. "Possessed by a heroic passion, he uses matter as symbols of it." The passage also poses the problem of philosophy, which is, says Emerson, "for all that exists conditionally to find a ground unconditioned and absolute." It further provides what Emerson calls "the first and last lesson of religion," which is "the things that are seen are temporal; the things that are unseen are eternal."[5]

The dazzling sentences through which *Nature* first reaches the reader are in fact just the high points of a carefully constructed manifesto of philosophical idealism. We are not to be argued into slow assent but startled into instant agreement by the self-evident quality of each proposition. *Nature* marks the arrival of Emerson's mature style, especially of the bold cartwheeling definitions that convince at the same time as they dramatically alter the reader's perceptions: "The imagination may be defined to be the use which the reason makes of the material world." "As the eye is the best composer, so light is the first of painters." "That which, intellectually considered, we call Reason, considered in relation to nature we call Spirit." "Ethics and religion differ herein; that the one is a system of human duties commencing from man; the other, from God." Toward the close of the essay Emerson constructs whole paragraphs by piling such sentences one on top of another with easy power. It is like the building of afternoon clouds over the hot plains of summer. "The ruin or the blank that we see when we look at nature, is in our own eye. The axis of vision is not coincident with the axis of things, and so they appear not transparent but opaque." Emerson is never better than when he is voicing the discontent that never left him despite his striving and optimism and enthusiasm. He strikes here, and throughout *Nature,* at the roots of modern alienation: "The reason why the world lacks unity and lies broken and in heaps, is because man is disunited with himself."[6]

Nature marks the beginning of Emerson's rethinking of classical Stoicism, an enterprise that will actively concern him for the next five or six years, reappearing in essay after essay. In the 1842 essay "The Transcendentalist" he will maintain that "this way of thinking [transcendentalism], falling on Roman times, made Stoic philosophers . . . on prelatical times, made Puritans and Quakers; and falling on Unitarian and commercial times makes the peculiar shades of idealism which we know." Stoicism had an enormous impact on Emerson and his circle, probably greater than that of Puritanism, whether direct or indirect. Stoicism, like Puritanism, is more than a matter of character traits; it is a body of thought underlying and giving coherence to certain character traits. It teaches that we must turn to nature as the primary source of moral principles. Stoicism was founded by Zeno, at the end of the fourth century B.C., after Alexander had shattered the Greek *polis,* which had been the traditional context for moral action. From Zeno to Marcus Aurelius, the Stoics aimed to provide a basis for moral action and a means of personal well-being in the natural endowments of any human being, irrespective of social status. The value of any particular theoretical inquiry depends on whether it has any significance for the moral life. Stoicism is not anti-intellectual. It insists that true morality is impossible without knowledge, especially scientific knowledge. Stoicism endorses Heraclitus's "All individual things in the world are manifestations of one primary substance" and insists that there is a law that governs the course of nature and should govern human action. Stoicism has been claimed as a Semitic element in Greek thought and as a pagan element in Christianity. In Emerson and Thoreau it takes on its modern form of self-reliance understood not as self-sufficiency but as self-respect.[7]

Dividing the world into those things one can change and those one cannot, Stoicism channels attention to the former. It cares always for ethics, almost never for metaphysics or epistemology. Its question is not "What can I know for certain?" but "How should I lead my life?" Stoicism asserts that since there is only one law for human beings and for nature, we should study nature to learn the law for us. Stoicism emphasizes individual will, self-rule, or autarchy, and Stoics believe that human beings are for the most part able to help themselves, that they have adequate resources if only they can be mobilized. A recent commentator has observed: "If stoicism is the recognition of the supremacy of conscience, yet with no projection of the desired life into any juster or sterner world, its appeal cannot but continue to hold."[8]

Nature has been read as a gospel of selfishness, illogic, optimism, and parochialism. Emerson's life and his reading while he worked on *Nature* show the book to be rooted in family life, formal logic, Greek tragedy, and Asian classics. Most of all, *Nature* is a modern Stoic handbook, Marcus Aurelius in New England. It is also a modern version of Plato, an American version of Kant. It is a brief for the priority of law over fact, aim over action, intent over outcome, pattern over print. The plan, idea, or concept of anything, whether a simple tool or the most complex piece of legislation, precedes the actual hammer or the actual voting rights act and determines it. In this sense, the plan or idea is more real—more important—than the physical product. This is the mainmast of idealism and Emerson lashed himself to it for life.

In the end Emerson would prove to be more than an American Plato since he would reject Plato's politics and would struggle to reconcile Platonism with democratic idealism. He is not just an American popularizer of Kant either, because he subjected German idealism to what may be called the critique of everyday life and because he brought life to Kant's acceptance of the authority of subjective knowledge by connecting it with the experiences of the great religious mystics and enthusiasts and with the passions and raptures of great poetry. Nor is Emerson merely an American Marcus Aurelius, because he reconciles classical Stoic insistence on self-rule with Dionysian wildness and a sweeping commitment to self-expression. Emerson is at last neither derivative nor eclectic. His insistence on grounding thought, action, ethics, religion, and art in individual experience is his center. He makes a modern case for the idea that the mind common to the universe is disclosed to each individual through his or her own nature. In this respect Plato is a Greek premonition of Emerson, Marcus Aurelius a Roman one, and Kant a German one.

But *Nature* was not conceived, and does not finally make sense, as just another document in the history of thought. Like the rose that pleases us not because it makes reference to earlier and other flowers but for itself, *Nature* is Emerson's personal witness, his "Here I stand." The book is intended to be self-validating. We are not asked to take it on faith, or on authority, or in a historical context. It is not argued or defended, just presented. To paraphrase Johnson, that book is true in vain that the reader cannot recognize as true. There is nothing in *Nature* that a reader cannot test. The best the past can do is confirm our hunch that our own innermost convictions lie beyond the reach of refutation or confirmation. This is also the best any writer can do. Emerson performs the ultimate act of helpfulness by handing his perceptions over to the reader and then removing himself: "Know then, that the world exists for you. For you is the phenomenon perfect. What we are, that only can we see. All that Adam had, all that Caesar could, you have and can do . . . build, therefore your own world."[9]

39. Margaret Fuller

ON JULY 21, AS EMERSON'S BOOK LAY ON HIS WRITING TABLE, almost finished, but still with "one crack in it, not easy to be soldered or welded," Margaret Fuller came to Concord to stay with the Emersons for a visit that stretched to three weeks. A modern historian has claimed that Fuller had "the only mind among her contemporaries that could have conversed on a plane of equality with Rousseau and Goethe." She had grown up on Cherry Street, near Harvard Yard in what was then Cambridgeport. Her father, Timothy Fuller, was an outspoken, cranky Jeffersonian Democrat and a lawyer; he took charge of Margaret's education from infancy. He pushed her unmercifully at her lessons, which included Latin from age six on, and he kept her up late in the evenings, sending her to bed at last overstimulated and unable to sleep. This pressure exacted fearful costs in frequent headaches, a nervous stomach, insomnia, and nightmares. But she also acquired a first-rate education, and later she gave credit to her father for holding her to the same standards he would have held a son. "He respected his child, however, too much to be an indulgent parent. He called on her for clear judgment, for courage, for honor and fidelity; in short for such virtues as he knew."[1]

Margaret spent her fourteenth and fifteenth years at the Misses Prescott's school in Groton. In 1826, when she was sixteen, she returned to Cambridge and became a close friend and intellectual companion of (Frederic) Henry Hedge, five years older than she and a student at Harvard Divinity School. She fell in love with a distant cousin, George Davis, but he did not reciprocate her feelings. She was closest to James Freeman Clarke, who, like Davis, graduated from Harvard in 1829. Clarke was enormously fond of her. He was also very much in awe of her and readily acknowledged her intellectual superiority. Beginning in 1832 they studied German together, fired, said Clarke, by the "wild bugle call" of Carlyle and determined to come to grips with Goethe.

But the wonderful life in Cambridge came to an end. In the spring of 1833 the Fuller family moved to rural Groton; in July Clarke went off to become a minister in Louisville; in 1834 Hedge went to Bangor to be a minister there. In 1835 Timothy Fuller died, leaving Margaret as the family breadwinner.

Fuller had been hoping to meet Emerson for several years. They had many friends in common. She met Harriet Martineau, who urged Emerson to get to know her. He read her translation of Goethe's *Tasso* and in early 1835 he became eager to meet her. When she arrived in Concord that July day in 1836, she was twenty-six, he thirty-three. Surviving pictures of her are more than ordinarily inadequate. From descriptions left by her friends, she was clearly attractive, though not conventionally beautiful. She had blonde, abundant hair, a quick smile, perfect teeth, and "sparkling, dancing busy" eyes that "overflowed with fun." It was her vivacity—which no portrait ever succeeded in suggesting—that struck everyone. She was always lively; her face was so mobile that isolating a single feature was difficult. People remembered her "graceful carriage of head and neck and her often half-closed eyes shooting "piercing glances at those with whom she conversed." Her forcefulness was obvious. Samuel Ward, who knew her well, said of her: "How can you describe a Force? How can you write the life of Margaret?"[2]

Margaret Fuller had force of mind as well as the often described force of personality. Hedge noted admiringly that she had both masculine and feminine traits, as these were then understood. The characteristic action of her mind was, he said, "determined by ideas rather than by sentiments. And yet with this masculine trait she combined a woman's appreciation of the beautiful." Her intellect, Hedge said, "was rather solid than graceful, yet no one was more alive to grace." Clarke said that

> the first and most striking element in the genius of Margaret [she encouraged people to call her Margaret] was the clear, sharp understanding, which keenly distinguished between things different, and kept every thought, opinion, person, character in its own place, not to be confounded with any other.

Clarke also testified to the unusual comprehensiveness of her mind: "Some persons see distinctions, others resemblances; but she saw both." She had a high opinion of herself and said so frankly. "I now know all the people worth knowing in America," she said one day to Emerson, "and I find no intellect comparable to my own." It may have been the simple truth. If not, it was close. Emerson himself never gainsaid her remark, even in the privacy of his journal.[3]

Fuller's thought has a strong classical base, more Latin than Greek, but clearly marked by both. Her fundamental allegiance was, to use Matthew Arnold's terms, Hellenic, not Hebraic. She recalled that even as a child she had compared

> the Hebrew history, where every moral obliquity is shown out with such naiveté, and the Greek history, full of sparkling deeds and brilliant sayings, and their gods and goddesses, the types of beauty and power, with the dazzling veil of flowery language and poetical imagery cast over their vices and failings.

Her education was more in literature than in philosophy or religion, but with friends like Hedge and Clarke, she was soon exploring the latter with her own pronounced clarity and energy.[4]

When Margaret was twenty-one, she had a powerful life-shaping experience. The moment has some of the earmarks of a religious conversion and some elements of a mystical experience. It is strikingly similar to the experiences Emerson reports in *Nature,* and the effect stayed with Fuller a long time. The experience occurred on Thanksgiving Day, 1831, after a church service, which she disliked, she said, "from a feeling of disunion with the hearers and dissent from the preacher." In a mood of childlike sadness, she says, "I felt within myself great power, and generosity and tenderness; but it seemed to me as if they were all unrecognized. . . . I was only one and twenty; the past was worthless, the future hopeless." She went walking out over the fields.

> It was a sad and sallow day of the late autumn. Slow processions of sad clouds were passing over a cold blue sky; the hues of earth were dull, and gray, and brown, with sickly struggles of late green here and there: sometimes a moaning gust of wind drove late, reluctant leaves across the path—there was no life else.

She stopped beside a stream. "It was shrunken, voiceless, choked with withered leaves." She sat down, thinking of nothing; "all was dark, and cold, and still. Suddenly the sun shone out with that transparent sweetness, like the last smile of a dying lover." At that moment, she says, there "passed into my thought a beam from its true sun . . . which has never since departed from me." This was a moment of self-revelation, a moment that showed her not only who she was but in what relation she stood to the world. "How is it that I seem to be this Margaret Fuller? What does it mean? What shall

I do about it? . . . I saw how long it must be before the soul can learn to act under these limitations of time and space, and human nature; but I saw also, that it *must* do it." Like Emerson's moment standing on the bare hillside, Fuller's moment of self-affirmation was accompanied at once by a sense that one is not an isolate self but a part of a central, all-pervading consciousness. "I saw," she goes on, in her Ecclesiastes-like way, "that there was no self: that selfishness was all folly, and the result of circumstance; that it was only because I thought self real that I suffered."[5]

Seven years later the experience was still vividly with her. "I felt," she wrote a friend,

> how true it was that nothing in any being which was fit for me, could long be kept from me, and that if separation could be, intimacy had never been. All the future seemed to drop from my existence and I was sure that I should never stand alone in this desert world, but that manna would drop from heaven, if I would but rise with every rising sun to gather it.[6]

At sixteen, five years before her crucial revelation, Fuller was reading de Staël, Epictetus, Milton, and Racine. In 1830, when she was twenty, the list included Byron, Novalis, Goethe (*Wilhelm Meister*), Combe, and Coleridge. In 1833 she read Richter, Disraeli, Lessing, and Plato—especially the *Crito,* the *Phaedo,* and the *Apology.* In 1834 she translated Goethe's *Tasso* and Hedge showed it to Emerson. By now she was also studying Eichhorn and the general problem of the evidences of Christianity. By 1835 she knew herself well enough to say, "I am Germanico, not transcendental." She planned to write a series of six historical tragedies. The year she met Emerson she was working on Herschel, Martineau, Southey, Heine's letters, Fichte, Jacobi, histories of philosophy by Buhle and Tennemann, and the Scottish Common Sense writers Brown and Stewart. For many years, however, her reading had been dominated by Goethe, whose mind she thought had more adequately grasped the nature of things than anyone else. Even more than Emerson, Fuller was Goethe's reader in America.

Fuller's chief strength, by all accounts, was not in writing but in conversation. Her formal conversation classes (each of which cost a participant the equivalent of half a year's tuition at Harvard) became famous. Hedge noted that "she wrote with difficulty." She herself said: "My voice excites me, my pen never." Though the testimony is universal that her conversation—never adequately reported—was better than her writing, still her force of mind comes clearly through her writing, especially in her best book, *Woman in the Nineteenth Century.* Here she makes good her claim to a permanent place in what she herself calls "the world of mind."[7]

Margaret Fuller argues for self-dependence for women. A woman needs what a man needs, that is, autonomy, or "a standard within herself." She conceives of life as a process of self-development and of history as the evolution of human beings toward a more complete humanity through the dialectic interplay of male and female. She presents a clear theory, long before Malinowski, that the myths of any given people are the cultural and social charter of that people. She expressed mythologically her conviction that masculine and feminine qualities exist side by side in every individual: "Man partakes of the Feminine in the Apollo, woman of the Masculine as Minerva." She was herself often said to have a "masculine mind," but she wittily turned the edge of that dubious compliment. There is no special virtue, she says, in a "merely mannish mind." She was convinced that persistence and courage are the most womanly, no less than the most manly, qualities. The empathic energy of her own mind can be seen in, for example, the flash of insight into the figural nature of Greek myth. "The Greeks," she said, "saw everything in forms which we are trying to ascertain as law, and classify as cause."[8]

Before Fuller and Emerson met, she knew him as a speaker. Indeed, there was nothing of his she could have read that had anything other than local interest. But she had been strongly affected by his "great powers as a speaker," observing that his "general manner was that of the reader, occasionally rising into direct address or invocation in passages where tenderness or majesty demanded more energy." When in later years she reviewed his *Essays,* she called him "a man whose only aim is the discernment and interpretation of the spiritual laws by which we live, and move, and have our being, all whose objects are permanent, and whose every word stands for a fact." She told Clarke that Emerson's

> influence has been more beneficial to me than that of any American [Goethe came first for her] and that from him I first learned what is meant by the inward life. . . . That the mind is its own place was a dead phrase to me till he cast light upon my mind. . . . It would take a volume to tell what this one influence did for me, but perhaps I shall some time see that it was best to be forced to help myself.[9]

Along with this handsome acknowledgment, there is a faint reservation in those little words "only" and "perhaps." Fuller took less from Emerson than either Thoreau or Whitman, and she probably gave him more than either of them. After an uncertain start, Emerson and Fuller got on very well. When she left after this first long visit he noted with elegant simplicity, "Yesterday Margaret Fuller returned home after making us a visit of three weeks—a very accomplished and very intelligent person." Their relationship would go through many turns, some of them painful, but all of them vital. He thought her a new Corinne, "more variously gifted, wise, sportive, eloquent . . . magnificent, prophetic, reading my life at her will, and puzzling me with riddles like this; 'yours is an example of a destiny springing from character.'" Their first meeting set a tone that was to persist. She would push a little too much, he would defend a little too quickly. "'I know not what you think of me,' said my friend," Emerson wrote in his journal, with this reply, which was doubtless better phrased than it had been in actual conversation. "Are you sure? You know all I think of you by those things I say to you. You know all which can be of any use to you."[10]

If Emerson guarded his heart with her, it was because he had to. He loved her, and he knew he loved her. More than any other person—except possibly Ellen—Margaret Fuller got through to Emerson's emotional life. She could always touch the quick. Seven years later, à propos her trip to Sault Sainte Marie he wrote:

> She came to me
> And turned on me those azure orbs
> And steeped me in their lavish light . . .
> I think I could spend the longest day
> In unfolding all was folded in that ray.[11]

Intellectually, her enthusiasm for Goethe was a stimulating corroboration for Emerson. She believed, with a force at least as great as his, that ideas are ideas of particular persons. It seems altogether likely that Fuller, even in this first meeting, pushed Emerson away from the abstract and theoretical idealism toward which *Nature* kept drifting and pushed him toward what may be called biographical idealism—idealism that is concerned with ideas only as they can be lived, with laws only as they can be seen in events, with the word only when it becomes flesh, with the spiritual only when it animates the material. "Man is the point wherein matter and spirit meet and marry," wrote Emerson in his journal nine days after Fuller's arrival. They talked too about self-reliance and about new scriptures for new people. "Respect yourself," he wrote, also during her visit. "Trust the instinct to the end, though you cannot tell why or see why." "Make your own Bible. Select and collect all those words and sentences that in all your reading have been to you like the blast of a trumpet out of Shakespeare, Seneca, Moses, John and Paul." Best of all, she was as interested as he was in how the mind works. Immediately after her departure, Emerson worked out in his journal a startlingly modern explanation of Coleridge's saying "Every object rightly seen unlocks a new faculty of the Soul." "That is to say," Emerson comments, "it becomes a part of the domain of consciousness; before it was unconscious truth, now is available knowledge."[12]

Emerson's 1836 meeting with Fuller started one of the important relationships of his life. For the next ten years they were in close and sometimes almost continuous touch with each other. They were friends and colleagues, but there was more than intellectual comradeship in their give and take. Emerson learned from her something about the possibilities of self-reliance against long odds. She undertook to educate his art sense, and she introduced him to such writers as George Sand. She helped him understand Goethe; she made him aware of the peculiar power of mythology, and she gave him new standards for friendship and for a kind of social openness that he found attractive but difficult. She taught him something about the situation of women in the nineteenth century.

After Fuller left, Emerson swiftly finished *Nature* with the section "Prospects," which returns the argument to the living present, and we hear no more of a sequel to be called "Spirit." Emerson went for a long walk at Walden Pond. At the end of August the first of the proofsheets of *Nature* arrived. On September 8 he went to an alumni dinner at Harvard which was part of Harvard's two-hundredth anniversary celebration. But he saw mainly its pathos. He was thinking no doubt of Charles and Edward. The next day his little book was published.

Go Alone

40. The Symposium

On September 8, 1836, the day of the Harvard bicen-
tennial celebration and the day before the publication of *Nature,* Henry
Hedge, George Putnam (the Unitarian minister in Roxbury), George Ripley, and Emerson met at Willard's Hotel in Cambridge to plan a symposium
or periodic gathering of persons who, like themselves, found the present
state of thought in America "very unsatisfactory." What came to be called
the Transcendental Club was thus born "in the way of protest" on behalf
of "deeper and broader views" than obtained at present.[1]

More specifically, the impulse behind the Transcendental Club was a
protest against the arid intellectual climate of Harvard and Cambridge.
President Quincy had his eye on the past. His commemorative speech soon
grew into a two-volume history of Harvard University. Andrews Norton,
the leading theologian of the school, was about to bring out the first volume
of his *Evidences of the Genuineness of the Gospels* (1837), a huge, shallow,
tendentious volume that takes the novel approach of simply ignoring the
vast majority of serious work on the subject for the preceding seventy-five
years. No one at Harvard was equipped or inclined for modern thought in
this area. "There is," said Hedge, "a rigid, cautious, circumspect, conservative *tang* in the very air of Cambridge which no one, who has resided there
for any considerable time, can escape." The club never met in Cambridge.
Harvard at this time had a president, eleven professors, and seven instructors. An average meeting of the club drew eleven members; on occasion it
could draw seventeen. The intellectual and literary candlepower of the club
easily exceeded that of the college.[2]

Eleven days after the first meeting at Willard's Hotel, the group held a
second meeting, this time at Ripley's house in Boston. Ten persons attended; besides Hedge, Ripley, and Emerson, there were Bronson Alcott,
James Clarke, Orestes Brownson, Convers Francis, and several divinity
students. The Club, as it was sometimes called, was now a reality.

Emerson had been leery of the whole undertaking, as he told Hedge.
Fresh from the stimulus of Margaret Fuller's three-week visit, he preferred,

245

he said, "the society of one faithful person" to a confident crowd of "menacing rapid trenchant talkers" who "cut me short—they drive me into a corner—I must not suggest, I must define." But the first meeting went well. "The conversation was earnest and hopeful," he noted. It was decided that no one should be admitted "whose presence excluded any one topic." Pains were taken to avoid a cozy tone of self-congratulation. Early in the afternoon Emerson commented how "twas pity that in this Titanic continent where nature is so grand, Genius should be so tame. Not one unchallengeable reputation." Present company not excluded.[3]

The symposium, or club, or whatever it was (Emerson called it something different almost every time he mentioned it—Hedge's Club, the Aesthetic Club, the Transcendental Club), was gathered at a pivotal moment, just as a number of its members were breaking into print. The club was a forum for new ideas, a clearinghouse, full of yeast and ferment, informal, open-ended, far from the usual exclusive social clique conveyed by the word *club*. The meetings often centered on a single topic; any list of their subjects conveys the tone of the group. On October 3, 1836, at Alcott's in Boston the topic was "American Genius—the causes which hinder its growth, and give us no first rate productions." On October 18, 1836, at Brownson's house in Boston it was "Education of Humanity." On May 29, 1837, at Ripley's in Boston it was "What is the essence of Religion as distinct from morality?" In the summer of 1837 at Emerson's house it was "Does the species advance beyond the individual?" On May 20, 1838, at Stetson's house in Medford it was "Is Mysticism an element of Christianity?" In June of 1838 at Bartol's house in Boston it was "On the character and genius of Goethe"; in December of 1838 at the same place it was "Pantheism." On May 13, 1840, at Emerson's it was on "the Inspiration of the Prophet and Bard, the nature of Poetry, and the causes of sterility of poetic Inspiration in our Age and country."[4]

"The life of a man is a self-evolving circle," Emerson says in "Circles," "which, from a ring imperceptibly small, rushes on all sides outward to new and larger circles, and that without end." The Transcendental Club, so-called, served its members in this manner. The club had been Hedge's idea. Emerson, who attended at least twenty of the thirty meetings over the next four years, was always a leading spirit, but the group contained a number of other remarkable and forceful individuals, whose lives were now deeply intertwined with Emerson's.

246

George Ripley was one year older than Emerson, a native of Greenfield, Massachusetts, and now a Boston minister. He had a library full of philosophy and biblical criticism, including Kant, Fichte, Schleiermacher, Herder, Cousin, Hegel, Schopenhauer, Eichhorn, Paulus, Bauer, and Tholuck. He read Vico and Giordano Bruno as well as Goethe and Schiller. Between 1830 and 1837 he published ten major articles in *The Christian Examiner*. In 1836 he published a discussion of James Martineau's "Rationale of Religious Enquiry" which produced quite a stir and was abused by Andrews Norton as "infidelity." Ripley was slender—in his early years— with a full head of close-curling brown hair. He had bright black eyes and always wore gold-rimmed glasses. He was an irrepressible spirit, a punster with a sort of "constitutional hilarity." He relished Carlyle's wry description of him as "a Socinian minister who left his pulpit to reform the world by cultivating onions." Ripley founded and edited the series of books called *Specimens of Foreign Standard Literature,* and he did indeed leave his pulpit to found and lead the Brook Farm experiment in communal living. Above all, Ripley is the great American translator, commentator, and disciple of Schleiermacher, whom he regarded as "the greatest thinker who ever undertook to fathom the philosophy of religion."[5]

Then there was Orestes Brownson, the same age as Emerson, born in Stockbridge, Vermont, and self-educated. He was ordained a Universalist minister in 1826, but he became too liberal for the Universalists and went on to take up the radical free thought and socialism of Robert Dale Owen and Frances Wright. He had been a corresponding editor of *The Free Enquirer* and had helped found the Workingman's Party in New York. In 1832 he became a Unitarian and in 1836 he was a minister at Canton, Massachusetts. During the winter of 1835–1836 Henry Thoreau, then in his junior year, came and taught school and studied German with Brownson. During that same year Brownson organized a new church among the working people of Boston, and he brought out a book called *New Views of the Church and Society.* Brownson was over six feet tall, his large face was framed by chin whiskers. He was a vigorous thinker and prolific writer. In 1838 he founded and for years wrote most of *The Boston Quarterly Magazine.* The election of 1840 drove him to political conservatism; in 1844 he converted to Catholicism. For the rest of his life he championed these two causes, becoming the most eminent Catholic lay person in nineteenth-century America. Speaking of his passionate and strongly written *The*

Laboring Classes, A. M. Schlesinger, Jr., calls Brownson Marx's most important American forerunner. Of Brownson's later career, Russell Kirk says he became the first writer to describe Marxism as a Christian heresy and "is perhaps the most convincing American opponent of Marxism."[6]

Convers Francis, then forty-one, was the oldest of the club regulars before Caleb Stetson of Medford became a steady member. Francis was a minister at Watertown. The year the club was gathered, he published a *Life of John Eliot* and a short tract called "Christianity as a Purely Internal System." He was a moderate Unitarian, a liberal trusted by most radicals and most conservatives. For his diplomatic skills and his seniority, he was chosen moderator of the new club.[7]

The gathering certainly filled a need. There were three more meetings this fall of 1836 and five or six a year for the next four years. The group expanded rapidly. There was Theodore Parker, son of a Lexington farmer, just graduated from Harvard Divinity School. Parker was a short, powerful, balding man with a massive forehead. His most striking feature was a pair of steel-blue eyes that were somewhat obscured by his gold-rimmed spectacles. He was an effective speaker with a great career as a reformer ahead of him. In 1836 he had been writing innumerable articles for *The Scriptural Interpreter,* including a landmark early translation of Jean Astruc's *Conjectures on Genesis.* He was already at work on his monumental edition and enlargement of De Wette's *Introduction to the Old Testament,* the most important (and most neglected) work of American biblical scholarship before the Civil War. There was John S. Dwight, later a Brook Farmer, and after that a well-known music critic whose mission was bringing Beethoven's music to Americans. There was Caleb Stetson, an older man, a wit, the minister at Medford; he hosted the club twice. There was Chandler Robbins, Emerson's successor at Boston's Second Church. Margaret Fuller attended, as did Elizabeth Hoar, Charles Emerson's "widow," now a close friend of Emerson's and an intellectual in her own right.[8]

Membership was not rigidly defined. The "members" of the club were those who attended. A list of the people who attended reads like a who's who of the liberal intellectuals of the time. These included Ephraim Peabody, Boston minister and later editor of *The Western Messenger,* Sarah A. Ripley, an accomplished classicist and teacher from Watertown, Sarah Clarke, an artist, sister of James Clarke, and Elizabeth Peabody, later publisher of *The Dial.* Over time at least twenty-three others came to a few meetings; these included Jones Very the poet, Charles Follen, teacher of

German at Harvard, Henry Bellows, leader of the anti-Emersonian institutional Unitarians and Melville's New York pastor later in life. There was William Adams, visiting from his mission in Calcutta. William Ellery Channing, grand old man of Unitarianism, came once. Still others included George Bancroft the historian, Shobal Clevinger the sculptor, Christopher Cranch, a poet (famous later for his witty satirical cartoons of Emerson), Samuel Ward, a friend of Fuller's, Henry Thoreau, Edward Taylor the sailor-preacher, and Sophia Ripley, married to George and author of the brilliant and stirring piece "Woman" in *The Dial.*

These people came from a variety of backgrounds and educations, but they came together now because they were in general if not complete agreement on a number of points. They were dissatisfied, individually and as a group, with the present state of philosophy, religion, and literature in America. They looked for hope to Europe, especially to Germany, to Kant in philosophy, to Schleiermacher in religion, and to Goethe in literature. They were mostly anti-Lockean; most believed in intuition. They were romanticists, not classicists or philosophes. They were radicals or liberals rather than conservatives in politics and almost all followed the logic of their belief in freedom and autonomy into one or another arena of social action. Margaret Fuller ended up in newspaper journalism, the women's movement, and the Roman revolution. Parker devoted his life to antislavery work. Peabody was active in the kindergarten movement and in the movement for American Indian rights. Emerson and Thoreau came out strongly for abolition, Ripley founded Brook Farm, Brownson became a powerful voice first for labor, then for Catholicism.[9]

No one knows who first called the group the Transcendental Club, but the name has stuck, despite a hundred and fifty years of qualification, refinement, and hindsight. Emerson's 1842 piece "The Transcendentalist" is still the defining statement: "It is well known to most of my audience that the Idealism of the present day acquired the name Transcendental, from the use of that term by Immanuel Kant." Emerson goes on to praise Kant's profundity and precision and notes that Kant's influence has become so pervasive "that whatever belongs to the class of intuitive thought is popularly called at the present day transcendental." Few of those assembled in 1836 would have disagreed with this or with Alcott's saying that transcendentalism "means that there is more in the mind than enters it through the senses." They would also have agreed with what Nathaniel H. Whiting, a mechanic from South Marshfield, Massachusetts, told a Bible convention in 1842: "Truths which pertain to the soul cannot be proved by any external testimony whatsoever."[10]

Whatever transcendentalism was, it was not suited to institutionalizing. It gave birth to no academy; it flourished in no college or seminary. It had two collective expressions during its heyday (the club and the magazine called *The Dial*) but could only manage one at a time. The last meeting of the club was in 1840, the year *The Dial* was founded. For better or worse, American transcendentalism was uncohesive, preferring to unravel rather than compromise its belief in the sovereign worth of each separate strand of yarn.

Transcendentalism did not transform American life, but it did change— and continues to change—individual American lives. Transcendentalism was not only a literary, philosophical, and religious movement; it was also, inescapably, a social and political movement as well. In philosophy transcendentalism taught—teaches—that even in a world of objective knowledge, the subjective consciousness and the conscious subject can never be left out of the reckoning. Thoreau could say "the purest science is still biographical," or, as Emerson might have said, there is finally no science, there are only scientists.[11]

In religion transcendentalism teaches that the religious spirit is a necessary aspect of human nature—or of the human condition—and that the religious spirit does not reside in external forms, words, ceremonies, or institutions. In Emerson's words, "The one thing of value in the universe is the active soul." In literature transcendentalism holds that it is a built-in necessity of human nature to express itself, that self-expression, like self-development, is one of the purposes of life itself. The social imperative of transcendentalism is twofold. It insists, first, that the well-being of the individual—of all the individuals—is the basic purpose and ultimate justification for all social organizations and second that autonomous individuals cannot exist apart from others. In the transcendentalist vocabulary "association" is just as charged a word as "self." Transcendentalism believes that the purpose of education is to facilitate the self-development of each individual. The political trajectory of transcendentalism begins in philosophical freedom and ends in democratic individualism.[12]

By virtue of its openness to science (understood as the study of nature), transcendentalism avoids divorcing itself from the mainstream of modern science and technology. But it affirms that "not he is great who can alter matter, but who can alter my state of mind." Some say that modern liberalism is without a soul. Transcendentalism in general and Emersonian idealism in particular offer an alternative to utilitarian liberalism, to leader worship, and to collectivism. Transcendentalism's commitment to the individual and to the principle of individuation is a commitment to the soul or spirit that each person possesses in common with all other human beings. It is the ambition, if it has not yet been the fate, of transcendentalism to provide a soul for modern liberalism and thereby to enlarge the possibilities of modern life.[13]

41. The Forging of the Anchor

FROM THE SECOND HALF OF SEPTEMBER 1836 TO EARLY MARCH
1837 Emerson was reading, thinking, writing, and talking at white heat.
Perhaps the reason was the reception and sale of *Nature*, which went very
well. Perhaps it was in part the stimulus of the new discussion group, or
perhaps it was the prospect of a child, for Lidian was in her eighth month.
Whatever the cause or conjunction of causes, Emerson was euphoric, full
of energy. His journal is exuberant, brilliant, expansive. He was pursuing
the line laid out in *Nature*, boldly cutting off his retreat, burning his bridges,
and setting out on his own: "Shall I write on the tendency of the modern
mind to lop off all superfluity and tradition and fall back on the nature of
things?" His language is strong, dismissive, physical. "The Romantic ate up
the doric letters and life of the old nations," he observed. He thought the
new "democratic element" had "shown the nullity" and "given a hollow
sound to the name of king and earl and lord." In sweeping language
Emerson notes how "vast quantities of the stock literature of the past, the
pastoral poems, the essays, the sermons, the politics, the novels turning on
merely local and phenomenal questions" are perishing.[1]

As he often did when excited, he tossed off lists and catalogs. They are
the inventories of his many worlds. "An ampitheatre is a cup of men, the
pagoda is a tent, the pyramid a mound, the Gothic aisle a festal grove, the
Parthenon a cabin." Image crowds on image in a tumbling heap of inventive
abundance. "We scare ourselves by the names we give, death watch, earwig,
deaths-head moth, St. Anthony's fire, St. Vitus' dance." He loved "the
eight-rowed corn, and the twelve-rowed, and the brindled, and the badger
corn, and the Canada corn, and the sweet, the white, and the Missouri."
Sometimes he turned his verbal torrent on himself. He wrote once of the
"sad, estranged, misadventured, estrayed Waldo Emerson." More often
though the impulse was a Homeric, a Goethean reaching out to the world.

Let us paint the agitator, and the man of the old school, and the
member of Congress, and the college professor, the formidable editor,

the priest, the reformer, the contemplative girl, and the fair aspirant for fashion and opportunity, the woman of the world who has tried and knows.

He was like his admired Carlyle who, Emerson once said, uses the language "like a protean engine which can cut, thrust, saw, rasp, tickle or pulverize as occasion may require."[2]

Emerson's lists are an expression of overflowing plenty, of energy, of impatient haste. "We peddle, we truck, we sail, we row, we ride in cars, we creep in teams, we go in canals, to market, and for the sale of goods." Emerson managed to sustain his creative outburst for several months while he planned, wrote, and delivered the most intellectually coherent and thematically unified set of lectures he would ever do, lectures that were the foundation—and much of the substance—of the best work of the next five or six years.[3]

His writing these new lectures is all the more remarkable because of the increasing number of pressing calls on his time. There was the large house and the growing family. In January of 1837 William ran into severe financial problems and Emerson spent much time and money helping him out. He was also in charge of supplying the pulpit of the East Lexington church. He did all his own arrangements for lectures, all his own correspondence. There were requests for lectures, for verses, for articles. Knowing bereavement himself, he wrote long letters of condolence. When the Boston press attacked Alcott for his radical educational ideas, Emerson did what he could, writing letters to the papers in protest. He pursued and brokered new projects, such as the idea of translating Eckermann's *Conversations with Goethe.*

Emerson kept working, however, and by early October he was calling his projected series "The Philosophy of Modern History." He kept the title broad, partly to give himself elbowroom, partly because he was still trying to storm the main gate, as he had in *Nature.* He intended to treat religion, literature, science, and art "directly" and to "indicate the foundation of them in the nature of things." He had always written out his lectures and, before that, his sermons. Although he acknowledged the extempory brilliance of an Alcott or a Fuller, he thought written composition able "to surpass any unwritten effusion of however profound genius, for what is writ is a foundation of a new superstructure, and a guide to the eye for a new foundation, so that the work rises tower upon tower with ever new and total strength of the builder." His journal sparkles with casual brilliance. Among the pleasures of architecture he listed "the cobweb, the bird's nest, the silver counterpane of the stonespider, the cocoon, the honeycomb, the beaver dam." He chided science for too much concentration on "marrowless particulars." He rephrases Newton: "The motion of the moon is nothing but an apple-fall." He plays with time, writing that "a moment is a concentrated eternity." Years of practice at recording first impressions, dreams, nuances, and unbidden objections were paying off. His journal becomes remarkably alive now—even transparent. He is able to set down everything going on around him as well as inside him, and he was deeply in tune with Lidian. In early January, as he sat before his journal and fretted about the problem of genius, Lidian came in and wrote her name, her son's, and her husband's to "warm my cold page."[4]

Emerson was reading Charles Lyell's *Principles of Geology* but was disappointed to find it "only a catalogue of facts." He was also reading Sir Humphry Davy, but he was most excited about a poem called "The Forging of the Anchor" by the Irish poet Samuel Ferguson. Ferguson's poem, which Emerson read "with delight," was cast in the poetic mold of Schiller's *Song of the Bell* and Longfellow's *The Building of the Ship*. Ferguson describes with hammerlike realism the heating and shaping of a great ship's anchor weighing several tons. He focuses on the moment when the white-hot lump of rough metal is winched up from the charcoal pit in which it has been heated:

> The windlass strains the tackle chains, the black mound heaves below
> And red and deep a hundred veins burst out at every throe
> It rises, roars, rends all outright . . .

The scene becomes, in Ferguson's vivid narrative, a volcanic moment of creation: "The high sun sees not, on the earth, such a fiery fearful show." The poem is about style, about the shaping of power, written in the dark diction of chthonic energies: "The roof ribs swarth, the candent hearth, the ruddy, lurid row / Of smiths that stand, an ardent band, like men before the foe."[5]

On October 15 Emerson walked out eastward from Concord center to Goose Pond, which is near Walden Pond. "Amid the many coloured trees I thought what principles I might lay down as the foundation of this course of lectures I shall read to my fellow citizens." This was what Emerson called elsewhere a "casting moment," a moment in which he saw with unaccustomed force and clarity the cardinal points of what he recognized both as his own convictions and the "perennial philosophy." Amid the many-colored trees, he jotted down eight basic propositions. He begins with the idea that will underlie "History," "Self-Reliance," and the other great essays: "There is one mind common to all individual men." This is Platonism; Emerson means we all have reason in common. Communication is possible because all human minds are, in important respects, similarly constituted. The second of Emerson's Goose Pond principles is the Stoic ground law: "There is a relation between man and nature so that whatever is in matter is in mind." This is the basis for language and for what the writer does. The third point is that expression is as basic a human drive as sex: "It is a necessity of the human nature that it should express itself outwardly and embody its thought." "As all creatures are allured to reproduce themselves, so must the thought be imparted in speech." He adds, as a corollary, "Action is as great a pleasure and cannot be foreborne." Point four says, "It is the constant endeavor of the mind to idealize the actual, to accommodate the shows of things to the desires of the mind." He gives architecture and art as examples.[6]

Point five is the theory of classification: "It is the constant tendency of the mind to unify all it beholds, or to reduce the remotest facts to a single law." Point six extends point five and is a specific application of point two: "There is a parallel tendency/corresponding unity in nature which makes this [unification] just, as in the composition of a compound shell or leaf or animal from few elements." Point seven describes, in Baconian fashion, an idol of the mind, the tendency to "separate particulars" and magnify them, from which come "all false views and particular sects." Emerson's last point is the intellectual parallax or corrective postulate for the previous point: "The remedy for all abuses, all error in thought or practice, is the conviction that underneath all appearances and causing all appearances are certain eternal laws which we call the Nature of Things." When Emerson speaks of fate or necessity, he means these eternal laws. The last of his principles points back to the first; both are restatements of basic Platonism in modern terms.[7]

These principles are Emerson's categories, his list of primary powers of the mind, considered apart from the contents of any given mind or the objects of thought. Taken together, these principles form the molten core of Emerson's thought, and his work of the next few months was to hammer them out in convincing detail.

The year 1836 is a great year for Emerson. Everywhere in his writing there are images of forging and birth. And capping the new friendships with Alcott and Fuller, the publication of *Nature,* and the gathering of the club was the birth of his first child, Waldo, on October 31. Emerson took to calling him Wallie at first and commented with vast satisfaction on how he was a "troublesome comfort unspeakable." The pregnancy had been hard; Lidian had been ill for months and was confined to her room for two weeks after the birth. The week Waldo was born, Emerson went scrambling in the woods with a neighbor, Peter Howe, bringing back "six hemlock trees to plant in my yard which may grow while my boy is sleeping." He proudly reported Waldo's progress. Lidian noted that Emerson was "a most attentive observer of nursery phenomena." He told William that at two and a half months Wallie could "suck, cry, laugh, coo, warble, and jump"; at just under four months "Waldo struggles, leaps, studies manipulation and palmistry, and optics." Whenever the baby fell sick, fear descended on the household. The child touched something deep inside Emerson. There is in some of his comments a defenseless, prayerful nakedness that had not been there since the days of Ellen. When Waldo caught a cold in April Emerson wrote, "Ah! my darling boy, so lately received out of heaven, leave me not now."[8]

42. We Are Not Children of Time

THE LECTURES ON THE PHILOSOPHY OF HISTORY WERE THE
first Emerson had ever given entirely on his own management. No organization sponsored him; he was part of no series. This was his own venture
and his own responsibility. The series was long, consisting of twelve lectures
in all. After the introductory lecture, which took place on December 8,
1836, at Boston's Masonic Temple, Emerson gave talks on the humanity
of science, art, literature, politics, society, trades and professions (Emerson's
best lecture on labor), manners, ethics, the present age, and, on March 2,
1837, the final lecture, on the individual. Emerson did not publish these
lectures because he later appropriated substantial sections for "History,"
"Self-Reliance," "The Oversoul," "Art," "Thoughts on Modern Literature," "Spiritual Laws," and "Compensation." What often appear as scattered insights in these better-known essays appear here in this set of lectures
as parts of a major and coherent phase in Emerson's development, the
moment when his thought reached its most systematic.

The lectures return again and again to two main points. One is a radical
dechronologized conception of history; the other is an insistence on the
subordination of the individual to the whole. Emerson begins by deprecating the "battles and leaders" view of history, the "barren and wearisome
chronicle" in which "the unity of the story is secured by concentrating
attention to the man or woman on the throne." Emerson now insists that
human history can be understood only as the expression of that human
nature that is common to all men and women. There is one mind, in
which we all share, and "of this one mind, History is the record." It follows
that "all the facts of history pre-exist in the mind as laws." That is, they
exist in each mind, so that the whole of history is in each mind. History
"is all to be explained from individual experience." It may no longer be
true that man is the measure of all things, but for purposes of understanding history, "the nature of man *is* the measure of all facts attributed to it,"
says Emerson. "The fact narrated must correspond to something in me to
be credible."[1]

257

Emerson's radical redefinition of history is not so much a new concept of history as a new way of reading history. His great essay "History" is in fact an essay on *reading* history. At the start of his new series of lectures he says—and one can hear the vehemence in the imperative phrasing—"We, as we read, must become Greeks, Romans, Turks, priest and king, martyr and executioner, that is, must fasten these images to some reality in our secret experience, or we shall see nothing, learn nothing, keep nothing." Like Walt Whitman later, Emerson feels a kinship with whomever he reads about, a kinship made possible by the "perfect identity" of us all: "I see the same features,—I catch the sparkle of the same eye,—I identify the smile, and the frown, the air, and the voice, alike whether humanity appears in a helmet, or a cowl, or a fillet, or a hat, in a golden crown or a braided palmleaf." This identity holds across space and time. The only way to understand the past is to imagine it—and everyone in it—as the present: "When a thought of Plato becomes a thought to me, when a truth that fired the soul of St. John, fires mine, time is no more." This "stupendous fact of the radical identity of all men," this mandatory full membership in the human race, means that in this respect at least "we are not children of time."[2]

The inescapable corollary of this insistence on one mind and common humanity is a repeated and consistent attack on individualism as commonly understood. In these lectures we see Emerson working through a remarkably complete critique of romantic individualism. The critique is a necessary preparation for Emerson's new kind of self-trust. In the opening lecture Emerson says in one breath that "we early arrive at the great discovery that there is one mind common to all individual men: that what is individual is less than what is universal . . . that error, vice and disease have their seat in the superficial or individual nature." He comes back to this point again and again. He says approvingly that "all our education aims to sink what is individual or personal in us." "Nothing but God is self-dependent," he says carefully. "Every being in nature has its existence so connected with other beings that if set apart from them it would instantly perish."[3]

Emerson insisted on this point. "Insulate a man and you annihilate him. He cannot unfold, he cannot live without a world." In the lecture "Art" Emerson goes so far as to say that the artist who wishes to create a work that will be generally admired "must disindividualize himself." And in the lecture "Politics" he asserts that "the foundation of equality is this, that they [persons] are all possessed by one mind . . . in virtue of the access of all to Reason." In the lecture "Religion" Emerson starts by saying that what he has been calling the universal mind is now called reason by philosophers. He then bluntly concedes that "the antagonistic nature to the Universal mind is the Individual, the personal."[4]

In the "Society" lecture Emerson makes a similar distinction, saying that "besides this generic nature every man has an individual nature." Finally, in the "Ethics" lecture Emerson reached the formulation of this relationship between the individual and the collective mind which was to remain with him permanently. He called it "self-trust" and described it as "the one maxim which makes the whole ethics of the mind." He defined self-trust now—with a balance he was never later to improve on—as "not a faith in a man's own whim or conceit as if he were quite severed from all other beings and acted on his own private account, but a perception that the mind common to the universe is disclosed to the individual through his own nature." This is the culminating statement in the best lecture of the series. Henceforward the perception that each is an expression of all will be the immovable anchor of Emerson's thought.[5]

43. The American Scholar

THE FINANCIAL PANIC OF 1837 AFFECTED EMERSON MOST SE-
verely through his brother William. The supply of paper money had tripled
in the United States between 1830 and 1837 as part of the general boom
that had begun in 1825. Hoping to strengthen the central bank, President
Jackson stipulated that all obligations to the United States be paid in specie.
Overseas creditors made similar demands. Then the wheat crop failed in
1836 and the price of cotton fell as well. Bank after bank suspended
payment. All the banks in Boston had suspended payment by May of 1837.
Many failed outright. That portion of Emerson's money in bank stock
produced little or no income. Hard money was in very short supply. By
December of 1836 William needed, he said, $6,500. He offered 20 percent
interest but could find no lender in New York even at that rate. He turned
to Waldo for help. Waldo transferred enough assets to William to cover
$6,400 worth of debts, and for the next several years the two brothers' affairs
were closely intertwined as they worked to raise a few hundred dollars on
a second mortgage here and a few hundred as an advance there, all to keep
William from losing various properties and investments altogether. Year
after year the brothers covered scores of pages with anxious—and for
Emerson dispiriting—calculations.[1]

In March Emerson gave up the idea of editing a volume of Charles's
writings. Emerson found the darkness in Charles's work very painful. "I
withdraw myself from the influence," he confessed in his journal. "So much
contrition, so much questioning, so little hope, so much sorrow harrowed
me. I could not stay to see my noble brother tortured even by himself."
Deeply enmeshed in the family calamities and surrounded by his own busy
household, Emerson read Goethe, wrote in his journal, and kept up a busy
life. Fuller came to visit again, as did Alcott. There were frequent trips to
Boston and to East Lexington. The club continued to meet. There were
more trees to plant. At times Emerson was in quite a different mood and
could revel "in the high joys of perfect wedlock." When Jonathan Philips
and William Ellery Channing paid the club the honor of a visit, Emerson

observed shrewdly that "sages are like kings so environed with deference and ceremony" that their appearance "gives no true word for mind or heart."[2]

Emerson was thirty-four in May 1837. In his journal he reasserted his sense that life is symbolic and went on to specify the ways in which people class themselves according to their perception of this fact. Most persons live "to the utility of the symbol," as though the apparent world were the real one and as though the world were chiefly meant to be useful to us. Some few, poets and artists, live "to the beauty of the symbol." They too live as though the visible world were all there is. And some, those who possess some spiritual perception, manage to live "to the beauty of the thing signified." This was not just theory for Emerson. He read the increasingly hard times, the "emphatic and universal calamity," as a failure of modern materialism and an indictment of American society. "The world has failed," he said simply. Even Carlyle, he noted, had a disturbing tendency to worship strength, "heedless much whether its present phase be divine or diabolic."[3]

Adversity often gave Emerson a strange elation. All through this spring and summer he was living on the stretch; he had frequent moments of almost visionary intensity. The end of April witnessed one such quick updraft of Emerson's spirits. He was reading Goethe's translation of Plotinus on art. Plotinus wants us to see the artistry behind and shaping the artifact. Emerson gives the idea sudden life by saying the art of shipbuilding is "all of the ship but the wood." As artistry is more important than artifact, so, Emerson now concludes, "character is higher than intellect."[4]

Emerson was so sick in June that he could not study and he thought seriously of travel. He nevertheless gave a talk in Providence at the opening of a school to be run on Bronson Alcott's principles. Margaret Fuller was one of the new teachers. The talk was predictably on education, but the tone is one of radical dissatisfaction. Emerson had in mind both the financial crisis of the country and the local, Bostonian attack on Alcott's school—an attack that effectively ended the school—as he told his audience that a commercial revolution had shattered the frame of society and that "a desperate conservatism clings with both hands to every dead form in the schools, in the state, in the church." The address is a call for reform both of society and of education. "What," he asks, "is the end of human life? It is not, believe me, the chief end of man that he should make a fortune and beget children whose end is likewise to make a fortune, but it is, in few words, that he should explore himself."[5]

If the month of June was lost to study, Emerson did find time to read Donne's "Second Anniversary" and Boswell's *Life of Johnson*. He was particularly delighted with the latter. This month he wrote a letter—now lost—to Harvard president Quincy in support of Henry Thoreau, currently a senior planning to graduate at the end of August. Thoreau had fallen in the esteem of his instructors; Quincy thought him rebellious, and it seemed that he might be passed over when it came to class awards and prizes. During the third week in June Emerson was asked to deliver the address at the annual meeting of Harvard's Phi Beta Kappa Society. Emerson was a stopgap. The society's first choice was the Reverend Jonathan Mayhew Wainwright, an Episcopalian and the author of a book of hymns, but Wainwright declined the Phi Beta Kappa offer.[6]

Emerson had just recently written some verses for Concord's Fourth of July celebration and the unveiling of the North Bridge Battle Monument, which commemorated one of the opening battles of the American Revolution. Emerson's lines have become his own best known monument. "By the rude bridge that arched the flood, / Their flag to April's breeze unfurled, / Here once the embattled farmers stood / And fired the shot heard round the world." All through the summer months of July and August Emerson looked to his own powder and priming as he worked out his "theory of the scholar's office" for the Phi Beta Kappa assembly.[7]

On August 31 Emerson and Lidian drove to Cambridge for the event. Commencement had been the day before, but there was still an overflow crowd gathered at noon in the old wooden church that still stands in Harvard Square across the street from Massachusetts Hall and just outside the main gate to Harvard Yard. The outside of the Brattle Street Church was—and still is—an awkward monument of Carpenter Gothic that never seems able to hold a coat of paint through the winter. The sanctuary inside is of an entirely different character. It is a graceful example of Jeffersonian classicism and Federal simplicity. Emerson's audience in 1837 included U.S. Supreme Court Justice Joseph Story and Massachusetts Supreme Court Chief Justice Lemuel Shaw. Also present were Oliver Wendell Holmes, James Russell Lowell, Richard Henry Dana, Wendell Phillips, and Edward Everett. There were other former teachers such as Edward Channing, colleagues such as Henry Ware, Sr., and Unitarian heavyweights such as Andrews Norton. It was a good audience, and Emerson's shot, if he fired one, would at least be heard around the little world of eastern Massachusetts. Not everybody was there. Henry Thoreau had graduated the day before (with a part in the commencement and some of the prize money), but it seems he had already vanished from Cambridge.

Emerson spoke for a hour and a quarter, in what one perennial attender of commencements called "the misty, dreamy, unintelligible style of Swedenborg, Carlyle, and Coleridge." Emerson's friends urged him to publish the talk, which he quickly did, at his own expense. The edition of five hundred copies of "The American Scholar" was sold out in a month. There may have been some small sense of moment when he gave the speech. As time passed, however, the talk became famous, even legendary. Fifty years later Oliver Wendell Holmes was calling it "our Intellectual Declaration of Independence."[8]

But the most famous point in the talk is not only the least original part but the least characteristic of Emerson. Bliss Perry noted in 1923 that for a quarter century before 1837 speaker after speaker at Harvard had issued ritual warnings about listening too long to the courtly muses of Europe and ritual prophecies that our day of dependence, our long apprenticeship to the learning of other lands, was drawing to a close. Perhaps none of the previous warnings or prophecies had been so forcefully put, but the general subject was so common that it had become a standard undergraduate theme topic. What is remarkable is that Emerson fell so tamely into line, since he was himself deeply and openly indebted to European thought and literature. He was also, despite occasional moments of national enthusiasm, not much interested in literary nationalism or a strictly national criticism. When he came to write *Representative Men,* not one of his models was an American. "The American Scholar" was written by a man who read daily in Goethe, Plutarch, Montaigne, Shakespeare, and Wordsworth, a man who would later say,

> It will hereafter be noted that the events of culture in the nineteenth century were, the new importance of the genius of Dante, Michel Angelo, and Raffael to America: the reading of Shakespeare, and above all the reading of Goethe. Goethe was the cow from which all their milk was drawn.[9]

At the time he wrote the address, however, Emerson was in a rebellious, challenging mood. He was dismayed and angry about the public attack that was driving Alcott's school under; he was reacting to Charles's despair. He was recoiling from the financial panic that kept everyone bent over their account books day and night. He was also moving to correct the extreme

Eurocentrism of the club. Ripley's current projects were his Foreign Standard Authors series and Schleiermacher. Hedge and Brownson were as "Germanico" as Fuller. Emerson himself valued Goethe above all others. Still, and despite a lifelong interest in foreign literature of all kinds, Emerson entered a significant dissent this spring. "On the whole what have these German Weimarish art-friends done?" Emerson asked. "They have rejected all the traditions and connections, have sought to come thereby one step nearer to absolute truth. But still they are not nearer than others." He found them not heroic, not holy, with an inadequate view of nature and with no power to illuminate or rectify. Finally, they are too exalted: "The roots of what is great and high must still be in the common life." And even when the genius of a European writer could not be denied or discounted, the problem of the burden of the past remained. "Genius is always the enemy of genius by overinfluence," Emerson told his Phi Beta Kappa audience. As evidence he adduced the English dramatic poets who "have Shakespearized now for two hundred years."[10]

The reason for this sudden and in some ways uncharacteristic disparagement of Europe was not so much to boost America as to argue for the practical adequacy of the individual, the imperative of self-reliance, the superiority of the whole person to the specialist who accepts the divided self as a necessary effect of the division of labor. He was interested not in the bookworm, not even in the thinker, only in Man Thinking. He was not so much interested in separating America from its European past as he was in separating the individual from his incapacitating education, most of which happened to be European.

To praise individualism was one thing, but when Emerson went so far as to disparage the institutional forces that undermine autonomy, part of his audience was offended. His speech had no praise for Harvard, no paean to the long tradition of scholarly learning that was even then silting up the rivers of thought, no comfortable references to progress. Emerson had no good word for the Bible ("Books are for the scholar's idle times") or the church or Christ ("The man has not been born who can feed us ever"). Instead, he offered an explicit critique of institutions, including, of course, American institutions: "The book, the college, the school of art, the institution of any kind, stop with some past utterance of genius. . . . They pin me down. They look backward and not forward."[11]

"The American Scholar" is only the first of a long series of lectures and addresses Emerson wrote on "the duties of the scholar." He returned to the subject again and again, at Middlebury in Vermont, at Wesleyan in Connecticut, and at the University of Virginia many years later. This first audience may well have wondered what he meant by "scholar." Certainly it was not what he once called "the book-learned class, who value books as such." Nor was it what another time he called "the restorers of readings, the emendators, the bibliomaniacs of all degrees." Emerson's comments on scholars as the term is now understood are almost always disparaging or satirical. Scholars, he said, "are found to make very shabby sentences out of the weakest words because of exclusive attention to the word." A year hence he would be dismissing "the learned class" and "half-witted persons" in the same breath. Emerson always preferred a reader to an annotator and a writer to a reader. By *scholar* he means, in this address, something of what we mean by *student,* something of *intellectual,* and most, perhaps, of what we mean by *writer.*[12]

"The American Scholar" is perennially fresh because what is being liberated here is not America—not American literature or the American intelligentsia—but the single person. In fact, it is Emerson himself who is being freed. The address is a personal statement of faith. When Emerson promises that "if the single man plant himself indomitably on his instincts, and there abide, the huge world will come round to him," he is hoping to convince himself. Perhaps for this reason the essay has always had the capacity to kindle readers. And why not? Emerson intended the address to be incendiary; he openly acknowledges the common fire that warms us all. Explaining why the perpetual worship of even the very great is finally useless, Emerson says:

> It is one central fire, which, flaming now out of the lips of Etna, lightens the capes of Sicily, and, now out of the throat of Vesuvius, illuminates the towers and vineyards of Naples. It is one light which beams out of a thousand stars. It is one soul which animates all men.[13]

Emerson's audience on that last day of August was not the assembly of judges, professors, ministers, school-board members, and other persons who had been institutionalized. It was, as it would henceforward be, the single hearer, the solitary reader, the friend—unknown but always singular—who felt and still may feel personally addressed and shaken by the collar when encountering Emerson's startling observation that meek young persons "grow up in libraries, believing it their duty to accept the views which Cicero, which Locke, which Bacon have given, forgetful that Cicero, Locke and Bacon were only young men in libraries when they wrote those books."[14]

44. Casting Off

ON THE DAY AFTER THE PHI BETA KAPPA ADDRESS THE TRAN-scendental Club was due to meet at Emerson's house in Concord. The gathering had originally been composed of ministers and divinity students. Emerson had successfully urged the inclusion of Alcott and now he cooked up a scheme with Margaret Fuller to expand the group further. He invited Fuller, Elizabeth Hoar, and Sarah Ripley to the dinner at his house before the meeting. He couldn't promise anything, he told Fuller, "but you shall gentilize their dinner with Mrs. Ripley if I can get her, and what can you not mould them into in an hour!" The plan worked and henceforward there often were women present at the meetings of the club.[1]

Emerson now took a breather, doing no intellectual work for ten days. The weather was glorious. He enjoyed the "lukewarm milky dog-days of common village life," basking in the "warm and yellow light of these pearly days—corn, beans, and squashes ripening every hour, the garden, the field an Indian paradise." Carlyle sent him a copy of his new book, *The French Revolution*. Emerson was warm in his praise. He liked its unconventional side, its emphasis on ordinary people and events: "You have recognized the existence of other persons than officers and of other relations than civism." Best of all, he told Carlyle, "You have broken away from all books, and written a mind." What he praised in Carlyle was what he wanted for himself and had tried to do in the Phi Beta Kappa speech. "We were socially and intellectually moored to English thought," said James Russell Lowell, "till Emerson cut the cable and gave us a chance at the dangers and glories of blue water."[2]

Emerson had in mind both a book and another set of lectures. Lidian thought he inclined just now toward the book. Perhaps for financial reasons he determined to do the lectures first. He tried to find a subject "large enough to hold all I might be forced to put in," and he settled on "The Principles, the Means, and the End of Human Culture." His journals for October and November are correspondingly full and varied. He brooded on the problem of being versus seeming. Conversations with some of his

266

close women friends forced him to consider some of the implications of his ideas. "In company with a lady it sometimes seems a bitterness and unnecessary wound to insist, as I incline to, on this self-sufficiency of man." Too many courses of action, too many paths were, he saw, shut to women, "and the fine women I think of who have had genius and cultivation who have not been wives but muses have something tragic in their lot." He concluded that a woman was doing herself an injustice to compare herself to historical women. "It needs that she feel that a new woman has a new and yet inviolate problem to solve; perchance the happiest nature that yet has bloomed is hers; let it not be ruined beforehand on despair grounded on their failure."[3]

Emerson's senses were all alive and open this fall of 1837. As always, his sense of sight led the others. The world is full of what he calls "eyetraps." Any fact, such as a coat lacking the haunch button, "pricks attention" and draws our eye. He recommends taking a walk with a painter "and you shall see, for the first time, groups, colors, clouds and keepings." In the golden October season, which Thoreau once said would by itself make the reputation of any climate, Emerson thought out his reply to those who considered miracles to have ceased. "Have they indeed? When? They had not ceased this afternoon when I walked into the wood and got into bright miraculous sunshine in shelter from the roaring wind."[4]

Wildness attracted him now, as it always did when his senses were stirring and he felt wide awake. "As the contemporaries of Columbus hungered to see the wild man, so undoubtedly we should have the liveliest interest in a wild man, but men in society do not interest us because they are tame," he wrote in October. Emerson did not think of wildness as an extreme but as the norm. "Culture," he insisted, "is not the trimming and turfing of gardens, but the showing the true harmony of the unshorn landscape with horrid thickets and bold mountains and the balance of the land and sea."[5]

However serene and self-sure he may have seemed to others, Emerson's own feelings varied widely and changed quickly. He hated sickness, talk of sickness, and letters about sickness, and he almost frantically repeated his advice to himself to be self-reliant. At one moment he could be filled with chagrin, regret, a sense of loss, or a feeling that "after thirty a man wakes up sad every morning." At other times he lived in a euphoric trance, like a man in love. When he found himself wondering about animal magnetism one day, he caught himself up short, saying, "There is wonder enough in my thumbnail already." He thought everyone's life had something startling in it somewhere: "The hints we have, the dreams, the coincidences, do make each man stare once or twice in a lifetime." He knew also that falling in love is, even more than wildness, a departure from tameness and a subject of avid interest to others: "There walks not on this planet the man, sage or savage, who is passionately in love whose deportment and thoughts, could they be witnessed or reported, would not instantly engage our interest."[6]

In such moods, with such interests, it is little wonder that Emerson found his antipathy to the logic-chopping of formal theology growing. He felt a physical, almost a visceral revulsion from it: "I looked over the few books in the young clergyman's study yesterday till I shivered with cold. Priestley, Noyes, Rosenmuller, Joseph Allen . . . Schleusner, Norton." His own reading this fall was wildly eclectic. He read John Forster's *Life of John Pym* and the second volume of George Bancroft's *History of the United States*. His interest in Asia continued strong. He read Calidasa's *Meshaduta* and "a sketch of Lord Napier's negotiations with the authorities at Canton" in the *Asiatic Journal*. He also read John McClelland's *Some Inquiries in the Province of Kemaon,* a book about Indic geology. He reread old friends; there was Aeschylus, Ben Jonson, and Goethe. He admired Sir Humphry Davy's *Consolations of Travel* and took extensive notes on William Gardiner's *The Music of Nature.*[7]

While Emerson was working on his new lectures in November, he was interrupted by an extraordinary event, the violent death of Elijah Lovejoy in Alton, Illinois, at the hands of a mob. Emerson did not know Lovejoy, but the event shocked and stirred him as it did all abolitionists. Lovejoy, thirty-five, was a crusading abolitionist and Presbyterian minister who had already been driven out of St. Louis. At Alton, just north of East St. Louis, antiabolitionist mobs had thrown Lovejoy's press in the river three times. When a fourth arrived on a Mississippi steamboat, Lovejoy got the consent of the mayor and recruited about fifty men to help him take delivery and guard the new press in a stone warehouse near the river. The next night an opposing crowd came to seize the press. There was shooting on both sides and one of the attackers was killed. The mayor arrived, affirmed Lovejoy's right to protect his property, and tried unsuccessfully to send the mob home. A ladder was placed against the warehouse and a man with a torch climbed it and set fire to the wood shingle roof. Lovejoy came out and took aim at the man but was himself shot before he could fire.[8]

John Quincy Adams said Lovejoy's death "sent a shock as of any earth-quake throughout this continent." But the public response was complex. Many abolitionists, including William Lloyd Garrison, were firmly opposed to the use of force, both in principle and because they thought the cause of abolition would gain wider support if it disavowed insurrectionary violence. Garrison considered Lovejoy to have set a dangerous precedent. Newspapers all over the North treated the incident as a free-speech and freedom-of-the-press issue. Efforts were made to rent a hall for an "indignation meeting" in Boston, but abolition was still in such general disfavor that not until December 8 could a hall be found. Meanwhile, in Concord, which was considered a hotbed of abolitionist sentiment (though it was far from universal among Concordians), a meeting was got together in late November and Emerson was asked to address it.[9]

The talk has not survived, but from Emerson's journal outlines and notes we can get some sense of his argument. He was firmly antislavery and had been so for many years. "No man," he now wrote, "can hold property in man. . . . Reason is not a chattel; cannot be bought and sold; and every pretended traffic in such stock is invalid and criminal." Though he was firmly opposed to slavery, he still was not free of the casual racism of white society of the time. He now doubted, as he said, that "the African race have ever occupied or do promise ever to occupy any very high place in the human family." He was not yet ready to call himself an abolitionist, but his defense of the movement was strong: "The professed aim of the abolitionists is to awaken the conscience of the Northern States in the hope thereby to awaken the conscience of the Southern States: a hope just and sublime." But Emerson too emphasized the free-speech aspect of the case, saying, "Our great duty in this matter is to open our halls to the discussion of the question steadily day after day year after year," and he distanced himself from the abolitionist party by this language. After setting out the abolitionist plan he discussed "its aspect to us." The outline for this part of the talk emphasizes the freedom-of-speech issue, but it goes further, advocating political action. The abolitionist plan is, to "us," "a question for discussion" and "a question for action." For New England, specifically, he thought the importance of the discussion was to get people "by voting, to assert the slave's right."[10]

Emerson had been deeply involved in social and political matters for years. He served on the school committee, the cemetery committee, the library committee, and the Lyceum committee. On specific issues he wrote letters, collared friends, addressed meetings, and signed petitions. While he was not himself an organizer, he gave the abolitionist cause more than silent sympathy or money. He spoke out now, in 1837, as he would later, again and again. Behind the public support, his journals show him engaged in a long struggle between the logic of his belief that there is one mind common to all humans and the endemic racist condescension of white America toward black and Native American people.

Lidian Emerson was at this time ahead of her husband on the subject of abolition. She was ahead of him too in her lively, imaginative sympathy with the sufferings of the middle passage and other horrors of slavery. In early September 1837 Sarah and Angelina Grimke spent a week in Concord, dined and took tea with Lidian, and left her determined not to "turn away my attention from the abolition cause till I have found whether there is not something for me personally to do and bear to forward it."[11]

The Grimke sisters had also written manifestos in 1836, the year of Emerson's *Nature*. Angelina Grimke's *Appeal to the Christian Women of the South* and Sarah Grimke's *Epistle to the Clergy of the Southern States* as well as Angelina's later *Appeal to the Women of the Nominally Free States* made it clear that the North was no more innocent than the South, that "the women of the North were deeply involved in slavery by their prejudice against color, by their use of slave products, and by their support of the colonization [Liberia] movement." As the Grimke sisters got to Lidian, so she undoubtedly got to her husband. But he was speaking for himself when he concluded that "when we have settled the right and wrong of this question I think we have done all we can. A man can only extend his active attention to a certain finite amount of claims." This was an honest conclusion, even if it disappointed some. His active attention was just now committed to his lecture series on human culture.[12]

45. Human Culture

On December 3 little Waldo took his first steps by himself. He was thirteen months old. Three days later, on December 6, 1837, Emerson gave the first lecture of his new series. He spoke about it with a deprecating air; he told William his subject was "all divine and human matters and some others." In fact, however, the series he called "Human Culture" was, like the preceding one, carefully focused. The "Philosophy of History" series had begun with history and ended with the constitutive unit of history, the individual. The new series began with the individual and showed how each part of the individual human being provides us with the key, or even the gateway, to some larger, more general aspect of human life.

The opening lecture set up Emerson's general themes. The political note that later came out in *Representative Men* is already strong: "The modern mind teaches that the nation exists for the individual." But the subject of the series is not the individual and the state but self-cultivation. "His own culture—the unfolding of his nature, is the chief end of man." By culture, Emerson does not mean official culture—what the Germans call *Kultur*, of museums, theater, and symphony performances—but self-development, education, *Bildung*. As always, Emerson is the philosophical idealist, but now he is at pains to emphasize the practical side of idealism, which he pointedly defines not as the pursuit of the best but of the better: "That Better we call the Ideal. Ideal is not opposed to Real, but to Actual. The Ideal is the Real. The Actual is but the apparent and the temporary." He also makes it clear that he is very much interested in expanding the serious claims of subjectivity: "The obscure attractions which natural objects have for [each person] are only indications of the truth which appears at last, that the *laws of nature pre-existed in his mind*."[1]

These 1837 lectures present Emerson's phenomenology. "In the philosophical view of Human Culture, we look at all things in a new point of view from the popular one, viz. we consider mainly not the things but their effect on the beholder." The second lecture, called "Doctrine of the Hands," is similar to the "Commodity" chapter in *Nature,* showing how we are educated and formed by daily work and daily life. "It is by the properties of light and fire that all nations have described their idea of God. It is chiefly from the gardener's bulb that they have described the growth of the mind." Every trade has its discipline and its vocabulary. There is no knowledge that is useless. Every trade has something to teach. The carpenter lives by "the stern ethics which sparkle on his chisel edge."[2]

Lecture three, "The Head," is Emerson's first attempt at "a natural history of the intellect." He presents a sketch of the development of consciousness, which he puts in quasi-theological terms. Creation is the discovery that one exists. "As soon as the youth of the universe has felt and uttered the great fact of being ["I am"] he transfers this me from that which it really is, to the frontier region of effects in which he dwells, to his body and its appurtenances, to home and land." This is the cost of consciousness, this is the Fall.[3]

Lecture four, "The Eye and Ear," is about beauty; lecture five, "The Heart" or "The Affections," treats love, friendship, kindness, and courage. On the last of these Emerson now has a radical view, very much that of Krishna's advice to Arjuna in the Bhagavad Gita. "Courage," says Emerson,

> is grounded always on a belief in the identity of the nature of my enemy with my own [nature], that he with whom you contend is no more than you. If we believed in the existence of strict individuals, natures, that is not radically identical but unknown, unmeasurable, we should never dare to fight.

Lecture six treats intellectual integrity. Its main point is the Quaker one that the inner light or the still small voice is not whim or personal preference but a person's own and only window on the real light, the molten core, the one deep well of life.

> It is the character of all great and good action, speech, and thinking that it proceeds from Necessity; that the doer feels it must be. It is done by such relinquishment of caprice and self will, such abandonment to the promptings of nature and instinct, that the individual agent holds himself no wise accountable. He followed a thread of divine leading and the world is guarantee for his deed.

This sixth lecture is the best of the series. Parts of it ended up later in the essays "Spiritual Laws" and "Experience." It is full of bold connections. Is not our interest in genius an interest in what is wild and not tame, Emerson asks, and is not our interest in the wild an interest in what is real?[4]

After the seventh lecture, "Prudence," which is again, like "The Hands," a return to practical daily concerns, Emerson reached out to summarize the series in a pair of lectures called "Heroism" and "Holiness." When Emerson repeated this series of lectures, somewhat shortened, in Concord and in Framingham, he used "Heroism" as the concluding lecture, and he later printed it in his first book of essays. By *hero* Emerson did not mean warrior or strong man in the sense in which, say, Carlyle did. Heroism as Emerson understood it was a necessary quality of the self-reliant person: "The hero is a mind of such balance that no disturbance can shake his will, but pleasantly, and, as it were, merrily, he advances to his own music."[5]

Yet if Emerson gave heroism a subtle new emphasis, he did not completely discard the older view. He invoked Aunt Mary's advice to "always do what you are afraid to do." He knew that there is a ferocity in life that must be confronted; he instanced the lockjaw "that bends a man's head back to his heels" or the hydrophobia "that makes him bark at his wife and babes." Harder to overcome, in some ways, are the wearing effects of daily life. "Time," he said, "is slit and peddled into trifles and tatters. A door is to be painted; a lock to be repaired; a cord of wood is wanted; the house smokes; or I have a headache; then the tax . . . these eat up the hours." It is easy for Emerson to say loftily that "every heroic act measures itself by its contempt of some external good." It is by saying what heroism is not that Emerson gives vividness and energy to his characterization. "What shall it say, then, to the sugar-plums and cats-cradles, to the toilet, compliments, quarrels, cards, and custard which rack the wit of all human society?" He invokes Elijah Lovejoy, killed two and a half months earlier. Beneath the splendid, unexceptionable insistence that "the essence of greatness is the perception that virtue is enough" runs a subtheme of savagery in nature and in man. The essay expects violence, is prepared for it, and is, in an oblique way, a long-range forecast of civil war.[6]

But still Emerson keeps the individual, not the nation, in mind, and he ends the lecture series with the lecture "Holiness" and a summary lecture, much of which is now lost. "Holiness," first given on January 3, 1838, is a forecast of the "Divinity School Address" Emerson wrote and delivered later this year. The lecture describes the "moral sentiment" as a fundamental aspect of human nature, in religious and not just in philosophical terms. Somewhere between superstition and atheism, Emerson says, a person "begins to ask if . . . he shall not best attain the true mark in science and in life by a reliance on the Divine in himself." Emerson is not so much interested in a reasoned acceptance of religion as in conveying the felt experience of it. He rests his case by describing high, brief moments of sight. "The highest state of which we have any experience," he says, "is the act of adoration." When we have learned that the sources of nature are in our own souls, then we will see that "the world is the perennial miracle which the soul worketh," and we will understand that "there is no profane history, that all history is sacred."[7]

Realism as well as soaring exuberance characterizes these closing lectures. It is significant that the sequence of "Prudence," "Heroism," and "Holiness" would be replicated some years hence in Emerson's first book of essays with the sequence "Prudence," "Heroism," and "The Oversoul." This is the mature Emerson who knows that there are forces at work that can utterly and majestically defeat any individual effort. It is not imagination that commonly masks reality; it is routine. "Captain Franklin, after six months travelling on the ice to the North Pole, found himself two hundred miles south of the spot he had set out from. The ice had floated." But perhaps the sense of perfectly articulated aspiration that breathes through all these lectures is best conveyed in an image that came to Emerson one day in Concord when he saw a "fair girl . . . in town expressing so decided and proud a choice of influences, so careless of pleasing, so wilful and so lofty a will." It occurred to him that "so shall we be ennobled also" and he wanted to say to her: "Never strike sail to any. Come into port greatly, or sail with God the seas."[8]

46. The Peace Principle
and the Cherokee Trail of Tears

THE ANTISLAVERY MOVEMENT WAS NOT THE ONLY SOCIAL issue that made a successful claim on Emerson's time in 1837 and 1838. There was also the peace movement, long an issue with Quakers and now expanding under such names as "Non-resistance," "Christian non-resistance," and "non-violence." After Lovejoy's death, Garrison put out a new prospectus for *The Liberator* saying that in addition to supporting abolition the paper would now equally support nonresistance. Garrison arrived at pacifism by a curious route. Insurrection was wrong, he thought. If the slaves cannot justifiably use violence to free themselves, he argued, then no one in less difficult circumstances could properly use force either. Later, when significant numbers of abolitionists began to endorse the use of force, the peace movement broke away and formed a separate movement. Meanwhile, in March 1838, before the split, the American Peace Society sponsored a series of lectures in Boston, and on March 12, 1838, Emerson gave the seventh lecture, "The Peace Principle." The written version appeared later in his collected works as "War."

Emerson does not deal with current events in the lecture. He makes no reference to the Seminole War. He treats the subject in a philosophical or theoretical way. He must have startled his audience when he began not by attacking war but by praising it. The uses of war, he said, are to "educate the senses, call into action the will, and perfect the physical constitution." War is the "subject of all history" and the "principal employment of the most conspicuous men." War stands for—we might say it is a trope for—the "great and beneficent principle of self-help." "Nature implants with life the instinct of self-help, perpetual struggle to be, to resist opposition, to attain to freedom, to attain to mastery and the security of a permanently self-defended being."[1]

But the essay veers sharply as Emerson next insists that war reflects only the primitive and early part of human development: "The sympathy with war is a juvenile and temporary state." To thoughtful people of the present day, war "begins to look like an epidemic insanity." Emerson expects the future to bring an end to war and a new era of international law and cooperation to replace the era of nationalism and competition. Emerson looks forward to an international "congress of Nations" as a forum for settling disputes, and he challenges his audience to look on peace as an even more heroic endeavor than war. What he calls the peace principle is not to be manifested chiefly by organizing a society and passing resolutions. Nor will it be "carried into effect by fear." "The cause of peace is not the cause of cowardice," he says, it is a positive and greater principle than that of war. If war forms a person to a kind of self-dependence, peace forms him or her to a greater self-dependence. "If peace is to be maintained," he says, "it must be by brave men who have come up to the same height as the hero, namely the will to carry their life in their hand, and stake it at any instant for their principle, but who have gone one step beyond the hero, and will not seek another man's life." Peace, in short, can be maintained only by persons who have "attained such a perception of their own intrinsic worth that they do not think property or their own body a sufficient good to be saved by such dereliction of principle as treating a man like a sheep." As a statement of principle, the Quakers themselves could scarcely have done better. Garrison was delighted with the speech and henceforward considered Emerson "a man of the new age."[2]

In April 1838, about a month after Emerson's peace lecture, the last act of the tragic expulsion of the Cherokees from their homeland was beginning. On April 6, 1838, General Winfield Scott was put in charge of the Cherokee country, given reinforcements and orders to evict the Cherokees, by force, if necessary, and transport them to the west side of the Mississippi River. There was a good deal of opposition to the government policy. Meetings were called, one of them in Concord on April 22. Emerson was the first speaker, outlining the situation, reading the "appeal of the Cherokees," and voicing his own strong disapproval of the government's position.

The Cherokees had originally lived on about forty thousand square miles bounded on the north by the Ohio River and including most of what is now Kentucky and Tennessee along with parts of what are now Alabama, Georgia, North and South Carolina, Virginia, and West Virginia. Over time they had ceded lands to the United States government until they occupied about one-tenth the original area. The remaining land was located mostly in northwestern Georgia and northeastern Alabama and included bits of Tennessee and North Carolina. The Cherokees were no band of roaming savages surrounded by civilization. The Cherokee Nation was a complex, highly evolved civilization by any standard. It had a bicameral legislature, a principal chief who was popularly elected, and a national supreme court at the apex of a network of eight judicial districts. The Cherokee census of 1835 reported 16,532 Cherokees and 1,592 slaves of Cherokees. Leading Cherokees lived in showplace mansions. Joseph Vann had 110 slaves, George Waters 100, John Ross, the principal chief for almost forty years, had 19 slaves, his brother 41. They kept fine carriages, thoroughbred racehorses, immense libraries, and old silver. The children of well-to-do Cherokee families were educated at seminaries or academies in South Carolina, Tennessee, and Connecticut.[3]

Literacy was fairly high among the Cherokees. Not many spoke or read English, but over half could read and write using the Cherokee alphabet devised by the Cherokee scholar Sequoya in 1821. The nation had a press that turned out a newspaper, hymnbooks, and pamphlets in Cherokee. They were essentially an agricultural people, living by the plow, the spinning wheel, and the anvil. The inventory of 1825 shows 17,531 cattle, 7,653 horses, 47,732 swine, 752 looms, 2,486 spinning wheels, 72 wagons, 921 plows, 10 sawmills, 31 gristmills, 62 blacksmith shops, 8 cotton machines, and 12 schools.[4]

United States policy had long been to move all Indian tribes living east of the Mississippi to new lands on the west side of the river. Jackson's removal bill had been narrowly passed in 1830. In 1832 in a flurry of activity the government signed removal treaties with the Creeks on April 4, the Seminoles on May 9, the Appalachicolas on October 11, the Chickasaws on October 20, the Kickapoos on October 24, the Pottawattomies on October 26, the Shawnees, Delawares, Piankashaws, and Peorias on October 26, and the Weas and Senecas on October 29. The Cherokees, under Chief Ross, refused. They had made twenty-eight previous treaties, each one guaranteed in perpetuity. All twenty-eight had been broken. Jackson's men, working with Georgia politicians, found a minority faction of the Cherokees to sign a removal treaty. The faction included Major Ridge, his son John, and Elias Boudinot and his brother Stand Watie, later a Confederate brigadier general. The Ridge party reasoned that the nation would be forced to move eventually, so they signed a treaty at New Echota in March of 1835 ceding their eastern lands in return for five million dollars and land in the west. But the Ridge party was at most a few hundred people; the majority of the tribe, led by Ross, expressly repudiated the treaty. The protest was signed by 15,964 Cherokees.

The United States government knew perfectly well that the treaty was a fraud but went ahead with the plan for removal. Opposition was substantial, even impressive, and it had been building for years. Daniel Webster was against the plan, Chief Justice John Marshall of the U.S. Supreme Court had ruled in 1832 in favor of Cherokee sovereignty and against the claims of the State of Georgia. Marshall held that "the principle of Discovery by which a discoverer took possession of discovered territory in the name of his country, did not convey ownership nor impair the rights of the occupants to sell or not sell their land." What a discovering nation obtained was merely the "exclusive right of purchase." General Wool, in charge of all U.S. troops in the Cherokee Nation, was opposed to relocation. So was William Wirt, a great constitutional lawyer, former U.S. attorney general, and partner in a Baltimore law firm retained by Chief Ross. But the president, now Van Buren, was determined to proceed. He replaced General Wool with Scott and ordered him to proceed with the eviction of the Cherokees.[5]

The April meeting in Concord was part of the final wave of protest. Emerson did more than open the meeting and read the Cherokee appeal. He composed an open letter to President Van Buren which was printed in newspapers in Concord, Washington, and elsewhere. In this letter Emerson abandons his usual tone of high moral argument pitched to the solitary reader or hearer. The letter is angry, direct, outraged. He describes the "sham treaty" engineered by Ridge and Boudinot, whom he had earlier heard and admired when they were touring the country in 1831 to build support for the Cherokees. Emerson details the Cherokee Nation's rejection of the treaty and then cites the order fixing "a month from this day as the hour for this doleful removal." Emerson calls on Van Buren to stop it, protesting: "Such a dereliction of all faith and virtue, such a denial of justice, and such deafness to screams for mercy were never heard of in times of peace and in the dealing of a nation with its own allies and wards, since the earth was made."[6]

If all that the newspapers said was true, Emerson thundered, the country stood on the brink of a terrible crime, a "crime that really deprives us as well as the Cherokees of a country; for how can we call the conspiracy that should crush these poor Indians our government, or the land that was cursed by their parting and dying imprecations our country any more?" His journal records his bitter, heartsick feelings about the impending disaster. On April 26 he wrote, "Yesterday went the letter to Van Buren, a letter hated of me." Not that he had doubts about the matter. When first brought to his attention on April 19, the news served "to blacken my days and nights."

He had bad dreams. It was not the cause that bothered him but the way it had to be addressed. Time was short, what was needed was not light but action. Emerson was not a professional agitator like Garrison or Lovejoy. His work addressed the individual conscience. He disliked the threat-producing atmosphere of crisis. Worst of all, he was afraid it would be of no use. He called the letter a "deliverance that does not deliver the soul." "Why shriek?" he wrote in his journal. "Why strike ineffectual blows?" But much as he hated mass meetings and demagogic rhetorical appeals, he went through with them. "I stir in it for the sad reason that no other mortal will move and if I do not, why it is left undone. The amount of it, be sure, is merely a scream, but sometimes a scream is better than a thesis."[7]

General Scott began rounding up the Cherokees, forcing them into hastily constructed concentration camps, on May 23, right on schedule. Eleven months later the last contingent arrived in the west. Transport was inadequate, as was water, food, clothing, and shelter. Disease ran unchecked through the crowded stockades. The weather was hot, the roads bad. People died every day along the trail. It was a death march. The commissioner of Indian affairs wrote in his report: "Good feeling has been preserved, and we have quietly and gently transported 18,000 friends to the west bank of the Mississippi."[8]

47. Henry Thoreau

On May 25, 1838, Emerson turned thirty-five, the age that for centuries had been regarded as the halfway point of a full life. Elizabeth Hoar described to him one evening "the apathy from which she suffers." Emerson declared himself at a loss, "as I did not sufficiently understand the state of mind she paints." But if he seldom knew apathy, he was not free from personal regrets or from the entailed sadness of the Emerson family. After a "remembering talk" with Lidian in March he noted that he could "go back to no part of youth, no past relation, without shrinking." Thinking of Ellen, Edward, and Charles, he added that "infinite compunctions embitter each of those dear names." It is hard to know exactly what he had in mind. He wrote that he was remorseful that he might have shortened Ellen's already short life by offering her the "uneasy uncentered joy" of one who had been presented with an undeserved good instead of "the heart of a man humble and wise," and he reproached himself now, as he often did, with a "superficial coldness and prudence." He could write, surprisingly, that "after thirty a man wakes up sad every morning." To mark his midlife melancholy he composed a dirge in memory of his brothers, his "strong, star-bright companions." Many of the lines have a moving simplicity: "In the long sunny afternoon / The plain was full of ghosts." So much of Emerson's emotional life was spent in family relationships that he could end the poem saying to himself: "You cannot unlock your heart, / The key is gone with them." Still, there were counterbalancing joys. Little Waldo, now a year and a half old, built a tower in his father's study one day "of two spools, a card, an awl case, and a flour-box top." Lidian came in, saw it, and "then fell in such a fit of affection that she lay down by the structure and kissed it down." She then rushed off to the nursery to see "the lovely creature."[1]

An important new presence in Emerson's life this year was Henry Thoreau. They had become acquainted the previous year, in 1837, when Emerson was thirty-four and Thoreau a twenty-year-old senior at college. In April Thoreau read *Nature;* in June he read it again. That same month

Emerson was writing Harvard president Quincy to plead Thoreau's case for honors. Shortly after graduation late in summer of 1837, about the time he began a short-lived teaching job with the Concord public schools, Thoreau also began a journal, evidently at Emerson's urging. Emerson's first journal entry about Thoreau comes in February 1838. Emerson delighted in his young friend; he noted how "every thing that boy says makes merry with society." He approved of Thoreau's being, as he said, "spiced through with rebellion." The two of them went for a walk in late April to the Cliff, a high spot with a spectacular view over the valley of the Sudbury river: "Warm, pleasant, misty weather which the great mountain amphitheatre seemed to drink in with gladness. A crow's voice filled all the motes of air with sound."[2]

Emerson and Thoreau were alike in many ways. Thoreau at twenty was of medium height, with sloping shoulders. He moved with unusual energy. He walked with his eyes on the ground, watching for leaves, flowers, and arrowheads. Like Emerson, he had a large nose and his most remarkable feature was his eyes, which were large, deep-set, and alive with intelligence. The relations between the two men were close, changeable, and beset with difficulties. Thoreau was neither son nor brother but something of each. He came to have a special place in the Emerson family. He adored Lidian, writing her extravagant, moonstruck letters that look very much like love letters. Thoreau also loved the Emerson children and was loved in return by them. When Emerson was away for long trips Thoreau came to stay and help out. When Emerson's mother died, Thoreau was delegated to take charge of the feeble-minded Bulkeley at the funeral.

A visitor in 1852 named John Albee has left the fullest description of how Emerson and Thoreau got along together in public. Thoreau was already at Emerson's when Albee arrived. "He was much at home with Emerson: and as he remained through the afternoon and evening, and I left him still at the fire side, he appeared to me to belong in some way to the household." Emerson continually deferred to Thoreau, Albee recalled, "and seemed to anticipate his views, preparing himself obviously for a quiet laugh at Thoreau's negative and biting criticisms, especially in regard to education and educational institutions." Albee had come to find out how to get the best kind of education.

Emerson pleaded always for the college; said he himself had entered at fourteen. This aroused the wrath of Thoreau, who would not allow any good to the college course. And here it seemed to me Emerson said things on purpose to draw Thoreau's fire and to amuse himself. When the curriculum at Cambridge was alluded to, and Emerson casually remarked that most of the branches of learning were taught there, Thoreau seized one of his opportunities and replied "Yes indeed, all the branches and none of the roots." At this Emerson laughed heartily.

Albee noted that "in the evening Thoreau devoted himself wholly to the children and the parching of corn by the open fire."[3]

The Thoreau Emerson was seeing in the spring of 1838 was a young poet who was reading Goethe's *Italian Journey,* who found in Virgil confirmation of the idea that human nature is essentially the same in all times and places, and who was interested in crystal formation. He looked a little like Emerson and people would say later that he came to have some of Emerson's speech mannerisms. He was a disciple who was incapable of fawning or of uncritical admiration. He was brash, irreverent, rebellious, and amusing. But he was a disciple. Emerson once wrote: "Thoreau gives me, in flesh and blood and pertinaceous Saxon belief, my own ethics. He is far more real, and daily practically obeying them, than I; and fortifies my memory at all times with an affirmative experience which refuses to be set aside."[4]

The Emerson Thoreau came to know in 1838 was still a young man himself, very much involved in the natural world and fond of walking. "If I go into the forest, I find all new and undescribed," Emerson wrote.

> Nothing has been told me. The screaming of wild geese never heard; the thin note of the titmouse and his bold ignoring of the bystander; the fall of the flies that patter on the leaves like rain, the angry hiss of some bird that crepitated at me yesterday. The formation of turpentine and indeed any vegetation, any animation, any and all, are alike undescribed. Each man that goes into the wood seems to be the first man that ever went into a wood.

With keen senses and an even keener sense of the transformations of everyday life, Emerson had strange depths. "Come out of your warm angular house resounding with few voices into the chill grand instantaneous night," he wrote.

> In the instant you leave far behind all human relation, wife, mother and child, and live only with the savages—water, air, light, carbon,

lime and granite. . . . I become a moist cold element. Nature grows over me. Frogs pipe; waters far off tinkle; dry leaves hiss; grass bends and rustles; and I have died out of the human world and come to feel a strange, cold, aqueous terraqueous, aerial etherial sympathy and existence. I sow the sun and moon for seeds.[5]

Best of all, Emerson believed and could persuade others that the world was indeed new for each person.

You think in your idle hours that there is literature, history, science, behind you so accumulated as to exhaust thought and prescribe your own future . . . In your sane hour you shall see that not a line has yet been written; that for all the poetry that is in the world your first sensation on entering a wood or standing on the shore of a lake has not been chaunted yet. It remains for you; so does all thought, all objects, all life remain unwritten still.

Thoreau found in Emerson a person for whom ideas were as real as things. Thoreau once told a mutual friend that "he found in Emerson a world where truth existed with the same perfection as the objects he studied in external nature, his ideas real and exact as antennae or stamina."[6]

Thoreau got his start from Emerson but became his own man. They shared such things as their obvious interest in Concord, in nature, in walks, and in Walden Pond. They were both modern Stoics, interested in self-rule and autonomy. Both believed in the stability of human nature, in the essential equivalence of all times and places, and in Kantian rather than in Lockean theories of mind. Both believed in the process of individuation and in the authority of individual conscience. Emerson's ideas on poetry, history, self-reliance, and friendship show up in Thoreau's journals and many of Thoreau's subjects appear in Emerson's journals. It is sometimes impossible to say who took what from whom. Emerson was talking about "sauntering" just as he came to know Thoreau. Emerson owned land at Walden Pond, took almost daily walks there, and felt a sort of proprietary interest in the place. Shortly after Thoreau's "Ktaadn" was published, Emerson returned to the theme of wildness. Not long after the first version of *Walden* was written, Emerson was meditating on the flowing sand in the recently cut railroad embankment. Thoreau's late unfinished projects have analogies if not roots in Emerson. As early as 1835 Emerson thought he would write a "natural history of the woods around my shifting camp for every month of the year." Emerson also found (via George Fox) a powerful metaphor in the dispersion of seeds: "George Fox's chosen expression of the God manifest in the mind is the seed. He means the seed of which the Beauty of the world is the flower and goodness the fruit."[7]

But their many similar subjects could not obscure the fact that the temper and grain of their minds were very different. What in Emerson was an interest in originality—meaning the power to originate—was in Thoreau an emphasis on the wildness that is the fundamental building block of everything, including civilization. Emerson's inclination to pacifism, as seen in "War," is quite at odds with the combativeness and the military spirit of Thoreau's "The Service." Emerson was much less interested in the classics than Thoreau. Emerson was strongly affected by Plato, Marcus Aurelius, and Plutarch, but he was happy to use translations. Thoreau often read his classics in the original languages. Insisting on reading books in the original when translations were available seemed to Emerson perverse, like insisting on swimming across the Charles River instead of taking a bridge to Boston. Emerson was much less scholarly than Thoreau and not just in languages. Emerson came to detest conventional scholarship; he called it "books written by the dead for the dead." Thoreau is not only more classical and more scholarly but he is also more methodical, more interested in science, more committed to close observation. Emerson is more open emotionally, more social. He lived more in a world of strong friendships and was increasingly at the center of a large family that had many claims on him. He was more deeply grounded in Christian thought and feeling. Thoreau preferred Aristotle, Emerson Plato.

Emerson prepared the way for his own disappearance into his text. He wrote no memoir, he distrusted chronology, and he aimed for the timeless. Thoreau wrote about himself and his own excursions, and he almost always wrote narrative. Emerson did neither. His writings are distillations on different topics, deliberately detached from time and place, except through illustration, anecdote, imagery, and diction. Emerson was working for a completely different kind of expression than was Thoreau, though they had one important emphasis in common. Both were writing firsthand accounts of personal experience, not what they knew of the opinions of others, not commentary. Thoreau went in for narrative, Emerson for epiphanic aphorism. Emerson made his topical and abstract essays live by metaphor, anecdote, and other narrative devices. Thoreau gave his narratives depth and resonance by making them include and encapsulate moments of high insight. Both were only fair to middling as letter writers but splendid as journal writers. Both had very elaborate notebook systems for keeping track of material and for treasuring up their moments of illumination and insight. Both were capable of living with astonishing intensity for months at a stretch, though Emerson seems to have had more great moments, more experiences of pure "contact," to use Thoreau's word for his great moment on top of Mt. Katahdin.

Both Emerson and Thoreau used the figure of Apollo for personal symbolism. Both understood that the Apollonian spirit loves clarity and form and so is obliged to keep its distance, that it dislikes "whatever is too near, entanglement in things, the melting gaze, and equally, soulful merging, mystical inebriation and its ecstatic vision." The Apollonian spirit is "capable of looking on the world and existence as form, with a glance free alike of greed and of yearning for redemption." Thoreau thought of himself as the Apollo who was obliged to keep the sheep of King Admetis. Emerson was moved by the Apollo to whom Orestes comes pleading to be released from the Furies. Thoreau saw himself as superior brilliance forced for his sins to do unworthy labor. Emerson felt himself pursued by a steady stream of suppliants, each of whom wanted something from him, each one a further threat to his own hard-won self-possession. Both felt set apart from the ordinary, living for insight, aware always of the laws and forms that govern and drive process. Each was hungry for clarity, eager for form. And in the end both men were cursed by the resulting, inevitable, unbridgeable need to stand apart.[8]

48. Go Alone: Refuse the Great Models

IN FEBRUARY 1838 LIDIAN WENT TO PLYMOUTH—THE "OLD natal nest and eggshell of us all," her husband called it—for a two-week stay. Emerson wrote nearly every day to report Waldo's newest words, "Mamma gor," "beedy beedy," "din din." He was also involved in the complicated planning for an edition of Carlyle's essays. He wrote Margaret Fuller inviting her to Concord again. He was getting to know Henry Thoreau and Caroline Sturgis, the latter a close friend of Margaret Fuller's. Sturgis had wit and beauty, she was nineteen, and she wanted to be a poet. When she visited Concord with Fuller this summer Emerson was struck with her lively questions and independent spirit.[1]

Emerson was also laboring on Alcott's behalf again. Alcott had completely rewritten *Psyche,* and Emerson now read it through again twice. It was still impossible. Emerson wrote a gentle, brilliant critique of it, a critique that illuminates Emerson's own pursuit of a style. The main problems with Alcott's writing were with tone, style, point of view, and voice. The manuscript had too much prophetic pretension to be "a book of thought addressed to cultivated men." But it was too fanciful, playful, ambitious, and periphrastic to be "a gospel, a book of exhortation and popular devotion." Emerson recommended revision, "the most resolute compression almost to a numbering of the sentences 1,2,3,4 as they are things," and modification of personal passages "until they speak to the condition of all, or at least of a class. The author's Ego must be the human Ego, and not that of his name and town."[2]

William's business affairs were worse than ever. Emerson went to the banks, improved his knowledge of how the credit markets worked, and schemed to raise a few hundred more dollars by moving collateral around and by signing notes on other notes. At the same time he was writing and giving a long course of lectures in Boston and repeating many of them in Concord, Framingham, and Cambridge. On top of all this were the insistent protest meetings, letters to be written, and special talks to be given. There had been the antislavery talk the previous fall. Now there was the peace lecture and the Cherokee removal business. In late March, in between these last two talks, at the height of Emerson's immersion in the pressing worlds of family, friends, business, and politics, came an invitation to address the graduating seniors at the Harvard Divinity School. He accepted and began planning his address; it was yet another protest piece, this time against the failures of what he called "historical Christianity."[3]

The invitation was timely. On March 18 Emerson had noted in his journal that "there is no better subject for effective writing than the Clergy," and he proposed to himself, "I ought to sit and think and then write a discourse to the American clergy showing the ugliness and unprofitableness of theology and churches at this present day." Three days later, as if on cue, a committee of students, which included H. G. O. Blake, who later became a good friend of both Emerson and Thoreau, wrote to ask Emerson to speak. Emerson knew these young men. He had been to Cambridge to talk with them from time to time. Emerson found it difficult to refuse requests from earnest young people. The students were much interested in theism, a hot topic at least in part because the trial of Abner Kneeland for atheism was coming to a head in the Massachusetts courts.[4]

Kneeland was sixty-four, a former Universalist minister and biblical scholar. He was now a professed freethinker and had since 1831 been editor of the *Boston Investigator*. He had been under indictment in the Massachusetts courts since 1833. In June of 1838, a month before Emerson's "Divinity School Address," Kneeland began to serve a two-month jail term for blasphemy. Though Emerson did not find Kneeland's rough, Paine-like language congenial, he nevertheless signed the petition opposing Kneeland's sentence. Somewhere between the dogmatic slumbers of the orthodox and the "brutality of indiscriminate skepticism"—in Melville's nice phrase—there was room for a bold new statement of the power of live belief.[5]

Emerson went seriously to work. He thought that the time was ripe for a "natural history of reason"—an affirmation of Kantian and Coleridgean reason—which might offset the cold, dismissive rationalism of such books as Isaac Taylor's *Natural History of Enthusiasm* and the scornful Voltairean diatribes of Abner Kneeland. He knew the meaninglessness of the merely well-meant. He wrote a comic form letter of advice to himself in his journal: "Read and think. Study now and now garden. Go alone, then go abroad. Speculate awhile, then work in the field. Yours affectionately . . ." As he planned the talk, he felt again the gathering weight of the past: "A man now comes into the world a slave, saddled with twenty or forty centuries." The theological schools "pick out for emulation of the young men the Oberlins, the Wesleys, Dr. Lowell, and Dr. Ware. But with worst effect. All this excellence kills beforehand their own." He now knew, as he would later say, "the only path of escape known in all the worlds of God is performance." He was now reveling in the approach of summer, the "creative deluge of light and heat." When the thermometer hit ninety degrees Fahrenheit on June 10, he remarked, "Man in summer is man intensated."[6]

The address was given on July 15 to the tiny senior divinity class of six students together with their families, friends, and teachers. It was taken to be an attack on the Unitarian establishment—the denomination had been founded thirteen years earlier—and it was. Emerson was long past the point of giving lip service to even a liberal version of formal Christianity. Like Aunt Mary, whose letters he was reading again this spring, he wanted no more secondhand God, even on the best authority. He professed "reverence unfeigned" for Jesus but denied his perfection and made a little list of his defects: "I do not see in him the love of Natural Science: I see in him no kindness for Art; I see in him nothing of Socrates, of Laplace, of Shakespeare." He thought that the New Testament, while admirable, lacked epic integrity. Some years later when the publisher James Munroe asked him seriously what he believed of Jesus and prophets, Emerson gave the answer he had already reached in 1838:

> It seemed to me an impiety to be listening to one and another, when the pure Heaven was pouring itself into each of us, on the simple condition of obedience. To listen to any secondhand gospel is perdition of the first gospel. Jesus was Jesus because he refused to listen to another, and listened at home.[7]

Emerson's address was indeed an attack on formal historical Christianity, but the talk was even more dangerous than that, for Emerson proposed as a counterweight to formal religion not atheism but a personal religious consciousness. "I deny personality to God because it is too little not too much," he said. What Emerson produced for this occasion is a modern confession of faith, an announcement of the gospel according to the present moment, a belief not so much in pantheism as hypertheism, a declaration of the divinity of the human. Never content just to attack what he disapproved, Emerson puts the case for positive religious feeling.[8]

The opening sentence of the address ("In this refulgent summer, it has been a luxury to draw the breath of life") is not a casual allusion to the weather or a clearing of the throat. It is the central theological point of the talk. Divinity surrounds the living every day. The first part of the address is a description of the religious impulse in human beings. Emerson says that the "religious sentiment," the religious feeling, is universal and that it derives from or is awakened by the "moral sentiment," which is the even more fundamental perception that the world has an essential balance and wholeness. The feeling of veneration or reverence that arises from this perception is the basic building block of all religion. That feeling is an intuition, revealed to each person; it cannot be had at second hand.[9]

The divine nature is present in all persons. The mischief begins, says Emerson, when the divine nature is attributed to one or two persons, denied to all the rest, and "denied with fury." Jesus' life illustrates his central teaching, which is that the divine manifests itself in the human, much as the Hegelians say spirit manifests itself in matter. But when Jesus is separated from the human, mythologized and treated as a god, this crucial point is lost. Emerson's account emphasizes the irrationality and violence of theological dispute. He satirizes those who shout, "This was Jehovah come down out of heaven. I will kill you if you say he was a man." Like Bernard Shaw later, Emerson has come to distrust the person whose God is in heaven. The two great errors of historical Christianity are, says Emerson, the misunderstanding and mythologizing of Jesus and the fetishistic worship of the canonical Bible, a blind adoration driven by the assumption that revelation is over and miracles ceased, "as if God were dead." The first error removed divinity from us: "That which shows God in me, fortifies me. That which shows God out of me, makes me a wart and a wen." The second error denies us our own firsthand revelation and the miracle of every summer day.[10]

Emerson turns swiftly from the attack on organized Christianity back to the more difficult matter of what to do about it. He had recently had to endure the lifeless preaching of Concord's new assistant minister, Barzillai Frost. Frost's style was abstract and dull; his preaching amounted only to grinding "in the mill of a truism and nothing comes out but what was put in." Emerson was driven frantic as he sat and listened. Eventually he found himself watching the snow falling outside the church windows. The frost outside was more interesting than that inside. "The snowstorm was real," he noted, "the preacher merely spectral." There was no connection between Frost's abstractions and real life; there was nothing of Frost himself. "He had lived in vain," Emerson grumbled. "He had no word intimating that ever he had laughed or wept, was married or enamoured, had been cheated or voted for, or chagrined. If he had ever lived and acted we were none the wiser for it."[11]

Taking Frost as his example, though not by name, Emerson now argued that religion is not served by this sort of conventional preaching but only by living discourse. The preacher—if indeed even the name can still be endured—must declare the wonder of the world as revealed to him. In biblical terms Emerson insisted that each preacher must be a new prophet. In post-Kantian terms Emerson set out for his audience Schleiermacher's theology of communication. The soul has "a desire and need to impart to others the same knowledge and love" it has itself experienced, Emerson said. "If utterance is denied, the thought lies like a burden on the man." In the fourth chapter of his *Talks on Religion* Schleiermacher describes "the social element in religion." Religious man, he says, is impelled by his nature to speak. That same nature also makes him a hearer when a group is voluntarily gathered together. It is not gossip or common conversation Schleiermacher has in mind. Nor is solitary utterance sufficient: "He whose heart is over-flowing with emotion can open his heart only before an auditory." Fortunately this communication is something everyone, not just priests, can do. For Schleiermacher, as for Emerson now, the religious impulse in human nature demands not only expression but communication with others. Great truths demand great utterance. The highest truths need the highest utterance, which means poetry. The religious nature finds its full expression only in communication between people. When poetry (or preaching or lecturing) achieves this, it is doing its job. Only when live religious feeling has been driven out of a society must it take refuge under the dead letter of a canonical bible.[12]

"It is the office of a true teacher to show us that God is, not was; that he speaketh, not spake," said Emerson. Not that he seems to have held out much hope for the modern church: "I think no man can go with his thoughts about him into one of our churches, without feeling that what hold the public worship had on men is gone, or going." He quoted Lidian's saying "On Sundays, it seems wicked to go to church." He thought "the true Christianity—a faith like Christ's in the infinitude of man—is lost." He could see no point in founding a new church, a new "cultus." It was not this form or that to which he objected. It was not even the process of formalization that bothered him. The point was that each person had to follow the curve of his own faith into his own form of worship. If art is the path of the creator to his work, as Emerson would say in "The Poet," then religion is the path of the believer to his God. Emerson believed it even more important to recognize, as he now told his Divinity School audience, that "Faith makes us, not we it."[13]

Emerson rounded off his talk with the only advice possible, even if he held out little hope of its being possible within the forms of any organized religion. "Let me admonish you," he said, "to go alone; to refuse the good models, even those which are sacred to the imagination of men, and dare to love God without mediator or veil." He was asking a lot, even of the young and idealistic: "Yourself a newborn bard of the Holy Ghost, cast behind you all conformity, and acquaint men at first hand with Deity."[14]

The Divinity School address was Emerson's last face-off with formal or organized religion, though he remained a deeply religious man with a thoroughly spiritual view of human life and the world. Had he continued to contend with denominational Christianity, he might have written a book about representative religious thinkers. Ever since his days at divinity school, he had regarded the prophets as fellow writers. When he became interested in Paul or Jesus or John, or in later figures such as Luther, Fox, Fénelon, and Swedenborg, it was because he recognized something of himself in each. Each represented some aspect of *homo religiosus* writ large, but the point was that each new person had the same or similar qualities waiting for development and expression. "Why should not we also have a poetry and philosophy of insight and not of tradition," he had asked in *Nature*, "and a religion by revelation to us?" His conclusion then in 1836 still held now in 1838: "The sun shines today also. There is more wool and flax in the field. There are new lands, new men, new thoughts. Let us demand our own work and laws and worship."

Emerson's temper was never Calvinist. He does not belong in the Augustinian strain of religious feeling—confessional, guilt-driven, egocentric, legislative—so much as in the Erasmian, with its tolerance, its belief in free will, its reformist (rather than revolutionist) attitude, its refusal to put form first, its love of literature, its respect for learning, and its pragmatic emphasis on human and humane matters. The Erasmian-Arminian strain is older and stronger than Calvinism. Indeed Calvinism can be seen, as Hugh Trevor-Roper has argued, as a temporary aberration, a heresy, if you like, which caught on and has had an unusually long life in America. Just as Jonathan Edwards rethought Calvinism in the light of Newton and Locke, so Emerson rethought Erasmianism and Arminianism in the light of Kant, Schelling, and Lyell. Speaking of his differences with the whole range of what he called historical Christianity, from orthodox Calvinism to orthodox Unitarianism, Emerson considered himself to have accepted the truth of Christianity. Where he differed was in his conviction that Christianity was founded on human nature, not on the Bible. "They call it Christianity. I call it consciousness."[15]

These Flying Days

49. New Books, New Problems

A WEEK AFTER THE "DIVINITY SCHOOL ADDRESS" EMERSON traveled to Hanover, New Hampshire, to give a lecture on literary ethics at Dartmouth. The talk was the second of what was to become a long series of talks on the American scholar and on what he now called for the first time the American mind. Emerson noted again the failure of America to produce major imaginative work. He complained anew about "feudal straps and bandages." The scholar he called for at Dartmouth is very nearly the same person as the poet-prophet he had called for in Cambridge. He was more enthusiastic now about biography, which he called the "fortification of hope." Still, he continued to downplay individual idiosyncrasy and to place great emphasis on common humanity. "The impoverishing philosophy of ages has laid stress on the distinction of the individual, and not on the universal attributes of man," he said. He insisted that he was tasting "the self-same life, its sweetness and greatness, its pain, which I so admire in other men." He was eloquent on the dangers of a too private life: "The condition of our incarnation in a private self, seems to be a perpetual tendency to prefer the private law, to obey the private impulse, to the exclusion of the law of universal being."[1]

But he expected that the young writers of the coming generation would find a fresh field before them, a world in which "all literature is yet to be written." In language that forecasts Thoreau's work so strongly that one suspects the intellectual energy was already flowing both ways between the two men on their walks, Emerson says, "The man who stands on the sea-shore, or who rambles in the woods, seems to be the first man that ever stood on a shore, or entered a grove, his sensations and his world are so novel and strange." And that feeling of newness, he added, "that is morning." The Dartmouth talk was not all easy optimism. A new life has new conditions and new costs. One must go it alone and "embrace solitude as a bride" in order to become acquainted with one's own thoughts. Yet Emerson recommends no hermitage, no withdrawal from the world. "Not insulation of place, but independence of spirit is essential," he said. Emerson's urging the young men to hold on to their early visions and romantic expectations had an edge to it. He told them that abandoning those expectations meant death: "Then once more perish the buds of art, and poetry, and science, as they have died already in a thousand thousand men."[2]

Beside keeping up with new books, such as Furness's *Jesus and His Biographers,* a new translation of *The Institutes of Menu,* a volume of Tennyson, and rereading old favorites such as Herschel and Las Casas on Napoleon, Emerson was now reading out-of-the-way books that gave him new language, new vocabularies, and new ways of seeing. He thought James O'Connell's *A Residence of Eleven Years in New Holland and the Caroline Islands* one of the best books of recent years. In a lively, unpretentious, and engaging narrative, O'Connell recounts his travels on a ship carrying female convicts from England to Australia. His report of their street talk or "flash" is especially vivid. "The rum cove of this vile is up to lushing max" seems hopelessly impoverished when translated for us as "the king of this place drinks gin." One of O'Connell's characters says of a person in particularly filthy clothes: "his kelp [hat] and his tug [coat], stewed down, would fill the doctor's coppers [cooking kettles] with soup." Emerson loved the vigor of common speech and common objects, not just for themselves but because they directed him outward: "Is not the beauty that piques us in every object, in a straw, in an old nail, a cobblestone in the road, the announcement that always one road lies *out* into nature?"[3]

Emerson also now read an absorbing and imaginative book by William Gardiner called *The Music of Nature: or, an Attempt to Prove That What Is Passionate and Pleasing in the Art of Singing, Speaking, and Performing upon Musical Instruments, Is Derived from the Sounds of the Animated World.* The book is stuffed with arcane and delightful information. English half-crowns have the sound of high A, an octave above the tuning fork. "Gamblers can perceive the difference in the sound [of a coin] whether it falls on one side or the other." Emerson noted Gardiner's claim that "Beethoven in his Pastoral Symphony has given us the warm hum of the insects by the side of a babbling brook." Gardiner observes that children have voices, in proportion to their size, ten times louder than those of adults. He gives musical notations, some of them quite elaborate, for oxen, cows, calves, yelping curs, cross children, geese, and Newfoundland dogs. He notices that "dogs in a state of nature never bark, they simply whine, howl, and growl." He gives colors for the sounds made by common instruments (the trombone is deep red, the flute sky blue, the oboe yellow) and describes the moods of different keys (A is golden, warm, and sunny, E minor is persuasive, soft, and tender). Emerson took careful notes on Gardiner's argument that the shapes of many of our letters derive from the shape of the mouth in uttering them. "The two semicircles in the letter B represent the lips as closely pressed together in the act of forcing that explosive sound."[4]

A third book, which offered Emerson a fresh, detailed, and concrete way of seeing and appreciating painting, was Charles Bell's *Essays on the Anatomy of Expression in Painting* (1806). Bell was a distinguished anatomist who did important work in mapping the nervous system. This book, an early effort, undertakes to persuade the reader that anatomy is "the grammar of that language" in which the arts of design address us. Bell is concerned mostly with facial expression.

> The expression, attitudes, and movements of the human figure are the characters of this language, which is adapted to convey the effect of historical narration, as well as to show the working of human passion, and give the most striking and lively indication of intellectual power and energy.

Through careful description and numerous engraved plates, Bell tries explicitly to "lay a foundation for studying the influence of the mind upon the body." He is not much interested in anatomically inaccurate classical works. He is not at all interested in stillness and tranquillity. Instead, he discusses and illustrates the anatomical expression of madness, rage, jealousy, grief, anguish, weeping, laughter, and sorrow. Bell's interest in this book is not medical; he is concerned with expression in painting, and his point is that anatomy is "the true basis of the art of design" and its benefit is to bestow on the painter "a minuteness of observation."[5]

The effect of Emerson's reading of Bell is apparent in the comments he was now making in the summer of 1838 as he renewed his interest in art and architecture. He was reading Heeren and Belzoni on Egypt and was newly impressed with the great monuments of Karnak. He was reading Goethe's *Farbenlehre,* a remarkable book on how the human eye sees color. The *Farbenlehre* has been scorned as anti-Newtonian, but it has been of great interest to painters. Emerson's new interest in the subject was probably a result of the interest Margaret Fuller was now taking in Emerson's art education. Early in June she brought by a portfolio with work by Guercino and Lucas van Leyden and some of Piranesi's "Carceri Imaginari." Emerson was particularly affected by what he called Piranesi's "infernal architecture."[6]

Emerson had laid eyes on a vast amount of European art during his Italian trip. But it was Margaret Fuller and her friend Sam Ward the painter who now showed Emerson how really to see a work of art. It took him a long time, he said, to know what he thought of a picture, but he was gaining confidence. In the middle of August Fuller brought a portfolio of Ward's copies of works by Raphael, Thorwaldsen, and Guercino. One can feel the influence of Charles Bell on Emerson's eye when he says of Raphael's "Angel Driving Out Heliodorus" that "the crest of the angel's helmet is so remarkable, that, but for the extraordinary energy of the face, it would draw the eye too much." The study of painting sharpened Emerson's already keen visual sense. There seems to be an actual link between his visual acuity and increased articulation. He wrote to Fuller about "how entirely the value of facts is in the classification of the eye that sees them." He noted how the "power of the eye to charm down insanity or ferocity in beasts is a power behind the eye." And he described a September sunset now in fresh Luminist terms. He was standing on top of "Dr. Ripley's hill." "In the west, where the sun was sinking behind clouds, one pit of splendor lay as in a desert of space, a deposit of still light, not radiant. Then I beheld the river . . . journeying out of the grey past on into the green future." Despite the beauty of the September scene Emerson felt himself, he said, "a stranger in nature," tangential to its beauty. "And yet," he concludes this strangely powerful account, "the dictate of the hour is to forget all I have mislearned; to cease from man, and to cast myself again into the vast mould of nature."[7]

It would be a mistake to overread this passage, but Emerson was in fact deeply troubled by September 1838. His disquiet had to do with the reception of the address at the divinity school. On August 27, about five weeks after the talk, Andrews Norton published a violent attack on Emerson in a Boston newspaper. Norton accused "the new school in Literature and Religion" of a "restless craving for notoriety and excitement" and sneered that its origins could be attributed "to ill-understood notions obtained by blundering through the crabbed and disgusting obscurity of some of the worst German speculatists." He attacked Cousin, "that hyper-Germanized Englishman, Carlyle," and "the German pantheist Schleiermacher." Norton accused the transcendentalists of "great ignorance and incapacity for reasoning." He singled out Emerson, saying—accurately enough—that Emerson "professes to reject all belief in Christianity as revelation" and that "he makes a general attack upon the Clergy on the ground that they preach what he calls 'Historical Christianity.'" Norton considered Emerson's address an "incoherent rhapsody" and an "insult to religion." He accused Emerson of perpetrating "a great offense" and observed that "the highly respectable officers" of the university had heard the speech with disgust. Norton's own position was crystal clear: "There can be no intuition, no direct perception of the truths of Christianity." We must have Christianity through the Bible and its miracles, through the church and its authorities, or not at all.[8]

Norton was a dedicated teacher, a selfless and, some thought, a charming man. He knew exactly what was true and what false and he willingly took it on himself to decide what should and should not be said at Harvard or printed in Unitarian journals. He was as sure of himself as was Emerson and as little disposed to argue or plead. Norton's vehemence, his abusiveness, and his desire to conduct the dressing-down in as public a manner as possible were all provocative. Some of Emerson's friends, such as Parker and Peabody, rallied to his defense. Some, like Chandler Robbins, sat on the fence. There were attacks and counterattacks in the newspapers, the magazines, and the religious journals. The address—and Norton's spirited response— called forth far more public notice than anything Emerson had ever done or said. *Nature* received some eight notices by the end of 1839, the "American Scholar" address eleven. The "Divinity School Address" provoked thirty-six—not counting reprints—in a much shorter time. Emerson was accused of vagueness, inconsistency, impiety, nonsense, infidelity, blasphemy, and "foulest atheism." His friend and successor at Boston's Second Church, Chandler Robbins, now editor of the *Christian Register,* waffled helplessly, editorializing about Emerson as a good man and valuable friend despite his "unphilosophical and erroneous speculations." Henry Ware, Jr., delivered and published a response critical of Emerson's address but did it graciously and the two remained friends.[9]

Emerson was first dismayed and then appalled as the dispute rolled on. He himself took no further part in it. He refused to defend or explain himself. He was unaccustomed to the publicity and chagrined that he was unable to ignore it. The controversy drew him "out of equilibrium," he said, "putting me for a time in a false position to people." Being so conspicuous "spoils thought," he said. He was rueful at first and rather shocked by it all. But as the fuss continued—"the very mud boils," he wrote in late September—he became hurt and even bitter. In early September he wrote a comment that later found its way into "Self-Reliance." As soon as a person "has once spoken or acted with *éclat,* he is a committed man, watched by the sympathy or the hatred of hundreds." Support was in some ways as bad as attack. "I hate to be defended in a newspaper," he wrote in his journal. "As long as all that is said is said against me, I feel a certain sublime assurance of success, but as soon as honied words of praise are spoken for me, I feel as one that lies unprotected before his enemies." He even wrote Carlyle advising him not to think of an American lecture tour just now because the public was so stirred up against anyone associated with Emerson.[10]

Emerson was so shocked by the outcry that he overreacted. Neither Channing nor Walker, the senior intellectuals of Unitarianism, had sided with Norton. Indeed, Channing was known to be sympathetic to the new views. Norton made fresh enemies by his tone and methods. Norton saw himself as the hammer of orthodoxy, specially appointed to pulverize a new heresy. But he accomplished no such thing. Controversy over Emerson's "Divinity School Address" continued, as did controversies over miracles, for many years, and the liberals have never been clearly defeated. Indeed, the modern split between conservative and liberal Unitarians dates to this time. Meanwhile, when Emerson announced and began a new lecture series late in 1838, he was surprised to find that his audience had not dropped off as he feared. Still, the intemperate public fuss over the address left a lasting mark on Emerson. He felt—quite rightly—cut off from Harvard and from the Unitarian church. More important, he felt himself standing in a new relation to the public. He no longer spoke with ease about how the individual must sink his private self in the general human nature. His fundamental ideas had not changed, but now he was impressed with how society could whip an individual for not conforming. The difference between the strongly pro-community language of earlier lectures and the strident defense of individualism in "Self-Reliance" is the result of Emerson's first prolonged exposure to public censure.

50. Jones Very

MANY OF THE NEW PEOPLE IN EMERSON'S LIFE WERE NOW
associated with reform movements. He wrote approvingly to Aunt Mary
about the "variety and velocity" of the new movements: "War, Slavery,
Alcohol, Animal Food, Domestic Hired Service, Colleges, Creeds, and now
at last Money also, have their spirited and unweariable assailants, and must
pass out of use or must learn a law." He wrote to Fuller that he began to
be proud of his contemporaries even though the zealots, many of them
young men, could be tiresome on occasion. Their manners "are perchance
disagreeable; their whole being seems rough and unmelodious, but have a
little patience," Emerson told himself. He was thinking not so much of the
bright young people such as Henry Thoreau, Caroline Sturgis, or H. G. O.
Blake (who first came for a visit in November 1838) as of the single-issue
reformers who now began to flock to the Emerson home in Concord.
Elizabeth Hoar called them Waldo's menagerie. Lidian looked in the parlor
one day and got a "feeling of horror" from the circle of "men with long
beards, men with bare feet."[1]

There was William Henry Channing, a nephew of Dr. Channing, who
came in July 1838 and who was already on his way to becoming a critic of
transcendental individualism and a proponent of socialism. There was a
nameless health-food convert—possibly a disciple of Silvester Graham,
whom Emerson called the "prophet of bran-bread and pumpkins." Lidian
offered the man a cup of tea one day. "Tea! I!" he exclaimed. The next
minute Emerson undertook to help him to butter. "Butter! I!" he exclaimed
again. There was Edward Palmer, whose pamphlet "A Letter to Those Who
Think" attacked the use of money. Lidian observed that while Palmer's
principles prevented him from providing himself with a handkerchief, they
did not prevent his accepting one of Emerson's from her.[2]

The oddest, most compelling, and most trying of the new acquaintances
was Jones Very, who came in late October for a five-day visit. Very now took
himself—apparently literally—to be the "new born bard of the Holy Ghost"
Emerson had called for in his "Divinity School Address." Very had decided

that Emerson himself "was *prepared* but not yet quite arrived at the Father's mansion." He undertook to become Emerson's spiritual director and came to Concord to lay his ax at Emerson's root.[3]

Very was twenty-five, ten years younger than Emerson. He was now a student at Harvard Divinity School and until recently Greek tutor at Harvard. His "tall angular figure" moved with a "long, stately" stride. His manner was solemn and fervent. His skin was stretched tightly over his face, which was thin and smooth with a high forehead. He wore a large black hat, a black suit and frock coat, and he carried a black walking stick. A photograph shows his small rigid mouth set in a straight line, his eyes locked in a stare and fixed on a spot just past the viewer's left ear.[4]

Very came from Salem. His mother, Lydia Very, was a forceful, outspoken materialist, an atheist and a disciple of Frances Wright. Elizabeth Peabody, who was no social dainty, remarked on the vehemence of Lydia Very and called her "a tiger of a woman." Lydia Very did not believe in marriage as a legal arrangement but only as a moral one. Captain Jones Very, the boy's father, took him at age ten on a voyage to the North Sea, where he twice visited Kronborg Castle, the Elsinore of Hamlet. His biographer observes that not long before his own father's death, the eleven-year-old Jones Very "walked the parapet on which Hamlet was said to have seen the ghost of his father."[5]

Very entered Harvard in 1833, at age twenty, as a second-semester sophomore. He won the Bowdoin Prize twice and graduated second in his class in August 1836. In the fall he enrolled in the divinity school, serving at the same time as Greek tutor in the college. His religious feelings had deepened in college and by the fall of 1836 he was in a state of religious exaltation. He had read Emerson's *Nature,* taking it as a literal testament. Not only did he believe that God is the origin of the poet's inspiration, he also believed, as the Quietists do, that authentic religion requires a complete surrender of all conscious thought, a denial of all private will, so that one becomes a perfect vessel or conduit for the Holy Spirit. In other language Very was trying to abandon all reliance on the senses and the "understanding" in order to live exclusively by what the Kantians were calling pure reason. From Channing and from Emerson, Very learned to look for the God within.

In August of 1837 Very was riding a B & M train from Boston to Lowell when he was suddenly struck by a sense of terror at how fast he was moving through the countryside. The terror subsided when he realized that he habitually stood "amid movements far more worthy of alarm yet with perfect safety." Exalted now by the sense of being in God's care and by a simultaneous "sense of man's power and gifts," he felt himself "borne along by a divine engine and undertaking his life-journey." The trip "passed on for a while as without time." When he returned from the trip he felt purged, exhilarated, and encouraged in his seeking.[6]

In December 1837 Very gave a lecture in Salem entitled "Why There Cannot Be Another Epic Poem." His argument was that the old objective external world of action that created the epic had been succeeded by a Christian subjective inward world of tensions appropriate to the drama rather than to the epic. Elizabeth Peabody heard the lecture, was profoundly impressed, and wrote Emerson urging him to invite Very to Concord to lecture. Emerson responded, and on April 4 Very came to Concord and gave his lecture. Very's ramrod-straight inner-directedness and obvious brilliance cheered Emerson up just as he was meditating his forthcoming divinity school address. The example of Very was one reason why Emerson could so confidently call for a new "teacher" and could assure his audience that they were, each and all, newborn bards of the Holy Ghost.

Emerson saw Very again this spring of 1838. In May Very attended a meeting of the Transcendental Club at Stetson's house in Medford. There, in the old eighteenth-century parsonage at 141 High Street, with its massive twin chimneys, beneath the cavernous attic with its twelve-inch-square hand-hewn oak beams pegged together with long oak spikes, in the front parlor with its inside shutters and the "HL" hinges (standing, so I was told as a boy growing up in that house, for Holy Lord), the subject of the day was mysticism. Very took part vigorously. Emerson said little and was disappointed in himself.

Very heard Emerson's address to the graduating class in divinity in July 1838. His intensity and sense of mission seem to have been heightened by hearing the address his own example had helped to fire. Very now considered himself the spokesperson for the Holy Ghost. He did not share Emerson's view of the symbolic or representative nature of great teachers and prophets. Very still had one foot in the forms and mythology of historical Christianity. As a result he considered himself to be *literally* a vehicle for the Holy Ghost, to be the only such vehicle, and at the same time to be—personally—the second coming, the Messiah.

In class he cried out to his astonished undergraduate students, "Flee to the mountains, for the end of all things is at hand." The Harvard authorities could no more tolerate this sort of challenge than they could Emerson's, and Very was relieved of his duties as Greek tutor. As he departed for Salem, he sent to Emerson an essay on Shakespeare he had been working on since April. He also sent a letter in which he told Emerson flatly that "the hour is past of which I have often spoken to you and you hear not mine own words but the teachings of the Holy Spirit." Very's state of mind at this time may be seen in Elizabeth Peabody's account of what happened next.

> One morning [Sept. 16, 1838] I answered a ring at a door and Mr. Very walked in. He looked much flushed and his eyes very brilliant and unwinking. It struck me at once that there was something unnatural—and dangerous in his air—As soon as we were within the parlor door he laid his hand on my head—and said "I come to baptize you with the Holy Ghost and with fire"—and then he prayed. I cannot remember his words [she was remembering this in 1880] but they were thrilling—and as I stood under his hand, I trembled to the center.[7]

Very then made the tactical error of trying similarly to baptize several Salem ministers, including the Rev. Charles W. Upham, an avowed enemy of Emerson's, and these unconvertible gentlemen got Very committed to McLean's Asylum for a month. While at McLean's, Very wrote an essay on *Hamlet*, which is anything but insane. For Very the play is about "the great reality of a soul unsatisfied in its longings after immortality." Shakespeare "chains us with awe." "The great foreplane of adversity has been driven over [Hamlet] and his soul laid bare to the very foundation." Very observes that "Hamlet has been called mad, but as we think, Shakespeare thought more of his madness than he did of the wisdom of the rest of the play." With a powerful Melvillean lunge, Very goes for the heart of Hamlet's mystery,

> the mystery which hangs over our being, and which Shakespeare felt more strongly perhaps than any other of our race ever did, that enabled him to cast so deep the dark foundations of his supernatural beings, and give them all but that power over us which their actual visitation would have.[8]

Very left McLean's on October 17 and returned to Salem. Elizabeth Peabody was sympathetic but thought him "manifestly insane" as she wrote to Emerson to warn him that Very intended to visit Concord again. On

October 24 Very arrived at Emerson's door for a five-day visit. He was somewhat calmer now. Lidian later recalled that he had been "restored to a state of childlike simplicity. How he sat there with a piece of gingerbread in each hand so innocent and unconscious." He had come to show Emerson the Hamlet essay and to preside over the rebirth of his host and hostess. He declared the Second Coming to be at hand. Very's biographer describes Very's state of mind at this time:

> Christ is in every man, not only in Jones Very, and needs only to be set free in them, as He had already been set free in himself. The Second Advent consists in the freeing of Christ. Therefore the Second Advent could be brought about, even in Emerson—provided he agree to follow the directions of John the Baptist as he (Very) interpreted them.[9]

On the fifth day of his stay with the Emersons this unusual guest declared it a "day of hate," a day when "he discerns the bad element in every person he meets." He answered some comment of Lidian's with "Your thought speaks there and not your life." To Emerson he said, "You do not disobey because you do the wrong act, but you do the wrong act because you disobey." The tolerance of the Emersons seems amazing at this distance. But Very was witty and in a way charming, and he was completely—devastatingly—in earnest. Emerson recorded in his journal: "He felt it an honor, he said, to wash his face, being as it was the temple of the Spirit." Emerson could no longer reach or be reached by Very, but he was nevertheless impressed, and he had vastly more sympathy for Very than Cambridge had for Emerson. Emerson, to his credit, recognized and honored the religious visionary in Jones Very. "He is gone into the multitude as solitary as Jesus," said Emerson as Very left. "In dismissing him I seem to have discharged an arrow into the heart of society."[10]

Alcott—to whom Very wrote in December—answered the question of Very's sanity by saying, "He is insane with God—diswitted in the contemplation of the holiness of Divinity." William Ellery Channing put it in modern Coleridgean terms. He said Very had not lost his reason, "he has only lost his Senses." "Men in general," Channing went on, "have lost or never found this higher mind. *Their* insanity is profound, *his* is only superficial." Emerson agreed. He thought Very discredited himself "by a certain violence I may say of thought and speech." Nevertheless, he considered him "profoundly sane." "Talk with him a few hours," he wrote Fuller, "and you will think all insane but he. Monomania or mono sania he is a very remarkable person and though his mind is not in a natural and probably not in a permanent state, he is a treasure of a companion."[11]

About a month after his departure Very sent Emerson two poems he had just published, "Enoch" and "In Him We Live." Emerson's response was warm and immediate. Apparently he had not until now known the other chief thing about Jones Very, which is that he is, with Longfellow, the finest writer of sonnets in all of nineteenth-century American poetry. With immense formal control, Very creates strong, sweet devotional poetry recalling that of George Herbert. "Enoch" begins: "I looked to find a man who walked with God," and it rises skillfully to this close:

> For Him no heart-built temple open stood,
> The soul forgetful of her nobler birth
> Had hewn Him lofty shrines of stone and wood,
> And left unfinished and in ruins still
> The only temple he delights to fill.

When he learned that Very had two hundred such poems, Emerson urged him to bring out a book. Emerson himself undertook to select and edit the volume, which appeared in 1839. The book begins with Very's essays on epic poetry, Shakespeare, and Hamlet, followed by sixty-five poems. Shortly thereafter, the Holy Spirit departed from Very, no longer speaking through or even to him. The exalted state of 1837 and 1838 was too intense to be sustained, as Emerson foresaw. Very's vision clouded, his rapture drained away. His hunger had devoured him from inside. Like Faust with the Erd-Geist, he had been for a short time host to a power he could not in the end control. He lived on until 1880, a mild Unitarian minister. He held positions briefly in Eastport, Maine, and North Beverly, Massachusetts, but he was too shy to be a good preacher; from age forty-five he was virtually retired, living in his native town. He lived in the shadow of lost rapture, with only the memory of his almost saintlike radiance. A friend observed that "he moved in Salem like Dante among the Florentines: a man who had seen God."[12]

51. *The Attainable Self*

LIDIAN BROKE OUT INTO "WILD HOSPITALITY" IN NOVEMBER 1838 and gave two elaborate parties. She was pregnant again, often feeling sick, and there were times in December when she could eat nothing for days except rice water. Emerson was struggling to assemble a new series of lectures to be called "Human Life." He was worried that the public reaction against the "Divinity School Address" might have cost him his lecture audience. Nervously, he gave away more than his usual number of free tickets. He told his brother on November 16 that he was "floating, drifting far and wide in the sea of 'Human Life,' without port without chart and even with a glass so thick on the compass that it is only once in a while I can see sharply where it points."[1]

The metaphor was apt. Not only was he exploring new subjects, he was recharting old ones. He had, for example, come to a new understanding of the evolution of modern Protestantism. Instead of tracing the Protestant movement back to Luther and Calvin, he now saw that the real Reformation—or at least that part of it that interested him—stemmed from the English Commonwealth period and came not from the Puritans but from their enemies, the Quakers. He quotes an account from Sewel's *History of the Quakers:* "About this time there were abundance of people in England who having searched all sects could nowhere find satisfaction for their hungry souls. And these now understanding that God by his light was so near in their hearts began to take heed thereunto." Starting then with George Fox and the reassertion of the inner light, "the subsequent history of western Europe and of America has been the slow unfolding of the higher elements of the human nature."[2]

But the more Emerson emphasized the appeal to the light or spirit within the individual, the more he was appalled by the crippling burden of the past each individual is obliged to carry. "Man has encumbered himself with aged errors, with usages and ceremonies, with law, property, church, customs, and books till he is almost smothered under his own institutions," he told his large audience at the opening lecture in Boston on December 5, 1838.

The lecture, the "Doctrine of the Soul," contains much that Emerson later used in "The Oversoul." The taut spiritual tone of the lecture owes something to Emerson's recent encounter with Jones Very, though Emerson is at pains to provide a clear, unmystical definition of soul as "not an organ but [that] which animates and exercizes all the organs . . . not a faculty but a light . . . not the Intellect or a Will but the master of the Intellect and the Will."[3]

The lecture series as a whole shows Emerson's increasing preference for process over result. Indeed, now, for Emerson life *is* process. "The one thing of value in the world is the active soul," he would say, with the emphasis on the word "active." At the end of the first lecture he said flatly, "The presence of this element [soul] is constant creation." In the second lecture he defined growth as the constant effort of the soul to find outside itself that which is within, and he characterized culture as the "constant progress of the heart." Forgetting what he had told Alcott about verbs ending in *eth,* he said, "As a man thinketh, so is he: and as a man chooseth, so is he, and so is nature . . . A man is a method, a progressive arrangement; a selecting principle."[4]

Emerson's first lecture took up where his previous series had ended, with the decisive importance of the individual soul. The next lectures set out to apply the lesson to common aspects of life in a common-sense order. The second lecture considered home. "The instinct of the mind requires ever some thing permanent—permanent as itself—to be its outward object: to be its home." Eventually, he says, "the rest or home of the mind comes to be in the perceived order and perfection of nature as the great fact which all changes do publish." Just as he had argued for a dechronologized concept of history, so now in "Home," this subtle and neglected talk, he argues for a nongeographical sense of place: "Having found his home in that which affirms itself to be the cause of all . . . all places are alike to him for that which is with him constitutes place. He *is* place."[5]

The third lecture, "School," was another in the series of lectures on the American scholar which Emerson was to develop and refine over his entire working life. This lecture shows his current preoccupation with mind rather than nature; he lists the teachers or influences on us. First comes instinct. The "primary wisdom is intuition, whilst all subordinate teachings are tuitions." Next comes "condition," by which Emerson means nature and our situation in it: space, time, sun, moon, climate, want, sleep, dualism, growth, death. Then come, in order, persons, books, and facts. Though much of the lecture is about influences on the mind—a necessarily passive subject—its best parts, as usual, are about the activity of the mind.[6]

The lecture "Love" follows, half of which was still to be written the day before he was scheduled to deliver it, while Lidian, seven months' pregnant, was feeling unusually weak and low-spirited. He then gave the lecture "Genius," which was similarly unfocused but which sparkles with aphoristic bits: "Genius is the activity that repairs the decay of things." "To believe your own thought, that is genius." "Genius is always representative . . . the man of genius apprises us not of his wealth but of the commonwealth." This he followed by the lecture "Protest," which begins with a long, convincingly written account of the dissonances, the violations, the penalties, the losses, the "confessedly bad pass" of things as they are: "This old age; this ossification of this fat in the brain; this degeneracy; is the Fall of man." Protest is born as revolt against the standing order. "To every young man and young woman the world puts the same question, 'Wilt thou become one of us?' And to this question the soul in each one of them says heartily, 'no.'" "Protest" is a very Thoreauvian essay. Emerson was already calling him "my protester" in letters, and the lecture recounts incidents from their walks. "I must not get over the fence? But to the building of that fence, I was no party. Suppose some great proprietor, before I was born, had bought up the whole globe. So had I been hustled out of nature."[7]

"He has seen but half the universe who never has been shown the House of Pain," Emerson begins his lecture on "Tragedy." "No theory of life can have any solidity which leaves out of account the value of Vice, Pain, Disease, Poverty, Insecurity, Disunion . . . Fear, and Death." In his lectures "Tragedy" and "Comedy," Emerson is not interested in literary forms so much as in the forces and qualities that shape lives. Emerson turns first to what he calls the "terrible idea that lies at the foundation of the old Greek Tragedy," namely, the

> belief in Fate or Destiny; that the order of nature and events is constrained by a law not adapted to man nor man to that, but which holds on its way to the end, blessing him if his wishes chance to lie in the same course—crushing him if his wishes lie contrary to it—and careless whether it cheers or crushes him.

After reviewing the demoralizing effects of poverty, inequality ("the radical tragedy of nature seems to be the distinction of more and less"), disease, and insecurity, Emerson settles toward the center of the subject, toward "the proper tragic element, which is terror." His interest is not so much in the usual occasions for terror, such as a storm or the sight of a mountain lion raking open a deer, as in those people "who move the profoundest pity," who are terrorized by life, by the "power of the imagination to dislocate things." Thinking perhaps of Charles, Emerson says, "There are people who have an appetite for grief . . . there are natures so doomed that no prosperity can soothe the ragged and dishevelled desolation. They mishear; and misbehold; they suspect; and dread." Although tragedy was not one of Emerson's more congenial topics—as his son and editor later noted—the lecture on tragedy is far better than that on comedy, which unpersuasively develops the truism that "a perception of the comic seems to be a balance wheel in the metaphysical structure of man."[8]

Emerson originally planned to conclude the series with two lectures, one on "the limitations of human activity by the laws of the world," the other on the resources, tendencies, and prospects of human activity. But poor health, including a prolonged bout of insomnia, forced him to cut the series short, finishing with the lectures "Duty" and "Demonology." In effect "Duty" is the conclusion and "Demonology" is a lecture-length footnote. "Demonology is the shadow of theology," says Emerson. He defends the subject, to a point, on the same grounds Goethe used to defend astrology, that it is an uninformed premonition of a greater order in nature than is now apparent. But Emerson is most concerned to warn against the invisible world, which he does best when he notes how "this obscure class of facts has great interest for some minds. They run eagerly into the twilight and cry 'there's more than is dreamed of in your philosophy.'" "All nature is rich," he concludes, but demon lore is "her least valuable and productive part."[9]

Many passages from "Duty" ended up later in "Compensation," in "Spiritual Laws," and in "Self-Reliance." Against the gigantic facts and forces of history, historical religion, and social pressure, against "creeds and classifications that are thrust on the soul from Botany to Calvinism," and against the weight of the past, of the tragic, and of the demonic, Emerson asserts the essential adequacy of the individual, the possibility of action, and the accusing sufficiency of every day. He complains once more that we lack faith to utter things directly, and that we instead "wrench to present ends the old Hebrew language and borrow of David, Jeremiah and Paul." In words that will echo in the writings of Thoreau, Whitman, and Dickinson, Emerson now insists that "the primary word will be that now spoken." New people need new scriptures. As we grow up we leave behind the words we have learned because "we can use words as good when occasion comes." Once more Emerson comes back to his own enterprise, to the work of the writer in the present age, to the perception that "utterance is place enough" and to the importance of adequate primary expression for the project that is closest to each young or still-growing person in his audience, that is, the drive to reach his or her own "unattained but attainable self."[10]

52. Home and Family

By late February 1839 Lidian had put "every inch of her house and all her possessions in absolute perfect order." February 23 was a mild winter day and Lidian used it to go out and clean up the barn. At ten o'clock that evening she announced that "the baby had sent compliments." At six the next morning the baby was born. Lidian said firmly to her husband, "Her name is Ellen." As Ellen later told the story, Lidian had planned for some time to present Emerson with another Ellen. Lidian knew it was impossible to compete with the memory of Ellen Tucker. Lidian had even had a dream in which she and Emerson were together in heaven when Ellen came up. Lidian had bowed out, leaving Emerson with his first wife. If she did not feel that she was everything Emerson wanted, perhaps she could provide what he wanted in this way. Emerson was moved by Lidian's magnanimity. As Ellen Tucker had become Emerson's Beatrice, so his blessing on the newborn Ellen has a Dantean grace. In his journal he wrote: "I can scarce ask more for thee, my babe, than that name implies. Be that vision and remain with us and after us." To Lidian's sister he wrote the news, ending, "Fair fall the name and every beautiful vision it recalls on this new dreamer of the Dream of Human Life."[1]

Lidian made numerous friends among the many visitors to Concord. She was much taken with Jones Very. She also became a close friend of Alcott's and of Margaret Fuller's. She sometimes got up while it was still dark, took an ice-cold bath, and caught the early coach to Boston in order to attend one of Fuller's celebrated "Conversations." She was horrified and amused by the flock of high-minded reformers and talkers which now fluttered around Emerson during the "transcendental times," and she satirized them all in a short piece called the "Transcendental Bible." Here is Lidian's whole duty of man for these new aspirants to moral perfection:

Never hint at a providence, Particular or Universal . . .
Never speak of sin. It is of no consequence to "The Being" whether *you* are
　　good or bad.

Never confess a fault. You should not have committed it and who cares
    whether you are sorry?
Never speak of Happiness as the consequence of Holiness . . .
Never speak of the hope of immortality. What do you know about it? . . .
Never speak of affliction being sent and sent in kindness; that is an old wives'
    fable.

Under "Duty to your Neighbor" Lidian listed the following transcendental commandments:

Loathe and shun the sick. They are in bad taste and may untune us for
    writing the poem floating through our mind.
Scorn the infirm of character and omit no opportunity of insulting and
    exposing them.
Despise the unintellectual and make them feel that you do by not noticing
    their remark.
Abhor those who commit certain crimes because they indicate stupidity . . .
Justify those who commit certain other crimes. Their commission is con-
    sistent with the possession of intellect.

The whole piece runs to less than two printed pages. Emerson relished it,
called it "the Queen's Bible," and laughed all the way through when it was
read in the family.[2]

    Theirs was a spirited household. Lidian told her husband "that when she
gives any new direction in the kitchen she feels like a boy who throws a stone
and runs." One visitor recorded that Emerson would come to the back stairs
and holler out, "The dinner waits, O Queen!" and Lidian would answer,
"One moment, O King, and I will come." Lidian was a meticulous, anxious
housekeeper. She took her cares to bed and beyond. She once dreamed that
she had died and was in her coffin in the parlor. The funeral hour approached; the room needed tidying up and the housemaids were leaning on
their brooms and talking. Since no one else seemed capable of action, Lidian
finally sat up in the coffin and took charge. One of Lidian's campaigns was
for fresh air. Not only windows but chamber doors and even outside doors
were flung open at night even in winter. Lidian exulted in the health she
was bringing her family. Emerson hated the cold. Lidian loved inventions
and by 1844 or 1845 had installed the new air-tight stoves in every room
in the house. Emerson was then, according to his daughter, comfortable in
winter for the first time in his life. But it took repeated visits by Uncle

William to change Lidian's ways. William would begin his visits by marching through the house shutting outside doors before taking off his hat. Ellen recalled that her mother's hands were "so hot that she left a door handle warm just by turning it."[3]

Emerson's study was on the ground floor in the front room, just to the right of the front door. One wall was solid books. The others were covered with pictures. In the center of the room was his writing table; in later years it was a round table, four feet in diameter. Here Emerson sat in his rocker, the chair in which, as his daughter says, "he really spent his whole indoor life." Those who saw him only on the lecture platform did not guess that he could be either physically restless or extremely relaxed, but Walt Whitman once watched Emerson in a room full of people and observed how his legs were all braided up under his chair, and Henry Longfellow found him one day on a Boston wharf, waiting for the Portland steamer, dozing inside a coil of rope with his hat pulled over his ears.[4]

Waldo was two and a half when Ellen, the "February Flower," was born. Emerson described the boy as "handsome as Walden Pond at sunrise." He was learning to talk: "little flower" came out "liddle powup." His own name came out "Waddow." He slept on a trundle bed in the same room with his father and mother. In the fall, when he was three, watching Emerson dig potatoes with a less than perfect attitude, Waldo said, "I wish you would not dig your leg." He had the pure grammar of the preschooler. The past tense of bite was, naturally, bited. He had his share of the legal genius of childhood. When he was almost five he was asked once to account for his sister Ellen's sudden loud cries. He replied that Ellen "put her foot into his sand and got pushed." The children had a dog named Bingo and a large rocking horse with long runners and stirrups called Diamond, a lovely detailed muscular carving with legs extended in a gallop. Lidian had bought it in Woods Hole one day thinking to use it for her own exercise.[5]

Emerson liked to have the children sit on his knee. Ellen used to climb up and then ask questions. "I remember not only the immense pleasure I was having . . . but the standing off, so to speak, in my mind to consider it and to think what a full and fit use of a father and his study it was." The children helped him with garden chores. Emerson had an erratic and clumsy passion for trees. He planted shade trees and ornamentals. Most of all, he loved fruit trees. He planted apples and pears of many varieties, keeping a book to record their progress. Gardening touched an exotic chord in his romantic nature. "Plant the Banian," he once wrote, "the Sandal-tree, the

Lotus, the Upas, Ebony, Century Aloes, the Soma of the Vedas, Asclepius, Viminalis, the Mandrake and Papyrus, Dittany, Asphodel, Nepenthe, Haemony, Moly, Spikenard, Amonium." But he never had much luck growing things. One visitor recalled that if Emerson planted corn it was sure to come up tulips. A committee of the Massachusetts Horticultural Society made a special trip to the Emerson place to investigate how Emerson managed to get such poor fruit from such excellent stock.[6]

Most of all, Ellen later remembered the walks with her father:

> Whenever we walked with him, he told us the name of every flower and showed us how many pine-needles in each sheath the two kinds of pines had, and how the lichens grew thickest on the north side of every tree, how the ferns came up crozier-shaped, and how their seeds were on their leaves.

He would also show them

> how pretty the milk-weed seeds were with the silver fish inside, and how the goldfinches surrounded the thistles. He told us every time what bird it was that was singing . . . and when the brown thrasher sang he said the Indian came one day in old times and said that bird had said Indian Indian Go White Man, white man give corn, beer, beer, beer, beer.

He pointed out the red cup-moss, loosestrife, and goldenrod, and he liked the name Lespedeza so well he said it over and over. He recited poetry too on his walks with the children. He taught them Latin and Greek. He also taught them that life was exhilarating.

> We all remember his taking us up on the hills on the other side of the road and running down the back of them with us. . . . When we ran down the hills with him it was a fearful delight; it seemed as if we shouldn't be able to keep our feet, but we always did, and the speed was something glorious.[7]

Emerson's friendship with Margaret Fuller warmed rapidly in early 1839. She had been translating some of Goethe's poems—notably "Prometheus"—and was bringing out an American translation of Eckermann's *Conversations with Goethe*. She sent Emerson a mischievously curt one-page summary of Alcott's ideas. She was teaching school in Providence, Rhode

Island, when her father died, and she began to plan another move, possibly, she thought, to Concord. Emerson's correspondence with Carlyle began to expand dramatically this year also. Emerson had been minding Carlyle's American publishing affairs for several years and now was engaged in editing a four-volume edition of his *Miscellaneous Essays.* As Carlyle's American ventures prospered and Emerson began to send substantial earnings to Carlyle, the latter's somewhat condescending tone changed abruptly. For the next few years it would be Carlyle who took the initiative, writing so frequently that letters kept crossing in the mail. Emerson began to daydream about assembling "my college" in Concord. He would have "Allston, Greenough, Bryant, Irving, Webster, [and] Alcott summoned for its domestic professors" while from abroad he would invite Carlyle, Hallam, and Campbell. What he wanted, he said, was not schoolteaching but "living learning."[8]

His own learning was winding through several new paths during the first four months of 1839. He read Augustine's *Confessions,* Landor's *Pericles and Aspasia,* and Sterling's *Onyx Ring.* He made a first try at Dante's *La vita nuova.* In Plutarch's essay on Socrates' daemon he recognized a Greek precursor of the Quaker's inner light. He admired the stern Saxon language and manners of Fletcher's *Bonduca,* noting that Fletcher fell short only of "Shakespeare's *dire* style" (as in the scene between Hamlet and his mother). He read Roger's *Italy,* with its many illustrations by J. M. W. Turner. It was the book that Ruskin said determined the course of his life. Emerson did not have Ruskin as a guide, and he missed the power of the Turners, preferring the drawings of Salvatore Rosa.

Perhaps the most interesting book Emerson read in early 1839 is William L. Stone's *Life of Joseph Brant-Thayendanegea,* a two-volume biography in nine hundred closely printed pages. This is the masterpiece of a journalist who wrote on many subjects but who spent years in careful research and painstaking documentation for his life of the principal war-chief of the Five Nations and ally of the English during the American Revolution. What is remarkable about Stone's book is its stance. Completely devoid of "savagism," the condescending praise of the noble savage, appropriately self-conscious about who is writing the history of the Indian, and aware also of how hitherto "the white historian has drawn them with the characteristics of demons," Stone avoids generalities and stereotypes. He gives us instead a detailed, sober, documented biography. He treats Brant as a major figure in his own right, as a Napoleon or Washington. Stone takes great care to investigate all claims, especially those of Indian "atrocities." Not long after reading this impressive biography Emerson wrote the startling sentence that later was pulled into the essay "History": "There is no history, only biography."[9]

Emerson would go even further in his repudiation of conventional history, to a belief that the great turning points in a life are not events but moments of illumination. In mid-May he wrote that "the epochs of our life are not in the visible facts of our choice of a calling; our marriage, our acquisition of an office and the like, but . . . in a thought which reverses our entire manner of life." He was himself growing—and he was aware of it—and his life was now marked by frequent moments of thought that swept sudden shafts of light backward and forward. He was conscious that every day saw the unlocking of "new magazines of power and enjoyment." Never had his rock-bottom conviction of identity, of the "all-in-each" principle, been clearer or stronger. In mid-April he wrote:

> I believe in the omni-presence; that is; that the all is in each particle; that entire Nature reappears in every leaf and moss. I believe in Eternity—that is that I can find Greece and Palestine and Italy and England and the Islands—the genius and creative principle of each and all eras in my own mind.[10]

53. Writing Essays

In July 1839 Emerson was putting together a selection of Jones Very's poems for a volume. "I have selected sixty-six that really possess rare merit," he told Fuller. At the end of the month Henry Thoreau showed Emerson his poem "Sympathy" ("Lately alas I knew a gentle boy . . .") and Emerson responded with the generosity of spirit that drew so many young people to him. In his journal Emerson called Thoreau's poetry "the purest strain and the loftiest, I think, that has yet pealed from this unpoetic American forest." Later this year Emerson was introduced to the manuscript poetry of Ellery Channing. Here he was more guarded. He wrote Samuel Ward that Channing "goes to the very end of the poetic license, and defies a little too disdainfully his dictionary and logic." He conceded that "his lines betray a highly poetical temperament," but, as he grumbled to himself, "I do not wish to read the verses of a poetic mind, but only of a poet. I do not wish to be shown early poems."[1]

Emerson's own poetry was not going well. "I pine to write verses and cannot," he told Fuller. But this inability did not prevent him from thinking about poetry. His notes on a walk with Caroline Sturgis catch very well the associative, connective way his mind worked on the subject of poetry. He noticed

> the iteration which delights us in so many parts of nature, as the reflection of the shore and the trees in water; in architecture, in the repetition of posts in a fence, or windows or doors or rosettes in the wall, or still finer the pillars of a colonnade—in poetry rhymes and still better the iteration of the sense as in Milton's "Though fallen on evil days / On evil days though fallen and evil tongues."

What he himself wanted was "not tinkling rhyme but grand Pindaric strokes as firm as the tread of a horse. . . . I wish to write such rhymes as shall not suggest a restraint but contrariwise the wildest freedom." The only poem he wrote this year, 1839, was "The Problem," which suggests again his old impatience with forms and roles. "I like a church, I like a cowl; / I love a prophet of the soul / . . . Yet not for all his faith can see / Would I that cowled churchman be." What he wants is not just poems but contact with the original force from which poems come. "The burdens of the Bible old; / The litanies of Nations come, / Like the volcano's tongue of flame, / Up from the burning core below."[2]

His daily energies were now mostly directed to prose, some of which was not even his own. In 1837 he had "contracted for, financed, advertised, promoted and reviewed" an American edition of Carlyle's *French Revolution*. The project had been so successful that another much larger one was undertaken, a four-volume collection of Carlyle's early magazine pieces. Emerson made the selection, worked with the publishers, advanced hundreds of dollars to cover the cost of paper, printing, and binding, arranged for proofing, and sent agonizingly detailed accountings to Carlyle. Emerson kept track of every penny and every free copy; he oversaw type size, format, binding colors, distribution, advertising, author's copies, and postage. Emerson was committing an amazing act of friendship, and it must have given him pause to see the four substantial volumes of Carlyle's *Miscellaneous Essays* (to say nothing of *The French Revolution, Sartor Resartus, The Life of Schiller,* and the translation of *Wilhelm Meister*) alongside his own meager published output, which consisted of *Nature,* a pamphlet-sized book that was shorter than John Sterling's current article on Carlyle in the *Westminster Review,* and two even smaller pamphlets, the "American Scholar" and the "Divinity School Address." Emerson had published less than half a volume, all told, even if we include the address at Concord's bicentennial and a couple of lectures printed in the *North American Review,* which Emerson was by no means willing to do. True, Carlyle was eight years older, but the contrast was still humbling.[3]

Of course, Emerson had mountains of material. He had the equivalent of six volumes of sermons and lectures and he had filled dozens of notebook journals. He wrote easily, much faster than his ink could dry. He was just now trying the new steel pens. When it came to publishing, though, he agonized, revised endlessly, tinkered with words and sentences. He would spend months on an essay. Later on it would take him years to get together a book, and the gaps between books got longer and longer. But now, in the late spring and summer of 1839, he went to work in earnest on his long planned book of essays. He had wanted for years to write essays that could stand comparison with Montaigne or Bacon on topics of general human interest. The scope of his ambition is revealed in a letter this year to Alcott in which Emerson says he is at work on what he hopes will be "a shapely book of Genesis."[4]

In preparing the book Emerson now discarded the various schemes and outlines he had adopted for his earlier lecture series. He also refused to take the easy path of selecting some of his better lectures and working them up. He reached instead for the large diachronic themes that were woven through dozens of lectures and sermons, themes that in some cases went back to his schoolteaching days. This was a new enterprise and called for a whole new resurvey of his available materials and a new way of organizing those materials.

When Emerson had started keeping journals many years before, he had tried to be systematic:

> I fancied that by keeping a manuscript journal by me, over whose pages I wrote a list of the great topics of human study, as, Religion, Poetry, Politics, Love, Etc., in the course of a few years I should be able to complete a sort of encyclopedia containing the net value of all the definitions at which the world had yet arrived.

Finding that this plan did not work, he shifted to another, whereby he used the journals to record his thoughts and impressions as they first struck him, and he assigned the thoughts to categories later on. He was intrigued to read that "Sheridan made a good deal of experimental writing with a view to take what might fall, if any wit should transpire in all the waste pages." As a result, Emerson told Carlyle, "my journals, which I dot here at home day by day, are full of disjointed dreams, audacities, unsystematic, irresponsible lampoons of systems, and all manner of rambling reveries, the poor chupes and berries I find in my basket after endless and aimless rambles in woods and pastures."[5]

In a less self-deprecating mood Emerson noted how a journal full of highlights and notable quotations, one that leaves out the chaff and dross of daily routine and dull reading, tends to move from one great passage to the next. Such a journal "converts the heights you have reached into table land." The essays Emerson now projected were the ultimate product of this heightening through selectivity, as each essay would represent the best of the journal comments, which were themselves the best of each day and its thought and reading.

Emerson's journals were now numerous. There were perhaps as many as a hundred by 1839, and just finding specific entries in the shelves of notebooks was a problem that increased with time. He made an index of each journal's contents in the back of it. By 1838 he began making lists of topics, entering under each topic a list of passages that might apply, giving location symbols and page numbers by which he could locate each passage. By 1843 he had a separate notebook with a topic at the head of each page and for each topic dozens of one-sentence references to passages in the journals. By 1847 he had a 400-page master index of topics, each followed by scores, even by hundreds of short quotes and location symbols. He could open the master index to, say, "Intellect" and there find a list of 96 references, each given in brief form and with precise indications as to where in his journals each passage was to be found. As the years passed and material continued to pile up, Emerson kept up the old indexes and made new ones. He had separate indexes for "Platoniana" and for "Swedenborg"; he had a huge biographical index that listed 839 men and women whose lives or work interested him, together with notations for all the places in his journals where he discussed or quoted each one. These indexes themselves, never printed—with one exception—represent many months and perhaps years of work all by themselves. But without elaborate indexes neither Emerson nor anyone else would ever have been able to locate particular passages in this collection of notebooks, which eventually came to over 263 volumes.

Emerson's earliest notebooks had flung themselves outward with grandiose titles such as "Wide World" and "Universe." And in the end he came back to that plan and to the encyclopedic ambition they suggest. "A journal," he wrote, "is to the author a book of constants, each mind requiring to write the whole of literature and science for itself." And under the heading "Writer" in one of his grand synoptic indexes he wrote, "Great should his apparatus be: big as the solar system."[6]

By July 8 Emerson had three essays in more or less finished form. Work went so well that he expected to be done by autumn. He tried out different sequences, but in all his plans the essay "History" came first. The piece is not really about history but about how to convert the burden of the past into a survival kit for the present. It could equally well be called "On Reading History." "The fact narrated must correspond to something in me to be credible or intelligible. We, as we read, must become Greeks, Romans, Turks, priest and king, martyr and executioner, must fasten the images to some reality in our secret experience, or we shall learn nothing rightly." The past cannot be ignored. Emerson read as much history as anyone. But the past can be understood only if we imagine each moment of it as present, with ourselves as the actors in it. Not knowledge of the past but sympathy with it is what matters. And no aspect of the past, however grand it may appear, is to be regarded as superior to the present moment. For the purpose of historical reading is the education of the reader: "The student is to read history actively and not passively, to esteem his own life the text and books the commentary." "We are always coming up with the emphatic facts of history in our private experience and verifying them there," he says. When we once accept our own ability to experience and to judge everything in history, then "all history becomes subjective," says Emerson. He pounds his phrases home now like well-hit nails, and the prose moves with the vehemence of undeniable conviction: "In other words, there is properly no history, only biography. Every mind must know the whole lesson for itself, must go over the whole ground. What it does not see, what it does not live, it will not know."[7]

"History" is followed by "Self-Reliance," perhaps the one essay for which Emerson is most often remembered. Not only has its title entered common speech, but it is still the single best place to see how the self-rule of classical Stoicism, the *Bildung* of Goethe, the subjective theology of Schleiermacher, and the revolution of Kant and his successors came to be translated into accessible language by Emerson and—what is much more important—shown to have a constant bearing on everyday life. "Self-Reliance," like *Hamlet,* is now too familiar to seem fresh or revolutionary: "Society everywhere is in conspiracy against the manhood of every one of its members." "Nothing is at last sacred but the integrity of your own mind." "A foolish consistency is the hobgoblin of little minds." "Self-Reliance" is Emerson's essay on the unalienated human being. The essay is not a blueprint for selfishness or withdrawal; it is not anti-community. It recommends self-reliance as a starting point—indeed *the* starting point—not as a goal. When a better society evolves, it will not, in Emerson's view, come about through a suppression of the process of individuation but through a voluntary association of fulfilled individuals.

The ideas in "History" and in "Self-Reliance" were not new to Emerson in 1839; they may be traced back through many years, through lectures, journals, and sermons. The same is true for "Compensation," which goes back, as Emerson himself tells us in the essay, all the way to boyhood. He called it his essay on "offsets." It might even better be titled "On Justice," for this is Emerson's foundational essay on the balance of nature, the idea of the universe as a whole, no part of which can be changed without affecting the other parts. Starting from Newton's law that every action has an equal and opposite reaction, Emerson extends the idea to intellectual, moral, and religious realms and to daily life. He acknowledges that both good and bad things happen. "Fear for ages has boded and mowed and gibbered," he says. "There is a crack in everything"; we face not only opportunity but "this running sea of circumstance." The essay ends with a direct assault on "the natural history of calamity" and with an extraordinary metaphor, an extension and deepening of the famous "transparent eyeball" image into a startling answer to the "old-clothes" imagery of Swift and Carlyle. The passage bears witness also to Emerson's by now pervasive awareness of change, growth, process, metamorphosis. We are all subject to time and change, says Emerson, but

> in proportion to the vigor of the individual, these revolutions [changes] are frequent, until in some happier mind they are incessant, and all worldly relations hang very loosely about him, becoming, as it were, a transparent fluid membrane through which the living form is seen, and not, as in most men, an indurated heterogenous fabric of many dates and of no settled character, in which the man is imprisoned. Then there can be no enlargement, and the man of today scarcely recognizes the man of yesterday. And such should be the outward biography of a man in time, a putting off of dead circumstance day by day, as he renews his raiment day by day.

This is Ovid in Concord. The idea of metamorphosis is now as important to Emerson's work as the great passage on the flowing sand in the railroad cut in *Walden* is to Thoreau's. This is Emerson's new myth of the growth of consciousness.

54. The Heart Has Its Jubilees

EMERSON'S ALREADY BUSY LIFE BECAME EVEN BUSIER THIS SUMmer of 1839. There were new books, new friends, new lectures, new projects. His correspondence increased, his journal grew. He seemed to have unlimited energy. For about the next two and a half years there is a tone of workaday exaltation to everything Emerson did. Exhilaration became a habit. He was living at the apogee of his own orbit of possibility. And since he was capable of sustained effort on many projects at once, there are now, more than ever, multiple contexts for everything he was writing. During the second half of 1839, he worked on the essays "Love" and "Friendship" for his book. He also began a new lecture series called "The Present Age" with two lectures on literature, followed by "Politics," "Private Life," "Reforms," "Religion," and "Education." Emerson was closely involved in the planning for a new magazine. He went with George Bradford on a sightseeing trip to the White Mountains just as Henry Thoreau and his brother John were setting off for their boat trip on the Concord and Merrimack rivers. Emerson liked the "savage and stern" New Hampshire landscape and thought the Flume "as wild a piece of scenery as I ever chanced to see." He packed off a bushel of potatoes to William in New York. The shipping directions got lost, but the potatoes arrived anyway. When William asked what kind they were, Emerson said they were automatic potatoes, "learned, self-relying," knowing their own destination and opening "a new science, Potato Magnetism."[1]

Emerson's reading ranged widely as usual. He read Keats's "Eve of St. Agnes" and "Hyperion." He read Dickens's *Oliver Twist,* George Sand's *Spiridion,* Balzac's *Le livre mystique,* and Victor Hugo's *Hunchback of Notre-Dame.* He read Gilbert White's *Natural History of Selborne* and Linnaeus's account in *Lachesis Lapponica* of his travels in Lapland. He read John Forster's *Life of Oliver Cromwell* in Dionysius Lardner's *Cabinet Encyclopedia* edition. Lardner's volumes were small and handy—true pocket books—which were useful in several ways. A soldier at the siege of Lucknow found that one of the volumes could stop a musket ball after passing through 120 pages. Emerson was also reading Burton's *Anatomy of Melancholy* and

Plutarch's *Isis and Osiris,* and he dipped into the new twelve-volume set of Victor Cousin's Plato which had been given him by his Concord Lyceum audience as a token of appreciation. By far the most unusual book in his new reading was *Goethe's Correspondence with a Child* by Bettina von Arnim. This book not only influenced his ideas of friendship, it raised the temperature of his social relations in a curious way.[2]

In 1839 Emerson was making new friendships even as his older ones continued to ripen. His correspondence with Carlyle and his labors as his American agent increased. He was becoming closer to Margaret Fuller, who was educating him now in modern fiction. In June she brought out her translation of Eckermann's *Conversations with Goethe.* Fuller was getting ready to leave Providence. She decided against Concord and settled instead for Boston, where in the fall of 1839 she began to give the public "Conversations" that first made her famous. Also in 1839 and 1840 George Ripley came riding publicly to the defense of Emerson (and Spinoza and Schleiermacher) in a series of three letters directed against Andrews Norton's *The Latest Form of Infidelity.* "Letters" gives the wrong impression. Ripley's three pieces together fill four hundred printed pages. Never gathered together or properly published as a unit, the work remains the unacknowledged high point of the influence of Schleiermacher in American thought in the nineteenth century and a declaration, for those who could see it, that Emersonian transcendentalism was not an aberration, as Norton claimed, but proceeded in one of the main currents of modern thought.[3]

Horace Mann came to Concord to speak; there were increasingly frequent walks with Henry Thoreau. There was a new English admirer, a writer, a protégé of Carlyle's named John Sterling. Elizabeth Hoar went through a troubled period from which she emerged to become even closer to Emerson and to the family. Emerson called her "sister," and when his daughter Ellen asked whether she should study Greek, Emerson said yes, citing Aunt Lizzy as a model and praising her "Greek mind." There were other new friends this fall, making new claims on Emerson. Sam Ward, a painter and student of art history, Anna Barker, a New Orleans socialite and beauty who came from a New England Quaker family, and Caroline Sturgis, the young free-spirited poet, all became friends of Emerson now through Fuller. Like Fuller, they dispensed with the traditional reserved manner associated with New Englanders and required both candor about and continuing discussion of emotional matters. They were impatient with the ordinary forms of social life; they prized intensity and strove toward ever greater intimacy with one another. All three wanted to get to know Emerson. He in turn seemed eager to clinch and deepen these new relationships. In "Friendship" he writes feelingly of how we rise to meet new people. When a much commended stranger arrives,

> we talk better than we are wont. We have the nimblest fancy, a richer memory, and our dumb devil has taken leave for the time. For long hours we can continue a series of sincere, graceful, rich communications, drawn from the oldest, secretest experience so that they who sit by, of our own kinfolk and acquaintance, shall feel a lively surprize at our unusual powers.[4]

Emerson borrowed Ward's portfolio and admired Michelangelo with him. They recommended books to each other. Some of the best letters Emerson ever wrote were those to Ward. He seems to have allowed Ward to get as near him as his brother Charles had been. "But who are you that wrote me this letter—and how came you to know all this? I thought you were younger. I love you very much," Emerson wrote the twenty-one-year-old Ward.[5]

In early October Emerson finally met Anna Barker. Fuller had been trying to introduce the two since September of 1836. Barker was very beautiful by all accounts and she also had a gift for intimacy, a way of bestowing her "frank and generous confidence" that was irresistible. "Anna's miracle, next to the *amount* of her life, seems to be the intimacy of her approach to us," Emerson once observed.

> The moment she fastens her eyes on you, her unique gentleness unbars all doors, and with such easy and frolic sway she advances and advances and advances on you, with that one look, that no brother or sister or father or mother of life-long acquaintance ever seemed to arrive quite so near as this now first seen maiden.

Emerson was a little smitten. She visited Concord. "She came and covenanted with me that we two should speak the truth to each [other]," he told Caroline Sturgis later. Then Emerson found out that Barker had already been engaged to be married to Sam Ward before her visit to Concord. Emerson's response to the news seems unusual, as does his telling all this to Sturgis. "The news which Anna told me at Cambridge offended me at first with a certain terror," Emerson wrote Sturgis.

> I thought that the whole spirit of our intercourse at Concord implied another resolution. I thought she had looked the world through for

326

a man as universal as herself and finding none, had said, "I will compensate myself for my great renunciation as a woman by establishing ideal relations; not only Raphael [Ward] shall be my brother, but that Puritan at Concord. . . . I will elect him also."

Emerson was disappointed and a little miffed. Clearly he thought Anna Barker was offering him more than she was. She did marry Sam Ward in 1840 and the two moved off, away from Emerson and art to their own world of business.[6]

Emerson's friendship with Caroline Sturgis, which began at the same time he was getting to know Barker and Ward, was a more interesting one, stronger, longer lasting, and harder to understand. Sturgis was twenty, Emerson thirty-six when they became friends. Their friendship was colored, if not actually created by Bettina von Arnim's *Goethe's Correspondence with a Child.* This book, published in Germany in 1835 and translated into English by the author the following year, is a loose transcript of the letters back and forth between the fifty-eight-year-old Goethe and the twenty-year-old "child" Bettina. Bettina's letters are lively, perceptive, and full of entertaining description. But their principal note is one of headlong romantic adoration, passionate yearning, and intimate badinage. Goethe encouraged his young correspondent's letters and returned her ardor with genuine affection. The following is Bettina's account, in a letter to Goethe's mother (with whom she had been on close terms for years), of her first meeting the great man: "The door opened and there *he* stood, solemnly grave, and looked with fixed eyes upon me. I stretched my hands towards him—I believe—I soon lost all consciousness. Goethe quickly caught me to his heart. 'Poor child, have I frightened you?'" Goethe leads her into his room, to a sofa. After a little talk about the death of the Duchess Amalia, Bettina goes on:

> I suddenly said "cant stay here upon the sofa," and sprang up. "Well," said he, "make yourself at home." Then I flew to his neck—he drew me upon his knee, and locked me to his heart. Still, quite still it was—everything vanished. I had not slept for so long—years had passed in sighing after him. I fell asleep on his breast: and when I awoke I began a new life.[7]

When she writes to Goethe, Bettina is completely open. She is alarmingly articulate about her feelings: "A dam within my heart has, as it were, broken up:—a child of man, alone on a rock, surrounded by rushing storms, uncertain of itself, wavering here and there, like the thorns and thistles around it,—such am I; such I was before I knew my master." "Thou, who hast knowledge of love," she writes in another letter, "and the spirituality of senses, ah, how beautiful is everything in thee. . . . O God, how fain would I now be with thee." There is nothing to separate these from love letters. The book was skillfully translated by Bettina herself and soon attracted a following. Emerson told Fuller the book "moves all my admiration. . . . She is the only formidable test that was applied to Goethe's genius. . . . Hers was genius purer than his own."[8]

Now Caroline Sturgis read Bettina and began writing similar letters to Emerson. It was life imitating art. Sturgis too has verve, charm, lyric grace, and a kind of literary coquettishness that drew strength from Bettina (who in turn had modeled her own persona on that of Mignon, a character in *Wilhelm Meister*). Emerson himself was very enthusiastic about Bettina. He made extravagant claims. He called Bettina "the most imaginative person in our day," and he thought *Goethe's Correspondence with a Child* "the most remarkable book ever written by a woman." Over the next few years the correspondence between Sturgis and Emerson reads very much like that between Bettina and Goethe.

After Emerson visited Sturgis at Newburyport, she wrote him: "Do you know that you vanished through a rainbow trebly arched and radiantly painted upon the dark clouds, beneath the center of it the white steeples gleamed forth from over the brown fields?" Her letters are both charming and intimate. "I know I have never been anything but a child," she wrote, "but perhaps I shall sometime learn to be a woman. I wish to have the actual thing as it stands, neither more nor less, will you not give it to me as far as you can, and not throw tint and clouds into the shining sky?" Her letters question, invite, challenge. "I shall stay at home every morning until you come till one or half past," she wrote him. "Walk down to the edge of the pond a little to the right of the house to see if you cannot find me there under the trees reading Beckford's Travels with my eyes shut." Many of her letters have no salutation and no closing. One begins "and you my dearest brother, shall be my saint and purify me, for this is the joy of friendship." The same letter closes "I never knew a day more full of sweetness and glory than this. May you be happy in it, is the wish of one who loves you."[9]

Emerson's response to Sturgis was like Goethe's to Bettina. He did not try to stop or change things, and he probably assumed it could all be kept under control. And he was undoubtedly fond of her. They stood out in the summer night and looked up together at the stars with their "broad edges of glory." He wrote to her as "my true sister," and he assured her that he recognized the link between their souls. Their time together made "golden days." He wrote to her, "And now you have another claim on me which I hasten to own, for are you not my dear sister and am I not your brother? I cannot write to you *with others,* any more than I can talk with you at a round table."[10]

Emerson had always been an emotional person privately, but the emotional openness—amounting even to a sort of public openness—of his relationships with Barker, Ward, Sturgis, and Fuller was something new. The effect on Emerson of these new relationships may be gauged from an extraordinary passage he wrote in November 1839, just as all these new friendships were blooming. In a fragmentary manuscript autobiography that has never been printed he describes his new condition in terms that recall both his dream of eating the world and the "transparent eyeball" experience. "I plunge with eagerness," Emerson wrote,

> into the pleasant element of affection, with its hopes and harms. It seemed to me swimming in an Iris where I am rudely knocked ever and anon by a ray of fiercer red, or even dazzled by a momentary blindness by a casual beam of white light. The weal and wo are all poetic. I float all the time nor once grazed the old orb.[11]

As he wrote to Elizabeth Hoar in September of 1840, he was somewhat amazed at his suddenly having "a roomful of friends." "So consider me as now quite friendsick and lovesick, a writer of letters and sonnets."

There is no question but that Emerson was attracted to Caroline Sturgis, and even though this, like all his new friendships, was conducted with the language and under the flag of honorary sibling relations and Platonic soul-mating, the charade was not empty. It is not too much to say that in the early 1840s Emerson was living emotionally, though not physically, in what would now be called an open marriage. There is nothing to suggest any physical intimacies between Emerson and Sturgis (or Barker or Fuller). Nor were any of the new friendships clandestine. Lidian knew all about them, was herself often present, frequently copied Emerson's letters, and counted both Fuller and Sturgis among her own friends. Perhaps the warmth of the correspondence between Sturgis and Emerson can be explained by their shared commitment to enthusiasm or by their fascination with German romantic friendship. Whatever the explanation, there was an undeniable current of affection between them at this time. Late in life Emerson returned all of Caroline Sturgis Tappan's letters to her; they were wrapped in a bundle and were discreetly labeled "To be sent unopened to Caroline Tappan."

Lidian's tone toward her husband shows no cooling at this time, nor does his toward her. But two further bits of evidence indicate that all was not well with their marriage now. Their daughter Ellen noted that sometime in 1841 Lidian "waked to a sense that she had been losing—had lost—that blessed nearness to God in which she had lived so long, and she never regained it." Perhaps it was also her nearness to Emerson that she feared losing. The other indication of trouble is that Emerson began now to voice in his journal serious doubts about the institution of marriage. Writing in November of 1840 he said he thought "Swedenborg exaggerates the circumstance of marriage." He went on:

> All lives, all friendships are momentary. *Do you love me?* means at last *Do you see the same truth I see?* If you do, we are happy together: but when presently one of us passes into the perception of new truth, we are divorced and the force of all nature cannot hold us to each other . . .

The passage is a long one, rising in feeling as Emerson rejects the idea of permanently fixed relationships. "But one to one, married and chained through the eternity of ages is frightful beyond the binding of dead and living together." In December he dreamt that a convention had assembled to debate the institution of marriage. After many "grave and alarming objections" were raised, a defender arose

> and turned on the audience the spout of an engine which was copiously supplied from within the wall by water . . . whilst I stood watching astonished and amused at the malice and vigor of the orator [with the fire hose]. I saw the spout lengthened by a supply of hose behind, and the man suddenly brought it round a corner and drenched me as I gazed.

Passion overwhelmed institutions and discussions. Emerson himself was no longer just an observer. He now found himself completely involved in emotional matters and drenched in their reality.[12]

In August of 1841 Emerson was still protesting that "it is not in the plan or prospect of the soul, this fast union of one to one." In September of 1841 he repeated that "plainly marriage should be a temporary relation, it should have its natural birth, climax and decay, without violence of any kind,— violence to bind or violence to rend." The same year, he made a note, "I marry you for better, not for worse." In 1843 he was still upset by what he called "the vitriolic acid of marriage," and in 1852, after his trip to England, he was still thinking (as he wrote) that "everything is free but marriage." He wrote a long, bitter comment on how it is that the youth marries and has children and then is asked what he thinks about marriage. "'Too late,' [says the not-quite-autobiographical "youth,"] 'too late.' I should have much to say if the question were open. I have a wife and five children and all question is closed for me."[13]

Emerson and Lidian stayed married. They displayed, both in public and in private, tenderness, solicitude, and esteem for each other. But the love that makes marriages in the first place was no longer, in Emerson's case, focused solely on his wife. His slowly forming book of essays has no essay on marriage, though it does have essays entitled "Friendship" and "Love." Emerson's essay "Love" is not interested in *caritas,* or caring, but in *eros,* in being in love. The original opening of the essay is a strong straightforward celebration of Eros. "Every soul is a celestial Venus to every other soul. The heart has its sabbath and jubilees in which the world appears as a hymeneal feast, and all natural sounds and the circle of the seasons are erotic odes and dances." Emerson later toned down the openly erotic note of this passage, but the rewritten opening has an equally insistent emphasis on desire as well as a certain wisdom about the human heart: "Every promise of the soul has innumerable fulfillments: each of its joys ripens into a new want."[14]

55. Identity and Metamorphosis

EMERSON HAD THOUGHT ABOUT STARTING AND EDITING A MAG-
azine since at least his days at divinity school. More recently the transcendentalists as a group—especially Alcott, Ripley, Parker, Fuller, and Emerson—had been feeling the lack of a proper place to publish their new views.
Even the most liberal of the Christian magazines were unsympathetic. The
ladies magazines and the light literature magazines were utterly unsuitable.
The Knickerbocker in New York was hostile; there was no serious literary
magazine in New England. That there had been a transcendentalist peri-
odical in Louisville (*The Western Messenger*) since 1835 only made the lack
in New England more keenly felt. In October 1839 Orestes Brownson, no
longer a transcendentalist but editor of the best general journal then going
in Boston (*The Boston Quarterly Review*), invited the transcendentalists to
write for him. Faced with protective assimilation, their collective will came
together and Emerson, Alcott, Ripley, and Fuller decided to launch their
own magazine with Fuller as editor, Ripley as business manager, and
Emerson pledged to help out in all necessary ways. He worked to find a
publisher, he read manuscripts, and he solicited contributions.[1]

Emerson was in constant communication with Fuller, who had now
moved to Jamaica Plain. In late March the Alcotts moved to Concord.
Everything seemed to go in a headlong rush. Emerson talked about these
months as his "days of passion." He wrote many letters a day, often with
a throw-away brilliance. He told Fuller he had been reading "one of Lord
Brougham's superficial, indigent, disorderly, unbuttoned, penny-a-page
books called *Times of George III.*" Fuller was urging him to pay more
attention to such books as Firdusi's *Shah Nameh,* an eleventh-century book
of kings and a major document of Iranian national sentiment.[2]

On February 21 the bluebirds came back to the box on Emerson's barn.
In March baby Ellen learned to stand. In April Sophia Peabody was finishing
a portrait medallion of Charles Emerson. Emerson himself spent April
working on "The Oversoul" and trying to decide whether to buy a cow. On
May 4 the prospectus for *The Dial* was issued.

Emerson's main daily preoccupation during February 1840 was with his lecture series "The Present Age." His deeper concern was with the volume of essays he was still trying to assemble. The tone in the lectures is bright, declarative, decisive. There is a clear note of announcement, of setting forth. "There are two parties," Emerson said in the opening lecture, "the party of the Past and the party of the Future." The former he called "the Establishment," the latter "the Movement." He was increasingly conscious of the public and political contexts of the Movement this year. "The modern mind teaches that the nation exists for the individual—for the guardianship and education of every man," he said. Now was the time to break new ground. "This is the age of severance, of dissociation, of freedom, of analysis, of detachment." Above all, he insisted in lecture after lecture, "it is the age of the first person singular."[3]

Emerson's sense of what was important and his growing reservations about science may be seen in the two lectures on literature in this series and in the way in which he now classified his reading. The highest class of books expresses the moral element—what ought to be. The next class includes works of imagination—what really is. The last class includes works of science—or what appears. But he was skeptical that even the highest kind of books could have any permanent canonical value. "What are books?" he asked his audience. "They can have no permanent value. . . . When we are aroused to a life in ourselves, these traditional splendors of letters grow very pale and cold." Literature, he said "is a heap of nouns and verbs enclosing an intuition or two." But the main subject of the lectures, the theme that runs through them all, is the idea of the new age of subjectivity, of the first person singular.[4]

Even in the lectures on politics—of which he observes "there are some subjects that have a kind of prescriptive right to dull treatment"—he is continually attracted by the idea of "the thousand or the million stranded cord which my being and every man's being is." He insisted, "I am an aggregate of infinitesimal parts." Emerson now proposes a complex, many-sided subjectivity, no longer a simple affirmation of the self: "What is man but a congress of nations?" The multifaceted, fractionated self is now a given, a starting point, though the goal of thought and perception remains the same. As he explains in the lecture on religion, we live for those rare (one might say Yeatsian) moments when "this deep power in which we lie and whose beautitude is all accessible to us, is not only self-sufficing and perfect in every hour, but the act of seeing and the thing seen, the seer and the spectacle, the subject and the object are one."[5]

This is the mature form of Emerson's fundamental conviction of the essential oneness of all things. The idea has been variously expressed. It appears as the *atman* of the Bhagavad Gita, the true self we all share. It is also the leading idea of the "identity-philosophy" of Schelling: "The Absolute is the pure identity of subjectivity and objectivity, of the ideal and the real . . . the conviction that the philosophy of nature and the system of transcendental idealism are mutually complementary." Coleridge takes up the idea in chapter 12 of the *Biographia Literaria.* The transcendental philosopher holds that nature is unconsciously involved in the existence of our own being, "that it [nature] is not only coherent but identical, and one and the same with our own immediate self-consciousness. To demonstrate this identity is the office and subject of his philosophy."[6]

Emerson's point of view, his procedures, his method of composition, and his main convictions all rest on the perception that the world of differences can and must be resolved into a world not only of similarity but of identity. In Emerson's cosmos difference is hell, similarity purgatory. Identity alone constitutes paradise. This idea reaches its first full expression in 1840, although it occurs all through Emerson's work. Identity is the leading idea of the "Present Age" lecture series in 1840. This spring he also worked it out in the poem "The Sphinx" and in the essay "The Oversoul." Even this last essay did not exhaust the subject. "Identity" appears as a major heading in all the indexes and lists of subjects Emerson made during the 1840s.[7]

At the conclusion of "The Sphinx" the secret that all is in each is articulated by the thousand voices of nature: "Who telleth one of my meanings, / Is master of all I am." Emerson considered "The Sphinx" so central to his work that he always put it first in his own volume of poems. And in 1859, almost twenty years after it was written, he was still sufficiently interested in having the poem understood to descend to a very uncharacteristic explanation. "I have often been asked the meaning of 'The Sphinx,'" he wrote.

> It is this—the perception of identity unites all things and explains one by another, and the most rare and strange is equally facile as the most common. But if the mind live only in particulars, and see only difference, (wanting the power to see the whole—all in each) then the world addresses to this mind a question it cannot answer, and each new fact tears it in pieces . . .[8]

"The Sphinx" was written in April 1840, while Emerson was also at work on "The Oversoul," which is his essay on identity. In all previous sets of lectures Emerson chose to deal with the idea that the individual gains entrance to the common mind of humankind through his or her own nature as if it were a single perception. But in the volume of essays he was now preparing he took this idea up twice, once with the emphasis on the individual, in "Self-Reliance," and once with the focus on the general or common mind, in "The Oversoul." This formal division suggests that Emerson now saw the all-in-each idea as two overlapping but still discrete tendencies. "Self-Reliance" affirms the tendency toward individuation. "The Oversoul" affirms the existence of "that great nature in which we rest." This nature is variously called a unity "within which every man's particular being is contained and made one with all others," a "common nature," "the great heart of nature," "the common heart," and "the great, the universal mind." What links these two essays is Emerson's perception that the power available to the self-reliant individual is ultimately the power of the common nature described in "The Oversoul."[9]

May was a great month for Emerson this year. The earth was gay with the blossoming of fruit trees. His spirits soared as he worked. "Success depends on the aim, not on the means," he reminded himself. "Look at the mark, not at your arrow." As the world was full of latent heat, so he felt "latent joy" everywhere. "In the thought of tomorrow there is a power to upheave all thy creed, all the creeds, all the literatures of the nations . . ." In May George Ripley resigned from his pulpit in order to devote himself full-time to setting up a commune, a first step in the reformation of the competitive and selfish society he saw America becoming. Father Taylor came and spoke at a meeting of the Transcendental Club. Emerson wrote a long and glowing private tribute to the man and to the "exhilaration and cheer of so much love poured out through so much imagination."[10]

In June Emerson was working again on his essays "Love" and "Friendship." On July 1, 1840, the first number of *The Dial* appeared, the "bold bible for the Young America" from which so much was expected. It had strong material by Fuller on Jean Paul Richter, on critics, and on Washington Allston. There was a good piece by Parker. There was Thoreau's poem "Sympathy" and his essay "Persius" as well as Alcott's "Orphic Sayings." There was a fine poem by Christopher Cranch which made of the aurora borealis a symbol of the imagination. The magazine as a whole was forward-looking and reform-minded. The contributions were self-consciously part of "the newness." Yet the magazine also had another side, a memorial quality, containing as it did the voices of the dead, of Emerson's dead. Fuller had printed verses by Ellen Tucker Emerson, a poem by Edward Bliss Emerson, and a piece of Charles Emerson's writing called "Notes from the Journal of a Scholar." If Emerson rarely talked about the past, he nevertheless had a powerful impulse to memorialize those friends and relations he had loved. He could at least keep their voices alive.[11]

The editorial statement had been written by Emerson. It took issue forcefully with present conventions of religion and education, which, he said, were "turning us to stone." He looked for a revolution in thought and presented the magazine as a "protest against usage." The statement was also careful not to claim too much. "There is somewhat [something] in all life untranslatable into language," he wrote. "Every thought has a certain imprisoning as well as uplifting quality, and in proportion to its energy on the will, refuses to become an object of intellectual contemplation." At the moment when the group had finally found a collective means of expression, Emerson was warning readers of the residual inadequacy of all expression. It was his old fear that form—any form—might mean the death of the spirit. There would be no transcendentalist orthodoxy, no canon of permanently true scriptures. Emerson's strongest convictions about the nature of things forbade it.

> The Greek sculpture is all melted away as if it had been statues of snow, here and there a solitary figure or fragment remaining, as we see flecks and scraps of snow left in cold dells or mountain clefts in June and July. It is so with all things. Permanence is but a word of degrees, every thing is medial.[12]

Individuation was a fact and identity was a fact. But above and governing both of these processes now, in Emerson's imagination and in his writing, is the sense of flux, the conviction that all things change. In "The Present Age" he had used an image reminiscent of a famous trope from Bede's *Ecclesiastical History:*

> As the wandering seabird which crossing the ocean lights on some rock or islet to rest for a moment its wings, and to look back on the wilderness of waves behind, and onward to the wilderness of waters before, so stand we perched on this rock or shoal of time, arrived out of the immensity of the Past and bound and roadready to plunge into immensity again.

With stabbing verbal energy he wrote in his journal in late May: "All things unfix, dispart, flee."[13]

Emerson at 43.
(Original in Carlyle home in London; photo by
permission of Concord Free Public Library.)

Ruth Haskins Emerson (1768-1853), Emerson's mother.
(Photo by permission of Concord Free Public Library.)

William Emerson (1769-1811), Emerson's father.
(Engraving from David G. Haskins's, *Ralph Waldo Emerson.*)

William Emerson (1801-1868), Emerson's elder brother.
(Original miniature in Massachusetts Historical Society Library;
photo by permission of the Massachusetts Historical Society Library.)

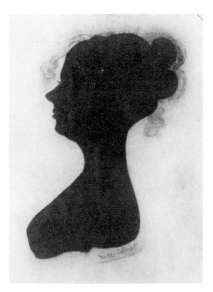

Mary Moody Emerson (1774-1863),
Emerson's aunt, as a young woman.
(Photo by permission of Concord Free Public Library.)

Emerson's younger brothers (top, left, right):
Bulkeley (1807-1859), Edward (1805-1834), Charles (1808-1836).
(Top: Original daguerreotype in Houghton Library; photo by permission of the Houghton
Library, Harvard University. Left, right: From David G. Haskins's, *Ralph Waldo Emerson.*)

Ellen Tucker Emerson (1811-1831), Emerson's first wife.
(Original miniature in Concord Museum; photo by permission
of The Concord Museum.)

Lidian Jackson Emerson (1802-1892),
Emerson's second wife and the mother of his children,
with Edward (1844-1930), their second son, in 1847.

*Waldo (1836-1842), the first child of Lidian and
R. W. Emerson, taken a few months before his death at age 5.*
(Original in Houghton Library; photo by permission of the
Houghton Library, Harvard University.)

*Ellen (1839-1909), elder daughter of Lidian and R. W. Emerson (left).
Edith (1841-1929), younger daughter of Lidian and R. W. Emerson (right).*
(Photos by permission of Concord Free Public Library.)

Emerson in 1848, at age 45.
(Original in Houghton Library; photo by permission of the
Houghton Library, Harvard University.)

Emerson in the 1850s.
(Photo by permission of Concord Free Public Library.)

Thomas Carlyle and Elizabeth Hoar.
(Left: Original in Houghton Library; photo by permission of the Houghton Library,
Harvard University. Right: Photo by permission of Concord Free Public Library.)

Henry Thoreau.
(Original in Concord Free Public Library; photo by permission
of Concord Free Public Library.)

Margaret Fuller.
(Original in Museum of Fine Arts, Boston; photo courtesy
Museum of Fine Arts, Boston.)

A. Bronson Alcott.
(Photo by permission of Concord Free Public Library.)

Emerson at 50.

(Original in Houghton Library; photo by permission
of the Houghton Library, Harvard University.)

Emerson at 56. Photo from a carte de visite,
derived in turn from a photo made by Matthew Brady in 1859.
(Original in author's possession; print made by Daniel Jones and
reproduced by his permission.)

"Bush," the Emerson home, on Lexington Road in Concord.
(Photo by permission of Concord Free Public Library.)

"Tumbledown Hall," Emerson's garden house, designed by Bronson Alcott and built by Alcott and Henry Thoreau. The sketch is by May Alcott.
(Original drawing in *Concord Sketches*; photo by permission of Concord Free Public Library.)

Emerson at 67, holding his first grandson, Ralph Waldo Forbes (1866-1937).
Also shown is John Forbes, whose son William married Edith Emerson.
(Original in Massachusetts Historical Society; photo by permission
of Massachusetts Historical Society.)

Emerson at 74, shown with his son Edward
and Edward's son Charles L. Emerson (1876-1880).
(Photo by permission of Concord Free Public Library.)

56. Brook Farm and Margaret Fuller

LATE JUNE AND EARLY JULY OF 1840 BROUGHT A SEARING drought, a full month of punishing weather with temperatures in the nineties every day. Emerson wilted in the "red hot noon," watched the crops drying up, and longed for coolness and shade. "In the sleep of the great heats," he told Ward, "there was nothing for me but to read the Veda, the bible of the tropics, which I find I come back upon every three or four years." He read again Sir William Jones's translation of the *Laws of Menu* (sometimes translated as the *Institutes of Menu*), the Pentateuch of India, and again it satisfied his thirst for origins, for the grand simplicity of the early lawgivers. "It is sublime as heat and night and a breathless ocean," he wrote. "It contains every religious sentiment, all the grand ethics." It taught him peace and purity and "absolute abandonment." It also taught him what nature taught him, "eternal necessity, eternal compensation, unfathomable power, unbroken silence."[1]

George Ripley had left his pulpit in May. He and Sophia were determined to find a more concrete means of reforming American society, which Ripley considered "vicious in its foundations." The Ripleys were spending the summer on a milk farm in West Roxbury. Ripley and Emerson and Alcott were all dreaming of forming a community of like-minded souls. In August Emerson was talking—it seems seriously—about creating a sort of free university "without charter, diploma, corporation, or steward." From, say, October to April each year Hedge would teach poetry, metaphysics, and the philosophy of history, Parker would teach ecclesiastical history, and Alcott would teach psychology, ethics, and the ideal life. Emerson would teach literature. He broached it to Ripley; he invited Fuller to join. "What society shall we not have! . . . We shall sleep no more and we shall concert better houses, economies, and social modes than any we have seen." What Emerson called "our University" was one expression of the communitarian impulse that was felt all over America in the early and middle 1840s. More specifically, this "university" was a

337

premonition of Brook Farm, which Ripley would have up and going by April of 1841.[2]

Emerson's hospitable invitation to Fuller to settle in Concord came just two days after a sharp personal challenge from Fuller. Emerson and Fuller had ridden together to Jamaica Plain on August 14. During the ride Fuller accused Emerson of "inhospitality of soul" on her own behalf as well as that of Caroline Sturgis. "She and Caroline would gladly be my friends, yet our intercourse is not friendship, but literary gossip" is the way Emerson recorded the indictment. He was nettled by this criticism. Doubtless he felt there was some justice to it, and it is interesting that his response was not to shrink or withdraw but to reach out again immediately to both women. He explained to Sturgis that he was holding back from yet further intimacy with her through fear of being rejected as he had been by Anna Barker: "I dare not engage my peace so far as to make you necessary to me, when the first news I may hear is that you have found in some heaven foreign to me your mate, and my beautiful castle is exploded to shivers." He defended himself vigorously and in plain language: "If I count and weigh, I love also." He stepped up the already brisk pace of his correspondence with Sturgis. They discussed their feelings for each other. "You are a brave dear child," he wrote her, "and your letter is truer than mine. It is not for me to fear that any other can bereave me of my part in you." She replied, "If my letter were truer than yours it was only because I loved you so much that I could easily see how I could love you and others also . . . if my friend gives me thought more lofty and beautiful than my own, it seems that he must for the time, be my God."[3]

Fuller was less easily mollified. She wanted a closer relationship with Emerson and she made it clear that there was more at issue than professionalism, more than comradeship, more even than the cult of friendship these New Englanders were collectively drawing from Goethe, Bettina, and de Staël. As he had not retreated with Sturgis, Emerson was not inclined to retreat with Fuller. "I shall never go quite back to my old arctic habits," he wrote her. "I shall believe that nobleness is loving, and delights in sharing itself." Fuller pushed for more. In late September she wrote to press a new relation. As he interpreted it, she had claimed "that I am yours and yours shall be, let me dally how long soever in this or that other temporary relation." Emerson tried to resist the claim without rejecting the claimant. He was married, after all—though he never used it as a reason—but he was at great pains not to give offense, and above all not to break off with Fuller. He talked it out in his journal:

> You would have me love you. What shall I love? Your body? The supposition disgusts you. What you have thought and said? well, whilst you were thinking and saying them, but not now. I see no possibility of loving anything but what now is, and is becoming. Your courage, your enterprise, your budding affection, your opening thought, your prayer, I can love, but what else?[4]

Fuller replied, maintaining the correspondence at the same temperature, yet knowing she would not get Emerson to agree to a closer relationship. "But did you not ask for a 'foe' in your friend? Did you not ask for a 'large, formidable nature'? But a beautiful foe, I am not yet, to you. Shall I ever be?" Emerson would awkwardly close down the language of personal intimacy with Fuller in late October. But until then—and even then—his impulse was to embrace, not to retreat. As summer turned to fall, Emerson's emotional life was remarkably close to the surface as he swept through what he called "these flying days."[5]

So too was he open and vulnerable on the subject of "The Community." Ripley's plans for a joint-stock commune devoted to farming and education were now taking concrete form. Ripley hoped that Emerson would take a leading role, as he had with those other manifestations of transcendentalism, the club and *The Dial*. Never had Emerson lived so much in the present, never had he been less settled in his plans, his home, or his marriage. And never had he been able to sustain such a pace in his writing as well as in his life. In September he read Ockley's *Conquest of the Saracens*. His Asian and Middle Eastern interests were growing, thanks at least partly to Fuller. He completed the essay "Spiritual Laws," his Thoreauvian essay on simplicity. "Our life might be much easier and simpler than we make it," he says.

He also finished the great essay "Circles," perhaps his best expression of the endlessly open and unfixed nature of things. "Our life is an apprenticeship to the truth that around every circle another can be drawn: that there is no end in nature, that every end is a beginning, that there is always another dawn risen on mid-noon, and under every deep a lower deep opens." "Circles" denigrates the permanent, the final, the fixed. It praises "life, transition, the energizing spirit." Nothing is truly permanent. Thus there can be "no sleep, no pause, no preservation, but all things renew, germinate, and spring." The essay itself spins outward in sweeping centrifugal circles of excitement and acceptance. The central energizing spirit he now praised was a wild spirit. The end of the essay emphasizes this passion as though mirroring Emerson's inner life at this time: "Dream and drunkenness, the use of opium and alcohol are the semblance and counterfeit of the oracular genius." These things therefore attract us and we "ask the aid of wild passions, as in gaming and war, to ape in some manner these flames and generosities of the heart." "Nothing great was ever achieved without enthusiasm. The way of life is wonderful. It is by abandonment."[6]

October 1840 was another extraordinary month for Emerson. His book of essays was coming together; he was not going to have to tie himself to a new lecture series. *The Dial* was getting mixed, mostly negative, reviews that seem only to have whetted the group's determination and tightened its grip on its convictions. The children were flourishing. Waldo had been sick but was recovering. Ellen was blossoming into language. Emerson's new friendships and his passion for friendship were giving him new depth and a greater ease of access to his own best thought. Ripley was proposing to start the community on the West Roxbury milk farm. He discussed his plans with Emerson and eventually, on November 9, sent Emerson a long letter setting out exactly what he hoped to do and urging Emerson to join him:

> Our objects, as you know, are to insure a more natural union between intellectual and manual labor than now exists; to combine the thinker and the worker, as far as possible, in the same individual; to guarantee the highest mental freedom, by providing all with labor, adapted to their tastes and talents, and securing to them the fruits of their industry; to do away with the necessity of menial services, by opening the benefits of education and the profits of labor to all; and thus to prepare a society of liberal, intelligent, and cultivated persons, whose relations with each other would permit a more simple and wholesome life, than can be led amidst the pressures of our competitive institutions.

The bright declarative mode of Ripley's "Declaration of Dependence," with its echoes of Jefferson and of the U.S. Constitution, is a perfect barometer of the hopefulness and fervency of the reform fever sweeping the country in the 1840s. With dozens of communes being founded, with abolition, temperance, peace, and the women's movements on the rise, and with repeated waves of interest in phrenology, mesmerism, and clairvoyance, it was an emotionally charged and politically turbulent decade similar to the 1790s and the 1960s. All three were decades of utopian euphoria fueled by a widely shared and wildly exciting conviction that the structure of society could really be fundamentally and rapidly changed. The Transcendental Club, *The Dial,* and the Brook Farm community all rode the first crest of this new wave. "We are all a little wild here," Emerson wrote Carlyle, "with numberless projects of social reform. Not a reading man but has a draft of a new Community in his waistcoat pocket. I am gently mad myself," he added with Falstaffian irony, "and am resolved to live cleanly."[7]

While his tone in the letter suggests a detached amusement, he was in fact as wild as any of them. "I am only an experimenter," he wrote, first in his journal and then in "Circles." "I unsettle all things. No facts are to me sacred, none are profane. I simply experiment, an endless seeker, with no past at my back." This is the Emerson John Burroughs called "the arch radical of the world." In his journal Emerson wrote:

In the history of the world the doctrine of reform had never such scope as at the present hour. Herrnhuters, Quakers, monks, Swedenborgians all respected something: the church or the state, literature, history, the market town, the ways of living, the dinner table, coined money. But now all these are gone and all else hears the trumpet and are rushing to judgement.

It was life alone, the business of living, that interested him: "The life of man is the true romance when it is valiantly conducted, and, all stops of the instrument opened, will go nigh to craze the reader with anxiety, wonder, and love. I am losing all relish for books and for feats of skill in my delight in this power." He saw process everywhere. Reflecting on the Hindu classics, he observed, "Transmigration of souls: that too is no fable." He accepted the idea that we can change or evolve downward as well as upward. Nature itself, as Heraclitus had said, was change. "The method of advance in nature is perpetual transformation," he now wrote, and the same perception is repeated over and over in phrases he would work into the essays he kept retouching and revising. "Life only avails, not the having lived," he concluded in a passage that went into "Self-Reliance." "Happiness is only in the moment of transition from a past to a new state, the shooting of the gulf, the darting onward."[8]

Emerson was now living as intensely as he ever would; his expressive channels were all wide open. His soaring moods—all constellated around the central perception that every day is both the day of creation and the day of judgment—found form in parables, poems, and dreams. His mythogenetic imagination, stirred to its core, brought out, for example, this central statement of his poem "Days" in a letter to Fuller in October: "Heaven walks among us ordinarily muffled in such triple or tenfold disguises that the wisest are deceived and no one suspects the days to be gods." And nothing expresses better than the following dream Emerson's new ease of access to his own inner universe, his cramping hunger for experience, and the fundamental sense of appetency and adequacy he felt during these flying days: "I dreamed that I floated at will in the great Ether, and I saw this world floating also not far off, but diminished to the size of an apple. Then an angel took it in his hand and brought it to me and said, 'This must thou eat.' And I ate the world."[9]

This is Emerson's global Eucharist; he had come to take Communion at last. The apple that Adam and Eve ate brought sin and death into the world. Newton saw that the moon was only a larger apple and its orbit a larger Fall. The story of the third apple, the world Emerson ate, marks the coming of the new American individual, the plain man or woman, cosmos in a workshirt, the self-reliant person who, as Virginia Woolf said years later in a review of Emerson's *Journals,* has discovered that "he cannot be rejected because he carries the universe within him."[10]

November 1840 saw the completion of the essay "Art," which is Emerson's piece on creativity. It is also the shortest of the major essays. He was pressing harder and harder, interested not in epiphenomena but in springs and sources. For Emerson art now is not the finished product, it is not even the creative process: "Art is the need to create." November also saw the arrival of George Ripley's lengthy and eloquent invitation to join Brook Farm and, at the end of the month, the Chardon Street Convention, a sort of carnival of the reform movements that were creating a giddy air of sweeping change and renovation.[11]

Late in 1840, as he was finishing off his volume of essays for the printer, Emerson wrote finis to two of the ventures that had helped sustain his soaring mood this year. In late October he tried to reground his friendship with Fuller by concentrating on things other than their personal involvement. "I ought never to have suffered you to lead me into any conversation or writing on our relation," he chided her in one last personal outburst. He admitted that for all their ups and down, they were "all the time a little nearer." But, he ended, "I see very dimly in writing on this topic. It will not prosper with me. Perhaps all my words are wrong. Do not expect it of me again for a very long time." There was no loss of esteem, no denial of affection. But Fuller's claim to exclusive occupancy of the inner chamber of Emerson's affections had to be rejected if it was not to be accepted. No neutral state was possible.[12]

A month and a half later Emerson wrote Ripley to say he would not join the Brook Farmers. He had been a long time deciding, for the move had been a very real option, the people involved were his people, and his letter to Ripley was hard for him to write. The letter shows evidence of uncharacteristic indecision and more than usual painstaking revision. "I have decided not to join it and yet very slowly and I may almost say penitentially," he wrote. His reasons were personal. He was convinced that "the Community is not good for me" and he was unwilling to put to the community "the task of my emancipation which I ought to take on myself." Ripley's plan, which was already being colored by his reading of Fourier, was full of intricate social "arrangements and combinations." Emerson distrusted this organizational complexity, and he added to his letter a critique of communal farming drawn from discussing the new project with Edmund Hosmer, a Concord farmer and neighbor. Hosmer distrusted the idea of everyone's cooperating in everything, and he disliked the idea of uniform pay. Hosmer thought, "As a general rule nothing was gained by cooperation on a farm, except in those few pieces of work which cannot be done alone, like getting in a load of hay, which takes three men." Hosmer also did not believe "that good work will continue to be done for the community if the worker is not directly benefitted."[13]

But these cavils were not the point. The decision about whether to join Brook Farm forced Emerson to make a hard choice. Between the community of others, which he believed in and which he was always trying to gather or foster around him, and the self-determination and independence of his present way of life, he took the latter. He did not disapprove of the community or its ideals. But he did question its methods. He could join no association that was not based on the recognition that each person is the center of his or her own world. As he was rejecting participation in Brook

343

Farm, he was also reading Orestes Brownson's "The Laboring Classes." Brownson had now moved on from transcendentalism to become its sharpest critic. "The truth is," Brownson wrote,

> the evil we have pointed out [the miserable condition of the working class] is not merely individual in its character. . . . The evil we speak of is inherent in all our social arrangements, and cannot be cured without a radical change of those arrangements. . . . The only way to get rid of those evils is to change the system.[14]

To Brownson, as to Ripley, Emerson simply said no. His faith in the power and the infinitude of the individual was greater than his faith in collective action, and he would not confuse the issue by compromise or by what he once called "a mush of concession." His sense of the need to address problems at the level of the individual was bolstered this month, as it had been all year, by his own case. With somewhat surprising clarity, like Thoreau's Chanticleer on his roof, he set out to wake his neighbors. "Do not imagine that the Universe is somewhat so vague and aloof that a man cannot be willing to die for it. If that lives, I live; I am the universe," he wrote in his journal. And the self with which he was so surely in touch at the moment was not an isolated figure but was connected through all things and persons to nature. "A man is a compendium of nature, an indomitable savage," he wrote in a remarkable passage.

> Take the smoothest curled courtier in London or Paris . . . [he] lives, makes, [and] alters, by omnipotent modes, and is directly related there, amid essences and billets doux, to Himmaleh mountain chains, wild cedar swamps, and the interior fire, the molten core of the globe.[15]

57. *Pythagoras and Plotinus*

ON THE FIRST OF JANUARY 1841 EMERSON SENT OFF HIS BOOK of essays to the printer. Both now and again in late March after *Essays* was published, Emerson was in low spirits. He complained that "lately it is sort of general winter with me." In March he grumbled that "March always comes [even] if it do not come till May." He added, "May generally does not come at all." His depression this year has been read as a personal crisis, but it may equally well have been the inevitable letdown after the long push to get *Essays* finished. The book was what Emerson had been aiming at all along, his serious bid to do something notable. He could no longer think of himself as probationary, full of promise. In a good mood now he thought of calling the book "Forest Essays." In a bad mood he felt revolted by his "poor cramp arid essays."[1]

He turned to other projects. In late January he delivered a lecture called "Man the Reformer" which was his answer to the challenge of George Ripley's Brook Farm commune and to Orestes Brownson's critique of transcendentalism. This talk is Emerson's essay on economics and economy. "How can the man who has learned but one art, procure all the conveniences of life honestly? Shall we say all we think? Perhaps with his own hands." "Let us learn the meaning of economy," Emerson says. "Can anything be so elegant as to have few wants and to serve them oneself?" The lecture, quickly published in the fourth issue of *The Dial*, asks the same questions Thoreau would later ask in the first chapter of *Walden*. Emerson was committed to the belief that unless individual reformation preceded social reorganization, nothing would change for the better. The answer was neither pat nor easy, and it is clear that Emerson continued to feel a strong pull toward liberal reform projects that were more than individual in scope.[2]

In March 1841 there was much talk of new domestic arrangements at the Emersons. A plan to merge households with the Alcotts fell through because although Bronson favored it, his wife Abigail did not. At the end of March the Emersons tried having one table for meals. Instead of having Louisa the maid and Lydia the cook eat in the kitchen, they were to eat, Brook Farm style, with the family. The cook refused, knowing perhaps what Hawthorne would point out later in *The Blithedale Romance,* that it is easier to condescend than to accept condescension. In April Henry Thoreau came to live with the Emersons. He occupied a special position, being neither family nor servant but closer to family than not. All these changes show a strong impulse in the Emerson family to expand the little domestic circle into a larger family, even if Lidian and Emerson could not go all the way to the communal life of Brook Farm, which at this moment was just coming into existence in West Roxbury.

Emerson's *Essays* finally appeared on March 20, 1841. Emerson made a long list of people to send complimentary copies to. He noted to his brother William that a new chapter on nature had been left out of the volume because he was not satisfied with it. His thinking about nature was undergoing a sea-change this year. In January he had been rereading Scott's *Quentin Durward* and reading the third volume of Bancroft's *History of the United States* and Goethe's *Farbenlehre,* but he had also gone to work on Neoplatonism and related ideas, this time in a serious and extended way. He read Plotinus. In March he read Iamblichus's *Life of Pythagoras.* In April he read Porphyry, the Neoplatonic opponent of Christianity who was Plotinus's student and editor and Iamblichus's teacher. In June he was studying Zoroaster again and looking forward to seeing Thomas Taylor's translation of Proclus. Also in June he read the *Hitopades of Vishnu Sarma,* he reread Plato's *Phaedrus, Meno,* and *Symposium* in Cousin's edition, and he read Taylor's six books of Proclus, Ocellus Lucanus *On the Nature of the Universe,* and a book called *Political Fragments of the Pythagoreans.* Beyond Emerson's constant hunger for original books, primitive truth, and personal witness and beyond his by now established habit of turning to Asian scripture and his equally established habit of reading for confirmation, there was a new motive in Emerson's renewed interest in classical and Asian transcendentalism. A talk he gave in August called "The Method of Nature" shows that his essentially Germanic idealism (Kant and Schelling filtered through Carlyle and Coleridge) was changing into a dynamic pantheism with strong parallels in the Pythagorean, Neoplatonic, and Zoroastrian traditions.[3]

Emerson was learning now to regard Pythagoras as the father of philosophy, "the first who called himself a 'philosopher' or lover of wisdom." Plato was to be seen as "the most genuine and best of all his disciples." Giordano Bruno was a modern Pythagoras, the "second Pythagoras." The core of Pythagorean teaching (it is called neo-Pythagoreanism in modern histories of philosophy), as Emerson now got it from Iamblichus, is that the essential nature of things, the fundamental reality, is number: "The eternal essence of number is the most providential principle of the universe, heaven and earth, and the intermediate nature." Another way to put it is to say that "things derive their beauty and order from participation in the first and intelligible essence. That first essence is the nature of number." Neo-Pythagoreanism is not so much concerned to quantify the world or reduce it to number as to see the essence of number as the ordering principle of the soul as well as the world. Pythagoreans also believed that there are some things that cannot be said or written directly, things that must be learned by reading between the lines or by the use of symbols. The Pythagoreans taught by symbols, and the teaching was extremely thorough, bearing on all aspects of life and conduct. Students passed through long, arduous periods of apprenticeship. Pythagoras himself has been described as "a charismatic figure with the typical traits of a Guru."[4]

Pythagorean teaching emphasizes vegetable diet and puts great emphasis on the power of music to teach the harmonies inherent in nature. Emerson was reading Iamblichus on Pythagoras in March. In April, as Hawthorne was taking up residence to start his new life at Brook Farm in a huge, unseasonable snowstorm, as Thoreau was coming to live with the Emersons, and as Emerson was looking over Carlyle's new book *Heroes, Hero-Worship and the Heroic in History*, and as his correspondence with Caroline Sturgis was continuing at its warmest, Emerson was moving seriously into Neoplatonism.

A major project of Neoplatonism was the reconciliation between paganism and Christianity. Neoplatonists built on Plato, to be sure, but the important aspect for Emerson now was that they were Pythagoreans; even Plato himself was to be understood as a Pythagorean. Most of Emerson's Neoplatonism was brokered for him by Thomas Taylor, the indefatigable eighteenth-century scholar who produced an endless stream of translations, commentaries, and editions and whose complete Plato, with the commentaries of Proclus, was *the* romantic Plato. Taylor believed that "all which the moderns possess of moral science consists in nothing else than small and broken, though splendid, fragments of the great Platonic vision of the universe." Taylor had nothing but contempt for what he called the "nugatory and fungous productions of the present." In reprisal the moderns, especially the Scottish Common Sense philosophers, had violently repu-

347

diated Taylor's new Platonism, and Emerson's interest shows him self-consciously going back to pick up the Platonic-Pythagorean thread that Stewart and Reid and Macintosh had studiously dropped.[5]

Emerson was particularly struck by two Neoplatonic teachings: the idea of the world as emanation and the idea of the ecstatic union with the One. For Plotinus everything emanates, or flows out, from the One, the ultimate power and unity of things. The first emanation is thought or mind, meaning the whole range of ideas from which in turn the whole range of tangible things and beings emanate. In a piece of visionary writing of this year Emerson says:

> As the river flows, and the plant flows (or emits odors), and the sun flows (or radiates), and the mind is a stream of thoughts, so was the universe an emanation of God. Everything is an emanation, and from every emanation is a new emanation, and that from which it emanates is an emanation also. If anything could stand still, it would be instantly crushed and dissipated by the torrent which it resisted.

This is not a pure or Berkeleyan idealism but a dynamic conception of reality consistent with idealism. Emerson's master metaphor now is metamorphosis, a metaphor that for the next ten years will increasingly dominate his thinking and writing. Now in his journal he writes boldly, "Metamorphosis is nature," and he balances this bold statement by saying that while life is "a flux of moods," there is "that which changes not, and which ranks all sensations and states of mind."[6]

The other idea Emerson took from Plotinus, an idea that blazed up in Emerson like fire in a dry forest, is Plotinus's conception of the final stage in the developing self-consciousness of the individual soul. This last stage is a mystical union of the self with the One "in an ecstasy characterized by the absence of all duality. In thought *of* God or *about* God the Subject is separated from the Object, but in ecstatic union there is no such separation." Such moments of ecstatic union are rare, brief, and overpoweringly intense, leading us to a "life beyond earthly pleasures." Such union is also the supreme experience, as Plotinus famously put it and as Emerson copied it out in April, "a flight of the alone to the alone."[7]

58. Osman's Ring: A Work of Ecstasy

MAY DID COME FOR EMERSON THIS YEAR AND IT WAS YET another fruitful month. One can see Emerson's mental and, if we may use the word, spiritual growth in his letters and journals and above all in the strange new essay, "The Method of Nature." The month that would see his thirty-eighth birthday began with an extended rereading of his aunt Mary Moody Emerson's letters and journals. His way forward often began with a step backward. He read over her letters and those of his brothers Charles and Edward, and he now wrote his most discerning pages on his aunt's originality. He especially admired her unpredictability: "Her wit is the wild horse of the desert who snuffs the sirocco and scours the palm grove without having learned his paces in the stadium." As much as any other trait, her freedom from conventional book learning made her unusual in Emerson's eyes: "Nothing can excell the freedom and felicity of her letters—such nobility is in this self-rule, this absence of all reference to style or standard: it is the march of the mountain winds, the waving of flowers, or the flight of birds."[1]

Emerson's admiring absorption in his aunt's creativity triggered his own. Recognizing that he was himself a reader of many books who could therefore hardly help "acquiring their average tone, as one who walks with a military procession involuntarily falls into step," he drew inward, as he often did, to a sort of alter ego or Socratic daemon, a free prophetic poetic voice or persona who was, of course, himself and yet was not his daylight self. When young he had adopted a voice named "Guy" for such purposes. He had used the figure of Uriel in a similar way. Now he wrote a long poem, "Woodnotes II," in which a pine tree is the principal speaker and teacher. And in his journal he wrote out a long vision that he said came from a dream in which he walked with a pundit to whom he gave the name Osman. It was as Osman he wrote the sentences already quoted about the world flowing out as emanation. At the end of *Nature,* when he was reaching for the highest, most authoritative voice he could, Emerson invoked "a certain poet," who was this Osman-self, a sort of interior "other." This phenomenon is familiar enough to poets. In our own day Czeslaw Milosz began his lectures *The Witness of Poetry* by saying: "All my life I have been in the power of a daimonion, and how the poems dictated by him came into being I do not quite understand."[2]

The name of Emerson's daemon apparently derives from the Turkish form of Othman, transliterated as Osman. Othman or Osman was the founder of the Ottoman empire in the thirteenth century. When he was a very young man, the historical Osman had a remarkable dream in which he saw a tree spring from his loins. The tree, "always growing and becoming greener and more beautiful, covered with the shade of its branches both land and sea, as far as the horizon of the three parts of the world." Beneath the tree rose the Caucasus mountains, from its roots flowed out the Tigris, the Euphrates, the Nile, and the Danube. A vast troop of birds

> sang and twittered beneath the fresh and perfumed roof, formed of interleaved branches, the leaves of which lengthened out into sword shapes. At this moment, a violent wind arose which turned the points of these leaves toward the different cities of the universe, and mainly towards Constantinople, which, situated at the juncture of two seas and two continents, resembled an enchased diamond between two sapphires and two emeralds, and seemed thus to form the precious stone of the ring of a vast dominion which embraced the entire world. Osman was going to put the ring on his finger when he woke up.

Besides the sexual suggestion and the prophecy of empire, Osman's dream is a vision of metamorphosis and emanation. In Emerson's visionary mode he was always trying—in his own way and for his own purposes—to put on the ring of Osman. Emerson's Osman says, for example, in the vision already quoted: "Let a man not resist the law of his mind and he will be filled with the divinity which flows through all things. He must emanate; he must give all he takes, nor desire to appropriate and to stand still."[3]

The immediate literary fruit of this reconnection to the wellhead of his poetry was "Woodnotes II," in which the pine tree speaks for a life in nature, away from the ordinary world in which "The Lord is the peasant that was, / The peasant the lord that shall be." Amid lines of remarkable freshness ("The shadows shake on the rock behind") the tree's essential aim is to teach us to recognize "The rushing metamorphosis / Dissolving all that fixture is" and melting "things that be to things that seem, / And solid nature to a dream."[4]

In June Emerson was rereading Dante's *La vita nuova,* he had found a copy of Taylor's *Proclus,* and he was dipping again into Zoroastrianism. The key to Emerson's interest in Zoroaster is also Pythagoreanism. Pythagoras was thought to have traveled in the East and to have learned the wisdom of the Zoroastrian mages. Plotinus was interested in Zoroaster as well. Emerson was familiar with Anquetil-Duperron's "Exposition du système théologique des Perses," which he read in April of 1832, and with his magisterial three-volume edition of the Zend-Avesta, a Zoroastrian text and the first major non-Western scripture apart from the Koran to be introduced to the West. Emerson understood from Goethe that Zoroaster—also called Zarathustra—was the first person to have institutionalized the pure and noble religion of nature in a cult or church. He also thought of Zoroaster as the first to teach through allegories. The already celebrated Zoroastrian dualism had a strange appeal for Emerson, whom we usually think of as strictly monistic. The tales of Ormazd (Ahuramazda) and Ahriman are very much like the long story of the good and bad brothers in another obscure book Emerson was puzzlingly fond of, Synesius's *On Providence.* Perhaps the dualism illuminated some aspect of the sad Emerson family history, though there were other appeals in Zoroastrianism for Emerson, as there were for Nietzsche. Emerson was drawn to Zoroaster's identification of the good principle with the idea of original fire. He liked the frank nature worship of Zoroastrianism as well as its interest in the purification and general health of nature itself. Here was a religion that aimed at more than the redemption of individuals.[5]

In July 1841 Emerson went off to Cohasset and the then deserted beach of Nantasket on the south shore of Massachusetts Bay. Here was a chance to rest, make his peace with the sea, and above all to try to capture something of the new worlds of thought whirling through his head for the address he had promised to give in August. Even Emerson's use of landscape was changing, as he himself recognized. From childhood he had held a sort of grudge against the sea, which had kept him penned in the streets of Boston. For many years and despite several voyages he considered any landscape that included the sea "a little vulgarized," as he told Fuller. Now he wrote Lidian from Nantasket that he found the sea "very satiating to the eye . . . this vastness and roar—the rubbing of the sea on the land so ancient and pleasant a sound, the color and curve of the same do fill and content the eye as mountains and woods do not—which we always wish higher or wilder." He was reading Proclus, Ocellus Lucanus (one of the earliest of the neo-Pythagoreans), Plato, and Pythagoras.[6]

Emerson was hoping for a "visitation of the high muse," for a visionary experience of life-altering intensity. He was after the sort of experience with which he could lift the reader or hearer "by a happy violence into a religious beatitude, or into a Socratic trance and imparadise him in ideas." Emerson knew precisely what kind of experience he was seeking. He had had them before. The experience at Mt. Auburn was one such and evidence of others is scattered through his journals. "My faith," he said this year,

> is some brief affecting experience which surprised me on the highway or in the market place—in some place at some time whether in the body or out of the body, I cannot tell, God knoweth, and made me aware that I had played the fool with fools all this time, but that there was, for me and for all, law, and ineffable sweetness of child-like carriage—and I should never be fool more.

Such experiences were invariably short. "In the space of an hour probably I was let down from this height," Emerson's account continues. "I was at my old tricks, the selfish member of a selfish society."[7]

Emerson had experienced just such a moment back in June. Henry Thoreau had taken him out on the Concord River: "Through one field only we went to the boat and then left all time, all science, all history behind us, and entered into nature with one stroke of the paddle." The time was sunset and Emerson was acutely aware of it as an extraordinary moment.

> Take care, good friend! I said as I looked west into the sunset overhead and underneath, and he with his face toward me rowed toward it—take care; you know not what you do, dipping your wooden oar into this enchanted liquid, painted with all reds and purples and yellows which glow under and behind you.

As the sunset glory faded, the stars came out "and began to cast such private and ineffable beams as to stop all conversation.

> A holiday, a villegiatura, a royal revel, the proudest, most magnificent, most heart-rejoicing festival that valor and beauty, power and poetry ever decked and enjoyed—it is here, it is this. These stars signify it and proffer it: they gave the idea and the invitation, not kings, not

palaces, not men, not women, but these tender, poetic, clear, and auspicious stars, so eloquent of secret promises . . . All experience is against them, yet their word is hope.[8]

The kind of experience for which Emerson is always reaching is the ecstatic state, an experience that gives a person the feeling of being outside time. The word *ecstasy* means "a displacement," a standing outside oneself. Ecstasy names "a range of experiences characterized by being joyful, transitory, unexpected, rare, valued, and extraordinary to the point of seeming as if derived from a preternatural source." Such experiences are marked by great intensity of feeling, by a sense of contact, which Marghanita Laski says in her study of ecstasy "is often spoken of as if it were the keynote of religious experience." Evelyn Underhill, whose classic, *Mysticism,* describes how to induce a kind of ecstasy, emphasizes the role of the eyes, of vision: "Do not think, but pour out your personality toward it; let your soul be in your eyes." Such moments are not exclusive to religious mystics. They occur also in literature. Proust's *Jean Santeuil,* for example, concerns itself with such experiences in the life of the title character: "The experiences that really count in Jean's life are the many occasions when, by the seaside, in a garden, or a wood, he is penetrated entirely by a sense of the unique, individual mystery of a setting, a particular beauty that awakes in him a sense of wonder and a great surge of happiness."[9]

For Emerson similar experiences were a source of vision, a confirmation of power: "The one thing we wish to know is where is power to be bought. We would give any price for condensation, concentration, and the recalling at will high mental energy." Emerson was also convinced that ecstatic states were experiences everyone has, much as Jorge Luis Borges has insisted that there are two or three occasions in everyone's life when he or she is capable of writing poetry. "Every man has had one or two moments of extraordinary experience," Emerson writes, "has met his soul, has thought of something which he never afterward forgot, and which revised all his speech, and moulded all his forms of thought." He was further convinced that ecstatic states were natural, not supernatural, and he took pains to demystify them. He once wrote: "I hold that ecstasy will be found mechanical, if you please to say so, or, nothing but an example on a higher field of the same gentle gravitation by which rivers run."[10]

"The Method of Nature" was written to be delivered at Waterville College in Maine for an occasion when Emerson knew his aunt would be present. The talk was considered a failure at the time, but if it was, it was one of those failures that are more interesting than most successes. "The Method of Nature" is Emerson's essay on ecstasy, an attempt to link that quintessentially personal experience of ecstasy with the metamorphic processes by which he understood nature to work.

> The metamorphosis of nature shows itself in nothing more than this; that there is no word in our language that cannot become typical to us of nature by giving it emphasis. The world is a dancer: it is a Rosary; it is a torrent: it is a Boat: a Mist, a Spider's Snare; it is what you will; and the metaphor will hold. . . . Swifter than light the World transforms itself into that thing you name.

Emerson emphasized this sense of process in the talk. Nature, he said, is a rushing stream that "will not stop to be observed."[11]

Emerson further argued, drawing from his new Neoplatonists, that "every natural fact is an emanation," and he tried to suggest the link between personal experience and the processes of nature by declaring flatly that "the power or genius of nature is ecstatic." He may well have been thinking of the famous experience recounted in *Nature,* in which the seer dissolves into a mere instrument of sight. For the new essay, however, Emerson had no single central incandescent moment, nothing half so vivid as the transparent eye. Nonetheless, as a recent commentator has pointed out, "The Method of Nature" marks the point at which the ecstatic experience of nature replaces Emerson's previous conception of human moral progress as nature's end. He now conceives of himself as a "professor of the joyous science." He is concerned now with the actions of the mind, with actual states, and he was less inclined than ever to waste time on what might have been, on what he gayly and superbly dismisses as "the waste abyss of possibility."[12]

59. The Frightful Hollows of Space

ON SEPTEMBER 21, 1841, EMERSON'S STEPGRANDFATHER EZRA Ripley died. It was the passing of more than a season. Ripley had been born in 1751. He belonged to and he stood for the revolutionary generation. Emerson said in his eulogy that Ripley "was identified with the ideas and forms of the New England Church, which expired about the same time with him." In 1841 the old meeting house of the First Parish in Concord was disassembled, reoriented ninety degrees to face as it now does, and enlarged and modernized inside and out in a graceful, airy, Greek Revival style. Old Dr. Ripley had never been reoriented or modernized. He was a loyalist at heart, no democrat, and a believer in particular providences. Emerson illustrated Ripley's beliefs with funny anecdotes about an eighteenth-century preacher and his ostentatious new one-horse shay that kept breaking down as a message to him. Ripley was credulous, opinioned, and a great kisser of women. One of his targets told Emerson it "seemed as if he were going to make a meal of you." Ripley was a man of anecdote, had no literature or art, knew everybody's grandfather, and was good at fires. His body, when it was laid out, seemed to Emerson "a handsome and noble spectacle . . . like a sachem fallen in the forest." Emerson said all the correct things in his tribute, but he was not much moved now or ever by the deaths of the fathers. He brought his son, Waldo, now almost five, to see the old man's body where he lay. The boy "walked round and round the couch, and at last asked, 'Why didn't they keep him for a statue?'"[1]

Waldo turned five in October. Concord was visited by its first traveling daguerreotypist this month, and it was John Thoreau, Henry's brother, who had the idea of taking Waldo to have his picture taken. The print shows a handsome little boy with large eyes, expressive eyebrows, and a full mouth. His dark hair is slicked down and parted in the middle and he is frowning from the long pose in bright sunlight which daguerreotypy then required. He was the apple of his father's eye and his constant companion. He played quietly in Emerson's study for hours. He slept in a trundle bed in his parents' bedroom. Lidian thought he was much like other little boys until he was nearly five, when he began "to seem wiser and more angelic all the time." Taken to visit friends in Boston, Waldo gazed at the splendid parlor and finally said to his mother, "How glass their knobs are."[2]

In August of 1841 Waldo was old enough to write a letter to his sister Ellen, then two and a half, but not old enough to go to the post office to ask for Daddy's letter. Emerson noted, without anxiety, that Waldo could be a bit timid: "He does not want to go to school alone, no, not at all, no, never." He played endlessly with a toy house he and Henry Thoreau were building for Ellen. It was to have grand features called "interspiglions." It was to have a bell "louder than ten thousand bells, that could be heard in all the countries." His grandmother gave him reading lessons every day. Margaret Fuller and Caroline Sturgis "caressed and conversed" with him whenever they were at the house. One night when he was almost four and when he and baby Ellen were just recovering from colds, Waldo told his mother he had just prayed a little prayer all himself. Lidian asked what he had said. "I asked God that I might be good—that Ellen might live and grow up."[3]

When Waldo was five in late October 1841 Lidian was in the last month of her third pregnancy. It was difficult and she felt ill much of the time. On November 18 she had a strange dream about a statue that looked "so beautiful that the blooming child who was in the room looked pale and sallow beside it." The statue spoke to the child—a girl—about life and being, "and then, by a few slight movements of the head and body, it gave the most forcible picture of decay and death and corruption, and then became all radiant again with the signs of resurrection." Whether the message from the statuesque older generation was hopeful or ominous was hard to say. Perhaps death, decay, and resurrection were grown-up matters, having little to do with children. Four days later Lidian gave birth to her second daughter. Emerson wanted to call her Lidian, but Lidian would not agree and it was some little time before Edith had a name.[4]

Early in October Emerson had learned that the City Bank was to pay no dividend. This left him six hundred dollars short, with no alternative but to go back to lecturing. Not that he was reluctant. He enjoyed the rapid composition that lecturing forced on him. He preferred such writing to the slow and difficult job of editing and condensing material for printed essays, and he both enjoyed and was confident about his speaking skills. He became interested in the new art of photography about the time his son's picture was taken this fall. Emerson liked the idea of an art in which light was the painter and he thought the new process represented "the true republican style of painting. The Artist stands aside and lets you paint yourself." He especially liked the idea that photography gave a straightforward, unidealized image, and he considered writing a set of lecture-portraits inspired by the new art. But this topic would have meant lectures on particular people, and he was not yet ready to do that. Still, the idea of portraits of types was much on his mind as he designed the series of talks called "The Times." Beginning on December 2 he delivered eight lectures in Boston, including "The Conservative," "The Poet," and "The Transcendentalist" among them.[5]

The opening talk, "The Conservative," set the tone and overall theme of the series. Its subject was the party of the past versus the party of the future, conservatism versus reform. He thought the modern reformers who were leading the crusades against war, slavery, alcohol, and "government based on force" were the true successors of Luther and Knox. He warned his hearers against separating religion and daily life, against becoming "dividuals," as he put it.

He described the roots of both reform and conservation in human nature. "Innovation is the salient energy, Conservation the pause on the last movement." He set up the argument in dialogue form, making up a Blake-like conversation between "Saturn" and "Uranus." Later in the same piece there is another dialogue between Youth and Property. Emerson's dialogue form is meant to convey two points of view simultaneously, as are the aphorisms of this essay. "There is always a certain meanness in the argument of conservatives, joined with a certain superiority in its facts." Emerson's habit of seeing the world as a system of compensations had brought him to a kind of binary structure, with emphasis falling more on the interaction between the poles of an argument than on the poles themselves.[6]

The talk "The Poet" focuses on the human need for expression, which Emerson insists is "a primary impulse of nature." Happiness itself depends, he says, not on property but on expression. "All that we do, or say or see is expression or for expression." And if poetry is usually considered the highest form of verbal expression, Emerson now puts in a word for modern prose: "I think even now, that the very finest and sweetest closes and falls are not in our meter, but in the measures of prose eloquence which have greater variety and richness than verse."[7]

In "The Transcendentalist" Emerson pits the materialists, who believe in experience, against the idealists, who believe in consciousness. "The

Transcendentalist" is about consciousness and constitutes a defining statement of the new movement. It cites Kant, Jacobi, and Coleridge and explains that the experience of the transcendentalist inclines him "to behold the procession and facts you call the world as flowing perpetually outward from an invisible unsounded centre in himself."[8]

In the last talk of the series, called at different times "Prospects" and "Duties," Emerson announced himself as a "professor of the joyous science" and vowed not to build "dungeons in the air." He aimed to exhilarate, and he insisted on the large view. "Our warm commodious houses and spacious towns are built on a planet swimming unpiloted in the frightful hollows of space," he told his audience. All we can do is be prepared.

> A man who has accustomed himself to look at all his circumstances as very mutable; to carry his possessions, his relations to persons, and even his opinions in his hand as a bird flieth, and in all these to pierce to the principle and moral law and everywhere to find that, has put himself out of the reach of skepticism.[9]

But not out of the reach of tragedy. January 1842 was a terrible month. On New Year's Day Henry Thoreau's older brother, John, cut himself while stropping his razor. On the ninth lockjaw set in. A Boston doctor pronounced the case hopeless. Henry, who had been living with the Emersons, returned to his father's house to nurse John, who died two days later. On January 20 Emerson finished his Boston lecture series with the image of the lonely pilotless planet and the Stoic preparatory meditation. Two days later, on January 22, to the shock and uncomprehending horror of his friends and family, Henry Thoreau came down with the symptoms of lockjaw. By the morning of the twenty-fourth, however, he was better. He turned out to have had a severe sympathetic reaction, not an infection.

That evening, at the Emerson's, little Waldo came down with scarlatina. Fever set in and increased quickly. On January 27 he was delirious. Lidian left him briefly to get some rest, but he called out for her; as she came back down she asked Dr. Bartlett if he would soon be better. "I had hoped to be spared this" was his response. Not until that moment had she considered he might not live. A few hours later, at 8:15 in the evening, the boy was dead.

Little Ellen was just coming down with the same disease. That night she took her father's place in Lidian's bed, so Lidian could watch her. Lidian had felt able to endure it all while she and Emerson and Emerson's mother talked together late that dreadful evening, but once she was alone she broke down. "Grief, desolating grief came over me like a flood," she wrote later, "and I feared that the charm of earthly life was forever destroyed." Nine-year-old Louisa May Alcott came to the door next morning to ask how Waldo was. Years later she remembered how "his father came to me, so worn with watching and changed by sorrow that I was startled and could only stammer out my message. "Child, he is dead" was the answer. "That was my first glimpse of a great grief," Alcott recalled.[10]

Emerson wrote four short letters to friends and family the night Waldo died and he wrote six or seven more the next day. He was reduced to a stuttering and helpless repetition. "Farewell and farewell," "my darling my darling," "my boy, my boy is gone." To Margaret Fuller he wrote, "Shall I ever dare to love anything again?" To Carlyle he wrote a month later, "You can never know how much of me such a young child can take away." Lidian, who knew that her husband's dismissal of misery was largely "in theory," who had said earlier that she scarcely knew anyone for whom the suffering of others was so real and who had her own hopeless and heartsick grief to contend with, now said of her husband: "How intensely his heart yearns over every memento of his boy I cannot express to you. Never was a greater hope disappointed—a more devoted love bereaved."[11]

The grief of both Emersons was deep, real, and immediate. It was also expressed—in letters, in talking, and above all, for him, in poetry. Over time he wrote the long elegy "Threnody," one of the great elegies in English and a poem in which Emerson rivals the Milton whose "Lycidas" he had known by heart for so long. Emerson felt anger and shock and bitterness. He did not believe in a conventional afterlife. He was bereft alike of his son and of the usual consolation. But he was able to mourn, and, perhaps largely for that reason, the worst of the grief passed more quickly for him than for Lidian. He was far from being the stereotype of the stolid Yankee (as in the joke, "Sam died Friday. He didn't want much said about it"). When he wrote Caroline Sturgis that he "grieved chiefly that I cannot grieve," the Thoreauvian contrariness and paradox may only signify some chagrin that he was not so utterly prostrated by grief as Henry was by John Thoreau's death.

Waldo's death made a deep wound in the entire Emerson family, one that never completely healed. Ellen, who was almost three at the time, noted painfully many years later how Margaret Fuller could not get over the fact that Waldo had died and she, Ellen, was left. The decline of Lidian during the next few years probably had several causes, but the most immediate and shocking was Waldo's death. Only one of Lidian's letters survives from the period 1843–1847, and it is a sad and troubled letter to Emerson, reading in part: "I have lost Ellen's most important years. The other children are of softer material as well as of more tender years. Perhaps I can yet take care of them. Waldo is safe."[12]

Six months after Waldo's death, Emerson wrote to a well-wisher in Baltimore, one Solomon Corner, that "the powers of the soul are commensurate with its needs." If there is affirmation in the first half of that sentence, there is a world of pain in the last word. Emerson's capacity for expression gave him the capacity to mourn. "The South wind brings / Life, sunshine and desire," he says at the beginning of "Threnody":

> But over the dead he has no power,
> The lost, the lost he cannot restore;
> And, looking over the hills, I mourn
> The darling who shall not return.[13]

Children of the Fire

60. The Dream of Community

EMERSON PULLED HIMSELF TOGETHER IN EARLY FEBRUARY. There were Lidian and the two remaining children to be considered. There was a lecture series he had promised to give in Providence, and there was Alcott. On February 12, writing from Providence, he guaranteed Alcott that he should have five hundred dollars to go to England to visit English admirers. The Providence series had not been successful as a money-maker, so he now decided to try his luck in New York. From February 26 through the middle of March Emerson lectured in New York. His almost daily letters to Lidian have a careworn, anxious quality, but they also have a strong strain of affection and dependence—as do hers to him at this time. Their correspondence has above all a kind of household realism that is in striking contrast to the high-flown, almost make-believe tone of his letters to Caroline Sturgis. The tragedy pulled Lidian and Emerson closer. And there was much for him to be anxious about. Henry Thoreau was still very ill and weak, unable to work or even get out of bed. Lidian suffered a spell of poor health, as did baby Edith. Emerson sent off letter after letter, begging for news.

The lectures in New York went well—though they netted only two hundred dollars—and Emerson was meeting new people. He met Charles King Newcomb, a twenty-two-year-old Brown graduate and friend of Margaret Fuller's. Emerson met him in Concord, between engagements. Newcomb had long curly black hair and a shy, uncertain, ardent, and somewhat mysterious manner. He had a little romantic interest in Fuller, which she discouraged. Later he was drawn to Caroline Sturgis. He was an early member of Brook Farm, where he lived in aesthetic semi-isolation. Lindsay Swift, historian of Brook Farm, called Newcomb "a sentimental devotee of unattached Catholicism." His room was filled with crosses and saints and over a sort of altar were pictures of Jesus and Loyola. After he saw the dancer Fanny Elssler, he put up her picture between them. Newcomb copied passages from Fuller's journal which Fuller had copied from Emerson's journal.[1]

When Newcomb met Emerson, Newcomb read to him from a piece called "Dolon," a dreamy Pre-Raphaelitish story about a sensitive boy who is awakening to the world around him. The tale has a fin-de-siècle languor; it is heavy with tragical premonition and with a strange druidical menace. The boy Dolon hears

> a sound behind him of something ascending the rock, and looking, he saw just rising from the rock, in the face of the moon, the man, whom he instantly recognized as if he knew, dressed in a surplice-like robe, gathered in at the waist by a white tasselled girdle, and a wreath of laurel and wild lilies on his left arm.

This figure kills the boy with a sacrificial knife and the piece ends abruptly. "Dolon" is about the preternatural sensibilities of an unusual child who is mysteriously sacrificed. It may have been inspired by the death of Waldo. Certainly the piece affected Emerson as nothing had since his son's death. With forgivable charity he praised Newcomb, worked with him on "Dolon," published it, and encouraged him to further work. But nothing more ever came. Newcomb was a momentary writer. He was able just once to write sentences that Emerson said *The Dial* was specifically created in order to publish. The vatic, nearly lucid "all forms are facts to youth and recognized by them as beings, not as persons" is typical Newcomb. And while Newcomb later proved a disappointment, Emerson felt more kinship with him just now than with the worldly New Yorkers he was meeting.[2]

He met Julia Ward, then twenty-three, and Catherine Sedgewick, whom he found sensible and pleasant. He also met Henry Bellows, who at age twenty-eight was just beginning his ministry at what would become All Souls Unitarian church on the upper east side of Manhattan. Bellows later became the leader of those Unitarians who wished to create a solid institutional base for Unitarianism. He was also Herman Melville's pastor in later years. Bellows became a kind of polar opposite of Emerson, but at this time Bellows was much interested in Emerson and helped arrange lectures. There was also William Cullen Bryant, now forty-eight, editor of the *New York Evening Post*. Even though he had a new book of poems out this year (*The Fountain and Other Poems*) and was fashionably interested in homeopathy, Bryant was already a figure out of the literary past.

Of more interest to Emerson was Henry James, the thirty-two-year-old Swedenborgian whose son, William, was born this year. James paid Emerson a visit after his first lecture and Emerson found him a "manlike thorough seeing person." James was also interested in the ideas of Charles Fourier, as were the other men Emerson saw a good deal of in New York, Horace Greeley and Albert Brisbane. Greeley was thirty-one. He had soft white hair, wore shapeless trousers, a crooked tie, white coat, and broad-brimmed hat. Emerson said Greeley "listens after all new thoughts and things but with the indispensable New York condition that they can be made available." Greeley had launched the *New York Tribune* just a year earlier, setting a new and elevated tone for a city newspaper. Police reports, scandals, dubious medical advertisements, and "flippant personalities" were all banned from its pages. Greeley was an egalitarian who opposed capital punishment, favored free speech—even for abolitionists—and supported labor unions. He was the first president of the New York Printers Union, he printed articles by Marx, his paper had the best political news in the city, and he lived in a Grahamite boarding house, as did Brisbane.[3]

Albert Brisbane was thirty-three in 1842. He had gone to Paris when he was eighteen to study with the philosopher Victor Cousin and the historian François-Pierre-Guillaume Guizot. He went on to Berlin where he studied social philosophy with Hegel. He visited Constantinople, then returned to Paris just after the revolution of 1830. In Paris, at age twenty-one, he read Fourier's *Traité de l'association domestique-agricole* (1821–1822). He immediately sought out Fourier and quickly became the leading disciple of the French utopian. Brisbane returned to America, wrote a book called *The Social Destiny of Man*—which is as much a translation as a discussion of Fourier's work—and labored tirelessly to advance the Fourierian cause. Brisbane got to Greeley early. Greeley gave him a front-page column in the *Tribune* on a regular basis. Mainly on account of Brisbane's efforts, over forty Fourierian communes were formed in the United States during the 1840s, among them Brook Farm.[4]

Brisbane's lofty dismissal of Hegel reveals the scale of Brisbane's expectations: "I found in Hegel and among his disciples no idea of a higher social order than the European Civilization." Fourier, by contrast, did have a higher vision. He thought the human race had passed through three social eras—the savage, the patriarchal, and the barbarian—and had arrived at the fourth stage, the still imperfect era of civilization. Fourier considered it his mission to lead the human race to the next and final stage of social organization, that which he called harmony. Fourier understood the term *civilization* to mean the "social system in which we live, as it is now, with all its defects and the little good it may possess." Fourier and Brisbane and the Brook Farmers referred contemptuously to "civilisées" much as Marxists refer to "the bourgeoisie." The present social system, that is, civilization, is "not adapted to the nature of man and his passions." Civilization's incoherence lies "in our system of separate households, or as many distinct houses as there are families." This state of affairs "absorbs the time . . . of one half of the human race, in an unproductive function, which has to be gone through with as many times as there are families."[5]

To avoid such waste and duplication of effort, Fourier planned to rearrange the human race into communes called phalanxes, with 1,680 persons to a phalanx. For further economies of scale all 1,680 would live in a single, large all-purpose building called a phalanstery. Fourier considered the present social order dominated by what he called "repulsive industry" and by wholesale repression of the passionate impulses natural to a human being. Fourier proposed to remedy this repressed misery by implementing a system of "attractive industry" based on a full recognition of "passional attraction" as the main motivating force of human nature. Fourier's estimate of his own role in this process is not handicapped by false modesty. "I alone," he wrote,

> shall have confounded twenty centuries of political imbecility, and it is to me alone that present and future generations will owe the beginning of their boundless happiness. Before me, mankind lost several thousand years by fighting madly against Nature. I am the first who has bowed before her, by studying attraction. . . . Possessor of the book of fate, I come to dissipate political and moral darkness, and upon the ruins of the uncertain sciences I erect the theory of universal harmony.[6]

In the phalanstery people would work at half a dozen different tasks each day, each task being one the person liked doing. Short stretches of work at gardening, orchard tending, or greenhouse maintenance (for example) would replace the assignment of masses of people to hateful jobs in factories. A worker might do a little shoemaking between ten and eleven thirty instead of slaving twelve hours a day in a shoe factory. Highest wages would go to those who did the least pleasant tasks. Careful attention would be paid to proclivities. Thus children, who naturally love dirt, would be assigned the garbage collection duties. By careful mating of people with work, a community of 1,680 persons ought to be more or less self-sufficient. Eventually the whole world would be similarly organized.

The very possibility of "attractive industry" itself rested on Fourier's theory of "passional attraction." Brisbane's book and other English accounts mentioned the theory, tantalizingly, but never went beyond saying in rather general terms that what was *really* wrong with modern civilized industrial society was that everyone is either taught or forced to repress most of his passions. Fourier's hopes for reform rested at bottom on a belief that human passions—emotions—were all naturally good, since they had been given us by God, and that if all passions were systematically and continually gratified life would become a beautiful round of fulfilling pleasure and work. Well before Freud, Fourier was maintaining that the two most important things in life were love and work and he had formulated a master critique of modern society's principal evil as that of repression.[7]

What Fourier had to say about work was readily available in English after 1840. What he had to say about love was not, even though the system of attractive labor depended on the theory of passional attraction. Brisbane was thoroughly familiar with Fourier's work on attraction. Indeed, he possessed the master's own annotated copy of the six-hundred-page treatise.[8]

Fourier recognized a total of twelve passions. First there were the five senses. Next came four affective passions: friendship, love, ambition, and paternity. Then came the three distributive passions: the cabalist, or love of intrigue, the butterfly, or love of variety, and the composite, a passion in which the spiritual and the physical were joined. Finally, the twelfth, last, and highest of the passions was unityism, a passion for harmonizing the self with all the rest of humankind.

Fourier's system of attractive labor undertook to fulfill all these passions. Hence arise the most famous units of the Fourierian scheme, the groups and the series. A group was composed of a minimum of seven persons and was divided into a center and two wings in such a way that the center was numerically stronger than either wing. A series was made up of three groups, also with the center group the strongest. One wing did the heaviest or largest aspect of a given job, the center did the most elegant or attractive part, and the other wing did the lightest or smallest. The idea was that the two wings would join to compete against the center, the two wings outnumbering the center but with the center having the edge in quality. By such dynamics Fourier expected both to stimulate competition and to avoid the dangers of easily resolved or ineffective competition. So important was this group dynamic of controlled competition that Fourier had carved on his tomb-stone the propositions: "The series distribute the harmonies; attractions are proportional to destinies." When Brook Farm went openly Fourierist in its later years—it was always Fourierist to some degree—it declared "the law of groups and series is, we are convinced, the law of human nature."[9]

Fourier would reform love too. Bourgeois society, he said, was dominated by false love, by amorous contraband, and he outlined a grammar of love progressing from *fidélité simple* to *infidélité composée;* he described the antics of what he called erotic quadrilles—four people involved in a web of amorous desire and deceit—and he sketched whole gamuts of desire, mu-sical scales of love, one of which works upward from monogamy to plurig-amy to cryptogamy to delphigamy to omnigamy, with quite a few inter-mediate stages.[10]

Fourier's intent was to create a world in which no desire went unmet or had to be repressed. In the new world of love in a proper Fourierist society, all false love would be swept away. Monogamous marriage would be scrapped, just as having one job would be scrapped. Everyone would become involved in a complex network of liaisons; everyone would wear a badge indicating his or her special characteristics. The major preoccupation of individuals would be the tending of relationships, which was, for Fourier, the only worthwhile human concern. In order to gratify all the passions, everyone would have a full range of relationships. For a man, say, one woman would be a platonic friend, another a work companion, a third a conventional lover, a fourth a spiritual companion. Women, of course, would have the same range of relationships. Furthermore, a full scale of sexual relations would also be available, both heterosexual and homosexual, in groups from two to ten, emphasizing everything from mere general lusts to specialized cravings to fully integrated combinations of physical and spiritual desire.[11]

Brisbane had already won over Greeley to Fourierism. Greeley and his wife in turn both became very interested in Brook Farm. Now Brisbane applied himself to Emerson. Finding that Emerson was not up on Fourier, Brisbane went to Emerson's hotel to educate him on the matter "by full illimitable personal explanation." Night after night there was animated conversation at Brisbane's boardinghouse. "What palaces! what concerts! what pictures, lectures, poetry, and flowers," Emerson wrote home. "Con-stantinople is to be the metropolis and we poets and miscellaneous tran-scendental persons who are too great for your Concords and New Yorks will gravitate to that point for music and architecture and society such as wit cannot paint nowadays."[12]

Emerson sensed that he would never be able to satisfy Brisbane or Greeley, with their expectation of total commitment, their demands for immediate, practical implementation of communal life, and their indifference or hostility to individual effort and the inner life. But Emerson was not indifferent to the dream of community, and his report on Fourierism for *The Dial* is respectful of Fourierian goals: "In a day of small, sour, and fierce schemes, one is admonished and cheered by a project of such friendly aims, and of such bold and generous proportion." Emerson was, however, skeptical about Fourierian means. He thought "that Fourier had skipped no fact but one, namely life. He treats man as a plastic thing, something that may be put up or down, ripened or retarded, moulded, polished, made into a solid, or fluid, or gas, at the will of the leader."[13]

Fourierism was too shallow, too optimistic, and too mechanical, especially now when Emerson was still shaken by the tragedy of Waldo's death. Just after his New York trip, he wrote to Sarah Clarke,

> I have no skill, no illumination, no "nearness" to the power which has bereaved me of the most beautiful of the children of men. I apprehend nothing of that fact but its bitterness. . . . It is nothing to me but the gloomiest sensible experience to which I have no key, and no consolation, nothing but oblivion and diversion.

And in his dreams there were jumbled images of a madman in the attic, a crib, animation reduced to magic, and a witchcraft-working will to evil:

> I found myself in a garret disturbed by the noise of some one sawing wood. On walking toward the sound, I saw lying in a crib an insane person whom I very well knew, and the noise instantly stopped: there was no saw, a mere stirring among several trumpery matters, furmuffs, and empty baskets that lay on the floor. As I tried to approach, the muffs swelled themselves a little as with wind, and whirled off into a corner of the garret, as if alive. . . . Seeing this and instantly aware that here was witchcraft, that here was a devilish will . . . I was unable to move: my limbs were frozen with fear . . . I mowed the defiance I could not articulate and woke with the ugly sound I made.

At these levels, and about such matters, Fourier had nothing to say.[14]

61. Children of the Fire

By mid-March 1842 Margaret Fuller had decided she could no longer remain editor of *The Dial*. Four days after getting her letter Emerson decided to take over the job himself rather than let the magazine die. "Let there be rotation in martyrdom," he wrote Fuller. On March 29 he attended the last meeting of the Chardon Street Convention, a loose gathering of radicals and reformers who met to debate the credibility and authority of the Old and New Testaments. Alcott and Brownson both attended, as did a working-class speaker named Nathaniel H. Whiting from South Marshfield, Massachusetts, who distinguished himself with a strong speech and a plain man's view of transcendentalism. Whiting said simply that truths pertaining to the soul could not be proved or disproved by external testimony.[1]

Again in April the City Bank failed to pay and again Emerson had to scramble for funds. Hard times contracted his income but not his commitments. It was thanks to Emerson that Alcott was about to sail for England to visit the school that had been named there for him. To Thoreau Emerson proposed a long review essay on a pile of recent scientific reports on the flora and fauna of Massachusetts, a subject that "admits of the narrative of all his woodcraft, boatcraft, and fishcraft," as he told Fuller. Emerson also talked with his friend and neighbor Edmund Hosmer about Colman's agricultural report on the state and about model farms and farmers. Of one such farmer—named Elias Phinney, a wealthy Lexington man—Hosmer said he "would starve in two years on any one of fifty poor farms in this neighborhood on each of which now a farmer gets a good living."[2]

Emerson's answer to Brook Farm and community was Concord and neighborhood. He was always scheming and inviting and making inquiries about houses to rent. Now in 1842 he hoped to get Hedge, Hawthorne, George Bradford, and Sarah Ripley to Concord. "Who knows but Margaret Fuller and Charles Newcomb would presently be added," he noted to himself. Although Emerson was always trying to improve his neighborhood, he knew and loved the ordinary parts of it. The East primary school was fifty paces away from Emerson's house, across the road from his front gate. The Concord Asylum, painted red, was just across the brook in his back yard. From it could be heard the hollering of mad Nancy Barron, for whom Emerson once took up a collection. Once when a man pulled into Emerson's yard with a load of wood, Emerson broke away from the earnest group of talkers gathered in his study and rushed into the yard, saying, "We have to attend to these things just as if they were real." He delighted in Hosmer's conversation and company, though probably not in that of another neighbor, John Richardson, who owned land adjacent to Emerson's at Walden Pond and who, by Emerson's account, "got a living by buying odd bits of land near good dwelling houses and removing on to them some old crazy barn or wretched shop and keeping it there until the proprietor of the house paid him a round sum for the land."[3]

He did his annual stock-taking in April, in the annual funk that seemed to come about a month before his birthday: "I have not yet adjusted my relations to my fellows on the planet, or to my own work. Always too young or too old, I do not satisfy myself; how can I satisfy others?" Beneath this by now ritualized lament, however, there is something else, a fear this spring that love itself is not part of the permanent order of things but is evanescent like most other things in nature. In a poem written this spring he confessed that he believed in expression not possession and that he was tormented by "the fear that love / Died in its last expression."[4]

Through all this trouble Emerson was now working on his essay "The Poet." The essay is about the nature of poetry and the function of the poet. This topic was Emerson's oldest and at some level his most urgent. For all his success as a preacher, a lecturer, and a writer of essays, he had always wanted most to be a poet. He had only recently written yet another lecture on the subject, but eloquent as it may have been on poetry as expression, he put it aside now and began to assemble material for a really definitive piece.

"The Poet" is arguably the best piece ever written on literature as literary process, and it is the major statement of international romantic expressionism, the idea that expressing our thoughts and feelings is not only one of the fundamental and given aspects about human nature—a basic drive, like sex—but also one of the main *purposes* of human life. The essay is full of verve and fire—fire is one of its four main metaphors—and it has a bright clarity born of Emerson's new enthusiasm for establishing boundaries and recognizing limits.

"The Poet" begins by brushing aside the kind of critic who sets up as a superior person by having "acquired some knowledge of admired pictures or sculptures" but whose own life has nothing beautiful in it. Poetry is not an acquisition, a possession, a skill, or a trade. Its forms are nothing except as they reflect the spirit, the inner fire. The forms of poetry by themselves do not matter. What matters is the source of poetry: "For we are not pans and barrows, nor even porters of the fire and torch bearers, but children of the fire, made of it."[5]

Czeslaw Milosz has noted with clear disapproval how "one of the basic tenets of modern poetics is the belief that true art cannot be understood by ordinary people." Emerson's whole enterprise, like that of Milosz, is set against this aesthetic. "The Poet" pursues the literary consequences of Schleiermacher's theology of communication. The shared human core that makes communion possible makes communication possible. "The poet," says Emerson, "is representative. He stands among partial men for the complete man, and apprises us not of his wealth, but of the common wealth." Emerson rejects the idea that the poet is in any way a superior person. The concept of the representative poet is the cornerstone of a democratic aesthetic Emerson was to work out over the next ten years.[6]

With equal clarity and logic Emerson also insists that the poet is a sayer, a namer, and not a maker. A poem is the result of seeing and saying; the art is in the process. The final product marks the end, the death, of the process, the point at which fossilization sets in, culminating in what E. A. Robinson calls "anthological pickle." Poetry for Emerson is not a collection of finished poems but the process that produces poems. This is why he can insist that

> poetry was all written before time was, and whenever we are so finely organized that we can penetrate into that region where the air is music, we hear those primal warblings, and attempt to write them down, but we lose ever and anon a word, or a verse, and substitute something of our own, and thus miswrite the poem.

The poetry is in the world, in people, in things. It is the poet's job to catch it and set it down. Thus originality (in the sense of novelty), so important to most romantics, is not of much interest to Emerson. "Nature's first green is gold," says Robert Frost, and, sure enough, when we look at the first day's tender leafing out of lilac buds, we see that Frost is simply watching things closely.[7]

With remarkable consistency Emerson condenses his antiformalism and restates his own theory of poetic process in a single sentence: "For it is not metres but a metre-making argument, that makes a poem." His explanation recalls Coleridge's distinction between mechanical form—for example, clay shaped on a potter's wheel—versus organic form—for example, a pear growing on a tree. Behind a poem and responsible for a poem, says Emerson, is "a thought so passionate and alive, that, like the spirit of a plant or an animal, it has an architecture of its own, and adorns nature with a new thing." Important poetry will be original only in the sense that it leads us back to origins, focusing attention on the originating spirit or idea. By such focusing poetry invites us "into the science of the real."[8]

Emerson's explanation in "The Poet" of how symbols work is a refinement of what he had said in *Nature:* "Things admit of being used as symbols because nature is a symbol, in the whole and in every part." Putting this in its most succinct form he says, "The universe is the externalization of the soul." Whatever problems this formulation may present as metaphysics, it is an apt and a liberating description of the world of the writer, for whom nature provides the language with which he talks about everything, including nature. But Emerson also insists that not only poets—by which he means writers—but all persons are drawn to the use of emblems. "Witness the cider-barrel, the log-cabin, the hickory-stick, the palmetto, and all the cognizances of party. . . . The people fancy they hate poetry, and they are all poets and mystics."[9]

What is new in the treatment of symbolism in "The Poet" is a distinction between confining and liberating symbols. A confining symbol—we might say an allegorical symbol—occurs when, for example, Boehme uses the morning redness of dawn to stand for truth and faith. "Mysticism," says Emerson, "consists in the mistake of an accidental and individual symbol for a universal one." True symbols are to be held lightly, to be understood as vehicular and transitive, good "as ferries and horses are, for conveyance, not as farms and houses are, for homestead." Emerson insists that the true symbol does not constrict but liberates because it is based on a full understanding of nature as something neither static nor fixed. "What we call nature," he says, "is a certain self-regulated motion or change." The poet enters this dance of the changes not as a passive spectator but as a liberating guide. "The use of symbols has a certain power of emancipation and exhilaration for all men. We seem to be touched by a wand, which makes us dance and run about happily like children." Emerson would have loved the children's book that suggested alternative ways to count to ten, such as "ounce, dice, trice, quartz, quince, sego, serpent, oxygen, nitrogen, denim." What Emerson has seized on is the power of symbols to suggest connections that did not appear before. Any new symbol is a certificate of "departure from routine." Where there is one connection there may be many. "The young man who wishes to remain a sound atheist cannot be too careful of his reading," says C. S. Lewis. And Emerson maintains that because of "tropes, fables, oracles and all poetic forms" we get a new sense and find within our world "another world or nest of worlds: for the metamorphosis once seen, we divine that it does not stop."[10]

A brief but much-quoted paragraph in "The Poet" laments the absence, as yet, of a great American poet. "We have yet had no genius in America, with tyrannous eye, which knew the value of our incomparable materials, and saw, in the barbarism and materialism of the times, another carnival of the same gods whose picture he so much admires in Homer." The whole paragraph reads like a cue for the entrance of Walt Whitman. "Yet America is a poem in our eyes; its ample geography dazzles the imagination and it will not wait long for metres." But it is significant that Emerson's call for a specifically American poetry is confined to this one paragraph, which ends, "But I am not wise enough for a national criticism, and must use the old largeness a little longer."

The essay finishes not with a call for national poetry but with a coda on the theme of preferring process over product, origins over ends, expression over possession. Poetry is not finally an end in itself. Emerson packs his essay now into one grand simple sentence: "Art is the path of the creator to his work." This is the transitive and vehicular wisdom of Emerson, it is what keeps him interested more in the present than in the future or the past. "To find the journey's end in every step of the road," he says in "Experience," "to live the greatest number of good hours, is wisdom."[11]

There is a new world of health in Emerson's remark in "The Poet" that "genius is the activity that repairs the decay of things." During the dark, busy, confusing days and months after Waldo's death, Emerson went searching for qualities in himself that might be capable of fighting back against death and decay. He groped downward and inward for the central fires of life, "the world-warming spark" he called it in a poem written this spring. He was seeking reconnection, rededication, his own self-regulating center. In another poem, written in April 1843 and called "The World-Soul," he testified that "Spring still makes spring in the mind." The death of his son did not put an end to Emerson's idealism; it did not shake his oldest and firmest convictions. Nor would his steady gaze permit him to indulge in the wish-fulfillment of belief in personal immortality. Waldo's death may have permanently saddened Emerson by removing part of his capacity for hope, but the evidence of "The Poet" is that the loss of Waldo forced Emerson back into a kind of activity that heals. Lewis Mumford has remarked that Emerson is better than Marcus Aurelius at last because of "his sense of life's capacity for self-renewal." If death is the end of everything, then living is everything. Or as Emerson stubbornly puts it this spring, "I am defeated all the time; yet to victory I am born."[12]

62. *Emerson's* Dial

WHEN EMERSON TOOK OVER THE EDITORSHIP OF *THE DIAL* IN
what he called an act of "petty literary patriotism," the magazine had three
hundred subscribers and its publisher had just gone out of business. Sales
brought in just enough money to pay for printing and binding; there was
nothing left over to pay an editor. The heartlessness of most literary
publishers ("wretched hungerstruck hyenas," Carlyle called them) was epitomized for Emerson by the sale in June 1842 of 750 copies of Alcott's
Conversations on the Gospels to some trunk makers, at five cents a pound,
for lining trunks. *The Dial* had been hospitable to new ideas, to young
unpublished writers, to idealism, to experimentation, and Emerson was
unwilling to see it die. For the next two years he put something between
a third and a half of his literary energies into *The Dial.*

At the same time Emerson was working on a new volume of essays and
spending much time with friends. Thoreau became a sort of editorial
assistant. Caroline Sturgis came for four days as the "wide warmth of June"
spread over Concord. Also this summer of 1842 Margaret Fuller came for
an extended stay. She hoped, she told Emerson, not to make a visit but to
try the business of actually living with the Emersons. Emerson took walks
with her, with Thoreau, and with Ellery Channing. In September he tried
to get to know Hawthorne by proposing (successfully) a forty-mile, two-day
walk to visit the Shakers at Harvard, Massachusetts, out past Stowe.

Emerson was reading Wordsworth, Proclus, and Plato as he worked on
"The Poet." He also read Tytler's *Life of Raleigh,* much of Sir Philip Sidney,
Pope's *Odyssey,* and Eliza B. Lee's *Life of Richter.* Though he hoped for much
from American literature to come, he accepted the then current dependence
on European literature. He made another of his periodic forays into fiction,
reading Balzac's *La peau de chagrin* (1831), Disraeli's *Vivian Grey,* and
Bulwer Lytton's *Ernest Maltravers, Zanoni,* and *Alice, or The Mysteries.*
Balzac, he said, had two merits, "talent and Paris." Of Bulwer Lytton he
said that "he really has seen London Society and does not give us ignorant
caricatures."[1]

Much of Emerson's time now was spent sweeping the field of his acquaintance for contributions to the magazine. He drew heavily on the
dependables, Parker and Fuller. He prodded Newcomb and Thoreau. He
coaxed poems out of the Sturgis sisters. Emerson was remarkably open to
new work, especially by young people, but he had little patience with those
who promised but never produced. There was, he noted "an American
disease, a paralysis of the active faculties, which falls on young men in this
country, as soon as they have finished their college education." Victims of
Vivian Grey,

> they discuss sun and moon, liberty and fate, love and death, and ask
> you to eat baked fish. They never sleep, go nowhere, stay nowhere,
> eat nothing, and know nothing, but are up to anything,—Festus-like,
> Faust-like, Jove-like, and could write an *Iliad* any rainy morning, if
> Fame were not such a bore.[2]

Parker had told Emerson that one way to make the magazine succeed
would be for the editor to write much of it himself. Over the next two years
Emerson published his lectures "The Times," "The Conservative," "The
Transcendentalist," "The Comic," "The Tragic," and "The Young American." He also printed a number of his poems, including "Saadi," "To
Rhea," and "Blight." He did articles on Fourierism, on the Chardon Street
Convention, on English reformers, on European books, on Carlyle's *Past
and Present,* to say nothing of numerous book reviews, literary notices,
introductions, letters from the editor, and so on. Joel Myerson lists seventy-
six contributions to *The Dial* by Emerson. Fifty-three of these were during
The Dial's last two years.[3]

Even so, Emerson's writing provided only a fraction of the magazine's
material. Emerson was an active editor, inventing departments and trying
to make the magazine a useful clearinghouse for new ideas. In his first issue
as editor Emerson printed Brisbane on Fourierian socialism, Newcomb's
strange story "Dolon," poetry by himself, Thoreau, Sturgis, Very, Channing, Hedge, Dana, and Eliza Clapp. There was a piece on Massachusetts
agriculture by Emerson. There was Thoreau's "Natural History of Massachusetts." There was a budget of scientific news: about the Wilkes expedition to Antarctica, about a meeting of state geologists, about Asa Gray's
appointment at Harvard. There were notices of a translation of Novalis's
Henry of Ofterdingen, of Fuller's *Gunderode* (published by Peabody); there
were reviews of Hawthorne's *Twice-told Tales* (by Fuller) and George

Borrow's *The Zincali—or Spanish Gypsies*. Fuller also did a retrospective called "Entertainments of the Past Winter," covering Lyell's lectures in Boston, performances of Handel's "Creation" and "Messiah," Beethoven's Fifth and Sixth symphonies, the ballet, and the dancing of Fanny Elssler. There was an editorial urging Harvard to get out of the parietal business and concentrate on instruction. There was news of Tennyson and Wordsworth and announcements of books by Henry Taylor, John Sterling, and Thomas Carlyle. A separate section was devoted to news from Berlin, the main item being the invitation to Schelling to lecture in Berlin on the philosophy of Revelation as an offset to the Hegelians. The last item in the magazine was an account of recent schisms in the Swedenborgian church in Germany.

With its pale covers and decorous typeface, *The Dial* looked like many other nineteenth-century periodicals. Physically it was not much different from, say, *The Christian Examiner*. But even a quick summary of the contents suggests the strength, range, and liveliness of the little circle that wrote and read *The Dial*. From July 1843 to the last number in April 1844 Emerson included various pieces by Parker, Thoreau's "Prometheus Bound," his "A Winter Walk," and many of his best poems. There were contributions by Lydia Child on aesthetic theory, by James Clarke on John Keats's brother George, by Emerson's dead brother Charles on Puerto Rico, by his old student Benjamin Peter Hunt on Jamaica. James Elliot Cabot, who later helped Emerson edit *Letters and Social Aims* (1876) and who wrote a still valuable memoir of Emerson, wrote an excellent piece on Kant. Charles Lane, who had come from England with Alcott when the latter returned home, wrote on Brook Farm and modern reform. There were poems by Christopher Cranch, Ellen and Caroline Sturgis, George W. Curtis, Samuel Ward, and Charles A. Dana. Hedge translated Schelling's inaugural Berlin lecture. The July issue for 1843 opened with Fuller's "The Great Lawsuit," the brilliant feminist piece that Fuller later expanded and published as *Woman in the Nineteenth Century*.

Emerson's *Dial* was different from Fuller's. The clearinghouse or noticeboard aspect was more pronounced. There was less space given to music and art, more to literature. Emerson valued and sought out the plain spokesperson, printing Nathaniel Whiting's speech at Chardon Street instead of, say, Alcott's. Emerson paid more attention to nature and science, at least partly because of Thoreau's interests. But the boldest new feature was the series "Ethnical Scriptures" on which Emerson and Thoreau collaborated. Each issue devoted several pages to a careful presentation of excerpts from the scriptures of a major world religion. The July 1842 issue had passages from the Hindu *Vishnu Sarma*. The January 1843 issue had selections from the Hindu *Laws of Menu;* the April 1843 selection was from Confucius. The July 1843 selection was from the Persian *Desatir,* quoting various Persian prophets including Zoroaster. The October 1843 issue had selections from the classic *Chinese Four Books.* The January 1844 issue had two sets of selections, one from the sayings of Buddha, the other from Hermes Trismegistus. In the last issue Emerson returned to Zoroaster, as brokered by Thomas Taylor. This feature, the "Ethnical Scriptures," anticipating the ecumenical movement and the modern history-of-religions point of view, was devoted to identifying the fundamental religious and ethical teachings that lie behind mythology and unite many religions that are separated by their mythologies. "Each nation has its bible more or less pure," Emerson observed in presenting the Hindu Stoicism of the *Vishnu Sarma.* "None has yet been willing or able in a wise and devout spirit to collate its own worth with those of other nations, and sinking the civil-historical and the ritual portions, to bring together the grand expressions of the moral sentiment in different ages and races."[4]

Emerson also put more emphasis on poetry. He had the printer set verse more generously, which meant fewer lines per page and made the poems easier to read. He also began—even before he became editor—a new department dedicated to what he called verses of the portfolio, by which he meant verses not designed for publication. The immediate occasion was a sheaf of Ellery Channing's poems, but Emerson had been interested for a long time in poetic first impressions, in what Melville would call half-formed foetal suggestions, in the latent, the promising, the first unselfconscious flowers of the mind, in informal rather than formal and finished verse. Emerson strove to get his own first impressions down on paper, and he valued the same hints of insight in others, even if they were partial, obscure, difficult, or elusive.

At first glance, editing seems out of character for a man who made such a point of doing only his own work. But Emerson had been editing the work of others for years. Early in the 1830s he began to assemble what would eventually be four manuscript volumes of the writings and sayings of his aunt Mary. Never intended for publication, the collection was one of Emerson's most important books. He also tried several times to edit his brother Charles's writings. He spent many hours trying to free Bronson Alcott's gospels of childhood from their author's attenuated prose. He did bold and extensive editing of Very's poems and prose, of Newcomb's "Dolon," and of Thoreau's "A Winter Walk." In all these he was trying to save the personal, the unconventional, the intimation before the deposition.

Editing was in fact deeply congenial to Emerson. For one thing he was more and more involved, as time went on, in editing himself. While new lectures could sometimes be written out hurriedly, the essays he now increasingly cared to write were assembled and edited from his journals and from earlier lectures and sermons and letters. From the 1840s onward Emerson used two quite different writing techniques. One produced the forty-page lecture, which he could write (if he had to) in a couple of days. The other produced the essay for publication, which could be any length and which could take a couple of years to finish. In Emerson's case, this latter process may fairly be called self-editing.[5]

The other reason editing came so easily to Emerson is that he conceived of the writer, the poet, as an editor of nature. If poetry was all written before time began, then the poet—and the critic and the editor—were all engaged in the same enterprise of trying to get the thing to express itself, free of its accidental, idiosyncratic, and individual baggage. If this makes the authorial function less original and creative than usually supposed, it makes the editorial function more important. Seen from this point of view, there is not such a great difference between writing, rewriting, and editing. Practically, however, there is a substantial difference. As Emerson began his two-year stint as editor of *The Dial,* he was moving into a phase of his own work in which he was to do proportionally less original writing and proportionally more editing of the rich materials he had already collected or written and stored up in his notebooks.

63. New Views

Steam was bringing new prosperity to Boston in the early 1840s. Boston was two days closer by steamship to Le Havre and Liverpool than was New York, and Boston had not yet lost the race to connect the new western railroads with the sea. Cunard had picked Boston as its American terminus, and a Boston merchant named Frederic Tudor was having prodigious success cutting ice on Walden and other ponds and shipping the ice packed in pine sawdust from Boston to the American South and eventually all the way to Calcutta. As the age of steam consolidated its hold, so the eighteenth century finally came to a close in New England in the 1840s—as Henry Adams acutely remarked. William Ellery Channing died in early October 1842. Emerson called him "the star of the American Church" and lamented that "he could not be reported, for his eye and voice cannot be printed, and his discourses lose what was best in wanting them." Ellen was now three and a half, Edith a year. Emerson had said this was the era of the first person singular. Lidian watched the baby kicking up both feet into the air and said Edie seemed to be saying "The world was made on purpose to carry round the little baby."[1]

Emerson met the sculptor Horatio Greenough. He read new books. He thought there might be six or seven good sentences in Cornelius Agrippa's *Vanity of the Arts and Sciences.* Of Capell Lofft's *Earnest, or Political Regeneration,* he said, "It is good for a Chartist epic, good for a bookstall, as much worth as a novel,—but no poem." His work on *The Dial* and on his own essays ("The Poet," "Character," and "Experience" were all under way by fall of 1842) was giving him a new respect for clarity and limits. "The intellect," he observes in "The Poet," "delights in detachment or boundary." Alcott returned from England with two kindred spirits, Charles Lane and Henry Wright. They proposed to found a new communal society to live an innocent life based on high Platonic conversation and the nonexploitation of animals; they would eat no meat, use no wool or leather, harness no plow-horse or ox. They intended to make no use of anything that resulted from or remotely supported slavery—no cotton—and they intended to eat only "aspiring" vegetables and fruits, that is, those that grew upward. They disapproved of potatoes, carrots, and other root crops because of their incorrigible downward tendencies.[2]

The implementation of so pure a life posed problems. Alcott maintained that "there should be found a farm of a hundred acres in excellent condition with good buildings, a good orchard, and grounds which admitted of being laid out with great beauty: and this should be purchased and given them in the first place." Emerson replied, "You ask too much. This is not solving the problem; there are hundreds of innocent young persons, whom, if you will thus stablish and endow and protect, will find it no hard matter to keep their innocency." Emerson went on to say that he would feel strengthened and instructed by someone (like the Brook Farmers or like neighbor Hosmer or, in his own way, Henry Thoreau) who "there where he is, unaided, in the midst of poverty, toil, and traffic, extricates himself from the corruptions of the same and builds on his land a house of peace and benefit, good customs and free thoughts."[3]

Alcott asked, "How is this to be done? How can I do it who have a wife and family to maintain?" Emerson's reply comes from his new respect for experience, not from any hostility to innocence. "I answered that he was not the man to do it, or he would not ask the question." The response was stiff but not unfair.

Emerson's moral idealism did not decline in the 1840s or even waver, but on questions of politics, social action, science, and metaphysics there is a new note of this-worldliness and practicality that grew on him in the months after the death of Waldo. When Sampson Reed answered Emerson's reservations about Swedenborg with "It is not so in your experience, but is so in the other world," Emerson shot back: "Other world? There is no other world; here or nowhere is the whole fact." Though he still cared about essences, he was increasingly ready to accept the reality of surfaces. He noted this year that "this new molecular philosophy goes to show that there are astronomical interspaces betwixt atom and atom; that the world is all outside; it has no inside."[4]

Out of doors he kept up his botany. "The mere names of reeds and grasses, of the milk weeds, of the mint tribe and the gentians, of mallows and trefoils, are a lively pleasure," he wrote. He much preferred plantain, houstonia, fire-weed, gnaphilium, lespedeza, and epigae to the cold mineral heavens of Swedenborg. "What I pray thee, O Emmanuel Swedenborg, have I to do with jasper, sardonyx, beryl, and chalcedony? what with tabernacles, arks, ephaphs and ephods . . . with chariots of fire? with dragons crowned and horned, or Behemoths or Unicorns?"[5]

He could now see the basis even for witchcraft in human nature, or, as he called it, character. So strong had his belief in character become that he could now say, "There ought to be no such thing as Fate. As long as we use this word, it is a sign of our impotence and that we are not ourselves." But if there was no fate, there was gender. Emerson believed in a male and a female principle in nature and he makes distinctions on that basis. "Women see better than men," he once noted. "Men see lazily if they do not expect to act. Women see quite without any wish to act." He also believed, as did Fuller, that the best, most interesting natures had both elements: "A highly endowed man with good intellect and good conscience is a man-woman." "Hermaphrodite is then the symbol of the finished soul." American men seemed to him to incline toward the female. "All the notable Americans, except Webster . . . are female minds. Channing, Irving, Everett, Greenough, Allston." He had good friends to tell him that woman's life was tragic, that women were slaves, that he needed to add the rights of women to his list of needed reforms. "Jane Carlyle suffers like all good women of my acquaintance from cruel headaches." Through Lidian, Aunt Mary, Elizabeth Hoar, and Margaret Fuller he learned something of the condition of women in the nineteenth century, and while he most often uses "man" to mean "human" and the masculine pronoun to refer to both men and women, he also made an occasional attempt to balance his language. He might use a female example: "We want the fortification of an acknowledgement of the good in us. The girl is the least part of herself. God is in the girl." He even uses, on occasion, double-shotted syntax: "Whoso blesseth all things, to him, to her, bend all the world of spirits." "A great boy, a great girl with good sense is a Greek." "The moment he acts from himself, tossing the laws, the books, the idolatries, the customs out the window, we pity him, we pity her no more." He also knew that there were limits. "Man can never tell woman what her duties are," he wrote in 1843.[6]

Emerson's commitment to individualism now had to face a rising tide of thought that was skeptical about the importance of the individual. "The young people, like Brownson, [W. H.] Channing, Greene, Peabody and possibly Bancroft think that the vice of the age is to exaggerate individualism, and they adopt the word *l'humanité* from Le Roux, and go for 'the race.' Hence the phalanx, Owenism, Simonianism, the Communities." He observed that "many voices call for it [union], Fourier, Owen, Alcott,

Channing. And its effect will be magical." He thought the new movement toward union or community "would rewrite institutions and destroy drudgery." But, he added pointedly, "not in the way these men think, in none of their ways. But only as a method that confirms union with isolation, silent union, actual separateness; ideal union, actual independence." Emerson was still committed to individualism, though he now put less emphasis on the mind common to all individuals and more on individual differences and on the process of individuation. He was still as committed as ever to the idea of freedom and self-liberation, though he was now aware of a variety of false or hollow freedoms.

> A man cannot free himself by any self-denying ordinances, neither by water nor potatoes, nor by violent possibilities, by refusing to swear, refusing to pay taxes, by going to jail, or by taking another man's crops or squatting on his land. By none of these ways can he free himself; no, nor by paying his debts with money; only by obedience to his own genius.[7]

Emerson's optimism, his idealism, his prospective, future-seeking point of view are still very much intact in late 1842, but they are no longer innocent, unmenaced beliefs. There is now a haunted, driven quality to his affirmations. It is as though he was never more than a step ahead of the soul-shriveling negations he so feared. Looking backward was not just a mistake, it was perdition: "A new day, a new harvest, new duties, new men, new fields of thought, new powers call you, and an eye fastened on the past unsuns nature, bereaves me of hope, and ruins me with a squalid indigence which nothing but death can adequately symbolize."[8]

64. The World

EMERSON'S DOWN-TO-EARTH STREAK IN COMBINATION WITH his almost unreachably austere idealism led James Russell Lowell to call him "a Plotinus Montaigne" and Edwin Whipple to think of him as a "Hindoo-Yankee,—a cross between Brahma and Poor Richard." And indeed almost any period of Emerson's adult life seems to have been half epiphany and half cordwood. He needed both ecstatic experience and pie for breakfast. During the fall of 1842 and the spring and summer of 1843 the realistic or worldly part of his life was constantly threatening to submerge the other side of his nature.[1]

In late October 1842 Alcott returned from England with Charles Lane and Henry Wright, two disciples of a man named James Pierrepont Greaves, an educational reformer who Pestalozzi said "best understood the spirit from which he was working." Emerson found himself making comparisons between England and America. The English had greater repose, he now thought. He read Browning's *Paracelsus* and Dickens's popular *American Notes,* which he thought "lively rattle, readable enough, and very quotable."[2]

Emerson spent January, February, and half of March on a lecture tour that took him to Baltimore, Washington, D.C., Philadelphia, New York, Newark, and Hartford. He had a new set of five lectures on New England, which he listed in a letter to Carlyle: "1) Religion; 2) Trade; 3) Genius, Manners, and Customs; 4) Recent literary and spiritual influences from abroad; 5) Spiritual History." The lectures are a preview of *English Traits.* They were designed as a new venture in regionalism not as provincial defensiveness. Emerson was still wrestling with the question of American identity. He traced the New England character back to Puritan times, remarking in his first lecture that the religious aspirations of the seventeenth century are "the most creative energy in our experience." Emerson acknowledged America's debt to European and especially English culture, but he had come to think that English culture was in some ways profoundly unsuited to Americans. "Our people have their intellectual culture from one

385

country and their duties from another. . . . we are sent to a feudal school to learn democracy."[3]

There seemed to be no end to the new demands on Emerson's time and energy. In addition to writing and delivering lectures, traveling from city to city, and making endless arrangements for halls, dates, and advertising, he was heavily committed to editing *The Dial.* He wrote many letters home and to old friends and he kept making new friends who quickly demanded their letters too. The after-shocks following Waldo's death and the long lecture trip seem to have renewed the bond of domestic intimacy between Emerson and Lidian. They wrote each other long, gentle, newsy letters, and each clearly craved more. Emerson's public orbit kept expanding. He had met the sculptor Horatio Greenough and now in Washington he watched Greenough's attempt to light his great statue of Washington with torches. He marveled at the exhibits brought back by the Wilkes expedition from Antarctica and the South Seas. He came to know and greatly admire Lucretia Mott, the Quaker abolitionist and feminist who was related to Mary Rotch. Two young men, Giles Waldo and William Tappan, made strong impressions on Emerson and, along with Louise Weston of Maine, were added to the list of promising young people with whom he kept in constant touch.

Emerson found travel difficult, but there were rewards, especially in New York. He admired energy and found himself impressed by the New York merchants, who he thought put the scholars to shame. The merchants "understand and do their work greatly better," he observed, and "they take up and consume a great deal more vital force." He also saw the other side of mercantile prosperity, noting years before Henry Mayhew's famous book *London Labour and the London Poor* how some men made a living by

> collecting ends of cigars which have been thrown away by the smoker, cutting off the unconsumed part and selling it to the tobacconist for pipe tobacco . . . others by collecting cinders out of coal ashes, others by raking for rags and dish cloth in the gutters which they sell to the papermakers. Others by collecting dog and hog manure.

New York held a sort of fascination for Emerson. The city represented the actual material world, much as Daniel Webster had now come to represent for Emerson the man of practical, material affairs.[4]

In August of 1843 the sixty-one-year-old Webster was one of the team of lawyers defending a bank president named William Wyman against charges of embezzlement. The case was tried in Concord. Webster captured all eyes. His personal presence was commanding; he radiated energy. The impression he made was physical, even visceral. His glance fell like a tree across one's path; he seemed driven by dark forces. Carlyle thought him "a magnificent specimen," the Yankee Englishman par excellence. "The tanned complexion, that amorphous craglike face, the dull black eyes under their precipice of brows, like dull anthracite furnaces needing only to be *blown:* the mastiff mouth, accurately closed. I have not," said Carlyle, "traced as much of silent berserkir rage, that I remember of, in any other man." Webster's words, said Emerson, "are like blows of an axe. His force of personal attack is terrible." This "Natural Emperor of men" had once courted Thoreau's aunt Louisa Dunbar in vain. Yet his mere glance was irresistible in the courtroom. He demoralized and annihilated witnesses. He appeared like "a great cannon loaded to the lips." He adjourned the court in Concord every day "by rising and taking his hat and looking the Judge coolly in the face: who then bade the crier adjourn the Court." Webster stood, in Emerson's imagination, in the same relation to other American notables as Napoleon stands in *Representative Men* against the figures of Plato, Swedenborg, and Shakespeare. Webster was the man of daylight practicality, modernity, business, and politics and stood in Emerson's imagination as the antithesis of the men of thought, faith, and art.[5]

Standing now in the greatest possible contrast to Webster was the triumvirate of Alcott, Lane, and Wright. The wise men, or the Sages, as Lidian called them, met in Emerson's house even when he was away in New York. Lidian kept him informed when Charles Lane announced that the only possible clothing for a person who wished to retain his innocence would be self-spun linen. One day Alcott was "descanting on the iniquity of formal exchange" (money), saying that we are all brothers and "brother should be free to take whatever he wanted of brother when he could find it." Lidian objected, saying, "That might do, if there were but two people in the world." Then Lane broke in with "a most inspiring animation" to announce "there *are* but two people in the world, the me and the *not* me." Caught up in the world as Emerson was, editing, lecturing, writing, and trying to tend to his family, he felt increasingly impatient with the Alcotts, the Lanes, the Newcombs, who promised much but performed little. If Webster was as real as a blast furnace, Alcott and his friends now seemed feather-light, insubstantial as air.[6]

If Emerson drew closer to the world as he approached his fortieth birthday in May 1843 and if Webster seemed now superior in some ways to Alcott,

Emerson's own way lay with neither. During his greatest immersion to date in workaday America, his most important writings are three poems and a translation that show him pointed in other directions entirely.

"Blight" is a moving, sometimes angry poem that contrasts the young scholars, whose feeling for nature is cold and whose botany is all Latin names, with the older generation, who preferred things to names and sought to be "a part of the round day, related to the sun." The moderns, he said, may have an armed vision, but they are essentially "strangers to the stars" and to all of nature. Therefore, says Emerson, in the Shakespearian coda,

> . . . to our sick eyes
> The stunted trees look sick, the summer short,
> Clouds shade the sun, which will not tan our hay,
> And nothing thrives to reach its natural term.[7]

"Blight" describes an alienation that is not cured but is made even worse by expression, at least by the kind of expression represented by scientific terminology. This poem and "To Rhea" are among Emerson's darker writings, suggesting as they do that expression itself, the poet's art, is of no real help.

"To Rhea" offers the following advice (one cannot help wondering to whom):

> If with love thy heart has burst,
> If thy love is unreturned:
> Hide thy grief within thy heart
> Though it tear thee unexpressed.[8]

"Saadi," which Emerson called a "poem on poetical ethics," marks the beginning of Emerson's long fascination with Persian poetry, but the unmistakable main point of the poem is that the true poet must keep to his own affairs.

> . . . he has no companion.
> Come ten, or come a million,
> Good Saadi dwells alone.[9]

In the summer of 1843 Emerson translated Dante's *La vita nuova*. He and Margaret Fuller had talked about it for some time. She had thought of translating it herself. No English version existed. Emerson was intrigued by the work. "Dante's praise is that he dared to write his autobiography in colossal cipher, or into universality," he says in "The Poet." The *Vita nuova* was, he thought, "like the book of Genesis, as if written before literature, while truth yet existed . . . It is the Bible of Love." It reminded him of his love for Ellen Tucker, about whom he was still writing in his journal. He still thought of her as "the angel who walked with me in my younger days" and observed, "I can never think of women without gratitude for the bright revelations of her best nature which have been made to me unworthy."[10]

But the *Vita nuova*'s powerful psychological treatment of the act of falling in love was also associated for Emerson with Margaret Fuller. She had recently told him at length a story about two days of her life which made him refer to her "novissima vita," and this year he wrote out his most enthusiastic and emotional appreciation of her. She inspired faith, he said. She made all other natures seem poor beside hers, and she had a "wonderful generosity." He had never known anyone to grow as she had. "She rose before me at times into heroical and god-like regions, and I could remember no superior women, but thought of Ceres, Minerva, Proserpina, and the august ideal forms of the Foreworld." He called the piece "Margaret"; it is a prose poem of unconcealed admiration and affectionate praise, and it was written in the shadow of the *Vita nuova*. Dante's *Vita nuova* tells the story of the young Dante's meeting Beatrice—whom he first sees in blood-red garments—of his great love for her, of her death, and of the poet's struggle to get his feelings into adequate words. The work is lofty, Christian, idealizing; it is at the same time psychologically realistic and searchingly honest in its portrait of what falling in love feels like. In Emerson's translation the born-again, conversion aspect of Dante's original comes through in repeated images of the "sweetness" that marks the experience of love, redeeming all the accompanying grief, weeping, and pains. "How is the populous city become solitary!" exclaims the newly reborn lover. The concerns at the heart of the *Vita nuova* are love and the expressing of love; they are the problems with which Emerson himself was now freshly struggling.[11]

There are many other signs of struggle beneath Emerson's apparently prosperous and smooth surface this year. He was restless and dissatisfied. "I have much thrust upon me," he told Fuller. "I know and see far too many people." He envied Fuller her trip west to Niagara. "We have all been East too long," he said. Lidian found the anniversary of Waldo's death difficult to bear. "Flowers grow over the grave," she said, "yet it is a grave no less." She reached her lowest ebb this year, writing her husband the grim passage that he copied into his journal and that someone tried later to obliterate. "Dear husband, I wish I had never been born. I do not see how God can compensate me for the sorrow of existence."[12]

Emerson's activity kept him from such despair, but he sometimes felt used up. "We are all dying of miscellany," he wrote in his journal. "I write a good deal," he wrote his English friend John Sterling, "but it is for the most part without connexion on a thousand topics." But even at his worst he knew what he should do:

> A man must do the work with that faculty he has now. But that faculty is the accumulation of past days. No rival can rival backwards. What you have learned and done is safe and fruitful. Work and learn in evil days, in insulted days, in days of debt and depression and calamity. Fight best in the shade of the cloud of arrows.

This is the fighting faith of the American scholar.[13]

65. The Young American

IN MID-SEPTEMBER 1843 MARGARET FULLER RETURNED FROM the western trip she would write up as *Summer on the Lakes*. Emerson told Elizabeth Hoar that his hopes for what he lightly called "Concord Socialism" lay in recruiting "half a dozen rare persons" to the town, but everywhere he looked, rare persons were leaving Concord and even the country. Thoreau was in New York, tutoring William Emerson's children and trying to make money writing. Henry James was off for Europe, as was Theodore Parker. Late in September Aunt Mary became gravely ill with erysipelas. She was still courting death in her seriocomic fashion. She dismissed her first doctor because, she said, "she wished to die in the presence of a superior and intelligent man." She then inquired of the new physician so selected "whether there were any *hopes* of the malady's ending fatally." She was in Newburyport, Massachusetts, and for a while relished the fact that none of her family knew where she was. Emerson heard of her condition, however, and rushed to Newburyport where he stayed until she was better. He wrote Fuller that it was hard to be with his aunt now, "for she suffers more than she enjoys," and he was sadly struck by "how much spur I have lost by the entire loss of her society for these last years." He went back to reading her letters and thought about working them up "with a little selection and compiling and a little narrative."[1]

He did a little lecturing, mostly from his New England series. He had visitors (Caroline Sturgis, Charles Lane) and he worked on his book of essays, but there was an atmosphere of endings as 1844 began. He planned to end *The Dial* with the April 1844 number. He looked forward to the last issue as a deliverance, but he was angry about the lack of support the magazine had elicited. Also in January Alcott's Fruitlands venture fell apart. Alcott and Lane had tried "to initiate a family in harmony with the primitive instincts in man." But by mid-December Lane told Emerson that he and Alcott had come to "think that they had been wrong in all these years with Pestalozzi in lauding the maternal instinct, and the Family etc. These, they now think, are the very mischief. These are selfish and oppose the establishment of the community which stands on universal love." The failure of Fruitlands was a terrible blow for Alcott. As the community broke up in the dark cold days of January, Alcott took to his bed, turned his face to the wall and hoped, like Aunt Mary, for death. "Very sad indeed it was to see this half-god driven to the wall," Emerson wrote in his journal. "I was quite ashamed to have just revised and printed last week the old paper denying the existence of tragedy, when this modern Prometheus was in the heat of his quarrel with the gods."[2]

Emerson continued to read without system and in all directions at once. "It makes no difference what I read," he once noted. "If it is irrelevant, I read it deeper. I read it until it is pertinent to me and mine." He reread Ben Jonson, paying special attention to his "admirable songs." Newly interested in medieval love poetry because of Dante, he now read the *Roman de la rose.* He went back to Montaigne, now first reading *Journey into Germany and Italy.* He kept up in French literature, reading Eugene Sue's *Les mystères de Paris.* He liked George Sand's *Consuelo* and thought Fourier's *Théorie de l'unité universelle* "the most entertaining of French romances." He read part 2 of Goethe's *Faust* and especially admired the Helena section. He thought the second part of *Faust* generally the "grandest enterprise of literature that has been attempted since the *Paradise Lost*" because "it enlarges the known powers of the human mind."[3]

He continued to read outside the Western tradition. His interest in Saadi led him to James Ross's translation of *The Gulistan.* Emerson liked Saadi's humanity and his wit. He enjoyed the description of "a schoolmaster so ugly and crabbed that the sight of him would derange the ecstasies of the orthodox." He also read and took notes on a volume called *The Chinese Classical Work Commonly Called the Four Books.* This work, published in Malacca in 1828 by David Collie, contained translations of a number of Confucian classics, namely, the four books of the so-called Second Order. There was the *Ta heo,* or *Great Learning,* by Tsang Sin, who was the greatest disciple of Kung Fu-tse, or Confucius. There was also the *Chung Yung,* or *Middle Way,* by the grandson of Kung Fu-tse, the *Lun Yi,* or *Book of Sentences* (sometimes called the *Analects*), and the *Meng Tsu,* or *Book of Mencius.* Emerson was attracted by the pithy, epigrammatic Chinese style and by the Confucian emphasis on the moral education and qualities of the superior person or great man, though not by the emphasis on filial piety. Emerson had long been familiar with Confucius, but Meng Tsu (Mencius) was new to him. The *Book of Mencius,* he told Fuller, is "in its quiet sunshine a dangerous foil to Carlyle's storm lights."[4]

Emerson was becoming increasingly interested in Buddhism. He either read or read about Burnouf's *Introduction à l'histoire du Buddhisme indien* (1844), an admiring book that was wholly free of missionary revisionism and that located the origins of Buddhism firmly in India. Emerson made admiring references to Buddhism in two of the essays for his new book, "Gifts" and "Nominalist and Realist." Despite the scarcity of major texts and sympathetic accounts in languages he could read, Emerson came quickly to value the importance and appeal of Buddhism. "Trace these colossal conceptions of Buddhism and Vedantism home, and they are always the necessary or structural action of the human mind," he wrote in his journal in 1845. "Buddhism read literally is the tenet of Fate."[5]

Emerson also read in December of 1844 Lydia Child's *Letters from New York,* which he considered an important contribution to and "a most salutary infusion of love into American literature." It is a lively, readable book, a vivid book of popular transcendentalism, quoting Coleridge and Carlyle and Bettina von Arnim, and filled with sharply observed scenes of city life, with special attention to street life and the poor.[6]

In "The Poet" Emerson says he is not wise enough for a national criticism. But in February 1844, while still putting finishing touches on that essay, he gave a talk in Boston called "The Young American," which is indeed national and not general in its focus. The essay has often been read as a harbinger and an endorsement of American expansionism under Polk, and it is true that Emerson was impressed by such signs of growth as the twelve to fifteen hundred new buildings a year going up in Boston. He did say that "this rage of road building is beneficent" and that America is "the country of the future." It is further true that while he opposed the annexation of Texas, he believed history would show the annexation inevitable. Emerson says in "The Young American" that "there is a sublime and friendly Destiny by which the human race is guided." This meant, in the case of the Irish railroad workers, that "we devise sumptuary laws, and relief laws, but the principle of population is always reducing wages to the lowest pittance on which human life can be sustained." This is where Emerson's logic takes him, and he is not content with it, nor with a country in which business is all important. "This is the good and the evil of trade, that it would put everything into market; talent, beauty, virtue, and man himself."[7]

Though Emerson was alive to the abuses of commerce and at times to its potential for a new kind of tyranny, he praised the commercial spirit in "The Young American" because it also represented a new, more democratic form of social organization than feudalism. Emerson is virtually alone among American writers in his endorsement of the principle of commerce. Most American writers have been antibusiness, many—including Thoreau—vehemently so. Emerson acknowledged the antibusiness sentiment of his friends; he was himself aware of the defects of a society in which everything and everybody had to endure what Robert Frost would call "trial by market." But he thought that eventually "the historian of the world will see that trade was the principle of liberty, that trade planted America and destroyed feudalism, that it makes peace and keeps peace, and it will abolish slavery."[8]

66. Emerson's Emancipation Address

ON AUGUST 1, 1844, EMERSON DELIVERED A FIERY, EMO-
tional speech in Concord calling for the abolition of slavery. He had always
been opposed to slavery; that was not in question. Now he was ready to
work actively and openly for abolition. His new willingness to get involved
had emerged since March of this same year. On March 3 he had given the
lecture "New England Reformers" in Boston's Amory Hall, wrapping his
general approval of reform movements in light irony and speaking from the
cool Apollonian distance of the observing intellectual. He traced the "sol-
diery of dissent" back to the Reformation and observed that "in these
movements nothing was more remarkable than the discontent they begot
in the movers." He insisted, as always, that "society gains nothing whilst
a man, not himself renovated, attempts to renovate things around him."
He was impatient with piecemeal, specific reforms. In his March speech the
antislavery movement was not even on his list. Among the "fertility of
projects for the salvation of the world," he mentions vegetarianism, temperance, animal rights, communal farming, and the abolition of money.
His affirmation is calm and qualified. Despite vaporing and backsliding, he
said, "in each of these movements emerged a good result, a tendency to the
adoption of simpler methods and an assertion of the sufficiency of the
private man."[1]

What exactly made Emerson change his tone is difficult to say. His outer
life rolled on eventfully but without any great watershed. Lidian, who was
almost forty-two, was reaching the end of another difficult pregnancy. On
July 10 she gave birth to a baby boy they named Edward. In June Emerson
had visited the Shakers again. Also in June the new Boston and Fitchburg
railway had begun service, giving Concord four trains a day to Boston and
making the town for the first time a suburb of Boston. Emerson read
Chambers's *Vestiges of Creation* and disliked its theology. He read Beckford's
Travels in Italy, John Evelyn's *Kalendarium Hortense.* He dipped again into
Boehme and Plato, worked with Fuller on the publication of *Summer on the
Lakes,* and read Thomas Clarkson's *History of the Abolition of the African*

Slave Trade and James Thome and J. H. Kimball's *Emancipation in the British West Indies.*[2]

Perhaps the vividness of these last two books jarred Emerson from observer to activist. Clarkson's two large volumes trace the rise, progress, and course of antislavery feeling among white reformers. One volume has a large fold-out engraving showing in heavily inked black and white the deck plan of a loaded slave ship. Another engraving graphs the course of abolition as a series of interlocking streams and rivers—a fluvial family tree—in which each person or movement is seen as a tributary to one of the great rivers of abolition. Thome and Kimball, the latter a former editor of the New Hampshire *Herald of Freedom,* wrote a short report detailing their firsthand experiences in the newly emancipated British West Indies, concentrating on Antigua and Barbados. Perhaps Emerson was swayed by the already perceptible defection of Daniel Webster. "Could Mr. Webster have given himself to the cause of abolition of Slavery, in Congress, he would have been the darling of this continent," Emerson wrote in his journal in May. Perhaps what swayed Emerson now was the influence of Lucretia Mott, the powerful abolitionist and women's rights advocate he had recently come to know and admire. She had been aware of Emerson since at least 1840, and she was urging Americans to "examine the history of emancipation in the West Indies," the better to "strike off the fetters from our bondmen."[3]

More likely Emerson felt the continual influence at home of Lidian, who had been a strong abolitionist since 1837, when she met and was inspired by the Grimke sisters. By the early 1840s the proslavery tone of the newspapers "made her hate her country," her daughter recalled. "She learned all the horrors of slavery and dwelt upon them, so that it was as if she continually witnessed the whippings and the selling away of little children from their mothers." Later, in the 1850s, when she "considered her country wholly lost to any sense of righteousness," she mounted her own protest against the celebration of the Fourth of July. She cast a literal pall on the day by covering the front gate and gateposts of the Emerson house—which lies prominently along Paul Revere's famous route—with large quantities of black cambric cloth. And in 1861, when war broke out, she felt "nothing but gladness" as she announced, "This is the beginning of the end of slavery."[4]

Emerson had been asked to speak on the tenth anniversary of the British emancipation of all slaves in the British West Indies; the sponsor was the

Women's Anti-Slavery Association, to which both Lidian and Cynthia Thoreau belonged. Because abolition was a controversial subject on which the people of Concord were divided, none of the local churches would open their doors to them. The event was scheduled for the courthouse. Henry Thoreau went from door to door urging Concord residents to attend. When the sexton of the First Parish Church refused to ring the bell to announce the meeting, Henry rushed to the church and rang the bell himself.

The speech itself was a departure from Emerson's usual style in three ways. It is mainly a long chronological narrative, it is full of the oratorical devices the young Emerson had learned from Everett, and it is intended as agitprop, like Antony's speech over the body of Caesar. Emerson intended to arouse, to inflame, to move his audience to action: "If any cannot speak, or cannot hear the words of freedom, let him go hence,—I had almost said, creep into your grave, the Universe has no need of you." He recounted the horrors of slavery, "pregnant women set in the treadmill for refusing to work," "men's necks flayed with cowhide, and hot rum poured on, superinduced with brine or pickle, rubbed in with a cornhusk, in the scorching heat of the sun." He told of "a planter throwing his negro into a copper of boiling cane-juice." He adds heavy irony to the horrors: "The sugar they raised was excellent. Nobody tasted blood in it." Emerson continued for page after page, giving the history of slavery and the history of efforts to stop it, culminating in the act of Parliament of August 1, 1834, by which "slavery shall be and is hereby utterly and forever abolished and declared unlawful throughout the British colonies, plantations and possessions abroad." The reason for celebrating this British act was, of course, to shame the Americans who had no such act on their books.[5]

Emerson was very much alive to the economic argument against slavery by which British manufacturers were encouraged to regard the West Indian blacks as so many potential customers. But he was also aware of the insidious psychology of slavery, and he commented on "the love of power, the voluptuousness of holding a human being in his absolute control." For those who feared emancipation might unleash a terrible retribution and bring massive civil disorder, Emerson stressed the mild and orderly transition to freedom that occurred in the West Indies. Then, at last, he turned from the British to the Americans, who were now seen to be lagging woefully behind the times. At this point Emerson turns from his warm historical survey to the present moment and to a tone of plain anger. He was personally shocked and outraged by reports of northern blacks arrested on the decks of Massachusetts ships lying in southern ports.

> I have learned that a citizen of Nantucket, walking in New Orleans, found a freeborn citizen of Nantucket, a man, too, of great personal worth, and, as it happened, very dear to him, as having saved his own life, working chained in the streets of that city, kidnapped by such a process as this.

Emerson was outraged that Massachusetts seemed to be able to do nothing to help its citizens, and he said so in blunt, provocative language: "If such a damnable outrage can be committed on the person of a citizen with impunity, let the Governor break the broad seal of the State; he bears the sword in vain." The congressional delegation from Massachusetts felt that unilateral action by Massachusetts or by the North would endanger the Union. Emerson's reply was, "The Union is already at an end when the first citizen of Massachusetts is thus outraged."[6]

The solution was not to be sought in further compromise and political juggling. America must follow England's lead and free the slaves. And if Emerson had been able in his private life until now to accept some of the condescending and muddy racism that undercut the urgency of abolition by declaring the blacks an inferior race, he now explicitly broke with that rationale. He declared to his audience that "the negro race is, more than any other, susceptible of rapid civilization." He also saw that abolition was not simply something conceded by white people, which was the view of Clarkson's book. "I add," said Emerson, "that in part it is the earning of the blacks." He was deeply impressed by the abilities of Toussaint L'Ouverture and of Frederick Douglass. His private journal comments are just as strong as his public language. Referring specifically to his own conviction of the sufficiency of the individual, he said, "Here is the Anti-Slave. Here is Man; and if you have man, black or white is an insignificance. Why, at night all men are black." It was also in his journal that he said, "The negro has saved himself, and the white man very patronizingly says I have saved you." To his Concord audience Emerson said, "The black man carries in his bosom an indispensable element of a new and coming civilization." And he ended the speech not with a graceful appeal to history or good will but with a stiff and polarizing insistence that "there have been moments, I said, when men might be forgiven who doubted. Those moments are past."[7]

The speech delighted the friends of abolition in the North. Henry Thoreau helped with arrangements to publish the address. Soon the Quaker poet John Greenleaf Whittier was writing to solicit Emerson's further help at an antislavery convention. A letter from William Lloyd Garrison a few years later suggests what Emerson's conversion meant to the cause: "You exercise a strong influence over many minds in this country which are not yet sufficiently committed to the side of the slave. . . . You are not afraid publicly and pointedly to testify against the enslavement of three million of our countrymen." Emerson was solidly committed to abolition both personally and publicly from now on. His speeches on the subject would, if gathered together, fill a good-sized volume. He appeared on many platforms, but he was not now or ever comfortable as an activist, an advocate. As in the matter of the Cherokee removal, he would speak because he must, because no one else would, because he had convictions, because he believed in action. But it was just not congenial work.[8]

Soon after the emancipation address Emerson fell to work on the printer's proofs of the new volume stodgily called *Essays: Second Series*. Neither "The Young American," his warmest defense of America to date, nor "Emancipation in the British West Indies," his sharpest attack on America to date, was scheduled for inclusion in the volume. The much cooler essay on "New England Reformers" was to be included. The book would also include "Experience," a magnificent breaking of new ground, the opening image of which says a great deal about Emerson's "position" at the moment: "Where do we find ourselves? In a series of which we do not know the extremes, and believe that it has none." Emerson's image is right out of Piranesi's *Imaginary Prisons*. "We awake and find ourselves on a stair; there are stairs below us, which we seem to have ascended: there are stairs above us, many a one, which go upward and out of sight."[9]

There was still a great deal he wished to do with the personal essay. "I have joyful dreams which I cannot bring to paper," he told Carlyle. And the natural world still beckoned. He bought "a pretty pasture and woodlot" of some fourteen acres on Walden Pond, a place he had visited almost daily for years. One of these days, he wrote Carlyle, "I may build me a cabin or a turret there high in the treetops and spend my nights as well as days in the midst of a beauty which never fades for me."[10]

67. Essays on Power

EMERSON SPENT MOST OF AUGUST AND SEPTEMBER 1844 COR-
recting proofs for his new volume of essays. He hated the work. He told
Fuller that it "bewilders my brain with its concentration on nothings." He
grumbled that "the impracticability and tough unalterableness of sentences
which must not stand as they are, demonstrates past a doubt the inherent
vice of my writing." He had trouble ending things. He was never quite
finished with an essay, and as time went on, completing a book-length
project became ever harder for him. There were interruptions too. Early in
September the address on emancipation was published separately as a
pamphlet. On the same day, September 9, someone knocked over a glue-pot
lamp in Benjamin Bradley's bookbindery on Washington Street in Boston;
the ensuing fire put all Boston bookbinding about a month behind schedule.
Finally, on October 19 *Essays: Second Series* appeared; it was three days before
the end of the world according to the Millerites, who were gathering on
hilltops and removing the roofs from their churches to expedite their ascent
into heaven on the Day of Judgment, which they had concluded was set for
October 22. Emerson's own conclusion on the matter was that "no man
has learned anything until he knows that every day is the judgment day."[1]

Emerson had thought of calling the book *The Poet and Other Essays*. In
fact, almost all the essays are about power and most were also about the
authority of subjective knowledge. "As I am, so I see," he said in "Experience." "Use what language we will, we can never say anything but what
we are." *Essays: Second Series* is an uneven volume, with light, short pieces
such as "Gifts," in which Emerson shows his awareness of the emotional
reversals that beset both giving and receiving. "It is a great happiness to get
off without injury and heartburning from one who has had the ill luck to
be served by you. It is a very onerous business, this of being served, and the
debtor naturally wishes to give you a slap." "Politics" is about the relation
of the state to its constituent members. Emerson believed, as did Jefferson
and Thoreau, that "the less government we have, the better." He was
explicitly egalitarian: "Of persons, all have equal rights, in virtue of being

identical in nature." He accepted the inevitability of private property and the inequality of means. He liked the Spartan principle of calling that which is just equal, not that which is equal just. He warned that "only young people believe anything can be imposed on a people," and he further believed that the antidote to abuses of formal government lay in the "influence of private character." "Every actual State is corrupt," he wrote. "Good men must not obey the laws too well."[2]

If politics leads us back to the individual, so do manners. The essay of that name asserts that "there is nothing settled in manners, but the laws of behaviour yield to the energy of the individual."[3]

There was a new essay on nature. Emerson's 1836 book had emphasized his philosophy of nature; his Waterbury address, "The Method of Nature," had emphasized ecstatic experience. Now he wrote an essay on the green world itself. "It seems as if the day was not wholly profane in which we have given heed to some natural object," he wrote. He described the "bald, dazzling white and deadly poles" of the earth's extremities and the "tempered light of the woods" around Concord. "The difference between landscape and landscape is small," he says, "but there is a great difference in the beholders." He insists that "nature is loved by what is best in us," much as Richard Nelson has said of his island in the Pacific Northwest that it is "no more inherently beautiful or meaningful than any other place on earth. What makes a place special is the way it buries itself inside the heart."[4]

Essays: Second Series shows no falling off in Emerson's own powers. The book contains two of the best essays he ever wrote, "The Poet" and "Experience." His language is fresh, full of epigrammatic force. Of expectation he says, "Every ship is a romantic object, except that we sail in. Embark, and the romance quits our vessel, and hangs on every other sail on the horizon." The brio with which he writes about routine gives even complaint a lively edge: "So much of our time is preparation, so much is routine, and so much retrospect, that the pith of each man's genius contracts itself to a few hours."

Most of Emerson's books contain one essay on doubt: it is "Circles" in the first volume of essays, "Montaigne" in *Representative Men,* and "Experience" here. The Emerson of this essay, like Thoreau on Katahdin, is avid for "contact" with "reality." "There are moods," he says, "in which we court suffering, in the hope that here at least we shall find reality, sharp peaks and edges of truth." But, he says, the hope is not borne out. Not even the death of his son, he says, has taught him anything about "truth" or "reality." It is not that Emerson rejects pain, loss, or grief. What he rejects is the idea put forward by the chorus of villagers in Sophocles' *Oedipus Rex* that in suffering is wisdom. The classical view of tragedy, the view of choruses of villagers in all times and places, is that this wisdom *redeems* the suffering. Emerson says no. Suffering brought him misery, not wisdom: "I grieve that grief can teach me nothing, nor carry me one step into real nature."[5]

"Experience" confronts and accepts a world in which "dream delivers us to dream, and there is no end to illusion" without clamoring for redemption or quick deliverance. "Life is a train of moods like a string of beads, and as we pass through them, they prove to be many-colored lenses which paint the world their own hue, and each shows only what lies in its focus." "The secret of the illusoriness," he adds, "is in the necessity of a succession of moods and objects." There is no place to anchor, no resting point. "We live amid surfaces, and the true art of life is to skate well on them." There is no answer to this dilemma, no solution, but there is a best course of action. We have nothing but our conviction of the adequacy of the present moment to throw into the uneven balance. "We must set up the strong present tense against all the rumors of wrath, past or to come." Life is possible only as a balance between power and form—a balance that depends on a paradox and exists only as a pull of opposites. "A man is a golden impossibility. The line he must walk is a hair's breadth. The wise through excess of wisdom is made a fool." We are obliged to live within "the beautiful limits," and we cannot have power simply at will. Emerson now concedes that "power keeps quite another road than the turnpike of choice and will, namely the subterranean and invisible tunnels and channels of life."[6]

"Experience" is not a despairing essay. If Emerson accepts no one vision, no one set of facts, he proposes an entirely new order of fact. "It is not what we believe concerning the immortality of the soul or the like, but the universal impulse to *believe* [his emphasis], that is the material circumstance and is the principal fact in the history of the globe." The essay builds to a powerful acceptance of subjectivity, which Emerson calls the "Fall of Man." We learn, he says, "that we do not see directly, but mediately, and that we have no means of correcting these colored and distorting lenses which we are, or of computing the amount of their error." This new awareness, this subjective self-awareness, is like a black hole, ravenously threatening to absorb all things. "Nature, art, persons, letters, religions, objects, successively tumble in, and God is but one of its ideas. Nature and literature are subjective phenomena, every evil and every good thing is a shadow which

402

we cast." The same subjectivity that gives authority to us as individuals sentences us to a world of relative truth. "People forget that it is the eye which makes the horizon." As he accepts subjectivity and uncertainty, so he can now accept disunity: "I am a fragment and this [essay] is a fragment of me."[7]

But Emerson will not settle for Fichtean solipsism or the sophist's shrug. He knows what the Stoic has always known. Real knowledge may be unattainable; the question therefore is not "What can I know?" but "How should I live?" Sartre said of the prison experiences of members of the French Résistance, "It is not what they do to you, it is what you do with what they do to you that matters." Emerson ends with a similar assertion: "I know that the world I converse with in the city and in the farm is not the world I *think*." The last sentence of the essay is his bridge back: "The true romance, which the world exists to realize, will be the transformation of genius into practical power." His own drive for practical power brought him to this: "To finish the moment, to find the journey's end in every step of the road, to live the greatest number of good hours, is wisdom." "Experience" is about the impossibilities, miscarriages, and mortgagings of power. Emerson conceded now for the first time that nature may have been very "sparing of her fire" in making us. But "Experience" is not a flaccid or defeated essay because Emerson's tough articulateness and awareness are also weapons. The arsenal of power is larger than we think, and the fire within may be modest, but it is still sufficient.[8]

68. Ex Oriente Lux

THE COMBINATION OF A COMMITMENT TO THE WORK OF ABolition and the publication of the new book of essays had a revitalizing effect on Emerson, enlivening his reading and sending him ranging ever farther afield. New readings overlapped old, familiar books yielded fresh connections with the present, and books from one culture or era became newly applicable in another. This sort of cross-fertilization happened frequently for Emerson. This year, 1844, he gave it a name, "croisements," crossings or crossbreeding. Its startling symbols for Emerson were "the seashore, and the taste of two metals in contact, and our enlarged powers . . . at the approach and at the departure of a friend." He felt these crossings or intersections most strongly perhaps in the "experience of poetic creativeness which is not found in staying at home, nor yet in travelling, but in transitions from one to the other." As he tried to court this crossroads experience, so he tried now to manage his whole life so as "to present as much transitional surface as possible."[1]

The pace of his life kept quickening, like a metronome notched up to an ever faster beat. In December 1844 he was praising Concord's Social Circle, a group of twenty-five of "our citizens, doctor, lawyer, farmer, trader, miller, mechanic." This, like the various other clubs he would become associated with, was less a vehicle for exclusion and social snobbery than a gathering that fed Emerson's constant hunger for village society, for "association" and friendship. He now came to know James Elliot Cabot, who had written one of the papers in the last number of *The Dial* and who would become Emerson's friend, editor, and biographer.

Also in December 1844 Samuel Hoar, one of Concord's leading citizens—Elizabeth's father and a man who looked quite a bit like John Brown—was expelled with Elizabeth from South Carolina for trying to investigate that state's treatment of free Massachusetts persons of color. Though Emerson was horrified at the violence offered to this friend and neighbor, he was, he said, almost glad of the incident and hoped it would not dissipate in personal outrage but would stiffen the political resolve of Massachusetts.

In December Emerson read Alexander Henry's account of his travels in Canada among various Indian tribes. The book, almost pure narrative, is artless, vivid, detailed, concrete. It is utterly without rhetorical posturing, educated inflation, self-aggrandizement or special pleading. Events seem to speak for themselves. The book relies almost entirely on personal observation. Here is Henry's description of the eight-person Canadian freight canoes that could carry eight thousand pounds: "The canoes, which I provided for my undertaking were, as usual, five fathom and a half in length, and four feet and a half in the extreme breadth, and formed of birch-tree bark a quarter of an inch in thickness. The bark was lined with small splints of cedar-wood, and the vessel is further strengthened with ribs of the same wood." Emerson thought it the best book he had read on the Indians.[2]

In January 1845, in a sudden concentration of focus, Emerson read a whole shelf of books about Napoleon. March was a month of decision. The Concord Lyceum invited the noted abolitionist Wendell Phillips to speak. The curators of the Lyceum resigned in protest. Emerson, Thoreau, and Sam Barrett were elected instead and Phillips spoke on March eleventh. By mid-month the snow was gone and people had got their feet back on the ground. Henry Thoreau borrowed an ax and went out to Walden Pond to cut down some white pines to build himself a cabin on a piece of Emerson's land. By month's end Emerson was elated to have found a new subject for a series of lectures, the uses of great men. By April he was also planning to bring out a volume of his poems.

During the summer Emerson gave a talk at Middlebury College in Vermont and—with some changes—at Wesleyan in Connecticut. The talk, which was not published until many years later (and then not in complete form), was another of Emerson's ongoing assessments of the American scholar. This summer the topic has a new and quite practical urgency. "The cant of the time inquires superciliously after the new ideas," he told the young men. "It believes that ideas do not lead to the owning of stocks." Emerson insisted that it was the other way round, that idealism is the origin of action. "For as the solidest rocks are made up of invisible gasses, as the world is made of thickened light and arrested electricity, so men below know that ideas are the parents of men and things." The link between idea and act is crucial and Emerson restates it: "There was never any thing that did not proceed from a thought." Emerson is most interested now in outcomes: "There is no power in the mind but in turn becomes an instrument. The descent of genius into talents is part of the natural order and history of the world." He quoted Burke's comment that "it is not only our duty to make the right known, but to make it prevalent." He also demanded some positive steps by his hearers: "We have seen to weariness what you cannot do; now show us what you can and will."[3]

Emerson himself took an active role in a series of meetings held in September and October in Concord and Cambridge to organize opposition to the annexation of Texas. At one meeting he spoke, urging the voters of Massachusetts to break silence and voice their opposition to the proposed annexation. To another meeting he carried a public letter to himself from Whittier.[4]

During the same time as his steadily growing interest in active protest, Emerson was also—characteristically—pushing his reading into ever wider circles. He read Kohl's account of Russia. He began to grasp the importance of Schelling (this was Cabot's influence), and in September 1845 he began to read Humboldt's ambitious *Kosmos*. Emerson felt an excited sympathy for the vast intellectual unification projects of the last two. He also did sustained reading this year in Islamic religion, culture, and literature—with special attention to Persia—and in major Indic texts.[5]

Emerson's starting point for Islam was a book called the *Akhlak-I-Jalaly*, translated by W. F. Thompson as *The Practical Philosophy of the Muhammedan People*. Published in London in 1839, the book has an enthusiastic preface that sets its tone in declaring that "depreciation of the Muhammedan system should now be at an end." The *Akhlak* was drawn in part from a tenth-century source, though it was actually assembled in the fifteenth century at a period when cosmopolitan Arab scholars were taking ideas from Plato and Aristotle as well as from the Koran. The resulting work, says Thompson, is superior to anything produced in the West at that time. He also argues that the *Akhlak* should be translated as "Transcendental Ethics." The book was Emerson's introduction to Sufism, the mystical wisdom of Islam. Thompson calls Sufism the "practical pantheism of Asia." He also describes it as a pure idealism, for, "holding all visible and conceivable objects to be portions of the divine nature, it was impossible that they should admit the imperfection observable in them to have any real existence." The book itself has the tough density of, say, the *Nicomachean Ethics,* and it treats major ideas with a certain freshness. It enumerates seven kinds of wisdom: penetration, quickness of intellect, clearness of understanding, facility of acquirement, propriety of discrimination, retention, recollection. The book goes on to insist on the Muslim preference for justice (equity) over wisdom and for affection over equity: "Affection then is the paramount sovereign, and equity is his vice-regent." Emerson particularly liked the book's commitment to learning and teaching; its conclusion says: "Let it be the object of your constant endeavor to instruct both others and yourself."[6]

Emerson also knew Firdusi's *Shah Nameh,* or Book of Kings, the "*Iliad* of the East," a book seven times longer than the *Iliad* and one of the great expressions of Iranian national sentiment. Its main hero is Rustum, the chief event of whose life was the unwitting killing of his son Sohrab. The episode, a resonant reversal of the Oedipal situation, fascinated the late Victorians and was the subject of one of Matthew Arnold's best poems. The *Shah Nameh* was attractively translated and abridged by James Atkins and published in London in 1838. Margaret Fuller was reading it by 1840 and through her Emerson first came to it.[7]

Emerson also owned a book called *The Desatir: or Sacred Writings of the Ancient Persian Prophets,* which had been published in 1818. He and Fuller were both reading it in November of 1844. Partly through this work Emerson was able to connect his old interest in ancient Persia and Zoroaster with his newer interest in medieval Persia and its great poets. Emerson now also read a book called *Specimens of the Popular Poetry of Persia as Found in the Adventures and Improvisations of Kurroglou, the Bandit-Minstrel of Northern Persia.* The names of Firdusi, Saadi, Hafez, Jami, Rumi, and Omar Khayyam will recur through his reading, thinking, note-taking, and poetry from now on. Beginning in 1844 and 1845 Islam had a major impact on Emerson, especially but not exclusively through Sufi poetry.[8]

Emerson also returned to his interest in Indic wisdom during 1844 and 1845. He read new books such as H. T. Colebrook's *Miscellaneous Essays,* and he reread old favorites such as the Vishnu Purana and the Bhagavad Gita with a new sense of familiarity and recognition. From the Vishnu Purana now came the key insights for his poems "Hamatreya" and "Brahma." "I will repeat to you, Maitreya, the stanzas that were chanted by the Earth," Emerson copied out in his journal. Those who said "the earth is mine,—it is my son's—it belongs to my dynasty,—have all passed away. . . . Earth laughs, as if smiling with autumnal flowers to behold her kings unable to effect the subjugation of themselves." From another part of the same book Emerson copied out: "What living creature slays or is slain? What living creature preserves or is preserved? Each is his own destroyer or preserver, as he follows evil or good."[9]

What Emerson was really getting now from the Vishnu Purana was a fresh sense of the power of the idea of identity, a word that had for Emerson the visceral kick that the word "contact" had for Thoreau. "Identity, identity! friend and foe are one stuff, and the stuff is such and so much that the variations of surface are unimportant," he exclaimed in his journal. It is what Schelling was driving at, as Emerson now began to see.

Western admiration of the East—"orientalism"—has often been denigrating, condescending, reductionist, preemptive, or plain imperialist. The modern historian of orientalism, Edward Said, has claimed that a politics of difference lay at the heart of the West's imperial cultural enterprise, "that politics needed to assume, indeed needed finally to believe, that what was true about Orientals or Africans was *not* however true about or for Europeans." The extreme version of this is the modern view that differences are all there is; we are constituted by our differences. Emerson understood the vast consequences of the differences-versus-identity dispute and he threw his whole weight onto the side of identity. "Some men," he wrote,

> have the perception of difference predominant, and are conversant
> with surfaces and trifles, with coats and watches, and faces and cities
> . . . And other men abide by the perception of identity. These are the
> orientals, the philosophers, the men of faith and divinity.

Emerson's absorption in Asian religion and literature cannot be understood unless one sees that for him the East was the proof—persuasive precisely because it was non-Western—that at the deep end of the pool, where it matters, Westerner and Easterner are profoundly alike, indeed identical. Nor does this perception in any way lessen the importance and the delight of the shallow differences that separate us from one another. Emerson's politics of identity validated both East and West, declined subordination or dismissal, and committed him to a constant and ever widening radar-sweep of inquiry.[10]

There was new power for Emerson again in the Bhagavad Gita as well. It was, he said, "a transnational book." He admired its teaching that worship is the height of right conduct, "because the sailor and the ship and the sea are of one stuff, because though the bases of things are divided, the summits are united." Emerson could now accept, as Thoreau could not yet, the central necessity Krishna lays upon Arjuna, the necessity of fighting. The perception of identity does not excuse us from acting; quietism is not the answer. "Children only and not the learned speak of the speculative and the practical doctrines as two."[11]

The Natural History
of Intellect

69. Representative Men

WHAT EMERSON CALLED HIS "PANTHEON COURSE OF LEC-
tures" had its roots way back in Emerson's early interest in biography. But
his immersion in books about Napoleon seems to have catalyzed his new
interest in the idea. "I have found a subject," he wrote in his journal, "*On
the use of great men*." He would do a modern Plutarch, but with a difference. He was not interested in the usual worshipful bowing down before
the unreachable great ones. Emerson took the idea of a pantheon seriously—even literally; he thought his subject was one "which might serve a
Schleiermacher for monologues to his friends." He considered doing one
of the lectures on Jesus. But he was interested from the start not in the
absolute greatness of his chosen figures but in "the great value of these
individuals as counterweights, checks on each other." His concern was not
so much with the great ones themselves as with the use of the great in our
education.[1]

Emerson's lectures on representative men and the book he eventually
made of them are in the strongest possible contrast to Carlyle's view of
heroes in *Heroes, Hero-Worship and the Heroic in History* or in his vast just-
concluded work on Cromwell. In 1846 Carlyle told the American abolitionist Elizur Wright that "men ought to be thankful to get themselves
governed, if it is only done in a strong and resolute way." The subject was
one of major disagreement between Emerson and Carlyle; there is nothing
Carlylean about *Representative Men*. Just when Carlyle was urging Emerson
to "take an American hero, one whom you really love, and give us a history
of him," Emerson was assembling something quite different. Emerson's
book included no Americans. The final selection was Plato, Swedenborg,
Montaigne, Shakespeare, Napoleon, and Goethe, standing respectively for
man as philosopher, mystic, skeptic, poet, materialist, and writer. By contrast, when Charles Sumner gave the 1846 Phi Beta Kappa address at
Harvard on "The Scholar, the Jurist, the Artist, the Philanthropist," his
examples were John Pickering, Joseph Storey, Washington Allston, and
William Ellery Channing.[2]

Emerson's list was pretty firmly fixed from the beginning. He considered using Saadi instead of Shakespeare and he once thought of having a chapter on Fourier after that on Napoleon. He was conscious of having left out Jesus, but he felt unable to "render historic justice to the world's chief saint." Baudelaire noted that Emerson had left out Voltaire, the antipoet. *Representative Men* has been widely admired, especially by writers. Emily Dickinson called it "a little granite book you can lean on." Robert Frost admired the language of "Montaigne, or the Skeptic." "Cut these words and they bleed," Frost quoted, not quite accurately, adding, "I am not submissive enough to want to be a follower, but he had me there. I never got over that." Jorge Luis Borges also cites Emerson's essay on Montaigne as representative of the work of a great critic, where "you feel . . . that his criticism comes from his personal experience of him" as opposed to the criticism of such critics as T. S. Eliot, in whose case "you always think—at least I always feel—that he is agreeing with some professor or slightly disagreeing with another."[3]

Representative Men is Emerson's major effort to reconcile the reality of the unequal distribution of talent with a democratic belief in the fundamental equality of all persons. Emerson believed in equality because he believed in the adequacy of the individual, of each individual. Each great person represents, for Emerson, the full flowering of some one aspect of our common nature. Great persons are not superior to us; they are exemplary, symbolic, or representative of us. "What can Shakespeare tell in any way but to the Shakespeare in us?" Emerson is a leveler, but he believes in leveling up. "As to what we call the masses, and common men," he says toward the close of the introductory lecture, "The Uses of Great Men," "there are no common men. All men are at last of a size, and true art is only possible on the conviction that every talent has its apotheosis somewhere." This conviction is the basis not only of art but of the interpretation of art. "The possibility of interpretation," he says, "lies in the identity of the observer with the observed."[4]

So the lecture on Plato is not on Plato himself so much as on the Platonic element in us all. Emerson found in Plato's work the plenitude—the sense of the miraculous fullness and multiplicity—of the world, which is itself a Platonic notion. "Out of Plato come all things that are still written and debated among men of thought," Emerson says. "Plato is philosophy and philosophy Plato." "Philosophy," he adds by way of definition, "is the account which the human mind gives to itself of the constitution of the world." From Plato we learn that there are "two cardinal facts . . . 1) Unity or Identity, and 2) Variety." "We unite all things by perceiving the law which pervades them; by perceiving the superficial differences and the profound resemblances. But every mental act—the very perception of identity or oneness, recognizes the differences of things. Oneness and otherness."[5]

Plato is for Emerson the great philosopher of identity, the great monist, though Emerson makes it plain that he himself has not lost interest in what is different and other. Not only do we seek others, we seek "the otherest" we can find, he says. This impulse is sufficiently strong to lead Emerson to conclude with a consideration of Plato's defects, which are that after all he left no system and that he is too "literary." "His writings have not the note of authority which the screams of prophets and the sermons of unlettered Arabs and Jews possess." Each essay in *Representative Men* concludes with a cool assessment of the subject's shortcomings. This tactic was deliberate and indeed necessary to Emerson's design. Since he thought that the use of great persons is to educate the present generation, not to stun it with superiority, he had no wish to intimidate his readers and hearers by describing the unmatchable perfections of his subjects. Perhaps this salutory denigration was added partly at Thoreau's urging, for Emerson noted in his journal that "Henry Thoreau objected to my 'Shakespeare,' that the eulogy impoverished the race. Shakespeare ought to be praised, as the sun is, so that all shall be rejoiced."[6]

Swedenborg is Emerson's representative mystic, the person who *sees* all that the philosopher *knows*. The mystics proceed via "ecstasy or absence,—a getting out of their bodies to think." Emerson profoundly respects this path, which is, he warns, "difficult, secret, and beset with terror." The praise of Swedenborg is that he understands that metamorphosis is the law of the universe and that things are representative. In Swedenborg's writings the Ovidian and Hindu ideas of metamorphosis and transmigration cease to be understood in the old way as objective phenomena, becoming instead subjective: "All things in the universe arrange themselves to each person anew, according to his ruling love." At the center of Swedenborg Emerson found the idea of correspondence, "the fine secret that little explains large, and large little." For Emerson Swedenborg is an experimentalist who has been led by his work to the identity theory, to a belief that

> nature iterates her means perpetually on successive planes. In an old aphorism, *nature is always self-similar.* In the plant, the eye or germinative point opens to a leaf, with a power of transforming the leaf

into radicle, stamen, pistil, petal, bract, sepal, or seed. The whole art of the plant is still to repeat leaf on leaf without end.[7]

If his admiration for Swedenborg is heartfelt, so is the subtraction. "The vice of Swedenborg's mind," says Emerson, "is theologic determinism." Emerson also lamented that Swedenborg, who understood symbols, who "saw the poetic construction of things," and who therefore grasped the "primary relation of mind to matter," could himself be so utterly devoid of poetry: "In his profuse and accurate imagery is no pleasure, for there is no beauty. We wander forlorn in a lack-lustre landscape. No bird ever sang in all those gardens of the dead."[8]

In the essay "Montaigne, or the Skeptic" Emerson argues that the value of skepticism is in its "resistance to premature conclusions." The proper ground of the skeptic is that "of consideration, of self-containing, not at all of unbelief, not at all of universal denying, nor of universal doubting." This essay on doubt is finally an essay on residual belief, which Emerson says "consists in accepting the affirmations of the soul; unbelief, in denying them." The wise skeptic does not teach doubt at last but how "to look for the permanent in the mutable and fleeting."[9]

Emerson explores Shakespeare's lack of interest in originality and how he "esteemed the mass of old plays waste stock, in which any experiment could be freely tried." Emerson concludes, as did Keats, that "great genial power, one would almost say, consists in not being original at all,—in being altogether receptive; in letting the world do all, and suffering the spirit of the hour to pass unobstructed through the mind." Shakespeare thus stands for "this power of expression, or of transferring the inmost truth of things into music and verse."[10]

The idea for *Representative Men* seems to have begun with Emerson's interest in Napoleon, whom he considered by far the best known and most powerful figure of the nineteenth century. "The history of Bonaparte is the commanding romance of modern times because every reader studies in it his own history." In other words, Napoleon became "the idol of common men because he had in transcendent degrees the qualities and powers of common men." These qualities were all in Napoleon's favor, for Emerson, and it is for different reasons that Napoleon becomes the infernal figure in this pantheon of half-gods. He is the perfect representative of the business class, he is thoroughly modern, he is no saint. He once ordered Bourrienne, his secretary, to hold all letters unopened for three weeks, by which time most of them had taken care of themselves. Above all, Napoleon is pure materialism, "pointing at a sensual success and employing the richest and most varied means to that end ... subordinating all intellectual and spiritual forces into means to a material success." Emerson was always happy to concede that "whatever appeals to the imagination, by transcending the ordinary limits of human ability, wonderfully encourages and liberates us." But Napoleon's glory "passed away like the smoke of his artillery, and left no trace. He left France smaller, poorer, feebler than he found it."[11]

The essay on Goethe comes last, so as not to leave Napoleon in possession of the field. Where Napoleon destroyed a world, Goethe created one. Goethe stands, says Emerson, "for the class of scholars and writers who see connections where the multitude see fragments, and who are impelled to exhibit the facts in order, and so to supply the axis on which the frame of things turn." Although he lived "in a small town, in a petty state, in a defeated state"—as did Plutarch—he "flung into literature, in his Mephistopheles, the first organic figure that has been added for some ages and which will remain as long as the Prometheus." Emerson also credits Goethe with suggesting the leading idea of modern botany, that a leaf or the eye of a leaf is the unit of botany, and that every part of a plant is only a transformed leaf to meet a new condition. As Napoleon brought desolation, so Goethe brought hope. Emerson gives his highest praise when he credits Goethe with lightening the burden of our past:

> Goethe, coming into an over-civilized time and country, when original talent was oppressed under the load of books and mechanical auxiliaries and the distracting variety of claims, taught men how to dispose of this mountainous miscellany and make it subservient.[12]

Emerson says on the last page of the essay that Goethe "teaches courage and the equivalence of all times." The same could be said of Emerson. The last paragraph of the Goethe essay is in the same brash chanticleer voice as the opening paragraph of *Nature*, written almost ten years earlier: "We too must write Bibles." Above all, we must put what we know into practice, and "first, last, middle and without end . . . honor every truth by use."[13]

70. The Lecturer

THE YEAR 1845 BROUGHT NEW FACES AND TOOK AWAY OLD. IN January Poe's "The Raven" made the greatest stir yet created by an American poem. Napoleon's brother Joseph died this year. Ireland suffered the Great Hunger. Frederick Douglass was on the abolitionist lecture circuit and talking about writing his autobiography. Margaret Fuller, now living in New York, fell in love with James Nathan. Brook Farm was nearing its end. Robert Owen, of New Harmony fame, came to visit the Alcotts. Henry Thoreau moved into his cabin at Walden. In October Nathaniel and Sophia Hawthorne left the Old Manse and Concord. Starting on December 11 in Boston Emerson began his new series of lectures with "On the Uses of Great Men."

Emerson repeated the series many times in many places over the next few years; it did not appear in book form until five years later in 1850. With this series Emerson's lecturing career took a marked upward turn. He had begun public lecturing in 1833, seven years after Josiah Holbrook had started the American Lyceum, a network of local lecture series designed to promote "the universal diffusion of knowledge." Emerson gave 1 lecture in 1833 and 7 in 1834. Each year he gave more until by 1838 he was doing 30 a year, almost all of them in eastern Massachusetts and southern New Hampshire. Between 1838 and 1845, when he was working on books and on *The Dial*, he gave fewer lectures but expanded his territory, addressing audiences in Providence, New York, Philadelphia, and other eastern cities. By 1846 he was giving 54 lectures a year; he maintained this pace until the early 1850s, when he began to give as many as 78 or even 80 a year.[1]

Over his active career of four decades, Emerson gave some 1,500 public lectures. Lecturing was a major part of his life and a major source of income. For twenty-five years he was out and away from home lecturing for four, five, or even six months out of each year, every year. He traveled as far west as St. Louis, Des Moines, Minneapolis, and eventually California; he gave 17 lectures in Canada but almost none south of the Ohio River. He delivered the great majority of his lectures in Massachusetts. He gave 157 lectures in New York state. He gave more lectures in Maine than in New Hampshire

(35 to 27) and many more in Illinois (49), Ohio (56), Pennsylvania (42), and Wisconsin (29) than in Connecticut, the land of steady habits, where he spoke only 18 times in his entire career.[2]

On a typical trip he either lectured or traveled by train to the next town almost every day for months on end. One two-week stretch in the winter of 1855 had him in Rochester, New York, on February 15, in Syracuse on the sixteenth, Rome on the seventeenth, Oneida on the nineteenth, Vernon on the twentieth. Then he went back to Rochester on the twenty-first, to Lockport on the twenty-second, Hamilton, Ontario, on the twenty-third, back to Syracuse on the twenty-fourth, to Canandaigua on the twenty-sixth, Watertown on the twenty-eighth, and Cazenovia on the first of March. That makes 12 speaking engagements in two weeks, each one involving a train trip.[3]

In the beginning Emerson made all his own arrangements. In the 1850s he made use of nonprofit lyceum bureaus to schedule lectures along established routes. In the sixties he began to use the newly established commercial booking agents. Though he had ever more friends in most of his stops, he preferred to stay in hotels. Like many a veteran lecturer, he prized a bit of calm and privacy even at the cost of some dreariness and loneliness.

Lecturing was Emerson's job, as he and his family and friends all understood it. The work was demanding, physically taxing as well as emotionally draining. Sometimes he caught colds or lost his voice, but he generally kept engagements even so. He refused to talk down to his audiences; if a lecture did not go well, he always assumed the problem was with him, not with the audience. He tried conscientiously to reach the mixed public that attended lyceum lectures. The lyceums were a working-class institution. They were founded, supported, and directed by local boards made up originally of working people intent on bettering themselves through practical education. Lyceums provided then what YMCAs and community colleges provide now. Emerson did not in general give talks at colleges and universities. He never spoke at Yale; after the "Divinity School Address" he was not welcome—not even invited—to speak at Harvard until after the Civil War. It is ironic that the American Plato had his greatest impact not through the academy—named in honor of Plato's place of instruction—but through the institution named for the walk where the practical Aristotle taught, the Lyceum.[4]

Emerson was often received rather coolly at first. But as time passed, he became more popular, for example, in Wisconsin. He always drew mixed reviews. He was one of the very few literary lecturers from the East to remain a steady lyceum attraction in Ohio for twenty years. Yet the historian of Ohio's lyceum movement noted that "no other cultural speaker from the East evoked so much adverse criticism." People were almost never tepid in their response to Emerson. Some years before her marriage to Nathaniel Hawthorne, Sophia Peabody thought Emerson was "the greatest man—the most complete man—that ever lived." The Wisconsin *Kenosha Democrat* thought him "an infidel, an abolitionist, a monarchist" and traced to him and his friends "all of the social, political, and moral abominations which threaten, disturb, and degrade the Northern states." Often he was badly praised. The *Toledo Commercial* told its readers that Emerson's lecture "Table Talk" would contain none "of the loose garbage" often found in the work of American writers. A person whose letter was signed "A German" insisted that Emerson "was entirely Celtic in his philosophy." In Quincy, Illinois, the editor of the *Daily Herald,* Burrell Taylor, attacked Emerson's lecture "The Man of the World" as "a hash." Taylor thought anyone "who has access to any of the standard encyclopedias . . . can get up just as good a lecture." What really bothered the Quincy editor was Emerson's "omission of all reference to the Bible, as the foundation of all moral excellence." When Emerson spoke against the Fugitive Slave Act in Cambridge, Massachusetts, he was hissed, as Edwin Whipple recalled, by "a score or two of foolish Harvard Students" who turned up for the occasion. The same observer noted that the students were "the rowdiest, noisiest, most brainless set of young gentlemen that ever pretended to be engaged in studying 'the humanities.'"[5]

In 1845 the students at Wesleyan invited Emerson to speak. The college president, Stephen Olin, prepared the way by denouncing transcendental-ism in his baccalaureate sermon and set an example by laughing out loud at various points during Emerson's talk. In 1841 Emerson delivered "The Method of Nature" in Waterville, Maine. He arrived late at night and there was some doubt as to where he was to stay. The stage driver knocked at house after house, saying "he had inside a man who *said* he was to deliver the lit-ra-rye oration tomorrow." Finally the right house was found. Next day "I delivered my oration," Emerson recalled, "which was heard with cold silent unresponsive attention, in which there seemed to be a continuous unuttered rebuke and protest."[6]

Hawthorne's son Julian remembered Emerson as "ungainly in build, with narrow, sloping shoulders, large feet and hands and a projecting carriage of the head which enhanced the eagle-like expression of his glance and features." One night, Julian goes on, "Emerson had the misfortune to wear a pair of abominably creaking boots; every slightest change of posture would be followed by an outcry from the sole leather, and the audience soon became nervously pre-occupied in expecting them." Julian remembered the sound of the boots long after he had forgotten what the lecture was about. Boots seem to have been a general problem. When Emerson's lecture "The Conduct of Life" was announced in Cleveland for January 29, 1857, the notice said "the hour of the lecture is eight o-clock, on or before which time it is expected that men with heavy boots, or 'creaky' ones will have located themselves."[7]

The Illinois *Bloomington Pantagraph* mocked him in print as "Ralph Cold-Dough Simmerson." In Warren, Ohio, he was introduced by a man who tried three times but could only bring out "Walph Raldo Emerson" each time. One lecture in Rock Island in January 1866 was held on the second floor of a large building on the ground floor of which was a wagon depot. The talk was praised by the local paper. "The only drawback was the really painful sensation produced by the slamming of doors, the tramp of heavy feet on stairs and aisles, the rattling of stoves, and the thunder produced by the driving of teams on the noisy planks under the hall."[8]

The lyceum season came during the winter. Travel was hard, hotels and lecture halls were cold. It was common to hear people "slambanging the stoves and coal scuttles during the lecture." Winter also created competing attractions. One town in Illinois canceled ice skating to try to swell an Emerson audience. In February of 1857 he was lecturing in Cincinnati. The weather had been warm and crowds went out to the riverbank every day expecting to see the ice break up. Finally, on the night Emerson gave "Works and Days," the ice let go; six steamers were wrecked and much other damage done. The papers observed that Emerson had spoken and the ice gave way.[9]

As he toured the country year after year, Emerson became a familiar—and memorable—figure. If we make allowances for illness and later for age, the descriptions of his lecturing style are remarkably consistent. An 1857 description in the *Cincinnati Times* is typical, though unusually well written. Emerson is described as

> tall, angular, loose-limbed, with an olive complexion, large features, especially the nose, and a blue or grey eye that has a mysterious and undefinable light in its depth. . . . He is not graceful, but he carries a weight grace and culture alone could never supply. He stands at an

acute angle towards his audience, and limberly, and has barely a gesture beyond the motion of the left hand at his side, as if the intensity of his thoughts was escaping, like the electricity of a battery, at that point.[10]

At the height of his powers Emerson held audiences rapt. His daughter Ellen, who plainly adored him, went to hear him and reported, "Not a word was lost, the whole company responded by movement, by smile, by breaths, by utter silence followed by some expressive sound from moment to moment through the whole lecture." Several accounts make it clear that it was common at the time to applaud during as well as after a lecture. Emerson worked to produce effects. He would read over funny stories and remarks as much as twenty times at home "to get through laughing at them himself that he might be sure not to laugh at the lecture." Though he often used a plain speaking style, he was capable of dramatic strokes. In his lecture on Swedenborg this year, 1845, he began with a fifteen-minute "compact statement of the opinions of the Swedish Sage," according to one listener. It became monotonous; the audience was lulled into assuming Emerson to be a converted Swedenborgian. "At the conclusion of his exposition he paused for half a minute, and then in his highest, most piercing tones he put the question, 'Who *is* EMMANUEL *SWEDENBORG?*' his voice rising as he accented every syllable. The effect was electric."[11]

Emerson enjoyed giving lectures. He was good at it, he followed it as a sort of calling, and he was excited by the presence of a crowd. He loved the emotional bond between a good speaker and an appreciative audience. "Precisely what the painter or the sculptor or the epic rhapsodist feels, I feel in the presence of this house, which stands to me for the human race, the desire, namely to express myself fully, symmetrically, gigantically to them, not dwarfishly and fragmentarily." He liked "being agitated to agitate." Much of Emerson's success as a lecturer derives from this close connection he felt with his audience, from his perpetually renewed acquaintance with failure, and from the fact that those nightly audiences were to him representative of the whole human race.[12]

71. Persia and Poetry

THE EARLY MONTHS OF 1846 WERE CONSUMED BY LECTURING. Emerson shuttled from Gloucester to Lowell to Worcester to Providence to Boston. On March 3 the new, unfinished central building at Brook Farm burned down, effectively ending the most successful, most interesting, and surely the sunniest of the communal enterprises of the period. It was symptomatic that the fire broke out in the grandiose new Fourierian "phalanstery" while the Brook Farmers were at a dance in the comfortable old farmhouse headquarters known as "the Hive." On the same day Ellery Channing left for Europe on funds raised and provided by Emerson.

The great event of Emerson's April was his discovery of the Persian poet Hafez. He bought a copy of Joseph von Hammer's excellent German edition, the two-volume *Der Diwan von Mohammed Schemsed-din Hafis* (Shams od-din Mohammed Hafez) at Elizabeth Peabody's bookshop, the point of entry into American intellectual life for much new German work. He soon became enthralled with the work of Hafez, the fourteenth-century Sufi master and greatest of Persian lyric poets. Emerson had known of Hafez for some time, but this was his first real encounter with him. Almost everything about Hafez appealed to Emerson: his directness, his fondness for short forms, his wit, his imagery, his lack of preachiness, his sensuousness, his ecstatic, joy-filled lyric celebration of life. Emerson recognized now that Hafez was for him, and he bent to the labor of getting something of him into English.[1]

Hafez's habits of mind were congenial to Emerson in part because Hafez was a Sufi. Emerson may have known only very little about the mystical transcendentalism of Islam and Persia. He rarely used the word Sufi. Still, it was the Sufism in Hafiz to which he responded so deeply and so quickly. Sufism, according to a modern authority, "is believed by its followers to be the inner, 'secret' teaching that is concealed in every religion." Its bases are in every human mind. Sufism has no mythology, no scripture, no church. The Sufis say, "This is not a religion, it *is* religion." Sufism is not monastic or aescetic. One must live in the world, among people. Sufis believe that

> the world is a fashioning instrument, which polishes mankind. They, by identification with the processes of continuous creation, are themselves fashioners of other complete men. . . . To understand them, you must bring into action an intelligence which is an intuitive one, normally held down by its friendly enemy, the intelligence of the logical mind.

Sufis believe in the symbolic nature of the world; they teach through symbols and parables. They are thus the heirs of Zarathustra, as Emerson recognized. "The Sufi speaks of wine, the product of the grape, and its secret potential, as his means of attaining 'inebriation.' The grape is seen as the raw form of the wine. Grapes then mean ordinary religion, while wine is the real essence of the fruit." The Sufi says, "Before garden, vine, or grape was in the world, our soul was drunken with immortal wine."[2]

All this was in Hafez, in a language of lips, wine, and roses; every line of every poem testified that the spiritual appears to us only through the senses. Emerson recognized this teaching in Hafez's lines, though it was for him half-buried in German, like a statue congealed in a block of marble. Emerson eventually filled a 250-page notebook with translations from Persian poets, mostly Hafez. It was difficult work, quarrying the poems out of black-letter gothic type. Emerson kept at translating over many years, and we can glimpse the process when he says, in another context, "We see the law gleaming through like the sense of a half-translated ode of Hafiz."[3]

A journal comment of this year gives a glimpse of what Emerson recognized in Hafez: "Hafez, whom at first I thought a cross of Anacreon and Horace, I find now to have the best blood of Pindar also in his veins. Also of Burns." Emerson translated hundreds of lines of Hafez; almost all are poems of love, wine, fire, and desire. Emerson especially liked the four line *rubai* form, with its compression and pith. It is a verse equivalent of his aphoristic prose.

> Lo! where from heaven's high roof
> Misfortune staggers down.
> We, just from harm to stand aloof
> Will to the wineshop run.

* * *

They say, through patience, chalk
Becomes a ruby stone.
Ah yes, but by the heart's true blood
The chalk is crimson grown.

* * *

The East wind and I
Are an amorous pair
O the spark of thine eye
Oh the scent of thy hair.

* * *

See how the roses burn
Bring wine to quench the fire.
Alas! the flames came up with us
We perish with desire.

* * *

In the midnight of thy locks
I renounce the day
In the ring of thy rose lips
My heart forgets to pray.

* * *

The chemist of fire
will thy perishing mould
Were it made out of mire
transmute into gold.[4]

Emerson also included a number of *rubai* from Omar Khayyam in his
"Orientalist" notebook. His clear favorite, however, is Hafez, who from now
on becomes a symbol and standard for Emerson of the highest poet,
comparable to Shakespeare.[5]

Persian poetry had a major impact on Emerson's own poetry this year;
it focused his efforts and even redirected them. Emerson had been thinking
for some years of gathering his poems together in a volume. Now, under
the intoxicating spell of Hafez, he wrote several new poems, reworked his
earlier ones, and arranged for publication. When the volume came out in
December, it also contained two translations from Hafez, one of them eight
pages long. These poems from Hafez were never reprinted after the first
edition, perhaps because Emerson reverted to his vow to do only his own
work. Or perhaps it was because Fitzgerald's English version of Omar

Khayyam (1859) was better than Emerson's Hafez, though the latter certainly has its moments, such as

> Every clod of loam beneath us
> Is a skull of Alexander;
> Oceans are the blood of princes;
> Desert sands the dust of beauties.

Or perhaps Emerson never reprinted his Hafez translations because later on he became unwilling to stand by the poetry of intoxication, which now fascinated him for the same reason it would fascinate William James. "The sway of alcohol over mankind," James wrote,

> is unquestionably due to its power to stimulate the mystical faculties of human nature, usually crushed to earth by the cold facts and dry criticism of the sober hours. Sobriety diminishes, discriminates, and says no: drunkenness expands, unites, and says yes. It is in fact the great exciter of the yes function in man.[6]

The Hafez translations are Emerson's buried *Rubaiyat,* eloquent testimony to the attraction Hafez had for him at this time. So is the poem "Bacchus," which, when set side by side with the first of Emerson's translations from Hafez, reveals itself to be a Hafez-inspired rhapsody on the power of inspiration symbolized by intoxication. Emerson has poured his new Persian wine in an old Greek bottle, creating a deliberate opposition and alternative to his earlier, Apollonian strain. Emerson's translation from Hafez begins:

> Butler, fetch the ruby wine
> Which with sudden greatness fills us.

"Bacchus" begins:

> Bring me wine, but wine which never grew
> In the belly of the grape.

"Bacchus" is one of Emerson's best poems. Its imagery has the skylark boldness and the swallow-tail grace of Hafez or Omar Khayyam:

> Wine that is shed
> Like the torrent of the sun
> Up the horizon walls

Or like the Atlantic streams, which run
When the South Sea calls.[7]

Emerson's own poetry has a marked Persian strain from now on. He wrote about Hafez in 1858 in a piece called "Persian Poetry" and about Saadi in an 1865 preface to a new edition of *The Gulistan*. In the latter he said of the Persians that "their superior intelligence, their esteem for men of learning, their welcome to Western travellers, and their tolerance of Christian sects in their territories . . . would seem to derive from the rich culture of this great choir of poets."

Emerson kept up with French, German, and English translations of the Persian poets. He continued to read Persian history and he pursued the work of European commentators such as Silvestre de Sacy, the Abbé Remusat, Ernest Renan, Max Müller, and Sir William Jones. He was interested in the great cities of Persia's romantic past, cities such as Shiraz, where both Saadi and Hafez were buried. Shiraz had once had forty colleges; it still had eleven, the largest of which had a hundred rooms. Even in its decline, Shiraz seemed a wondrous seat of learning and poetry, especially compared to prosaic Boston and the few pinched little colleges of New England.[8]

Persian poetry was a new homeland for Emerson. It gave him the form, the imagery, and the tone for a poetry of ecstasy, a poetry to express his strong emotional non-Apollonian side, a poetry that did justice to the sweetness of life lived in the senses as well as to the spiritual enjoyments to which such a life corresponded.[9]

Emerson's interest in Hafez in 1846 rekindled his interest in other arts. He bought a group of prints—most of which can still be seen on the walls of the house in Concord, and most of which are representative of various sibyls by Michelangelo, Raphael, and Guercino. The sibyls were the female prophets of the classical world. According to Varro there were ten of them; the most famous was the sibyl of Cumae. They were understood to be inspired by heaven and were in the habit of writing down their utterances on leaves in front of their caves. Great care had to be taken to gather up the leaves in order, quickly, before a wind could scatter and scramble them. Emerson hung the pictures partly out of interest in the Old Masters and partly from interest in the sibyls themselves, corresponding as they did, perhaps, with some of the strongest influences in his own life.[10]

Emerson was again interested in music too this spring of 1846. "We have not done with music," he wrote. "We wish to be ravished, inspired and taught; we do not want prison melodies or modern antiques or Jim Crow songs, but the Godhead in music, as we have the godhead in the sky and the creation."[11]

In May he was walking to Walden every day with Ellen and Edith, who were seven and (almost) five. It was now in the glow of enjoying his daughters and Hafez and the spring that he made his famous crack about Boston's "corpse-cold Unitarianism" after he went to hear Edward Everett sworn in as the new president of Harvard.[12]

In June Emerson wrote "Bacchus" and put final touches on "The World Soul," a poem that signals the most recent shift in Emerson's habitual patterns of imagery. He had made striking use of the imagery of eyes and vision in his early work. A great deal of his mature work draws figural energy from fire, volcanoes, and lava. Now the fascination with Persian poetry begins to bring images of wine and roses to his verse. Perhaps his new interest in Persian poetry had something to do with his feelings for Caroline Sturgis or with revived feelings for Lidian. It is hard to imagine that the passion for Persian poetry is just an interest in metaphor for strictly spiritual feelings about divinity. Passion was awakening in him again, and, though he was only forty-three, the emotion seems to have caught him by surprise, as if he had been a much older man.

> Spring still makes spring in the mind
>   When sixty years are told;
> Love wakes anew this throbbing heart,
>   And we are never old.
> Over the winter glaciers
>   I see the summer glow
> And through the wild-piled snow-drift
>   The warm rosebuds below.[13]

72. The New Domestic Order. Poems

In July 1846 the Emersons revolutionized their house-keeping. They brought in a Mrs. E. C. Goodwin to run their home as a boardinghouse. The Emersons contracted themselves into four rooms, the rest being given to Mrs. Goodwin to use for her own family or to rent to other lodgers. The Emersons were literally boarders in their own house.

Less than a year earlier, in the fall of 1845, they had taken a first step toward lightening those burdens that fell mainly on Lidian. They had hired a woman named Sophia Foord or Ford to be the children's teacher and governess. The Emersons did not do things by halves. They now converted the west end of the first floor of the barn into a schoolroom, painting it and putting in a chimney. Miss Ford taught Lizzy and Abby Alcott, Lizzy and Barry Goodwin, and Caroline Pratt as well as the Emerson children. Lidian and her husband had strong convictions about raising children. Ellen and Edith were raised on a strict vegetarian diet. Ellen later recalled that she never ate meat or chicken until she was eighteen. She also recalled that "we were to have a pail of cold water splashed over us every morning. We were to be made active and hardy, trained to write a diary and taught sewing as well as lessons."[1]

Sophia Ford's coming was some relief to Lidian, but not enough. She felt unable to keep house at all now, and so Mrs. Goodwin was invited to take over. The Emersons had long entertained hopes for domestic reform and they had tried repeatedly to expand their family group. Emerson loved having a large clan around him; he recalled fondly the busyness of his boyhood home. He had been seriously tempted by Brook Farm; the Alcotts had almost come to live with them; Margaret Fuller had tried it, and Henry Thoreau would spend as much time living with them as he had spent in his cabin at Walden. Having decided to put the house in someone else's hands, Lidian now went to work to get the house clean enough to turn over. She "set out upon a tremendous upheaval of the whole house . . . to make over every carpet, to penetrate to every dark corner and bring all things to judgement." It was almost as bad as moving. Emerson thought it foolish,

Miss Ford disapproved, Ruth Emerson, Lidian's mother-in-law, understood but felt sorry. It was a task that would have daunted a healthy strong woman and Lidian soon "fell beside the way," as Ellen told the story. But "there was nothing for it but to get up and go on. The tragedy darkened every day."[2]

Somehow the house was made ready and Mrs. Goodwin arrived, probably in July, with her four children. Other "summer boarders" followed. The new arrangement lasted about a year and a half. It was at least a partial success, for there was a new note of gaiety and bustle everywhere. The barn schoolroom was full of children. Henry Thoreau and Sophia Ford took the whole family huckleberrying. (Ford later proposed marriage to Thoreau, who responded with an emphatic refusal.) There were other comings and goings. Ellery Channing returned from Europe and Margaret Fuller left for Europe. This was the summer Thoreau spent a night in jail for not paying his poll tax. He was living out at Walden now, where he had gone partly in order to escape the din and crowding of the boardinghouse his mother was running in their home. Emerson had dreamed of building a hut of his own at Walden Pond for some time. Now he began actively to plan a retreat similar to Thoreau's on the other side of the same pond—also on his own land—and for much the same reason. But Emerson never built his shack by the pond, for at bottom he rather enjoyed the crowding and activity of his Bush Community.[3]

He kept working on his book of poems. He added "Mithridates," "Merlin II," "Alphonso of Castille," and "Bacchus." He sent the manuscript off to the printers in the fall. There must have been a certain exhilaration in finishing up. He wrote to Aunt Mary, he read Marcus Aurelius. But even as he finished his volume of poems, he was haunted by what he had left unsaid. He wrote to Lidian, who was visiting Plymouth, "But though days go smoothly enough they do not bring me in their fine timely wallets the alms I incessantly beg of them. Where are the melodies, where the unattainable words?" The poems would speak for themselves, and the journal testifies to a renewed forcefulness and sense of conviction this fall. In a comment that Baudelaire would much admire, he wrote, "The one good in life is concentration; the one evil is dissipation." He had also learned to give everything he had to each project in turn, to hold nothing back: "What a discovery I made one day that the more I spent the more I grew." He thought now that it was the poet—a certain kind of poet—who had the best claim to lasting fame.

I think that he only is rightly immortal to whom all things are immortal; he who witnesses personally the creation of the world; he who enunciates profoundly the names of Pan, of Jove, of Pallas, of Bacchus, of Proteus, of Baal, of Ahriman, of Hari, of Satan, of Hell, of Nemesis, of the Furies, of Odin, and of Hertha.

He reaffirmed both detail and pattern. He admired people "who know the beauty of a quince-orchard, of a heron, of a wood pigeon, of a lonesome pasture," and he admired the fact that "the world is saturated with deity or law."[4]

Poems came out in December 1846; the American edition was issued on Christmas Day. This was the only one of Emerson's books to be bound in white boards. His fourth book, it was the first to set him before the public in the role he had most longed for ever since he was a child. The volume begins with "The Sphinx," a difficult but important poem that gives Emerson's original turn to the classic riddle of the Sphinx, in which the answer (humankind) finds unity where the question (what goes on four legs, then two, then three?) assumes multiplicity. "The Sphinx" is Emerson's poetic declaration of the fundamental identity of all things. At the end of the poem the figure of the Sphinx suddenly expands like Pan into all of nature:

> Through a thousand voices
>   Spoke the universal dame:
> Who telleth one of my meanings
>   Is master of all I am.

It is unfortunate that later editors decided this poem was too difficult and so removed it from its place at the start of the volume, thus directing attention away from the sibylline, ecstatic, prophetic note that is so pronounced in many of the poems. Because later editors omitted the Hafez translations and repositioned "The Sphinx," they obscured the original shape and content of Emerson's first book of poems.[5]

The volume shows the breadth of Emerson's poetic interests. "Ode: Inscribed to W. H. Channing" raises the problem of art and political engagement. Its denunciation of materialism—"Things are in the saddle / And ride mankind"—is more often quoted than the ending, in which 1848 and Whitman's "Resurgemus" seem to loom dimly:

The Cossack eats Poland
Like stolen fruit,
Her last noble is ruined,
Her last poet mute:
Straight, into double band
the victors divide.
Half for Freedom strike and stand:
The Astonished muse finds thousands at her side.[6]

Perhaps the most striking aspect of the volume as a whole is the voice it gives to the extravagant, wild, ecstatic side of Emerson. For despite the aura of sobriety and calm that has settled on the common conception of the man, there was another side to Emerson, the side that had been addressed first by his aunt Mary Moody Emerson, the side that wanted to be daring, to take risks. Only outsiders thought him detached. Emerson had a hunger for friendship and a delight in affection. What had expressed itself as silliness when he was a boy expressed itself in fits of exuberance when he was grown. And there was always a side of him that sought intensity, moments of insight, moments of life-changing experience, descents of power for which poetry alone provided adequate expression. Emerson's poems are the record of his Dionysian or Hafezian side.

What Emerson really hoped for in this volume of poems is suggested in a journal entry written around this time:

O Bacchus, make them drunk, drive them mad, this multitude of vagabonds, hungry for eloquence, hungry for poetry, starving for symbols, perishing for want of electricity to vitalize this too much pastime; and in the long delay, indemnifying themselves with the false wine of alcohol, of politics, or of money. Pour for them, O Bacchus, the wine of wine. Give them, at last, Poetry.[7]

73. The Orchard Keeper

THE SENSE OF FRUITION EMERSON FELT TOWARD THE END OF
1846 may have arisen partly from the publication of his poems, but the
feeling also had another quite literal source, which was a new interest in fruit
trees. Emerson had been mildly interested in orchards for years. He had
planted fifteen apple trees in 1836. Now, in November 1846, his brother
William sent him a box of young grapevines. Emerson carefully unpacked
them into a tub of earth and next day replanted them into good soil in the
garden. With his finances now improving, he had recently bought a two-acre
field east of his house. He began keeping an orchard book in which he
recorded the names of the varieties of his new fruit trees.[1]

This new interest in fruit was partly a result of Emerson's discovery of
Andrew Jackson Downing's *The Fruits and Fruit Trees of America* (1845).
Emerson's son Edward later noted that this had been an important book
for his father, who was especially pleased by those pages in the introduction
that talked about Van Mons's theory of amelioration. Downing's volume
is appealing, well written, even urgent; it is a book with a mission. Downing
was a landscape gardener and nurseryman, one of the teachers of Frederick
Law Olmsted and Calvert Vaux, and arguably the greatest single figure in
American horticulture. With this book Downing aimed to "increase the
taste for the planting and cultivation of fruit trees" and to "furnish a manual
for those who, already more or less informed upon the subject, desire some
work of reference to guide them in the operations of culture and in the
selection of varieties." The book focuses on the development and nurturing
of varieties under domestication, a subject much discussed by Darwin.
Downing's 1845 book taught the Concord transcendentalists the working
vocabulary of Darwin's great book of 1859. Downing could have called his
book "The Origin of Domestic Varieties."[2]

"It will be remarked," says Downing, "that our garden varieties of fruits
are not natural forms. They are the artificial productions of our culture.
They have always a tendency to improve, but they have also another and
stronger tendency to return to a natural or wild state." Downing quotes John

Lindley's comment that "there can be no doubt that if the arts of cultivation were abandoned for only a few years, all the annual varieties of plants in our gardens would disappear and be replaced by a few original wild forms."[3]

Downing becomes lyrical as he considers the improvement or amelioration of fruit trees.

> Transplanted into a warmer aspect, stimulated by a richer soil, reared from selected seeds, carefully pruned, sheltered, and watered, by slow degrees the sour and bitter crab expands into a Golden Pippin, the wild pear loses its thorns and becomes a Bergamotte or a Beure, the almond is deprived of its bitterness, and the dry and flavorless peach is at length a tempting and delicious fruit. It is thus only in the face of obstacles, in a climate where nature is not prodigal of perfections, and in the midst of thorns and aloes that man the gardener arises and forces nature to yield to his art.

This description is worthy to stand beside John Smith's famous description of the delights of easy fishing in the teeming waters of the New World.[4]

Downing's book is interesting not only for its detail but for its steady interest in the power of cultivation and of creation. To the person

> who views with a more than common eye the crimson cheek of a peach, the delicate bloom of a plum, or understands the epithets rich, melting, buttery as applied to a pear, nothing in the circle of culture can give more lively and unmixed pleasure, than thus to produce and to create—for it is a sort of creation—an entirely new sort, which he believes will prove handsomer and better than anything that has gone before.[5]

Downing's book is a practical vindication of the transcendentalist's emphasis on cultivation; it revives the concept of culture both as a process and as a metaphor by reconnecting it to its roots in agriculture and arboriculture. It calls attention to the efficacy of culture—of grafting and pruning and training—and it offers itself as a vast metaphor for human culture. The book invigorated Emerson and sent him back to his own proper projects refreshed. His late writings are filled with the imagery of orchards and fruit-tree culture. Downing's book was proof that one could change things. No orchard keeper can be a believer in fate.

Emerson soon had more than a hundred fruit trees whose names had their own poetry. There were plums, such as Damson, Green Gage, Plymouth, and Coe's Golden Drop. There were peaches, including Early Rose, Early York, Gross Mignon, and President. He had over thirty apple trees, among them Golden Russet, Gravenstein, Spitzenberg, Baldwin, Wine-apple, Jonathan, Hightop, Bellflower, Tallman Sweet, Dutch Coddling, and Sopsavine. One apple in the orchard list is named Thoreau and in all probability was developed by his young friend. Of the four hundred varieties of pear grown at the time in eastern Massachusetts, Emerson had Duchesse d'Angoulême, St. Ghislaine, Glout Morceau, Iron, Seckel, Fulton, Bloodgood, Bartlett, Dunmore, and Dix. He also put in a dozen quince trees. The quince is a close relative of the pear and is often used for root stock in the grafting of pears. Emerson's quinces included Long Green, Beurre Diel, Catilac, and Pound. Tart and austere as it comes from the tree but wonderful when cooked and mixed with apples, the nearly forgotten quince was another native of Persia that came to flourish in Concord.[6]

Parts of Emerson's land were later sold off; much of what remains has run wild. Only a few steps from the house the land is densely overgrown, essentially abandoned and thoroughly impenetrable. Recent efforts have carved out a garden space behind the house. Emerson's own fruit trees are gone, though a few descendents remain. The real crop of the orchard is in his late writings. But simply to stand in his backyard and say "apple" or "quince" is to miss entirely the rich cornucopia of varietal names, the once valued separate qualities of each of Emerson's more than a hundred trees, the everyday connection between the cultivation of the soil and the life of the mind which has vanished. That lost orchard also haunts the biographer, since it stands for everything that was common and lively and is now unrecoverable in Emerson's life.

74. I Shall Never Graduate

DURING THE FIRST TWO-THIRDS OF 1847 EMERSON WAS MORE restless and dissatisfied than he had been for many years. On the surface his life was going well. He was forty-three now, settled and successful. His children were thriving. He had published four books; he had his next one clearly in mind. He had a large and still increasing audience for his lectures. But there was a clear lull or pause after the appearance of *Poems.* Perhaps he felt the postpartum letdown that often follows the publication of a book. Certainly his domestic situation was troubling, dominated as it was by Lidian's continued illness and indisposition. The new living arrangements with Mrs. Goodwin were more expensive than the old way, and he was still carrying William, who now owed him more than five thousand dollars. Money was always a concern, yet he felt obliged to bail out a cousin, Robert Haskins, and also Aunt Mary, who had unwisely signed away part of her farm.

Emerson still read with the contented nonchalance of one who never knows from what direction inspiration will appear but who knows that it will appear. He read more in Hafez and Kurroglou; he read Swedenborg's *Animal Kingdom* with the same half-fascinated, half-repelled attention that marked his other encounters with the Swedish scientist-mystic. He read the *Heimskringla* and the prose *Edda.* He read Boeckh's *Public Economy of Athens,* Alfieri's *Autobiography,* and Aristophanes. He read Machiavelli's *The Florentine Histories* and complained that "the Florentine factions are as tiresome as the history of the Philadelphia Fire Companies."[1]

His literary work was equally miscellaneous. He wrote letters trying to find a publisher for Thoreau's *A Week on the Concord and Merrimack Rivers.* He tried to help a Danish novelist, Harro Harring, with the publication of a novel called *Dolores: A Novel of South America.* Theodore Parker was eager to launch a new journal. Emerson was interested but not really enthusiastic. He was making minor corrections for a new edition of *Essays: First Series,* but the main work of the year seems to have been indexing his journals, a job dull and fussy enough to depress a dervish even while it was an incomparable preparation for new work. Two enormous 400-page indexes, one built on the other, bear the date 1847, testifying to hours of exacting labor.[2]

If the tide was out for Emerson this year, it was in for Thoreau, who was conducting his own experiment in the reformation of domestic economy at Walden. On February 10 Thoreau gave a talk at the Concord Lyceum on how he lived at the pond, a lecture that was to grow eventually into *Walden*. Meantime, Emerson was coming quickly to regret having bought additional land and having set out ambitious plantings. "No land is bad, but land is worse," he wrote in his journal.

> I delight in long free walks. These free my brain and serve my body. . . .
> But these stoopings and scrapings and figurings in a few square yards
> of garden are dispiriting, driveling, and I seem to have eaten lotus,
> to be robbed of all energy, and I have a sort of catalepsy, or unwill-
> ingness to move, and have grown peevish and poor-spirited.

He needed stimulation, as he told Carlyle. He noted to himself, "I have wished for a professorship. Much as I hate the church, I have wished [for] the pulpit that I might have the stimulus of a stated task." He had at times almost a frantic sense of unused or dissipated energy, and his images took on the quality of a powerful and urgent summons. "A snowflake will go through a pine board, if projected with force enough," he told himself in late March.[3]

Emerson's dissatisfaction extended to the country at large, to America "the ungirt, the diffuse, the profuse, procumbent." "We live in Lilliput," he complained. He thought the "American mind a wilderness of capabil-ities," and he took a grim pleasure in his friend Ellery Channing's proposal that

> there should be a magnified Dollar, say as big as a barrel head, made
> of silver or gold, in each village and Colonel Shattuck or other priest
> appointed to take care of it and not let it be stolen; then we should
> be provided with a local deity and could bring it baked beans or other
> offerings.

So sharp was Emerson's feeling of alienation now that he could write: "Who has society! people to talk to? people who stimulate? Boston has 120,000 and I cannot now find one."[4]

His life seemed full of isolated details, some interesting enough, but without connections one to the other or to a larger coherence. He heard of an eleven-year-old boy in Vermont named Henry Safford who performed astonishing feats of math. Asked one day during a public examination to multiply 365,365,365,365,365,365 by itself,

> he flew round the room like a top, pulled his pantaloons over the top of his boots, bit his hand, rolled his eyes in their sockets sometimes smiling and talking and then seeming to be in agony until in not more than one minute, he said "133,491,850,208,566,925,016,658,299, 941,583,225."[5]

In July and August Alcott and Thoreau entertained themselves and the town by putting up an elaborate rustic summerhouse in the middle of Emerson's new land. The structure was designed by Alcott to have "peristyle gables, dormer windows etc." In late August Emerson described it to Lidian who was off for a rest in Maine: "Mr. Alcott and Henry are laboring at the summer house, which, in spite of their joint activity has not yet fallen. A few more spikes would to all appearances shatter the supporters. I think to call it Tumbledown Hall."[6]

Emerson's correspondence writhes with malaise in March. To Samuel Ward he wrote that he was getting "a little modern imagination in books I need not name for the same quality may be sucked indifferently from any bundle of railroad literature." By June the sense of desiccation had become pronounced. He wrote George Bradford that he had "no news or visitor from abroad, no lion roars, no mouse cheeps, we have discovered no new book, but the old atrophy inanition and drying up proceeds at an accelerated rate." In September he replied to a request for information about his life with curt distaste: "I have no history that would make the smallest figure in a narrative. . . . We will really say no more on a topic so sterile." The old image of a procession of days returned to taunt him; it was his habitual image for his recurring sense that he was missing out: "The days come and go like muffled and veiled figures sent from a distant friendly party, but they say nothing, and if we do not use the gifts they bring, they carry them as silently away."[7]

Toward the end of July 1847 Emerson decided to accept one of those offered gifts, an invitation to go to England. The proposal had been made first by an English journalist and bibliographer named Alexander Ireland in

438

the fall of the preceding year. Emerson was wary of undertaking a full-dress lecture tour, but he was willing to speak to appropriate audiences, if such could be found. He wished to see paintings and statues, and the more lonely and sad he found Concord, the more he liked the idea of an extended trip. Around August 30 Lidian invited Henry Thoreau to come stay with her and the children during Emerson's projected absence. A week later Thoreau left his hut, bringing to an end his two-year, two-month, and two-day stay at Walden Pond.

Emerson found even the arrangements for travel dispiriting. He wrote contemptuously to his brother about "my little fuss of preparation." "All my life is a sort of College examination," he told William. "I shall never graduate. I have always some torments ahead." He now threw himself into preparing lectures for delivery in England but without his usual pleasure in a new task. There is an almost panicky determination in Emerson's resolution now, reminding one of Samuel Johnson's endless efforts at self-reform.

Perhaps one reason for Emerson's mood in early 1847 is the change in his relationship with Caroline Sturgis. Back in September of the previous year he had sent her some of the poems that were to appear in his volume. With her usual bright outspokenness, Sturgis replied in October, saying she liked the poems, although she was put off, she said, because "they had all the old words in them." She liked "Bacchus" best. She still had a touch of the quality that caused her to be called "the American Bettina," saying at the end of her letter: "I wish some days you could come and make me a visit as at Concord last winter, or I could come into your study and make all the essays flutter about."[8]

Later, apparently on February 11, 1847, they met again and Sturgis made some comment about being surprised to find real "personalities" in some of the poems Emerson had sent her, poems that were by now published. Emerson quickly said that the poems "were not historical etc," meaning, one gathers, that they were not based on real people or events or feelings. But three days later he wrote her a long, intricate letter in which he tried to make it clear that he regretted his positive denial and that he did not wish to repudiate the events or feelings that had given rise to the poems in question but that they were, in their present form, just poems and as such "consciously fabulous to any actual life and purposes of mine, when I write them." Sturgis regarded poetry as something personal. She had always been sensitive about publishing her own poems under her own name, and now

Emerson went to considerable lengths in this letter to defend the poems as poems, without repudiating the private circumstances from which they had come. "But the seeing you—suggested that these poems, which the day before were poems,—were personalities, and they instantly became unspeakably odious to me. I seem to have surprised myself in an offense which I never forgive in another. And that offense too against you."[9]

This seems to be both an admission that the poems in question—perhaps "Rhea" among them—were based on their relationship and an apology for printing them. We do not know which poems Caroline Sturgis was referring to; we can only guess, therefore, at the circumstances in question. Emerson closed his letter with a declaration that seems determined to be warm and emphatic:

> The calling in by trumpeting poetry, of millions of witnesses, though it may be very idle, would be indifferent, so long as I am what I say I am and do not equivocate to myself. This friendship has been the solidest social good I have known, and it is my meaning to be true to it.

It is the word "social" that stands out here. Whatever they had been to one another—and there was probably never anything more than a kind of reckless epistolary passion—their relation to each other was henceforth solidly "social." They stopped writing. Sturgis, living now in Lenox, Massachusetts, was moving in circles other than Emerson's. She no longer wrote Fuller either, who complained in 1847 that she never heard from Caroline and no one wrote about her.[10]

Caroline Sturgis had been interested since 1843 in a man named William Tappan. Emerson had introduced them. Before 1847 was out Sturgis and Tappan were married.

75. England

ON OCTOBER 5, 1847, IN BOSTON EMERSON BOARDED THE
packet *Washington Irving* for Liverpool. The fifteen-day passage was un-
eventful. The ship encountered large floating drifts of boards, logs, and chips
that came down from the rivers of Maine and New Brunswick after every
high tide. They saw whales and blackfish. Dolphins swam in the bow wave
and huge schools of mackerel tore the surface of the sea.

England jolted Emerson. Everything seemed different, bigger, faster,
heavier. "Everything in England bespeaks its immense population," he
wrote. "The buildings are on a scale of size and wealth out of all proportion
to ours." The people were large-bodied and hard-eyed; they passed each
other in the street with "complete incuriosity and stony neglect each of every
other." The best one could say of the climate was that it was temperate and
good for work. The Midlands, where Emerson spent a good deal of time,
were blanketed in coal smoke that made night and day almost indistin-
guishable. Sheep turned black, trees turned black, spit turned black. In
London too the sun rarely penetrated the smoke, and it rained a little every
day, or as Emerson put it, "on every tide."[1]

All was bustle and activity in England. At home in Concord, before
leaving, Emerson had noted how the river was "decorated with nymphaea,
the cardinal flower, and the button bush, asclepias, and eupatoriums." In
England he saw mostly cities where all life moved on machinery. "The
Englishman never touches the ground. The steamer delivers him to the cab,
the cab to the railway train, the train to the cab, the cab to the hotel, and
so onward." Railroads connected everything. It was symbolic of the new
forces that on December 1, 1847, while Emerson was in Liverpool, the time
all over England was reduced and standardized to Greenwich Mean Time.
Until that day the time for each village or town had been regulated by local
solar observation, noon being the moment when the sun reached its highest
point overhead.[2]

There was too much of everything. Poets "lie three, six, or ten deep
instead of single as in America." The British Museum housed 420,000

volumes on twelve miles of shelves. "It is impossible to read from the glut of books," said Emerson. He noted with amusement how the English mangled the language, saying "Idersay" for "I dare say" and clipping every word. "Dr. Cook Taylor who wrote for the Athenaeum I never doubted was Dr. Coutell." They said "Yer-up" for "Europe," "kyer-ious" for "curious," and "steeryerd" for "steward."[3]

Emerson had a hard eye himself for the extremes of wealth and poverty. "The Marquis of Breadalbane rides out of his house a hundred miles in a straight line to the sea, on his own property. The Duke of Sutherland owns the county of Sutherland, stretching across Scotland from sea to sea." "The possessions of the Earl of Lonsdale gave him eight seats in Parliament." Primogeniture still reigned. Its theory, according to a Colonel Thomas, was "to make one son strong enough to force the public to support all the rest."[4]

Literacy was alarmingly low. Forty percent of the English people could not write their names, compared to one half of one percent in Massachusetts. Nor was English scholarship impressive. Emerson was shocked that Thomas Taylor's name was essentially unknown. When Friedrich Tholuck, a professor of theology at Halle, said to Thomas Chalmers, professor at St. Andrews and Edinburgh, "that he was astonished that none of the theologians here [England] had had the candour to read Strauss," Chalmers replied, "Sir, I will read it on your recommendation, but is it a big book? for I am old."[5]

This was the England of *Oliver Twist*. There were beggars of all ages in the cities. They stood "barefooted in the mud on a bridge in the rain all day to beg of passengers." The children reminded him of his own at home, as he told his wife:

> I cannot go up the street but I shall see some woman in rags with a little creature just of Edie's age and size, but in coarsest ragged clothes, and barefooted, stepping beside her, and I look curiously into *her* Edie's face, with some terror lest it resemble *mine,* and the far-off Edie wins from me the half-pence for this near one.

The problem of poverty was beginning to attract organized attention. A *General Report on the Sanitary Conditions of the Laboring Population* appeared in 1842. Emerson noted that "among the trades of despair is the searching the filth of the sewers for rings, shillings, teaspoons etc, which have been washed out of the sinks. These sewers are so large that you can go underground great distances."[6]

Emerson was a shrewd observer of what massive industrialization was doing to the workers. His critique of the factory system of production is tough and unsentimental.

> The incessant repetition of the same hand-work dwarfs the man, robs him of his strength, wit, and versatility, to make a pin-polisher, a buckle maker, or any other specialty; and presently, in a change of industry, whole towns are sacrificed like ant-hills, when the fashion of shoe-strings supersedes buckles.

The system was not working as it was supposed to. Competition led to shoddy goods and to fraud rather than to lower prices for higher quality.

> England is aghast at the disclosure of her fraud in the adulteration of food, of drugs, and of almost every fabric in her mills and shops; finding that milk will not nourish, nor sugar sweeten, nor bread satisfy, nor pepper bite the tongue, nor glue stick. . . . 'Tis not, I suppose, want of probity so much as the tyranny of trade, which necessitates a perpetual competition of underselling, and that again a perpetual deterioration of the fabric.[7]

When Emerson first landed in England, he took rooms and generally dined alone. He made a dash to Manchester to confer with Alexander Ireland, who was arranging lecture engagements for him, and another to London to see Carlyle. He was soon swept up in a busy schedule. During all of November he shuttled back and forth between Liverpool and Manchester, where he was giving concurrent lecture series. Somewhat to his surprise he was a great success. His Liverpool audiences averaged 750 persons. He found that *The Dial* was "absurdly well-known." People lionized him; hostesses gave dinners for him; the clergy attacked him every Sunday from Anglican pulpits. He gave some sixty-seven public lectures in England and Scotland during his stay, and he met Thackeray, Tennyson, Macaulay, Disraeli, Palmerston, Wordsworth (again), Dickens, George Eliot, Matthew Arnold, Thomas DeQuincy, Samuel Rogers, Leigh Hunt, Crabbe Robinson, Harriet Martineau (again), and Arthur Hugh Clough, who became a good friend. He met critics and journalists such as John Payne Collier, the Shakespearian critic, Archibald Alison, John Wilson ("Christopher North"), and Francis Jeffrey, the original editor of the *Edinburgh Review*. He heard Richard Cobden, who, he told Thoreau, was "the best man in England." He went to see Turner's paintings, which he thought justified Ruskin's praise, and he was impressed by Turner's effort to paint what he saw, not what he knew. He met George Stephenson, the engineer who created the modern railroad, Charles Lyell, the geologist, Robert Chambers, author of *Vestiges of Creation,* and Richard Owen, the anatomist and curator of the Hunterian museum. He met J. J. Garth Wilkinson, the Swedenborgian turned Fourierist, and Charles Babbage, the mathematician and inventor of the calculating machine. He heard Faraday; he met Chopin and heard him play. When the Pre-Raphaelite brotherhood of Holman Hunt, John Millais, and Dante Gabriel Rossetti drew up a list of immortals "which constitutes the whole of our creed," Emerson was one of four Americans on the list. (The others were Poe, Longfellow, and Washington.)[8]

In July of 1848, when he had boarded the ship that was to take him home, Emerson was talking on deck with Arthur Hugh Clough, his new English friend, who was a poet. "You leave all us young Englishmen without a leader," said Clough. "Carlyle has led us into the desert, and he has left us there." Emerson said to him, "This is what all the young men in England have said to me." The exchange points to the one aspect of the trip that had not gone well in England—Emerson's friendship with Carlyle. When they first sat down in October 1847 to talk, Emerson found that neither his meeting with Carlyle fifteen years earlier nor all their correspondence had adequately prepared him. "I have now at last been taken by surprise by him," he wrote Lidian. "He is not mainly a scholar, like the most of my acquaintances, but a very practical Scotchman, such as you would find in any sadler's or iron dealer's shop, and then only accidentally and by a surprising addition the admirable scholar and writer he is." His ingrained pessimism quickly wore on Emerson: "He talks like a very unhappy man, profoundly solitary, displeased and hindered by all men and things about him, and plainly biding his time, and meditating how to undermine and explode the whole world of nonsense which torments him."[9]

Carlyle's opinions on most subjects were now the opposite of Emerson's. Carlyle disapproved of abolition. He snarled at welfare.

> They gather up six millions of money every year to give to the poor, and yet the people starve. He [Carlyle] thinks if they would give it to him to provide the poor with labour and with authority to make them work or shoot them, and he to be hanged if he did not do it, he could find them in plenty of Indian meal.

Emerson agreed with a Mr. Forster who called Carlyle's main passion "musket-worship." Emerson observed that all Carlyle's methods "include a good deal of killing," and he confessed to Lidian in April 1848 that he saw Carlyle seldom and without much pleasure. Emerson saw with dismay that Carlyle now was "protectionist in political economy, aristocrat in politics, epicure in diet, goes for murder, money, punishment by death, slavery, and all the petty abominations, tempering them with epigrams."[10]

In December there was even a minor explosion. As Emerson told one of his English admirers shortly before leaving for America, he and Carlyle had been talking about Cromwell one day. Carlyle "had grown impatient of opposition, especially when talking of Cromwell. I differed from him," Emerson told George Searle Phillips,

> in his estimate of Cromwell's character and he rose like a great Norse giant from his chair—and, drawing a line with his finger across the table, said, with terrible fierceness, "Then sir, there is a line of separation between you and me as wide as that, and as deep as the pit."[11]

Emerson and Carlyle did not break off. They corresponded, and while Carlyle was catty and backbiting in his private comments about Emerson to others, he made arrangements for him and came loyally to all his London lectures. Emerson had, after all, gone to enormous trouble to get Carlyle published in America, reading his proofs and getting royalties to him. Before going home to America Emerson took one last excursion with Carlyle to see Stonehenge, and there seems to have been a reconciliation of sorts on Salisbury Plain. The memory of their glorious first meeting, the years of solid mutual aid with each other's books, and the habits and assumptions of friendship carried them through where the actual basis for a friendship no longer existed.[12]

76. The Natural History of Intellect

THE INNER HISTORY OF EMERSON'S SECOND TRIP TO EN-
gland—the story told by his journal and lectures—is more complicated and
less triumphant than were his busy and colorful days. When he was still in
New England, preparing for his trip to England, he drew up a list of the
"superstitions of our age." He cited "the fear of Catholicism, the fear of
Pauperism, the fear of immigration, the fear of manufacturing interests, the
fear of radicalism or democracy, [and] faith in the steam engine." If he had
been drawing up a personal account, he might have noted his own fear of
conformity, of not tending to his own affairs, of aiming too low, of not living
to the full, and his faith in the individual as the engine of history. He tried
again to characterize this faith, this time in a dream image of "the central
man": "We shall one day talk with the central man, and see again in the
varying play of his features all the features which have characterized our
darlings, and stamped themselves in fire on the heart."[1]

Even as he crossed the Atlantic toward the Old World, Emerson knew,
as he had known before in 1832, that England and Europe would challenge
him, would displace his central man and make him feel peripheral, provincial, and derivative. The serenity and self-sureness that others saw in
Emerson was not an illusion, but it was a state of mind that required constant
encouragement. Emerson said several times that he was going to England
to find a whip for his top. Most often he had to do the job himself. "Do
it," he wrote this year, "bridge the gulf well and truly from edge to edge
and the dunces will find it out. There is but one verdict needful and that
is mine. If I do it, I shall know it." He also recognized that the best way
to maintain his own equanimity while abroad was to keep busy at his own
work. As he was getting caught up in the whirl of English life, he noted in
his journal that "the only girth or belt that can enable one to face these
Patagonians of beef and beer, is an absorbing work of your own."[2]

Emerson was not getting much from his reading just now. He had read
Rousseau's *Confessions* while still in New England. The ship's library had
included books by Dickens, Dumas, and Marryat. Emerson brought along

his great-grandfather Joseph Emerson's diary on this trip. He had been reading Laing's translation of Snorri Sturluson's *Heimskringla* and also Mallet's *Northern Antiquities,* a compendium of Norse myth and legend, together with a translation of the prose *Edda.* Norse myth was to England what Homer was to Greece. Emerson never got caught up in the Ossian craze, preferring the rough but genuine texts of the Eddas. He was also preparing for modern England by reading the second volume of the much discussed *Modern Painters,* published anonymously but known to be by John Ruskin, who was at the time twenty-eight.

Emerson seems to have done much more writing than reading on this trip. He brought with him a number of lectures and a good deal of material out of which to make lectures. While in England Emerson quarried lectures from four different mines. He depended heavily at first on his "Representative Men" series. Occasionally he read older lectures, such as the 1836 "The Humanity of Science." He was also, even at the start of the trip, working up a new group of lectures, including "Eloquence," "Domestic Life," "Reading," "The Superlative," and "Natural Aristocracy." There is no clear organizing theme to these talks; perhaps they were the fruit of his recent labor of reindexing his journals. He published none of these lectures until much later. He did not publish "Eloquence," "Domestic Life," and "Reading" until 1870 in the volume called *Society and Solitude.* "The Superlative" and "Natural Aristocracy" appeared posthumously in the 1884 volume *Lectures and Biographical Sketches.* This does not mean that Emerson did not value the lectures. On the contrary, it means that these lectures were among his working stock of available lectures for decades, precisely because they had not appeared in print.

Eloquence was an old topic and one as basic to Emerson as poetry. In one way his whole career can be defined as a striving for eloquence. For "Eloquence" he went back to materials first collected in 1827. His approach now was to consider eloquence not as a goal for a gifted few but as a shared human quality. "I suppose every man is eloquent once in his life," he said, going on to use a metaphor that would have appealed to Walt Whitman. "The difference between us is that we boil at different degrees of the thermometer."[3]

Emerson had treated domestic life in 1838 in a talk called "Home." Now, spurred perhaps by his experience with Mrs. Goodwin's boardinghouse, he wrote a gentle and moving piece on childhood, drawn from his times with his children and lighted also by a nostalgia for his own childhood. "If a man wishes to acquaint himself with the real history of the world, with the spirit of the age, he must not go first to the state-house or the courtroom," he wrote. The events of the household "are more near and affecting to us than those which are sought in senates and academies." Emerson gave this talk sixteen times in northern England, Glasgow, and London in 1847–1848. A recognition of the centrality of domestic life was now a major part of what he had to say.[4]

The vigorous essay "Reading" reveals another of Emerson's current preoccupations. The essay begins briskly with the observation that most books are good for nothing: "They work no redemption in us." He also admits that he has learned from "a surly bank director, that in bank parlours they estimate all stocks of this kind [books] as rubbish." The first part of the talk is about reading in general and is summed up in three rules: "1. Never read a book that is not a year old [because only good books survive]. 2. Never read any but famed books [same reason]. 3. Never read any but what you like." The essay goes on to suggest a reading list of "famed books" that Emerson found repaid the effort of reading. This is also the essay in which Emerson made a crack about translations which is guaranteed to nettle any teacher of foreign language: "I should as soon think of swimming across Charles River when I wish to go to Boston, as of reading all my books in originals when I have them rendered for me in my mother tongue."[5]

"Natural Aristocracy" is devoted to the Jeffersonian concept of an aristocracy of virtue and talent. Aristocracy for Emerson is a symbol of any natural excellence or unusual daring or striking effort. He was dismissive of modern landed and titled nobodies, and he stuck to his opinion that "the true aristocrat is he who is at the head of his own order."[6]

The most intriguing of the new group of miscellaneous lectures this year is one called "The Superlative," only a few scraps from which have been printed. The fragment published in *Lectures and Biographical Sketches* (1883) suggests an essay on the plain style, an essay against superlatives. Only inexperienced writers use superlatives, says Emerson, since they do not perceive "that superlatives are diminutives, and weaken, that the positive is the sinew of speech, the superlative, the fat." Emerson quotes approvingly from a French journalist who said of the Duke of Wellington's papers, "Here are twelve volumes of military dispatches and the word glory is not found in them." But the original 1847 lecture on the superlative was much different. Emerson called it his lecture on Hafez; it was a lecture in praise of enthusiasm, a sequel to his lecture on ecstasy called "The Method of

Nature." It distinguished between a false or hollow superlative ("Je suis desolée," "my blood froze") and the genuine superlative, which was now for Emerson best represented by Hafez, "the model of lyric grace and felicity,—the Aeolian harp hung in grapevines and harem windows,—Hafez,—the foam of the cup, the sheen of the waterfall, all whose poetry is a superlative yet in whom it is native."[7]

The positive degree consists in "calling things by their right names." The superlative degree derives from an exalted state, common to prophets and poets, which sees or names things "representatively, for those interior facts which they signify." The superlative is that state in which "the mind strings worlds like beads upon its thought."[8]

If there is no obvious center or single method common to these new lectures, apart from the idea that objects and qualities as well as persons are representative, there is rather too much method to the other set of lectures Emerson gave this year. By April of 1848 he was working on a project he called "a kind of Natural History of Intellect." In June of 1848, after he had returned to England from a quick trip to Paris, Emerson gave a set of lectures called "Mind in the Nineteenth Century" to raise money for his passage home. The lectures were rewritten and delivered again in 1849, in 1850, and finally in Emerson's course of lectures at Harvard in 1870 (repeated in 1871). After Emerson's death, his editor, James Elliott Cabot, published the first three of these lectures in *Natural History of Intellect* (1893). The "Natural History of Intellect" lectures were never completed to Emerson's satisfaction, but even so they represent one pole of his thought, the frequently recurring impulse to set transcendental idealism on a solid, professional, respectable, philosophical basis.[9]

In "Natural History of Intellect" Emerson tried to imbue the study of mind with some of the exactness and certainty of the physical sciences. He admired the "security and happiness of the naturalist's attitude, sure of admiration for his facts, of their sufficiency." "Could not," he wondered, "a similar enumeration be made of the laws and powers of the intellect?" and he answered his own question: "It can be done because these powers and laws are also facts in a Natural History. They also are objects of science, and do suffer themselves to be numbered and recorded as readily as the stamens of a plant or the vertebrae of a fish." This had been the project of Kant and his followers, to bring the rigor of scientific method to the subject of mind. Emerson knew this, just as he knew the difficulty of studying the instrument with which we study. For the purposes of these lectures the human mind was both object and subject. Aware that Kant, Fichte, and Schelling tried to describe the mind in books intended to be read by other philosophers, Emerson set out to do a similar job in a language accessible to ordinary people. "This is my design," he said: "to make sketches of the laws of the intellect." He was still convinced that there was a point-by-point correspondence between the world of mind and the world of nature. "The conclusion is irresistible," he wrote, "that what is a truth or idea in the mind is a power out there in nature."[10]

The "Natural History of Intellect" lectures represent Emerson's answer to the challenge of bluff British empiricism and the pervasive materialism of modern England. In one way these lectures were a false step for Emerson. He had no real patience or gift for the kind of painstaking logical structure implied by his working title. But there is no doubt that the project was of great importance to him. He kept working on it, off and on, for the rest of his life. That his powers were failing him when he returned to the subject in his lectures at Harvard in 1870 should not blind us to the importance Emerson gave to the effort. In many ways the "Natural History of Intellect" lectures continue and deepen the problems raised in *Nature*. The lectures also continue Emerson's lifelong eagerness to join the arts with the sciences, and if he never brought this project to a conclusion or a fulfillment that satisfied him, he nevertheless reached some remarkable conclusions. Emerson was by now aware of the problems in the philosopher's desire to achieve certain knowledge and of the problems inherent in the Stoic's reply, which is to worry about action, not about knowledge. "What we really want," he says in the "Natural History of Intellect," "is not a haste to act, but a certain piety toward the source of action and knowledge." This is very close to Thoreau's saying in "Walking" that "the highest that we can attain to is not knowledge, but sympathy with intelligence." What matters at last is neither intention nor results. "What is life," Emerson concludes, "but the angle of vision. A man is measured by the angle at which he looks at objects."[11]

77. Chartism and Revolution

OF THE REVOLUTIONS THAT ERUPTED THROUGHOUT EUROPE IN 1848 like a chain of volcanoes, Emerson actually witnessed two. He was more in sympathy with one than the other, but both pointed him back to his own subject.

"Suddenly out of its stale and drowsy lair, the lair of slaves, like lightning Europe leapt forth," wrote Walt Whitman of the events of 1848. Ireland boiled with revolt. Italy chafed under the Austrians. In February the weak bourgeois king Louis Philippe was overthrown and the victors proclaimed a republic in Paris. In the Netherlands and in Denmark terrified monarchs granted new democratic constitutions almost before they were asked. Ludwig of Bavaria abdicated; Metternich's Vienna system disintegrated in March. The king of Prussia promulgated a constitution, Kossuth demanded one for Hungary, and the Austrian empire fell apart in just days. Metternich fled. Venice proclaimed itself again a republic. The suddenness of revolt was astonishing, even though there had been a long buildup of reformist pressure all over Europe during the preceding two decades.

In England as on the Continent 1848 was the culmination of a long period of radicalism. On April 10, 1848, agitation in England came to a head with a large Chartist demonstration in London. The Chartist movement aimed to enfranchise the working class. Emerson was sympathetic to the general aims of the Chartists, which he associated with democratic currents in his own country. "The English dislike the American structure of society," he wrote in *English Traits,* "whilst yet trade, mills, public education and Chartism are doing what they can to create in England the same social condition."[1]

On the night before the march Emerson had dinner outside London with J. J. Garth Wilkinson (the Swedenborgian after whom Henry James named two of his sons) and afterward walked into London with Thomas Cooper, a veteran Chartist leader and a poet. Cooper was not involved in the next day's demonstration. He did not like the idea of armed revolt, which was being talked about in some quarters, and he was setting up a separate

Chartist league that was to work by moral suasion alone. Cooper noted that during their long evening walk, Emerson "seemed eager to learn all he could, and willing to communicate all he could."[2]

The Reform Bill of 1832 had enlarged the franchise and put the government firmly in the hands of the middle class. In the chapter "Reform and Chartism" designed for *English Traits* but omitted from that book, Emerson explained 1832: "The reform Bill took away the right of election from a stone wall, a green mound, and a ruined house. Birmingham and Manchester, which had no member whilst their mills paid [for] the coalitions of Europe, were allowed to return two members each." But the bill only enfranchised about a million voters in a population of thirty million. The Chartist movement was named after the charter they wished to see adopted; it had six points: universal male suffrage, equal-sized constituencies, no property qualification for members of Parliament, a secret ballot, annual Parliaments, and salaries for MPs. Emerson wrote of the Chartists, "They gain and hope, gain by each fright they give. So many of the nobility and gentry carried their jewels to market in 1848 as to depress the price." He noted that the Chartist demands were "resisted by the Egyptian stiffness of England," but he thought "they will have it at last."[3]

On April 10 a crowd estimated at around thirty thousand unarmed Chartists gathered at Kennington Common, south of the Thames, to march on Westminster and the houses of Parliament. Their leaders called themselves the "Convention" and seemed to think they were in France. Feargus O'Connor, the undisputed leader of the movement, apparently had no clear plan, apart from presenting his petition with its 5.7 million signatures to the House of Commons. O'Connor told a cheering crowd that the House of Commons was now of less importance than the Convention.[4]

The Duke of Wellington took charge of defending London. The Iron Duke posted seven regiments of British regulars throughout London, keeping them hidden. These were tough troops, much like those of whom the duke once said he could well believe they might frighten Bonaparte because, "by God, they frighten me." The government closed all offices. Employees of the General Post Office barricaded the building and took up arms. The Bank of England was fortified with sandbags. Palmerston himself barricaded the Foreign Office with bound copies of the *Times* and armed the clerks with cutlasses and ancient muskets. The authorities put a hundred and seventy thousand hastily deputized "special constables" in the streets. As soon as Feargus O'Connor showed up at Kennington Common, the London chief of police sent a messenger to him. O'Connor met with the chief, who told him not to march and warned him of the forces arrayed against him. O'Connor immediately caved in, agreeing to come alone to Parliament to present his petition and agreeing also to abandon the march. He went back to the crowd, and in a long, rambling, self-serving speech gradually revealed what he had just agreed to. As the crowd was dispersing in uncertainty, a few fights broke out. Then it began to rain, a "steady, heavy London rain," and the demonstration was over.[5]

Emerson observed that the Chartists were poorly represented. In his notes he describes O'Connor as a "swindling leader" and Cooper as a "fustian Poet," both of them ready to "betray them [the people] in public and cheat them in private." Emerson was disappointed too in the English writers who were "bold and democratic" until the event. "The moment revolution comes, are they Chartists and Montagnards? No, but they talk and sit with the rich and sympathize with them. Should they go with the Chartists? Alas they cannot. . . . The scholar recoils—and joins the rich. That he should not do." Even if one could not wholeheartedly endorse the Chartists, even if one objected to the "gross and bloody" Chartist chiefs, Emerson thought a writer should at least stay neutral. Emerson's own low opinion of the chiefs and his reading of their motives led him to this summary of the event:

> People here expect a revolution. There will be no revolution, none that deserves to be called so. There may be a scramble for money. But as all the people we see want the things we now have and not better things, it is very certain that they will, under whatever change of forms, keep the old system.[6]

Early in May 1848 Emerson made a trip to Paris. He went again to the Jardin des Plantes, but what caught his attention on this trip was not museum displays but the shops and streets and above all the books. "Everything odd and rare and rich can be bought in Paris," he wrote. Emerson was in Paris with Arthur Clough; they had dinner together most nights. Emerson was also invited to dinner at de Tocqueville's where he met Marie de Flavigny, comtesse d'Agoult (whose pen name was Daniel Stern), who had recently written the first major French piece on Emerson. He also met the historian and writer Edgar Quinet, who had already been strongly influenced by Emerson's writings. He heard Jules Michelet lecture. Michelet was a well-known historian whose book *The People* had just been translated into English and was to have a major impact on Walt Whitman. Emerson heard Alphonse-Marie-Louis Lamartine, an eminent man of letters who was now taking a prominent part in the provisional government of the moment, and he went three times to see performances by the great actress known simply as Rachel. But all this was dramatically overshadowed by the revolt of May 15, which Emerson witnessed at street level.[7]

Louis Philippe had been turned out in the February Revolution and a provisional government had been established, composed of both the middle (or bourgeois) class and the socialists who represented the "blouses," or working class. By May elections had been held, the bourgeois had won heavy majorities, and the socialists had suffered a considerable defeat. The socialists now began to agitate in the political clubs for some sort of counterstroke. Emerson visited several of the clubs, including the Club des Droits de l'Homme, which was that of Louis Auguste Blanqui, who made common cause with his rival Armand Barbès in the uprising on May 15. Blanqui, the man who first formulated the concept of the "dictatorship of the proletariat" was a terrifying figure; de Tocqueville described him as a "fanatic who looked like a corpse." He had spent much of his life in prison for his radical views, which favored violent overthrow of the bourgeois government, the systematic reorganizing of labor and society, attending to the social causes of poverty, and communism. He was a strong speaker; he frightened Parisians more than anyone since Hébert in 1794.[8]

Emerson reported on the tone in Blanqui's club, which he visited on May 14, the day before the uprising. One orator said, "Why should the rich fear that we should not protect their property?—we shall guard it with the utmost care, in the belief that it will soon be our own." Emerson found the clubs fascinating.

> The men are in terrible earnest. The fire and fury of the people, when they are interrupted or thwarted, are inconceivable to New England. The costumes are formidable. All France is bearded like goats and lions, then most of Paris is in some kind of uniform, red sash, red cap, blouse perhaps bound by red sash, brass helmet and sword, and everybody is supposed to have a pistol in his pocket.[9]

On May 15 at one o'clock in the afternoon a crowd of several thousand, led by Blanqui, overran the National Assembly. The pretext was a demonstration of behalf of Poland, but the demonstrators disrupted the proceedings and broke up the assembly. A part of the crowd, led by Barbès, then rushed off to the Hôtel de Ville, the traditional place to proclaim a new government. Meanwhile the existing government managed to call out the National Guard. "I saw the sudden and immense display of arms when the rappel [the fall-in] was beaten on Monday afternoon," Emerson wrote home, "the street full of bayonets, and the furious driving of the horses dragging cannon toward the National Assembly."[10]

There was tremendous confusion. Emerson observed "the rapid succession of proclamations proceeding from the government, and posted on the walks at the corners of all streets, eagerly read by crowds of people—and, not waiting for this, the rapid passage of messengers with proclamations in their hands which they read to knots of people, and then ran on to another knot and so on, down a street." The existing government prevailed quickly. "Before night, all was safe," Emerson wrote Lidian, "and our new government, who had held the seals for a quarter of an hour, were fast in jail."[11]

The May uprising Emerson witnessed was just a preliminary to the much more serious revolt in Paris in June and July, when huge barricades, four times the height of a man, were thrown up at the entrance to the Faubourg St. Antoine and elsewhere, and there was prolonged fighting and much loss of life. Emerson was appalled by the spectacle of riotous revolutionary Paris. "Torchlight processions have a seek and slay look," he noted, "dripping burning oil drops, and the bearers now and then smiting the torch on the ground, and then lifting it into the air." He noted too that the boulevards had "lost their fine trees, which were all cut down for barricades in February. At the end of a year we shall take account, and see if the Revolution was worth the trees."[12]

Emerson's sympathies were with the existing government on this occasion, that is, with the bourgeois government that had replaced Louis Philippe in February and in which the poet Lamartine held a major position. "I am heartily glad of the shopkeepers' victory," Emerson wrote on May 17. He understood that "this revolution has a feature new to history, that of socialism," but he had little faith in socialism by now. "For the matter of socialism," he wrote, "there are no oracles. The oracle is dumb. When we would pronounce anything truly of man, we retreat instantly on the individual."[13]

The events of 1848 gave Emerson a important lesson in politics. Even mass demonstrations and revolutionary crowds led him back to the problem of the individual. He left Paris, returned to London, and began giving the lectures he had been working on called "Mind in the Nineteenth Century," the first three of which were published much later as *Natural History of*

Intellect. As the Jardin des Plantes had shown him his way fifteen years earlier, so the revolutions of 1848 now showed him that his way had nothing to do with current events. "The world is always childish," he wrote in his journal, "and with each gewgaw of a revolution or a new constitution that it finds, thinks it shall never cry any more." What Emerson had to say was true only at the level of the individual, but he insisted that that level was the only one that mattered in the long run. "It is always becoming evident that the permanent good is for the soul only and cannot be retained in any society or system. This is like Naphtha which must be kept in a close[d] vessel."[14]

The Science of Liberty

78. Return: Quarrel with Thoreau

ON HIS WAY HOME EMERSON TRIED TO BALANCE HIS BOOKS ON England. Carlyle was still, he thought, the most interesting person, Clough the most promising young poet, the *Heimskringla* the best clue to English character. He had written Lidian that he could not regret making the trip but that it had been too costly in every way. He was sorry to have missed so many weeks and months of his children. He had allowed himself "freely to be dazzled by the various brilliancy of men of talent," but "in calm hours I found myself no way helped." Despite all his contact with the great and the energetic, he felt that he had "scarcely had a good conversation, a solid dealing, man with man, in England."[1]

Emerson had intended to be unimpressed by England. But, as he wrote Carlyle, "England is the country of success, and success has a great charm for me, more than for those I talk with at home." England had not only impressed him, it had made him feel personally slight, displaced from his own center. While still aboard ship on his return voyage he wrote his brother William a list of his "intellectual poverties" that included "weak eyes . . . no animal spirits, an immense and fatal negative with our Anglican race. No Greek, no mathematics, no politics."[2]

He felt he had lost control of his own life. He wrote soberly to Sam Ward, saying he now thought that "we belong to our life, not that it belongs to us." It was the nadir of Emerson's self-reliance and self-esteem. He even felt faintly fraudulent.

> The secret of Guy [one of Emerson's old literary alter egos], the lucky and famous, was, to conceal from all mankind that he was a bore. It was wonderful how often and how long by skilful dispositions and timings he managed to make it believed, by clever people too, that he was witty and agreeable.

Even his dreams suggest that beneath the surface calm there was plenty of unexpressed—almost Carlylean—anger.

All night I was scarifying with my wrath some conjuring miscreant, but unhappily I had an old age in my toothless gums, I was old as Priam, could not articulate, and the edge of all my taunts and sarcasms, it is to be feared, was quite lost. Yet spite of my dumb palsy, I defied and roared after him, rattled in my throat until wifey waked me.[3]

Emerson was glad to be home; he was American, not English, after all, but he felt uncharacteristically inarticulate about it. When asked in England to produce an American with an American idea, Emerson described the liberal reform ideas of Boston, probably Alcott's school and Brook Farm. "The merits of America were not presentable," he wrote in his journal. "The tristesse of the landscape, the quiet stealing in of nature like a religion, how could that be told?" It occurred to neither Emerson nor his English questioner that Emerson himself was the article being sought. Comparisons between England and America continued to force themselves on Emerson. This was a subject he would not be done with for many years to come.[4]

Lidian had been very sick while Emerson was away. She had a severe case of jaundice and continual nausea. Thoreau wrote to Emerson that she had a general sickliness that made her life intolerable to her. She had been bedridden for a month, Thoreau wrote, and was "as yellow as saffron." She was ill again when Emerson arrived home, as were his son and his mother. Within two weeks of his return, by mid-August, all three were much better; Lidian was planning a trip to Lynn. Other pressing matters awaited Emerson. He was obliged to think about lectures for the coming season. He had promised to find an American publisher for Carlyle's brother's translation of Dante. In England John Chapman had talked much about a new magazine to be published in Boston and London to give expression to what the English perceived to be a new Atlantic civilization. New magazines were now more interested in Emerson than he in them. Theodore Parker had launched the *Massachusetts Quarterly Review* listing Emerson as an editor and promising contributions from him. Knowing Parker's energy and determination, Emerson mustered all the arguments he could think of for not starting a new magazine, then pressed Parker to "write me immediately why this thing should not stop."[5]

Returning from almost a year abroad, Emerson saw his old friends with new eyes. Charles Newcomb showed up "with his fine perceptions, his excellent instincts, his beautiful learning, his catholic mind," but Emerson was impatient with him. "He has become the spoiled child of culture, the *roué* of Art and Letters, *blasé* with too much Plato, Dante, Calderon and Goethe" and so fearful of losing his exquisite balance of mind that he had written nothing for three years. "Farewell, my once beautiful genius," Emerson wrote in his journal. "I have learned a sordid respect for uses and values . . . Are we to say a man shall not go out to the shed to bring an armful of wood, lest this violence of action hurt the balance of his mind?" But as he wrote off Newcomb, he could not say enough about Alcott. Alcott's faith was perfect, his aim unchanged, his standards the highest: "Alcott declares that a teacher is one who can assist the child in obeying his own mind. . . . He believes that from a circle of twenty well-selected children he could draw, in their conversation, everything that is in Plato."[6]

Emerson's return from England also marked the beginning of a serious rift between him and Henry Thoreau. Thoreau was now thirty-one. He had spent most of the past year in Emerson's house, taking Emerson's place in his own family. Thoreau was fond of the children—who adored him—and he was emotionally attached to Lidian, who was some sixteen years older than he was. He had written her lofty, ardent letters from New York a few years earlier and his journals have passages that have led a number of people to believe that in some complicated and never quite fully acknowledged way he was in love with her. "Others are of my kindred by blood or of my acquaintance but you are mine," Thoreau wrote in his journal for 1848–1849. "You are of me and I of you. I can not tell where I leave off and you begin—there is such harmony when your sphere meets mine." Thoreau's few letters to the absent Emerson this year are prickly and defensive. Thoreau was skeptical about English success, materialism, steam, speed, talk, and books, and he was contemptuous of Emerson's apparent relish of it all.[7]

Thoreau was writing a long piece on friendship just now, a piece that went into *A Week on the Concord and Merrimack Rivers.* "Friendship is evanescent in every man's experience, and remembered like heat lightning in past summers," he wrote. "All men are dreaming of it, and its drama, which is always a tragedy, is enacted daily." The essay, which fills thirty printed pages, is more about what is now called intimacy than about what is usually called friendship. The true friend, says Thoreau, addresses his friend like this:

I never asked thy leave to let me love thee—I have a right. I love thee not as something private and personal, which is *your own,* but as

461

something universal and worthy of love, which I have found. O how I think of you . . . Consent only to be what you are. I alone will never stand in your way.

The essay reads like an open letter, sometimes addressed to Lidian, sometimes to Emerson. It sets very high standards. Friends must meet on grounds of complete honesty. "Beware lest the friend learn at last to tolerate one frailty of thine, and so an obstacle be raised to the progress of thy love."[8]

The strained relationship seems to have broken for Thoreau over the publication of *A Week*. Despite his and Emerson's efforts to get it published in 1847, the book did not come out until 1849. It sold very badly, and what was worse, Emerson seems to have made some offhand criticism of its weaknesses. "I had a friend," Thoreau writes in his petulant past tense, "I wrote a book. I asked my friend's criticism, I never got but praise for what was good in it—my friend became estranged from me and then I got blame for all that was bad." Whatever the exact incident or exchange, Thoreau was stung by it. "While my friend was my friend he flattered me, and I never heard the truth from him—but when he became my enemy he shot it to me on a poisoned arrow."[9]

The estrangement was more profound than just one incident. Thoreau had no sympathy for Emerson's new worldliness. He disapproved of his European travels; he seems to have enjoyed being in Emerson's home and he must have felt displaced when Emerson returned. Emerson was now equally out of sympathy with Thoreau's renunciations and withdrawals. If Thoreau uses the strong language of enemy and poison, Emerson was equally damaging as he wrote about Thoreau in his journal: "I spoke of friendship, but friends and I are fishes in their habit. As for taking Thoreau's arm, I should as soon take the arm of an elm tree." The trouble was more than undemonstrativeness:

> Henry Thoreau is like the wood god who solicits the wandering poet and draws him into antres [caverns; the allusion is to a speech in *Othello*] vast and deserts idle, and bereaves him of his memory, and leaves him naked, plaiting vine and with twigs in his hand. Very seductive are the first steps from the town to the woods, but the end is want and madness.[10]

Emerson was not alone in seeing this dark quality in Thoreau. Although Thoreau was capable of high spirits, playfulness, loyalty, sincerity, high ardor and although he had friends, was close to his family and had disciples, there was an austere, Bartleby-like calm—the calm of a tomb—in him. He was also capable of bitter all-out negation; in this he was more like Carlyle than Emerson. He had little ordinary warmth, not much of the common touch, no concessions to ordinary human weakness and appetite. An important part of his inner core was a deep capacity for renunciation, an ability to do without, which was all the more impressive for seeming to be effortless. The ability to say no, to prefer not to, created a wall around Thoreau. Emerson admired him; he called him *the* man of Concord. Emerson defended him; their quarrels were always made up—even the ones that lasted a long time. The two men shared a sympathy with a certain kind of intellectual anarchy that Santayana says "is full of lights. Its blindness is made up of dazzling survivals, revivals, and fresh beginnings." Yet there was always this unapproachableness in Thoreau, and a number of people shared Emerson's lurking sense that Thoreau's anarchic vitality was poisoned because it was drawn from a well of isolation that was ultimately destructive. Moncure Conway said he suspected "that a perilous Erl-King's daughter lurked in the heart of Walden Water, and drew away the life of Thoreau." H. G. O. Blake, to whom Thoreau wrote the best letters of his life, began his correspondence with Thoreau by recognizing the strong negations in him. "When I was last in Concord, you spoke of retiring further from our civilization," he wrote Thoreau in March 1848. "I asked you if you would feel no longings for the society of your friends. Your reply was, in substance, 'No, I am nothing.'" And much as Emerson cared for Thoreau, praising his wit, his writing, and his love and knowledge of nature, he could not shut out this side of his character. "It is a misfortune of Thoreau's that he has no appetite," he noted. "He neither eats nor drinks. What can you have in common with a man who does not know the difference between ice cream and cabbage and who has no experience of wine or ale?" The exasperated Emerson observed that Thoreau "avoided commonplace, and talks birch-bark to all comers, and reduces them all to the same insignificance." He was only partly entertained that "he has no more use for a railroad than a bird has." There was a rigidity in Thoreau that led his pupils to call him "the trainer"; it was like the rigidity that had marked Emerson's brother Edward. One day in 1854 when Thoreau was talking, Emerson was suddenly struck "with a surprising resemblance in him to my brother Edward."[11]

Their expectations for each other were terrifyingly high. They spent many years in each other's company. Rifts and even breaks were to be expected.

Fortunately for both none of the breaks proved final; they were reconciled and remained friends, though the degree of intimacy would change significantly. The hard names, the sense that each had poisoned as well as inspired the other, even the word "enemy," testifies to the importance of this friendship for both men. And after anger, unnecessary honesty, bitterness, and impossibly high standards, finally there was forgiveness in both of them. Emerson at the end of his life still thought of Thoreau as having been his best friend. Thoreau ends his long essay on friendship by quoting "an oriental philosopher" who said: "Although friendship between good men is interrupted, their principles remain unaltered. The stalk of the lotus may be broken, and the fibres remain connected."[12]

79. The Walden Sierras. Quetelet

RETURNING FROM ENGLAND EMERSON'S SHIP HAD ENTERED
Halifax harbor in a fog. When the fog rolled up like a theater curtain
revealing the high hills, large bays, and wooded shores of that splendid
harbor, the ship's company burst into spontaneous applause. Nature was still
the New World's best act. Once home, Emerson tried to reroot himself in
his native New England. He went walking twice a week in Concord with
Ellery Channing, the poet, ne'er-do-well, and, as Emerson said, "the incomparable companion."

Walking with Channing one day near Walden, across the railroad tracks
from Thoreau's hut site and by the Andromeda Ponds, Channing admired
the landscape and suggested that they hold a water-color exhibition. Emerson countered that it would be better to

> have water color tried in the art of writing; let our troubadors have
> one of these Spanish slopes of the dry ponds or basins which run from
> Walden to the river at Fairhaven, in this September dress of color,
> under this glowering sky—the Walden Sierras in September, given as
> a theme, and they required to daguerreotype that in good words.

A bit later, sitting high on the cliff at Conantum overlooking the spectacular
river valley, Emerson was home again at last and the landscape reignited
around him. "Is all this beauty to perish?" he wrote.

> Shall none remake this sun and wind, the skyblue river, the riverblue
> sky, the yellow meadow spotted with sacks and sheets of cranberry
> pickers, the red bushes, the iron gray house with the color of the
> granite rock, the paths of the thicket, in which the only engineers are
> the cattle grazing on yonder hill; the wide straggling wild orchard in
> which nature has deposited every possible flavor in the apples of
> different trees?[1]

Channing and Emerson took walks to Flint's Pond, where the "crows
filled the landscape with a savage sound" and where the ground was covered
with dry leaves that rustled as they walked. They tried White Pond, "a

pretty little Indian basin, lovely now as Walden once was." In late November they walked over the Lincoln hills, seeing "golden willows, savins with two foliages, old chestnuts, apples as ever." They walked the seasons through. November was the coldest month Emerson could remember. The following July was so hot "the day is dangerous, the sun acts like a burning glass on the naked skin, and the very slugs on the pear leaves seem broiled in their own fat."[2]

In between walks Emerson's affairs swamped him. He tried to collect money owing on the Fruitlands property on behalf of Charles Lane. He wrote telegrams to Washington on behalf of Lidian's brother, the feisty and litigious Dr. Charles Jackson, who claimed to have used ether as an anesthesia before Morton. (Jackson also claimed to have pointed out to Samuel F. B. Morse the basic principle of the telegraph.) Emerson now undertook the sale of a family property on his own and William's behalf. He negotiated for a farm for G. P. Bradford. He sent corn and information on its use to Jane and Thomas Carlyle because potatoes had disappeared from England. He had his own orchard to attend. He tried to start a club to be called the Town and Country Club. He hired a new housekeeper; he wrote warm recommendations for the former housekeeper, Mrs. Goodwin. He even tried to sue the Fitchburg Railway for setting fire to his woods near Walden.[3]

Emerson worked up lectures on "Why England Is England" and he fed his reading as well as his observations into the work. He read Robert Lowth's *Life of William of Wyckham,* William Gilpin's *Forest Scenery,* the poetry of Fulke Greville, and Arthur Hugh Clough's new long modern poem in hexameters, *The Bothie of Tober-na-vuolich.* He also reread the old Norse *Heimskringla.* William of Wyckham was the prototypical Englishman, a cleric, founder of Winchester School, whose motto "Manners maketh men" Emerson had seen on the gates. He had also noted that the students were locked up every night. So much for manners. The *Heimskringla, or Chronicle of the Kings of Norway,* by Snorri Sturluson, stands in relation to England much as Homer does to modern Greece. It is the epic of the ice-lands of Norway, Sweden, Iceland, and Greenland, the salt saga of the northern sea-kings. Emerson copied out a description of Olaf Trygvyson that was also admired by Thoreau:

> King Olaf could run across the oars outside of the vessel while his men were rowing the "Serpent" [Olaf's ship]. He could play with three daggers, so that one was always in the air, and he took the one falling

by the handle. He could walk all around upon the ship's rails; could strike and cut equally well with both hands, and could cast two spears at once.[4]

Emerson now prepared the "Representative Men" lectures for book publication. For the Plato essay he went back over all the editions—versions, really—of Plato he knew. These included Thomas Taylor's edition, Victor Cousin's, Schleiermacher's, Ast's, Dacier's (via Sewall's), and the new one then appearing by Cary and others in Bohn's Library. Emerson also read proofs now for a volume to be called *Nature, Addresses and Lectures* which would reprint such early essays as "The Divinity School Address" and "The American Scholar" along with his first book. Like King Olaf, Emerson kept his old interests up and kept adding new ones. He liked Thoreau's "Ktaadn" and Horace Bushnell's "An Argument for 'Discourses on Christian Nurture'" best among new American writing. He read more Swedenborg, more Proclus, more George Sand. He read Stanley's *History of Philosophy* and in May 1849 he began to read J. B. Stallo's *Principles of Nature*. He read Joseph von Hammer Purgstall's *History of the Fine Arts of Persia*. There was a new translation of Marcus Aurelius by Henry M'Cormac and a book by Arthur Helps called *The Conquerors of the New World and Their Bondmen* (London: W. Pickering, 1848). This early revisionist history made a strong impression on Emerson. "Columbus seems to have been the principal introducer of American slavery," he wrote after reading it. Helps's crisply focused study also affected the way Emerson would treat New World "discoverers" in *English Traits*.[5]

Emerson lectured in 1848 and 1849 on England and he gave the "Natural History of Intellect" lectures again. As he repeated the latter set of lectures year after year, his compass needle swung back once again toward science and its claims. He observed that an important feature of the age "is the paramount place of natural history." He wished to make a contribution to what he now called "ethical science." He had visited the Hunterian museum in London. In New England his friend Thoreau was one of a network of field agents for the formidable Louis Agassiz, the most important figure in the new professionalizing of American science. In Emerson's view science was now as important as theology had once been, and he quoted Swedenborg with approval: "As large a demand is made upon our faith by nature as by miracles."[6]

The book that made the deepest impression on Emerson at this time was L. A. J. Quetelet's *A Treatise on Man*, published in France in 1835 and in

English translation in 1841. Quetelet, who has been called the "father of social statistics," invented the idea of the average man. Statistics had been gathered before. In America there was Samuel Blodget's *Economica: A Statistical Manual for the United States of America* (Washington, D.C., 1806). But Quetelet went well beyond the tabulation of physical data in his pursuit of what he called "social physics." He collected data on crimes, for example, as part of the "moral statistics" of the average man, and he forced his critics to confront his prediction that since there had been between thirty-four and forty-six reported knife murders in France each year from 1826 to 1831, the same number could confidently be expected in future years if conditions remained the same.[7]

Quetelet was accused of being a fatalist, of denying free will. But he was not concerned with the individual, only with the statistical average. Indeed, any given individual appeared to Quetelet an accidental deviation from the norm. He laid down that "the greater the number of individuals involved, the more do individual peculiarities, whether physical or moral, become effaced." Quetelet thus opposes the "great person" theory of history. He understands genius as arising out of historical process, not as determining it.

> A man can have no real influence on masses—he cannot comprehend them and put them in action—except as he is infused with the spirit which animates them, and shares their passions, sentiments, and necessities, and finally sympathizes completely with them. It is in this manner that he is a great man, a great poet, a great artist. It is because he is the best representative of his age, that he is proclaimed to be its greatest genius.

Quetelet here pushes Emerson's democratic idea of representative greatness to an extreme that annihilates the individual. It was Quetelet who said: "Give me the series of all the great men, and I will give you the known history of the human race." But Emerson could have said it. In pursuit of the average person, who is, "in a nation, what the center of gravity is in a body," Quetelet is unyielding about the role of the individual: "The greater the number of individuals, the more does the influence of individual wills disappear." "It is of primary importance," Quetelet insists, "to keep out of view man as he exists in an insulated, separate, or in an individual state, and to regard him only as a fraction of the species. In thus setting aside his individual nature, we get quit of all that is accidental." This seems easy enough to grasp when put in a general way. But Quetelet's focus on crime, for example, brought him to some very modern conclusions: "Society includes within itself the germs of all the crimes committed. . . . It is the social state, in some measure, which prepares the crimes, and the criminal is merely the instrument to execute them."[8]

Emerson read Quetelet just as he was working on *Representative Men* and he was prepared to follow Quetelet a surprising distance in his disregard for the individual. Emerson quotes Quetelet in his 1849 journal: "Every thing which pertains to the human species considered as a whole, belongs to the order of physical facts." Emerson liked Quetelet's quoting Napoleon, who said, "View man as we may, he is as much the result of his physical and moral atmosphere as of his own organization." Emerson kept referring to Quetelet and his work: "One must study Quetelet to know the limits of human freedom. In 20,000 population, just so many men will marry their grandmothers." Though one could not predict the actions of any single individual, one could be dismayingly accurate in predicting the actions of a large number of individuals. Five years later Emerson wrote, "Fourier was right in his 1,760 men to make one man. I accept the Quetelet statistics." Such acceptance had consequences. Even in 1849 Emerson could say, "We should kill ourselves if we thought men were free, and could derange the order of nature." He had come to think that the correct inference to be drawn from nature was of a "beautiful necessity."[9]

Emerson still believed—or at least he kept repeating—that "life is an ecstasy" and that "each man is a jet of flame." But his dreams now suggest that he knew he had lost something important in Europe and that he felt that he himself was not at all what he seemed to the casual observer. Late in August of 1849, just a week before the publication of *Nature, Addresses and Lectures,* he had "a long, sad, strange dream last night in which I carried E[llen] to Naples and lost her." And sometime in September, after the book was published, he had another dream in which

> a certain instructive race-horse was quite elaborately shown off, which seemed marvelously constructed for violent running, and so mighty to go, that he stood up continually on his hind feet in impatience and triumphant power. But my admiration was checked by some one else's remarking behind me, that "in New York, they could not get up the smallest plate for him." Then I noticed, for the first time, that he was a show horse, and had not run forward at all.[10]

80. Therienism and
the Hegelian Moment

EMERSON HAD COME HOME FROM ENGLAND FEELING DISPLACED
and uncertain. During the fall of 1849 and the winter of 1849–1850 he
gradually recovered his balance. Newly kindled by Hegelian notions about
history, the role of ideas in history, and the processes of consciousness, he
set out on a strenuous reexamination of many of his old convictions. This
reformulation will reach its full expression in Emerson's great essay "Fate."
Here idealism, freedom, and melioration are only put forward after the
claims of materialism, determinism, and inertia have been exhausted. This
new idealism was so tempered, qualified, and intertwined with the always
increasing cares of Emerson's daily life, with his experience of innumerable
live audiences, and with the growing materialism of the times, that it
amounts in places to a new position. It is a refracted idealism, a new idealism
born of the struggle between the old idealism and the new materialism.

This fall Emerson and Lidian reached a new understanding and a new
ease with each other. Emerson admired Lidian's scheme for educating the
local deliveryman, which was to pay him his usual fee for an errand but to
send him to go and sit through a Thursday Lecture in Boston and bring her
a report of it. They read Swedenborg together. And instead of his chafing
at marriage, he now praised it without cant or sentimentality. "Love is
temporary and ends with marriage," he wrote. "Marriage is the perfection
love aimed at, ignorant of what it sought. Marriage is a good known only
to the parties. A relation of perfect understanding, aid, contentment, possession of themselves and of the world,—which dwarfs love to green fruit."
Other aspects of his life reknit themselves. His walks with Channing and
Thoreau were so productive he began to think of a collaborative project, and
he began a new notebook ("AZ") in November with epigraphs from Horace
and Thoreau. He got word that Margaret Fuller was headed for home. He
prepared a book list for Caroline Sturgis Tappan which included the cream
of his recent reading.[1]

Emerson's main work for the fall of 1849 was preparing the manuscript
of *Representative Men* for publication. He chafed at the task less than usual;

it was still a live subject for him and he kept on revising in his head after he sent off the book. One of these afterthoughts was that he had failed to mention Swedenborg's main defect, "that he does not awaken the sentiment of piety," or what we would now call the religious sense. He also thought later that he had failed to do justice to "the unexpressed greatness of the common farmer and laborer."[2]

From an unpublished manuscript in Harvard's Houghton library it is evident that Emerson made a start on an essay on the latter subject this fall of 1849. The manuscript is variously headed "Therienism" or "Indian Therien." Taking the Canadian woodcutter and friend of Henry Thoreau's as his central figure, Emerson sketched out a representative natural man based on Alec Therien.[3]

Emerson admired Therien's heroic solidity.

> Among the test questions at the Egyptian funeral is the question, How did he stand in the world? The brave Therien stands well in the world—very inconspicuous in Beacon Street or the precincts of Union Park, nay absolutely unknown and inadmissable, living and dying, he never shall be known there. But he stands well in the world, as Adam did, as an Indian does, as a lion or a bull, or as one of Homer's heroes, Agamemnon or Ulysses do, very fitly likened to bull or lion.

The praise of Therien is precisely that he is close to nature, "comparable to sun and moon, to rainbow and flood, to tiger and lightning, because he is, as all natural persons are, only metamorphoses of these things."[4]

Therien is another model of the self-reliant person. "He has so much out-of-doors nature and life and so much self-subsistency" that he does not need any elaborate social or literary introduction. Emerson's representative natural man is, in this strongly Thoreauvian fragment, a rebuke to the economics of Adam Smith. "Society pays heavily for the economy it derives from the division of labor," Emerson writes. "Compare the Indian with his plenitude of power and his courage and cheer, and equality to all his duties, with the emaciated broken-hearted pin or buckle or stocking-maker, more helpless the further the division is carried."[5]

The "Therienism" sketch, brief as it is, suggests that Emerson intended the natural man to have a high place in his pantheon. His image of "these New Hampshire and Canada norsemen," these country people so far removed from the "lees and rinsings of cities," has as much potential for myth as Shakespeare or Napoleon. "As the ancients mended men by brute forms in order to make gods," Emerson writes, "as when they drew lines from the bull to make the neck of Hercules, or of the lion's head to form the head of Jove, so the cultivated man admires the massive and Nilotic attitudes of farmers and Indian hunters."[6]

Finishing *Representative Men* had left Emerson in a state of high energy and the next couple of months saw a burst of vigorous and creative thinking. Just as he had been finishing up the book, two incidents influenced his direction. A new Concord neighbor named Emmanuel Scherb spent an evening talking Hegel to Emerson. At about the same time Emerson obtained and read a copy of J. B. Stallo's *General Principles of the Philosophy of Nature* (Boston, 1848), which is a strongly Hegelian book. The result was that Emerson now came to his first serious reckoning with the thought of Hegel. The integrative energy of Hegelian thought, its assimilative power, and its fierce drive to grasp the *processes* of history and mind were deeply congenial to Emerson.

He arrived at Hegel via Stallo, who had been born in Germany in 1823 and had arrived in Cincinnati when he was sixteen. At twenty-one he became professor of physics, chemistry, and mathematics at Fordham in New York. When his book came out in 1848 he was twenty-five. He immediately went back to Cincinnati and turned to the practice of law. Stallo was a key figure in a group called the Ohio Hegelians which included Peter Kaufman, Moncure Conway, and August Willich. These Ohio Hegelians preceded the more famous St. Louis Hegelians who formed around W. T. Harris and his *Journal of Speculative Philosophy* (founded in 1867). Stallo's 560-page book is divided into two parts; the first is Stallo's programmatic review of the philosophy of nature, the second summarizes the thought of Fichte, Schelling, Oken, and Hegel. The Hegel section is by far the longest and the whole book is openly Hegelian. A modern commentator notes that it was "a more complete analysis of Hegel's philosophy than had yet appeared in English."[7]

The guiding idea of Stallo's Hegel is that "mind or thought is fundamentally identical with the forces which activate the whole natural world." Whatever Emerson's grasp of details may have been and however little he studied Hegel in the original German, it is clear that Emerson now found Hegelian philosophy congenial. His Hegel strongly resembles other nineteenth-century interpretations. Moncure Conway, who first waked to intellectual life through Emerson's "History," wrote of Hegel's thought: "Its essence is the conception of an absolute idea which has represented itself in Nature, in order that by a progressive development through Nature it may gain consciousness in man, and return as mind to a deeper union with itself." Carl Michelet, writing in 1837, claimed that Hegel's absolute idealism was a union of subjective and objective idealisms. Hegel, said Michelet, "combined idealism with realism by means of his dialectical method in which the thought of the philosopher becomes identical with the objective development of reality." A modern commentator suggests further why Hegel was attractive to Emerson and to Whitman. Hegel's is "a philosophy in which mind is fundamental to the world, in which freedom is the essence of mind, and in which freedom shows itself in thought as self-development, by contrast with mere conformity to fixed and uncritical categories."[8]

Hegel's thought not only gave Emerson a new road to an old destination, it pushed him to new efforts in his own search for the processes of life. He copied a number of sentences out of Stallo: "The configurations of nature are more than a symbol, they are the gesticular expression of nature's inner life." "Whatever exists, exists only in virtue of the life of which it is the expression." "The quantitative and qualitative existence of matter is an uninterrupted flight from itself, a never terminating whirl of evanescence."[9]

At least three important new developments in Emerson's thought this winter of 1849–1850 can be traced to his new enthusiasm for Hegel and his reabsorption in German idealism. One was a view of the history of modern (non-Darwinian) scientific thought, a view that can also be described as descended from biblical, typological thinking. Emerson takes the idea that "the form or type became transparent in the actual forms of successive ages as presented in geology," and he traces this view from Schelling to Oken to Hegel, Goethe, Geoffroi St. Hilaire, and finally to Louis Agassiz, who had "tried it in popular lectures on the times."

The second new Hegelian development in Emerson's thought is his new interest in the idea of freedom. In another recent Hegel text that Emerson knew, the "Introduction to the Philosophy of History" translated and printed in Hedge's *Prose Writers of Germany* (1847), Hegel says that "the history of the world is the progress in the consciousness of freedom." Hegel summarizes the section of his introduction labeled "History as the Interpretation of Spirit" this way: "The scheme is this; the Oriental world only knew that *one* is free [the Emperor]; the Greek and Roman world knew that *some* are free [the ruling class]; but we know that all men, in their true nature, are free,—that man, as man, is free."[10]

Emerson now drew up a similarly grand theory of historical development. His scheme has different ages and a different emphasis but is no less Hegelian in its movement. Emerson recognized a Greek era "when man deified nature," a Christian era "when the Soul becomes pronounced, and craved a heaven out of nature and above it,—looking on nature now as evil," and a third era, the modern, when we retraced our steps and rallied again to nature. "But now the tendency is to marry mind to nature," Emerson says, "to put nature under the mind." "Man goes forth to the dominion of the world by commerce, by science, and by philosophy."[11]

Hegel also forced Emerson to face the fact that he had not found a satisfactory way to reconcile the old but still troublesome conflict between freedom and determinism:

> My geometry cannot span the extreme points which I see. I affirm melioration,—which nature teaches, in pears, in the domesticated animals, and in her secular geology, and this development of complex races. I affirm also the self-equality of nature; or that only that is true which is always true, and, that, in California, or in Greece, or in Jewry, or in Arcadia, existed the same amounts of private power, as now, and the same deductions, however differently distributed.

The world of melioration admits choice, which in turn admits some freedom. The second world, that of "the self-equality of nature," is the world of equilibrium and natural law; elms are not free to become birches. There was much to be said for each position, and Emerson was candid enough to add, "but I cannot reconcile these two statements."[12]

Emerson's journal for February 1850 is full and excited. There is a sense of fresh energy as Emerson tested old convictions with new observations. The idea that there is fundamental order in the physical world, that when we get to the bottom of things reality will be found to be constructed in a manner that excludes mere randomness, took on new life for Emerson from the work of Ernst Chladni. "Chladni's experiments seemed to me central," wrote Emerson. "He strewed sand on glass, and then struck the glass with tuneful accords, and the sand assumed symmetrical figures. With discords, the sand was thrown about amorphously. It seems then, that Orpheus is no fable. You have only to sing, and the rocks will crystallize."[13]

The primacy of mind affirmed by Hegel had been suggested by Proclus. In his journal Emerson noted Proclus's saying, "Knowledge subsists according to the nature of that which knows, and not according to the nature of that which is known." The idea that the mind is active rather than passive had been put by Sallust, the Roman historian and ally of Julius Caesar: "Animus habet, non habetur" (the mind possesses, it is not possessed). Emerson also found a proto-Hegelian concept of how the mind relates to its object in the writing of the seventeenth-century physician Jean Baptiste van Helmont, whom he paraphrases as saying: "The understanding transforms itself into the image of the thing understood." Further corroboration of Hegel came from Goethe's premonition that the function of human beings is to give nature self-consciousness. Emerson found the following passage in Goethe's "Winckelmann":

> When the healthy nature of man works as a whole, when he feels himself, in this world, as in a large, beautiful, worthy and solid whole; when the harmonious well-being assures him a clear free joy, then would the universe, if it could be conscious, exult as arrived at its aim, and admire the summit of its own becoming and being.[14]

There is a celebrated image in George Eliot's *Middlemarch* (1871–1872) of how the mind makes order.

> Your pier glass or extensive surface of polished steel made to be rubbed by a housemaid, will be minutely and multitudinously scratched in all directions; but place now against it a lighted candle as a centre of illumination, and lo! the scratches will seem to arrange themselves in a fine series of concentric circles round that little sun. It is demonstrable that the scratches are going everywhere impartially, and it is only your candle which produces the flattering illusion of a concentric arrangement, its light falling with an exclusive optical selection. These things are a parable. The scratches are events, and the candle is the egoism of any person.

A modern philosopher says, "We know what we make. We make order. The Greeks thought order was there." By 1850 Emerson had already reached an understanding like George Eliot's sense of the transient self, but in common with the Greeks and with modern science, he also knew order was there in nature. Now he put it in an image:

> I figure to myself the world as a hollow temple, and every individual mind as an exponent of some sacred part therein, as if each man was

a jet of flame affixed to some capital, or node, or angle, or triglyph, or rosette, or spandyl, bringing out its beauty and symmetry to the eye by his shining. But when the jet of light is gone, the groined arch and fluted column remain beautiful, and can in an instant be lighted again and vindicated.[15]

81. The West

THERE WAS ALWAYS A RESTLESS QUALITY IN EMERSON. Although he was deeply attached to Concord and missed home terribly when he was away, he traveled a good deal outside Concord. A year and a half after he returned from England, he made his first trip to the American West. The country was growing rapidly and in interesting ways. Educated and liberal-minded Germans were settling in the Midwest, having left Europe after the failed uprisings of 1848. Gold had been discovered in California. In 1849 Yerba Buena became San Francisco. In 1850 California would become a state. Cholera had also reached the American West, getting as far as St. Louis by 1850. Among some Canadians there was a movement to annex Canada to the United States.

March 1850 was a pivotal moment. In January Henry Clay had introduced his compromise program, which included a new and stringent fugitive slave law. The debate in the Senate and in the country was prolonged and dramatic. Not until September would it finally pass. Feeling ran high. Calhoun led a group that wanted to see a country with two presidents—one northern, one southern—each with a veto. Clay was trying to save the Union but insisted on a bill that would allow runaway slaves to be chased and caught in free states. On March 2 a strongly stirred Walt Whitman wrote the last rhymed poem of his youth, "The Dough Face Song," a bitter attack on southern politicians: "We are all docile dough-faces, / They knead us with the fist." Five days later Daniel Webster, also trying to save the Union, joined Clay and lent his massive prestige to a fugitive slave law. Northern abolitionists were appalled. Whittier wrote a withering poem about Webster's "treachery" called "Ichabod." And on March 22, writing under the extraordinary pressure of events and seething at what he saw as Webster's betrayal, Whitman abandoned conventional metrical rhymed verse forms—forever—and wrote the first of his poems in the free verse that completely transformed his own work and would transform modern American poetry as much as the Civil War would transform American life. The poem appeared in the *New York Tribune;* it was called "Blood Money" and it cast Webster as Judas:

Of olden time, when it came to pass
That the beautiful God Jesus, should finish his work on earth
Then went Judas and sold the divine youth
And took pay for his body.[1]

In the middle of the controversy Emerson wrote asking his friend Henry James to arrange some New York lectures. He gave his current set of nonpolitical lectures: "Natural Aristocracy," "The Superlative," "Eloquence," and "Books." They were very well received. Ex-president Van Buren came to two. From New York Emerson wrote Furness in Philadelphia asking if lectures could be arranged there. He wrote home wearily from both cities. The tour was mainly a money-making endeavor. In May Emerson received an offer to lecture in Cincinnati. He seized the occasion and left for the West within a week. His long, vivid letters home clearly convey his excitement as he went by train to Buffalo, then boarded the steamer *America* for Sandusky, Ohio. The boat caught fire, made an emergency landing at Cleveland, and sent all the passengers ashore while firemen fought the flames in the hold for three hours and saved the ship. When it was found that Emerson was among the passengers, he was invited to deliver a talk on the spur of the moment, which he did that very evening.[2]

From Sandusky Emerson took a train all the way across Ohio down to Cincinnati in the southwest corner of the state on the Ohio River. He noticed that the forests were very different from those of New England, full of "beeches, immense black walnuts, oaks, rock maples, buckeyes in bloom, cornels in white flower, and red-buds." The farms in western Ohio were mostly "log-huts, with log-barns." Fields of more than a hundred acres each were common; he heard of one that was a thousand acres. The bottomland was so rich that the farmers used no manure.[3]

Cincinnati was a booming city of 120,000 persons, having grown from 36,000 a decade earlier. Emerson stayed in a "magnificent hotel, the best and largest building of that kind I have ever seen." He gave his current set of lectures, was pressed for more, and gave additional lectures on the "Natural History of Intellect." The newspapers gave him mixed reviews as usual. Emerson was buoyed by the experience and he returned to Cincinnati many times over the years.[4]

Thirty-five miles northeast of Cincinnati lies one of the grandest of the old Hopewell Indian monuments, Fort Ancient. Emerson went with a group to see this hill fort, one of the most remarkable of the more than ten thousand prehistoric structures to be found in the Ohio and Mississippi river valleys. It is a late Hopewell fort, dating from around A.D. 500. The fort sits on a long narrow plateau 230 feet above the Little Miami River in Warren County. Its walls, from six to twenty feet high and many feet thick, run more than three and a half miles overall, enclosing about a hundred acres in three linked areas. Early white settlers had reasoned that the savage Indians they met could not have built such works and so a mound-builder mythology had grown up around the idea that an earlier race—a lost tribe of Israel perhaps—had built them.[5]

Emerson visited Fort Ancient two years after the publication of Squier and Davis's *Ancient Monuments of the Mississippi Valley*, the first book published by the new Smithsonian Institution. Squier suggested there were links between the Mound Builders and native South American cultures. When Emerson visited "the old mounds of the old race who inhabited this country 3000 years ago" and gazed out at the old trees standing "on the very summit of this long-drawn parapet," on his forty-seventh birthday, he wrote that he was "often reminded of my visit to Stonehenge." He said nothing about the fair-skinned mound builders of myth. He may have known the Squier and Davis volume, but he could not have known that modern archaeology would link the Hopewell and Adena cultures so closely with those of Stonehenge and Avebury that artifacts from the former would be used to illuminate the latter.[6]

After the Cincinnati lectures Emerson was free to return home. He decided, however, to make a trip of it and see more of the country. "I learn Western geography," he wrote home, "buy maps, and shall see a prairie before I die." He set out with a party of seventeen to visit Mammoth Cave in Kentucky. The group went by boat 315 miles down the Ohio, past Louisville, to Evansville, Indiana, then by another boat 150 miles up the Green and Barren rivers to Bowling Green, then by coach 30 miles to the cave. On the Green River

> we disturbed the ducks all the way . . . and wild turkeys flew before us from tree to tree. Where the river widened occasionally, lay long strata of dried leaves solidly matted together, deserted by the water, and when these are disturbed by thrusting a pole into them, carburetted hydrogen comes out in quantity, and if lighted burns all over the river.[7]

Emerson had never been so purely the sightseer since his early trip to Italy, and his description of the Mammoth Cave has all the wonder and admiration he had once lavished on the Capitoline Museum. He walked eighteen miles in fourteen hours in the cave. They fired Bengal lights and Roman candles; they admired the Bottomless Pit, the Coffin Room, Echo River, Purgatory, and a long passage called Cleveland's Cabinet where, Emerson said,

> the walls of the cave are profusely decorated with beautiful flowers and rosettes of wonderful elegance, and where I learned one thing plain and clear—that the volutes and foliation of the capitols of columns were not learned from any basket of acanthus, but from the efflorescence of caves.

The party stayed underground the entire day. "When we emerged into the warm night, at half past nine o'clock, it was raining fast, and a long and violent thunderstorm had passed over us whereof we nothing knew. We had lost one of the 'days of our bright lives.'"[8]

From the cave Emerson went by stage to Eddyville, Kentucky, then down the Cumberland river to Paducah, Illinois, on the Ohio. He passed Cairo, a town of "sailor shops, ten pin alleys and faro tables," where "the only habitable place seemed to be . . . an old steamboat whose engine had been taken out and the boat moored and fitted up into the dirtiest of Ann Street boarding houses." River life was rough and makeshift. "The boats are very cheaply and poorly built, no 'palaces' at all, just made to keep above water from port to port, and generally disabled of one wheel." Steamboat disasters were "as common as mosquitoes. At St. Louis, 47 boats were burned between the 17 May 1849 and 17 May 1850."[9]

Just past Cairo the Ohio runs into the Mississippi: Emerson marveled at the scene, the "wide, wide eddying waters" and the low shores. He described the "great sweeps of the Mississippi," the large islands, the long distances from either shore. He found it "the loveliest river, no towns, no houses, no dents in the forest, no boats almost. We met, I believe but one steam-boat in the first hundred miles."[10]

He arrived at St. Louis, at the same time as the cholera, which had come from Asia, breaking out in Turkestan in 1844, reaching Baghdad in 1846, Russia in 1847, and Edinburgh in 1848. Thence the pestilence spread to Belfast and within a month to Staten Island. By December of 1848 it was in New Orleans and starting upriver. Treatment was ineffective. The disease began with diarrhea and vomiting. A cholera patient had an unmistakable and frightful appearance: "Dark circles ringed his eyes, his skin was cold and clammy, he writhed in muscular cramps, he lay moaning in helpless prostraton, his pulse almost disappeared. . . . Often he died of a 'dry collapse' his body desiccated, while his bowels were found full of fluid."[11]

Emerson said of the disease simply: "Cholera and death in my hotel at St. Louis; cholera and death in my steamboat on the river." He went back on the river, took a boat—the *Excelsior*—450 miles upstream, past Hannibal on the Missouri shore, past Quincy and Nauvoo on the Illinois shore, past Keokuk, Iowa, all the way to Galena, Illinois, near the Wisconsin border. From here Emerson went overland to Chicago, then to Detroit, then by steamer to Buffalo and so home by rail.[12]

The West fascinated Emerson. It continued to grow on him and soon became a major counterweight to old England in his imagination. Emerson embraced the West, returning nearly every year on his lecture circuits. He was interested in the riverboat gamblers, the hard professionals "who professed to be entire strangers to each other, and, if asked any question respecting the river, 'had never been on these waters before.'" People at St. Louis "already smell the Pacific," Emerson noted. He also observed "a certain largeness in the design and enterprise of the people," to say nothing of their language. "They had a boat," he said, "drawing so little water that they said it would sail in a heavy dew." Elsewhere he heard about a tornado that carried a child for miles. "This was too good to leave alone. So we presently heard of a tornado that drove a plough through a field, and turned as pretty a furrow all round the field as you ever saw."[13]

The West was messy, no doubt. "Everyone has the mud up to his knees, and the coal of the country dinges his shirt collar." But it was also grand. "The people are all kings," he wrote. "Out on the prairie the sceptre is the driving whip. And I notice an extraordinary firmness in the face of many a drover, an air of independence and inevitable lips, which are worth a hundred thousand dollars." He passed a field belonging, he was told, to a man named Jacob Strawn, who seemed to epitomize this new westerner. Strawn owned forty thousand acres, lived in the saddle, and ate mush and milk with two spoons; his idea of a great man was not Plato or Shakespeare but "the man who stands in the gap when a great herd of cattle are to be separated."[14]

82. The Matter of Margaret

AFTER FOUR YEARS ABROAD MARGARET FULLER SET OUT FOR home on May 17, 1850, sailing from Livorno in the American brig *Elizabeth*. She may have been married to the Italian nobleman named Ossoli who accompanied her. She had a two-year-old son, she had taken an active part in the (unsuccessful) revolution in Rome in 1848, and she had written a book about it. She had repeated premonitions of disaster about this trip. "I am absurdly fearful," she wrote, "and various omens have combined to give me a dark feeling." Her only consolation was that if disaster did strike, "I shall perish with my husband and my child and so may be transferred to some happier state." She saw her life as from a distant shore, proceeding as regularly as the acts of a Greek tragedy, and, she wrote, "I can but accept the pages as they turn."[1]

On July 18 the ship was approaching the New Jersey coast. The weather was thick; the wind was 17 to 21 knots from the southeast. As evening wore on the wind increased until by midnight it reached hurricane velocity. The skipper, a man named Bangs, reefed the sails but kept the ship driving, confident that he would see Navesink light and then slip into New York harbor. But he was too far north and going faster than he supposed. At about four in the morning of the nineteenth, the ship slammed into a sandbar just off Fire Island with a jolt that threw the passengers out of their bunks. The next wave lifted the stern, turned the ship sideways, and smashed it against the bar. The Carrara marble in the hold broke loose and went through the side of the ship. The masts were now cut away as the ship lay pinned against the bar by crashing seas in a hurricane. The tide was rising, which meant that each wave hit the ship with more weight than the one before it.[2]

When day broke it became clear that they were only a few hundred yards from the beach. But no surf-boat was launched and no line-gun fired. Instead, the passengers and crew on the wreck—a few of whom were to survive—could see the local wreck-pickers carrying off the first spoils from the not-yet-consummated disaster. Margaret Fuller Ossoli refused to be separated from her husband and son. She could not be persuaded to grab a plank and try to save herself. Her two-year-old son Nino stood next to no chance in the surf. At the last minute, as the forecastle was breaking up in a wild smother of spray, the steward grabbed Nino and leaped over the side to swim for it. Neither made it alive. Margaret and her husband died in the wreck. Their bodies were never recovered. Margaret was last seen "seated at the foot of the foremast, still clad in her white night-dress, with her hair fallen loose upon her shoulders."[3]

Emerson later wrote in his journal that she had died "within sight of and within 60 rods of the shore. To the last her country proves inhospitable to her; brave, eloquent, subtle, accomplished, devoted, constant soul." He noted that the rumors about her marriage and child were raising eyebrows. "The timorous said what shall we do? how shall she be received, now that she brings a husband and child home. But she had only to open her mouth, and a triumphant success awaited her. . . . For she had the impulse and they wanted it." He copied with approval Elizabeth Hoar's saying that Fuller "was the largest woman, and not a woman who wanted to be a man." Her death affected Emerson almost like a death in the family. "I have lost my audience," he wrote. "I hurry now to my work admonished that I have few days left."[4]

William Henry Channing proposed that a memorial volume be put out and Emerson warmed to the project at once. "O Yes 'Margaret and Her Friends' must be written, but not post haste. It is an essential line of American History." Emerson was sharply aware of the loss of her manuscript history of the 1848 Roman revolution. He had dispatched Thoreau to the scene of the fatal wreck in part to see if any manuscripts could be recovered. The proposed memorial volume could not take the place of her lost history, of course, but it might present a personal portrait of her that was not to be found in her four published books. Horace Greeley also thought a memorial volume should be got out. The hurry-up New York publisher wanted the volume by September.[5]

Emerson immediately began a new notebook for recording details and motifs of Fuller's life and writings. The notebook begins with a recognition of the last public passion of her life. The motto for the notebook is from Virgil's first Eclogue: "Et quae tanto fuit Romam tibi causa videndi? Libertas" (And what was the urgent business that brought you to Rome? Freedom). Fuller had been much interested in how masculine and feminine traits coexisted in most natures. Emerson copied out part of an 1844 poem of hers: "But if I steadfast gaze upon thy face [the moon], / A human secret

like my own I trace, / For through the woman's smile looks the male eye."
He shared her interest in the daemonic, which she defined as "energy for
energy's sake." He also shared Sam Ward's exasperated sense of inadequacy
at the task before them. Ward said, "How can you describe a Force? How
can you write a life of Margaret?" and Emerson replied, "Well, the question
itself is some description of her." As Emerson understood her, Fuller had
a genius for friendship; she was

> this joyful guest who brought wit, anecdotes, love-stories, tragedies,
> oracles with her, and with her broad web of relations to so many fine
> friends, seemed like the Queen of some parliament of love, who
> carried the key to all confidences, and to whom every question had
> been finally referred.

Above all Emerson was sensitive to the sense of total intimacy she both
required and bestowed. "An absolute all-confiding intimacy between her
and another, which seemed to make them both sharers of the whole horizon
of each others' and of all truth, did not make her false to any other friend."
The tone he wished to convey was one of plenitude, of inexhaustible riches
and an endless horizon of promise. "For her opulent mind the day was never
long enough to exhaust, and I who have known her intimately for ten years
from July 1836 till August 1846 when she left this country never saw her
without some surprise at her new powers."[6]

The *Memoirs of Margaret Fuller Ossoli*, which finally appeared in two
volumes in February 1852, edited by Emerson, J. F. Clarke, and W. H.
Channing, is our indispensable source for Fuller's life. Recent critics have
complained that the editors "repressed her sexuality, her brooding sense of
incompleteness, and her increasingly radical political point of view." Channing, Clarke, and Emerson together made Fuller "intellectually safer and
sexually acceptable, her marriage normal, her son legitimate." But there was
nothing rascally or malicious in their work—nothing like Rufus Griswold's
pathological misrepresentation of Poe or Oliver Wendell Holmes's later
effort to falsify Emerson's views on abolition. Fuller's editors lacked basic
archival respect and were shockingly destructive as they cut and pasted her
own manuscripts for the printer, yet Emerson in particular took care to
quote her accurately and his editorial selectiveness was well within then
current standards. Their work was comparable to Fuller's own editing of
Eckermann's *Conversations with Goethe* (which Emerson thought Fuller's

best book in some ways) in which she removed all trace of Eckermann's visit to Italy, frequently condensed Eckermann's remarks, and sometimes condensed Goethe's. Imperfect as the *Memoirs of Margaret Fuller Ossoli* is, the project was a labor of love.[7]

Emerson had ambitious hopes for the book. It was widely agreed that Fuller talked better than she wrote; she herself thought so and said so, as Emerson was aware. His idea was to produce, from her journals and writings, from conversation, table talk, letters, and autobiographical fragments, a vivid portrait of Margaret Fuller at her best. It would have to be written, he told Sam Ward, "tête exaltée, and in the tone of *Spiridion,* or even Bettine, with the coolest ignoring of Mr. Willis, Mr. Carlyle and Boston and London." The next day he wrote Caroline Sturgis Tappan to say that the book "must be written in the bravest mood of *Spiridion,* or of Bettine, better yet of Dante,—mystically in Novelis' sense, that is, as if the world were one pair of lovers." These comments and comparisons are our best indication of what Emerson wanted the memorial volume to be. Novalis here means *Heinrich von Ofterdingen,* the famous romantic *Bildungsroman* in which the hero is initiated not into the world but into the higher truths whose language is myth. By Dante Emerson meant the *Vita nuova;* he is thinking of spiritual autobiographies in narrative—sometimes fictional—form, of life journeys in which love and friendship play the central roles. The *Vita nuova* is the great poem about the emotional intensity of being in love. "Bettine" was shorthand for the ultimate in the articulation of personal intimacy and for hypertrophic powers of expression in correspondence. *Spiridion* is George Sand's strangely powerful novel about spiritual rebirth, another favorite of Fuller's. Set in a Franciscan monastery, it tells of the secret discovery and reconcealment of a new religion of humanity born from within but at war with Christian institutions. What all these books have in common—what Emerson clearly wanted for the Fuller volume—was a pervasive tone of emotional and spiritual intensity and an irresistible, all-risking thirst for personal intimacy and spiritual truth.[8]

83. The Tragic

THE DEATH OF MARGARET FULLER WHEN SHE WAS ONLY FORTY was a shock to Emerson. The deaths of his first wife, his younger brothers, and his first child had also been shocking, of course, but he had rebounded from them. Somehow, Margaret's death caught him unprepared and undefended. Her loss drove him in on himself and made him intensely conscious of a side of life he usually tended to rush over. It is easy to call this consciousness a sense of tragedy, but in Emerson's case it did not have the clear form and redemptive lift of classical tragedy. He had rather a sense that something was fundamentally wrong with the universe, an awareness of some elemental lack at the core of things. Emerson's friend the elder Henry James once gave this account of his awareness of emptiness at the center:

> Every man who has reached even his intellectual teens begins to suspect that life is no farce; that it is not genteel comedy even; that it flowers and fructifies on the contrary out of the profoundest tragic depths—the depths of an essential dearth in which its subjects roots are plunged. . . . The natural inheritance of everyone who is capable of spiritual life is an unsubdued forest where the wolf howls and the obscene bird of night chatters.

This sense of dearth is the opposite of the sense of fullness and possibility. Even memory was now a burden for Emerson: "Happy those, say I, who can live in the present moment! who do not use their memories, or sulkily reflect, 'Well, I shall have my revenge by and by.'"[1]

Emerson watched his children with vast pride and fondness, of course, but also now with apprehension. Ellen was eleven, Edith nine, Edward six. They had all made it past five, Waldo's age when he died. But daily life took its own toll. "The one thing we watch with pathetic interest in our children is the degree in which they possess recuperative force," Emerson wrote. He was thinking of the times when they were "wounded by us, or by each other, when they go down at school to the bottom of the class, when they fail in competition of study or of play with their mates." He could have been thinking about his own brothers.

> If they lose their spirit and remember the mischance in their chamber at home,—it is all over with them, they have a check for life. But if they have that degree of buoyancy and resistance that makes light of these mishaps . . . the scars rapidly cicatrize and the fibre is all the tougher for the wound.[2]

Emerson's own recuperative power was unusual, but the oftener it was called upon, the more slowly it responded. The losses were cumulative too and no longer so easily sloughed off as when he was younger. No longer close to Aunt Mary, with Fuller gone, Emerson now felt "my chief want in life is somebody who shall make me do what I can do." He admired the energy and success of a man like Julius Caesar, of whom the Roman poet Lucan said, "He thought nothing done while anything remained to be done." For years now Emerson had looked upon the days as gods, each one bringing gifts according to our ability to receive. But there were also times when he could say, "You think another day another scream of the eternal wail."[3]

Emerson's reading this year covered a huge range of subjects as usual, and some of it fed into his growing willingness to deal with the unhandsome, unsmiling side of life. From his Ozymandian distance he read Wilhelm Zahn's elegant volume, *Les plus beaux ornaments de Pompeii et Herculaneum* (Berlin 1829–1842), C. Fellows's *Account of Ionic Trophy Monuments,* and Austin Layard's *Nineveh.* During his western trip he worked on F. T. Vischer's *Aesthetik oder Wissenschaft des Schonen,* 5 vols. (Reutlingen and Leipzig, 1846–1854). (When English translations were unavailable, he could, of course, read books in both French and German.) His expanding American interests can be seen in his reading of J. C. Fremont, of Agassiz's *Lake Superior* (for which Cabot had written the main narrative), and the 1849 *Report of the Commissioner on Indian Affairs* (published in 1850). He read Charlotte Bronte's *Jane Eyre* and *Shirley* and Thackeray's *Vanity Fair.* He found Tennyson's *In Memoriam* lacking in real consolatory power; it is, he said, "the commonplaces of condolence among good unitarians in the first week of mourning."[4]

Only a few new books caught his attention in a serious way. One was J. A. Froude's grim little novel, *The Nemesis of Faith.* The book is a short, bleak attack on Christianity; the irreligion of the book cost Froude his Oxford post. The tone ranges from angry to weary despairing; the arguments are drawn from the long deist tradition, from Paine, and from D. F. Strauss. The book is the essence of Victorian doubt. Froude derides what he calls "talismanic materialism" and cynically acknowledges the "grave moral deterioration which follows an empty exchequer." Froude's protagonist is a man ruined by his faith, by his desire for faith, by his pretense of faith. Froude writes well and we can taste the disillusion when he says, "Neither good enough for heaven, nor bad enough for the other place, we oscillate in the temperate inertia of folly." Falling in love with a married woman, the protagonist behaves badly and weakly. His subsequent life is destroyed by "remorse not for what he had done, but for what he had not done." His life and the book end with unrelieved Hawthornian gloom:

> Amidst the wasted ruins of his life, where the bare bleak soil was strewed with wrecked purposes and shattered creeds, with no hope to stay him, with no fear to raise the most dreary phantom beyond the grave, he sunk down into the barren waste, and the dry sands rolled over him where he lay.[5]

Emerson was also reading a volume of the letters of Christopher Columbus. He took a number of notes about the fourth voyage, that of 1503, which show Columbus's gifts as a letter writer and his skill in dramatizing his feelings of bitterness, neglect, and despair: "Solitary in my trouble, sick, and in daily expectation of death, surrounded by millions of hostile savages, full of cruelty, and thus separated from the Sacraments of our Holy Church, weep for me, whoever has charity, truth and justice." Another, later letter to the king and queen of Spain tells of his situation at Veragua.

> I was alone on that dangerous coast suffering from a fever and worn with fatigue. All hope of escape was gone. I toiled up to the highest part of the ship, and with a quivering voice and fast-falling tears, I called upon your highnesses' war-captains from each point of the compass, to come to my succour; but there was no reply. At length, groaning with exhaustion, I fell asleep, and heard a compassionate voice address me thus. "O fool, and slow to believe and serve thy God, the God of all. What did he do more for Moses or for David than he has done for thee?"

Emerson was struck both by Columbus's clamorous self-pity and by his comparison of himself to other great figures with a mandate from God.

Emerson's reading in Columbus and Froude offered him scenes and attitudes that ran counter to everything one thinks of as Emersonian. His interest in these books shows his growing willingness to face that other world of experience, the world of defeat and despair, the world that was more determined and less free than Emerson hoped.[6]

Emerson increasingly saw determinism through a scientific rather than a theological lens. The premise of science was that there are discoverable laws governing phenomena. Quetelet's statistics were the fruit of one such attempt to discover the laws governing human life. Now, in 1850, Emerson was reading Linnaeus's *Philosophia Botanica* (Stockholm, 1751), another major effort to understand the order in the apparent chaos of nature. Emerson was alert to the debate in botanical circles between the "natural" and "artificial" methods of plant classification. Linnaeus was constantly invoked as the great champion of the artificial (that is, the arbitrary) method of classifying plants according to the number of stamens a flower possessed. But Linnaeus himself had guessed in 1751 what Darwin would confirm in 1859. Emerson copied out Linnaeus's comment: "Methodus naturalis ultimus finis Botanica est et erit" (the natural method [that is, grouping plants by considering all their characteristics and differences] is and will be the ultimate goal in botany). The more strongly Emerson felt the case for tragedy, for waste, for chance, for loss, the more he looked to science as well as to his own convictions for proof of underlying order. Emerson observed that Linnaeus claimed that "all plants show a relationship, similar to a territory on a map, to each other." Goethe claimed that the leaf is the key to botanical morphology. As Emerson read it, Linnaeus and Goethe were both affirming that there was a real, if undiscovered order in things. The observation gave one hope for the human world, appearances notwithstanding. If there was less freedom in the world than appeared, there was also more order.[7]

84. The Conduct of Life

IN THE EARLY MONTHS OF 1851, WHILE EMERSON WAS STILL AT work on the Margaret Fuller memoir and still mulling over the relation between England and America—and his book on that subject—he was also at work on a third new project. This was a course of lectures to be called "The Conduct of Life," which he first gave in Pittsburgh on a trial run. He arrived in Pittsburgh on March 20, 1851, after a long trip from Philadelphia, "two nights being spent in the railcars and the third on the floor of a canal-boat, where the cushion allowed me for a bed was crossed at the knees by another tier of sleepers as long legged as I,—so that the air was a wreath of legs." He had been invited by the Young Men's Mercantile Library Association. He found his hotel, the Monongahela House, very good, and his hosts agreeable people.[1]

The Pittsburgh Emerson saw was a coal city, not a steel city, and it rivaled the English Midlands both in vitality and in coal smoke. Everywhere he looked he saw "black houses, black air, black faces and clothes of men and women." He was taken to see a coal mine by Thomas McElrath; he was shown coal seams five feet thick on land worth a thousand dollars an acre. The coal sold for a dollar forty cents a ton delivered or three to five cents a basket at the mine. Under his hotel window a row of steamboats lay tied up on the Monongahela, a quarter-mile above the confluence where it forms the Ohio. He learned that one in every six coal boats was lost getting to New Orleans.

Because he had not finished writing the opening remarks for "The Conduct of Life" lectures and because his hosts wanted his first lecture just a few hours after his 4 P.M. arrival, Emerson gave first an old lecture on "England," then on subsequent days he presented his new talks, "The Laws of Success," "Wealth," "Economy," "Culture," and "Worship." The subjects and even the order in which they were treated are very much the same as they would appear about ten years later in the volume called *The Conduct of Life*.

This volume was the one Carlyle liked best of all Emerson's work. It was also, unfortunately, the favorite of Orison Swett Marden, author of innumerable how-to-succeed books such as *Pushing to the Front* (Boston, 1895) and *The Young Man Entering Business* (New York, 1903). Because Emerson's later work proved usable to the publicists of the Gilded Age and because he did not wholly repudiate American business and workaday success, critics have argued that Emerson's later thought abandons the idealism of his youth and embraces the materialism that was becoming intellectually as well as socially respectable so quickly in the 1850s with Marx, Comte, Darwin, and the rise of modern science, modern medicine, anthropology, and social statistics. But Emerson had always been an affirmer and an accepter. As he had accepted his outsider status when he was young, so he now accepted his own gathering success. His deepest beliefs and values remained unchanged, though now when he began a topic by considering the ordinary, worldly, useful view of a subject—the commodity view—he spent more time sympathetically exploring the pull of the mundane and the material and he took longer before dropping the other shoe.[2]

The talk "Success" was the Napoleon piece, the commodity chapter of the new series. Emerson explored the value of talent and superficial success plus what he called "personal ascendency," or individual force of personality, and the exercise of ordinary power. "All power is of one kind," he declared, "a sharing of the nature of the world." He had his eye on both spiritual power and brute force as he observed that "all kinds of power usually emerge at the same time, good energy and bad." He understood the growing strength of America as something new, and he warned that "as long as our people quote English standards, they will miss the sovereignty of power." He agreed with the painter Thomas Cole that "in history the great moment is when the savage is just ceasing to be a savage . . . not yet passed over into the Corinthian civility. . . . Every thing good in nature and in the world is in that moment of transition." The kind of power Emerson treats here is neither physical force nor spiritual strength; it is the force of will or character that produces success. Emerson is interested in the power of execution, the power to carry out what one designs or intends. "The step from knowing to doing is rarely taken," he says; "'tis a step out of a chalk circle of imbecility into fruitfulness."[3]

"The Conduct of Life" lectures contain what Emerson had learned about living in the world since the mid-1840s. The real crop of his orchard is also here in the frequently occurring imagery of tree-keeping. His metaphor now for concentration is the severe pruning that "forces the sap of the tree into one or two vigorous limbs, instead of suffering it to spindle into a sheaf of twigs." Elsewhere he compares successful people to "thrifty trees, which grow in spite of ice, lice, mice, and borers."[4]

The lecture on wealth was Emerson's piece that could be most easily twisted to suit the gospel of wealth in post–Civil War America. "Man was born to be rich" is the kind of statement that is easily turned into Russell Conwell's "Acres of Diamonds" (1861) speech with its message that since there are riches to be found everywhere (acres of diamonds in every backyard) it was morally wrong to insist on remaining poor. Emerson is at some pains to say that wealth is not worth but is symbolic or representative of worth. He is, of course, most interested in spiritual and social riches, but he does not repudiate worldly or individual wealth. Still, Emerson can be of comfort to exploiters only by agile selection of quotations. He does say, "He is the richest man who knows how to draw a benefit from the labors of the greatest number of men." He also said, in the same lecture, "He is the rich man in whom the people are rich, and he is the poor man in whom the people are poor." Both statements are as applicable to a union organizer as to a venture capitalist. He has it clearly in mind that money is not value but is representative of value. He insisted that the farmer "knows how many strokes of labor it [his dollar] represents. His bones ache with the day's work that earned it. He knows how much land it represents."[5]

Parts of "Wealth" read like a reply to Thoreau; this lecture is Emerson's chapter on economics. "Each man's expense must proceed from his character." "Nothing is beneath you, if it is in the direction of your life; nothing is great or desirable if it is off from that." Brook Farm, Fruitlands, and Thoreau's time at Walden have now receded into the past, into a time of what Emerson calls "arcadian fanaticism," marked by "a passionate desire to go upon the land, and unite farming to intellectual pursuits." Emerson's own experience provides him with a comic refutation:

> With brow bent, with fair intent, the pale scholar leaves his desk to draw freer breath and get a juster statement of his thought, in the garden walk. He stops to pull up a purslain or a dock that is choking the young corn, and finds that there are two; close behind the last is a third; he reaches out his hand to a fourth, behind that are four thousand and one.[6]

The Jeffersonian ideal of subsistence farming was already a dream of the past. Emerson noted that "when men now alive were born, the farm yielded everything that was consumed on it" but that now "the farmer buys almost all that he consumes." For Emerson as for Thoreau, economy means how to live. Failure to understand that means missing Emerson's main point. "The true thrift," he concludes, "is always to spend on the higher plane, to invest and spend, with keener avarice, that he may spend in spiritual creation, and not in augmenting animal existence."[7]

Emerson organized each book of essays—through *The Conduct of Life*—more explicitly than the one before it. The second sentence in the "Culture" essay gives the design of the Pittsburgh series: "Whilst all the world is in pursuit of power, and of wealth as a means of power, culture corrects the theory of success." By "culture" Emerson means neither "high culture" nor the anthropological definition of culture as the shared ways of a group or a people. Culture for Emerson still means cultivation, or, most simply, education. "Culture" is Emerson's essay on education. The goal of education is the fulfilled individual. "Individuality is not only not inconsistent with culture, but the basis of it," he says. "And the end of culture is not to destroy this [individual determination], God forbid! but to train away all impediment and mixture and leave nothing but pure power." Like most of the ideas in *The Conduct of Life*, this theme was an old and familiar one for Emerson. But there are important differences in the conclusions Emerson now draws. Though he still defends country life and morning solitude, he is now much more alive to what he calls the "commanding social benefits of cities," and he is shrewdly aware that solitude can easily become "the safeguard of mediocrity." What he really wants is a life of activity without bustle, a life of both power and repose. After all, as he observes, "Niagara falls without speed."[8]

The final lecture in Pittsburgh, presented April 1, was "Worship." The title is misleading, since the piece is not at all about rites, rituals, or other aspects of formal worship. It is a lecture on the religious impulse in human nature, on the human need to believe. This is Emerson's last major essay on the religious spirit. "Worship" contains almost no consideration of church religion. Emerson stoutly asserts that "God builds his temple in the heart on the ruins of churches and religions." We do not need formal religions because "we are born believing. A man bears beliefs as a tree bears apples." The essay argues for the existence of a religious impulse, which is related to, but not the same as, the "moral sentiment" or universal moral sense of the Scottish Enlightenment. The essay also tries to clarify the connection between the religious sentiment and the intellect: "Worship stands in some commanding relation to the health of man, and to his highest power, so as to be, in some manner, the source of intellect."[9]

The achievement of this essay is its demonstration that religion and science, far from being enemies, are at last similar and rest on similar grounds. "The true meaning of *spiritual* is *real*," Emerson says. Farther on he claims that "shallow men believe in luck . . . Strong men believe in cause and effect . . . The curve of the flight of the moth is pre-ordained, and all things go by number, rule, and weight." Looking ahead, Emerson calls for a religion that will have the same reality test as science. The religion of the future "must be intellectual," he says. "The scientific mind must have a faith which is science. . . . Let us have nothing now which is not its own evidence." Throwing off the weight of authority in science and religion as in politics does not, however, mean anarchy. "The last lesson of life," says Emerson, "is a voluntary obedience, a necessitated freedom." When a person's "mind is illuminated, when his heart is kind, he throws himself joyfully into the sublime order, and does, with knowledge, what the stones do by structure."[10]

85. The Fugitive Slave Act

ON FEBRUARY 15, 1851, FIVE MONTHS AFTER THE PASSAGE OF the new fugitive slave law, a black man named Shadrach Minkins, also known as Fredrick Jenkins, was arrested in Boston as a fugitive—in Taft's Cornhill Coffeehouse, where he was a waiter. He was immediately arraigned. Massachusetts Chief Justice Lemuel Shaw (Herman Melville's father-in-law) refused a request for a writ of habeas corpus; the court adjourned before noon, before finishing the case. As the court was breaking up, Lewis Hayden, a black member of the Boston Vigilance Committee organized by Theodore Parker, entered the courtroom with a group of about twenty other black men. When the group left, the prisoner Minkins was gone. That night, a stormy one, Minkins was driven first to Watertown, then to Concord, where he stayed in the home of Mary Brooks. He was next taken to North Ashburnham and put on the Fitchburg railway heading north.[1]

Minkins's was a classic trip on the underground railway, which in eastern Massachusetts was a well-organized and well-funded operation. Many fugitives arrived by ship in Boston. There a schooner—provocatively named *Moby Dick*—ostensibly engaged in sight-seeing and fishing trips, actually served the Boston Vigilance Committee. Once a fugitive was safely ashore, he had his choice of five different established "railroad" lines running out of Boston. One of these lines went to Concord, then west to Leominster and the Fitchburg railway. Sometimes fugitives arrived in Concord via Sudbury. In Concord the main agents of the underground railroad included Edwin Bigelow, the blacksmith, and his wife; Mary Merrick Brooks and her husband "Squire" Nathan Brooks; Mary Rice; Ephraim Allen; Stearns Wheeler and his wife; Bronson Alcott; Waldo and Lidian Emerson; and the entire Thoreau family. Henry's sister Sophia was on the executive committee of the Middlesex County antislavery society in 1851, as was Mary Brooks. The escape network kept busy. When the fugitive slave bill became law in September 1850, there were 8,975 persons of color in Massachusetts, according to Theodore Parker. Within sixty hours of the bill's passage forty of these had fled. As time passed, the network of safe houses grew. At a meeting on July 9, 1854, Waldo and Lidian Emerson were among a small group of Concordians who promised to aid and shelter any escaping slave who "should appear at their door."[2]

The escape of Minkins was widely noticed and the South was infuriated. A month and a half later another arrest in Boston gained wide publicity. On April 3, 1851, Thomas Sims, a young black man who had just arrived from Savannah as a stowaway on the *M and H Gilmore* was arrested. On April 7 Chief Justice Shaw declined to rule the Fugitive Slave Act unconstitutional. Sims's hearing lasted from April 7 to 11. This time the authorities left nothing to chance. Justice Shaw, like everyone else, had to duck under the heavy chains that were hung across the courthouse door. On April 10 Theodore Parker spoke out forcefully in a Fast Day sermon on the case. But nothing availed. Two days later three hundred policemen, formed into a hollow square, escorted Sims from the court house to a waiting ship, the *Acorn*. On the eighteenth *The Liberator* printed a letter from Emerson calling for "every lover of human rights" to "enter his protest for humanity against the detestable statute of the last congress." On the next day, April 19, the anniversary of the revolutionary battle of Concord, and the high holy day of liberty in the Concord calendar, Thomas Sims was taken ashore in Savannah and publicly whipped.[3]

The Sims affair snapped Emerson's equanimity. He had been a staunch abolitionist for some time; he now became an activist. His immediate response to the Sims affair was angry and exasperated. On April 26 thirty-six Concord citizens signed a petition asking Emerson to express publicly his "opinion upon the Fugitive Slave Law and upon the aspects of the times." A week later, on May 3, 1851, Emerson delivered the talk in Concord. Recognizing that "it is not possible to extricate oneself from the questions in which your age is involved," he began by saying "the last year has forced us all into politics."[4]

His talk was not aimed at the South or even at the federal government. Because the politicians in Washington had capitulated to the southern slave-owners and had passed an immoral law, Emerson now believed that effective resistance could come only from individual states. Treating the Fugitive Slave Act as an evil that had—like the Fall—darkened the world, Emerson called on Massachusetts to honor its revolutionary past by resisting this new law. He appealed to his fellow townsmen to "make this law inoperative. It must be abrogated and wiped out of the statute books." He scoffed at the tameness with which Boston hurried to help the federal marshalls; he sneered at the "hot haste of terror" that had overtaken "presidents of colleges and professors, saints and brokers, insurors, lawyers, importers, manufacturers." His tone is intemperate, goading: "The popular assumption that all men loved freedom, and believed in the Christian religion, was found hollow American brag." He attacked Webster in strong abusive terms, accusing him of "taking the bit in his mouth and the collar on his neck and harnessing himself to the chariot of the planters." He drove home what was meant to be an obituary shaft: "The fairest American name ends in this filthy law."[5]

The address was not all inflammatory rhetoric. Emerson was after the high ground. "If our resistance to this law is not right," he said, "there is no right." This is almost exactly the ground Lincoln claimed when he said, "If slavery is not wrong, nothing is wrong." Emerson took some trouble to clarify the concept of an immoral law, finding precedents both in Blackstone and in canon law. Blackstone acknowledged a "law of nature" that held "that we should live on, should hurt nobody, and should render unto every one his due," and he insisted that "no human laws are of any validity if contrary to this." Canon law simply said that "neither allegiance nor oath can bind to obey that which is wrong." Emerson piled example on precept, citing the reply of the governor of Bayonne to the order of Charles IX for the massacre of St. Bartholomew's Day:

I have communicated your majesty's command to your majesty's faithful inhabitants and warriors in the garrison, and I have found there only good citizens, and brave soldiers; not one hangman: therefore, both they and I most humbly entreat your majesty to be pleased to employ your arms and lives in things that are possible, however hazardous they may be, and we will exert ourselves to the last drop of our blood.[6]

This was, of course, civil disobedience. In the years just ahead Emerson issued repeated, overt, public incitements to break the law. His forceful confrontational politics of emancipation have been underestimated since his death for three reasons. First, his principal notebook on the subject ("WO Liberty") was lost from 1903 until 1966. Second, many of his antislavery talks are still in manuscript, and when those that were published were gathered together, they were put in a volume harmlessly called *Miscellanies*, when it might have been *The Fugitive Slave Law and Other Papers*. Finally, both Holmes and Cabot, the authors of the most influential Emerson biographies before Rusk's, made careful and conscious efforts to underplay Emerson's antislavery work, much to the distress of Emerson's family. Len Gougeon has recently shown that from 1851 Emerson was a committed abolitionist. His anger at Webster's about-face concerning the fugitive slave law and at the Sims affair never died down. It seeped into his journals and letters. It leaps out in speech after speech. "This has ceased to be a representative government," he wrote, "when the statute itself fastens penalties of treason on acts of common humanity. . . . I submit that all government is bankrupt, all law turned upside down; that the government itself is treason." In another journal he wrote, "This filthy enactment was made in the nineteenth century, by people who could read and write. I will not obey it by God." He thought the law was the "most detestable law that was ever enacted by a civilized state." His revulsion was physical, his language extreme: "We must put out this poison, this conflagration, this raging fever of slavery out of the constitution."[7]

Emerson's response has the depth of a conversion experience. The change was permanent. In May 1851 he campaigned for John G. Palfrey, a Free-Soil candidate, in a special election for Congress. Emerson repeated his fugitive slave law speech in Lexington, Fitchburg, Cambridge, and Waltham. Palfrey lost by 87 votes out of 13,000 cast, but he carried Concord by 68 votes out of 298 cast. In 1854 Emerson wrote and delivered a whole new speech against the Fugitive Slave Act in New York on the fourth anniversary of Webster's March 7 speech. That same year the Emersons joined the underground railway. In 1854–1855 Emerson made his annual lecture tour using mainly two lectures on slavery. In 1856 he spoke on affairs in Kansas: "Language has lost its meaning in the universal cant. Representative government is really misrepresentative. . . . Manifest Destiny, Democracy, Freedom, fine names for an ugly thing. They call it otto [attar] of rose and lavender—I call it bilge-water." "For the past few years," he observed, "the government has been the chief obstruction of the common weal."[8]

Still later Emerson entertained John Brown at his home, raised money for him, and spoke on his behalf. Whitman observed that when Emerson came out for John Brown, "it was with the power, the overwhelmingness, of an avalanche." Emerson recognized and approved of John Brown's apocalyptic finality and his intransigent moral absolutism and he quoted what John Brown had said to him privately about the Golden Rule and the Declaration of Independence: "Better that a whole generation of men, women and children should pass away by a violent death than that one word of either should be violated in this country." Emerson did not believe in the Union above all. He was cool toward Lincoln until the Emancipation Proclamation, after which he said: "[Lincoln] has been permitted to do more for America than any other American man."[9]

Over the years Emerson gave the most emotional speeches of his career in the crusade against slavery. And while he was far from immune to the rising war hysteria that was slowly but visibly gaining in the country from 1851, his opposition to slavery was not only a matter of feelings but was based on clearly articulated ideas. In some Hegelian way he saw America as an incarnation of the moral law that said that one may not deny to others what one finds essential for one's self. If I am free, all should be free. "America," he wrote, "is the idea of emancipation." He sketched the rest of this entry rapidly, barely bothering with sentence structure.

> Abolish kingcraft, slavery, feudalism, blackletter monopoly, pull down gallows, explode priestcraft, open the doors of the sea to all emigrants. Extemporize government, California, Texas. . . . All this covers self-government. All proceeds on the belief that as the people have made a government they can make another.

Emerson's long campaign against slavery is a practical validation and concrete result of his even longer habit of affirming freedom of will and action in opposition to determinism.[10]

86. The Science of Liberty

IN LATE JUNE 1851 EMERSON'S MOTHER FELL OUT OF HER BED in the middle of the night during a bad dream. "She lay there," Emerson wrote his brother, "unable to help herself for a long time, neither calling out nor able to reach her bell rope or so much as a shoe to make a noise with, and wake us in the next room." Doctor Bartlett diagnosed a broken hip. She was eighty-three or eighty-four. By mid-September her mind had become clouded. "Her memory is much broken, and she confounds things sadly," Emerson wrote William.[1]

It was a melancholy autumn as Emerson went back to working on the memorial volume for Fuller. He began to prepare for the coming lecture season, and he opened a new notebook for "The Conduct of Life" series. He had given many of the lectures in Pittsburgh the previous winter, but the series was incomplete. His main occupation during the fall of 1851 was working up the long essay "Fate," with which he began "The Conduct of Life" lectures in Boston and which comes first in the book of that name published in 1860.

"Fate" is not only the anchor of the series and the volume, it is one of Emerson's great essays, an important rethinking of major issues and themes reaching back at least to *Nature* and "Compensation." "Fate" is Emerson's last full exploration of the meaning of nature and of its processes. The essay has been read as signaling a change of heart, as Emerson's turning away from the bold defiance of his early work to an acquiescence in the standing order, in the world as it is. But he wrote the essay in the urgent shadow of the Fugitive Slave Act and by the light of his own newly increased political activity. "Fate" is, despite its title, a vigorous affirmation of freedom, more effective than earlier statements because it does not dismiss the power of circumstance, determinism, materialism, experience, Calvinism, and evil, and because Emerson now had a much subtler grasp of the interrelation of fate and freedom, involving processes vastly more complex than that of simple compensation.

500

The essay begins gently by deprecating our interest in such abstractions as "the spirit of the times" and by turning our attention instead to the "practical question of the conduct of life. How shall I live?" In the first place, says Emerson, there is something fixed and immovable that we might as well call fate and might as well accept. "Great men, great nations, have not been boasters or buffoons," he insists, "but perceivers of the terror of life." In this essay Emerson concedes at last the dignity of those American Calvinists who "felt that the weight of the universe held them down to their place." Instead of skipping over the dark and unpleasant side of life, Emerson now dwells on it at length. He cites the cold that, "inconsiderate of persons, tingles your blood, benumbs your feet, freezes a man like an apple." Providence is not benevolence. "The habit of snake and spider, the snap of the tiger and other leapers and bloody jumpers, the crackle of the bones of his prey in the coil of the anaconda,—these are in the system, and our habits are like theirs."[2]

Emerson cites earthquakes, shocks from comets, volcanic eruptions, and cholera; he looks beneath the ocean where "the forms of the shark, the *labrus,* the jaw of the sea-wolf paved with crushing teeth, the weapons of the grampus, and other warriors hidden in the sea, are hints of the ferocity of nature." Emerson drives on, page after page, insisting on the crippling power of circumstance and on the sinister ability of statistics to foretell the number and location of the most appalling crimes. Nature, from this point of view, is not only "red in tooth and claw," it is "what you may do." The book of nature is now the book of fate. Fate embraces limitations and the unbreakable laws of nature; it endorses Calvinist and Hindu conceptions of the permanent fixedness of all things. Fate is the reality of rock bottom, "cropping out in our planted gardens of the core of the world." Emerson nails it to our attention by every means at his disposal, including a dream that vividly recalls the death of Fuller:

> I seemed in the height of the tempest to see men overboard struggling in the waves, and driven about here and there. They glanced intelligently at each other, but it was little they could do for one another. 'Twas much if each could keep afloat alone. Well, they had a right to their eye-beams, and all the rest was Fate.[3]

"Fate" is Emerson's long deferred, full-dress confrontation with the dark side of life, with evil, with indifference, with violence and savagery, with entropy and cold obstruction and rot. But even though he spends half the essay on the subject of evil, giving it full weight and expression, he does not accept it as the last word. Earlier essays such as "The Poet" might begin with a sentence or two deprecating false views. Now his method is different. Now he lets half the essay go by before turning the tables. Finally he says, "Even limitation has its limits. In its last and loftiest ascension, insight itself, and the freedom of the will is one of [Fate's] obedient members." There is fate, but there is also freedom. We must accept the existence of freedom just as we accept that of fate. In a seeming paradox he later explores in detail Emerson insists that freedom is necessary. We can only lead moral lives if we can choose. We can only choose if we are free to do so. "Choosing or acting in the soul is freedom." What is more interesting, freedom is also associated with thought and insight. "So far as a man thinks, he is free," he says. Indeed freedom comes from thought. "Intellect annuls Fate," he says. Emerson reaches back to college days and to the language of the Scottish Enlightenment to affirm the connection between freedom and that part of the human mind able to make choices based on knowledge. "If thought makes free," he says, "so does the moral sentiment."[4]

Most importantly and most characteristically Emerson now associates freedom with power, and he places the two of them in opposition to fate. "There can be no driving force," he says, "except through the conversion of the man into his will . . . The one serious and formidable thing in nature is a will."[5]

At this point "Fate" takes its most interesting and original turn. Emerson asks whether "seeing these two things, fate and power, we are permitted to believe in unity?" He adds pointedly, "The bulk of mankind believe in two gods." Emerson rejects this middlebrow Manichaeism; his real answer comes as he describes the complex interplay of opposites. He describes a world in which fate opposes power, nature opposes thought, determinism opposes freedom, circumstances oppose will. Emerson would once have explained the relation between fate and freedom by the relatively crude notion of displacement—"compensation" in his earlier terminology—or correspondence, the idea that everything in the world corresponds to something in the mind, or even by the idea of metamorphosis, the idea that since all things are at bottom the same thing, apparent differences are a matter only of changing external forms.[6]

But now he sees a more complex web of relationships. "Relation and connection are not somewhere and sometime but everywhere and always," he says. "Fate follows and limits power, power attends and antagonizes fate."

Further, "a man must thank his defects, and stand in some terror of his talents. A transcendent talent draws so largely on his forces as to lame him." Both his journal and his essays are now full of images of oppositional tension, images of a seesaw, of centrifugal versus centripetal force, of the pendulum. He took particular delight in the discovery of Robert Hook that the way to build any kind of stable arch was to invert a catenary, a catenary being "the curve of a flexible chain hanging freely from two points of suspension." Only that which is allowed to be completely flexible will form the exact pattern for a stable construction of the same shape made of rigid materials.[7]

Emerson draws up two columns. In one there are fate, nature, determinism, and circumstance. In the second column stand power, thought, freedom, and will. The two columns relate in a process Emerson is now willing to call "history." "History," he says, "is the action and reaction of these two, Nature and Thought." It is, he says, like "two boys pushing each other on the curbstone of the pavement." But there is not only action and reaction, stroke and recoil. There is unity and there is advance. The unity lies in the fact that the entire second column—power, thought, freedom, and will—is just as necessary, as *fated,* as the first column. This is the "beautiful necessity," the real order of nature, the ultimate status quo, the conviction that nature bats last. The possibility of progress, amelioration, reform, and struggle arises from the fact that this unity is not static but in some rough Hegelian way dialectical, that is to say, oppositional *and* advancing at the same time. For Emerson is at last convinced that the universe can be understood as "advance out of fate into freedom." Merely to say "Hegelian" or "dialectical" is finally misleading too, since the main force of the essay is not so much a theory of history as a platform for present action. Emerson began by asking, "How should I lead my life?" The answer given by the essay "Fate" is "Pursue freedom." Freedom is as much the "beautiful necessity" as is the standing order.[8]

It is significant that the best summary of "Fate" is that contained in Emerson's second address on the Fugitive Slave Act, an address delivered in New York three years later. In this talk Emerson says: "There are two forces in Nature, by whose antagonism we exist; the power of Fate, Fortune, the laws of the world or however else we choose to phrase it, the material necessities on the one hand,—and Will and Duty and Freedom on the other." There can be no doubt about which hand he chooses: "The world exists, as I understand it, to teach the science of liberty."[9]

Fame

87. My Platoon

ONLY A FRACTION OF THE ACTIVITY IN EMERSON'S LIFE DURING the early 1850s involved his creative work. During January and February 1852 he gave "The Conduct of Life" lectures in Boston and New York. The *Memoirs of Margaret Fuller Ossoli* appeared early in February and the book was an immediate success. A second printing came out by the end of the month. Emerson's domestic establishment had now grown to include seven servants. William ventured to suggest that he might live more modestly. Emerson's brisk reply makes it clear that something besides his own wishes was responsible. Lidian was unwell most of the time. Even so, he told William, he *was* about to shrink the household. Church played less and less of a role in his life. In April Emerson wrote a note expressly stating that he no longer was a member of the First Church in Concord. He gave no reason, but his declaration may have had to do with the church's stand, or lack of one, on slavery.[1]

In May 1852 the famous Hungarian revolutionary Lajos Kossuth came to Concord. Kossuth, now fifty-one, had become the governor of Hungary during its brief moment of independence in 1848. In 1849 the Hungarian republic was crushed by Russian and Austrian armies after a conference between Emperor Franz Joseph and Czar Nicolas I at which they declared that the "interest of all European States demanded armed interference in Hungary." In his public welcome Emerson called Kossuth "the foremost soldier of freedom in this age" and reminded him "that everything great and excellent in the world is in minorities." Emerson addressed Kossuth as "the man of Freedom" and told him "you are also the man of Fate."[2]

Emerson's reading this year was mainly in three areas: aesthetics, England, and America as compared with England. He had been reading in German aesthetics during his western lecture tour. Now, in January of 1852, he read Edward Garbet's helpfully titled *Rudimentary Treatise on the Principles of Design in Architecture as Deducible from Nature and Exemplified in the Works of the Greeks and Gothic Architects* (1850). Garbet was a student of Ruskin's, whose *Seven Lamps of Architecture* and *The Stones of Venice* Emerson already knew. He had recently read the latter. By July 1852 he was reading William Gilpin's *Observations . . . on the Highlands of Scotland* and his *Observations . . . on the Western Islands*. In April of 1852 Emerson passed on to Carlyle the best of his American reading on Indians and the West. For the former he recommended Alexander Henry's *Travels in Canada* and the works of George Catlin. For the West he preferred F. A. Michaux's *Voyage à l'ouest des Monts Alleghanys* and John S. Fremont's *Narrative of the Exploring Expedition to the Rocky Mountains* (1845). He mentions Bayard Taylor's *Eldorado* (1850) and Parkman's *The Oregon Trail* (1847). He was also reading Jean Bernard Bossu's *Nouveaux voyages aux Indes occidentals*. As always he extracted concrete details from his reading. "The Indians make a split in a young tree and introduce a sharpened stone ax or hatchet head into the split. As the tree grows it forms a strong and inseparable handle to the weapon." He read Harriet Beecher Stowe's *Uncle Tom's Cabin* and noted with admiration that "it is read equally in the parlor and the kitchen and the nursery of every house."[3]

Emerson's only recorded contact with the writings of Karl Marx occurred this year. Emerson read a signed piece by Marx in the *New York Tribune* for March 22, 1853, called "Forced Emigration." It is an impassioned, detailed, prophetic piece. Marx begins by showing how in older societies the lack of productive capacity obliged society to limit population. But the "application of science to material production" has created a new situation in which increased productive power has led landlords and mill owners to seek to limit population. As machinery improves, fewer workers are needed. Anything more than the basic minimum work force now constituted a drain on profits. Marx describes how workers concentrated in the large manufacturing cities—the industrial proletariat—are unable to emigrate by themselves and are unlikely to be helped by the middle class. Marx asks:

> Who will prevent them from going a step further and appropriating these forces, to which they have been appropriated before? Where will be the power of resisting them? Nowhere! . . . The modern changes in the art of production have . . . expropriated the Scotch clansman, the Irish cottier and tenant, the English yeoman, the hand-loom weaver, numberless handicrafts, whole generations of factory children and women; they will expropriate, in due time, the landlord and the cotton lord.[4]

This is the gist of the article from which Emerson extracted the following: "The classes and races, too weak to master the new conditions of life, must give way." Emerson's grasp of the inevitable nature of social change and his sympathy with the Chartists, the laboring classes of England, made him receptive to Marx's reasoning, which is strongly echoed in the chapter "Wealth" in *English Traits*. After Arkwright had improved the spinning jenny so that one man could do the work of a hundred, other machines were similarly improved. Emerson outlines the results. "But the men would sometimes strike for wages and combine against the masters, and, about 1829–30, much fear was felt lest the trade would be drawn away by these interruptions and the emigration of the spinners to Belgium and the United States." What the mill owners wanted was a completely automated spinning machine. "At the solicitation of the masters, after a mob and riot at Staley Bridge, Mr. Roberts of Manchester undertook to create this peaceful fellow, instead of the quarrelsome fellow God had made. After a few trials, he succeeded and in 1830 procured a patent for his self-acting mule: a creation, the delight of mill owners, and 'destined,' they said, 'to restore order among the industrious classes,' a machine requiring only a child's hand to piece the broken yarns. As Arkwright had destroyed domestic spinning, so Roberts destroyed the factory spinner."[5]

The difference between Emerson and Marx is not in their assessment of modern industrial conditions, not in their grasp of the dynamics of industrial production, and not in their understanding of the alienation of the individual under the conditions of modern production but in the proposed remedy.

Four years had passed since Emerson's return from England. He had intended to make a book out of his trip, and now, in 1852, he began seriously to assemble notes. He supplemented and tested his personal experiences with heavy doses of reading about England. He read the eight-volume *Pictorial History of England* by George L. Craik and Charles MacFarlane (London, 1841–1849). He read Edward Davies's *Mythology and Rites of the British Druids* for background on the England of Stonehenge, and he read the beautiful illustrated travelogues of the great theorist of the picturesque, William Gilpin. He read Benjamin Thorpe's three-volume *Northern Mythology* (London, 1851–1852) to fill out his already extensive knowledge of the saga literature, the old Scandinavian and Icelandic literature that underlies Anglo-Saxon. He read Thomas Fuller and William Camden. He read Kemble's *The Saxons in England*. For modern England he read Bristed's *Five Years in an English University,* Taylor's *Life and Times of Peel,* Medwin's *Life of Shelley,* Jesse's *George Selwyn and His Contemporaries,* and the writings of Sheridan, Cobbett, and Brougham.[6]

Friendships were increasingly important to Emerson now. In October 1851 the rift between Emerson and Thoreau had begun to heal. In late October they had a long talk, stating "over again, to sadness, almost, the eternal loneliness." Even as they acknowledged "how insular and pathetically solitary are all the people we know" and the impossibility of telling "what we think of each other when we bow in the street," the bond between them was at least tacitly reacknowledged. All through 1852 Emerson resumed his old habit of noting Thoreau's sayings and doings in his journal. It was in midsummer of 1852 that Emerson made his most personal and most generous comment ever about his young friend, the comment about Thoreau giving him back in flesh and blood his own ethics and about Thoreau's being "far more real, and daily practically obeying them, than I."[7]

Channing too was newly valuable to Emerson, who said in June 1852 that Ellery "is grown an accomplished Professor of Walking, and leads like an Indian." Emerson was amused that since Channing had come to know Thoreau, Channing "carries a little pocketbook in his breast pocket in which he affects to write down the name of each new plant or the first day on which he finds the flower." Emerson also drew closer to Theodore Parker during the early 1850s. They were newly agreed in their active opposition to the Fugitive Slave Act. Parker dedicated a volume called *Ten Sermons* to Emerson, and Emerson replied, gracefully deflecting the dedication by noting Parker's "graceful air of laying on others your own untransferable laurels."[8]

Emerson also cultivated new friends made during his English trip. There was William Allingham, the Irish poet now remembered for "Up the airy mountain, / Down the rushy glen." Allingham put a poem called "The Pilot's Daughter" at the beginning of a volume because Emerson had liked it. There was Arthur Helps, privy secretary to Lord Morpeth and future editor for Queen Victoria and her husband Albert. Emerson had read Helps's *Conquerors of the New World and Their Bondmen* as well as his *Friends in Council;* the latter is a series of books of dialogues on general subjects. Emerson's reading of Helps's "A Letter on Uncle Tom's Cabin" seems to have led him to the novel. There was Arthur Hugh Clough, Emerson's friend at Oxford and his companion in France, who, after much correspondence, came to Cambridge, Massachusetts, in March 1853 to try his luck in America.[9]

Emerson took and gave, both generously. From Ainsworth Spofford, a new friend and correspondent living in Cincinnati, later Librarian of Congress, Emerson got important material for his Fugitive Slave Act speeches. Spofford's pamphlet "The Higher Law Tried by Reason and Authority" deserves to be better known—for its clear argument that "no law subversive of natural right has any binding obligation," for its equally clear call for civil disobedience, and for its explicit rejection of the argument that one should work within the system to repeal a bad law. This will not do, says Spofford, as he outlines "the *actual* method in which the world gets rid of its unrighteous laws; first they are disobeyed and then repealed; first the people have thrown them aside, and then the legislatures have abrogated them." Emerson told Spofford that he was "deeply indebted" to him and had in his Fugitive Slave Act speech "only succeeded I believe in reproducing yours."[10]

In May 1852 Emerson met Delia Bacon of Tallmadge, Ohio. She had been brought up and educated in Hartford, had written a book, *Tales of the Puritans* (1831), and had become a popular lecturer on history and literature. She was now convinced that the plays attributed to Shakespeare were the work of a syndicate of writers, headed by Bacon, Raleigh, and Spenser, who wrote the plays in order to set forth a liberal political philosophy they could not present openly. She made an impression of "radiant enthusiasm." Emerson and later Hawthorne tried to help her get her subversive argument into print. Whether Emerson was fully persuaded by her argument does not appear, but he did quote with approval her comment, "You see yourself how much this idea of the authorship controls our appreciation of the works themselves." After many ups and downs, which included Emerson's losing a part of her manuscript, her *Philosophy of the Plays of Shakespeare Unfolded* finally reached print in England in April 1857.[11]

Some of the new friends were essentially disciples who had discovered themselves in reading Emerson. His books brought him in very little money, but they did have a powerful effect on some young people. John Albee, who came to visit Emerson in May 1852 and who later wrote a reminiscence, is typical. Albee had gone into a bookshop and opened *Representative Men*. He read a few pages, "becoming more and more agitated, until I could read no more there. . . . A complete revolution was opened in those few pages, and I was no longer the same being that had entered the shop." Albee felt that the book had been written for him. He wrote Emerson, who responded warmly and invited the young man to come to Concord and talk.[12]

Moncure Conway was another young convert. Born in Stafford County, Virginia, to a slave-owning father, his spiritual crisis came when he was fifteen: "I was listless and unhappy. I had begun to feel a repugnance to the idea of being a country lawyer, and was interested only in literature." One day he took his old flintlock and a copy of *Blackwoods Magazine* and went outside. When he opened the magazine, his eye fell at once on a passage from Emerson's "History," beginning, "It is remarkable that involuntarily we always read as superior beings," and ending, "All that Shakespeare says of the king, yonder slip of a boy that reads in the corner feels to be true of him." Suddenly Conway wished to know, "What self was this?" Conway could never say precisely what it was that so moved him, but he clearly experienced a revelation, a "glimpse of a vault beyond the familiar sky." Conway turned to a serious reading of Emerson, decided to study for the ministry, and came to Harvard Divinity School in 1853 at the age of twenty-one. He wrote Emerson, who responded heartily, and so began a lifelong friendship. Conway became a minister, serving in Washington, D.C., then in Cincinnati, where he founded a new *Dial* in honor of the old one. Eventually he took a church in London. He was an active abolitionist, a southern one, and is remembered for a major life of Thomas Paine and an important edition of his works.[13]

The most interesting of the new friends of the early 1850s was the sculptor Horatio Greenough. Born in Boston, Greenough was two years younger than Emerson. In 1825 he had become the first American sculptor to settle in Florence. In 1851 Greenough returned to America, to Newport, Rhode Island. The next year he wrote Emerson that he wished to talk with him about his ideas of the importance of functionalism in art and architecture. "Here is my theory of structure," he wrote Emerson. "An emphasis of features proportioned to their *gradated* importance in function . . . the entire and immediate banishment of all make-shift and make-believe." Emerson responded to the rough energy of Greenough's stonecutter prose, welcoming Greenough's letter as a "beam of sunlight." Greenough got Emerson to help him with a book he was writing. It was called *The Travels, Observations, and Experience of a Yankee Stonecutter,* and it appeared in 1852 under the pseudonym Horace Bender. Emerson carefully worked over the book twice for style. He also tried to set Greenough straight on abolition, without success. The book was indeed printed, but most of the edition was evidently lost or destroyed; only one copy survived. It is a trenchant, surprising book, with the best discussion of obelisks ever written: "It says one word . . . it says Here!"[14]

Emerson turned forty-nine this year. The days still brought him their gifts, but increasingly they also took them away. During the summer of 1852 Emerson's mother was confined to a new gadget called a wheelchair, of which there were only one or two in Boston. Hawthorne's sister Louisa was drowned in July when the *Henry Clay* burned in the Hudson River. On October 24 Daniel Webster died at his home in Marshfield, Massachusetts. Emerson could not forgive Webster for his stand on the Fugitive Slave Act, but with a gathering sense of the tragedy that would reach act five in the Civil War, Emerson wrote a little journal obituary for Webster that sounds like Antony over the body of Brutus. Emerson had been in Plymouth the day Webster died. He stood on the beach and looked across the hazy water: "The seas, the rocks, the woods, gave no sign that America and the world had lost the completest man." Then in December Greenough came down with a "brain fever" and was confined to McLean's Asylum in Somerville, where he soon died.[15]

Emerson lived by his observation that "there is properly no history, only biography." When he stopped to make little lists of the great moments in his life, what he usually jotted down were lists of names. This year he listed in his "platoon" "my brothers, and Everett, and Caroline, and Margaret, and Elizabeth, and Jones Very, and Sam Ward, and Henry Thoreau, and Alcott, and Channing." The list changed from time to time, but usually people rather than events or experiences or books marked the epochs of Emerson's life as he thought of it. He yearned for some social grouping in which "each shall be responsible for the weal of the other," some community into which "we will weave our repulsive Saxon individualism." But with those to whom he felt closest, such association never worked. "I cannot coax my mates into clubs," he wrote in his journal. "Ah solidarity! Ah Comitatus! Ah Club!"[16]

88. *Country Walking and the Sea*

EMERSON WAS FIFTY IN 1853. HE WAS ACUTELY AWARE NOW OF external losses and inner subsidence, of fresh limitations and flagging energies. He told Carlyle that he wrote "much less than formerly." He told Furness that he thought of leaving the lyceum to the younger lecturers, and he told his daughter Ellen—who was now fourteen and just going to boarding school, "I seldom write verses." He still enjoyed being out of doors, but he had little interest in solitary withdrawal. "It is pleasant to go to the woods in good company," he wrote, "but who dare go to the woods [alone] to poverty, and necessity, and living alone, or with sick, sour, and dependent people, and to ask nothing and expect nothing further then to match the solitude you find, with the solitude you bring—desart with desart?"[1]

On June 9, 1853, Caroline Sturgis Tappan's sister Susan committed suicide, provoking one of the gloomiest letters Emerson ever wrote. "Friends are few," he wrote Caroline. "Thoughts are few, facts few—only one: one only fact, now tragically, now tenderly, now exultingly illustrated in sky, in earth, in men and women, Fate, Fate." With bitter pessimism he wondered if it was not now the turn of fatalism, "now that stoicism and Christianity have for two millenniums preached liberty." In his effort to share Caroline's grief and dismay, Emerson held out what he called an "intelligent fatalism": "All the great world call their thought fatalism, or concede that ninety-nine parts are nature and one part power." Yet even in the face of suicide, that most irrefutable argument against self-reliance, Emerson could not entirely close the door, not even for consolatory purposes. This letter represents the farthest swing of Emerson's pendulum away from his belief in growth, change, and freedom toward a fatal determinism. It must be taken seriously, even if it is in a letter of condolence and not in a public lecture. Yet even here he does not abandon freedom and self-reliance; what he does is recalculate and drastically reduce the odds operating in their favor.[2]

Emerson still enjoyed his walks with Ellery Channing. Henry Thoreau could at times be wearisome, with his captious paradoxes and general contentiousness, but Ellery was entertaining, even though he was filled to his back teeth with crotchets. Ellery was once officially listed in a Concord census as a "do-nothing." Of one landscape he complained that it had too many leaves, each one much like all the others and all of them "apt to be agitated by east wind." He had a dog named Professor who seemed to have a sense of humor and who certainly knew more about nature than his master: "The dog tastes, snuffs, rubs, feels, tries everything, everywhere, through miles of bush, brush, grass, water, mud, lilies, mountain and sky." Emerson, Channing, and Professor visited Conantum, a section of Concord, "where we found sassafras, bass, cornel, viburnum, ash, oak, and slippery elm in close vicinity." They took a long walk out by Bedford, and in one of his endless schemes to funnel money with dignity to his friends Emerson proposed that Channing work up, out of his experiences and Emerson's journals, a book to be called *Concord Walking*.[3]

William Emerson wrote from New York, proposing a walking trip to Cape Cod, which he thought would do his brother good. They went during the first week in September. Emerson found it a bleak place. "The starknakedness of the country could not be exaggerated," he said. The keeper of the Nauset light told him that "he found obstinate resistance on Cape Cod to the project of building a light house on this coast, as it would injure the wrecking business." Emerson thought the country looked like "one of the Newfoundland banks just emerged, a huge tract of sand half-covered with poverty grass and beach grass, and for trees abele [white poplar] and locust and plantations of pitchpine." When the wind blew, "a large part of the real estate was freely moving back and forth in the air." The back side of the Cape seemed composed entirely of "salt dust, gravel, and fishbones." He "fancied the people were only waiting for the railroad to reach them in order to evacuate the country."[4]

Recent travels had given Emerson a heightened awareness of the sea, which figures increasingly in his journal and letters. One Saturday in April 1852 he had walked across the frozen St. Lawrence at Montreal. A few days later "the ice *shoved,* as they call it." He stood on a quay and saw acres and acres of ice rolling swiftly downstream. "Presently my road came floating down with the rest, the well beaten black straight road I had traversed. Parts of it were making mad somersaults and revolutions like porpoises in the water." A year later he was writing Carlyle about the Mississippi, describing "the powers of the river, the insatiable craving for nations of men to reap and cure its harvests, the conditions it imposes, for it yields to no engineering." At Nahant, a tiny rocky peninsula on the north side of Boston

Harbor, Emerson watched "the eternal play of the sea" and thought it seemed "the anti-clock, or destroyer of the memory of time." The sea was everywhere in the *Heimskringla,* which Emerson was reading again and which he called "the *Iliad* and *Odyssey* of English History." The sea cropped up strikingly in Davies's book on the druids: "The heavy blue chain [of the sea] dids't thou o just man endure." And he noted that Alcuin, the Anglo-Saxon scholar and contemporary of Charlemagne, called the sea "the road of the bold, the frontier of the land; the hostelry of the rivers; and the source of the rains."[5]

On June 14, 1853, Emerson made a visit to the East Boston shipyard of Donald McKay to see the largest ship in the world, the majestic new clipper *Great Republic.* She was eighty feet longer than any of McKay's previous ships and she was twice as heavy. Her main yard was 120 feet long; her topmast skysail yard 40 feet long. Her main standing rigging was made of twelve-and-a-half-inch four-stranded Russian hemp. Even in the shipyard *Great Republic* was arrestingly beautiful, a grand example of Greenough's ideas about form following function.[6]

Though Emerson wrote little poetry now, he was moved this year to write a quatrain based on Alcuin's that starts, "The sea is the road of the bold," and another, about the Vikings, drawn from his reading in Thierry's *Norman Conquest:*

> The gale that wrecked you on the sand
> It helped my rowers to row
> The storm is my best galley hand
> And drives me where I go.[7]

89. English Traits

EMERSON'S MOTHER DIED ON NOVEMBER 16, 1853. DR. BART-
lett had seen her death coming, but neither Lidian nor her husband had
believed him, and so Emerson was out of town when it happened. "After
being with her so long," he told an old family friend, "I feel as if I might
have been present at the moment of her departure." Born in 1768, Ruth
Haskins Emerson had "lived through the whole history of this country,"
as Emerson observed to his brother. She had always been there. He told
Carlyle, "In my journeyings lately, when I think of home, the heart is taken
out."[1]

Emerson was caught up in a new lecture season. He gave a highly
successful series in Philadelphia, then went west again. He was using "The
Conduct of Life" lectures as well as lectures on America, England, and
France, the latter material being related to his "English Traits" project. In
a new lecture, "Poetry," this year (a lecture that would eventually grow into
his 1872 essay "Poetry and Imagination," a work nearly as long as *Nature*),
he reformulated his view of poetry as symbolic: "The value of a trope is that
the hearer is one, and indeed Nature itself is a vast trope, and all particular
natures are tropes." In the final version of the essay he quotes William Blake
enthusiastically and at length:

> He who does not imagine in stronger and better lineaments and in
> stronger and better light than his perishing mortal eye can see, does
> not imagine at all. . . . I question not my corporeal eye any more than
> I would question a window concerning a sight. I look through it, and
> not with it.

He emphasizes the role of poetry in making us understand the identity
philosophy, and his interest in myth has become an interest in mythogenetic
power:

> Tis easy to repaint the mythology of the Greeks . . . but to point out
> where the same creative force is now working in our own houses and

public assemblies; to connect the vivid energies acting at this hour in New York and Chicago and San Francisco with universal symbols requires a subtle and commanding thought.[2]

Another new lecture this year proved to be a dead end. Indeed, the full text of "France or Urbanity" has not been published yet. Emerson had once declared himself not wise enough for a national criticism. He still was not, but in the mid-1850s, when much of his time was spent in antislavery activities and on his book on England, Emerson read several books on race and nationality. These included Robert Knox, *The Races of Men*. He was reluctant to abandon his universal humanism and slow to accept the idea that race and nationality are major factors in human development. Some of his weakest and least enduring writing is on this set of issues. The subject brought out a snide, Gibbonian tone. The French, he wrote, "excell all other nations in dress, in cooking, in dancing and in police." He hated the "aggressive and importunate" attitude of the French that "France lies in light" and that "all that is not French is barbarous." He observed, "They have carried the common pride of nationality one step further than most people, in their proverb that the Good God belongs to their tribe. Le bon Dieu est français."[3]

In March 1854 Emerson delivered the second of his Fugitive Slave Act speeches, this one in New York. That occasion and the Anthony Burns affair in Boston in May 1854 shook him to write bluntly of the United States Constitution: "The Fathers made the fatal blunder in agreeing to this false basis of representation [to count only 3/5 of the slaves in reckoning population for congressional representation] and to this criminal complicity of restoring fugitive slaves."[4]

He was still reading Stallo. "The age is marked by this wondrous nature-philosophy," Emerson wrote in May 1854. He summarized Stallo's account of Schelling as a demonstration of the "identity of man's mind with nature's, for he is a part of nature." He also got from Stallo the idea that "all difference is quantitative," that is, there are no differences in kind, only in degree. Even at a practical level he hungered for unity: "If Minerva offered me a gift and an option, I would say give me continuity. I am tired of scraps."[5]

The main intellectual work of 1854 and 1855 for Emerson was to get his English scraps into some sort of continuous form. *English Traits* is Emerson's least characteristic book. Instead of treating a general human problem or quality, it treats a particular people and a particular place. *English*

Traits is closer to de Staël's *Germany* or de Tocqueville's *On America* than to Montaigne's or Bacon's or Plutarch's essays. To do the book at all meant that Emerson had to abandon his broad Erasmian humanism and deal extensively with current events, social surfaces, statistics, newspapers, and names. This concrete side of the book is also its great strength and attraction, but it obliged Emerson to go out on the thin ice of current assumptions about racial and national character. Working on the book also had a displacing effect on Emerson, taking him out of his own world once more. It is interesting to note that most of the tension and mutual disapproval between Emerson and Thoreau came while Emerson was working on *English Traits* and Thoreau was working on the final drafts of *Walden*. Originally Emerson seems to have conceived the book as a running comparison between England and America. This structure was dropped, but the comparative impulse is still strong in the finished book. *English Traits* is a final reckoning with England, an effort to make good on "The American Scholar." *English Traits* is in praise of England, but it is a valediction. By isolating and describing English life, Emerson finally succeeded in separating it from American life.

A modern English writer has called *English Traits* a better commentary on England than all the subsequent ones by outsiders whether American or European. The beginning and the end draw explicitly on Emerson's own visits and give the whole the shape of an excursion. Chapter 3 is Emerson's most direct, most level-headed statement about race. "Men gladly hear of the power of race or blood," he writes with gentle irony. "Everybody likes to know that his advantages cannot be attributed to air, soil, sea, or to local wealth . . . nor to fortune, but to superior brain, as it makes the praise more personal to him." But while Emerson will concede the importance we actually give to race, he is much less sure what importance we really should give it. He observes that "whilst race works immortally to keep its own, it is resisted by other forces." Among these are civilization, religion, trades and professions, "personal liberty, plenty of food, good ale and mutton, open market or good wages for every kind of labor." Emerson is not finally persuaded by racial determinism: "The fixity or inconvertibleness of races as we see them, is a weak argument for the eternity of these frail boundaries."[6]

Emerson's English prize self-sufficiency, they honor the individual, they worship common sense: "An Englishman must be treated with sincerity and reality; with muffins, and not the promise of muffins." In literature Emerson admires the English power of generalizing. He quotes Bacon's "Nature is commanded by obeying her" and Spenser's "Soul is form and doth the body make." The process of generalizing is one of the themes of *English Traits.* For all his tolerance of the Englishman's "coarse strength and rude exercise," his "invincible stoutness," his proclivity for "butcher's meat and sound sleep," the qualities Emerson most admires are less tangible. In a wonderful image he describes Milton as "the stair or high table-land to let down the English genius from the summits of Shakespeare." Wordsworth's "Immortality Ode" is, he says, "the high water mark which the intellect has reached in this age." England, he concludes, "is the land of patriots, martyrs, sages, and bards, and if the ocean out of which it emerged should wash it away, it will be remembered as an island famous for immortal laws, for the announcements of original right which make the stone tables of liberty."[7]

This is Emerson's praise of England, but the book as a whole lacks this adulatory tone. Indeed what makes the book is its tart, smart-alecky satire. As in *Representative Men* Emerson ended each chapter with a list of the subject's shortcomings, so every chapter in *English Traits* is alive to both sides. He thought England had already reached its high point: "The English interest us a little less within a few years." His view of English history is dark comedy. "These Norsemen," Emerson says in the chapter "Race," "are excellent persons in the main, with good sense, steadiness, wise speech, and prompt action. But they have a singular turn for homicide; their chief end of man is to murder, or to be murdered." Of the Norman conquest he writes: "Twenty thousand thieves landed at Hastings. These founders of the House of Lords were greedy and ferocious dragoons, sons of greedy and ferocious pirates." The spirit of filiopietism is not in Emerson. His portrait of the patron saint of England is worthy of Mark Twain:

> George of Cappodocia, born at Epiphania in Cilicia, was a low parasite, who got a lucrative contract to supply the army with bacon. A rogue and informer, he got rich, and was forced to run from justice. He saved his money, embraced Arianism, collected a library, and got promoted by a faction to the episcopal throne of Alexandria. When Julian came, A.D. 361, George was dragged to prison, the prison was burst open by the mob, and George was lynched, as he deserved. And this precious knave became in good time Saint George of England, patron of chivalry, emblem of victory and civility, and the pride of the best blood of the modern world.[8]

To show his impartiality Emerson added that the New World had no better luck. He lamented "that broad America must wear the name of a thief . . . Amerigo Vespucci, the pickle-dealer at Seville, who went out, in 1499, a subaltern with Hojeda, and whose highest naval rank was boatswain's mate in an expedition that never sailed." "Thus nobody can throw stones," he concludes. "We are equally badly off in our founders; and the false pickle-dealer is an offset to the false bacon-seller."[9]

In August of 1854 the East Coast was in the grip of a severe drought that, Emerson wrote his daughter, "grows more extreme every minute; not a cloud as big as your finger in the sky and every day the sirocco blows." On August 9 *Walden* was published. Emerson had written an English publisher, Richard Bentley, in March to recommend the book. Thoreau is "a man of genius and writes always with force, and sometimes with wonderful depth and beauty." Now Emerson wrote another overseas correspondent to say that "all American kind are delighted with *Walden* . . . it is cheerful, sparkling, readable, with all kinds of merit, and rising sometimes to very great heights." Emerson's enthusiasm is laced by amusement born of long acquaintance: "We account Henry the undoubted King of all American lions." He added that the Stoic Thoreau, usually so indifferent to the opinions of others, was "walking up and down Concord, firm-looking, but in a tremble of great expectation."

Emerson gave the commencement address at Williams College this year. The other notable production of this August was in Cambridge, where the young people were busy with a one-act comic opera called *Il Pesciaballo*—the Fishball—written by James Russell Lowell and Francis James Child, the ballad scholar. *Il Pesciaballo* is the direct ancestor of the modern ballad "One Meat Ball" ("You gets no bread with one meat ball").[10]

90. Fame

By the mid-1850s Emerson was dangerously famous. His reputation had been pretty much local through the 1830s. His 1836 book, *Nature*, was not widely reviewed, but the storm over the "Divinity School Address" two years later brought him general attention and set a pattern for what was to follow: strong objections and attacks from one side and personal, witness-bearing praise—almost adulation—from another. His fame grew rapidly during the 1840s, through lecturing and the publication of two volumes of essays, *The Dial*, and the 1847 volume *Poems*. His earliest English notice had come in 1839, and in 1840 Richard Monckton Milnes wrote an influential article in the *London and Westminster Review*. In 1842 Dickens discussed Emerson and transcendentalism in his widely read *American Notes*. New York was now paying attention; notices by Walter Whitman, Edgar A. Poe, Rufus Griswold, and William Cullen Bryant appeared in 1842. By 1845 William Gilmore Simms was writing about Emerson in the *Southern and Western Literary Messenger* and Emerson was beginning to have a reputation in France. The Polish poet Adam Mickiewicz, who was at the time studying in Paris, was apparently the first person in France to become enthusiastic about the work of the new American writer. In 1844 a notice by Philarete Chasles called Emerson "the most original man produced by the United States up to this day." Edgar Quinet, an important French writer, was deeply involved with Emerson's work by 1845, calling it "the most idealistic of the age." Notices by the Comtesse d'Agoult and Emile Montegut followed in 1846 and 1847.[1]

Emerson's trip to England in 1847 and 1848 brought him in touch with most of literary England. His fame spread even more quickly in the United States after his English success. By 1849 an English journal could refer to the "Emerson mania." In 1850 Theodore Parker wrote a fifty-five-page piece on Emerson; it was the most thoughtful commentary to date. Hawthorne had included Emerson in a tale called "The Hall of Fantasy" in 1843; Emerson is mentioned in *Mosses from an Old Manse* and he forms part of the hero's reading in *The Blithedale Romance*. Poe picked a quarrel with

Emerson. Melville's *Mardi* and *Moby Dick* were both reviewed in Emersonian contexts.[2]

By the 1850s Emerson was a conspicuous part of the literary landscape. He got more English notices than any other American. By 1854 644 review notices of Emerson's work had appeared. This figure does not include newspaper accounts of his lectures, which, if counted, would probably triple or quadruple the number. Everywhere he went the papers reported his lectures. This exposure became a serious problem for Emerson, since he expected to use a lecture over and over and it became stale goods if accurately reported in papers of any great circulation. He cajoled and pleaded with editors not to print verbatim transcripts.[3]

One measure of Emerson's fame was the amount of fun poked at him. It is difficult to satirize a nobody. There was a slender but steady stream of early satire, including a couplet by Oliver Wendell Holmes in 1844, the celebrated portrait of Emerson as a "Plotinus-Montaigne" in James Russell Lowell's *Fable for Critics* in 1848, and scattered parodies of "The Sphinx." The stream became a flood in 1857. Melville satirized Emerson as Mark Winsome in *The Confidence Man*. Emerson published "Brahma" in November 1857; in the next month the poem elicited twenty-six parodies. His son said that Emerson "never failed to be completely overcome with laughter" if anyone started to recite the one that began:

> If the grey tom-cat thinks he sings,
> Or if the song think it be sung,
> He little knows who boot-jacks flings
> How many bricks at him I've flung.[4]

Fame had its drawbacks, but it was a problem Emerson had been preparing for. He had never shunned it or affected to scorn it. There is a very early poem which begins by conceding that

> He pays too high a price
> For knowledge and fame
> Who sells his sinews to be wise
> His teeth and bones to buy a name.

But the poem concludes that fate does not permit us to hide "the world's light" and it therefore advises, "Go then sad youth and shine." One of Emerson's index entries under "Fame" is from Tacitus: "Contempt for fame is condemnation of virtue." He understood fame as a process and he considered its meaning to be a sympathy "by which the good become partners of the greatness of their superiors." He accepted the idea that a person's fame "characterizes those who give it, as much as him who receives it."[5]

Emerson never wrote an essay on fame, though he wrote several about qualities closely associated with it, such as eloquence, greatness, success, and immortality. He did collect materials on fame, which is one of 207 headings in his 1847 "Index Major." He listed Raleigh's comment that "fame is a ploughing-up of the air, and a sowing of the wind," and he was fond of the analogy between fame and a thunderbolt which "falls on one inch of ground but lights up the whole horizon."[6]

Fame came to Emerson relatively early, and while he generally handled it gracefully, his renown had a life of its own, tending to crowd out the real human being, sometimes in humorous ways. The young Sophia Peabody wrote her sister about Emerson in 1838: "I think Mr. Emerson is the greatest man—the most complete man that ever lived . . . He is indeed a 'supernal vision.' I often think that God and his holy angels must regard him with delight." In 1845 an English admirer, Henry Sutton, treated Emerson as a "living oracle" and put him in company with Paul, Boehme, Henry Agrippa, and the "old Brahminical writers." Moncure Conway, who met Emerson in the 1850s, saw him as a titanic iconoclast: "Emerson has the distinction of being the first repudiator of sacraments, supernaturalism, biblical authority, and of Christianity itself in every form, who suffered no kind of martyrdom." Another admirer named Andrew Jackson Davis went this one better in a book called *Arabula; or The Divine Guest.* Davis called for a new Bible in part 1 of his book and then helpfully provided one in part 2. He printed twenty new "books," each divided into chapter and verse; he included, among others, the gospel according to St. Theodore [Parker], the gospel according to St. Emma [Hardinge], and the gospel according to St. Ralph.[7]

By the early 1870s Emerson's reputation was so great that it had a life of its own. Eventually his fame effectively concealed him, especially from his admirers. When he was asked on the spur of the moment to address the law students of Howard University in 1872, Emerson improvised a talk on what books to read. What he said hardly mattered. A journalist who was present noted that the students "were all very much instructed by looking at Mr. Emerson's face and seeing him think." When the event was reported in the Boston papers, local bookstores quickly sold out of the titles Emerson had mentioned.[8]

Emerson's own best insight into fame is in his essay on "Character." The most dismaying aspect of fame, from the point of view of its possessor, is not just that fame is generally disproportionate to actual achievement but that the fame that we first assumed to be a reward for work well done becomes instead an impossible promise about future work. Fame casts an anticipatory chill over current efforts because it awakens expectations that can never fully be met.[9]

91. Whitman

THE SECOND HALF OF 1854 AND THE FIRST HALF OF 1855 WERE
very busy times for Emerson. From October 1854 to March 1855 he gave
seventy-three lectures. His reading ranged restlessly through time and space.
In June he read W. L. Herndon's *Exploration of the Amazon,* L. Sitgreaves's
Expedition down the Zuni and Colorado Rivers, and the census of 1850. In
July he read, besides French periodicals and ever more on England, Francis
Lieber's *Manual of Political Ethics* and he made plans to read T. F. Davis's
The Chinese and Father Huc's *Travels in China.* In September he was reading
the diaries of Pepys and Evelyn as well as Robert Southey's *Life of Nelson.*
He continued to translate Hafez and he began looking into the *Mahawanso,*
a classic of Pali Buddhism and the principal indigenous history of Sri Lanka.
In October he took up Sidney, Ben Jonson, and Chapman's Homer, and
he continued to read in St. Beuve's vast *Causeries de lundi.* In February 1855
he began reading the works of Barthold Niebuhr, the archrationalist historian of Rome who together with D. F. Strauss was the main force in the
new historiography. Niebuhr scorned the use of myth and legend for
historical research and insisted that history be constructed only from documents, inscriptions, and other physical remains. Niebuhr seems to have
antagonized Emerson, spurring him to a new interest in myth. In March
Emerson was rereading Iamblichus, Proclus, and Porphyry; in April he read
Pliny and in May the Rig-Veda and the *Mabinogion.*[1]

In March 1855 Emerson was arranging for young Frank Sanborn to teach
in Concord. Sanborn was twenty-four and had just graduated from Harvard.
He had first called on Emerson two years before. He was a hothead and a
political radical. By 1857 he would be John Brown's New England agent.
In later life he published many books about Emerson and Thoreau, and his
sloppy editorial methods have been the despair of later editors. Sanborn's
rash nature had an ugly side. In the summer of 1862 he courted Edith
Emerson. She rejected him; he refused to accept her rejection. He tried first
to cajole, then to bully Edith. He impugned her integrity and got himself
into a prickly, defensive, whining correspondence (never published) first

with Edith, then with Lidian. Finally Emerson himself wrote Sanborn an angry letter advising him to drop the entire matter, which he did.[2]

This winter Emerson heard the great revivalist Charles Grandison Finney ("I did not suppose such a style of preaching still survived") and Henry Ward Beecher, who Emerson thought had the vigor of ten men. An April letter to George Bradford is full of the labored gaiety of a harassed man. Emerson told Bradford that Alcott was thinking of doing an English tour: "I plant myself, of course, mastiff-like to bark against the plan. But he shuns me. Ellery Channing is always on tiptoe on the wharf ready to embark; but we shall bark in that direction too."[3]

Summer approached. Brother William was suffering from three head-aches a day. Lidian was ailing; Thoreau was alarmingly feeble. On July 4, 1855, Lidian draped the gate and fence posts in front of the house with black as a protest against the state of the Union. At precisely this low moment a thin anonymous book of poems arrived for Emerson from New York; it was called *Leaves of Grass*. Emerson read the book at once and found it "so extraordinary for its oriental largeness of generalization" that he sent his copy to Sam Ward for his immediate reaction. Emerson also wrote to Caroline Tappan, calling Whitman's book "the best piece of American Buddhism that anyone has had strength to write, American to the bone." Then on July 21 he sat down and wrote Whitman. "I am not blind to the worth of the wonderful gift of 'Leaves of Grass,'" he wrote. "I find it the most extraordinary piece of wit and wisdom that America has yet contributed." He admired the "courage of treatment" and much more. "I greet you at the beginning of a great career," he wrote, then closed by saying that he felt like "striking my tasks and visiting New York to pay you my respects."[4]

Walt Whitman was thirty-six when he received what has become the most famous letter in American literary history. He had learned the printing trade as a boy and had worked for years on various papers, writing, editing, and setting type. He had most recently been operating a printing office and stationery store, doing free-lance work, and speculating on houses. He was a strong free-soil poet who had been jolted out of conventional verse by the Fugitive Slave Act. In July of 1855 he had a ninety-five-page book of poems in his new free verse printed in New York. Whitman's father had died just ten days before Emerson's letter was written. The effect of the letter on Whitman can be imagined. He had heard Emerson lecture and had spe-cifically admired his ideas about the nature and function of the poet. "My ideas were simmering and simmering," Whitman told John T. Trowbridge, "and Emerson brought them to a boil." The letter—of which Whitman's friend Horace Traubel shrewdly said many years later that it was more important for Emerson to write than for Whitman to receive—now sent Whitman boiling into activity again. He got the *New York Tribune* to print Emerson's letter, he had it printed up as a flyer, and he quickly got up a second edition with a quotation from the letter and Emerson's name stamped in gold on the spine. Whitman neglected to ask Emerson's permission for all this and it raised a few eyebrows in Boston, but who can really blame Whitman? Emerson had responded to many people with generous enthusiasm, but none of his young friends—not Thoreau nor Fuller nor Channing nor Very nor Greenough—had ever received such a single bolt of jubilant approval out of a clear sky. Emerson said something to Samuel Longfellow, the poet's brother, about Whitman's rudeness in printing the letter, but Whitman's impulsiveness had no effect on Emerson's enthusiasm for his work. Emerson pushed *Leaves of Grass* on Thoreau, Alcott, Sanborn, Cabot, and Furness. Thoreau went around Concord waving the book like a red flag. Alcott was impressed, but almost everyone else in Concord and Boston and elsewhere recoiled from the powerful sexuality of Whitman's poetry. For years Emerson was nearly alone in his admiration for Whitman. He was for Emerson the poet who had grasped more clearly than anyone else the idea that the poet is representative. Whitman was indeed the poet Emerson had called for in "The Poet," the person who claimed little or nothing for himself but got his material and his strength by acting as the conduit and spokesman—the representative—of everyone he had ever met or heard or read about.[5]

Emerson's admiration for *Leaves of Grass,* which he called a mixture of the Bhagavad Gita and the *New York Herald,* led him to search out Whitman in New York in December 1855, to send Thoreau and Alcott to see him, to help him place his writing, and to write letters on his behalf to two members of Lincoln's cabinet, William Seward and Salmon P. Chase. Not only was Emerson's enthusiasm for Whitman's poetry undiminished but his later letters of recommendation outdo even his own original letter to Whitman. "If his writings are in certain points open to criticism," he wrote Secretary of State Seward, "they show extraordinary power, and are more deeply American, democratic, and in the interest of political liberty, than those of any other poet."[6]

On March 17, 1860, Whitman was in Boston arranging for the third edition of *Leaves of Grass.* Emerson spent the day with him. They took a long walk on Boston Common. Emerson tried to persuade Whitman to tone down some of the explicit references to sex in the "Children of Adam" section. He made it clear that his suggestions did not imply disapproval of the passages, the poems, or the poet but were made strictly with an eye to public acceptance. Whitman ignored the advice, but the day lived in his memory as the one on which the great issues of his poetry and his career became completely clear to him, a day after which he felt no more self-doubt.

The two met again, possibly a dozen times, but probably fewer. In letters and conversations with others Emerson admitted to various reservations about Whitman—hardly surprising for a man who had reservations about Jesus. Most of these have reached us at second hand, through people, including Emerson's own children, who disapproved of Whitman. It seems clear that Emerson never really changed his mind about Whitman. Whitman wrote one piece in 1880 in which he denied ever being seriously influenced by Emerson. In the conversations from which Horace Traubel constructed his splendid memoir *With Walt Whitman in Camden,* we get another story. Emerson is a constant, almost an obsessive presence in this record; there are over three hundred references to Emerson, many of them extended discussions, over a period of two and a half years. Whitman came back again and again to the letter and to the day in Boston when Emerson urged him to "cut the bits here and there that offended the censors." "He did not urge this for my sake but for the sake of the people," Whitman recalled, "He seemed to be arguing that I didn't need the people as much as the people needed me. I said: 'You think that if I cut the book there would be a book left?' He said 'Yes.' Then I asked, 'But would there be as good a book left?' He looked grave; this seemed to disturb him a bit. Then he smiled at me and said, 'I did not say as good a book—I said a good book.' That's where he left it."[7]

Whitman considered Emerson "a man who with all his culture and refinement, superficial and intrinsic, was elemental and a born democrat." This judgment was in strong contrast to his assessment of Thoreau, whose great failing, said Whitman, was his "disdain, contempt for average human beings; for the masses of men." A full portrait of Emerson emerges from Whitman's conversations with Traubel, in old age, years after Emerson's death.[8]

We learn from Traubel that Whitman advised Anne Montgomerie to "read all the Emerson you can—it is the best preparatory soil. Emerson is not conclusive on all points, but no man more helps to a conclusion."

Whitman admired the fact that one could not put a tag on Emerson: "They never could hold him; no province, no clique, no church." "I always go back to Emerson," he said on another occasion. "He was the one man to do a particular job wholly on his own account." Of the continuing popularity of Emerson's writings Whitman said, "Emerson never fails; he can't be rejected; even when he falls on stony ground he somehow eventuates in a harvest." Whitman's vivid conversational style was full of reported conversations. He quotes Emerson's saying, "I agree with you Mr. Whitman, that a man who does not live according to his lights—who trims his sails to the current breeze—is already dead." Another time Emerson told Whitman, "You have a great pack howling at your heels always, Mr. Whitman; I hope you show them all a proper contempt; they deserve no more than your heels." Whitman also reports moments of Emersonian self-criticism. "He said he felt that culture had done all it could for him—then it had done something for him which had better been left undone." Another time Whitman likened himself to Emerson, saying, "I am inclined to ask with the good Emerson in his later days whether I am I any more; whether I'm not in danger; whether opposition, cuffing, blows direct from the shoulder, antagonisms, would not be better, more bracing for me."[9]

Another recollection has the vanished presence of a physical touch.

> I remember Emerson said to me in one of our talks: "You have won far more plaudits, have many more friends, Mr. Whitman, than you are aware of; you will be patient I know; the world will come your way in the end because you have put it in your debt and such obligations are always acknowledged and met." The gentle Emerson. He would lay his hand on my coat sleeve when he was about to say something; touch me sort of half-apologetically as if saying, if I may be permitted![10]

Whitman felt Emerson's warmth and friendliness. "I never get tired of talking of him," he said one day. "I think everybody was fascinated by his personality."

> His usual manner carried with it something penetrating and sweet beyond mere description. There is in some men an indefinable something which flows out and over you like a flood of light—as if they possessed it illimitably—their whole being suffused with it. Being—in fact that is precisely the word. Emerson's whole attitude shed forth

such an impression. . . . Never a face more gifted with power to express, fascinate, maintain.[11]

Emerson found in Whitman the great modern poet he was seeking. Whitman found in Emerson the justification for literature itself.

> I often say of Emerson that the personality of the man—the wonderful heart and soul of the man, present in all he writes, thinks, does, hopes—goes far toward justifying the whole literary business—the whole raft good and bad—the whole system. You see, I find nothing in literature that is valuable simply for its professional quality; literature is only valuable in the measure of the passion—the blood and muscle—with which it is invested—which lies concealed and active in it.

It is a handsome tribute, fit to be stamped in gold letters on the next edition of Emerson's writings.[12]

92. The Remedy at the Hour of Need

AT THE CLOSE OF THE 1850 ANTI-SLAVERY CONVENTION IN Boston, a small group of the delegates gathered to consider the issue of women's rights. A call for a national convention resulted. Paulina Davis, a leader in the movement, invited Emerson to address the meeting, which was scheduled to be held in Worcester in the fall of 1850. He declined to speak but agreed to having his name included in the list of conveners. The following year Lucy Stone, an Oberlin graduate and an early activist in the women's rights movement, asked him to address the second annual convention. Again he declined, saying in extenuation that he was working on the memoir of Margaret Fuller. The *New York Tribune* printed his letter along with an account of the meeting. Finally, in September 1855, two months after reading *Leaves of Grass,* Emerson gave a lecture at the Second Annual New England Women's Rights Convention in Boston.

Many prominent leaders were there. The first day's speakers were the reformer Wendell Phillips, the Unitarian minister and active abolitionist Thomas W. Higginson, and Lucy Stone. On the second day Caroline Dall, Antoinette L. Brown, and Susan B. Anthony spoke during the day. Dall was a protégé of Margaret Fuller's; Brown—also from Oberlin—was one of the first women in America to be ordained as a minister; Susan B. Anthony was in 1855 still at the beginning of her career. She was a brilliant and tireless organizer who had held meetings in fifty-four of New York's sixty-one counties during the preceding year. In the evening there was the lecture by Emerson and a poem by Elizabeth Oakes Smith, a popular writer, author of *Woman and Her Needs* (1851).[1]

The purpose of the 1855 convention was to report, state by state, on the status of New England laws relating to women's property rights. A number of states, beginning with Rhode Island, and by 1853 including New Hampshire, Indiana, Wisconsin, and Iowa, had made moves toward guaranteeing these rights. Still, the new legislation guaranteed married women their property only "under certain regulations." Emerson's position on this issue was clear. Women "have an unquestionable right to their property," he said.[2]

His position on the whole range of women's rights was a good deal less clear. He did not give his audience anything as simple and direct as Theodore Parker had when in his 1853 sermon "The Public Function of Women" Parker said: "To make one-half the human race consume all their energies in the functions of housekeeper, wife, and mother, is a waste of the most precious material God ever made." Emerson's views on women are in general close to Fuller's early views and in many cases derive from hers. Her *Woman in the Nineteenth Century* was reprinted this year, 1855. Emerson accepted the idea—as had Fuller—that men and women have different qualities and different excellences. Fuller had written in "The Great Lawsuit": "Were they [women] free, were they wise fully to develop the strength and beauty of woman, they would never wish to be men, or man-like." Emerson, following Fuller, pulled back from assigning women a wholly separate sphere, the position endorsed by Catharine Beecher, Lydia Sigourney, and others. Fuller disliked the idea of different spheres of influence; she refused, for example, to limit domesticity to women, saying, "If men look straitly to it, they will find that unless their lives are domestic, those of the women will not be."[3]

In his evening lecture Emerson described woman's special qualities, among which he considered her interest in "the life of the affections," her skill in conversation, her civilizing social qualities, her role as tastemaker, and her more deeply religious nature. He thought that because women were "more exquisite," they were also "more vulnerable, more infirm, more mortal than men." After a lengthy consideration of differences and similarities, and a careful listing—and dismissal—of the usual charges against allowing women an active role in the world, Emerson concluded by emphasizing the common ground: "I think it is impossible to separate the interests and education of the sexes."[4]

Emerson seems to have believed in 1855 that women should have equal rights if they wanted them and that they did not want them. "I do not think it yet appears that women wish this equal share in public affairs," he told his audience, "but it is they and not we that are to determine it." Emerson's ambivalence showed in his talk. The newspapers, in reporting the speech, were not sure which side he was on. Paulina Davis wrote to thank him for the speech and to ask that it be published; this suggests that she thought it favorable. The lecture was not published until 1881, and the subject continued to be a sore one in the Emerson home. Lidian became a strong supporter of women's rights. In this cause, as in abolition, she was well ahead of her husband. Daughter Edith was in favor, daughter Ellen opposed. One day at tea in 1871 Ellen raised the subject, talking against suffrage for women and then writing down what happened.

> Mother mounts her most bolting and snorting warhorse and leaves us all nowhere in less than no time. Edith on a pony of the same breed charges valiantly on her presuming sister and tells her the least these inferior and selfish minds that cannot see the benefit and privilege of voting can do is to hold their idle tongues. Father won't speak one word till, particularly requested, he gives his views and as a reward has directly the fury of all his household levelled at them.[5]

Some time well after the Civil War, Emerson wrote another talk about women's rights. It is headed "Discourse Manqué" in his manuscript draft. It was never delivered and only printed in part as an end note to "Woman" (his 1855 speech) in the volume *Miscellanies* in the collected works edited by Emerson's son. "Discourse Manqué" is a short piece, showing the continuing influence of Fuller, as well as an increased sympathy with the women's rights movement, which Emerson now calls, without qualification or condescension, "an honor to the age." Ignoring the issue of the domestic sphere, Emerson concentrates on public life. He says that women "are better scholars than [men] at school, and the reason why they are not better than [men] twenty years later may be because men can turn their reading to account in the professions, and women are excluded from the professions." He echoes one of the main points of *Woman in the Nineteenth Century* when he says, "Superior women are rare anywhere, as are superior men . . . and every country, in its roll of honor, has as many women as men." He cites the work of American women in the abolition movement, in the hospitals of the Sanitary Commission during the Civil War, and in the Freedmen's Bureau after the war as proof of women's practical effectiveness in public affairs.

> They claim now her full rights of all kinds,—to education, to employment, to equal laws of property, equal rights in marriage, in the exercize of the professions, and of suffrage. . . . And now at the moment when Committees are investigating and reporting the election frauds, woman asks for her vote. It is the remedy at the hour of need.[6]

93. The Power and Terror of Thought

DURING THE MID-1850S EMERSON TOOK UP A NUMBER OF HIS oldest, most central themes and reconsidered them in the light of accrued experience. His speeches on affairs in Kansas, on the attack on Charles Sumner, and on John Brown and his raid—coupled with his disapproval of the national government—rekindled his old political radicalism. In a speech for a Kansas relief meeting in September 1856 he admitted, "I own I have little esteem for government. I esteem them only good in the moment when they were established." He was "glad to see that the terror at disunion and anarchy is disappearing. Massachusetts in its heroic day, had no government—was an anarchy." He does not mean chaos, of course. A better word for the anarchy Emerson has in mind would be "autarchy," rule by self. He went on to say, "Every man stood on his own feet, was his own governor."[1]

Emerson gave commencement addresses at Williams College in 1854 and at Amherst in 1855. He still had a deep distrust of institutions. Just when his brother's son, William Jr., was headed for Harvard Law School and when his own children were reaching college age (Ellen was sixteen in 1855, Edith fourteen, Edward ten), he wrote: "Universities are, of course, hostile to genius, which, seeing and using ways of their own, discredit the routine." In the address he gave at Williams Emerson took up his old subject, the American scholar. Time had sharpened his sense of the forces working against the independent mind. "Our Anglo-Saxon society is a great industrial corporation," he told the young men. "You must make *trade* everything. Trade is not to know friends or wife or child or country." He urged his hearers to resist, not to join the merchants. "It is the vulgarity of this country—it came to us, with commerce, out of England—to believe that naked wealth, unrelieved by any use or design, is merit." There is a new stridency and a new firmness here, as Emerson warns his audience—and they are not Sunday-morning warnings he has in mind—against the powerful pull of English cultural assumptions, American politics, trade and wealth, in short, against materialism.[2]

What the scholar, the intellectual, the writer should be doing was harder to say in positive terms. Emerson began to assemble material for a lecture to be called "The Power and Terror of Thought," the point of which was to be that ideas, not vested interests, were the great force in human history. "The architecture gives the value to all the stones." "Order is matter subdued by mind." Emerson reached for his old volcano metaphors to describe the forces that shape the earth: "As the invisible gas we breathe, if pent, has an elasticity that will lift the Appalachian Range as easily as a scrap of down, so a thought carries nations of men and ages of time on its shoulders." He never finished the essay; it was as if his own pent-up volcanic forces no longer had the strength to heave up a new mass.[3]

Emerson was still attracted to energy and to energetic figures. Another project of the 1850s was a piece on Father Taylor, the sailor-preacher, his old friend and a man whom Emerson continued to regard as one of the great poets of America, a man who "says touching things, plain things, cogent things." But this essay, which might have hastened critical attention to the salty Whitman of American pulpit oratory, he never completed either.[4]

Late in March 1855 Emerson gave a new lecture on beauty in Concord; he included it in *The Conduct of Life* five years later. "Beauty" by no means abandons the idea of beauty as *kosmos,* the notion that beauty is the world as it is, in all its endless forms and interrelationships. But now Emerson's friendship with Greenough bears fruit, as Emerson examines the anatomy of beauty and explicitly relates beauty to function. "Elegance of form . . . marks some excellence of structure," he writes. "All beauty must be organic . . . outside embellishment is deformity." A modern critic has observed that the compression Emerson gets into his speech is a compression he had attained in his life. "The line of beauty," says Emerson, "is the result of perfect economy. The cell of the bee is built at that angle which gives the most strength with the least wax."[5]

In the essay "Illusions," which ended *The Conduct of Life,* Emerson took up the subject he had last considered in "Experience," exploring now the extent to which experience teaches us that we live in a world of illusion. He opens with a detailed description of Mammoth Cave. He insists now on the role played by the senses, which "interfere everywhere, and mix their own structure with all things they report of. . . . In admiring the sunset, we do not yet deduct the rounding, coordinating, pictorial powers of the eye." "We live," he says, "by our imaginations, by our admiration, by our sentiment," and it is sobering to discover how much of what is most important to us is illusion. We are easy prey for these "deceptions of the senses, deceptions of the passions, and the structural beneficent illusions of sentiment and intellect." The phrase "the structural illusions of intellect" has a gloomy Baconian grandeur, but this is not the last word. Time too is an illusion: "What seems the *succession* of thought is only the distribution of wholes into causal series." Emerson recognizes that "science has come to treat space and time as simply forms of thought." Emerson in the mid-1850s had come to have a pervasive sense of the impermanence of all the visible surfaces of life, the same sense William James says Hegel had. "This dogging of everything by its negative, its fate, its undoing," James writes, "this is the Hegelian intuition of the essential provisionality, and consequent unreality, of everything empirical and finite."[6]

What then is not illusion? There are left for Emerson three realities or paths toward reality. The first is the reality of subjective affirmation: "Our first mistake is the belief that the circumstance gives the joy which we give to the circumstance. Life is an ecstasy." The second is the perception that every day holds all the reality there is. In an explicit repudiation of the biblical lament "Now we see through a glass darkly . . . ," Emerson says with his usual theological bravado, "We see God face to face every hour." The third reality is the assumption on which science rests, that "there is no chance, no anarchy in the universe. All is system and gradation."[7]

We are not at last locked in the splendid labyrinth of our own perceptions. The essay ends with a little victory, as when we climb once again a familiar and neighboring peak. "Illusions" ends also with the deliberate metaphor of a conscious mythmaker. The days are gods. "The young mortal enters the hall of the firmament; there he is alone with them [the days] alone, they pouring on him benedictions and gifts." Then come the whirling snowstorms, the illusions of life. "The mad crowd drives hither and thither, now furiously commanding this thing to be done, now that." But there always come moments of clarity and reckoning. And when "for an instant, the air clears and the cloud lifts a little, there are the gods still sitting around him on their thrones,—they alone with him alone."[8]

Optimism is a weak, almost useless word for this kind of perception. "There is," said Whitman,

> apart from intellect . . . an intuition of the absolute balance, in time and space, of the whole of this multifariousness, this revel of fools, and incredible make-believe and general unsettledness we call the world; a soul-light of that divine clue and unseen thread which holds

the whole congeries of things, all history and time and all events, however trivial, however momentous, like a leashed dog in the hand of a hunter. [Of] such soul-sight and root center for the mind, mere optimism explains only the surface.[9]

A major line of purpose in Emerson's mature work is to redeem the word *idea,* which had been devalued by Hume to mean only the faint shadow of a sense impression. For Emerson now as for Plato earlier, ideas are perceptions. They are the realities of which sense impressions are the shadows. At the center of Emerson's life and work is a core of these perceptions, bound together. They are not arguments or hypotheses. They are certainly not elements of a system, but neither are they opinions. When the storms of illusion clear, in the moments at the top of the mountain, these are the perceptions that Emerson retains:

The days are gods. That is, everything is divine.

Creation is continuous. There is no other world; this one is all there is.

Every day is the day of judgment.

The purpose of life is individual self-cultivation, self-expression, and fulfillment.

Poetry liberates. Thought is also free.

The powers of the soul are commensurate with its needs; each new day challenges us with its adequacy and our own.

Fundamental perceptions are intuitive and inarguable; all important truths, whether of physics or ethics, must at last be self-evident.

Nothing great is ever accomplished without enthusiasm.

Life is an ecstasy; Thoreau has it right when he says, "Surely joy is the condition of life."

Criticism and commentary, if they are not in the service of enthusiasm and ecstasy, are idle at best, destructive at worst. Your work, as Ruskin says, should be the praise of what you love.

There is nothing in this list that Emerson had not learned firsthand. These are not abstractions but practical rules for everyday life. The public consequences of such convictions for Emerson were a politics of social liberalism, abolitionism, women's suffrage, American Indian rights, opposition to the Mexican War, and civil disobedience when government was wrong. The personal consequence of such perceptions was an almost intolerable awareness that every morning began with infinite promise. Any book may be read, any idea thought, any action taken. Anything that has ever been possible to human beings is possible to most of us every time the clock says six in the morning. On a day no different from the one now breaking, Shakespeare sat down to begin *Hamlet* and Fuller began her history of the Roman revolution of 1848. Each of us has all the time there is; each accepts those invitations he can discern. By the same token, each evening brings a reckoning of infinite regret for the paths refused, openings not seen, and actions not taken.

On September 29, 1855, just a little more than a week after the Women's Rights Convention, Concord opened and dedicated a new cemetery called Sleepy Hollow. It was to be a garden cemetery in the new fashion, like Mt. Auburn in Cambridge. Inevitably, the persons in charge asked Emerson to speak. Inevitably, he accepted. In his talk, he acknowledged the human hunger for immortality but dismissed the mortuary materialism of the Egyptians and early Christians, who believed in and built for a physical resurrection of each individual body. He praised instead the Greeks, who "loved life and delighted in beauty" and who "built no more of those doleful mountainous tombs." He also spoke of the irresistible democracy of natural processes, of the chemistry which "recomposes for new life every decomposing particle."[10]

He particularly liked the idea that the new burial ground was to be an arboretum, planted with every tree that is native to—or able to grow in—Massachusetts, "so that every child may be shown growing, side by side, the eleven oaks of Massachusetts, and the twenty willows; the beech, which we have allowed to die out in the eastern counties; and . . . the vast firs of California and Oregon."[11]

Another lecture season was coming up. A new and uncharacteristic note of weariness appears in Emerson's letters. He dreaded the strenuous western trip. He apologized for not writing to his old friend and financial adviser Abel Adams, adding, "But one of these days, before I die, I still believe I shall do better." He noticed how "my son is coming to do without me." In July 1856 while reading a translation of the Upanishads, he was stirred to write one of his last great poems, "Brahma." He called it "Song of the Soul" in this first version. It is a poetic equivalent of "Illusions," an antiphonal response to Whitman, and an affirmation of the "identity-philosophy."

> If the red slayer think he slays
> Or if the slain think he is slain

They know not well the subtle ways
I keep and pass and turn again.

The poem is written from the point of view of Brahma, but the last two lines turn attention back to the earth-bound seeker. "But thou, meek lover of the good, / Find me and turn thy back on heaven."[12]

One year later, on July 8, 1857, Emerson moved the coffins of his mother and his son Waldo from the Ripley tomb up on the narrow ridge of the small crowded old burying ground in the center of Concord to a new plot in Sleepy Hollow. "The sun shone brightly on the coffins, of which Waldo's was well preserved—now fifteen years," he wrote later in his journal.

Once more Emerson did an extraordinary thing. Just as he had looked into the coffin of his dead wife Ellen twenty-five years ago, in 1832, so now he ventured to look into Waldo's. What he saw is not recorded. Waldo had been born in 1836; he was a few months past his fifth birthday when he died in 1842. Had he lived he would now, on this sunny day in July, be approaching his twenty-first birthday. His brothers and sisters were flourishing. Ellen was eighteen, Edith sixteen. It was two days before Edward's thirteenth birthday as Emerson stood looking down into little Waldo's coffin.

Virtually all of Emerson's creative life was lived in the twenty-five years between those glimpses not simply of death but of *his* dead, of Ellen in 1832 and of Waldo in 1857. No man was ever less inclined than Emerson to live in the past, nor was he doing so now. For Ellen and Waldo were not "the past." Dr. Ripley and his mother Ruth might perhaps be. Ellen and Waldo, dying so young and carrying down with them so much love and hope, represented a future that was never to come. Emerson had spoken of Sleepy Hollow as a place where "our children . . . shall come hither to read the dates of these lives." But this child would not.[13]

Before turning to go Emerson put a few white oak leaves on each coffin. The rugged, wide-spreading white oak is the greatest of the hardwoods in the eastern American woods; it was used by the early settlers for flooring, panels, and furniture that would defy time. When Emerson got home from Sleepy Hollow that evening, his daughter Ellen remembered, "He said he had looked into the coffin, but he said no more."[14]

Endings

94. Memory

MEMORY BEGAN TO INTEREST EMERSON IN THE MID-1850S. HE had never proposed to deal with the past by forgetting it; he had always insisted that the use of the past is to educate the present generation. But like Nietzsche Emerson knew the value of being able to forget. He told his daughter Ellen in 1854, "You must finish a term and finish every day, and be done with it. For manners, and for wise living, it is a vice to remember." He meant that one should not pick at the scabs of one's little mistakes, rudenesses, oversights, and failures. "This day for all that is good and fair. It is too dear with its hopes and invitations to waste a moment on the rotten yesterdays." His own memory was excellent. He was able when pressed to call up all of Milton's "Lycidas." He knew a great deal of Wordsworth by heart; he recited poetry to his children on their walks. Yet he set no great store on memory, and his work habits did not require much use of memory. His vast system of notebooks and indexes functioned as an external equivalent—a replacement really—of memory. And in one of those notebooks he wrote that "imagination is the morning, memory the evening of the mind." In the same notebook he observed that "the damages of forgetting are more than compensated by the immense value which new knowledge gives to what we already know."[1]

In 1857 Emerson wrote a lecture called "Memory." His "Natural History of Intellect" project obliged him to deal with this topic, but now he made an unusually strong statement. Memory is "the thread on which the beads of a man are strung, making the personal identity which is necessary to moral action." He saw special threats to memory in modern life. "If writing weakens the memory, we may say as much and more of printing. What is the newspaper but a sponge or invention for oblivion? The rule being that for every fact added to the memory, one is crowded out, and that only what the affection animates can be remembered." He consoled himself that "inventive men have bad memories" and he cited Newton as an example. There is no tone of irony or chagrin yet in his comments on memory, but the subject was sufficiently on his mind for him to notice mnemonic feats or aids in his reading. From Pepys's *Diary* he learned about Thomas Fuller's prodigious memory. Fuller had the best memory of his generation, could repeat back a list of five hundred random words after one hearing, knew more of Pepys's book by heart than Pepys himself, and could dictate in Latin to four scribes at one time and keep ahead of them all. And somewhere Emerson learned about the mnemonic system of Richard Grey, whose *Memoria Technica* was a well-known alternative to the many books on strengthening the memory which used the memory-house or palace system of recall.[2]

Grey's system was so elaborate that it nearly amounted to the creation of a new language. For remembering historical dates Grey used a table of numbers with letter equivalents. To remember a given date, one made up a new word, beginning with letters designed to recall the desired event, and ending with a date coded in letters. The table of letters for numbers was

a	e	i	o	u	au	oi	ei	ou	y	g	th	m
1	2	3	4	5	6	7	8	9	0	100	1000	1,000,000
b	d	t	f	l	s	p	k	n	z			

To remember that the creation of the world came in 4004, one remembered the word "crothf," "cr" being a tag for Creation, "othf" standing for 4004. Grey put together strings of events into lines of jabberwocky one was supposed to memorize. To remember the dates for Creation, the Deluge, the call of Abraham, the Exodus, and the foundation of Solomon's temple, one memorized the line "Crothf Deletok Abaneb Exasna Tembybe." Grey constructed many hundreds of such lines.[3]

Memory was increasingly not just a matter of utility for Emerson. It was a key to the future as well as to the past. "Memory is a presumption of a possession of the future," he wrote. He got his own future exactly reversed now when he said, "You may perish out of your senses, but not out of your memory or imagination."[4]

In November 1857 the first issue of the new magazine *Atlantic Monthly* appeared. It had several of Emerson's best poems, including "Days." "Days" is the parable of promise and failure which had been evolving through his notes and letters for well over twenty years. The poem opens with the procession of days, "Daughters of time, the hypocritic days / Muffled and dumb like barefoot dervishes . . ." The days offer us gifts. We can take as much as we will, but the speaker forgets his morning wishes and settles for "a few herbs and apples." "The Day / Turned and departed silent. I, too late, / Under her solemn fillet saw the scorn." This sequence—infinite promise followed by a sense of culpably meager performance—recurred with tidal regularity all through Emerson's life.[5]

Sometime in 1859 Emerson wrote, "I have now for more than a year, I believe, ceased to write in my journal, in which I formerly wrote almost daily—I see few intellectual persons, and even those to no purpose, and sometimes believe that I have no new thoughts, and that my life is quite at an end." Creative sparks could and did flame up on occasion, and Emerson had many active years ahead, but the general course of his life changed in the late 1850s, and a series of endings punctuated his last twenty-five years.[6]

The impression that there were two Emersons never quite goes away. James Russell Lowell discerned a dreamy seer living alongside a practical Yankee. Bliss Perry thought the two sides were physically reflected in the two quite different sides of Emerson's face. Alfred Kazin is nearer the mark when he speaks of a private self concealed behind the public Emerson, a lower-case person who continually made discoveries that the upper-case Emerson could use. Emerson's own sense of this crops out in his talk about his daemon and his attribution of certain home truths to "Guy" or "Osman." By the late 1850s a third and new layer of complexity emerged in Emerson's life. He was fast becoming an institution—his own lengthened shadow—and this growing reputation now preceded both the public and the private Emerson wherever he went.[7]

Just when it becomes harder for us to keep sight of the private Emerson, the public Emerson was busier than ever. As with most writers, his later life is much more fully documented than his earlier. After 1858 Emerson still had fourteen years of active lecturing left, during which he gave an average of forty-seven lectures a year. In 1858 he bought a gun and went on a camping and specimen-collecting trip in the Adirondacks with Louis Agassiz and a large party of Boston gentlemen. In October 1859 came John Brown's raid on Harper's Ferry. Within weeks Emerson created a minor furor by saying that Brown's execution "will make the gallows as glorious as the cross." Brown was hanged on December 2, 1859. Emerson gave one public eulogy in Concord and another in Salem.[8]

The Alcotts had returned to Concord in 1857. Elizabeth (Beth in *Little Women*) died the following year. By 1860 Louisa was having some success publishing her stories in the *Atlantic Monthly* and elsewhere. Also in 1860 Emerson's *The Conduct of Life* volume appeared. Emerson's old friend and ally Theodore Parker died of tuberculosis in Florence in April 1860. In the fall Abraham Lincoln was elected president.

Emerson was on a lecture tour when Darwin's *Origin of Species* appeared in America in the early months of 1860. He was impatient to see the book. His long interest in process in preference to taxonomy disposed him to believe in evolution, and despite his friendship with Agassiz, Emerson never said anything to suggest that he accepted Agassiz's ideas about special creation. Emerson understood evolutionary change, however, in Lamarckian and progressive terms. Neither he nor Thoreau was really interested in the problem of speciation that lay at the heart of the Darwin-Agassiz dispute. Still, Emerson was sympathetic to the idea of changing species. He thought of change—which he often called "the metamorphosis"—as a law of life. From Schelling, via Stallo, he copied—and repeated—that "all difference is quantitative." In other words, there are finally no differences of kind, only of degree. Emerson would have had no trouble with the heart of Darwin's argument, "that species are only strongly marked and permanent varieties, and that each species first existed as a variety."[9]

Emerson's reading in Goethe long ago had prepared him for some of Darwin's conclusions, for "the belief that all animals and plants have descended from some one prototype" and that "probably all the organic beings which have ever lived on this earth have descended from some one primordial form, into which life was first breathed."[10]

95. Civil War. Death of Thoreau

On April 12, 1861, came the bombardment of Fort Sumter. The war was on everyone's mind. Forty-five Concord volunteers left to go to war on April 19. In July the first battle of Bull Run (called the first battle of Manassas by the Confederates) was fought and it became clear that the war might be long. Emerson disapproved of the war as long as it was fought only to hold the Union together. He continued lecturing, mostly on nonwar subjects. In November he gave a talk called "Old Age," and while he energetically enumerated the advantages of age, it was evident that now at fifty-nine he began to feel himself old. One advantage of age, he said, is that "a success more or less signifies nothing." Another is that older people have generally found their means of expression. A minor advantage is that "sick-headaches" (migraines) generally diminish after fifty. The chief gain is that one need no longer be afraid of not living to a good age. We "have weathered the perilous capes and shoals in the sea whereon we sail, and the chief evil of life is taken away in removing the grounds of fear. The insurance of a ship expires as she enters the harbor at home."[1]

Characteristically, Emerson was attuned to the *way* in which we first—and belatedly—become aware of encroaching age. "That which does not decay is so central and controlling in us, that as long as one is alone by himself, he is not sensible of the inroads of time, which always begin at the surfaces and edges." Worst of all, as he noted in his journal, was that "now, only in rare moments and by happiest combination or concert of the elements do I attain those enlargements which once were a daily gift."[2]

The war came home to the North with the coffins. A boy from Amherst died in December 1861 from a wound at Annapolis; his body was put on a train, and Emily Dickinson wrote her cousin: "Poor little widow's boy, riding tonight in the mad wind, back to the village burying ground where he never thought of sleeping!" In January 1862 Emerson was invited to speak at the Smithsonian in Washington, D.C. He and Moncure Conway spoke on the same occasion, urging that immediate emancipation of the slaves was the best way to solidify the North and the best hope for a war that was not going very well. Lincoln may have heard the lectures; he was certainly aware of them. Emerson met Lincoln during this visit to Washington and was more impressed than he had expected to be. Lincoln told Conway, "I am not without hope that something of the desire of you and your friends may be accomplished."[3]

On March 9, 1862, the *Monitor* and the *Merrimack* fought to a draw, and the age of the wooden sailing warship was over. On April 6 and 7 twenty-three thousand men died in the bloody battle of Shiloh. A month later Concord suffered a nearer loss. Henry Thoreau died of tuberculosis; he was forty-four. Emerson wrote and delivered the eulogy for the man he would always remember as his best friend, even when his memory loss was so far advanced that he could not pull up the name. "Thoreau" is Emerson's last sustained major piece of writing. A great prose elegy, as good in its way as "Lycidas," this is Emerson's best, most personal biographical piece and it remains the best single piece yet written on Henry Thoreau.

Emerson outlined his subject with quick sharp strokes as with a mallet and chisel. Thoreau "was bred to no profession; he never married; he lived alone; he never went to church; he never voted; he refused to pay a tax to the state; he ate no flesh, he drank no wine, he never knew the use of tobacco; and though a naturalist, he used neither trap nor gun." Emerson understood Thoreau; he said there was something military in Thoreau's nature and that he only really felt himself when in opposition: "He wanted a fallacy to expose, a blunder to pillory, I may say required a little sense of victory, a roll of the drum, to call his powers into full exercise." Emerson insists on Thoreau's Americanness ("his aversation from English and European manners and tastes almost reached contempt") and on his originality. He had an eye for physical detail; Thoreau could "pace sixteen rods more accurately than another man could measure them with rod and chain." He invented a better pencil, and "from a box containing a bushel or more of loose pencils, he could take up with his hands fast enough just a dozen pencils at every grasp."[4]

Emerson gives his highest praise when he says Thoreau lived for the day; he insisted that Thoreau was industrious, highly organized, setting a high value on his time. Because he had not wasted his life at the needless toil of a steady job but would work odd jobs to make ends meet, he was the only really free person, "the only man of leisure in town."[5]

Emerson's Thoreau is a transcendentalist; he perceived "the material world as a means and a symbol." Emerson was famous for his own eagle-glance, but he seems to have stood in awe of Thoreau's, saying that Thoreau "saw the limitations and poverty of those he talked with, so that nothing seemed concealed from such terrible eyes." Emerson understood Thoreau's literary project, both its intent and its success. "Mr. Thoreau dedicated his genius with such entire love to the fields, hill and waters of his native town, that he made them known and interesting to all reading Americans, and to people over the sea." He gives Thoreau a mythic simplicity and roughness: "He wore a straw hat, stout shoes, strong grey trousers to brave scrub-oaks and smilax, and to climb a tree for a hawk's or a squirrel's nest."[6]

Both men knew that the quest is not always what it first seems and that what we hunt hunts us as we become the objects of our own obsessions. Thoreau said, "What you seek in vain for, half your life, one day you come upon, all the family at dinner. You seek it like a dream, and as soon as you find it you become its prey."

The Emerson who ended each essay in *Representative Men* with an inventory of the defects of Plato or Shakespeare or Goethe now did the same for Thoreau. "I cannot help counting it a fault in him that he had no ambition," Emerson says, meaning the desire to make a stir in his own times, like a Daniel Webster. This was a goal to which Emerson had devoted a great part—perhaps too great a part—of his own energy. But he has little else to say in dispraise, and the piece ends with a celebration of Thoreau's triumphs, with several pages of characteristic quotation, and with a reference to the vast unfinished projects Thoreau left behind. These projects, "The Dispersion of Seeds," "On Flowers and Fruits," a pre-Columbian history of North America, and a detailed calendar of an entire natural year remain mostly in manuscript and have baffled generations of scholars. If Thoreau had a master plan, it died with him. It seems as if he was aiming to parallel Humboldt's *Cosmos* without leaving Concord. It seems too that Emerson had some sense of what his friend was up to: "The country knows not yet, or in the least part, how great a son it has lost."[7]

Just about the time of Thoreau's death came the vexation of Frank Sanborn's proposal to Edith (now twenty), her refusal, and his unpleasant persistence. Lidian especially went to enormous length to explain everything to Sanborn; she kept the communication open, which eventually allowed him to repent, save face, and remain on friendly terms with the family.[8]

On September 17, 1862, the North and South fought to a draw at Antietam. Ten days later Lincoln issued the Emancipation Proclamation, which was to go into effect on January 1, 1863. Emerson hailed the proclamation; he gave a speech on October 12, which was published in November in the *Atlantic Monthly*. The abolitionist strategy was to give the proclamation so much publicity that Lincoln could not retract. "Done, it cannot be undone by a new administration. For slavery overpowers the disgust of the moral sentiment only through immemorial usage. It cannot be introduced as an improvement of the nineteenth century."[9]

The Emancipation Proclamation also had an immediate effect on the Emerson household. When war first broke out, Edward, who was eighteen, had wanted to enlist. Lidian forbade it; she and Emerson both regarded the preservation of the Union as insufficient reason for war. Only if the North would fight the war explicitly to free the slaves would they regard it as moral. Lidian hoped that other mothers would similarly obstruct and condition their sons' enlistment, thus forcing the president to declare emancipation in order to raise more men. When emancipation was proclaimed, Emerson and Lidian agreed, reluctantly, that Edward could now enlist. But Edward himself was now dissuaded by an old family friend, John Murray Forbes. One of Forbes's sons—the one who would eventually marry Edith—was away at war already. Forbes told Edward, "I am not half the man I was, since Will went to the war. If Malcolm should go too, I think my usefulness would be ended. You are your father's only son. I leave it to you to judge whether your father's services to the country or those that you could offer would be of most value." Edward gave up the idea of enlisting.[10]

96. Terminus

EMERSON HAD BECOME BY 1863 AN INESCAPABLE PART—A FIX-
ture—of American public life. At the huge meeting in Boston's Music Hall
on January 1 to celebrate the first day of emancipation, Emerson opened
the program, bringing the crowd shouting and singing to its feet with his
"Boston Hymn." Its eighteenth stanza, later taken up by the soldiers of
Higginson's regiment, the First South Carolina, pursued the logic of compensated emancipation with a startling turn.

> Pay ransom to the owner
> And fill the bag to the brim
> Who is the owner. The slave is owner
> And ever was. Pay him.[1]

There was now an enormous disparity between the thronged public
events at which Emerson was the ever more admired center and the private,
almost invisible events that recalled him to his origins. His aunt, Mary
Moody Emerson, died on May Day, 1863. She was not in her last years what
she had once been. "The present is ever too strong for the past, and in so
many late years she has been only a wreck," Emerson wrote his brother.
Emerson still clung to her writings and a simple funeral-day summary in
his letter to William has his old admiring grace and conviction: "Her genius
was the purest . . . her letters and journals charm me still as thirty years ago,
and honor the American air." A tiny knot of seven family members followed
the hearse to the grave in Sleepy Hollow on "a pleasant misty day such as
Aunt would have chosen, and the rain waited till we had laid her in the
ground an hour." When Emerson's own funeral came in 1882, it would be
a vast public affair. Special trains to Concord were laid on, and the floors
and balconies of the First Parish Church had to be specially shored up to
hold the anticipated crowds.[2]

Emerson turned sixty the month his aunt died. In June a committee of
which he was a member examined the curriculum at West Point. John
Burroughs heard that Emerson was in the neighborhood and came over to

meet him. In July Emerson wrote a poem, "Voluntaries," as a dirge for Colonel Robert Shaw and the Fifty-fourth Massachusetts Regiment. The Fifty-fourth Massachusetts was, like Higginson's First South Carolina, composed of black soldiers, and many were killed attacking Battery Wagner in the effort to retake Fort Sumter. This same month Emerson was busy with another memorial, editing the posthumous volume of Thoreau's *Excursions*. In December he was reading Thoreau's manuscript journals with, as he said, ever mounting estimation.[3]

The tide of the war turned in July 1863 at Gettysburg. In 1864 Grant took command of all the Union armies and pushed the war relentlessly south. Hawthorne died this year, on May 19. He was fifty-nine. At his funeral James Freeman Clarke compared him to Jesus in his sympathy for sinners and Oliver Wendell Holmes found the day so bright he thought it "looked like a happy meeting." It was Emerson who struck the dark note saying, "I thought there was a tragic element in the event . . . and in the painful solitude of the man, which, I suppose, could not longer be endured, and he died of it."[4]

There was at least a trace of the loneliness he described in Hawthorne in Emerson himself. There was a private side of Emerson that was inaccessible to others. Fuller and Sturgis both complained about it. His daughter Ellen said he was unable to talk about persons and events that were close to him. Once he began to tell her a story about a visit he and his first wife had made to a Mrs. Washburn, one of Ellen's family. He "could only make an exclamation, so to speak, and then another as a feeling from the heart came up to him. Again and again he said 'I can't.' Then he would read another poem perhaps, or I would ask a question." Many of the great moments in Emerson's writing came when this private self broke through to the surface. But now in 1865 so deeply was Emerson enmeshed in the war and in public life (he gave an astonishing seventy-seven lectures in 1865) that the public events and his reponses to them seem to have invaded and occupied his inner life. To Carolyn Tappan he wrote about Appomattox with the exuberance he usually showed only for the birth of a child: "But what a joyful day is this and proud to Allegheny ranges, Northern Lakes, Mississippi rivers and all lands and men between the two Oceans, between morning and evening stars." The tone here is of impersonal rapture or abstract enthusiasm, concealing as much as it reveals.[5]

Lincoln was shot on April 14 and died on the fifteenth. Emerson spoke on the nineteenth and his elegy tapped the deep vein of natural catastrophe that is evident in much of his best writing. This time, however, the occasion was commensurate with the language it called forth. "We meet," he began, "under the gloom of a calamity which darkens down over the minds of good men in all civil society, as the fearful tidings travel over sea, over land, from country to country, like the shadow of an uncalculated eclipse over the planet." But it is precisely because he could respond to public events with his own best resources that the public Emerson seemed more and more to be replacing the private one.[6]

Emerson's life with his family was lived in between his more public and more private lives. His daughter Edith was married in October 1865 to William H. Forbes. Emerson was sorry to see Edith leave home, but there were unexpected gains too. Forbes quickly overhauled Emerson's business affairs—at which he had never been much good—and made him more favorable publishing arrangements. The increased income eliminated some of the pressure to keep lecturing. His son, Edward, who turned twenty-one this year, was a student at Harvard. His daughter Ellen increasingly took on the responsibility for running the house as well as many of the duties of a general secretary.

Emerson's life was still very busy. He did a preface for a new edition of Saadi's *Gulistan* in 1865 and he brought out a volume of Thoreau's letters and poems. In 1866 Emerson undertook to raise money from his classmates for Harvard's Memorial Hall. His first grandchild, Ralph Emerson Forbes, arrived on July 10; Emerson's voice broke as he read out the message from Edith to the family. A week later he heard that he had been made an honorary Doctor of Laws from Harvard, with what emotion, if any, we do not know. In October Charles Eliot Norton asked him to become a regular contributor to the *North American Review*. Emerson still had a great deal of energy; he lectured and traveled and wrote and did committee work on the same demanding schedule as ever. But physical, social, editorial, or even performance energy is not the same as creative energy. By 1866 the best energy, the creative moments, came at greater and greater intervals. He wrote in March to Edith and her husband to apologize for not coming to visit: "I am always haunted by a dream of what might be done, perhaps this very day on some one of twenty unfinished tasks, and, though the power has not come in twenty weeks or days, I hesitate to budge, lest it should call in the moment I have stepped out."[7]

Toward the end of December 1866 Emerson was in New York, just starting his annual trip west. He was about to give his brisk, upbeat lecture on "Resources" for the twenty-fifth time when he arranged to meet his son Edward at the St. Denis Hotel. As they sat by the fire, Emerson read some of the poems for a new volume (*May-Day*) including one called "Terminus." Edward wrote later: "It almost startled me. No thought of his aging had ever come to me, and there he sat, with no apparent abatement of bodily vigor, and young in spirit, recognizing with serene acquiescence his failing forces." Edward reported that Emerson "smiled as he read. He recognized, as none of us did, that his working days were nearly done."[8]

"Terminus" is another poem that, like "Days," gives final expression to a long considered subject. "Terminus" is about boundaries and limits; drafts of parts of it date back to the mid-1840s. Recognizing that there are limits is one thing, accepting that one is reaching them is another. The main metaphor of the poem is not dying fire but the voyage:

> As the bird trims her to the gale,
> I trim myself to the storm of time,
> I man the rudder, reef the sail.

Emerson knew, as Auden knew, that the sea is the real situation and the voyage is the true human condition. He knew, as Kazantzakis reports, that

> the only thing that exists is the sea, and a barque as tiny as man's body, with mind as captain. This captain stands in his osseous cabin. Both male and female, he sows and gives birth; gives birth to the world's sorrows and joys, its beauties, virtues, adventures, all its bloody beloved phantasmagoria.

Earlier Emerson had raised his sails and—like a Gloucester fishing skipper racing for home with the catch—had tied off his halyards aloft so no one could lower sail in a blow even if he wanted to. "Never strike sail to any," that earlier Emerson had said. "Come into port greatly or sail with God the seas." Now he could end "Terminus" with:

> Right onward drive unharmed
> The port, well worth the cruise, is near
> And every wave is charmed.[9]

97. May-Day

As always Emerson was a little ahead of himself. Perhaps the direct acceptance of age gave him a momentary sense that he had overcome it. During 1867 he gave eighty lectures; he made two western trips through fourteen states. Only once before, in 1856, had he taken on so heavy a schedule. In January he was in Minnesota, where he visited one of the tiny remnants of the once powerful Santee Sioux. Little Crow had lost his war with the whites in 1863; in 1867, when Emerson went to Faribault to see a Sioux village, the battle of the Little Bighorn was nine years in the future. The Santee warriors had all been moved away to Dakota; the women, the children, and the aged were left behind in Minnesota. The village of eight tepees stood in a clearing in the middle of "a wild piece of timber." Emerson was able to visit two. In each the families were seated on the ground around a central fire. They were about to eat supper in one; they were singing in the other.[1]

In March Emerson was in St. Louis, where he renewed his acquaintance with the Hegel enthusiast William T. Harris and met Harris's group of young intellectuals, the St. Louis Hegelians. Emerson had been reading J. H. Stirling's *The Secret of Hegel* and he told Carlyle that despite difficulties he was not yet done with Hegel. (The nub of Stirling's irresistibly titled book is that "the universe is but a materialization, but an externization, but a heterization of certain thoughts; these may be named, these thoughts are the thoughts of God.") Emerson noted with wry amusement that Harris and his group "did not wish to see or hear me at all, but that I should see and hear them."[2]

The high point of 1867 for Emerson was the publication in late April of his second book of poetry, *May-Day and Other Poems*. The title poem, originally called "Spring," sets the tone of the volume. It is a thirty-six-page poem about the power of spring to "sweep ruins from the scarped mountains" and "cleanse the torrent at the fountain." The second poem, nineteen pages long, is a Wordsworthian excursion poem about the 1858 Adirondack trip during which Emerson and a party of aging gentlemen became boys again in the woods. The volume also contains a number of Emerson's best short poems. In addition to "Brahma," "Days," and "Terminus," there is "The Titmouse," "Two Rivers," and "Waldeinsamkeit." But the long poems, despite much reworking, show Emerson's waning poetic force. There is more real poetry in the sixteen lines of "The Rhodora" or in the last stanza of "The World Soul" than in the fifty-five pages of the two long poems that open *May-Day*.[3]

There is also a strong memorial strain in the book; Emerson printed his brother Edward's forty-five-line poem "The Last Farewell" and followed it with a seven-page poem, called "In Memoriam," about the brother who had died thirty-three years earlier. The volume looks backward in other ways too, for it deals extensively with old friends and old friendships. Emerson now called friendship "the fountain of my hidden life." Unable to profit artistically from Whitman's leap into free verse, Emerson in *May-Day* moves back toward Wordsworth and even toward the neoclassic diction he had once railed against in Alcott's work. Toward the end of the volume is a section called "Quatrains." Emerson had learned to take this form seriously from Persian poetry and he found it increasingly congenial. One quatrain is called "Memory."

> Night-Dreams trace on Memory's wall
> Shadows of the thoughts of day
> And thy fortunes as they fall
> The bias of the will betray.

There is real poetry elsewhere in the book as well, even in the overlong opening poem:

> I know the pretty almanac
> Of the punctual coming-back
> On their due-days, of the birds.

The last poem in the book, the "Song of Seid Nimetollah of Kuhistan," seeks to represent the song and the dance in which the dervish "imitates the movements of the heavenly bodies, by spinning on his own axis, whilst at the same time he revolves around the sheikh in the center, representing the sun." Emerson was only at rare intervals capable now of the whirling rapture, but it was still what he wanted and honored. "Spin the ball! I reel, I burn," it begins.[4]

Emerson was still reading actively. Besides rereading Hegel, he had gone back to Anquetil-Duperron and to Dante in a new translation. He was also reading this year F. Max Muller's *Science of Language*. His old boldness and phrase-making skill were there when a proper occasion called. In a speech at the founding of the Free Religious Association in late May 1867 he observed that the churches were no longer useful, that people no longer went to church, and that "a technical theology no longer suits." He enthusiastically reaffirmed enthusiasm as "the parent of everything good in history" and said that what was best in ancient religions was the sense of association, of community, of friendship they fostered. Two years later in the same forum he was rejecting supernaturalism and embracing ecumenism with his old energy, praising the Quakers and the Jews, and saying, acidly, "I think we might now relinquish our theological controversies to communities more idle and ignorant than we."[5]

In July 1867 Harvard appointed Emerson to its board of overseers and the Harvard chapter of Phi Beta Kappa asked him to deliver the annual address at commencement. Thirty years had passed since "The American Scholar"; now his topic was "The Progress of Culture." The occasion was a notable failure. Emerson suddenly found that he could not see his papers clearly. He had not until that moment needed glasses to read his lectures. He became flustered, his papers slipped away under his hands on the poorly contrived table he was using as a lectern. Finally one of his auditors got up and put a cushion under Emerson's papers for him. The audience was uneasy.[6]

July went badly this year in other ways. Emerson's old friend and benefactor Abel Adams died on the ninth. Sarah Ripley, one of the learned women to whom Emerson owed his education, died on the twenty-sixth. In late fall he set out on another western lecture tour.

As Emerson's powers and energies declined over the next few years, those of Lidian revived. The two processes were linked; it was a clear case of compensation. Emerson's decline made room for Lidian. As the grandchildren began to come and as she increasingly made her peace with the fact that Ellen was now running the house as well as acting as Emerson's secretary and editor, Lidian began to blossom. As Emerson went out less and less often in public, embarrassed by his failing memory, Lidian went out more and more. She wrote warm, affectionate, uncomplaining letters. By the midseventies, Ellen tells us, "the long lane had completely turned. At the Club Mother had made friends with all the people she had known slightly hitherto, she had actually become a belle and was invited out all the time. With the social life, her spirits rose, her ill health passed away, and she became a happy person."[7]

Everything that lives, said Santayana, is tragic in its fate, comic in its existence, and lyric in its ideal essence. So it was with Lidian now, and in 1867—if we may trust the manuscript record—she turned again to writing poetry. Freed now of all the conventions in which her early poetry was cast, she wrote a "Poem Composed in Sleep," a simple lyrical love poem, unpublished in her lifetime, which can only have been addressed to her husband and which does more than any single bit of writing to let us in behind the organic reticence they both habitually adopted.

> Will you walk in the fields, love?
>   Let us be gone.
> The tall grass will wave to thee
>   Fairest one.
>
> Will you walk in the meadows, love?
>   Let us be gone.
> The Flowrets will greet thee
>   Fairest one.
>
> Will you walk in the woods, love?
>   Let us be gone.
> The tall trees will bend to thee
>   Fairest one.
>
> Will you walk by the river, love?
>   Let us be gone.
> The stream will reflect thee
>   Fairest one.
>
> Will you walk on the hill, love?
>   Let us be gone.
> The blue sky will bend oer thee
>   Fairest one.[8]

And what of his feelings for her? They seem to have been renewed as well. For a New Year's present for 1868 Emerson had resilvered a pair of silver-plated candlesticks that Lidian treasured and that had worn down to copper. He wrote a little poem for her for the occasion, a poem just recently published. After telling how time "stole the silver, grain by grain" so that "nothing but copper could remain," the poem ends:

> But when Aladdin came to town
> Hiding his famed lamp in his gown
> Touched the old sticks with fingers new
> As if with star-shine riddled through
> And now they beam like her own feats
> Of mercy in the Concord streets.[9]

98. Harvard. California. Fire

IN 1868 CAME ANOTHER OF THE LOSSES THAT INCREASINGLY punctuated Emerson's life. His last surviving brother, William, had been suffering increasingly from headaches. On September 4 he wrote Emerson a letter full of the usual family chat, but adding, "Indeed, I am but poorly. The last two days I was not able to get down stairs." Nine days later he was dead. By chance Emerson arrived in New York on other business the day William died. The two brothers talked together for half an hour. William spoke with difficulty; he had not expected to see Waldo. When the end came, William's two sons lifted him to the bed. His last word was "Good-bye." "It was all a sad surprise to me," Emerson reported to Lidian. "I am glad to have come, if it was the last day."[1]

Honors, many of them ceremonial or conferred with an eye to publicity for the donor, continued to accumulate on Emerson's head. He was elected vice-president of the Massachusetts SPCA, an organization in which Lidian was active and for whose newspaper she wrote articles. In 1869 Emerson was elected vice-president of the New England Woman Suffrage Association.

Six years had passed since the death of Mary Moody Emerson and her nephew now wrote and delivered a long memorial piece on her. Emerson's exchanges with Aunt Mary had been a major part of his own development; his memorial to her is full of affection and the impulse to praise, though it no longer has the power of thought or the cold command of phrase that mark his best work. It is a biographical sketch, pieced out with a long string of quotations. She is Emerson's representative woman, and he insisted that hers was "a representative life . . . of an age now past, and of which I think no types survive." Years earlier he had idealized his first wife, Ellen, until she became a sort of Beatrice. Now, in a final reckoning, he set his aunt even higher—if such a thing is possible—recognizing in her some of the qualities of the creator of Beatrice. In an astonishing and moving passage he said, "When I read Dante the other day, and his paraphrases to signify with more adequateness Christ or Jehovah, whom do you think I was reminded of? Whom but Mary Emerson and her eloquent theology." Emerson had spent his life trying to live up to her expectations: "She gave high counsels. It was the privilege of certain boys to have this immeasurably high standard indicated to their childhood; a blessing which nothing else in education could supply." She stands, finally, said her nephew, apart from works, even from her own works, for "faith alone; faith alone."[2]

Emerson had aimed so high and wanted so much that he inevitably judged his own life a failure. He never quite became habituated to the disparity between promise and performance. "At certain happy hours," he said in a lecture,

> each man is conscious of a heaven within him, a realm of undiscovered sciences, of slumbering potencies, a heaven of which the feats of talent are no measure; it arches like a sky over all that it has done, all that has been done. All that is urged by the saint for the superiority of faith over works, is as truly urged for the highest state of intellectual perception over any intellectual performance.

And now, when it was too late to mount another major effort, Emerson's sense of the gap between perception and act was stronger than ever. This year he had a Prufrockian dream about it.

> I passed into a room where were ladies and gentlemen, some of whom I knew . . . One of the ladies was beautiful, and I, it seemed, had already seen her, and was her lover. She looked up from her painting and saw me, but did not recognize me;—which I thought wrong,—unpardonable. Later, I reflected that it was not so criminal in her, since I had never *proposed*.[3]

In the early months of 1870 Emerson was in the final stages of getting together the volume called *Society and Solitude*. Almost all the pieces in it had existed since the late 1850s, but the rearrangement of passages within each piece—always the hardest part of writing for Emerson—was giving him more trouble than usual. He wrote little that was new. His journals are meager and mostly undated. His correspondence with friends had now become fitful; there were long silences, mostly on his part, in his exchange with Carlyle. He complained of fits of "stupor," and his failing memory had driven him to construct mnemonics. He had been invited to lecture at Harvard in the spring, in the new graduate program in philosophy. It was to be a demanding series of eighteen lectures. Working on the book so long, Emerson left inadequate time to prepare the lectures.[4]

Harvard's new young president Charles Eliot wanted to expand the college beyond its traditional undergraduate curriculum. As a step toward graduate education, he took an existing program called University Lectures and reorganized it into two sequences of lectures. Each sequence ran a full year, cost one hundred fifty dollars—the same as a year's undergraduate tuition—and was made up of a series of courses that ran sequentially. The system was closer to extension courses or to adult education than to modern graduate school. There were seven lecture courses in the philosophy series; the other lecturers were Francis Bowen, John Fiske, Charles Sanders Peirce, James E. Cabot, Frederic Hedge, and George Fisher. Emerson was next to last; he gave three lectures a week starting April 26. Emerson called his course "The Natural History of Intellect."

The entire system of University Lecture courses was a failure. The total enrollment of "teachers and other competent persons" in both series (there was a modern languages and literature series in addition to the philosophy series) was nine. The scheme was dropped after the first year. Four people took the philosophy series through to the end. When Emerson gave the lectures again the following year, the lock-step sequence was abandoned, lower fees were set for each separate course, and some thirty people came to hear him.[5]

Because the whole system of University Lectures failed (Eliot replaced the program with the Graduate School of Arts and Sciences in 1872) and because Emerson's lectures have never been edited or even printed, we cannot yet be certain they were the trifles everyone has always assumed them to be. James Elliot Cabot, Emerson's friend, editor, and biographer who had as good a grasp of Emerson's papers as anyone after Emerson himself, said that Emerson "appears to have regarded ["The Natural History of Intellect"] as the chief task of his life." If Cabot is correct, this surprising judgment—no trace of which can be found in Emerson's own words—suggests that Emerson's editors, beginning with his friend Cabot and his son Edward, have not adequately represented Emerson's late work. Clearly Emerson had long considered such a project; something similar had been in his mind since the late 1830s. He had taken a major step toward its accomplishment in the English lectures of 1848, and he had seriously reworked the talks in the 1850s. Yet the very title, with its enlightenment, rationalist, Humean overtones, suggests a major conflict with *Nature,* "The Poet," and most of the early essays, which were born out of Emerson's challenge to Hume's destructive rationalism.[6]

At the very least Emerson's frequent return to this subject should warn us never to undervalue the rationalist, antisupernatural side of Emerson. In one important sense Emerson had been working on the "Natural History of Intellect" since his return from Europe in 1833; the course could also have been called "The Nature of Mind." These lectures above all reflect Emerson's long interest in science—not science as measurement, or replication, or induction, or data collecting but science as the study of nature and of the nature of things. Emerson had always had a keen interest in the imaginative and creative aspect of scientific discovery. He still did; he made lists of creative scientific ideas and of concepts that seemed to bridge science and art. He called the second lecture of his course "The Transcendency of Physics," and he insisted on the interdependency of fact and mind: "I think no metaphysical fact of any value which does not rest on a physical fact, and no physical fact important except as resting on metaphysical truth."[7]

Emerson's philosophical interest in science was now focused on the way science had restricted itself to self-evident truths. By self-evident he did not mean obvious or superficial but the opposite of supernatural, or occult, or miraculous, or handed down by authority. Science deals with matters that when probed provide their own evidence. Emerson thought that this test of self-evidence was also applicable to moral, religious, aesthetic, and political matters. He thus saw no necessary difference between science and other subjects. Prophecy too is concerned with self-evident truths; so is poetry. The other side of Emerson's lifelong aversion to the academic enterprises of buttress-building and commentary is his steady interest in the clear, impassioned expression of self-evident truths. He saw this as the task of scientist, prophet, and poet alike.

In his writing and lecturing since the early 1830s Emerson had really had only one subject, to which he now returned in the Harvard lectures, saying in his opening talk, "I hope to invite your attention to the laws of the mind." The subject was enormous. "There is nothing that does not belong to it,—not a science, not a word of man, speech of orator, hymn of poet, prayer of priest, witticism at table, but this sets us on the analysis to find wherein the power, wisdom, worth or fun lies." The inclusiveness of the subject appealed to Emerson, but its breadth also made his task unrealizable. No system could contain it:

> All these exhaustive theories appear indeed as false and vain attempts to analyse the primal thought. That is *up*-stream. And what a stream! Can you swim up Niagara Falls? My contribution will be merely historical. I write anecdotes of the intellect . . . a list or Farmer's Almanac of mental moods.[8]

Definitional aphorism was first and last for Emerson the supreme literary form for the self-evident. In these lectures, as in the entirely unknown and unedited 1868 lectures "Philosophy of the People," Emerson's aphoristic power was undiminished.

The mind is the center of things, so that theology, Nature, Astronomy, and history date from where the observer stands.
Without identity at base, chaos must be forever. On the initial forms or forces,—be they what they may,—we must have already all the properties which in any combination they afterwards exhibit.
Philosophy is insight into the necessity of things. The ground of everything lies in the thing itself.
The reality of things is thought. It is the secret of power. All superiority is this, or related to this.
Our whole existence is subjective. What we are, that we see, love, hate. A man externizes himself in his friends, and in his enemies, and parasites, and in his gods.
You are the book's book. Thus an intellectual man might say with some conviction, it makes no difference what I read.
The children [playing dress-up] have only the instinct of their race, the instinct of the universe—in which *becoming somewhat else* is the whole game of nature, and death the penalty of standing still.[9]

The Harvard Lectures represent Emerson's final say on his lifelong subject, the nature of mind; they are a rethinking of idealism in the light of the material gains of the nineteenth century. Emerson's position is clear enough, though his statement of it did not satisfy him or his audience or his early editors. The intensive format of the lectures was daunting. Ellen said they were "eating him all up." He was neither pleased with them nor able to improve them the second time around. He ended by giving fewer than the number of lectures advertised, and at the conclusion of the second set his son-in-law whisked him off to California to recuperate.[10]

The California trip was done in Forbes's showy style. The party of twelve included Edith, her husband William Forbes, and James Thayer, who later wrote up the trip. They left Chicago by private railroad car; George Pullman personally saw them off on April 13, 1871. Six days later Emerson met Brigham Young in Salt Lake City. Three days after that he reached San Francisco. He stood in the back of the car and watched the glorious western valleys roll out behind him. California clearly caught his imagination. He said he thought "no young man would come back from it." He learned that California wine was never adulterated because grapes, at a penny a pound, were cheaper than any additive. Emerson admired the great Sequoias and noticed that they generally bore marks of fire. Having lived thirteen hundred years they "must have met that danger and every other in turn. Yet they possess great power of resistance to fire." Emerson was reading Titus F. Cronise, *The Natural Wealth of California* (1868), and John S. Hittell, *The Resources of California* (1866). He was asked to name a tree in the Mariposa grove. Aware that the giant redwoods had been named in honor of the only man in history known to have invented a whole alphabet, the Cherokee Sequoya, Emerson offered the name Samoset (the Indian benefactor of the Plymouth colonists) to a tree that measured fifty feet around at two and a half feet from the ground.[11]

While at Yosemite, which would not be set aside as a national park until 1890, Emerson met John Muir, then thirty-three and working at a sawmill. Muir was already a great admirer of Emerson. He now showed him how to distinguish yellow pine, sugar pine, and silver fir. (Sugar pines have enormous cones fourteen to twenty inches long; the needles of silver fir *look* silver.) Emerson seemed to Muir "as serene as a sequoia." He tried to get Emerson to go camping and sleep out in the open. Muir was disappointed in Emerson, but he recognized, as not everyone did, that he was past his prime. Even so, Emerson recognized his man. At the end of the visit, Muir walked to the edge of the Mariposa grove and watched Emerson's party depart on horseback. "Emerson lingered in the rear ... and when he reached the top of the ridge, after all the rest of the party were over and out of sight, he turned his horse, took off his hat and waved me a last good-bye."[12]

Emerson did not know how to stop working. His habit of writing outlived his capacity to write. He kept accepting engagements, rearranging old talks for new occasions. After his return from California, he gave twenty-nine more lectures in late 1871 and early 1872, traveling as far west as Chicago and Quincy, Illinois, and as far south as Washington, D.C.

He kept reading, and from time to time he found a book that ignited his old enthusiasm. In the fall of 1871 he found John Ruskin's *The Two Paths*. Ruskin's starting point was one of Emerson's own. Every great school of art, said Ruskin, had as its main aim "the representation of some natural fact as truly as possible." The book is made up of lectures delivered in 1858 and 1859 on "art and its application to decoration and manufacture." Ruskin embraced the Goethean idea that the great artist turns outward and takes some small part of the world as his or her subject. This position put Ruskin squarely against the then rising doctrine of art for art's sake.

> Wherever art is practised for its own sake, and the delight of the workman is in what he *does* and *produces,* instead of in what he interprets or exhibits,—there art has an influence of the most fatal kind on brain and heart, and it issues, if long so pursued, in the *destruction both of intellectual power* and moral principle; whereas art devoted humbly and self-forgetfully to the clear statement and record of the facts of the universe, is always helpful and beneficent to mankind, full of comfort, strength and salvation.

Emerson read the book in September 1871 and praised it at every meal.[13]

On the night of July 23, 1872, a crackling sound inside the plastering waked Emerson in the upstairs bedroom of his Concord home. The house was on fire. He could see it through a crack between the plastering and the molding of a closet. Lidian ran to him; together they opened the waste-paper cupboard door and the fire flashed out. It had started in the garret and was working its way down. Aware now that he and Lidian could not put it out themselves, Emerson ran to the front gate and shouted, "Fire! Whitcomb! Staples! Fire!" Both neighboring houses were astir instantly. Sam Staples, Thoreau's onetime jailor, got to the garret door first, saw the smoke, smelled burnt carpets, and took charge. The garret door was closed; the fire could not be stopped, but there would be time to empty the house. The alarm had been raised; other neighbors came pouring in. They carried out what pictures, books, clothes, and furniture they could; the rest they threw out of the windows. The fire engine arrived and somehow the one-armed Ephraim Bull Jr. (son of the man who developed the Concord grape) got up on the roof with a hose. When the fire was put out, the house was still standing.

The front stairs were unburnt, as was Emerson's study, with all his books and papers. Elsewhere in the house, ceilings were down, and there were lakes on the floors. Outside there were mountains of clothes, books, and furnishings.[14]

The house would have to be rebuilt. Emerson had inadequate resources; he still depended heavily on lecture fees for living expenses. But thousands of dollars were raised now in Boston, Cambridge, and Concord to help the man and his family who had helped so many others. The fire constituted one more ending. After the fire Emerson virtually gave up public lecturing, appearing from then on only for very special occasions before familiar and already well-disposed audiences.

99. *Philae and Parnassus*

THE FIRE AFFECTED EMERSON PROFOUNDLY. HE WAS EX-
hausted; he became ill. His power of attention and his memory weakened
visibly. Enough money had been raised for him to take a trip as well as
rebuild the house. On October 23, 1872, he sailed with Ellen for England,
the Continent, and Egypt. This trip too was an ending. Reversing his first
European trip of forty years earlier, he and Ellen went from England through
Paris to Naples, where they took ship for Egypt. After seeing Alexandria and
Cairo, they set off by boat up the Nile. He found it "a wonderful country,
but easily seen. Egypt is practically nothing but a strip of land, only a green
ribbon on either side of the Nile, but 520 miles long." Emerson found it
humiliating not to know the language. Egypt put questions to which he had
no answers. "The Sphinxes scorn dunces," he wrote in his journal. He was
much interested in the organic foundation of Egyptian forms. "The lateen
sail is the shadow of a pyramid: and the pyramid is the simplest copy of a
mountain, or of the form which a pile of sand or earth takes when dropped
from a cart." He noted with dismay, as travelers still do, how all the children
"have flies roosting about their eyes, which they do not disturb." Oph-
thalmia, carried by the flies, was rampant; there were blind beggars at every
landing.[1]

The traditional goal of a trip to Egypt was the island of Philae, the jewel
of the Nile, situated near Aswan, where the Nile widens at the first cataract.
This point marks the edge of ancient Egypt and the beginning of ancient
Nubia, now Sudan. Philae was a small island, less than a thousand feet long
and five hundred feet wide. The Italian explorer Belzoni said it contained
"the most superb group of ruins I have ever beheld together in so small a
space of ground." The temple of Isis at Philae was the last place where the
ancient Egyptian religion had been practiced until it was closed down by
Justinian in the sixth century A.D.[2]

Emerson had always associated Philae with the tomb of Osiris. He knew
from Plutarch that Isis had opened the coffin of Osiris and that Osiris's body
had been torn apart and scattered. Isis later buried the pieces bit by bit as

she found them. Emerson was really attracted to Egypt by a wish to see the tomb of "him who lies buried at Philae," as his son noted. Some part of Emerson had died and been buried with each of his loved ones beginning with Ellen. Philae was the last station on Emerson's pilgrimage of losses. Afterward, retracing his steps through Italy, France, and England, he felt curiously lighter, relieved of a burden: "For the first time for many years you wake master of the bright day, in a bright world without claim on you, only leave to enjoy. This dropping for the first time the doleful bundle of duty creates, day after day, a health as of new youth."[3]

In France he met Taine and Turgenev; in England he saw old friends, declined offers to lecture, talked with Ruskin and with F. Max Muller, and breakfasted with Gladstone. He was welcomed everywhere as a celebrity. When he arrived home in Concord, the train carrying him blew its whistle all the way in from Walden Woods to the depot, where the whole town had turned out—school was canceled—to welcome him home. His working days were now over. At Ellen's suggestion he brought in James Elliot Cabot to finish a task he had started but could not finish, the book called *Letters and Social Aims,* a miscellany made up of old lectures and parts of lectures not previously published.

His memory was getting worse. In England he had been glad to have Edward (then going to medical school in England) beside him at dinner in case he could not bring up his wife's name. What he suffered from was aphasia; unable to call up a given word, he would resort to circumlocutions that sometimes came out like riddles. Once when he wanted the word "umbrella," Cabot remembered him saying: "I can't tell its name, but I can tell its history. Strangers take it away." The decay of memory was gradual, but unfortunately Emerson was also quite conscious of it. "We remember that we forget," he had once written. He observed that memory has a personality of its own. It "volunteers or refuses its informations at its will, not at mine." Someone told him that Alcott had once said "that as the child loses, as he comes into the world, his angelic memory, so the man, as he grows old, loses his memory of the world." His friend Max Muller sent him a birthday greeting in 1880: "The translator of the Upanishads, Moksha Mulara, sends greeting and best wishes to his American Guru, Amarasunu . . ." Accompanying this was a "newly discovered Upanishad" that said, among other things, "The self never forgets—the inscriptions on the memory fade and it is well that much should be forgotten." Emerson's son Edward later wrote a poem called "Memory, or the Gates," in which

he too invoked the Wordsworthian—and Hasidic—idea of the moment of
forgetting that precedes birth. Edward matches it with that other, later
moment when we pass through the second gate of forgetting before death.
Of the brief span in between, Edward wrote:

> Think again.
> Thousands of days were granted, and each one
> Gave thousand minutes between sun and sun
> And every one brought tribute, flowers or stars
> Or help unlooked for in the spirit's wars.[4]

As time passed, Emerson's memory worsened, becoming a serious em-
barrassment. Increasingly he avoided social situations and stayed home. In
1874 Edward finished his training as a physician, came home to America,
and married Annie Keyes. Late in 1874 Emerson brought out—with major
help from Edith—a poetry anthology called *Parnassus*. The selection is odd,
for the volume was not intended as a book of everyone's favorite poems, not
even of his own favorites, but a collection of family favorites for parlor
reading. Emerson left out himself, Poe, and Whitman. He included his
brother Edward, Lucy Larcom, Jones Very, Jean Ingelow, Sara H. Palfrey,
Thoreau, Harriet Spofford, David Wasson, Anna Barbauld, Julia Dorr, and
F. B. Sanborn. He included John Quincy Adams, Calidasa, and Simonides.
Many of the poems had personal, indeed private associations for him. Many
are about the sea, including one by Jean Ingelow that has a vivid scene
recalling the death of Margaret Fuller and her son:

> The Captain reeled on deck with two small things
> One in each arm—his little lad and lass
> Their hair was long and blew before his face
> . . . He fell
> But held them fast. The crew, poor luckless souls!
> The breakers licked them off; and some were crushed
> Some swallowed in the yeast, some flung up dead.[5]

Only an extraordinary event now could coax Emerson out in public. In
a spirit of reconciliation with the South, he went to the University of
Virginia in 1876, but he lacked the strength to make himself heard beyond
the front rows. He worked with Cabot and Ellen to get out a volume of his
own poems. *Selected Poems* appeared in 1876. He also worked with Ellen

on the preface to a coffee-table book to be called *The Hundred Greatest Men*. The slow evaporation of memory no longer fretted him; he was remarkably happy. In 1879 Edith wrote Carlyle: "Father is very well and very happy. Mother often says that he is the happiest person she ever knew—he is so uniformly in good spirits, and waking each morning in a joyful mood."[6]

Of the two old friendly antagonists, Carlyle died first. On February 10, 1881, as they were burying Carlyle in Ecclefechan, Emerson was delivering a paper on Carlyle at a Carlyle memorial meeting of the Massachusetts Historical Society. He sat with Ellen beside him at a small table in the Dowse Library in Boston. Joseph Slater describes the scene: "He stumbled over long words. When he seemed entirely defeated, Ellen would make the sounds silently and he would imitate her lips . . . his audience drew closer into a circle around him." It was his last public performance.[7]

100. Fire at the Core of the World

IN HIS 1842 JOURNAL EMERSON HAD WRITTEN:

> The tongue of flame, the picture the newspapers give, at the late fire in Liverpool, of the mountains of burning cotton over which the flames arose to twice their height, the volcano also, from which the conflagration rises toward the zenith an appreciable distance toward the stars—these are the most affecting symbols of what man should be. A spark of fire is infinitely deep, but a mass of fire reaching from earth upward into heaven, this is the sign of the robust, united, burning, radiant soul.

This was also Emerson's image for the energy behind the poetic impulse. Poetry was for him never just a matter of writing, of expression, but always of connecting one's own small flame to the great central fires of life. Our days demand fire: "We must have not only hydrogen in balloons and steel springs under coaches, but we must have fire under the Andes at the core of the world."[1]

Emerson's own life was now burning low. On the nineteenth of April, 1882, Emerson went walking, got soaked in a sudden shower, and made an already existing cold worse. The next morning, as he was coming down for breakfast, his daughter Ellen recalled, "He cried out and staggered as from a blow, just as we passed the rocking horse in the front entry." Emerson could give no satisfactory account of what he felt. After he had sat for a while, he said, "I hoped it would not come this way. I would rather fall down cellar." He slept most of the day.[2]

On the next day, April 21, six days before his death, Emerson was diagnosed as having pneumonia. Despite Edward's warning, Emerson got up, dressed, and went as usual to his study. After tea, he consented to go up to his bedroom early but would accept no help closing up his study for the night. He went from window to window, locking them and closing the shutters on each. Then, as was his custom, he went to the fireplace and took his fire apart, setting the sticks, one by one, on end on each side, and separating all the glowing coals. That done, he took his study lamp in his hand, left the room for the last time, and went upstairs.

Genealogies

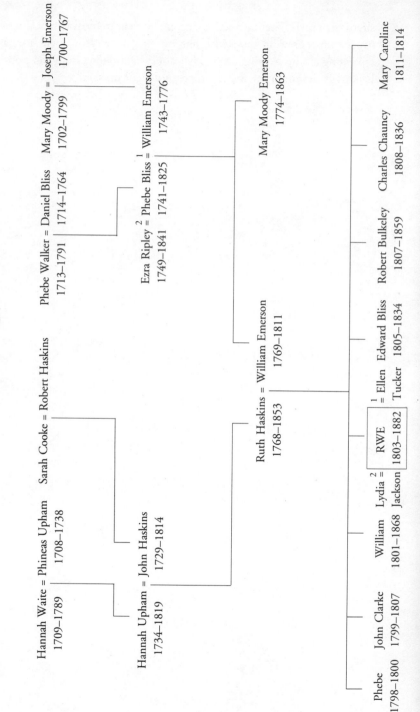

Hannah Waite = Phineas Upham
1709–1789   1708–1738

Sarah Cooke = Robert Haskins

Phebe Walker = Daniel Bliss
1713–1791   1714–1764

Mary Moody = Joseph Emerson
1702–1799   1700–1767

Hannah Upham = John Haskins
1734–1819   1729–1814

Ezra Ripley [2] Phebe Bliss [1] = William Emerson
1749–1841   1741–1825   1743–1776

Mary Moody Emerson
1774–1863

Ruth Haskins = William Emerson
1768–1853   1769–1811

Phebe   John Clarke   William   Lydia [2] = RWE = [1] Ellen   Edward Bliss   Robert Bulkeley   Charles Chauncy   Mary Caroline
1798–1800   1799–1807   1801–1868   Jackson   1803–1882   Tucker   1805–1834   1807–1859   1808–1836   1811–1814

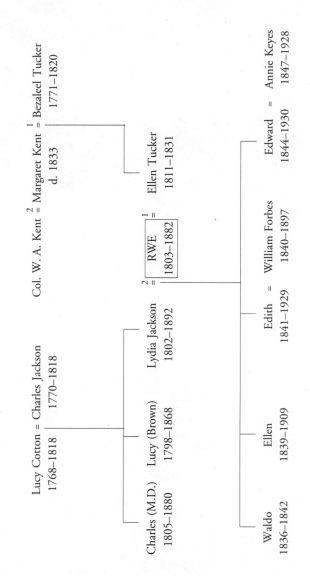

Lucy Cotton = Charles Jackson
1768–1818   1770–1818

Col. W. A. Kent [2] = Margaret Kent [1] = Bezaleel Tucker
                       d. 1833   1771–1820

Charles (M.D.)   Lucy (Brown)   Lydia Jackson   [2] = RWE [1] = Ellen Tucker
1805–1880   1798–1868   1802–1892   1803–1882   1811–1831

Waldo   Ellen   Edith = William Forbes   Edward = Annie Keyes
1836–1842   1839–1909   1841–1929   1840–1897   1844–1930   1847–1928

Chronology of the Life
of Ralph Waldo Emerson

1803	born May 25 in Boston
1811	father, William Emerson, dies
1812–17	attends Boston Latin School
1817–21	attends Harvard College
1821–25	teaches school
1826	trip to St. Augustine
1828	engaged to Ellen Tucker
1829	ordained minister of Second Church in Boston
	marries Ellen Tucker, September 10
1831	Ellen dies, February 8
1832	resigns from Second Church
	first trip to Europe and England
1834	starts new career lecturing
	brother Edward dies, October 1
1835	moves to Concord, Massachusetts
	marries Lydia Jackson, September 14
1836	brother Charles dies, May 9
	Nature published
	son Waldo born, October 30
1837	"The American Scholar" address at Harvard
1838	"Divinity School Address"
1839	daughter Ellen born, February 24
1840–44	*The Dial*
1841	*Essays* published
	daughter Edith born, November 22
1842	son Waldo dies, January 27
1844	son Edward born, July 10
1847–48	second trip to England and France
1850	*Representative Men* published

first western lecture tour
Margaret Fuller dies, July 19
1853 mother, Ruth Haskins Emerson, dies, November 16
1855 meets Whitman
1856 *English Traits* published
1859 brother Bulkeley dies, May 27
1860 *The Conduct of Life* published
1862 Henry Thoreau dies, May 6
1863 aunt Mary Moody Emerson dies, October 3
1867 *May-Day and Other Pieces* published
1868 brother William dies, September 13
1870 *Society and Solitude* published
 "Natural History of Intellect" lectures at Harvard
1871 trip to California
1872 house burns, July 24
1873 third trip to Europe, including England and Egypt
1874 *Parnassus* published
1875 *Letters and Social Aims* published
1882 dies in Concord, April 27

Principal Sources

Manuscripts

Most of Emerson's papers are in the Houghton Library at Harvard. Besides the notebooks that have been published in *JMN* and *PN,* and those currently being published in *TN,* there are still more than fifty unpublished notebooks. Especially useful are Emerson's various indexes, his four volumes of the writings of his aunt, Mary Moody Emerson, and various autobiographical fragments. There are dozens of unpublished late lectures. There are more than three thousand letters to Emerson. Houghton also has diaries of Ruth Haskins Emerson, Ellen Tucker, and Charles Chauncy Emerson. This library also has the poetry of Ellen Tucker and that of Lydia Jackson, Charles Chauncy Emerson, and Edward Bliss Emerson. Ellen Tucker Emerson's "What I Can Remember about Father" is especially valuable. I have also used Houghton's Longfellow papers and the Sturgis family correspondence.

A large collection of letters from Mary Moody Emerson, Ruth Haskins Emerson, Charles Chauncy Emerson, Edward Bliss Emerson, and William Emerson (RWE's brother), known as the Wortis Collection, has been recently deposited in the Massachusetts Historical Society Library. This library also has Edward Everett's translation of Eichhorn in its Everett Collection.

The Concord Free Public Library has Edward Waldo Emerson's notes on the Underground Railroad and a two-volume scrapbook of RWE's miscellaneous writings and notices as well as a wealth of materials for the history of Concord. W. E. Channing's Reading List in Divinity is at the Harvard Divinity School Library. Arthur Bestor's bibliography of Fourierism is at Columbia University. The Berg Collection of the New York Public Library has Peabody family correspondence. The Beinecke at Yale has a marked-up volume of Mary Moody Emerson's copy of de Staël's *Germany.*

George Goodspeed has a collection of letters concerning Frank Sanborn's proposal to Edith. The manuscripts concerning the controversy over the New-Light Quakers of New Bedford in the 1820s have disappeared. The trail stops at the Rhode Island Historical Society, where the Friends have a major archive.

The most important of the unpublished sources are listed below.

RWE	"Index Psi," Houghton b Ms Am 1280 H 110
RWE	"Old Index," includes "Platoniana" and "Index II" (1847), Houghton b Ms Am 1280 H 107
RWE	"Index Major," assembled after and based on "Index II," Houghton b Ms Am 1280 H 106
RWE	"Index Minor" (1843), Houghton b Ms Am 1280 H 104 and 104a
RWE	"Index Minor" (n.d.), Houghton b Ms Am 1280 H 131
RWE	"Biography" (1874), Houghton b Ms Am 1280 H 131
RWE	"Index Swedenborg," Houghton b Ms Am 1280 H 194f
RWE	"The Power and Terror of Thought," Houghton b Ms Am 1280.203 (11)
RWE	"Memory, 1858," Houghton b Ms Am 1280.203 (8, 9)
RWE	"France, or Urbanity," Houghton b Ms Am 1280.202 (6)
RWE	"Discourse Manqué," Houghton b Ms Am 1280.202 (3)
RWE	"MME I," Houghton b Ms Am 1280 H 146
RWE	"MME II," Houghton b Ms Am 1280 H 147
RWE	"MME III," Houghton b Ms Am 1280 H 148
RWE	"MME IV," Houghton b Ms Am 1280 H 149
RWE	"Autobiographical Sketch," Houghton b Ms Am 1280.245 (121)
RWE	"Autobiography," Houghton b Ms Am 1280.235 (127)
RWE	"Hecker and the Catholic Church," Houghton b Ms Am 1280.214 (110)
RWE	"Therienism," Houghton b Ms Am 1280.214 (123)
RWE	"Egypt," Houghton b Ms Am 1280.214 (221, 222)
RWE	"Philosophy of the People," Houghton b Ms Am 1280.209
RWE	"Chartism," Houghton b Ms Am 1280.201 (7)
RWE	"Suppressed Passages on English Literature," Houghton b Ms Am 1280.201 (8)
RWE	"Transcendency of Physics," Houghton b Ms Am 1280.212 (3)
RWE	"Identity," Houghton b Ms Am 1280.212 (13)
RWE	"Platonists," Houghton b Ms Am 1280.212 (16)
CCE	Diary, Houghton b Ms Am 1280.220 119
CCE	"Socrates," Houghton b Ms Am 1280.220 (121)
CCE	Letters, Massachusetts Historical Society Library

EBE	Letters, Massachusetts Historical Society Library
WmE	Letters, Massachusetts Historical Society Library
EE	"What I Can Remember about Father," Houghton b Ms Am 1280.227
ETE	"Commonplace Book," Houghton b Ms Am 1280.215 (74)
CS	Letters to RWE, Houghton b Ms Am 1280 (3159 to 3164)
CS	Letters to RWE, Houghton b Ms Am 1221 (271 to 279, 316 to 372)
CS	Letters to RWE, Houghton b Ms Am 1280.235 (610)
CS	Letters to RWE, Houghton b Ms Am 1465 (1215 to 1226)
LJE	Poems, Houghton b Ms Am 1280.235 (377 to 381)

Abbreviations

AL . . . . *American Literature.*

ARLR . . . . *American Renaissance Literary Report.* Ed. K. W. Cameron. Hartford, Conn.: Transcendental Books 1987–.

CW . . . . *The Complete Works of Ralph Waldo Emerson.* Centenary Edition, ed. E. W. Emerson. 12 vols. Boston: Houghton Mifflin, 1903–1904.

EL . . . . *The Early Lectures of Ralph Waldo Emerson.* Ed. Stephen E. Whicher, Robert E. Spiller, and Wallace E. Williams. 3 vols. Cambridge: Harvard University Press, 1959–1972.

ESQ . . . . *Emerson Society Quarterly.*

EtE . . . . K. W. Cameron. *Emerson the Essayist.* 2 vols. Raleigh, N.C.: Thistle Press, 1945.

EWE . . . . Edward Waldo Emerson. *Emerson in Concord.* Boston: Houghton Mifflin, 1889.

HW . . . . *The Collected Works of Ralph Waldo Emerson.* 5 vols. to date. Cambridge: Harvard University Press, 1971–.

J . . . . *Journals of Ralph Waldo Emerson.* Ed. E. W. Emerson and W. E. Forbes. 10 vols. Boston: Houghton Mifflin, 1909–1914.

JMN . . . . *The Journals and Miscellaneous Notebooks of Ralph Waldo Emerson.* Ed. William H. Gilman et al. 16 vols. Cambridge: Harvard University Press, 1960–1982.

L . . . . *The Letters of Ralph Waldo Emerson.* Vols. 1–6, ed. Ralph L. Rusk. Vols. 7 and 8, ed. Eleanor Tilton. New York: Columbia University Press, 1939–.

NEQ . . . . *New England Quarterly.*

PN . . . . *The Poetry Notebooks of Ralph Waldo Emerson.* Ed. Ralph H. Orth, Albert J. von Frank, Linda Allardt, and David W. Hill. Columbia: University of Missouri Press, 1986.

SAR . . . . *Studies in the American Renaissance.* Ed. Joel Myerson. Boston: Twayne, 1977–82; Charlottesville: University Press of Virginia, 1983–.

TN . . . . *The Topical Notebooks of Ralph Waldo Emerson.* Ed. Ralph H. Orth, Susan Sutton Smith, and Ronald A. Bosco. Columbia: University of Missouri Press, 1990–.

TSB . . . . *Thoreau Society Bulletin.*

Short Titles

McAleer . . . . . . John McAleer. *Ralph Waldo Emerson: Days of Encounter.* Boston: Little, Brown, 1984.

Allen . . . . Gay Wilson Allen. *Waldo Emerson: A Biography.* New York: Viking, 1981.

Bibl. . . . . Joel Myerson. *Ralph Waldo Emerson: A Descriptive Bibliography.* Pittsburgh: University of Pittsburgh Press, 1982.

Cabot . . . . James Elliot Cabot. *A Memoir of Ralph Waldo Emerson.* 2 vols. Boston: Houghton Mifflin, 1888.

Corr. HDT . . . . . *The Correspondence of Henry David Thoreau.* Ed. Walter Harding and Carl Bode. New York: New York University Press, 1958.

Dial . . . . *The Dial: A Magazine for Literature, Philosophy, and Religion.* 1840–1844. Reprint. New York: Russell and Russell, 1961.

E-C Corr. . . . . . . *The Correspondence of Emerson and Carlyle.* Ed. Joseph Slater. New York: Columbia University Press, 1964.

E's Library . . . . . Walter Harding. *Emerson's Library.* Charlottesville: University Press of Virginia, 1967.

E's Reading . . . . . Kenneth W. Cameron. *Ralph Waldo Emerson's Reading.* Raleigh, N.C.: Thistle Press, 1941.

Gougeon . . . . . . Len Gougeon. *Virtue's Hero: Emerson, Antislavery, and Reform.* Athens: University of Georgia Press, 1990.

Gregg . . . . *One First Love: The Letters of Ellen Louisa Tucker to Ralph Waldo Emerson.* Ed. Edith W. Gregg. Cambridge: Harvard University Press, 1962.

Haskins . . . . . . David Greene Haskins. *Ralph Waldo Emerson, His Maternal Ancestors.* Boston: Cupples Upham and Co., 1887.

Letters of EP .... *Letters of Elizabeth Palmer Peabody.* Ed. Bruce A. Ronda. Middletown: Wesleyan University Press, 1984.

Letters of ETE ... *The Letters of Ellen Tucker Emerson.* Ed. Edith W. Gregg. 2 vols. Kent, Ohio: Kent State University Press, 1982.

Letters of LE .... *The Selected Letters of Lidian Jackson Emerson.* Ed. Delores Bird Carpenter. Columbia: University of Missouri Press, 1987.

Letters of MF .... *The Letters of Margaret Fuller.* Ed. Robert Hudspeth. 5 vols. Ithaca, N.Y.: Cornell University Press, 1983–.

Life of LE ...... Ellen Tucker Emerson. *The Life of Lidian Jackson Emerson.* Ed. Delores Bird Carpenter. Boston: Twayne, 1981.

May-Day ...... Ralph Waldo Emerson. *May-Day and Other Pieces.* Boston: Ticknor and Fields, 1867.

Nature .... Ralph Waldo Emerson. *Nature.* Boston: James Munroe, 1836.

Parnassus ..... *Parnassus.* Ed. Ralph Waldo Emerson. Boston: Houghton Mifflin, 1874.

Poems .... Ralph Waldo Emerson. *Poems.* Boston: James Munroe, 1847.

Pommer ..... Henry F. Pommer. *Emerson's First Marriage.* Carbondale: Southern Illinois University Press, 1967.

Porte .... Joel Porte. *Representative Men.* New York: Oxford University Press, 1979.

Rusk .... Ralph L. Rusk. *The Life of Ralph Waldo Emerson.* New York: Scribner's, 1949.

Secondary Bibl. ... Robert E. Burkholder and Joel Myerson. *Emerson: An Annotated Secondary Bibliography.* Pittsburgh: University of Pittsburgh Press, 1985.

Sermons .... *The Complete Sermons of Ralph Waldo Emerson.* Ed. Albert J. von Frank, Teresa Toulouse, Andrew Delbanco, Ronald A. Bosco, and Wesley T. Mott. 4 vols. Columbia: University of Missouri Press, 1989–1992.

Uncoll. .... Ralph Waldo Emerson. *Uncollected Writings.* New York: Lamb, 1912.

Notes

The names of Emerson family members are abbreviated as follows: RWE = Ralph Waldo Emerson, WmE = William Emerson (RWE's brother), CCE = Charles Chauncy Emerson, EBE = Edward Bliss Emerson, EWE = Edward Waldo Emerson, MME = Mary Moody Emerson, ETE = Ellen Tucker Emerson (RWE's first wife), EE = Ellen Emerson (RWE's daughter). For other abbreviations in the notes see the lists of abbreviations and short titles under Principal Sources.

1. Prologue

1. See A. S. Bolster Jr., *James Freeman Clarke* (Boston, 1964), 65, and Joy Bayless, *Rufus Wilmot Griswold* (Nashville, Tenn.: Vanderbilt University Press, 1943), 64–66. *JMN* 4:7.

2. S. Freud, "Reflections upon War and Death," in his *Character and Culture* (New York: Macmillan, 1963), 128; *JMN* 8:149.

3. Ms. notebook "MME I," Houghton b Ms Am 1280 H 146, p. 10; Ms. notebook "MME II," Houghton b Ms Am 1280 H 147, p. 5.

4. *JMN* 4:7; Cabot 1:173, 174.

5. *JMN* 4:22, 26, 16.

2. Emerson at Harvard

1. Hugh Blair, *Lectures on Rhetoric,* 5th Am. ed. (1812), 285–286.

2. R. Bayne, introduction to Joseph Butler, *The Analogy of Religion,* Everyman ed. (London: J. M. Dent, 1906); *The Analogy,* pt. 1, p. 115; E. E. Hale, introduction to RWE, *Two Unpublished Essays: The Character of Socrates and the Present State of Ethical Philosophy* (Boston: Lamson Wolffe, 1896). For a modern view of Paley, see

R. Dawkins, *The Blind Watchmaker* (New York: Norton, 1987), 4–6, and J. Burrow, introduction to Charles Darwin, *The Origin of Species* (London: Penguin, 1968), 21–23.

3. Although there is now a wide consensus that the Gospel of St. Mark is the earliest, Griesbach's claim has recently been revived. See C. M. Tuckett, *The Revival of the Griesbach Hypothesis* (Cambridge: Cambridge University Press, 1983).

4. *JMN* 1:15. For RWE's view of history, see his uncollected "Thoughts on the Religion of the Middle Ages," in the *Christian Disciple,* n.s. 24 (Nov.–Dec. 1822): 401–408. For his view of Indic religion at this time see RWE, *Indian Superstition,* ed. K. W. Cameron (Hanover, N.H.: Friends of the Dartmouth Library, 1954).

5. *JMN* 1:19.

6. EWE 26

7. George Dangerfield, *The Era of Good Feelings* (New York: Harcourt Brace, 1952), 243.

3. The March of Mind

1. *JMN* 1:4.

2. *L* 1:89; for RWE's comments on *Samor* see *JMN* 1:7; for RWE's reading from 1819 to 1824 see *JMN* 1:395, 27, 55. For books RWE borrowed from the Boston Library Society 1815–1844 see *EtE* 2:149–186. For books RWE borrowed from the Harvard Library 1817–1868 see *E's Reading,* 44–49.

3. For Blackwell and Lowth, see B. Feldman and R. Richardson, *The Rise of Modern Mythology* (Evansville: Indiana University Press, 1972), 99–102, 144–146, and Murray Roston, *Prophet and Poet: The Bible and the Growth of Romanticism* (Evanston, Ill.: Northwestern University Press, 1965) 71ff., 82.

4. For RWE's early assessment of Everett see *JMN* 1:12–13; for a later view, RWE, "Historic Notes of Life and Letters in New England," in *CW,* vol. 10, *Lectures and Biographical Sketches,* p. 331. In 1814, the same year he was called to the Brattle Street Church, Everett published a reply to G. B. English's feisty *The Grounds of Christianity Examined* (1813), in which English had argued that the Old Testament had priority over the New, that Judaism was the true religion, and that Christianity was wrongly "built upon the prostrate necks of the Hebrew nation" (p. xviii).

5. For Everett's reading in Eichhorn, Warburton, Montfaucon, Caylus, Jones, Wolf, Anquetil-Duperron, Bayle, Vossius, Blackwell, Wood, and Heyne, see Edward Everett, "Synopsis of a Course of Lectures on the History of Greek Literature,"

Houghton Library manuscript. For Everett's appointment to Harvard in order "to connect Greek literature with biblical criticism," see P. R. Frothingham, *Edward Everett* (Boston 1925), 35. For Everett's knowledge of biblical criticism, see his ms. translation of Eichhorn's *Introduction to the Study of the Old Testament* and his own 365-page unpublished "Introduction to the Old Testament," both in the Massachusetts Historical Society Library. For Heyne, see Feldman and Richardson, *The Rise of Modern Mythology,* and C. Hartlich and W. Sachs, *Der Ursprung des Mythosbegriffes in der modernen Bibelwissenschaft* (Tübingen: Mohr, 1952).

6. RWE, "Historic Notes," *CW* 10:330; *JMN* 1:14, 235, 242.

7. RWE, *Two Unpublished Essays: The Character of Socrates and the Present State of Ethical Philosophy,* ed. with intro. by E. E. Hale (Boston: Lamson Wolffe, 1896), 14, 16.

8. E. T. Channing, "The Orator and His Times," in his *Lectures Read to the Seniors in Harvard College* (Boston: Ticknor and Fields, 1856); on rapid writing see "A Writer's Habits" in the same volume, p. 213; on the weight of the past see "A Writer's Preparation" in the same volume, pp. 198–200.

9. *JMN* 1:285. For "Uilsa" see Evelyn Barish, *Emerson: The Roots of Prophecy* (Princeton: Princeton University Press, 1989), 83–89.

10. RWE, *Two Unpublished Essays,* 50–51, 63, 53, 62.

11. *JMN* 1:242, 236.

12. Sampson Reed, "Oration on Genius," Aug. 21, 1821, in *EtE* 2:9–11. RWE and his brother Charles copied out the oration. See Houghton b Ms Am 1280.235 (509, 510, 511).

13. Reed, "Oration on Genius," 2:11; for RWE and Reed, see K. W. Cameron, "Sampson Reed, My Early Oracle," in *EtE* 1:253–294.

4. Home and Family

1. Mark Erlich, *With Our Hands: The Story of Carpenters in Massachusetts* (Philadelphia: Temple University Press, 1986).

2. *L* 2:427.

3. *JMN* 7:119; 5:438; Haskins 58.

4. Cabot 41; *JMN* 5:50.

5. See James Barnes, *Naval Actions of the War of 1812* (New York: Harpers, 1896), and C. S. Forester, *The Age of Fighting Sail* (Garden City, N.Y.: Doubleday, 1956).

6. *L* 4:179.

7. Joel Porte has plausibly connected Emerson's rebellious antinomianism to his father's tendentious and protracted indictment of Anne Hutchinson. See Porte 112–118; Wm. Emerson "Sermon, 21 July, 1808," in his *Historical Sketch of the First Church in Boston* (Boston: Munroe and Francis, 1812), 245.

8. Haskins 43; Cabot 35.

9. Haskins 78.

10. EWE 6; Haskins 71; for Ruth Emerson's interest in Fénelon see letter from Wm. Jr., 20 Mar. 1824. For Wogan see Haskins 71. For Flavel and Mason see EWE 25. Flavel's *On Keeping the Heart* (New York: American Tract Society in the Evangelical Library, vol. 7, 1819) is Christian self-cultivation; RWE's "Sursum Corda" may also be related to it. Teresa Toulouse also makes use of Flavel (1630–1691) in her *The Art of Prophesying: New England Sermons and the Shaping of Belief* (Athens: University of Georgia Press, 1987).

11. Flavel, *On Keeping the Heart*, 13; John Mason was a Methodist minister and botanist whose *Self-Knowledge* (1744–1745) was reprinted in Hartford, Conn., in 1814; Mason, *Self-Knowledge*, 20–21.

12. For Sarah Ripley see Elizabeth Hoar's "Mrs. Samuel Ripley" in *Worthy Women of Our First Century*, ed. Mrs. O. J. Wister and Miss Agnes Irwin (1877; reprint, Plainview, N.Y.: Books for Libraries Press, 1973). Soon after 1811 Sarah Alden Bradford Ripley was reading Griesbach's text of the Bible, "the critical preface to which was far more exciting than any reading can ever be to me again" (p. 179). She was reading Gesenius, via Convers Francis, by 1820. Before that she had read Robert Lowth's *Isaiah* and knew of "the general identification of poet and prophet among ancient nations" (p. 134).

5. The Angel of Death

1. For information on Mary Moody Emerson's life and reading, I am indebted to Phyllis Cole, who has generously shared her incomparable knowledge of the subject; *CW*, vol. 10, *Lectures and Biographical Sketches*, p. 404.

2. "Mary Moody Emerson" in *CW*, vol. 10, *Lectures and Biog. Sketches*, pp. 407, 428–429; Rosalie Feltenstein, "Mary Moody Emerson: The Gadfly of Concord," *American Quarterly* 5 (Fall 1953): 235. See also George Tolman, *Mary Moody Emerson* (1929), and Evelyn Barish, "Emerson and the Angel of Midnight: The Legacy of Mary Moody Emerson," in *Mothering the Mind*, ed. Ruth Perry and Martin Watson Brownley (Holmes and Meier, 1984, 218–237.) RWE's account of his aunt, written late, when he was no longer able to use his own

assembled materials with much force, appears in *CW*, vol. 10, *Lectures and Biog. Sketches.*

3. *CW* 10:379.

4. Ms. notebook "MME II," Houghton b Ms Am 1280.235 (147), p. 263; *CW* 10:385.

5. For MME on Marcus Aurelius, see ms. notebook "MME I," Houghton b Ms Am 1280 H 146, p. 33; on Wm. Law, see "MME II," 203; on Calvin, ms. notebook "MME III," Houghton b Ms Am 1280 H 148, p. 276; on de Staël, "MME I," 79–81; on Plato and Spinoza "MME I," 260; on Boehme, ms. notebook "MME IV," Houghton b Ms Am 1280 H 149, p. 22, on Eichhorn, see *JMN* 2:375. MME's marked-up copy of vol. 1 of de Staël's *Germany* (which she gave to RWE in 1830) is in the Beineke Library.

6. "MME III," 276.

7. *JMN* 7:442; "MME I," 113.

8. "MME I," 14, 33, 23.

9. "MME II," 228–229; 5; "MME I," 27.

10. "MME II," 200–203. We finally have a selection of letters by MME, *The Selected Letters of Mary Moody Emerson,* ed. Nancy Craig Simmons (Athens and London: University of Georgia Press, 1993), but the four notebooks of her writing that Emerson read and reread have never been published. Neither has the RWE-MME correspondence been put together and published as a unit, though it reveals more about the formation and workings of Emerson's mind than the twice-edited letters to and from Carlyle.

11. *CW,* vol. 3, *Essays: Second Series,* "Experience," p. 288.

6. Scottish Common Sense

1. Edward Everett thought Stewart "the greatest philosopher since Plato." See P. R. Frothingham, *Edward Everett* (Boston, 1925), 54; William Gass, "On Emerson and the Essay," in his *Habitations of the Word* (New York: Simon and Schuster, 1985). For Emerson's enthusiasm for Stewart, see *L* 1:125. Emerson was reading Stewart in Nov. 1822. He was reading the *Dissertation* in Dec. 1823, an *Edinburgh Review* article on Stewart in Jan. 1824, Stewart's *Philosophical Essays* the same month, Adam Smith's *Theory of Moral Sentiments* in July 1824, and Thomas Brown on cause and effect in Nov. 1824. The Swiss historian J. C. L. S. de Sismondi has been called a disciple of William Ellery Channing by J. Christopher Herold in *Mistress to an Age* (New York: Bobbs-Merrill, 1958). Detailed studies of

the impact of Scottish Common Sense on RWE include Merrell R. Davis, "Emerson's 'Reason' and the Scottish Philosophers," *NEQ* 17 (June 1944): 209–228, J. E. Schamberger, "The Influence of Dugald Stewart and Richard Price on Emerson's Concept of Reason," *ESQ* 18 (1972): 179–183, and S. Liebman, "The Origins of Emerson's Early Poetics: His Reading of the Scottish Common Sense Critics," *AL* 45 (Mar. 1973): 23–33.

2. Stewart's *Dissertation,* written for the *Encyclopedia Britannica Supplement,* is sometimes also called *A General View of the Progress of Metaphysical, Ethical, and Political Philosophy since the Revival of Letters;* on matter and mind see *Dissertation,* in *Collected Works of Dugald Stewart,* ed. Wm. Hamilton (Edinburgh, 1854), vol. 1, introduction, esp. p. 24.

3. Stewart, *Dissertation,* 113, 224ff.

4. Stewart, *Dissertation,* 436, 441, 447, 437.

5. Only recently has Emerson's encounter with Hume been adequately assessed. See Evelyn Barish, *Emerson: The Roots of Prophecy* (Princeton: Princeton University Press, 1989), and also John Michael, *Emerson and Skepticism: The Cipher of the World* (Baltimore: Johns Hopkins Press, 1988); anon., "Stewart's Introduction to the Encyclopedia," *Edinburgh Review* 36 (Oct. 1821): 259.

6. Dugald Stewart, *Elements of the Philosophy of the Human Mind,* vol. 1 (1792); vol. 2 (1814), vol. 3 (1827), in *Coll. Works,* 11:15; David S. Robinson, *The Story of Scottish Philosophy* (New York: Exposition Press, 1961), 29; Adam Smith, *The Theory of Moral Sentiments,* pt. 1, chap. 1, sec. 1.

7. See Dugald Stewart, "Concerning the Fundamental Laws of Human Belief," in *Coll. Works,* vol. 3; Robinson, *Scottish Philosophy,* 212.

8. Stewart, *Elements,* 8; *Dissertation,* 70; *Elements,* 22.

9. The concept of the moral sense had for the early nineteenth century something of the sweep and dignity the concept of dharma (the moral order of the universe) has in Hindu thought. The link between Western idealism and Hindu thought had already been much discussed in Emerson's day. See David S. Robinson's "Dugald Stewart and Hindu Philosophy" in his *The Story of Scottish Philosophy.* See also Thomas Brown's "The Sceptical System of Berkeley and Hindu Philosophy," in his *Lectures on the Philosophy of Mind,* 4 vols. (Edinburgh, 1851), 2:14–27. On the limits of Scottish Common Sense see Alasdair MacIntyre's *Whose Justice: Which Rationality* (Notre Dame, Ind.: University of Notre Dame Press, 1988). MacIntyre says that Common Sense failed in America when it could not provide a solution to the dispute over slavery. Kantianism, with its predication of the absolute value of freedom, could and did.

10. *JMN* 1:94.

7. The Brothers Emerson

1. *JMN* 1:99, 2:59; Joel Myerson, *The New England Transcendentalists and "The Dial"* (Rutherford, N.J.: Fairleigh Dickinson University Press, 1980), 194.

2. Haskins 51.

3. EWE 20; *JMN* 11:282.

4. Material for the life of William, Jr., is in his voluminous unpublished correspondence in the Wortis Collection in the Massachusetts Historical Society Library and in the unpublished dissertation by Karen Kalinevitch, "Ralph Waldo Emerson's Older Brother: The Letters and Journals of William Emerson," University of Tennessee, 1982. The letters of EBE and CCE are in the Wortis Collection. Other writings by EBE and CCE are in the Emerson Family papers at Houghton.

5. EWE 51.

6. EBE to CCE, Jan. 24, 1824.

7. EBE to WmE, Mar. 27, 1827; CCE to WmE, June 30, 1827; EBE to WmE, May 19, 1828.

8. CCE to WmE, May 29, 1828; see WmE to RHE, July 14, 1828.

9. EWE 51.

10. *L* 1:202; EBE to WmE, June 10, 1828; EBE to WmE, Nov. 1, 1824; WmE to RWE, Aug. 15, 1822. See also Allen 30, 44, 85, 105.

11. CCE to MME, Oct. 11, 1825; CCE to MME, Sept. 12, 1825; CCE to MME, May 18, 1828; CCE to MME, Feb. 11, 1827.

12. *L* 1:227, 239; CCE to MME, July 20, 1828.

13. CCE diary, May 19, 1831, Houghton b Ms Am 1280.220 (119); CCE to MME, Feb. 21, 1829.

14. CCE diary, 1835; *JMN* 5:107, 453.

15. CCE diary, Nov. 9, 1835.

16. CCE, "Thekla's Song," Houghton b Ms Am 1280.220 (126). Printed in *Parnassus*, p. 447, the lines are freely adapted from Schiller's "Thekla: Eine Geisterstimme."

8. The Young Writer

1. G. E. Woodbury, *Ralph Waldo Emerson* (New York: Macmillan, 1926), 21.

2. *JMN* 1:227.

3. *JMN* 1:93, 176, 97, 104, 102, 87, 139.

4. *JMN* 1:120, 117, 129, 113.

5. For MME on Eichhorn's *Apocaplyse,* see *JMN* 2:375, from a letter of June 26, 1822. Eichhorn argues that the Apocalypse of St. John is a drama intended to

show how Christian teaching would lead to the downfall of "the two false religions," those of Jerusalem and Rome. "The poet [of the Apocalypse] was resolved in his own mind to dramatise the prophecies of Jesus Christ concerning the triumph that his teaching was finally to have over Judaism and Paganism and by dramatic art to present it visually in the theatre." J. G. Eichhorn, *Apocalypsen* (Göttingen, 1791). I am indebted to an unpublished modern translation by Victor Castellani. Ram Mohan Roy, the founder of Vedanta and the man whom Gandhi called "the father of advanced liberal thought in Hinduism," believed that there is nothing profane and that "the profane is simply what has not yet been sanctified." See Roy, *Translation of an Abridgement of the Vedant or Resolution of All the Veds* (Calcutta, 1816). See also Spencer Lavan, *Unitarians and India* (Boston: Beacon, 1977), and S. C. Crawford, *Ram Mohan Roy* (New York: Paragon House, 1987). For RWE's dismissive comment on Roy see *L* 1:117. For Boston interest in Roy see the *Christian Register*, Nov. 23, 1821, and May 17 and June 7, 1822. For an argument that Roy had a real influence on the young Emerson, see Alan Hodder, "Emerson, Rammohan Roy, and the Unitarians," *SAR* (1988), 133–148.

6. RWE, "Thoughts on the Religion of the Middle Ages," *Christian Disciple*, n. s. 24 (Nov.–Dec. 1822): 401–408.

7. David Hume, *Enquiry Concerning Human Understanding*, in his *Works* (1826), 4:73, 74, 86–87.

8. *L* 1:127.

9. EWE 29; *JMN* 2:184.

10. *JMN* 2:153, 155.

9. The Paradise of Dictionaries and Critics

1. William Ellery Channing, "Unitarian Christianity," in the *Collected Works of William E. Channing*, rev. ed. (Boston: American Unitarian Assoc., 1886), 384.

2. Channing, "The Moral Argument against Calvinism." in the *Works*, 466.

3. Channing, "Evidences of Revealed Religion," in the *Works*, 226.

4. Karen Kalinevitch, "Ralph Waldo Emerson's Older Brother: The Letters and Journals of William Emerson," Ph.D. diss., Univ. of Tennessee, 1982, pp. 112, 124.

5. The standard account of the "Higher Criticism" is Christian Hartlich and Walter Sachs, *Der Ursprung des Mythosbegriffes der Bibelwissenschaft.* The reception of the new historical criticism of the Bible in America urgently needs study. One would not guess, from Albert Schweitzer's widely read *Quest of the Historical Jesus*, that England or America had any part in it. Jerry Wayne Brown's excellent pioneering study *Biblical Criticism in America* does not treat the formative years in sufficient

detail. Two thematic studies, useful within their stated limits, are Jurgen Herbst, *The German Historical School in American Scholarship* (Ithaca: Cornell University Press, 1965), and Carl Diehl, *American and German Scholarship 1770–1870* (New Haven: Yale University Press, 1978). Barbara Packer has made a contribution in her "Origin and Authority: Emerson and the Higher Criticism," in *Reconstructing American Literary History*, ed. Sacvan Bercovitch (Cambridge: Harvard University Press, 1986), 67–92. Evelyn Shaffer's *Kubla Khan and the Fall of Jerusalem* (Cambridge: Cambridge University Press, 1975) shows how intricately the new criticism was intertwined with the ambitions of the new generation of English romantic prophet-poets. Lowth's ideas got into the German universities via Michaelis and into English biblical criticism via his own *Isaiah* (1778), Blayney's *Jeremiah* (1784), and Newcomb's *Ezekiel* (1788). Edward Everett remarks that the English paid little attention to the German critics; Theodore Parker later discovered how little attention the Germans paid to Americans. But Herbert Marsh translated Michaelis's *Introduction to the New Testament*, 4 vols. (1793–1801), prefacing it with the long "Dissertation on the Origins of the First Three Gospels," which was much read in America.

6. F. A. Wolf (1759–1824), founder of the field of philology and of modern Homeric criticism, was a contemporary of Eichhorn's who studied at the same university, Göttingen, with one of the teachers of Eichhorn, C. G. Heyne.

7. Kalinevitch, "Ralph Waldo Emerson's Older Brother," 123; two of Eichhorn's books, *Einleitung in das Alte Testament* (1780) and *Die Hebraischen Propheten*, 3 vols. (Göttingen, 1816–1819), passed from William to RWE by 1828 (see *L* 1:250). MME was acquainted with Eichhorn's *Apocalypsen* (see *JMN* 2:375). Edward Everett's ms. translation of Eichhorn is in the Massachusetts Historical Society Library. Theodore Parker's review of D. F. Strauss's *Life of Jesus* gives an excellent account of the state of advanced American knowledge of the subject at the time. Eichhorn is virtually the only German taken seriously by Andrews Norton in his vast unread three-volume *Evidences of the Genuineness of the Gospels*, vol. 1 (Boston: John Russell, 1837), vols. 2 and 3 (Cambridge: John Owen, 1844).

8. *JMN* 2:162–163.

9. *JMN* 2:189–190.

10. *JMN* 2:190.

10. Mme. de Staël and the Other Germany. Divinity Studies

1. *Edinburgh Review* 30, no. 60 (Sept. 1818): 275. For RWE's reading, it is necessary to consult K. W. Cameron's "Emerson's Book Borrowings from the Boston Society Library," in *EtE* 2:149–186, as well as his *E's Reading*.

2. De Staël, *Germany* (London: John Murray, 1813; New York, O. W. Wight, 1859), 288, 289. Phyllis Cole kindly pointed out to me that MME's copy of *Germany* is in the Beineke. A thoughtful recent treatment of de Staël and Emerson is in Joel Porte's *In Respect to Egotism* (Cambridge: Cambridge University Press, 1991).

3. De Staël, *Germany,* 292.

4. De Staël, *Germany,* 388

5. Perry Miller's wartime essay "From Edwards to Emerson" (orig. title "Jonathan Edwards to Emerson," *NEQ,* Dec. 1940) has created a partly specious connection between the two men. Emerson's own interest in Edwards was quite limited. He knew Dugald Stewart's description of Edwards as "the most celebrated and indisputably the ablest champion of the scheme of necessity who has since appeared" (*Dissertation,* pt. 2, sec. 3). Edwards appears on the longer of Channing's two reading lists (see n. 11 below, this chapter) and it is clear that Emerson knew Edwards's *On the Freedom of the Will.* Despite Emerson's wholesale rejection of Calvinism, he refers to Edwards as one of the admirable old breed of Puritans. There may well be a connection between Edwards's *Freedom of the Will* (see p. 274) and Emerson's comment that "a thing affirming itself in words is not thereby affirmed." Sidney Ahlstrom has observed, "Emerson stands in the tradition of Thomas Shepard and Jonathan Edwards as an awakener of the sleeping spirit" (Ahlstrom, *A Religious History of the American People* [New Haven: Yale University Press, 1972], 598); see *JMN* 2:159, 197, 227, and *JMN* 4:257.

6. *JMN* 2:219, 230.

7. *JMN* 2:231, 6:229, 2:237, 241.

8. Channing's short reading list is among the Emerson papers at Houghton and has been printed in K. W. Cameron, *The Transcendentalists and Minerva* (Hartford, Conn.: Transcendental Books), 3:1010; Henry Scougal, *The Life of God in the Soul of Man,* in his *Works* (1677; reprint, Boston: Pierce and Williams, 1839), 15.

9. *JMN* 2:265.

10. RWE's "Letter to Plato" is printed in *JMN* 2:246ff. with no indication that it was addressed to MME, whose reply can be found in notebook "MME I," Houghton b Ms Am 1280 H 146, p. 165ff.; *JMN* 2:251.

11. Dr. Channing's "Course of Study for Students in Divinity" is a dense thirty-four-page bibliography. The ms. is at Harvard Divinity School; it has been published in facsimile by K. W. Cameron in *The Transcendentalists and Minerva,* 3:1010–1022. The evidence that Emerson was working from this list, or one much like it, is only that he was working with Channing on a weekly basis in late 1824 and that the books he was now studying are not contained in Channing's earlier, shorter list but are contained in this longer list (see n. 8 above, this chapter). For

Lardner see *JMN* 2:263 and 383, for LeClerc *JMN* 2:300. RWE's copy of Thomas Newton's *On the Prophecies* was acquired by me at a book giveaway at 25 Beacon Street in Boston in 1983.

12. For RWE's December 1824 work plan see *JMN* 2:300; on Calvinism see *J* 2:33 and *J* 1:373. For Griesbach, Rosenmuller, Prideaux, Macknight, Buckminster, West, and Butler (all on Channing's longer list) see *JMN* 3:354–357. For Schleiermacher see *JMN* 8:485.

13. The volcano image is in *JMN* 2:316, 319, 324.

14. *J* 2:64–65.

11. Pray without Ceasing

1. Evelyn Barish, *Emerson: The Roots of Prophecy* (Princeton: Princeton University Press, 1989).

2. Barish, *Emerson,* 156–157; *JMN* 2:414; ms. notebook "MME I," Houghton 0b Ms Am 1280 H 146, pp. 146–147.

3. *JMN* 2:419.

4. Cicero, *De natura deorum* (New York: Penguin), book 1, p. 69; *JMN* 2:315.

5. Cabot 1:111, 112.

6. Kalinevitch, "Ralph Waldo Emerson's Older Brother: The Letters and Journals of William Emerson" (Ph.D. diss., University of Tennessee, 1982), 214; WmE to MME Oct. 27, 1825; MME to RWE Sept. 27, 1825.

7. *L* 1:164.

8. For Emerson's Platonism see Stuart G. Brown, "Emerson's Platonism," *NEQ* 18 (Sept. 1945): 325–345, and Ray Benoit, "Emerson on Plato: The Fire's Center," *AL* 34 (Jan. 1963): 487–498. On RWE and the Cambridge Platonists see Vivian Hopkins, "Emerson and Cudworth," *AL* (1951), 80–98, and Daniel W. Howe, "The Cambridge Platonists of Old England and the Cambridge Platonists of New England," in *American Unitarianism 1805–1861,* ed. Conrad Wright (Boston: Northeastern University Press, 1989), 87–120. On RWE and Neoplatonism see John Harrison, *The Teachers of Emerson* (New York: Sturgis and Walton, 1910), George M. Harper, "Thomas Taylor in America," in *Thomas Taylor the Platonist,* ed. K. Raine and G. M. Harper (Princeton: Princeton University Press, 1969), 49–102, Arlene J. Hansen, "Plotinus: An Early Source of Emerson's View of Otherworldliness," *ESQ* 18 (1972): 184–185, and Stanley Brodwin, "Emerson's Version of Plotinus: The Flight to Beauty," *Journal of the History of Ideas* 35 (July 1974): 465–483. For RWE's familiarity with Moses Mendelssohn see *JMN* 4:211 and ms. notebook "S," Houghton b Ms Am 1280 H 122, p. 26.

9. J. J. Rousseau, *Emile,* trans. Barbara Foxley (London: Dent, 1911), 8. Emerson owned copies of a 1794 French edition and a 1763 English translation. *JMN* 2:414, 415.

10. Edmund G. Berry, *Emerson's Plutarch* (Cambridge: Harvard University Press, 1961), is the standard treatment of the subject. A more penetrating view of Plutarch is in Moses Hadas, *Ancilla to Classical Reading* (New York: Columbia University Press, 1954).

11. *JMN* 3:15, 36.

12. *Essays of Montaigne,* trans. C. Cotton (London, 1926), 1:xvii, 7.

13. The standard work on Emerson and Montaigne, Charles L. Young's *Emerson's Montaigne* (New York: Macmillan, 1941), is limited by the fact that Young was unaware that RWE read and was impressed by the "Apology for Raimonde de Sebonde." Emerson quotes from this masterpiece of natural theology in his sermon 28 given on March 15, 1829, printed in *Sermons* 1:232, and in *JMN* 6:30, 156. *CW,* vol. 4, *Representative Men,* pp. 154, 5.

14. *Essays of Montaigne* 1:360, 2:86–87; EWE 24.

15. *J* 2:105; William Ellery Channing, "The Religious Principle in Human Nature," in *The Works of William E. Channing* (Boston: American Unitarian Assoc., 1886) 931; see George Ripley on Schleiermacher in the *Christian Examiner* 73, 3d ser., no. 4 (March 1836).

16. *L* 1:173, 176.

17. Sampson Reed, *Observations on the Growth of the Mind* (Boston: Cummings, Hilliard, 1826), 17.

18. Reed, *Observations,* 65. Reed's law of criticism is very close to that of George Fox.

19. Reed, *Observations,* 75. Another likely source of RWE's imagery of sight is the Gospel of St. Luke.

20. *L* 1:174.

21. *JMN* 3:50. The line is adapted from Jeremiah. See Porte 142 for a suggestive discussion.

12. The Prince of Lipona

1. *JMN* 3:57.

2. Gamaliel Bradford, *Damaged Souls* (Boston: Houghton Mifflin, 1923), 130; J. R. Hanna, *A Prince in Their Midst* (Norman: University of Oklahoma Press, 1946), 59.

3. *JMN* 3:115; *L* 1:189.

4. *JMN* 3:87, 88, 89, 73.

5. *JMN* 3: 77. There is some question about whether RWE visited Murat's plantation in Tallahassee. The last word appears to be Alan J. Downes's "The Legendary Visit of Emerson to Tallahassee," in *Florida Historical Quarterly* (1956) 34:334–338.

6. Hanna, *A Prince*, 109; *JMN* 3:77.

7. Achille Murat, *The United States of North America*, 2d ed. (London: Effingham Wilson, 1833), xxxvii, xxviii, 5.

8. Murat, *The United States*, 91; *JMN* 3:117.

9. Rusk 121; Murat, *The United States*, 124–125.

10. Murat, *The United States*, 80; *L* 7:160. For hypertheism see the Rev. A. P. Peabody, in Haskins 131.

11. Murat, *The United States*, 135; *L* 7:162.

13. The Balance Beam

1. For RWE on Stabler see *JMN* 3:266; William Stabler, *A Memoir of the Life of Edward Stabler* (Philadelphia: John Richards, 1846), 8. The impact of Stabler on RWE is fully discussed by Elizabeth Addison, "Compensation and the Price of Purity: An Old Quaker Impresses the Young Emerson," *SAR* (1992), 107–120.

2. *JMN* 3:78–79.

3. *L* 7:160; *L* 1:210; See RWE to EBE, May 8, 1827, and RWE to MME June 2, 1827, in *L* 7:162.

4. *Sermons* 1:70, 88, 105, 110, 116. A thorough and discerning study of Emerson's sermons is Wesley Mott, *The Strains of Eloquence: Emerson and His Sermons* (University Park: Pennsylvania State Press, 1989); still of interest is the preface to A. C. McGiffert's *Young Emerson Speaks* (Boston: Houghton Mifflin, 1938). A full and persuasive account of how RWE's later work may be seen as growing out of his experiences as a minister is David Robinson's *Emerson, Apostle of Culture* (Philadelphia: University of Pennsylvania Press, 1982) supplemented now by his introduction to *Sermons*. The starting place for understanding how much RWE's later style owes to the sermon form is Lawrence Buell's deservedly well-known *Literary Transcendentalism: Style and Vision in the American Renaissance* (Ithaca: Cornell University Press, 1973).

5. *Sermons* 1:120.

6. *Sermons* 1:73.

7. *L* 1:207.

8. *PN* 8, 5, 6, 8.

9. *JMN* 3:88; *PN* 4.

10. *L* 7:162; *L* 1:208.

11. *L* 7:166–167. In quoting from modern editions of RWE's letters, I have silently changed "ye" to "the" and "yt" to "that" and so forth because RWE was using abbreviations based on the then understood Old English letter " Þ " (thorn), pronounced "th," even though these abbreviations are not always clear from RWE's handwriting.

14. Ellen Tucker

1. The two indispensable books for information on Ellen Tucker are Henry F. Pommer, *Emerson's First Marriage* (Carbondale: Southern Illinois University Press, 1967), and Edith Emerson Gregg, ed., *One First Love: The Letters of Ellen Louisa Tucker to Ralph Waldo Emerson* (Cambridge: Harvard University Press, 1962). Ellen's notebook, journal, and verse book are with the Emerson papers at Houghton b Ms Am 1280 H (157, 158, 158a). The notebook "ETE Verses," Houghton b Ms Am 1280 H 144, has been published in *PN*; Gregg 23. The stereotype of the bloodless Emerson is challenged by John McCormick's "The Heyday of the Blood: Ralph Waldo Emerson," in *American Declarations of Love,* ed. Ann Massa (New York: St Martin's Press, 1990), 35–45.

2. Gregg 46, 61, 73, 80.

3. Gregg 68, 70, 105.

4. Gregg 29, 152, 161, 96.

5. *L* 1:227; *JMN* 3:103; J. J. Rousseau, *Emile,* trans. Barbara Foxley (London: Dent, 1911), 7, 8.

6. *JMN* 3:107. Dr. Elisabeth F. Richardson has pointed out to me that Louis W. Tinnan's "Creativity and Mental Unity," in *Perspectives in Biology and Medicine* 34, no. 3 (Spring 1991): 347–354, provides an interesting new scientific account of the phenomenon of the daemon. See also Ida Walter's master's thesis, "Emerson and the Romantic Conception of Daemon," University of Denver, 1981.

7. *Sermons* 1:226, 230.

8. *L* 1:256; *JMN* 3:149; *L* 7:176–177.

15. Ordination and Marriage: Love and Reason

1. Henry Ware, *Hints for Extemporaneous Preaching* (Boston, 1826); *L* 1:261.

2. W. E. Channing, "Fénelon" in *The Works* of William E. Channing, D.D. rev. ed. (Boston: American Unitarian Assoc., 1886), 559–578; the book Channing

is reviewing is *Extracts from the Religious Works of La Mothe Fénelon,* 8th ed., trans. Louisa A. Marshall (London, 1831).

3. EBE to MME, Mar. 15, 1829.

4. *Sermons* 2:26; for Ware see *L* 1:257, 273 and Houghton b Ms Am 1280 (3362).

5. *L* 1:267, 270; The story about Greene is in EE's ms. "What I Can Remember about Father," pp. 47–48.

6. On RWE's chaplaincy see *L* 1:270, n. 40.

7. *L* 1:271, 277; Ellen's physician was Dr. James Jackson, not to be confused with Dr. Charles Jackson, the brother of RWE's second wife; *JMN* 3:153; *L* 1:277–278.

8. Gregg 101.

9. On Marsh see Peter Carafiol, *Transcendent Reason: James Marsh and the Forms of Romantic Thought* (Gainesville: University Presses of Florida, 1982), and his "James Marsh's American 'Aids to Reflection': Influence through Ambiguity,'" *NEQ* 49, no. 1 (Mar. 1976): 27–45. Carafiol has also edited the *Selected Works of James Marsh,* 3 vols. (Delmar, N.Y.: Scholars Facsimiles and Reprints, 1976); J. Marsh, "Introduction" to S. T. Coleridge, *Aids to Reflection* (Burlington, Vt.: Chauncy Goodrich, 1829), 11, 33.

10. Marsh, "Introduction," 36, 52. Perry Miller in his "Jonathan Edwards to Emerson" *NEQ* 13 (Dec. 1940): 589–617 and Rene Wellek in his "Emerson and German Philosophy," *NEQ* 16 (Mar. 1943): 41–62 have both minimized the impact of Kant on Emerson. For the opposite point of view, see O. B. Frothingham, *Transcendentalism in New England* (New York: Putnam's, 1976), and H. Pochmann, *German Culture in America* (Madison: University of Wisconsin Press, 1957).

11. J. G. Herder, *Outlines of a Philosophy of the History of Man,* trans. T. U. Churchill (London, 1801), 2, 3.

12. *JMN* 3:168; Virginia Woolf, "Emerson's Journals," in *Books and Portraits* (London: Hogarth Press, 1977), 69.

16. We Are What We Know

1. *JMN* 16:258. EWE published his father's sketch of Taylor in the *Atlantic Monthly* 98 (1906): 177–181 as "Father Taylor," by RWE. It has not been collected or reprinted.

2. Gilbert Haven and Thomas Russell, *Father Taylor, the Sailor Preacher* (Boston: B. B. Russell, 1872), 435, 226, 165, 175, 330; M. D. Conway, *Autobiography:*

Memories and Experiences, 2 vols. (Boston: Houghton Mifflin, 1904), 1:131. See the treatment of Taylor in David Reynolds's *Beneath the American Renaissance* (New York: Knopf, 1988).

3. *Sermons* 2:112, no. 61.

4. *JMN* 3:179, 182. The theological substitution of friendship for salvation may be traced in Coleridge's *The Friend,* in Channing's ms. "Course of Study for Students in Divinity" in the Harvard Theological School Library, and in Schleiermacher's *Dialogue on Christmas Eve,* trans. Terence Tice (1805; reprint, Richmond: John Knox Press, 1967), and his "The Social Element in Religion," which is chapter 4 of his *Lectures on Religion to Its Cultured Despisers,* trans. George Ripley, printed in F. H. Hedge, *Prose Works of Modern Germany* (1848). A modern treatment is Sally McFague, *Metaphorical Theology* (Philadelphia: Fortress Press, 1982).

5. *JMN* 3:181–182; *Sermons* 2, nos. 69, 71, 73.

6. *Sermons* 2, nos. 73, 74, 75; *L* 1:307 n. 71.

7. *Sermons* 2, no. 87.

8. *JMN* 8:134; *EL* 3:97; *CW,* vol. 1, *Nature, Addresses and Lectures; JMN* 6:113; *JMN* 8:157.

9. George Combe, *The Constitution of Man* (1828; reprint, Delmar, N.Y.: Scholars Facsimiles and Reprints, 1974); *JMN* 3:177.

10. For "Theoptics" see *JMN* 3:263, 304, 329.

17. Gerando and the First Philosophy

1. See "Blotting Book IV" in *JMN* 3:359–370; on Gerando see John B. Wilson, "A Fallen Idol of the Transcendentalists," in *Comparative Literature* 19 (1967): 334–340. H. H. Clark says RWE got his first idea of an evolutionary process in nature from Gerando. See H. H. Clark, "Emerson and Science," *Philological Quarterly* 10 (July 1931): 225–260. Gerando was a continuing influence on RWE; his *Du perfectionement moral* (Paris, 1824) has a chapter called "Society and Solitude."

2. Joseph de Gerando, *Self-Education,* trans. Elizabeth Peabody (Boston, 1830) 3, 41, 98; the French original is *Du perfectionement moral* (Paris, 1824). *JMN* 3:212.

3. *JMN* 3:362, 363, 364.

4. *JMN* 3:366, 369.

5. *JMN* 3:208.

6. *JMN* 3:205.

7. *JMN* 3:219; Vincent Scully has described the connection between death, burial, and the land in his *New World Visions of Household Gods and Sacred Places* (Boston: Little, Brown, 1988), 96–98.

8. William Lloyd Garrison, "The Liberator," vol. 1, no. 1 (1831), p. 1. *L* 1:316; *JMN* 3:225.

9. Henry Rowe Schoolcraft, *History of the Indian Tribes of the United States* (Philadelphia: Lippincott, 1857), 435; CCE to WmE, Jan. 30, 1831.

18. The Wreck of Earthly Good

1. CCE to WmE, Feb. 6–8, 1831.

2. CCE to WmE, Feb. 6–8, 1831.

3. *JMN* 3:227.

4. *L* 1:318.

5. *JMN* 3:226.

6. *Sermons* 3, no. 107, first preached Feb. 20, 1831.

7. *JMN* 3:227, 228.

8. *Sermons* 3, no. 107, Feb. 20, 1831; *JMN* 3:227; for Plotinus see *JMN* 3:235–236; *JMN* 3:231, 260.

9. Herbert Marsh's "Dissertation" is part of his four-volume English edition of J. D. Michaelis's *Einleitung in das Neue Testament.* Marsh translated and annotated Michaelis's fourth edition from 1793 to 1801 as *Introduction to the New Testament.* Michaelis studied in England in 1741 and translated Lowth's *De Sacra Poesia Hebraorum* into German. Other works of Michaelis in English include Sir John David Michaelis, *Commentaries on the Laws of Moses* (London: Rivington, 1814), and *The Burial and Resurrection of Jesus Christ According to the Four Evangelists* (Boston: J. Hatchard, 1827). Michaelis was Eichhorn's teacher. "Emerson's Gospel Lectures" have been edited by Karen Kalinevitch in *SAR* (1986), 69–112.

10. Kalinevitch, "Emerson's Gospel Lectures," lec. 3.

11. See John Jason Owen, *Commentary . . . on the Gospels,* 3 vols. (New York, 1857–1860), A. F. Buesching, *Die Vier Evangelisten* (Hamburg, 1766), Gottlob Christian Storr, *Opuscula acad. interpretationem librorum sacrorum,* 3 vols. (Tübingen, 1790–1803), and Daniel Veysie, *Examination of Mr. Marsh's Hypothesis* (1808); Kalinevitch, "Emerson's Gospel Lectures," 89.

12. Leslie Stephen, *A History of English Thought in the Eighteenth Century,* 3d ed. (1876; reprint, New York: Peter Smith, 1949), 2:405.

19. In My Study My Faith Is Perfect

1. For Vedanta see chap. 8 above, n. 5; untitled review essay on Cousin in *Edinburgh Review* (July 1834), 367, 363, 364.

2. For the view that Emerson's serious interest in India is earlier than his reading in Cousin, see K. W. Cameron, ed., *Indian Superstition,* Hanover, N.H.: Friends of the Dartmouth Library, 1954); V. Cousin, *Introduction to the History of Philosophy,* trans. H. G. Linberg (Boston: Hilliard, Grey, 1832), 72. The literature on RWE's "Brahma" is extensive. See esp. Andrew M. McLean, "Emerson's Brahma as an Expression of Brahmin," *NEQ* 42 (Mar. 1964): 115–122.

3. Yosef Yerushalmi has pointed out in his *Zakhor: Jewish Memory and Jewish Forgetting* (Seattle: University of Washington Press, 1982) how the absence of Western-style chronologically oriented historical narratives is not evidence of a gap, a lack, or of lost books but rather the natural result of a completely self-confident culture that lives exclusively in an all-sufficing present.

4. Cousin, *Introduction,* 293.

5. See Dale Riepe, *India in American Thought,* and the still valuable studies of Arthur Christie, *The Orient in American Transcendentalism* (New York: Columbia University Press, 1932), and F. I. Carpenter, *Emerson and Asia* (Cambridge: Harvard University Press, 1930). Emerson's importance for the understanding of India in America is also treated in Carl T. Jackson, *The Oriental Religions and American Thought in the Nineteenth Century* (New York: Greenwood, 1981).

6. *Poetical Works of William Wordsworth,* Oxford ed., ed. T. Hutchinson (London, 1904), 214; *JMN* 3:305.

7. *JMN* 3:270, 271, 298, 299.

8. *L* 1:334, 336.

9. *JMN* 3:314, 312; *L* 1:338, 341, 342.

20. Separation

1. *JMN* 3:316.

2. *JMN* 3:324.

3. For the theological extension of Communion into communication, see the fourth lecture of Schleiermacher's *Lectures on Religion to Its Cultured Despisers,* trans. George Ripley, in F. H. Hedge's *Prose Writers of Germany* (1848); for Ridge and Boudinot, see *L* 1:346.

4. See the article, with portrait, on John Ridge in Thomas L. McKenney and James Hall, *History of the Indian Tribes of North America* (Philadelphia: Rice and Hart, 1855), 2:77–102.

5. For Taylor's impact on RWE's style, see David Reynolds, *Beneath the American Renaissance* (New York: Knopf, 1988); *L* 1:347.

6. *JMN* 3:327, 316.

7. *E's Reading,* 19; for Brewster see *JMN* 3:326; for Child see *JMN* 4:40. A valuable index to RWE's reading at this time is his list of recommended books for Ellen's cousin Elizabeth Tucker, *L* 7:202–205. RWE's current interest in science had him reading the *Philosophical Transactions of the Royal Society of London.* The volumes for 1813 and 1816 contain difficult, often technical articles by both Herschels and by Humphry Davy, David Brewster, Everard Home, Joseph Banks, Charles Babbage, J. Berzelius, and many others. Emerson recorded opening Ellen's coffin in *JMN* 4:7.

8. *JMN* 4:11–12; RWE was reading Anquetil-Duperron's "Exposition du système théologique des Perses tiré des livres Zend, Pehlvis et Parsis," in vol. 37 of the *Histoire, avec mémoires de l'institut, Academie des inscriptions et belles lettres* (1767), 571–754. See *E's Reading,* 19.

9. *JMN* 4:13, 14, 16.

10. J. F. W. Herschel, *A Preliminary Discourse on the Study of Natural Philosophy* (London: Longman, 1831), was in RWE's library; Herschel, *Preliminary Discourse,* 3, 4.

11. Herschel, *Preliminary Discourse,* 5

12. Herschel, *Preliminary Discourse,* 8, 14, 15.

13. *Sermons* 4:157, May 27, 1832. A copy of Mary Somerville's *On the Connexion of the Physical Sciences* (London: John Murray, 1834) was in RWE's library.

21. A Terrible Freedom

1. RWE's letter of June 2(?), 1832, to the Second Church in Boston is missing. His views on Communion at this time may be traced in *L* 1:351–354 and *L* 7:207. His full treatment of the subject comes later in *Sermons* 4:185–194, no. 162, dated Sept. 9, 1832. Important accounts of RWE's break with the church include David Robinson, *Apostle of Culture* (Philadelphia: University of Pennsylvania Press, 1982), 30–47, and J. Frank Schulman, "Emerson's Reason for Leaving the Parish Ministry" (M. Div. thesis, Meadville-Lombard Theological School, 1974). For RWE's continuing interest in the Fall as a paradigm for life, see Barbara Packer, *Emerson's Fall* (New York: Continuum, 1982).

2. *L* 1:354; RWE was reading Penn's *Works* and Thomas Clarkson's *Portraiture of Quakerism,* 3 vols. (N.Y.: Samuel Stansbury, 1806), in June 1832 (see *E's Reading,* 19); in July he read William Sewel's *History of the Quakers* (1722), which is largely an account of the life and ministry of George Fox (see *JMN* 4:31–32). The Lord's

Supper (Communion) is treated at length by Clarkson, *Quakerism,* 2:338–382; see Mary C. Turpie, "A Quaker Source for Emerson's Sermon on the Lord's Supper," *NEQ* 17, no. 1 (1944).

3. *L* 7:189; MME to RWE, Feb. 24, 1832, in *L* 1:353n.; *JMN* 4:27.

4. CCE to WmE, July 6, 1832, in *L* 1:353n.; *JMN* 9:117; RWE's letter of resignation is in *L* 1:355; the poem is in *JMN* 4:47; *JMN* 4:51.

5. *JMN* 4:35; *L* 1:358; *JMN* 4:60.

6. *JMN* 4:46.

7. CCE to MME, Nov. 26, 1832; *L* 1:361; CCE to MME Dec. 10, 1832.

22. The American Eye

1. *JMN* 4:102–103.

2. Samuel Kettell, *Specimens of American Poetry,* 3 vols. (Boston: S. G. Goodrich, 1829); *JMN* 4:114, 65.

3. *JMN* 4:106, RWE added the "thereby" in his own later versions of this sentence; *JMN* 4:104.

4. *JMN* 4:104, 109.

5. *JMN* 4:116, 113, 118, 84.

6. A fuller account of Emerson in Sicily is R. D. Richardson, "Emerson in Sicily," *ESQ* 34 (1988): 23–36; *L* 1:362–363.

7. A graphic cross-section of Mt. Etna forms the frontispiece of Andrew Bigelow's *Travels in Malta and Sicily* (Boston: Carter, 1831), one of RWE's guidebooks. See *JMN* 4:106.

8. On RWE and Italy, see R. D. Richardson, "Emerson and Italy," in *Browning Institute Studies* 12 (1984): 21–131, and Evelyn Barish's handsome illustrated *Emerson in Italy* (New York: Henry Holt, 1989). RWE's two lectures on Italy, early examples of the illustrated lecture, have never been published; they are in Houghton b Ms Am 1280; *JMN* 4:141, 142, 148. A painting of Vesuvius in eruption, a gift from Lidian's brother Charles Jackson, still hangs in the front hall of the Emerson house in Concord.

9. For an imaginative treatment of the efficacy of San Zenobio, see Porte 64–65.

10. For American travelers in Italy see Van Wyck Brooks, *The Dream of Arcadia: American Writers and Artists in Italy, 1760–1915* (New York: E. P. Dutton, 1958), Paul R. Baker, *The Fortunate Pilgrims: Americans in Italy 1800–1860* (Cambridge:

Harvard University Press, 1964), and William L. Vance, *America's Rome,* 2 vols. (New Haven: Yale University Press, 1989).

11. *JMN* 4:150; perhaps one reason for RWE's admiration of the figure of "Justice" on Paul III's tomb was its strong suggestion of the features of Ellen Tucker.

12. "Letter from W. S. Landor to R. W. Emerson" (Bath, 1856); RWE's reaction to Southey was informed pique. He had been reading Southey since college days. See K. W. Cameron, "Emerson's Borrowings from the Boston Library Society," in *EtE* for June 1819 and December 1829 (*Thalaba the Destroyer*). See also *E's Reading,* 18, 20. He had also been reading Landor's *Imaginary Conversations,* 3 vols. (London, 1824–1828), since August 1825.

13. Julius Hare and Augustus Hare, *Guesses at Truth* (London, 1827), 4, 24; *JMN* 4:176; for RWE's knowledge of Italian literature, see Emilio Goggio, "Emerson's Interest in Italy and Italian Literature," in *Italica* 17 (Sept. 1940): 97–103.

14. *JMN* 4:165; a framed engraving of "Cypresses in the Villa d'Este in Tivoli," a gift from Margaret Fuller, hangs in the Emerson study in the Concord Museum. The books and pictures in the museum's fireproof re-creation of RWE's study are RWE's own; the books and pictures in his actual study in his house are replacements. It is often said that RWE had no eye for art. The evidence of his home suggests otherwise. The walls and shelves are crammed with pictures and objects. In RWE's own study Italian art predominates. The study has eleven Italian pictures. The work of Raphael and Michelangelo dominates the whole house. There are eight large engravings from Raphael, eight after Michelangelo, and one each from Reni, Correggio, da Vinci, and Lorenzo di Credi. There is no catalog of the art in the Emerson house and no full study of it has yet been made. See J. P. Brawner's "Emerson's Debt to Italian Art," in *West Virginia University Philological Papers* 8 (Oct. 1951): 49–58.

23. I Will Be a Naturalist

1. *JMN* 4:194.

2. *JMN* 4:75, 77.

3. *L* 1:390; *JMN* 4:76.

4. See J. W. von Goethe *Italian Journey,* trans. W. H. Auden and Elizabeth Mayer (1962; reprint, San Francisco: North Point, 1982).

5. See Marguerite Duval, *The King's Garden* (Charlottesville: University Press of Virginia, 1982); *JMN* 4:200.

6. See A. L. de Jussieu, "Exposition d'un nouvel ordre . . . ," in *Mémoires de l'academie royale des sciences* 76 (1774), and his *Genera Plantarum* (Paris, 1789); Charles Darwin, *The Origin of Species* ed. J. Barrow, (New York: Penguin, 1968). Kurt Sprengel and A. de Candolle, *Elements of the Philosophy of Plants* (1821).

7. *JMN* 4:198–199. Detailed accounts of RWE's visit to the Jardin des Plantes include H. H. Clark, "Emerson and Science," in *Philological Quarterly* 10 (July 1931): 225–260, and, especially, David Robinson's "Emerson's Natural Theology and the Paris Naturalists: Towards a Theory of Animated Nature," *Journal of the History of Ideas* 41 (1980): 69–88.

8. *JMN* 4:199, 198; Herschel, *A Preliminary Discourse on the Study of Natural Philosophy* (London: Longman et al., 1831), 135–136.

9. Herschel, *Preliminary Discourse,* 140, 141; *JMN* 4:200.

24. A White Day in My Years

1. *JMN* 4:78; RWE's exposure to the museum of John Hunter and his ideas about evolution were of particular interest to RWE's son Edward, who saw his father as an early and independent proponent of evolution.

2. *JMN* 4:408; I. A. Richards, introduction to *The Portable Coleridge* (New York: Viking), 6.

3. See *E's Reading,* 65; *L* 7:188.

4. *JMN* 4:408–411.

5. *JMN* 4:413; gerardia is an American genus belonging to the figwort family; Emerson's American eye must have seen something similar in England; *JMN* 4:219.

6. *CW,* vol. 5, *English Traits,* p. 15; R. Garnett, *Life of Thomas Carlyle* (London: W. Scott, 1887), 23; J. A. Froude, *Reminiscences of Thomas Carlyle* (New York: Scribner's, 1881), 328, 329, 330.

7. Thomas Carlyle, "Jean-Paul," in *Critical and Miscellaneous Essays* (Boston: Dana Estes, n.d.), 1:13.

8. Carlyle, "The State of German Literature," in *Critical and Miscellaneous Essays,* 1:20.

9. Carlyle, "The State of German Literature," in *Critical and Miscellaneous Essays,* 1:79.

10. *E-C Corr.,* June 1949; Carlyle, "Signs of the Times," in *Critical and Miscellaneous Essays,* 1:468–469, 473–474, 477, 485, 487.

11. Carlyle, "Characteristics," in *Critical and Miscellaneous Essays,* 1:381.

12. *CW,* vol. 5, *English Traits,* p. 18.

13. Carlyle, "Characteristics," 1:363; Fred Kaplan, *Thomas Carlyle: A Biography* (Ithaca, N.Y., 1983), 202; I. A. Richards, *The Portable Coleridge*, 6.

14. C. J. Woodbury, *Talks with Emerson* (New York: Baker and Taylor, 1890), 46; *JMN* 4:63.

15. *CW*, vol. 5, *English Traits*, p. 19; Emerson's notes on his visit to Wordsworth are in *JMN* 4:222–226.

25. The Instructed Eye

1. *JMN* 4:81.

2. *JMN* 4:83, 77, 84.

3. *JMN* 4:84.

4. *JMN* 4:242. Compare RWE's listing of what he thought America well rid of to the similar list Henry James drew up as an indictment in his *Hawthorne* (1879; reprint, Ithaca: Cornell University Press, 1956), 34. *JMN* 4:237.

5. *L* 1:397; *JMN* 4:93–94; *Sermons* 4:210.

6. Thomas Paine, *The Age of Reason,* in *Thomas Paine,* ed. H. H. Clark (New York: Hill and Wang, 1944), 262.

7. *JMN* 4:95. RWE's last major project, "The Natural History of Intellect," has almost exactly the same group of ideas at its core as his first major project.

8. *EL* 1:17.

9. *EL* 1:17, 21, 23.

10. *EL* 1:26.

11. *EL* 1:39, 44, 46.

26. Mary Rotch: Life without Choice

1. *JMN* 4:256; John M. Bullard, *The Rotches* (New Bedford, Mass., 1947), 92–97.

2. The best general treatment of RWE and Quakerism is Yukio Irie, *Emerson and Quakerism* (Tokyo: Kenkyusha, 1967). Crucial to the New Bedford background is Frederick B. Tolles, "The New Light Quakers of Lynn and New Bedford," *NEQ* (Sept. 1959), 291–316, and his "Emerson and Quakerism," *AL* 10 (May 1938): 142–165. Also helpful are Leonard B. Ellis's *History of New Bedford* (Syracuse, N.Y.: D. Mason, 1892), and *The Diary of Samuel Rodman: A New Bedford Chronicle of Thirty-seven Years 1821–1859,* ed. Zephaniah W. Pease (New Bedford, Mass.: Reynold, n.d.).

3. For Stabler, see above, chap. 13, n. 1; for Tuke see Irie, *Emerson and Quakerism,* 21. RWE's debt to Clarkson was discovered by Mary C. Turpie in her "A Quaker Source for Emerson's Sermon on the Lord's Supper," *NEQ* 17, no. 1 (1944).

4. Haskins 118.

5. Thomas Clarkson, *A Portraiture of Quakerism* (New York: Samuel Stansbury, 1806), 1:xxvii–xxviii, 2:v.

6. Clarkson, *Quakerism,* 2:v.

7. William C. Braithwaite and Henry T. Hodgkin, *The Message and Mission of Quakerism* (Philadelphia: Winston, 1912), 21, 24, 95, 26.

8. William Penn, *The Rise and Progress of the People Called Quakers* (1694; reprint, Philadelphia: Chapman, 1855), 45ff.

9. Tolles, "New Light Quakers," 315–316; *Autobiography and Letters of Orville Dewey,* ed. M. E. Dewey (Boston: Roberts, 1883), 67; Hale White, "What Mr. Emerson Owed to Bedfordshire," *Athenaeum* 2846 (1882): 602–603; see M. G. Hill, "A Rill Struck Out from the Rock: Mary Rotch of New Bedford," *The Bulletin of Friends Historical Association* (Philadelphia: The Association) 45 (1956); 8–23.

10. Tolles, "New Light Quakers," 307; *JMN* 4:263.

11. *JMN* 4:264, 267.

12. *JMN* 4:269.

13. *JMN* 4:273.

14. *EL* 1:165, 166, 172, 167, 181.

15. *EL* 1:174; William Sewel, *History of the Quakers,* 3d ed., 2 vols. (Philadelphia: Benjamin and Thomas Kite, 1832), 1:10–11.

16. *EL* 1:458.

27. A Living Leaping Logos

1. George B. Emerson (1797–1881) was a second cousin of RWE. He married Mary Rotch of New Bedford in Nov. 1834 and wrote a widely read *Report on the Trees and Shrubs Growing Naturally in the Forests of Massachusetts* (Boston: Dutton and Wentworth, 1846); *L* 1:401; *JMN* 4:253.

2. *E-C Corr.,* 428.

3. F. H. Hedge, article 7 in the *Christian Examiner* 15, n. s. 9 (1833): 119.

4. Ibid., 120, 121. This conception of the transcendental program is to be found also in Coleridge's *The Friend,* vol. 3, essay 5, and in the "Idealism" chapter of Emerson's *Nature,* where RWE says, "The problem of philosophy . . . is, for all that exists conditionally, to find a ground unconditioned and absolute."

5. Hedge, *Christian Examiner,* 124, 125. In the sentence beginning "In all science..." I have silently reversed Hedge's phrase "nature and Intelligence" in order to make his parallelism clear. The importance of Fichte and Schelling to the evolution of German idealism, later minimized by Hegel, is being reasserted. See esp. Jere Paul Surber's introduction to his *Hegel: The Difference between the Fichtean and Schellingian Systems of Philosophy* (Reseda, Calif.: Ridgeview, 1978).

6. *L* 1:412–413; Charles's unpublished lecture on "Socrates" is in Houghton b Ms Am 1280.220 (121).

7. *JMN* 5:371; *Life of LE,* 10.

8. *Life of LE,* 8, 17, 18, 42, 43.

9. The mss. of Lydia Jackson's poetry are in Houghton b Ms Am 1280.235 (377–381).

10. *JMN* 4:260; Mme. de Staël, *Corinne,* trans. A. H. Goldberger (New Jersey: Rutgers University Press, 1987), 54, 30, 45. Emerson knew this novel in a Boston edition of 1808.

11. *JMN* 4:279, 278, 276.

12. *JMN* 4:274.

28. A Theory of Animated Nature

1. *JMN* 4:281–282.

2. *EL* 1:71, 75.

3. See John Leslie, *Elements of Natural Philosophy* (Edinburgh, 1823), which RWE borrowed from the Boston Athenaeum in 1832; *JMN* 4:288–289.

4. See "Emerson's Borrowings from the Boston Society Library," in *EtE* 2:149–186; Thomas Carlyle, "Goethe," in his *Critical and Miscellaneous Essays* (Boston: Dana Estes, n.d.), 1:195, 198, 204. For the impact of Goethe on RWE see F. B. Wahr, *Emerson and Goethe* (Ann Arbor, Mich.: George Wahr, 1915), Henry Pochmann, *German Culture in America* (Madison: University of Wisconsin Press, 1957), and Gustaaf Van Cromphout, *Emerson's Modernity and the Example of Goethe* (Columbia: University of Missouri Press, 1990).

5. *JMN* 6:110; see J. W. von Goethe, *Italian Journey,* trans. W. H. Auden and Elizabeth Mayer (San Francisco: North Point, 1982), 251–363.

6. *CW,* vol. 5, *Representative Men,* p. 219; See Goethe's *Metamorphosis of Plants* in Bertha Mueller, *Goethe's Botanical Writings* (Honolulu: University of Hawaii Press, 1951); *JMN* 4:301.

7. *JMN* 6:113.

8. Charles Woodbury, *Talks with Emerson* (New York: Baker and Taylor, 1890), 27.

9. Ibid., 28, 29.

10. *E-C Corr.*, 99; T. Carlyle, *Sartor Resartus* (New York: Odyssey, 1937), 67, 27, 68.

11. Carlyle, *Sartor*, 66, 119, 72.

29. Each and All

1. *E-C Corr.*, 105; *L* 7:224–225, 229–230; W. H. Channing (1810–1884) was a nephew of the famous William Ellery Channing.

2. On RWE's inheritance from Ellen Tucker, see Evelyn Barish, *Emerson: The Roots of Prophecy* (Princeton: Princeton University Press, 1989), 224. In later years RWE maintained an ample household. He had enough money to be generous to Alcott, Channing, Thoreau, John Brown, and many others, yet when his house burned in 1871 he did not have the resources to rebuild and a collection was taken up in Concord and Boston to help him out. For the finances of Henry James, Sr., see Fred Kaplan, *Henry James* (New York: William Morrow, 1992), 10–11.

3. See George Wasson, *Sailing Days on the Penobscot* (1932; reprint, New York: Norton, 1949). *L* 7:277; *JMN* 4:390.

4. For Peabody's impression of RWE see *L* 1:417n.; Carl F. Strauch, "Emerson's Phi Beta Kappa Poem," in *NEQ* 23, no. 1 (Mar. 1950): 65–90, has the complete text of the poem.

5. "Fortus" is printed in *Records of a Lifelong Friendship* (Boston: Houghton Mifflin, 1910), 177–185; *L* 1:435.

6. Strauch, "Emerson's Phi Beta Kappa Poem," 89; *JMN* 4:341; *L* 1:435; *JMN* 4:340.

7. There is no modern edition of RWE's poetry. In addition to *CW*, vol. 9, *Poems*, it is necessary to consult the first editions of *Poems* (1847) and *May-Day* (1867), Carl Strauch's valuable unpublished dissertation, "A Critical and Variorum Edition of the Poems of RWE" (Yale, 1946), and the recently published *PN*.

8. *JMN* 4:263, 291.

9. *JMN* 4:382.

10. *L* 1:435.

11. See Carl F. Strauch, "The Year of Emerson's Poetic Maturity: 1834," in *Philological Quarterly* 34, no. 4 (Oct. 1955): 353–377; *JMN* 4:266–267, 287, 286, 307, 308, 310, 323.

12. *JMN* 4:324; Charles J. Woodbury, *Talks with Emerson* (New York: Baker and Taylor, 1890), 23; *JMN* 4:357.

13. CCE to EH, Aug. 30, 1834; *JMN* 4:315–316; G. E. Woodbury, *Ralph Waldo Emerson* (New York: Macmillan, 1926), 43; *CW*, vol. 8, *Letters and Social Aims*, 355n.; *JMN* 4:316.

30. Confluence

1. For RWE's grandfather, see *Diaries and Letters of William Emerson (1743–1776)*, ed. Amelia F. Emerson (Boston: privately printed, 1972).

2. *JMN* 4:349. RWE's published portrait of his stepgrandfather Ripley is much gentler: see *CW*, vol. 10, *Lectures and Biographical Sketches; E-C Corr.,* 109.

3. EBE to RWE, July 7, 1834; Cabot 1:221; *JMN* 4:325.

4. CCE to WmE, Sept. 12, 1834; CCE to EH, Sept. 14, 1834.

5. The notebook "MME I" (Houghton b Ms Am 1280.235 [146]) begins on p. 3 with an extract about MME from a letter of CCE dated Jan. 20, 1835. After this, the notebook works backward in time, picking up material from the 1820s before proceeding.

6. *JMN* 4:324, 357, 331, 377.

7. *JMN* 4:345.

8. Coleridge's letter is in *The Literary Gazette and Journal of the Belles Lettres* (London, Sept. 13, 1834; reprinted in *EtE* 155–156); *JMN* 4:335.

31. Lidian

1. *JMN* 4:328; Moses Hadas, *Ancilla to Classical Reading* (New York: Columbia University Press, 1954), 309; *JMN* 4:331.

2. *JMN* 4:333, 336, 348, 353.

3. *JMN* 4:353, 376.

4. *JMN* 5:11, 395, 8.

5. *JMN* 5:8, 10.

6. *L* 7:232; *Life of LE,* 48.

7. The familiar story about RWE changing Lydia's name to Lidian to avoid the Yankee dialect from changing it to Lydiar rests on a letter from Lidian's older daughter, Ellen, to her younger, Edith. See *Life of LE,* xliii; *Letters of LE,* 28, 29.

8. *Life of LE,* 48.

9. *Life of LE*, 47, 69.

10. *Life of LE*, 68, 42, 77.

11. *Life of LE*, 83, 79.

32. The New Jerusalem

1. EWE 156; Cabot 69, 678–679; George F. Train, *My Life in Many States* (New York: D. Appleton, 1902), 60; H. Hoeltje, "Emerson in Minnesota," in *Minnesota History* 2 (June, 1930): 145–159; *L* 2:203; *L* 3:221; *EL* 1:40, 41.

2. *EL* 1:99, 11, 110.

3. *EL* 1:120, 132.

4. *EL* 1:149, 150.

5. *EL* 1:166, 186.

6. *JMN* 5:5; *JMN* 4:360; *L* 1:425. See R. R. Niebuhr, *Schleiermacher on Christ and Religion* (New York: Scribner's, 1964).

7. *JMN* 5:6.

8. Czeslaw Milosz, "Swedenborg and Dostoevsky," in his *Beginning with My Streets* (New York: Farrar, Straus, and Giroux, 1991), 164. For the influence of Swedenborg on RWE, see the extensive and excellent treatment in *EtE*, and also Clarence Hotson, "Emerson's Philosophical Sources for 'Swedenborg,'" in *The New Philosophy* (Oct. 1828), 482ff. A helpful recent essay is Anders Hallengren's "The Importance of Swedenborg to Emerson's Ethics," in *Swedenborg and His Influence*, ed. E. J. Brock et al. (Bryn Athyn, Pa.: Academy of the New Church, 1988). RWE's grasp of Swedenborg depended not only on Reed and Oegger but on his friend Hedge's brilliant essay "Emmanuel Swedenborg" in *The Christian Examiner* 15 (1833):193–218.

9. Sampson Reed, *Observations of the Growth of the Mind* (Boston: Cummings, Hilliard, 1826), 4; see Guillaume Oegger, *The True Messiah* (French ed., orig. pub., 1832), trans. Elizabeth Peabody (Boston: E. Peabody, 1842). Emerson's interest in language is best described in Philip F. Gura, *The Wisdom of Words* (Middletown: Wesleyan University Press, 1981), chap. 3, "The Example of Emerson."

10. *EtE* 2:84–85

11. *EtE* 2:85; the idea of the world "flowing forth" in Oegger is very close to the Neoplatonic idea of emanations; *EtE* 87.

12. C. S. Lewis, *The Allegory of Love* (New York: Oxford University Press, 1936), 45; Alain Robbe-Grillet, "Nature, Humanism, and Tragedy," in his *Toward a New Novel* (New York: Grove Press, 1965).

13. *JMN* 5:18.

33. The Art of Writing. Jakob Boehme

1. *E-C Corr.,* 125.

2. *JMN* 5:40; *EL* 2:261.

3. *JMN* 10:315; *JMN* 7:302; "Intellect," in *CW,* vol. 2, *Essays: Second Series,* p. 340; EPP to GEP, June 18, 1836. For RWE's methods of journal-keeping, see Linda Allardt's excellent introduction to *JMN* 12.

4. *JMN* 9:341; see Laurence Rosenwald, *Emerson and the Art of the Diary* (New York: Oxford University Press, 1988). Rosenwald is particularly helpful on what he calls "the small discursive forms, the aphorism, the apothegm . . ." and "the small narrative forms, the many varieties of anecdote" (p. 22).

5. *L* 2:463.

6. C. J. Woodbury, *Talks with Emerson* (New York: Baker and Taylor, 1890), 149; *E-C Corr.,* Nov. 3, 1844; *JMN* 7:247; *JMN* 5:79; *E-C Corr.,* 185.

7. *JMN* 9:77.

8. Woodbury, *Talks with Emerson,* 23; *JMN* 7:24; *JMN* 10:320; *JMN* 8:400.

9. *JMN* 8:114; *JMN* 9:46, 250.

10. William Howitt, *The Book of the Seasons* (London, 1831), 129, 234; *JMN* 5:25.

11. *JMN* 5:270.

12. *JMN* 5:63, 40, 46.

13. *JMN* 5:56–57; John Norris, *Essay towards the Theory of the Ideal or Intelligible World* (London: Manship, 1701), 8; *JMN* 5:57.

14. *JMN* 5:58.

15. Jakob Boehme, *Aurora,* chap. 8, sec. 7, quoted in *Jakob Boehme: His Life and Thought,* ed. John J. Stoudt (New York: Seabury Press, 1968). For Stoudt's comment on Boehme and Luther, see p. 61.

16. Jakob Boehme, *Six Theosophic Points,* intro. Nicolas Berdyaev (Ann Arbor: University of Michigan Press, 1958), viii. Berdyaev notes that Boehme's importance to German idealism is his discovery "that a thing can be revealed only through another thing that resists it" (p. xi).

17. *JMN* 5:75.

18. *L* 3:418; *JMN* 4:303; *JMN* 5:51, 53.

34. Marriage and Concord

1. "Historical Discourse," in *CW,* vol. 11, *Miscellanies.* RWE's notes for the talk are in Journal "L 'Concord,'" pub. in *JMN* 12.

2. See Lemuel Shattuck, *History of Concord* (Boston: Russell Odiorne, 1835). See also *L* 1:451–456 for Shattuck's complaint that RWE had stolen his thunder.

3. *Life of LE,* 79.

4. Boston was shipping ice to Jamaica as early as 1805 and to Calcutta by 1833. See Josiah Quincy, *A Municipal History of Boston to 1830* (Boston, 1852).

5. *L* 1:395; *JMN* 5:420; Shattuck, *History of Concord,* chaps. 14, 15.

6. *Remembrances of Concord and the Thoreaus: Letters of Horace Hosmer to Dr. S. A. Jones,* ed. George Hendrick (1977), discussed in Alfred Kazin, *An American Procession* (New York, 1984), 28. For details of Concord libraries, including holdings, see Robert A. Gross, *Books and Libraries in Thoreau's Concord* (Worcester: American Antiquarian Society, 1988). On church and state see *The Meetinghouse on the Green: A History of the First Parish in Concord and Its Church,* ed. J. W. Teele (Concord: The First Parish in Concord, 1985), 109.

7. Shattuck, *History of Concord,* 217.

35. Alcott and English Literature

1. Odell Shepard, *Pedlar's Progress* (Boston: Little, Brown, 1937), 41, 34, 83.

2. For Alcott's reading in Pestalozzi see Shepard, *Pedlar's Progress,* 84–85. For Alcott's Quaker reading see Frederick C. Dahlstrand, *Amos Bronson Alcott: An Intellectual Biography* (Rutherford, N.J.: Fairleigh Dickinson University Press, 1982), 31–32.

3. Elizabeth Peabody, *Record of a School,* 2d ed. (Boston: James Munroe, 1836), 111; Shepard, *Pedlar's Progress,* 257, 258.

4. A. Bronson Alcott, *The Doctrine and Discipline of Human Culture* (Boston: James Munroe, 1836).

5. *JMN* 5:98–99; Peabody, *Record of a School,* 24; Jack Larkin, *The Reshaping of Everyday Life, 1790–1840* (New York: Harper and Row, 1988), 288.

6. A. Bronson Alcott, *Conversations with Children on the Gospels* [recorded by Elizabeth Peabody], 2 vols. (Boston: James Munroe, 1836–1837), 100.

7. *JMN* 5:98; *Journals of Bronson Alcott,* ed. Odell Shepard (Boston: Little, Brown, 1938), 69.

8. *EL* 1:215.

9. *EL* 1:233, 237.

10. *EL* 1:237; Sharon Turner, *History of the Anglo-Saxons,* 7th ed., 3 vols. (London: Longman, 1852; orig. ed., 1799–1805), 1:59, 61, 177; *JMN* 5:100. See Philip Nicoloff, *Emerson on Race and History* (New York: Columbia University Press, 1961).

11. *JMN* 5:106; S. T. Coleridge, *On the Constitution of Church and State,* ed. John Colmer (Princeton: Princeton University Press, 1976), 12.

12. *EL* 1:218, 219, 225, 226.

13. *EL* 1:256, 284.

14. RWE quotes from sonnets 15, 25, 33, 52, 70, 77, 107, 124. See *EL* 1:293–295; *EL* 1:328.

15. *EL* 1:358, 361.

36. All in Each: Writing Nature

1. For Russell's role in the publication of *Sartor,* see *L* 7:254–255.

2. CCE to EH, Apr. 3, 1836.

3. *JMN* 5:77, 83, 90, 76. Phyllis Cole has noted that the sphinx was a familiar emblem in the language of the Emerson family, applied at different times to E, to CCE, and to MME.

4. *JMN* 5:103, 110, 114, 118, 136.

5. *The Works of Confucius,* ed. J. Marshman (Serampore, 1809), 36, 68, 65. All of these except the last are recorded by RWE in *JMN* 5:120–122.

6. *JMN* 13:352; CCE to EH, Apr. 3, 1836.

7. A. B. Alcott, "Psyche: An Evangele," Houghton ms. *59M–306(9), p. 102.

8. Emerson read "Psyche; or the Breath of Childhood," Houghton ms. *59M–306(8), in 1836. Only the parts he marked for Alcott to save have been printed, in *EtE* 2:101. RWE read Alcott's rewritten version, "Psyche: An Evangele," in June 1838. RWE also read Alcott's 1835 Journal, Houghton ms. *59M–308(8), in 1836. Alcott also left in manuscript three accounts in 480 pages of Anna's early years, one account (332 pages) of Louisa's early years, and an account (Houghton ms. *59M–306[6]) called "Observations on the Spiritual Nature of My Children"; Alcott, "Psyche; or the Breath of Childhood," iii; Odell Shepard, *Pedlar's Progress* (Boston: Little, Brown, 1937), 73.

9. *JMN* 5:108, 107.

10. *JMN* 5:127, 136–137.

11. *JMN* 5:132, 134, 133.

37. Nature: The Laws of the World

1. *Life of LE,* 65; CCE diary, Houghton b Ms Am 1280.220 (119), n. p. The passage is dated June 10, 1836, which is an obvious error since Charles died on May 9 of this year.

2. *L* 2:19, 20, 25.

3. *JMN* 5:174.

4. *JMN* 5:160. Jonathan Phillips was a close friend of Dr. Channing; he unobtrusively provided funds for the Emerson brothers at crucial moments. See *L* 1:251, 429.

5. *JMN* 5:163, 166, 179; *L* 2:26.

6. Orestes Brownson, *New Views of Christianity, Society, and the Church* (Boston: James Munroe, 1836), 3; George Ripley, *Discourse on the Philosophy of Religion Addressed to Doubters Who Wish to Believe* (Boston: James Munroe, 1836), 9, 10; W. H. Furness, *Remarks on the Four Gospels* (Philadelphia: Carey, Lea, and Blanchard, 1836), 22, 146.

7. RWE, *Nature* (Boston: James Munroe, 1836), 5. Emerson's later changes in the text of *Nature*, not always improvements, are reflected in *CW*, vol. 1, *Nature, Addresses and Lectures*, and in *HW*, vol. 1, *Nature, Addresses and Lectures*. Emerson's *Nature* is parallel to Lucretius's *De rerum natura* in title, scope, and ambition, not in ideas. Lucretius is a radical materialist.

8. *Nature*, 5.

9. *Nature*, 6, 7.

10. *Nature*, 23–24, 21, 22.

11. *Nature*, *CW*, vol. 1, *Nature, Addresses and Lectures*, 9, 10; on the mystical experience see Evelyn Underhill, *Mysticism* (New York: Dutton, 1911), pt. 1, chap. 4, and pt 2, chap. 2.

38. Nature: *The Apocalypse of the Mind*

1. George Perkins Marsh, *Man and Nature, or, Physical Geography as Modified by Human Action* (New York, 1864). RWE read this book in 1869. See *E's Reading*, 89.

2. *Nature* (1836), 29, 30, 118.

3. *Nature*, 39.

4. *Nature*, 32.

5. *Nature*, 59–60, 61, 65, 72.

6. *Nature*, 65, 72, 91.

7. RWE, "The Transcendentalist," in *CW*, vol. 1, *Nature, Addresses and Lectures*, p. 339. RWE discusses Stoicism in "The Sovereignty of Ethics," in *CW*, vol. 10, *Lectures and Biographical Sketches*, in "Self-Reliance," *CW*, vol. 2, *Essays: First Series*, and in "Ethics," in *EL* 2. RWE is placed among modern Stoics by

Matthew Arnold in his "Emerson," *MacMillan's Magazine* (May 1884), 50:1–13, and by R. M. Wenley in his *Stoicism and Its Influence* (Boston, 1924). RWE read the great Stoic writers Marcus Aurelius, Epictetus, Cicero, Seneca, and Plutarch. RWE took the Jeremy Collier translation of Marcus Aurelius out of the Harvard Library on Nov. 16, 1826, and on Feb. 1, 1829. He owned the 1844 translation by Henry M'Cormac and the 1864 translation by George Lang. There is a chapter on religion, mysticism, and Stoicism by Victor Cousin in the *Philosophical Miscellanies,* ed. George Ripley (Boston: Hilliard Gray, 1838). See also *The Stoic Strain in American Literature,* ed. Duane J. MacMillan (Toronto: University of Toronto Press, 1979).

8. Wenley, *Stoicism,* 167.

9. *Nature,* 92.

39. Margaret Fuller

1. *L* 2:32; *Margaret Fuller: American Romantic,* ed. Perry Miller (Ithaca: Cornell University Press, 1963), xiii; Margaret Fuller, *Woman in the Nineteenth Century* (1845; reprint, New York: Norton, 1971), 38–39. See Charles Capper's excellent *Margaret Fuller: An American Romantic Life,* vol. 1, *The Private Years* (New York: Oxford University Press, 1992).

2. *Memoirs of Margaret Fuller Ossoli,* ed R. W. Emerson, W. H. Channing, and J. F. Clarke, 2 vols. (Boston: Phillips, Sampson, 1852), 482, 92, 488.

3. *Memoirs of Margaret Fuller Ossoli,* 95, 113.

4. *Letters of MF,* 1:219.

5. *Memoirs of Margaret Fuller Ossoli,* 139–141.

6. *Letters of MF,* 1:348.

7. *Memoirs of Margaret Fuller Ossoli,* 96, 471; the closest thing to an adequate account of MF's conversation is Caroline Healy Dall, *Margaret and Her Friends* (Boston: Roberts, 1895); Fuller, *Woman,* 39.

8. Fuller, *Woman,* 177, 116, 42, 105.

9. Margaret Fuller, "Emerson," in her *Life Without and Life Within,* ed. A. B. Fuller (Boston: Brown, Taggard, and Chase, 1860), 194, 193; M. D. Conway, *Emerson at Home and Abroad* (Boston: James R. Osgood, 1882), 89.

10. *Memoirs of Margaret Fuller Ossoli,* 107, 65; Miller, ed., *Margaret Fuller,* xix; *JMN* 5:187.

11. *JMN* 8:459.

12. *JMN* 5:187, 189.

40. The Symposium

1. Joel Myerson, "A Calendar of Transcendental Club Meetings," *AL* 44 (May 1972): 197–207.

2. Josiah Quincy, *The History of Harvard University* (Cambridge: J. Owen, 1840); Andrews Norton, *Evidences of the Genuineness of the Gospels,* vol. 1 (Boston: John B. Russell, 1837), vols. 2 and 3 (Cambridge: John Owen, 1844). Norton's learning, especially in German scholarship, does not compare well with that of Emerson, Ripley, or Parker. The *Evidences* should be compared with Ripley's three *Letters* (see chap. 54, n. 3) and with Parker's edition of De Wette's *Introduction to the Old Testament,* 2d ed. (Boston: Little, Brown, 1850; orig. ed., 1843), and with his review of D. F. Strauss's *Life of Jesus* in *The Critical and Miscellaneous Writings of Theodore Parker,* 2d ed. (Boston: Horace B. Fuller, 1867; orig. ed., 1843), 276–343; Joel Myerson, "Convers Francis and Emerson," *AL* 50 (Mar. 1978): 17–36.

3. *L* 2:29; *JMN* 5:194.

4. Myerson, "Calendar of Transcendental Club Meetings."

5. O. B. Frothingham, *George Ripley* (Boston: Houghton Mifflin, 1882), 290, 229.

6. A. M. Schlesinger, Jr., *Orestes A. Brownson: A Pilgrim's Progress* (Boston: Little, Brown, 1945), Russell Kirk, introduction to *Orestes Brownson: Selected Essays* (New York: Gateway, 1955).

7. T. W. Higginson, "Lydia Maria Child," in his *Contemporaries* (Boston: Houghton Mifflin, 1899), 110, 111. To compare Francis's ideas about nature to RWE's, see Guy R. Woodall "The Selected Sermons of Convers Francis (Part Two)," in *SAR* (1988), 76–82. Francis's sister, Lydia Maria Child, was a popular author who by 1836 had published more books than all the men in the transcendentalist circle put together.

8. William R. Hutchison, "Theodore Parker and the Confessional Question," in his *The Transcendentalist Ministers* (New Haven: Yale University Press, 1959; reprint, New York: Archon, 1972), 99.

9. See Anne C. Rose, *Transcendentalism as a Social Movement, 1830–1850* (New Haven: Yale University Press, 1981). Charles Capper has recently argued that at the heart of the transcendentalist movement was "a paradox very much like the one that defined Fuller's life—the ironic and surprising conversion of a subjectivist, alienated, elitist, and self-consciously "private" faith into an instrument of radically democratic cultural and (for some at least) social change." Charles Capper, *Margaret Fuller: An American Romantic Life,* vol. 1, *The Private Years* (New York: Oxford University Press, 1992), xi.

10. RWE, "The Transcendentalist," in *CW,* vol. 1, *Nature, Addresses and Lectures.*

11. H. D. Thoreau, *A Week on the Concord and Merrimack Rivers* (Princeton: Princeton University Press, 1980), 362.

12. Current discussions of Emersonian transcendentalism and modern political and social thought include Robert Bellah et al., *Habits of the Heart* (Berkeley, Los Angeles, London: University of California Press, 1985), Christopher Lasch, *The True and Only Heaven* (New York: Norton 1991), Judith Shklar, "Emerson and the Inhibitions of Democracy," in *Political Theory* 18, no. 4 (Nov. 1990), George Kateb, "Thinking about Human Extinction," in two parts in *Raritan* 6, no. 2 (Fall 1986), and 6, no. 3 (Winter 1987), and his *The Inner Ocean: Individualism and Democratic Culture* (Ithaca: Cornell University Press, 1992), David Marr, *American Worlds since Emerson* (Amherst: University of Massachusetts Press, 1988), Richard Poirier, *A World Elsewhere* (New York: Oxford University Press, 1966).

13. *JMN* 5:349; see Francis Fukayama, "The End of History?" in *The National Interest* (Summer 1989).

41. The Forging of the Anchor

1. *JMN* 5:200, 201.

2. *JMN* 5:207, 247; 8:70; *L* 3:22; RWE, "Lecture on the Times," in *The Dial* 3, no. 1 (July 1842): 4; *JMN* 7:387.

3. RWE, "Emancipation in the British West Indies," *CW,* vol. 11, *Miscellanies,* p. 123.

4. *JMN* 5:218; *L* 2:39; *JMN* 5:198, 206, 217, 220, 216–218.

5. *L* 2:41; RWE, *Parnassus* (Boston: Houghton Mifflin, 1874), 287.

6. *JMN* 5:221.

7. *JMN* 5:221.

8. *L* 2:54; *JMN* 5:241; *Letters of LE,* 54; *L* 2:55.

42. We Are Not Children of Time

1. *EL* 2:8, 13, 15. "History" may also be regarded as the theory of the historical novel. Paul Scott explicitly built the *Raj Quartet* on Emerson's "History."

2. *EL* 2:15, 14, 20.

3. *EL* 2:11, 12, 17.

4. *EL* 2:17, 48, 71, 83–84.

5. *EL* 2:99–100, 151.

43. The American Scholar

1. See WmE to RWE, Dec. 12, 1836, and July 1, 1839, for overview of RWE's loans to William.

2. *JMN* 5:288; Charles's papers have not been edited. Besides the long and moving correspondence with Elizabeth Hoar, there are essays, lectures, diaries, and poetry. His diary for 1831–1836 is at Houghton b Ms Am 1280.220 (126); RWE also kept a notebook for material on and by Charles called "CCE" and published in *JMN* 6:255–286; *JMN* 5:327.

3. *JMN* 5:331, 333, 291.

4. *JMN* 5:307.

5. *EL* 2:197, 199.

6. For RWE's letter to Quincy, see F. B. Sanborn, *Henry D. Thoreau* (Boston: Houghton Mifflin, 1882), 52, 57; Jonathan Wainwright was also the author of a recent election-day sermon, *Inequality of Individual Wealth the Ordinance of Providence, and Essential to Civilization* (Boston: Dutton and Wentworth, 1835).

7. *CW*, vol. 9, *Poems*, p. 158; *JMN* 5:347.

8. John Pierce, quoted by Bliss Perry in "Emerson's Most Famous Speech," in Perry's *The Praise of Folly and Other Papers* (Boston: Houghton Mifflin, 1923); Oliver Wendell Holmes, *Ralph Waldo Emerson* (Boston: Houghton Mifflin, 1884).

9. *JMN* 9:382.

10. *JMN* 5:288–289, 303, 306: "The American Scholar," in *CW*, vol. 1, *Nature, Addresses and Lectures*, p. 91.

11. Ibid.

12. *EL* 2:231; Orestes Brownson concluded that by "scholar" in this address Emerson meant "author." See Brownson's review of RWE's address in *The Boston Quarterly Review* 1, no. 1:106–120. A comprehensive treatment of Emerson's views of the scholar is Merton Sealts, *Emerson on the Scholar* (Columbia: University of Missouri Press, 1992).

13. "The American Scholar," in *CW*, vol. 1, *Nature*, p. 108.

14. Ibid., p. 89.

44. Casting Off

1. *L* 2:95.

2. *JMN* 5:420, 372; *EC Corr.* 167; Bliss Perry, "Emerson's Most Famous Speech," in Perry's *The Praise of Folly and Other Papers* (Boston: Houghton Mifflin, 1923), 95–96.

3. *L* 2:97; *JMN* 12:181; *JMN* 5:410.

4. *JMN* 5:396, 423.

5. *JMN* 5:405, 411.

6. *JMN* 5:388; *EL* 2:300.

7. *JMN* 5:398; *E's Reading,* 23, and *JMN* 5:432.

8. Carleton Mabee, *Black Freedom: The Nonviolent Abolitionists from 1830 through the Civil War* (New York: Macmillan, 1970), 41.

9. Alma Lutz, *Crusade for Freedom: Women of the Anti-Slavery Movement* (Boston: Beacon, 1968). The best treatment of Emerson's long interest in the abolition of slavery is Len Gougeon, *Virtue's Hero: Emerson, Antislavery, and Reform* (Athens: University of Georgia Press, 1990).

10. *JMN* 12:153–154, 152.

11. Lutz, *Crusade for Freedom,* 103–104.

12. *JMN* 12:154.

45. Human Culture

1. *EL* 2:213, 215, 217, 221.

2. *EL* 2:222, 232, 243.

3. *EL* 2:248; for the centrality of the Fall in Emerson see Barbara Packer's excellent book *Emerson's Fall* (New York: Continuum, 1982).

4. *EL* 2:285, 295, 306.

5. *EL* 2:331.

6. *EL* 2:330, 313, 332.

7. *EL* 2:343, 356, 355.

8. *JMN* 5:445.

46. The Peace Principle and the Cherokee Trail of Tears

1. *CW,* vol. 11, *Miscellanies,* pp. 154, 155.

2. *CW,* vol. 11, *Miscellanies,* pp. 171, 174, 578n.

3. See Glen Fleischman, *The Cherokee Removal, 1838* (New York: Franklin Watts, 1971), Emmer Starr, *Starr's History of the Cherokee Indians* (Fayetteville,

Ark.: Indian Heritage Assoc., 1967; orig. pub., Oklahoma City, Warden, 1921), and Thurman Wilkins, *Cherokee Tragedy: The Story of the Ridge Family and the Decimation of a People* (New York: Macmillan, 1970).

4. Fleischman, *Cherokee Removal,* 19–20.

5. Fleischman, *Cherokee Removal,* 21.

6. RWE's Cherokee Letter is in Cabot 697–702 and has been reprinted in *RWE: Selected Essays, Lectures, and Poems,* ed. R. D. Richardson (New York: Bantam, 1990).

7. Cabot 700; *JMN* 5:479, 475, 477.

8. Fleischman, *Cherokee Removal,* 73. Emerson spoke in Concord on April 22. Robert Gross has discovered in the National Archives a memorial or petition dated May 11, 1838, addressed to the second session of the Twenty-fifth Congress signed by "Ezra Ripley and 491 others of Concord, praying that the treaty made with the [Ridge Faction of the] Cherokees at New Echota, may not be enforced" (National Archives, Senate Petitions and Memorials, Tabled, regarding treaty with Cherokee Indians [25A-G21], 25th Cong., 2d sess., record group 46; ref. to petition in Journal of the Senate of the United States of America: The Second Session of the Twenty-Fifth Congress [Washington, D.C.: 1937], 393). This memorial, which Professor Gross has graciously allowed me to cite, shows either that Emerson's position on the Cherokee removal was a commonly held view or that his advocacy was at least locally effective.

47. Henry Thoreau

1. *JMN* 5:489, 456; *CW,* vol. 9, *Poems,* pp. 145–147.

2. Thoreau almost certainly started his journal before meeting Emerson. He had notes from his college courses, his early journal is evidently the edited residue of earlier notes, and the only detailed account of the first meeting of Emerson and Thoreau, that of Mary Miller Engel in *I Remember the Emersons* (Los Angeles: Times-Mirror, 1941), has Helen Thoreau hearing Emerson speak and being reminded of a passage in her brother's journal; *JMN* 5:452, 453, 460, 480. Recent additions to our knowledge of the Emerson-Thoreau friendship include Robert Sattelmeyer, "When He Became My Enemy," *NEQ* 62: 187–204, and David Robinson, "Emerson's Later Resistance to Thoreau," paper delivered at American Literature Association, 24 May 1991.

3. John Albee, *Remembrances of Emerson* (New York: Robert G. Cooke, 1901), 18–19, 22.

4. *JMN* 8:303.

5. *JMN* 5:469, 496–497.

6. *JMN* 7:17; Moncure Conway, *Emerson at Home and Abroad* (Boston: James B. Osgood, 1882).

7. *JMN* 5:25, 55.

8. Walter Otto, *The Homeric Gods* (1954; reprint, Boston: Beacon Press, 1965), 78, 79.

48. Go Alone: Refuse the Great Models

1. *L* 2:114, 115.

2. *L* 2:139, 140.

3. See WmE to RWE, May 9, 1838, and WmE to RWE, May 31, 1838, on WmE's financial situation.

4. *JMN* 5:464.

5. See Robert E. Burkholder, "Emerson, Kneeland, and the Divinity School Address," *AL* 58, no 1 (Mar. 1986): 1–14.

6. *JMN* 7:18; *JMN* 5:465, 500; "Wealth," in *CW,* vol. 6, *The Conduct of Life; JMN* 7:10.

7. *JMN* 5:72; *JMN* 13:406.

8. *JMN* 5:467; the Rev. A. P. Peabody, quoted in Haskins 131.

9. *CW,* vol. 1, *Nature, Addresses and Lectures,* pp. 119, 134.

10. *CW,* vol. 1, *Nature, Addresses and Lectures,* pp. 129, 134, 132; Wallace Stevens said "God is in me or is not at all," in "Adagia," in his *Opus Posthumous* (New York: Knopf, 1957), 172. For the Emersonian strain in Stevens, see esp. the essay "Two or Three Ideas," in his *Opus Posthumous,* 202–216.

11. *JMN* 5:481, 463; see David Robinson's "Poetry, Personality, and the Divinity School Address," in *Harvard Theological Review* 82, no. 2 (1984): 185–199.

12. "An Address," in *CW,* vol. 1, *Nature, Addresses and Lectures,* p. 134; F. Schleiermacher, "The Social Element in Religion," trans. George Ripley in F. H. Hedge, *Prose Writers of Germany* (Philadelphia: Carey and Hart, 1848), 441–445.

13. "An Address," in *CW,* vol. 1, *Nature, Addresses and Lectures,* pp. 142, 144, 150.

14. Ibid., pp. 145, 146.

15. *JMN* 7:28; Emerson's antipathy to the Augustinian strain was one reason the New Critics generally disliked him. As Harold Bloom has noted: "sin, error, time, history, a God external to the self, the visiting of the crimes of the fathers upon the sons; these are the topoi of the literary cosmos of Eliot and his Southern followers,

and they were precisely of no interest whatever to Ralph Waldo Emerson." *Modern Critical Views: RWE,* ed. Harold Bloom (New York: Chelsea House, 1985), 1; Hugh Trevor-Roper makes the case for Calvinism as an "obscurantist deviation" from the Arminian-Socinian movement, which, he says, has "a distinct origin, a continuous tradition, and a pedigree longer than that of Calvinism." See Trevor-Roper's "The Religious Origins of the Enlightenment," in his *Religion, the Reformation, and Social Change* (London: Macmillan, 1967), esp. 219ff.

49. New Books, New Problems

1. "Literary Ethics," in *CW,* vol. 1, *Nature, Addresses and Lectures,* pp. 156, 161, 162, 163, 165.

2. Ibid., pp. 167, 168, 173, 174, 185–186.

3. *Institutes of Hindu Law: or The Ordinances of Menu,* ed. Graves Chamney Haughton (London, 1825); *JMN* 7:60n.; see also *JMN* 7:53–54; for James O'Connell's *A Residence of Eleven Years in New Holland and the Caroline Islands* (Boston, 1836), see *L* 2:168–169; *JMN* 7:78.

4. For William Gardiner's *The Music of Nature* (London: Longmans, 1840), see *EtE* 2:164; Gardiner, *Music of Nature,* 18, 26, 24–25, 75, 42.

5. For Bell see *JMN* 7:53–54 and *E's Reading,* 23; Bell, *Essays on the Anatomy of Expression in Painting* (London: Longman, 1806), vi, vi-vii, viii, 12.

6. For Goethe's *Farbenlehre,* see *JMN* 7:85, *L* 2:164, and *L* 7:319; for Guercino, Piranesi, and van Leyden, see *JMN* 7:6–7.

7. *JMN* 7:47, 92, 52, 74.

8. Andrews Norton, "The New School in Literature and Religion," in *The Boston Daily Advertiser* (Aug. 27, 1838), reprinted in Perry Miller, *The Transcendentalists* (Cambridge: Harvard University Press, 1950), 193, 195; Andrews Norton, *A Discourse on the Latest Form of Infidelity* (Cambridge: John Owen, 1839), 32.

9. Chandler Robbins, editorial in *The Christian Register* 18 (Feb. 2, 1839): 18. The dispute set off by RWE's "Divinity School Address" can be followed in Miller's *The Transcendentalists* and in more detail in Robert E. Burkholder and Joel Myerson, *Emerson: An Annotated Secondary Bibliography* (Pittsburgh: University of Pittsburgh Press, 1985).

10. *JMN* 7:65, 66, 95; *E-C Corr.,* 196.

50. Jones Very

1. *L* 7:324; *Letters of LE,* 80.

2. *Life of LE,* 80–81.

3. *Letters of EP*, 215.

4. Edwin Gittleman, *Jones Very: The Effective Years* (New York: Columbia University Press, 1967), 22, 336.

5. *Letters of EP*, 219; Gittleman, *Jones Very*, 147.

6. Gittleman, *Jones Very*, 146–147.

7. Gittleman, *Jones Very*, 194; *Letters of EP*, 406.

8. Jones Very, *Essays and Poems* (Boston: Charles C. Little and James Brown, 1839), 101, 85.

9. *Life of LE*, 78; Gittleman, *Jones Very*, 243–244.

10. *JMN* 7:122, 123.

11. *The Journals of Bronson Alcott,* ed. Odell Shepard (Boston: Little, Brown, 1938), 108; Gittleman, *Jones Very*, 269; *L* 2:173.

12. E. A. Silsbee, quoted in *Poems by Jones Very,* ed. William P. Andrews (Boston: Houghton Mifflin, 1883), 30.

51. The Attainable Self

1. *L* 7:328; *L* 2:175.

2. *EL* 3:7, 8.

3. *EL* 3:15–16.

4. *EL* 3:36.

5. *EL* 3:26, 28, 29.

6. *EL* 3:45.

7. *EL* 3:22, 89, 90, 94.

8. *EL* 3:104, 110, 125.

9. *EL* 3:170, 168, 169.

10. *EL* 3:144, 21.

52. Home and Family

1. *Life of LE*, 77; *JMN* 7:170; *L* 2:189.

2. *Life of LE*, 81–83.

3. *JMN* 5:479; *Life of LE*, 92, 87.

4. *Life of LE*, 60; *E-C Corr.*, 136.

5. *L* 2:135; *JMN* 8:44.

6. Ellen Emerson ms., "What I Can Remember about Father," Houghton b Ms Am 1280.227, p. 36; "Concord Walks," in *CW,* vol. 12, *Natural History of Intellect,* p. 174; Mary Miller Engel, *I Remember the Emersons* (Los Angeles: Times-Mirror, 1941), 4; EWE 130.

7. Ellen Emerson, "What I Can Remember about Father," 32, 31.

8. *Letters of MF,* 1:336.

9. William L. Stone, *Life of Joseph Brant-Thayendanegea* (New York: George Dearborn, 1838), xiii; *JMN* 7:202.

10. *JMN* 7:195, 180, 186.

53. Writing Essays

1. *L* 2:204; *JMN* 7:230–231, 316.

2. *L* 2:212; *JMN* 7:210, 219; *CW,* vol. 9, *Poems,* pp. 6, 7.

3. Joseph Slater in *HW,* vol. 2, *Essays: First Series,* pp. xv-xvi; John Sterling's "Carlyle" in the *London and Westminster Review* for 1839 ran 128 pages.

4. *L* 2:194.

5. *JMN* 8:199; *E-C Corr.,* 272.

6. *JMN* 7:191; *JMN* 11:295; RWE ms., "Index II, 1847," Houghton b Ms Am 1280 H 107, p. 421.

7. "History," in *CW,* vol. 2, *Essays: First Series,* pp. 5, 7–8, 10.

54. The Heart Has Its Jubilees

1. *L* 2:221, 241.

2. Christopher Hibbert, *The Great Mutiny* (London: Penguin, 1980), 225.

3. George Ripley, *"The Latest Form of Infidelity" Examined: A Letter to Mr. Andrews Norton* (Boston: James Munroe, 1839); *Defense of "The Latest Form of Infidelity" Examined: A Second Letter to Mr. Andrews Norton* (Boston: James Munroe, 1840); *Defense of "The Latest Form of Infidelity" Examined: A Third Letter to Mr. Andrews Norton* (Boston: James Munroe, 1840).

4. For Elizabeth Hoar, see Elizabeth Maxfield-Miller, "Elizabeth of Concord: Selected Letters of Elizabeth Sherman Hoar to the Emersons, Family, and the Emerson Circle," part 1, *SAR* (1984), 229–298; part 2, *SAR* (1985), 95–156; part 3, *SAR* (1986), 113–198; "Friendship," in *CW,* vol. 2, *Essays: First Series,* pp. 192–193.

5. *L* 7:368.

6. *L* 2:333; *L* 7:404.

7. Bettina von Arnim, *Goethe's Correspondence with a Child* (Boston: Ticknor and Fields, 1836), 18–19. For the reception of this book in America see H. P. Collins and P. A. Shelley, "The Reception in England and America of Bettina von Arnim's Goethe's Correspondence with a Child," in *Anglo-German and American German Crosscurrents,* vol. 2, ed. P. A. Shelley and A. O. Lewis, Jr. (Chapel Hill: University of North Carolina Press, 1962).

8. Von Arnim, *Goethe's Corr.,* 71, 84; *L* 2:210; Margaret Fuller sent a copy of Emerson's praise to Bettina herself, who lived on until 1859.

9. *JMN* 11:342; *L* 3:77. An interesting sequel to the Bettina story is the long letter sent by Bettina's daughter Giselle to Emerson in 1858. See L. S. Luedke and W. Schleiner, "New Letters from the Grimm-Emerson Correspondence," *Harvard Library Bulletin* 25, no. 4 (Oct. 1977): 399–465; CS to RWE, Oct. 17, 184?; CS to RWE, Sept. 11, 1840; RWE's letters to Sturgis have only recently been printed, in *L* 7 and *L* 8. Sturgis's letters to RWE are in Houghton b Ms Am 1221. Only a few excerpts have been published, as footnotes to *L*. Sturgis's letters to Margaret Fuller have been published in *SAR* (1988), ed. F. Dedmond.

10. This was not the last time Emerson was made the object of Bettina-inspired adoration. Around 1847, when Louisa May Alcott was fifteen, she found a copy of *Goethe's Correspondence with a Child* while browsing in Emerson's library. She was, she says, "at once fired with a desire to be a Bettina, making my father's friend my Goethe. So I wrote letters to him, but never sent them; sat in a tall cherry-tree at midnight, singing to the moon till the owls scared me off to bed; left wildflowers on the doorstep of my 'Master,' and sung Mignon's song under his window in very bad German" (Ednah D. Cheney, *Louisa May Alcott: Her Life, Letters and Journals* [Boston: Little, Brown, 1917], 57). This story (and the story of Bettina's influence on Emily Dickinson) is told in Barton St. Armand's "Veiled Ladies: Dickinson, Bettine, and Transcendental Mediumship," in *SAR* (1987), 1–52; *JMN* 7:391; *L* 7:402.

11. *L* 2:330; *Life of LE,* 83; notebook "Autobiography" b Ms Am 1280 H 195.

12. *JMN* 7:532, 544.

13. *JMN* 8:34, 95, 144; *JMN* 13:258.

14. The original opening of "Love" is in RWE *Essays* (Boston: James Munroe, 1841) and in some modern reprints, such as that published by Thomas Y. Crowell in 1926, reissued as an Apollo edition in 1951. *CW* and *HW* give the later opening.

55. Identity and Metamorphosis

1. For *The Dial* see Joel Myerson, *The New England Transcendentalists and the Dial* (Rutherford, N.J.: Fairleigh Dickinson University Press, 1980).

2. *L* 2:262.

3. *EL* 3:187–188.

4. *EL* 3:230.

5. *EL* 3:240, 284.

6. F. Copleston, *A History of Philsophy,* vol. 7, part 1 (New York: Doubleday, 1965), 153; S. T. Coleridge, *Biographia Literaria,* ed. James Engell and W. Jackson Bate (Princeton: Princeton University Press, 1983), 260.

7. For RWE's continuing interest in identity, see the entries in "Index Minor," Houghton b Ms Am 1280 H 131, p. 44, "Index II," Houghton b Ms Am 1280 H 107, p. 177, and "Index Major," Houghton b Ms Am 1280 H 106, p. 161.

8. *CW,* vol. 9, *Poems,* p. 412.

9. "The Oversoul," *CW,* vol. 2, *Essays: First Series,* pp. 268, 276, 281, 296.

10. *JMN* 7:350, 354, 359.

11. *L* 2:287; a convenient index to everything in *The Dial* is the appendix to Myerson's *The New England Transcendentalists and the Dial,* 285–315.

12. *The Dial* 1, no. 1: 1–4; *JMN* 7:364.

13. *EL* 3:200; *JMN* 7:362.

56. Brook Farm and Margaret Fuller

1. *L* 7:398.

2. *Letters of EP,* 245; *L* 7:399; *L* 2:324.

3. *L* 2:325; *JMN* 7:509–510; *L* 7:403; CS to RWE, Sept. 11, 1840.

4. *L* 2:327, 336. It is not clear whether the "I" in "I am yours" is meant to refer to MF or RWE. For MF's response and her sense of frustration at what she took to be RWE's reserve see *Letters of MF,* 2:159–161, which includes a revealing journal entry; for RWE's response to MF's response see *JMN* 7:400.

5. *Letters of MF,* 2:160.

6. "Spiritual Laws," *CW,* vol. 2, *Essays: First Series,* p. 135; "Circles," *CW,* vol. 2, *Essays: First Series,* pp. 301, 320, 319, 321, 322.

7. O. B. Frothingham, *George Ripley* (Boston: Houghton Mifflin, 1888), 307–308; *EC Corr.,* 283–284.

8. *JMN* 7:395, 403, 404, 385, 518.

9. *L* 2:342; *JMN* 7:525.

10. Virginia Woolf, "Emerson's Journals," in *Books and Portraits,* ed. Mary Lyons (New York: Harcourt Brace Jovanovich, 1977), 69.

11. "Art," *CW,* vol. 2, *Essays: First Series,* p. 363.

12. *L* 2:353.

13. *L* 2:369. Hosmer's views on Brook Farm are printed in Frothingham's *George Ripley,* 317–318, and also in *L* 7:437–438n.

14. Orestes Brownson, "The Laboring Classes," in *The Boston Quarterly Review* 3, no. 11 (July 1840): 375.

15. *JMN* 7:542, 540.

57. Pythagoras and Plotinus

1. *JMN* 7:419, 422; *L* 2:444.

2. *The Dial* 1, no. 4: 532, 533.

3. Emerson read Porphyry's "On Abstinence from Animal Food" in *Select Works of Porphyry,* trans. Thomas Taylor (London, 1823). See *JMN* 7:429, 433. For the change in RWE's view of nature see Stephen E. Whicher's *Freedom and Fate* (Philadelphia: University of Pennsylvania Press, 1953), 141ff.

4. Iamblichus, *Life of Pythagoras,* trans. Thomas Taylor (1818; reprint, London: John M. Walkin, 1920), 28, 78; Peter Gorman, *Pythagoras: A Life* (London: Routledge, 1979), 2.

5. See *The Works of Plato,* trans. Floyer Sydenham and Thomas Taylor, 5 vols. (London: R. Wilks, 1804); quoted in Robert Blakey, *History of the Philosophy of Mind* (London: Longman, 1850), 37; *Select Works of Plotinus . . . and Extracts from the Treatise of Synesius on Providence,* trans. Thomas Taylor (London: Black and Son, 1817), vi.

6. *JMN* 7:449, 428–429; for RWE's interest in metamorphosis see Daniel Shea's excellent "Emerson and the American Metamorphosis," in *Emerson, Prophecy, Metamorphosis and Influence,* ed. David Levin (New York: Columbia University Press, 1975), 29–56.

7. F. Copleston, *A History of Philosophy,* vol. 1, part 2 (1946; reprint, Garden City, N.Y.: Doubleday, 1962); *JMN* 7:430.

58. Osman's Ring: A Work of Ecstasy

1. *JMN* 7:442.

2. Czeslaw Milosz, *The Witness of Poetry* (Cambridge: Harvard University Press), 3.

3. J. de Hammer [Joseph von Hammer-Purgstall], *Histoire de l'empire ottoman,* 13 vols. (Paris: Bellizar, 1835), 1:66–67, my translation; *JMN* 7:450.

4. *CW,* vol. 9, *Poems,* p. 52.

5. On April 18, 1832, RWE withdrew from the Boston Athenaeum volume 37 of the *Histoire de l'Académie des Inscriptions et Belles Lettres, avec les Mémoires de Littérature* (50 vols., Paris, 1736–1808). This volume contains Anquetil-Duperron's "Exposition du système théologique des Perses, tiré des livres Zends, Pehlvis, et Parsis," read before the institute in 1767. Since Anquetil-Duperron was an authoritative source, Emerson's subsequent readings in dubious texts were against a solid background. Frederick Carpenter was unaware of this; as a result the chapter on Zoroaster in *Emerson and Asia* (1930) is badly skewed. For RWE and Zoroaster see *JMN* 4:12, *JMN* 5:133, *JMN* 6:387–388, and *JMN* 7:456; RWE also knew "The Oracles of Zoroaster" printed in *The Phenix,* ed. William Gowan (New York, 1835). This book has two selections of Zoroastrian material. The "Oracles of Zoroaster" are translations from the Greek by J. P. Cory, with a biographical sketch by Pierre Bayle and an abstract of the theology by Edward Gibbon. The second selection, "The Chaldean Oracles of Zoroaster," is taken from Thomas Taylor's collection of oracles published in *The Classical Journal,* no. 22. RWE read Synesius's *On Providence,* in *Select Works of Plotinus . . . and Extracts from the Treatise of Synesius on Providence,* trans. Thomas Taylor (London: Black and Son, 1817).

6. *L* 2:422, 419.

7. *L* 2:427; *JMN* 8:116, 98–99.

8. *JMN* 7:454–455.

9. Marghanita Laski, *Ecstasy* (Bloomington: Indiana University Press, 1962), 5, 45, 49; see also Evelyn Underhill, *Mysticism* (New York: Dutton, 1911), 427–448; Germaine Bree, *The World of Marcel Proust* (Boston: Houghton Mifflin, 1966), 58.

10. *JMN* 11:437; *JMN* 8:10; *JMN* 11:53.

11. *JMN* 8:23; "The Method of Nature," in *CW,* vol. 2, *Nature, Addresses and Lectures,* p. 199. See David Robinson's excellent "The Method of Nature and Emerson's Period of Crisis," in *Emerson Centenary Essays,* ed. Joel Myerson (Carbondale: Southern Illinois University Press, 1982), 74–92.

12. *CW,* vol. 1, *Nature, Addresses and Lectures,* pp. 213, 215; David Robinson, "The Method of Nature and Emerson's Period of Crisis," 85.

59. The Frightful Hollows of Space

1. "Ezra Ripley, D.D.," *CW,* vol. 10, *Lectures and Biographical Sketches,* pp. 383, 389; *Life of LE,* 90.

2. *Life of LE,* 85.

3. *L* 2:437; *JMN* 8:165; *Letters of LE,* 89.

4. *JMN* 8:144–145.

5. *JMN* 8:142.

6. "The Conservative," *The Dial* 3:182.

7. "The Poet," *EL* 3:359.

8. "The Transcendentalist," *CW,* vol. 1, *Nature, Addresses and Lectures,* p. 334. On this line of thought, see Martin Bickman, *The Unsounded Centre* (Chapel Hill: University of North Carolina Press, 1980).

9. "Prospects," *EL* 2:379.

10. *Letters of LE,* 104; Louisa May Alcott's reaction is reported in Moncure Conway, *Emerson at Home and Abroad* (Boston: James R. Osgood, 1882), 141.

11. *L* 3:8; *E-C Corr.,* 317; *Letters of LE,* 82, 100.

12. *Letters of LE,* 135; *Life of LE,* 90.

13. Lewis Mumford, *The Conduct of Life* (New York: Harcourt, Brace, 1951), 298; *L* 7:502; "Threnody," *CW,* vol. 9, *Poems,* p. 148.

60. The Dream of Community

1. Lindsay Swift, *Brook Farm* (1900; reprint, New York: Corinth Books, 1961), 200.

2. C. K. Newcomb, "Dolon," *The Dial* (July 1842), 122.

3. *L* 3:23, 19.

4. Brisbane's column "Association" began to run in the *New York Tribune* on March 1, 1842, in vol. 1, no. 278.

5. Redelia Brisbane, *Albert Brisbane: A Mental Biography with a Character Study* (Boston, 1893), 96; Albert Brisbane, *The Social Destiny of Man* (Philadelphia: Stillmeyer, 1840; reprint, New York: Burt Franklin, 1968), xi, 2, 5, 6. RWE's copy of this book is in the Concord Free Public Library.

6. Charles Fourier, *Théorie des quatre mouvements et des destinées générales* (1808), quoted in Charles Gide's introduction to *Design for Utopia: Selected Writings of Charles Fourier* (1901; reprint, New York: Schocken, 1971), 14.

7. For a modern sympathetic account of Fourier and a convenient sample of his writings, see Mark Poster, *Harmonian Man* (Garden City, N.Y.: Doubleday, 1971).

8. For Brisbane's copies of Fourier's works, see the manuscript by Arthur E. Bestor, "Fourierist Books and Pamphlets Published in Great Britain and the United States," 39 pages, in the Columbia University library.

9. For the Fourierist aspect of Brook Farm, see Charles R. Crowe, "Fourierism and the Founding of Brook Farm," *Boston Public Library Quarterly* 12 (Apr. 1960): 79–88; J. T. Codman, *Brook Farm* (Boston, 1894), 74, 77, 84, 87, 152–153, and *Early Letters of G. W. Curtis and J. S. Dwight: Brook Farm and Concord,* ed. G. W. Cooke (New York: Harper and Bros., 1898), 154, 159, 164.

10. Fourier's views on love are in part 2 of the *Traité de l'association domestique-agricole* (Paris, 1822). The same book constitutes volume 4 of *Oeuvres complètes de Charles Fourier* (Paris, 1841–1843), where it is retitled *Théorie de l'unité universelle,* vol. 3; see esp. pp. 363–579. Caroline Sturgis Tappan had a copy in 1851 (see *The American Notebooks of Nathaniel Hawthorne,* ed. Claude Simpson [Columbus: Ohio State University Press, 1972], 446). Hawthorne also read it as part of his preparation for writing *The Blithedale Romance;* see Julian Hawthorne, *Nathaniel Hawthorne and His Wife* (Boston: James R. Osgood, 1884), 1:268–269.

11. C. Fourier, *Théorie de l'unité universelle,* 353.

12. *L* 3:20, 21.

13. RWE, "Fourierism and the Socialists," *The Dial* (July, 1842), 88, 89; Brisbane, *The Social Destiny of Man,* 30.

14. *L* 7:494; *JMN* 8:215–216.

61. Children of the Fire

1. *L* 3:35; *The Dial* 3:103.

2. *JMN* 8:239.

3. *JMN* 8:172; John McAleer, *Ralph Waldo Emerson: Days of Encounter* (Boston: Little, Brown, 1984), 209; Albee, quoted in *CW,* vol. 3, *Essays: Second Series,* p. 306; *JMN* 9:40.

4. *JMN* 7:458; "The Amulet," *CW,* vol. 9, *Poems,* p. 99.

5. "The Poet," *CW,* vol. 3, *Essays: Second Series,* p. 4.

6. Czeslaw Milosz, *The Witness of Poetry* (Cambridge: Harvard University Press); 27; "The Poet," *CW* 3:5.

7. "The Poet," *CW* 3:78.

8. "The Poet," *CW* 3:9–10, 12.

9. "The Poet," *CW* 3:14, 16–17.

10. "The Poet," *CW* 3:34, 30; Alistair Reed, *Ounce Dice Trice* (Boston: Little, Brown, 1958), 39; C. S. Lewis, *Surprised by Joy* (New York: Harcourt Brace Jovanovich, 1955), 191; "The Poet," *CW* 3:30.

11. "The Poet," *CW* 3:37, 38; "Experience," *CW* 3:60.

12. "The Poet," *CW* 3:22; "The World Soul," in *CW*, vol. 9, *Poems*, p. 19; *JMN* 8:228.

62. Emerson's Dial

1. *JMN* 7:459; *JMN* 8:195.

2. RWE, "A Letter," *The Dial* 4, no. 2 (Oct. 1843): 264; *JMN* 8:92.

3. Joel Myerson, *The New England Transcendentalists and the* Dial (Rutherford, N.J.: Fairleigh Dickinson University Press, 1980), 307–308.

4. *The Dial* (July 1842), 82.

5. Joseph Slater, in his introduction to *HW*, vol. 2, *Essays: First Series,* notes that "ninety-five percent of 'History' was drawn from the pages of the journals. . . . Even 'Circles,' the latest of the essays, which was not even begun until September 1840, is more than half made up of passages written in the journal as early as 1835" (p. xxv).

63. New Views

1. *L* 7:514; *JMN* 8:289.

2. *JMN* 8:306; "The Poet," in *CW*, vol. 3, *Essays: Second Series,* p. 21.

3. *JMN* 8:310.

4. *JMN* 8:245, 182–183.

5. *JMN* 8:232, 233.

6. *JMN* 8:228; *JMN* 7:310; *JMN* 8:175; *JMN* 10:392; *JMN* 8:380; *JMN* 9: 452; *JMN* 7:48; *L* 4:86; *JMN* 8:367, 450; *JMN* 7:202.

7. *JMN* 8:249. Le Roux was a Saint-Simonian who published *De l'humanité* in 1840 and was the first French writer to use the word *socialism.* See Carl J. Guarneri, *The Utopian Alternative: Fourierism in Nineteenth-Century America* (Ithaca: Cornell University Press, 1991), 55.

8. *JMN* 8:229.

64. The World

1. James Russell Lowell, *A Fable for Critics* (New York: Putnam's, 1848); Edwin P. Whipple, *Recollections of Eminent Men* (Boston: Houghton Mifflin, 1890), 124.

2. *JMN* 8:502; *L* 2:100..

3. *E-C Corr.,* 341; "Religion," Houghton b Ms Am 1280.199 (1), p. 16; Houghton b Ms Am 1280.199 (5), p. 1.

4. *L* 3:138; *JMN* 8:337–339.

5. *JMN* 8:327, 358, 359; *JMN* 9:250.

6. *Letters of LE,* 114.

7. "Blight," in *CW,* vol. 9, *Poems,* pp. 139, 141.

8. "To Rhea," in *CW,* vol. 9, *Poems,* p. 9.

9. "Saadi," in *CW,* vol. 9, *Poems,* p. 130.

10. "The Poet," in *CW,* vol. 3, *Essays: Second Series,* p. 37; *JMN* 8:430, 381.

11. "Margaret," *JMN* 8:368–369.

12. *L* 3:146, 176, 180; *Letters of LE,* 129; *JMN* 8:365.

13. *L* 7:549; *JMN* 8:400; *JMN* 10:41.

65. The Young American

1. *L* 3:210, 211; *JMN* 9:49, 46.

2. *The Dial* 4 (July 1843): 135; *L* 3:230; *JMN* 9:86.

3. *JMN* 10:35; *JMN* 9:43, 44.

4. *JMN* 9:38; Collie's work does not omit the subject of filial piety; see *The Chinese Classical Work Commonly Called the Four Books,* trans. David Collie (1828; reprint, Gainesville, Fla.: Scholars Facsimiles and Reprints, 1970), 75.

5. Eugene Burnouf, *Introduction à l'histoire du Buddhisme indien* (Paris: Imprimerie Royale, 1844); *JMN* 9:312, 323; Emerson was familiar with the treatment of Buddhism in Heinrich Ritter's *The History of Ancient Philosophy* (Oxford: Talboys, 1838) 1:63–64. He also read Edward Upham's *History and Doctrine of Buddhism* (London, 1829) in November 1846.

6. *L* 7:583.

7. "The Young American," in *CW,* vol. 1, *Nature, Addresses and Lectures,* pp. 363, 371, 374, 378.

8. "The Young American," in *CW,* vol. 1, *Nature, Addresses and Lectures,* p. 378; the journal passage in *JMN* 9:61 has slight variations.

66. Emerson's Emancipation Address

1. "New England Reformers," in *CW,* vol. 3, *Essays: Second Series,* pp. 251–252, 253–254. See Linck Johnson, "Reforming the Reformers: Emerson, Thoreau,

and the Society Lectures at Amory Hall, Boston," *ESQ* 37, no. 4 (1991): 245–289. Johnson shows that RWE's "New England Reformers" was really his considered answer to the communitarians.

2. On Concord as a suburb, see Robert Gross, "Transcendentalism and Urbanism: Concord, Boston, and the Wider World," paper given at the Nordic Association for American Studies, Copenhagen, June 27, 1982. See Thomas Clarkson, *The History of the Rise, Progress, and Accomplishment of the Abolition of the African Slave-Trade by the British Parliament,* 2 vols. (London: Longman, 1808), and James A. Thome and J. Horace Kimball, *Emancipation in the West Indies: A Six Month Tour in Antigua, Barbados, and Jamaica in the Year 1837* (New York: American Anti-Slavery Society, 1838), no. 7 of *The Anti-Slavery Examiner.* The best treatment, by far, of Emerson's antislavery activities is Len Gougeon's *Virtue's Hero: Emerson, Antislavery, and Reform* (Athens: University of Georgia Press, 1990).

3. *JMN* 9:90–91; see Lucretia Mott, *Slavery and the Woman Question,* ed. F. B. Tolles (Haverford, Pa.: Friends Historical Association), 54; Lucretia Mott, "Righteousness Gives Respect to Its Possessor," sermon delivered in Christ Church, Washington, D.C., Jan. 15, 1843, in *Lucretia Mott: Her Complete Speeches and Sermons,* ed. Dana Greene (New York: Edwin Mellen Press, 1980), 48.

4. *Life of LE,* 83–84.

5. "Emancipation in the British West Indies," in *CW,* vol. 11, *Miscellanies,* pp. 100, 104, 113.

6. "Emancipation," *CW* 11:118, 130, 131, 132–133.

7. "Emancipation," *CW* 11:141, 144, 147; *JMN* 9:125, 126.

8. W. L. Garrison to RWE, July 20, 1849, Houghton b Ms Am 1280.1184.

9. "Experience," in *CW,* vol. 3, *Essays: Second Series,* p. 45.

10. *E-C Corr.,* 359, 369; *L* 3:202.

67. Essays on Power

1. *L* 3:259; *HW,* vol. 3, *Essays: Second Series,* p. xxxi; *JMN* 9:97.

2. "Gifts," in *CW,* vol. 3, *Essays: Second Series,* p. 163; "Politics," in *CW,* vol. 3, *Essays: Second Series,* pp. 215, 201, 202, 203, 208.

3. "Manners," in *CW,* vol. 3, *Essays: Second Series,* p. 131.

4. "Nature," in *CW,* vol. 3, *Essays: Second Series,* pp. 172, 179, 170, 176, 178; Richard Nelson, *The Island Within* (San Francisco: North Point Press, 1989), xii.

5. "Experience," in *CW,* vol. 3, *Essays: Second Series,* pp. 40, 47, 49.

6. "Experience," *CW* 3:50, 55, 59, 64, 66, 67.

7. "Experience," *CW* 3:74, 75–76, 83.

8. "Experience," *CW* 3:84, 86, 60.

68. Ex Oriente Lux

1. *JMN* 9:296.

2. Alexander Henry, *Travels and Adventures in Canada and the Indian Territories between the Years 1760–1776,* in 2 parts (New York: I. Riley, 1809), 1:13–14.

3. "Discourse Read before the Philomathesian Society of Middlebury College, in Vermont, 22 July 1845," Houghton b Ms Am 1280.199 (9), pp. 13–14, 29, 41, 43, 51–52. Large parts of this talk were later incorporated into "The Scholar," in *CW,* vol. 10, *Lectures and Biographical Sketches,* see esp. pp. 212, 215, 216, 219.

4. See Cabot 2:752.

5. For RWE's reading of J. G. Kohl's *Russia: St. Petersburg, Moscow, Kharkoff, Riga, Odessa, the German Provinces on the Baltic, the Steppes, the Crimea, and the Interior of the Empire* (London: Chapman and Hall, 1844), see *JMN* 9:227; for Schelling see *L* 3:298 and *JMN* 9:188; for Humboldt see *JMN* 9:270 and "Humboldt," in *CW* vol. 11, *Miscellanies,* pp. 457–459.

6. *Practical Philosophy of the Muhammedan People, exhibited in its professed Connection with the European, so as to render either an introduction to the other; being a translation of the Akhlak-I-Jalaly, the most esteemed ethical work of Middle Persia, from the Persian of Fakir Jany Mohammed Asaad,* by W. F. Thompson (London: Oriental Translation Fund, 1839), lvii, 65, 68, 141, 351. For RWE's notes on the *Akhlak* see *JMN* 9:200, 263, 278, 284–288, 291, 385–386. See F. I. Carpenter, *Emerson and Asia* (Cambridge: Harvard University Press, 1930), chap. 7.

7. *Letters of MF,* 2:122.

8. For the *Desatir,* see *E's Library,* 79; for Kurroglou see *JMN* 9:359–361.

9. *JMN* 9:321, 319; the Vishnu Purana is extensively cited in *JMN* 9, esp. 9:288–290, 312–314, 318–322.

10. Edward Said, "The Politics of Knowledge," *Raritan* (Summer 1991), 21. For an argument that the term *orientalism* meant in the early nineteenth century just the opposite of what Said claims for it, see *Orientalism, Evangelicalism, and the Military Cantonment in Early Nineteenth Century India,* ed. Nancy G. Cassels (Lewiston, N.Y.: Edwin Mellen Press, 1991); *JMN* 9:72.

11. *JMN* 9:232, 231, quoting the Charles Wilkins translation of the Bhagavad Gita (*Bhagvat Geeta,* London: C. Nourse, 1785), 57.

69. Representative Men

1. *JMN* 9:188. Biography had been important to Emerson since his days as a minister. See Susan L. Roberson, "Young Emerson and the Mantle of Biography" *American Transcendental Quarterly,* n.s. 5:3 (Sept. 1991).

2. *E-C Corr.,* 396n., 381; *The Works of Charles Sumner,* 15 vols. (Boston, 1874–1883), 1:268–283.

3. *JMN* 12:580; *JMN* 9:139; Charles Baudelaire, "Intimate Journals," in Karl Shapiro, *Prose Keys to Modern Poetry* (Evanston, Ill.: Row Peterson, 1962), 35; *The Letters of Emily Dickinson,* ed. Thomas Johnson (Cambridge: Harvard University Press, 1958), 569; Robert Frost, "On Emerson," in *Daedalus* (Fall 1959), 712–718, reprinted in M. R. Konvitz and S. E. Whicher, *Emerson: A Collection of Critical Essays* (Englewood Cliffs, N.J.: Prentice-Hall, 1962), 13 (cf. "Montaigne," in *CW,* vol. 4, *Representative Men,* p. 168); "Jorge Luis Borges," in *Writers at Work: Paris Review Interviews,* 4th ser., ed. George Plympton (New York: Viking, 1976), 130.

4. For the relation of *Representative Men* to democratic idealism see Perry Miller, "Emersonian Genius and the American Democracy," in *Nature's Nation* (Cambridge: Harvard University Press, 1967), 163–174, and F. O. Matthiessen, *American Renaissance* (New York: Oxford, 1941), 631ff.; "The Uses of Great Men," in *CW,* vol. 4, *Rep. Men,* p. 6; *JMN* 9:315; "The Uses of Great Men," *CW* 4:31 (see *JMN* 9:246 for early version).

5. "Plato," in *CW,* vol. 4, *Rep. Men,* pp. 39, 49, 47, 48,

6. "The Uses of Great Men," *CW* 4:5; "Plato," *CW* 4:76; *JMN* 9:365.

7. "Swedenborg," in *CW,* vol. 4, *Rep. Men,* p. 97; *JMN* 9:301, 342; "Swedenborg," *CW* 4:124–125, 106, 107.

8. "Swedenborg," *CW* 4:134, 144.

9. *JMN* 9:343; "Montaigne," *CW* 4:159, 180, 186.

10. "Shakespeare," in *CW,* vol. 4, *Rep. Men,* pp. 191, 213,

11. *JMN* 9:152; "Napoleon," in *CW,* vol. 4, *Rep. Men,* p. 224.

12. "Goethe," in *CW,* vol. 4, *Rep. Men,* pp. 264, 277, 275, 289.

13. "Goethe," in *CW* 4:290.

70. The Lecturer

1. David Mead, *Yankee Eloquence in the Middle West: The Ohio Lyceum 1850–1870* (East Lansing: Michigan State College Press, 1951), 15; see William Charvat, *Emerson's American Lecture Engagements* (New York: New York Public

Library, 1961), and Eleanor Tilton, "Emerson's Lecture Schedule 1837–8 Revised," in *Harvard Library Bulletin* 21 (Oct. 1973).

2. See Charvat, *Emerson's American Lecture Engagements*, 8.

3. Rusk 385.

4. On the lyceum movement see Carl Bode, *The American Lyceum: Town Meeting of the Mind* (New York: Oxford, 1956).

5. C. E. Schorer, "Emerson and the Wisconsin Lyceum," *AL* 24 (Jan. 54): 473; Mead, *Yankee Eloquence*, 39, 61; Sophia Peabody to Elizabeth Palmer Peabody, 1838, Berg Collection, NYPL; Schorer, "Emerson and the Wisconsin Lyceum," 467; Mead, *Yankee Eloquence*, 55, 36; *Quincy Daily Herald*, Feb. 28, 1867, p. 2; E. P. Whipple, *Recollections of Eminent Men* (Boston: Houghton Mifflin, 1890), 140.

6. David Potts, *Wesleyan University 1831–1910* (New Haven, Conn.: Yale University Press, 1992), 50–61; Edwin P. Whipple, *Recollections of Eminent Men* (Boston: Houghton Mifflin, 1890), 146.

7. Julian Hawthorne, *Hawthorne and His Circle* (New York: Harper and Bros., 1903), 66; Mead, *Yankee Eloquence*, 44.

8. Eleanor Scott, "Emerson Wins the 900 Dollars," *AL* 17 (Mar. 1945): 84.

9. Louise Hastings, "Emerson in Cincinnati," *NEQ* 11, no. 3 (Sept. 1938).

10. Mead, *Yankee Eloquence*, 43.

11. Ellen Emerson, "What I Can Remember about Father," Houghton b Ms Am 1280.227, p. 40; Jeanne Kronman, "Three Unpublished Lectures by RWE," *NEQ* 19 (Mar. 1946): 109, and Louise Hastings, "Emerson in Cincinnati," 464; Ellen Emerson, "What I Can Remember," 41; Whipple, *Recollections*, 132.

12. *JMN* 9:70, 71.

71. Persia and Poetry

1. *Der Diwan von Mohammed Schemsed-Din Hafis*, trans. from the Persian by Joseph von Hammer (Stuttgart and Tübingen: Cotta, 1812–1813).

2. Idries Shah, *The Sufis* (London: Jonathan Cape, 1964), 25, 15; "From the Persian of Hafiz," in RWE, *Poems* (Boston: James Munroe, 1847), 209; Shah, *The Sufis*, 27. There are direct references to Sufism in Joseph von Hammer's introduction to *Der Diwan* and there is a clipping on p. 14 of RWE's "Orientalist" notebook, Houghton b Ms Am 1280 H 115, which refers to the "refined soofeeism of Persia." Emerson also makes reference to "the philosophical sect of the Sufis" in his "Orientalist" notebook, now published in *TN* 2:131. The allegorical approach to Hafez is discussed at length and in detail by Sir William Jones in "On the Mystical Poetry

of the Persians and Hindus," in *The Works of Sir William Jones* (London: J. Stockdale, 1807), reprinted in *The Works of Sir William Jones* (New York: Garland, 1984), vol. 2.

3. See notebook "Orientalist," Houghton b Ms Am 1280 H 115; *JMN* 9:352.

4. *JMN* 9:382; notebook "Orientalist," 9, 26, 54, 61, 136.

5. See notebook "Orientalist," 81, 117.

6. The Hafez translations Emerson included in his 1847 volume of *Poems* but did not reprint are "From the Persian of Hafiz" (pp. 209–216), Hafez's longest poem, and "Ghaselle: From the Persian of Hafiz" (pp. 217–218); these are translations of odes 686 and 61 in Jarrett's 1881 Persian text and W. H. Clarke's *The Divan-I-Hafiz* (1891; reprint, London: Octagon, 1974). Emerson translated them from the German of Joseph von Hammer. Von Hammer's introduction discusses Hafez's metrics. William James, *The Varieties of Religious Experience*, Library of America, p. 348.

7. "From the Persian of Hafiz," RWE, *Poems* (1847), 209; "Bacchus," in *CW*, vol. 9, *Poems*, pp. 125, 126.

8. Musle-Huddeen Sheik Saadi, *The Gulistan or Rose Garden,* trans. Francis Gladwin, with an essay on Saadi's life and genius by James Ross, and with a preface by R. W. Emerson (Boston: Ticknor and Fields, 1865); see clipping on Shiraz in notebook "Orientalist."

9. See J. D. Yohannon, "Emerson's Translations of Persian Poetry from German Sources," in *AL* 14 (Jan. 1943): 407–420, and his "The Influence of Persian Poetry upon Emerson's Work," in *AL* 15 (Mar. 1943): 25–41, as well as his *Persian Poetry in England and America* (Delmar, N.Y.: Caravan Books, 1977). See also Allen 431–431 and 470–472. Chapter 6 on "Persian Poetry" in F. I. Carpenter's *Emerson and Asia* (Cambridge: Harvard University Press) seriously underestimates the importance of the subject to RWE.

10. *JMN* 9:375.

11. *JMN* 9:379.

12. *JMN* 9:381.

13. *CW*, vol. 9, *Poems*, p. 19.

72. The New Domestic Order. Poems

1. M. M. Engel, *I Remember the Emersons* (Los Angeles: Times-Mirror, 1941), 116; *Life of LE,* 105.

2. *Life of LE,* 106.

3. *L* 3:362.

4. *L* 3:344; *JMN* 9:366; see Margaret Gilman, "Baudelaire and Emerson," *Romanic Review* 24 (Oct. 1943): 211–222; *JMN* 9:452.

5. "The Sphinx," in *CW*, vol. 9, *Poems*, p. 25; see Edward Waldo Emerson's comment on the placement of "The Sphinx," *CW* 9:403n.

6. "Ode: Inscribed to W. H. Channing," in *CW*, vol. 9, *Poems*, p. 79.

7. *JMN* 9:441.

73. The Orchard Keeper

1. See notebook "Trees" in *JMN* 8:518–549.

2. For RWE's interest in Downing, see *E's Library*, *JMN* 10:85, and *L* 8:112. EWE's comments are in *CW*, vol. 5, *English Traits*, pp. 336–337; Andrew Jackson Downing, *The Fruits and Fruit Trees of America*, rev. ed. (New York: John Wiley, 1864), vi.

3. Downing, *The Fruits*, 4.

4. Downing, *The Fruits*, 1–2.

5. Downing, *The Fruits*, 2, 3.

6. For the Colonel Wilder who had four hundred varieties of pear, see *JMN* 8:538. The English Horticultural Society listed six hundred varieties; see *A Description and History of Vegetable Substances Used in the Arts and in Domestic Economy* (Boston: Wells and Lilly, 1830; reprinted from the Library of Entertaining Knowledge published by the Society for the Diffusion of Useful Knowledge), 234.

74. I Shall Never Graduate

1. See *E's Reading*, and "List of Books" in *JMN* 10:17–18; *JMN* 9:466.

2. Houghton b Ms Am 1280 H 107, "Index II," the first page of which reads "Index to my manuscripts 1847," is clearly the first in time, and is in Emerson's handwriting. Houghton b Ms Am 1280 H 106, "Index Major," the first page of which reads "Index major to my manuscripts 1847," is based on "Index II" but has been considerably augmented and is in at least two hands.

3. *JMN* 10:93; *E-C Corr.*, 420; *JMN* 10:28.

4. *JMN* 10:79, 30, 77, 83, 97.

5. *JMN* 10:60.

6. *L* 3:411. There is a sketch of the summer house in A. B. Alcott's *Ralph Waldo Emerson: An Estimate of His Character and Genius* (1865; reprint, Boston: A.

Williams, 1882), 56. Two other sketches appear in May Alcott, *Concord Sketches* (Boston: Fields, Osgood, 1869).

7. *L* 3:387, 403, 418; *JMN* 10:61.

8. *L* 8:89, 91.

9. *L* 8:106, 107.

10. *L* 8:107.

75. England

1. *JMN* 10:178; *L* 3:425, 438.

2. *JMN* 10:217, 237, 185.

3. *JMN* 10:224, 215, 179, 218.

4. *CW*, vol. 5, *English Traits*, p. 182; *JMN* 10:182, 254.

5. *JMN* 10:251, 224.

6. *L* 2:442–443; *JMN* 10:257.

7. *CW*, vol. 5, *Eng. Traits*, pp. 167–168.

8. *L* 8:144; Raymond Postgate, *The Story of a Year: 1848* (London: Jonathan Cape, 1955), 139–140.

9. *L* 3:424.

10. *JMN* 10:230, 255; *L* 4:43, 49; *E-C Corr.*, 38.

11. January Searle [George Searle Phillips], *Emerson* (London: 1855), 47.

12. See Joseph Slater's introduction to *E-C Corr.*, 37–43.

76. The Natural History of Intellect

1. *JMN* 10:143–144, 395.

2. *JMN* 10:176, 156, 181.

3. "Eloquence," Feb. 10, 1847, Houghton b Ms Am 1280.199 (11).

4. "Domestic Life," in *CW*, vol. 7, *Society and Solitude*, p. 107.

5. "Reading," in *CW*, vol. 7, *Society and Solitude*, pp. 189, 196, 204.

6. "Natural Aristocracy etc 1848. Rough Notes," Houghton b Ms Am 1280.200 (2).

7. "The Superlative," in *CW*, vol. 10, *Lectures and Biog. Sketches*, pp. 164, 167; "Manchester Lectures, 1847, Fragments," Houghton b Ms Am 1280.199 (13).

8. "Manchester Lectures, 1847, Fragments," Houghton b Ms Am 1280.199 (13).

9. *L* 4:51.

10. "Powers and Laws of Thought I 1848," Houghton b Ms Am 1280.200 (3), pp. 6, 30.

11. "Powers and Laws of Thought I 1850," Houghton b Ms Am 1280.200 (5); H. D. Thoreau, "Walking," in *The Writings of Henry David Thoreau* (Boston: Houghton Mifflin, 1906), vol. 5, *Excursions and Poems,* p. 240.

77. Chartism and Revolution

1. See Louis Blanc, *The History of Ten Years: 1830–1840,* 2 vols. (London: Chapman and Hall, 1844–1845). *CW,* vol. 5, *English Traits,* p. 150.

2. Thomas Cooper, *The Life of Thomas Cooper* (London: Hodder and Stoughton, 1886), 312.

3. "Reform and Chartism," Houghton b Ms Am 1280.201 (7).

4. See the excellent account of the Chartist demonstration in Raymond Postgate, *Story of a Year: 1848* (London: Jonathan Cape, 1955), 112–128.

5. Postgate, *Story of a Year,* 125.

6. "Reform and Chartism," Houghton b Ms Am 1280.201 (7); *JMN* 10: 325, 311.

7. *JMN* 10:271. Interest in Emerson seems to have begun in France with the Polish poet Adam Mickiewicz, who lent Edgar Quinet his copy of *Nature* in 1838. Word then spread to Jules Michelet, Philarete Chasles, the Comtesse d'Agoult, and Lamartine. See Maurice Chazin, "Quinet, an Early Admirer of Emerson," *PMLA* 48 (Mar. 1933): 147–163, Besse D. Howard, "The First French Estimate of Emerson," *NEQ* 10 (Sept. 1937): 447–463, and C. M. Lombard, "Daniel Stern on Emerson," *Notes and Queries* 201 (May 1956): 217–218.

8. Postgate, *Story of a Year,* 150. A recent discussion of Emerson and socialism is Sacvan Bercovitch, "Emerson, Individualism, and the Ambiguities of Dissent," *South Atlantic Quarterly* 89, no. 3 (Summer 1990): 623–662; see also Larry J. Reynolds, *European Revolutions and the American Literary Renaissance* (New Haven: Yale University Press, 1988).

9. *JMN* 10:273: *L* 4:73.

10. *L* 4:73.

11. *L* 4:73.

12. *JMN* 10:266, 267.

13. *JMN* 10:310.

14. *JMN* 10:310, 328.

78. Return: Quarrel with Thoreau

1. *JMN* 10:339.

2. *E-C Corr.*, 442, 443; *L* 4:101.

3. *JMN* 10:322, 320.

4. *L* 8:184.

5. *Corr. HDT,* 207; *L* 4:108.

6. *JMN* 11:10–11.

7. R. Sattelmeyer, "When He Became My Enemy: Emerson and Thoreau 1848–49," *NEQ* 62 (June 1989): 187–204, 198. Delores Carpenter, who has done the most work on Lidian, believes that she and Henry were very close indeed. David Robinson has ably demonstrated the rift from Emerson's point of view in "Emerson's Later Resistance to Thoreau," paper presented at the American Literature Association Conference, Washington, D.C., May 1991.

8. H. D. Thoreau, *A Week on the Concord and Merrimack Rivers* (Princeton: Princeton University Press, 1980), 327, 330, 336, 339.

9. Sattelmeyer, "When He Became My Enemy," 189–190.

10. *JMN* 10:343, 344.

11. Moncure Conway, *Emerson at Home and Abroad* (Boston: James B. Osgood, 1882), 283; *Corr. HDT,* 213; notebook "OP Gulistan," Houghton b Ms Am 1280 H 108, pp. 123, 129, 127. See also Richard Bridgeman's *Dark Thoreau* (Lincoln: University of Nebraska Press, 1981).

12. Thoreau, *A Week,* 354.

79. The Walden Sierras. Quetelet

1. *JMN* 10:354, 358.

2. *JMN* 11:29, 36, 56, 132; *JMN* 11:358.

3. *JMN* 9:172; *L* 4:110.

4. *JMN* 10:246; *JMN* 11:104.

5. *JMN* 11:103, 108.

6. *JMN* 11:138; *L* 4:145: *JMN* 11:117.

7. See Solomon Diamond's introduction to the Scholars Facsimile and Reprints edition (Gainesville, Fla.: 1969) of Lambert A. J. Quetelet, *A Treatise on Man and the Development of His Faculties* (Edinburgh: William and Robert Chambers, 1842).

8. Quetelet, *A Treatise* (1969), 6, 101, 96, 5.

9. *JMN* 11:67, 91; *JMN* 13:340; *JMN* 10:105. The classic interpretation of the development of Emerson's thought from a belief in freedom to an acceptance of fate is Stephen E. Whicher, *Freedom and Fate: An Inner Life of Ralph Waldo Emerson* (Philadelphia: University of Pennsylvania Press, 1953).

10. *JMN* 11:85, 161, 147, 160.

80. Therienism and the Hegelian Moment

1. *JMN* 11:199, 213, 224–225.

2. *JMN* 11:192.

3. "Therienism," Houghton b Ms Am 1280.214 (123), pp. 3, 4.

4. "Therienism," 4, 5.

5. "Therienism," 5, 8.

6. "Therienism," 8, 9.

7. Loyd D. Easton, *Hegel's First American Followers: The Ohio Hegelians* (Athens: Ohio University Press, 1966), 44.

8. Easton, *Hegel's First American Followers,* 33, 310; H. B. Acton, "Hegelianism," in *Dictionary of the History of Ideas,* ed. Philip P. Weiner (New York: Scribner's, 1973), 2:407, 408.

9. *JMN* 11:200.

10. *JMN* 11:199; F. H. Hedge, *Prose Writers of Germany* (1848), 452.

11. *JMN* 11:201.

12. *JMN* 11:210.

13. *JMN* 11:203.

14. *JMN* 11:221, 240, 202, 221; the quotation from Goethe is from "Winckelmann" in Goethe's *Werke,* 55 vols. (Stuttgart and Tübingen: 1828–1833), 37:20.

15. George Eliot, *Middlemarch* (Boston: Houghton Mifflin, 1956), 195. I owe the formulation "We know what we make . . ." to Jere Surber, professor of Philosophy at the University of Denver; *JMN* 11:161.

81. The West

1. Walt Whitman, *The Early Poems and the Fiction,* ed. T. L. Brasher (New York: New York University Press, 1963), 44, 47

2. See Louise Hastings, "Emerson in Cincinnati," *NEQ* 11 (Spring 1938): 443–469.

3. *L* 4:203.

4. *L* 4:204.

5. Ephraim Squier and E. H. Davis, *Ancient Monuments of the Mississippi Valley* (Washington: Smithsonian Contributions to Knowledge, 1948), vol. 1; for the mythologizing of the Mound Builders see Robert Silverberg, *Mound Builders of Ancient America: The Archaeology of a Myth* (New York: N.Y. Graphic Society, 1968).

6. *L* 4:205; *JMN* 11:512; for the parallel between Hopewell and Stonehenge cultures, see Aubrey Burl, *Prehistoric Avebury* (New Haven: Yale University Press, 1979).

7. *L* 4:207, 211–212.

8. *L* 4:213.

9. *L* 4:209; *JMN* 11:518.

10. *L* 4:210.

11. Raymond Postgate, *Story of a Year: 1848* (London: Jonathan Cape, 1955), 225, 229.

12. *L* 4:216.

13. *L* 4:211; *JMN* 11:522, 512.

14. *L* 4:528.

82. The Matter of Margaret

1. *Memoirs of Margaret Fuller Ossoli,* ed. RWE, J. F. Clarke, and W. H. Channing (Boston: Phillips Sampson, 1852), 2:337.

2. *Memoirs of Margaret Fuller Ossoli,* 2:341–344; MF to Marcus Spring June 3, 1850, in F. B. Sanborn, "The Women of Concord," *The Critic* 48, no. 3 (1906): 254.

3. *Memoirs of Margaret Fuller Ossoli,* 2:349.

4. *JMN* 11:256, 257, 258.

5. *Memoirs of Margaret Fuller Ossoli,* 2:258; various schemes were put forward for editing the volume. At first it seemed that RWE, Ward, and Channing would do it. Single editors were proposed; Emerson thought Ward the best candidate. Eventually Ward dropped out entirely and the book, as it appeared, was edited by RWE, J. F. Clarke, and W. H. Channing.

6. The journal is called "Margaret Fuller Ossoli" and is printed in *JMN* 11; *JMN* 11:474, 477, 488, 494, 495, 415.

7. See, for example, Robert Hudspeth's introduction to the *Letters of Margaret Fuller* (Ithaca: Cornell University Press, 1983–), vol 1.

8. *JMN* 11:471; *L* 4:222; *L* 8:257; Emerson read George Sand's *Spiridion* when it appeared serially in the *Revue des Deux Mondes* 16 (1838).

83. The Tragic

1. *JMN* 11:309.

2. *JMN* 11:291–292.

3. *JMN* 11:302, 287.

4. *JMN* 11:322.

5. J. A. Froude, *The Nemesis of Faith,* 2d ed. (London: John Chapman, 1849), 22–23, 226–227.

6. RWE is quoting from *Select Letters of Christopher Columbus,* trans. R. H. Major (London, 1847); see *JMN* 11:290, 315.

7. *JMN* 11:293.

84. The Conduct of Life

1. *L* 4:246; *JMN* 11:523.

2. For O. S. Marden see Gail Thain Parker, *The Mind Cure in New England from the Civil War to World War I* (Hanover, N.H.: University Press of New England, 1973); a forceful and influential treatment of Emerson as the spokesman of a materialist, exploitative "rugged" individualism is Quentin Anderson's *The Imperial Self* (New York: Knopf, 1971).

3. "Power," in *CW,* vol. 6, *The Conduct of Life,* pp. 56, 62–63, 71, 74.

4. "Power," *CW* 6:73, 62. For other orchard images see *CW,* vol. 6, *Conduct of Life,* pp. 104, 115, 149, 203, 214.

5. "Wealth," in *CW,* vol. 6, *Conduct of Life,* pp. 99, 89, 97, 101. Conwell, a Baptist clergyman, delivered "Acres of Diamonds" some six thousand times for fees totaling eight million dollars.

6. "Wealth," *CW* 6:111–112, 114, 115.

7. "Wealth," *CW* 6:118, 119, 126.

8. "Culture," in *CW,* vol. 6, *Conduct of Life,* pp. 131, 134, 155, 159.

9. "Worship," in *CW,* vol. 6, *Conduct of Life,* pp. 204, 203, 216.

10. "Worship," *CW* 6:215, 220, 240, 241.

85. The Fugitive Slave Act

1. Wilbur H. Siebert, "The Under-Ground Railroad in Massachusetts," in *Proceedings of the American Antiquarian Society* n. s. 45 (1935): 67–68. Details on

Jenkins's stay in Concord are in EWE's manuscript notes (now in the Concord Free Public Library) on a conversation with Mrs. Bigelow in 1892.

2. Melvillian ironies abound in the "Shadrach" episode. As Emerson was making notes for his fugitive slave law speech, he insisted that old-fashioned uprightness seemed to have gone from Massachusetts. "Thomas Melville is gone," he wrote of Melville's grandfather in *JMN* 11:356; Theodore Parker, "The Boston Kidnapping," in *The Collected Works of Theodore Parker,* ed. F. P. Cobbe, vol. 5, *Discourses of Slavery* (London: Trubner, 1863), 187; Siebert, "The Under-Ground Railroad," 38.

3. *L* 8:273.

4. Len Gougeon, *Virtue's Hero: Emerson, Antislavery, and Reform* (Athens: University of Georgia Press, 1990), 159–160; *JMN* 14:385.

5. "The Fugitive Slave Law," in *CW,* vol. 11, *Miscellanies,* pp. 181, 183, 201.

6. Lord Charnwood, *Lincoln* (New York: Holt, 1917), 60; "The Fugitive Slave Law," *CW* 11:190, 191, 192.

7. John C. Broderick, "Emerson and Moorfield Storey: A Lost Journal Found," in *AL* 38, no. 2 (May 1966): 177–186. Gougeon has a penetrating analysis of the damage done by Holmes's distortions and by those of Harvard president Charles W. Eliot. See Gougeon's chapter "Abolition and the Biographers" and "Conclusion," pp. 342–343. Gougeon also has valuable notes, see esp. pp. 394–397; Gougeon, *Virtue's Hero,* 1–23; *JMN* 14:421, 423; *JMN* 11:412, 352, 363.

8. "Speech on Affairs in Kansas," in *CW,* vol. 11, *Misc.,* pp. 258, 259.

9. Horace Traubel, *With Walt Whitman in Camden,* vol. 4, Jan. 21 to Apr. 7, 1889 (Philadelphia: University of Pennsylvania Press, 1953), p. 293; "Remarks at a Meeting for the Relief of the Family of John Brown," in *CW,* vol. 11, *Misc.,* p. 268; "The Emancipation Proclamation," in *CW,* vol. 11, *Misc.,* p. 317.

10. *JMN* 11:406.

86. The Science of Liberty

1. *L* 4:252.
2. "Fate," in *CW,* vol. 6, *The Conduct of Life,* pp. 5, 6, 7.
3. "Fate," *CW* 6:8, 19.
4. "Fate," *CW* 6:22, 23, 28.
5. "Fate," *CW* 6:29, 30.
6. "Fate," *CW* 6:31.
7. "Fate," *CW* 6:31, 35; *JMN* 11:452.

8. "Fate," *CW* 6:43, 48.

9. "The Fugitive Slave Law" (second speech of that title, given in New York in 1854), in *CW*, vol. 11, *Miscellanies*, pp. 231, 232.

87. My Platoon

1. *L* 4:288, 289.

2. Edwin Emerson, Jr., *A History of the Nineteenth Century* (New York: Collier, 1902), 2:1108; "Address to Kossuth," in *CW*, vol. 11, *Miscellanies,* p. 399.

3. *E-C Corr.*, 476; *JMN* 12:17, 18, 121.

4. Karl Marx, "Forced Emigration . . . ," *New York Tribune* (March 22, 1853), reprinted in Karl Marx and Friedrich Engels, *Collected Works* (New York: International Publishers, 1979), 11:528–534.

5. RWE quotes Marx in *JMN* 13:127. He was sufficiently struck by the passage to make a short poem of it. See *CW*, vol. 9, *Poems*, p. 357. On RWE and Marx see Lewis S. Feuer, "Ralph Waldo Emerson's Reference to Karl Marx," *NEQ* 33 (Sept. 1960): 378–379; *CW*, vol. 5, *English Traits,* pp. 158–159.

6. See *E's Reading,* 27.

7. *JMN* 11:447; *JMN* 13:66.

8. *JMN* 13:61; *L* 4:347.

9. *L* 8:282.

10. Ainsworth Spofford, *The Higher Law Tried by Reason and Authority* (New York: S. W. Benedict, 1851), 21, 27; *L* 8:278.

11. *JMN* 13:79.

12. John Albee, *Reminiscences of Emerson* (New York: R. Cooke, 1901), 8.

13. Moncure Conway, *Autobiography: Memories and Experiences,* 2 vols. (Boston and New York: Houghton Mifflin, 1904), 2:77.

14. Horatio Greenough to RWE, Dec. 8, 1851, Houghton b Ms Am 1280 (1275); *L* 4:272; Horace Bender [Horatio Greenough], *The Travels, Observations, and Experience of a Yankee Stonecutter,* ed. Nathalia Wright (New York: G. P. Putnam, 1852; reprint, Gainesville Fla.: Scholars Facsimiles and Reprints, 1958), 37.

15. *L* 4:301; *JMN* 13:111.

16. *JMN* 13:28.

88. Country Walking and the Sea

1. *E-C Corr.,* 485; *L* 8:369; *L* 4:380, 365.

2. *L* 8:375.

3. Robert Sattelmeyer, "Ellery Channing in the 1855 Massachusetts Census," *Thoreau Research Newsletter,* vol. 2, no. 2, p. 8; *JMN* 13:177, 59, 61–62, *L* 8:365.

4. WE to RWE, Aug. 22, 1853, Wortis Coll.; *JMN* 13:41.

5. *L* 4: 290–291; *E-C Corr.,* 486; *JMN* 13:188, 134, 32; Edward Davies's volume is *Celtic Researches* (London: 1804); *JMN* 13:180.

6. See *JMN* 13:180.

7. *JMN* 13:180.

89. English Traits

1. *L* 4:398, 401; *E-C Corr.,* 498.

2. *JMN* 13:284; "Poetry and Imagination," in *CW,* vol. 8, *Letters and Social Aims,* pp. 11, 27–28, 34.

3. "France, or Urbanity," Houghton b Ms Am 1280.202 (6), pp. 46, 22, 22 1/2 (sic). Selections from this lecture were published as *Emerson's View of France and the French,* by Lestrois Parish (New York: American Society of the French Legion of Honor, 1935).

4. *JMN* 13:333.

5. *JMN* 13:292, 302, 314.

6. Alistair Cooke, *The American in England,* 1975 Rede Lecture (Cambridge: Cambridge University Press, 1975); "Race," in *CW,* vol. 5, *English Traits,* pp. 46, 48, 49–50.

7. "Ability," in *CW,* vol. 5, *Eng. Traits,* pp. 92, 94, 89; "Literature," in *CW,* vol. 5, *Eng. Traits,* pp. 233, 241, 242; "Character," in *CW,* vol. 5, *Eng. Traits,* p. 130; "Literature," *CW* 5:244; "Personal," in *CW,* vol. 5, *Eng. Traits,* p. 298; "Results," in *CW,* vol. 5, *Eng. Traits,* p. 308.

8. "Land," in *CW,* vol. 5, *Eng. Traits,* p. 37; "Race," *CW* 5:58, 60; "Cockayne," in *CW,* vol. 5, *Eng. Traits,* p. 152.

9. "Cockayne," *CW* 5:152.

10. *L* 4:457; *L* 8:399; *L* 4:460, 466.

90. Fame

1. RWE's reputation can be traced in detail in *Secondary Bibl.;* Philarete Chasles, *Anglo-American Literature and Manners* (New York: Scribner's, 1852); see Maurice Chazin, "Quinet: An Early Discoverer of Emerson," *PMLA* 48 (Mar.

1933): 147–163, B. D. Howard, "The First French Estimate of Emerson," *NEQ* 10 (Sept. 1937): 447–463, and Luther S. Luedke, "First Notices of Emerson in England and Germany, 1835–1852," *Notes and Queries* 22 (Mar. 1975): 106–108.

2. William J. Sowder, *Emerson's Impact on the British Isles and Canada* (Charlottesville: University Press of Virginia, 1960), 3, 45; Kenneth Silverman, *Edgar A. Poe: Mournful and Never-ending Remembrance* (New York: Harper Collins, 1992); *Secondary Bibl.*, 71, 100, 101.

3. The *Toronto Daily Leader* took a particularly gracious view of the matter, noting that the lectures were "the work that procures him the means of subsistence, and as such, entitled to the same protection that is afforded the inventor of a steam-plow." *The Daily Leader* (Toronto) (Sat., Jan. 28, 1860). I am indebted to Greg Gatenby for this account.

4. EWE 162; for parodies of "Brahma," see *Secondary Bibl.* and K. W. Cameron, "The Reception of Emerson's 'Brahma': Parodies and Paraphrases," *ARLR* 2 (1988): 165–190, and his "Emerson's 'Brahma': Early Explications and Commentary," *ARLR* 2 (1988): 197–223.

5. "Fame," in *CW*, vol. 9, *Poems*, p. 383; "Index Major," Houghton b Ms Am 1280 H 106, p. 107; "Greatness," in *CW*, vol. 8, *Letters and Social Aims*, p. 313; "Milton," in *CW*, vol. 12, *Natural History of Intellect*, p. 248.

6. "Index Major," 107.

7. SAP to EPP, Salem, 1838, Ms Berg; Henry Sutton, *The Evangel of Love* (London: C. A. Bartlett, 1847); Moncure Conway, "The Ministry of Emerson," *The Open Court* 17, no. 5 (May 1903): 258; A. J. Davis, *The Arabula* (Boston: William White, 1867). Henry Agrippa is Henricus Cornelius Agrippa von Nettesheim (1486?–1535), a Christian cabalist, mystic, and contemporary of Paracelsus.

8. *The Boston Evening Transcript*, Jan. 22, 1872.

9. "Character," in *CW*, vol. 3, *Essays: Second Series*, p. 89.

91. Whitman

1. RWE's planned reading on China is listed in *JMN* 13:339. RWE read George Turner's edition of *The Mahawanso, with an Introductory Essay on Pali Buddhistical Literature* (Ceylon: Cotta Church Mission Press, 1837). RWE read Barthold Niebuhr's *Life and Letters* (London: 1852), his *Lectures on the History of Rome* (London, 1849), and his *Lectures on Ancient Ethnography* (Boston, 1854). He read H. H. Wilson's edition of the *Rig-Veda-Sanhita: A Collection of Ancient Hindu Hymns*, 4 vols. (London, 1850–1866). He read Charlotte E. Guest's three-volume

translation of the Welsh classic, *The Mabinogion, from the Llyfr Coch o Hergest* (London, 1849). See *JMN* 13:485.

2. This 1862 correspondence between Sanborn and the Emersons is in the private collection of George Goodspeed, who kindly allowed me to read through it.

3. *L* 4:493, 497, 504–505.

4. *L* 8:442, 445, 446. The commentary on the Emerson-Whitman connection in *L* 4:520–521 is outdated. See esp. Justin Kaplan's *Walt Whitman* (New York: Simon and Schuster, 1980), and Jerome Loving's *Emerson, Whitman, and the American Muse* (Chapel Hill: University of North Carolina Press, 1982).

5. Whitman's comment to Trowbridge is discussed in Walt Whitman, *Daybooks and Notebooks*, 2 vols. (New York: New York University Press, 1978), 2:409. For Whitman's use of RWE's letter, see *L* 8:458n.

6. Walt Whitman, *The Correspondence*, vol. 1, ed. E. H. Miller (New York: New York University Press, 1961), 1:65.

7. Walt Whitman, "Emerson's Books, the Shadows of Them," in *Prose Works* (1892), *Collect and Other Pieces,* ed. Floyd Stovall (New York: New York University Press, 1964), 767–768. Horace Traubel, *With Walt Whitman in Camden,* vol. 3: Nov. 1, 1888, to Jan. 28, 1889 (reprint, New York: Rowman and Littlefield, 1961), 439.

8. Traubel, *With Walt Whitman in Camden,* vol. 1: Mar. 28–July 14, 1888 (reprint, New York: Rowman and Littlefield, 1961), 23, 285.

9. Traubel, *With Walt Whitman in Camden,* 1:256, 397; 2; July 16, 1888, to Oct. 31, 1888, p. 2; 3:52, 353, 318, 354; vol. 4: Jan. 21–Apr. 7, 1889; p. 289.

10. Traubel, *With Walt Whitman in Camden,* 4:413.

11. Traubel, *With Walt Whitman in Camden,* 4:167; vol. 5: Apr. 8–Sep. 14, 1889, p. 119.

12. Traubel, *With Walt Whitman in Camden,* 1:466.

92. The Remedy at the Hour of Need

1. See the accounts of the Second Annual New England Women's Rights Convention in Boston (1855) in *History of Woman Suffrage,* ed. Elizabeth Cady, Susan B. Anthony, and Matilda Joslyn Gage (New York: Fowler and Wells, 1881), vol. 1, and in *A History of the National Woman's Rights Movement from 1850 to 1870,* comp. Paulina W. Davis (New York: Journeyman Printers Cooperative Association, 1871; reprint, New York: Kraus, n.d.). On Lucy Stone see Elinor Rice Hays, *Morning Star: A Biography of Lucy Stone* (New York: Harcourt, Brace, 1961). Stone's

husband, Henry Blackwell, lived in Cincinnati. He helped arrange Emerson's lectures there and he put him up when he came to town. Parker's support for Antoinette Brown is expressed in his "Sermon of the Public Function of Women," Mar. 27, 1853, in *Collected Works of Theodore Parker*, ed. F. P. Cobb (London: Trubner, 1864), vol. 8, *Miscellaneous Discourses*.

2. "Woman," in *CW*, vol. 11, *Miscellanies*, p. 419.

3. Theodore Parker, "Sermon of the Public Function of Women," 88; Margaret Fuller, "The Great Lawsuit," in *The Dial* 4, no. 1 (July 1843): 23; Jill Ker Conway, *The Female Experience in Eighteenth- and Nineteenth-Century America* (Princeton: Princeton University Press, 1982), 207; Margaret Fuller, *Woman in the Nineteenth Century* (Boston, 1855; reprint, New York: Norton, 1971), 36.

4. "Woman," *CW* 11:425.

5. "Woman," *CW* 11:423–424. See Christina Zwarg's excellent "Emerson's 'Scene' before the Women: The Feminist Poetics of Paraphernalia," *Social Text* 18 (Winter 1987–1988): 129–144; *Letters of ETE*, 1:621.

6. "Discourse Manqué," Houghton b Ms Am 1280.202 (13), pp. 12, 16, 21.

93. The Power and Terror of Thought

1. "Speech on Affairs in Kansas," in *CW*, vol. 11, *Miscellanies*, pp. 258, 261–262.

2. "Address to the Adelphi Union of Williamstown College," Houghton b Ms Am 1280.202 (8), excerpts appear in Cabot 2:757–759.

3. "Power and Terror of Thought," Houghton b Ms Am 1280.203 (11), p. 3.

4. "Father Taylor," ed. Edward Waldo Emerson, *Atlantic Monthly* (1905), 177–181, never reprinted.

5. "Beauty," in *CW*, vol. 6, *The Conduct of Life*, pp. 290, 294; Alfred Kazin, "Dry Light and Hard Expressions," *Atlantic Monthly* (July 1957), 74.

6. "Illusions," in *CW*, vol. 6, *Conduct of Life*, pp. 311, 312, 319, 320; William James, *A Pluralistic Universe*, in his *Writings 1902–1910* (New York: Library of America), 670.

7. "Illusions," *CW* 6:311, 324, 325.

8. "Illusions," *CW* 6:325.

9. Quoted by William James in *The Varieties of Religious Experience*, in *Writings 1902–1910*, 357.

10. "Immortality," in *CW*, vol. 8, *Letters and Social Aims*, p. 325. A substantial part of "Immortality" was originally delivered as part of the dedication speech at

Sleepy Hollow. See "Consecration of Sleepy Hollow," *CW,* vol. 11, *Misc.,* pp. 429–430, for details.

11. "Consecration of Sleepy Hollow," *CW* 11:433.

12. *L* 4:538; "Brahma," in *CW,* vol. 9, *Poems,* p. 195, and first draft in *JMN* 14:100–103. Other drafts are in *TN* 2:96, 104.

13. "Consecration of Sleepy Hollow," *CW* 9:430.

14. Rutherford Platt, *The Great American Forest* (New York: Prentice-Hall, 1965), 8; *Life of LE,* 90.

94. Memory

1. *L* 4:439; "Notebook TO" 1855, Houghton b Ms Am 1280 H 87, p. 226.

2. "Memory," in *CW,* vol. 12, *Natural History of Intellect,* pp. 90, 99, 100; *JMN* 13:359. See *The Diary of Samuel Pepys,* ed. Robert Latham and William Mathews (Berkeley and Los Angeles: University of California Press, 1970), vol. 2, the entry for Jan. 22, 1661. For Gray see *JMN* 14:224–225. For other comments on memory see *JMN* 5:29, *JMN* 11:27, 28, 229. Frances A. Yates, *The Art of Memory* (Chicago: University of Chicago Press, 1966).

3. Richard Gray, *Memoria Technica,* new ed. (Dublin, 1796), 6.

4. *JMN* 14:225; "Memory," *CW* 12:110, 104.

5. "Days," in *CW,* vol. 9, *Poems,* p. 228.

6. *JMN* 14:248.

7. On the two Emersons see F. I. Carpenter, *The Emerson Handbook* (New York: Hendricks House, 1953), 1–3, and Alfred Kazin, "Dry Light and Hard Expression," *Atlantic Monthly* 200, (July 1957): 75.

8. Rusk 402.

9. *L* 5:195; "Poetry and Imagination," in *CW,* vol. 8, *Letters and Social Aims,* p. 7 and note; Charles Darwin, *The Origin of Species,* ed. J. W. Barrow (1859; reprint, London: Penguin, 1968), 443.

10. Darwin, *The Origin of Species,* 455.

95. Civil War. Death of Thoreau

1. "Old Age," in *CW,* vol. 7, *Society and Solitude,* p. 323.

2. "Old Age," *CW* 7:318, 445n.

3. *Letters of Emily Dickinson,* ed. Mabel Loomis Todd (New York: Grosset and Dunlap, 1951), 202; Moncure Conway, *Autobiography: Memories and Experiences,* 2 vols. (Boston: Houghton Mifflin, 1904), 1:345.

4. "Emerson's 'Thoreau': A New Edition from Manuscript," ed. Joel Myerson, *SAR* (1979), 37, 39, 40, 41. Myerson's text replaces that found in *CW,* vol. 10, *Lectures and Biographical Sketches.*

5. "Emerson's 'Thoreau,'" 43.

6. "Emerson's 'Thoreau,'" 43, 44, 46.

7. "Emerson's 'Thoreau,'" 46, 53, 54–55. The first step toward clarifying Thoreau's late work has recently been taken with the publication of "The Dispersion of Seeds," in *Faith in a Seed,* ed. Bradley P. Dean (Washington, D.C.: Island Press, 1993).

8. See above, chap. 91, n. 2.

9. "The Emancipation Proclamation," in *CW,* vol. 11, *Miscellanies,* p. 319.

10. *Life of LE,* p. 142.

96. Terminus

1. "Boston Hymn," in *CW,* vol. 9, *Poems,* pp. 201–204. For the Jan. 1 meeting in the Boston Music Hall see McAleer 573–574.

2. *L* 5:326.

3. *L* 5:344.

4. *J* 10:39–40.

5. Ellen Emerson, "What I Can Remember about Father," Houghton b Ms Am 1280–277, p. 46: *L* 5:412.

6. "Abraham Lincoln," in *CW,* vol. 11, *Miscellanies,* p. 329.

7. *L* 5:459.

8. See *CW,* vol. 9, *Poems,* pp. 489n. and 490n.

9. *PN* 222–227, 931–932; W. H. Auden, *The Enchafed Flood* (1950; reprint, New York: Knopf, 1967), 12; Nikos Kazantzakis, *Report to Greco* (New York: Simon and Schuster, 1965), 473; *JMN* 5:445; "Terminus," in *CW,* vol. 9, *Poems,* p. 252.

97. May-Day

1. *L* 5:492–494. For a contemporaneous view of the Santee Sioux see *Report of the Commissioners of Indian Affairs* (1866), 235, and *Report . . . of Indian Affairs* (1868), 264ff.

2. J. H. Stirling, *The Secret of Hegel*, 2 vols. (London: Longmans, Green, 1865), 1:126; *L* 5:514; see H. A. Pochmann, *New England Transcendentalism and the St. Louis Hegelians* (Philadelphia: Carl Schurz Foundation, 1948).

3. *May-Day and Other Pieces* (Boston: Ticknor and Fields, 1867), 38.

4. *May-Day*, 167, 188, 25, 203. For early drafts of "The Song of Seid Nimetollah," see *TN* 2:57–60.

5. *L* 5:496, 531; *JMN* 16:80 "Remarks at the Meeting for Organizing the Free Religious Association, Boston, May 30, 1867," in *CW*, vol. 11, *Miscellanies*, p. 478; "Speech at the Second Annual Meeting of the Free Religious Association," in *CW*, vol. 11, *Misc.*, p. 485.

6. Annie Adams Fields, *Authors and Friends* (Boston, 1897), 94.

7. *Life of LE*, 173, 182.

8. Lidian Emerson, "Poem Composed in Sleep," Houghton b Ms Am 1280.220 (132).

9. *PN* 504, 783n.

98. Harvard. California. Fire

1. WmE to RWE, Sept. 4, 1868; *L* 6:33.

2. "Mary Moody Emerson," in *CW*, vol. 10, *Lectures and Biographical Sketches*, pp. 399, 402–403, 432, 433.

3. "Introduction, Praise of Knowledge," Houghton b Ms Am 1280.212 (2), n.p.; *JMN* 16:165.

4. *JMN* 16:205.

5. Charles H. Haskins, "The Graduate School of Arts and Sciences," in *The Development of Harvard University since the Inauguration of President Eliot*, ed. S. E. Morison (Cambridge: Harvard University Press, 1930), 451–462, and S. E. Morison, *Three Centuries of Harvard* (Cambridge: Harvard University Press, 1936), 333–334.

6. Cabot 2:633.

7. "Transcendency of Physics," Houghton b Ms Am 1280.212 (3), p. 25.

8. "Introduction" to Harvard course, 1871, Houghton b Ms Am 1280.212 (1), p. 21.

9. "Philosophy of the People," lec. 1, Houghton b Ms Am 1280.209 (1), pp. 4, 18; "Philosophy of the People," lec. 1, folder 3, Houghton b Ms Am 1280.209 (3), p. 20; "Philosophy of the People," folder 12, Houghton b Ms Am 1280.209 (12), pp. 12, 14; "Philosophy of the People," folder 13, Houghton b Ms Am 1280.209 (13), p. 19.

10. *L of ETE,* 1:552.

11. Cabot 2:648; *JMN* 16:237–238.

12. John Muir, *Our National Parks* (Boston: Houghton Mifflin, 1901), 135.

13. John Ruskin, *The Two Paths* (New York: Maynard Merrell, 1893), 19, 16; *L* 6:239n. Though attributed to a letter of Ellen's the comment about praising Ruskin at every meal is not in *L of ETE.*

14. *L of ETE,* 1:677–682.

99. Philae and Parnassus

1. *L of ETE,* 1:688; "Egypt," Houghton b Ms Am 1280.214 (221); *JMN* 16:285, 290, 286.

2. Quoted in Peter A. Clayton, *The Rediscovery of Ancient Egypt: Artists and Travelers in the Nineteenth Century* (London: Thames and Hudson, 1982), 150.

3. *JMN* 16:292.

4. Cabot 2:652; "Journal TO," Houghton b Ms Am 1280 H 87; *JMN* 16:145; Max Müller to RWE, Apr. 19, 1880, in *Life and Letters of the Right Honorable Friedrich Max Muller* (New York: Longmans, Green, 1902); *Essays, Addresses, and Poems of Edward Waldo Emerson* (privately printed, 1930), 280.

5. Jean Ingelow, "Wreck of the Grace of Sunderland," in *Parnassus,* ed. R. W. Emerson (Boston: Houghton Mifflin, 1874), 320–321. On *Parnassus* see Ronald A. Bosco, "'Poetry for a World of Readers' and 'Poetry for Bards Proper': Theory and Textual Integrity in Emerson's Parnassus," *SAR* (1989), 257–312.

6. Quoted by Joseph Slater in his excellent introduction to *E-C Corr.,* 61.

7. *E-C Corr.,* 62–63.

100. Fire at the Core of the World

1. *JMN* 8:251, 329.

2. *L of ETE,* 2:672–674.

Index

659

Dacier, Andre, 11, 65

d'Agoult, Marie de Flavigny comtesse, 453, 522

Dall, Caroline, 532

Dana, Charles A., 378

Dana, R. H., 262

Dana, Richard Henry Jr., 14, 41

Dante Alighieri, 221, 312, 351, 388–389, 460, 486, 560; *La vita nuova,* 316

Dartmouth College, 295

Darwin, Charles, 140, 433, 489, 491; *Origin of Species,* 546

Davies, Edward, 509, 516

Davis, Andrew Jackson, 524

Davis, George, 235

Davis, Paulina W., 532, 533

Davis, T. F., 526

Davy, Sir Humphrey, 87, 123, 254, 268

DeQuincy, Thomas, 443

de Stael, Anne Marie Louise Necker, Baronne, 24, 25, 43, 52–54, 238, 519; *Corinne,* 25, 52, 168; and enthusiasm, 54; *On Germany,* 52

De Wette, W.M.L., 248

Dewey, Orville, 157, 160

Dial, The, 250, 339, 364, 369, 376, 376–380, 386, 332, 335–336; last number, 391

Dickens, Charles, 324, 385, 443, 446, 522

Dickinson, Emily, 310, 414, 547

Diderot, Denis, 30, 32

Diogenes, 216

Dion, 133

Disraeli, Isaac, 376, 443

Donne, John, 216, 262

Dorr, Julia, 570

Douglass, Frederick, 157, 398, 418

Downing, Andrew Jackson, 433

Drummond, James, 140, 142

Drummond, William, 123

Dunbar, Louisa, 387

Dwight, John S., 53, 175, 248

Edwards, Jonathan, 24, 54, 291, 594

Eichhorn, J. G., 13, 24, 43, 49–50, 111, 238, 247, 591–592, 593; and William Emerson, 49–50

Eliot, Charles William, 562

Eliot, George, 443, 475

Eliot, T. S., 101, 414

Elssler, Fanny, 363, 378

Emerson, Charles Chauncy, 4, 26, 35, 36, 38–40, 181, 209, 218–219, 241, 280, 310, 332, 336, 513; career after college, 183; death of, 224; and Elizabeth Hoar, 224; health collapses, 119; and Quakerism, 183; reads Sophocles, 220; shell collection, 122; "Thekla's Song," 40; and U.S. Indian policy, 106

Emerson, Edith, 193, 381, 428, 429, 486, 533, 535, 540, 549, 550; born, 356; marries William H. Forbes, 553; and *Parnassus,* 570; and Sanborn, 526–527

Emerson, Edward, 395, 433, 486, 535, 540; and Civil War, 550; at Harvard, 553; marries Annie Keyes, 570; "Memory, or the Gates," 569; and RWE's last days, 572; with RWE in England, 569; and "Terminus," 554

Emerson, Edward Bliss, 4, 35, 36–37, 164, 241, 280, 336, 513, 570; death of, 183; mental collapse, 86; resemblance to Thoreau, 463; "The Last Farewell," 556

Emerson, Ellen, 192, 325, 340, 355, 358, 381, 422, 428, 486, 533, 535, 540, 552, 569, 570; accompanies RWE to England, 568; born, 314; goes to boarding school, 514; on her mother, 557; and RWE's last days, 572; with RWE at Carlyle Memorial, 571; takes over housekeeping, 553; and vegetarian diet, 429

Emerson, Ellen Tucker, 3, 83, 191, 312, 336, 540, 552; as Beatrice, 109; death of, 108; estate settled, 175; meets Emerson, 84–88; and tuberculosis, 91–92, 98

Emerson, George B., 608

Emerson, George Barell, 164

Emerson, John Clarke, 21, 34

Emerson, Joseph, 447

Emerson, Lidian (Lydia Jackson), 167, 280, 286, 301, 305, 307, 363, 383, 387, 428, 527, 560; and abolition, 270, 396; birth of Ellen, 312; blossoming of, 557–558; and Edith, 356, 527; first meets Emerson, 99; ideas of, 192; illness, 436, 460; marriage to RWE, 330, 470; name change, 611; outlook of,

377; "Transcendency of Physics, The," 563; "Transcendentalist, The," 357, 377; "Two Rivers," 556; "Uilsa," 15; "Unity of God, The," 63; "Universe" (notebook), 42; "Uses of Great Men," 414, 418; "Uses of Natural History, The," 154; "Voluntaries," 552; "Waldeinsamkeit," 556; "Water," 167; "Why England is England," 466; "Woman," 534; "Woodnotes II," 349; "World-Soul, The," 374, 428, 556; "Worship," 490–493; "Young American, The," 377, 393

Emerson, Robert Bulkeley, 35, 37–38, 281

Emerson, Ruth Haskins, 20, 21–22, 34, 430, 513, 540; breaks hip, 500; death of, 517

Emerson, Waldo, 271, 286, 314, 340, 355–356; born, 256; death of, 358; physical description, 355

Emerson, William (brother of RWE), 8, 19, 35, 35–36, 313–314, 324, 391, 433, 527, 551; dies, 560; financial troubles of, 253, 260; returns from Germany, 64–65; studies in Germany, 49–50; teaches at Kennebunk Maine, 35

Emerson, William (father of RWE), 20, 34

Emerson, William (grandfather of RWE), 182

Emerson, William Jr., 535

English, G. B., 586

Enthusiasm, 54, 83

Epictetus, 216, 226

Epicurus, 63

Erasmus, Desiderius, 291

Etna, 133

Euripedes, 216

Evelyn, John, 395, 526

Everett, Alexander, 29

Everett, Edward, 13, 15, 29, 45, 46, 53, 79, 82, 262, 383, 428, 513, 589, 593; reading of, 586–587

Faraday, Michael, 444

Federalist Papers, The, 7

Fenelon, François de Salignac de La Moth, 21, 22, 39, 89, 90

Ferguson, Samuel, 254

Fichte, Johann Gottlieb, 146, 231, 238, 247, 450; and Quakerism, 161

Finney, Charles Grandison, 527

Firdusi, 407

Fisher, George, 562

Fiske, John, 562

Flaubert, Gustave, 121

Flavel, John, 21, 22, 184, 211

Fletcher, John, 316

Flint's Pond, 465

Follen, Charles, 248

Forbes, John Murray, 550

Forbes, Ralph Emerson, 553

Forbes, William H., 553, 565

Ford, Sophia, 429

Forster, John, 268, 324

Fort Ancient, Ohio, 478

Fourier, Charles, 365–369, 383, 392, 414

Fox, George, 189, 196, 284, 307, 158, 162–163

Francis, Convers, 245, 248

Franklin, Benjamin, 54

Franklin, Sir John, 274

Fremont, John S., 487, 508

Freud, Sigmund, 367

Frost, Barzillai, 289

Frost, Robert, 372, 414

Froude, James Anthony, 487

Fruitlands, 381–382, 391, 492

Fuller, Margaret, 3, 17, 26, 53, 235–241, 248, 261, 266, 297, 312, 315, 318, 325, 332, 359, 363, 370, 376, 377, 383, 388, 429, 470, 513, 532, 552, 570; death of, 482–483; education, 235, 237; influence on RWE, 239–240; on marriage, 193; on myth, 239; reading, 238; relationship with RWE, 240–241, 338–339; and *Shah Nameh,* 407; *Summer on the Lakes,* 391; "The Great Lawsuit," 378, 533; translates Goethe's *Tasso,* 238; *Woman in the Nineteenth Century,* 533

Fuller, Thomas, 509, 544

Fuller, Timothy, 235

Furness, William Henry, 78, 226, 296, 514

Garbet, Edward, 507

Gardiner, William, 268, 296

Sartre, Jean Paul, 403
Sattelmeyer, Robert, 622, 643, 649
Schelling, Friedrich Wilhelm Joseph von, 116, 166, 378, 406, 450, 473, 518, 546
Scherb, Emmanuel, 472
Schiller, J. C. F. von, 254
Schlegel, Friedrich, 116, 168
Schleiermacher, Friedrich, 49, 50, 65, 69, 79, 97, 111, 197, 225, 247, 249, 290, 298, 325, 372, 595, 600, 602; *Critical Essay on the Gospel of Luke,* 58, 111; and unbounded dependence, 88
Schlesinger, A. M., Jr., 248
Schulman, J. Frank, 603
Scott, General Winfield, 275
Scott, Paul, 619
Scott, Sir Walter, 11, 43, 168, 346
Scougal, Henry, 55, 184; Ellen Tucker reads, 85; *Life of God in the Soul of Man,* 55–56
Sealts, Merton, 620
Sedgewick, Catherine, 43
Seneca, 43, 216
Sequoya, 277, 565
Seward, William, 528
Sewel, William, 158, 307
Shaffer, Evelyn, 593
Shakers, 4
Shakespeare, William, 16, 24, 43, 214, 288, 316, 520
Shannon (frigate), 19–20
Shattuck, Lemuel, 206, 210
Shaw, Colonel Robert, 552
Shaw, Lemuel, 262, 495, 496
Shea, Daniel, 629
Sheridan, Richard Brinsley, 320
Sidney, Algernon, 216
Sigourney, Lydia, 533
Simms, William Gilmore, 522
Simonides, 570
Sims, Thomas, 496
Sismondi, J. C. L. S. de, 29, 42, 589
Sitgreaves, L., 526
Slater, Joseph, 571
Smith, Adam, 15, 29, 31, 32, 54, 211, 471
Smith, Elizabeth Oakes, 532
Smith, J. E., 87
Smith, John, 434

Smithsonian Institution, 479
Society for the Diffusion of Useful Knowledge, 189, 214
Socrates, 86, 216, 288
Somerville, Mary, 124
Sophocles, 199, 216, 402; *Antigone,* 220; *Electra,* 220
Southern Literary Messenger, 200
Southey, Robert, 136, 526
Souverain, Nicholas, 65
Sparks, Jared, 82
Spenser, Edmund, 520
Spinoza, Benedict, 24, 325
Spofford, Ainsworth, 511
Spofford, Harriet, 570
Squier, Ephraim, 645
St. Augustine, Florida, 73, 81–82
St. Hilaire, Geoffroi, 473
Stabler, Edward, 78, 157, 225, 597
Stackpole, Lewis, 135
Stallbaum, Johann Gottfried, 65
Stallo, J. B., 467, 472, 518, 546
Staples, Sam, 566
St. Armand, Barton, 627
Stephenson, George, 444
Sterling, John, 316, 325, 378
Stern, Daniel, 453
Stetson, Caleb, 164, 246, 248, 303
Stevens, Wallace, 623
Stevenson, Hannah, 41
Stewart, Dugald, 7, 15, 24, 29, 30–33, 54, 238
Stirling, J. H., 555
St. Laurence River, 515
Stoicism, 152, 379
Stone, Lucy, 532
Stone, William L., 316
Story, Joseph, 262, 413
Stowe, Harriet Beecher, 508
Strauss, David Friedrich, 488, 526, 593
Strawn, Jacob, 481
Stuart, Moses, 53
Sturgis, Caroline, 286, 301, 318, 325, 326, 327–331, 338, 347, 359, 363, 376, 378, 391, 428, 439–440, 470, 485, 513, 527, 552; marries Tappan, 440
Sturgis, Ellen, 378
Sturgis, Susan, 514

Very, Jones, 27, 248, 301–306, 312, 570; on "Hamlet," 304; poems, 306, 318; reads *Nature,* 302
Very, Lydia, 302
Vesuvius, 123, 134–134
Veysie, Daniel, 112
Vico, Giambattista, 247
Virgil, 282, 483
Voltaire, 138

Wainwright, Jonathan Mayhew, 262
Walden Pond, 399, 430, 465–466
Waldo, Giles, 386
Walker, James, 300
Walker, John, 7, 14
Wall, William, 135
Ward, Julia, 364
Ward, Samuel, 236, 249, 298, 318, 325, 326, 378, 438, 459, 513; on Fuller, 484
Ware, Henry, 86, 89, 90, 91, 262, 288, 299
Washington, George, 444
Wasson, David, 570
Waterford, Maine, 24
Waters, George, 277
Watie, Stand, 277
Webster, Daniel, 36, 39, 69, 177, 278, 316, 383, 386, 477; and abolition, 396; death of, 513; physical description, 387
Wellfleet, Massachusetts, 96
Wellington, Arthur Wellesley Duke of, 452
Welty, Eudora, 184
Wesley, John, 55
West, Benjamin, 78
Western Literary Messenger, 200, 332
Wharton, Thomas, 214
Wheeler, Stearns, 495
Whichcote, Benjamin, 65
Whicher, Stephen E., 644
Whipple, Edwin, 385, 420
White, Gilbert, 324

White's Pond, 465
Whiting, Nathaniel H., 249, 370, 378
Whitman, Walt, 12, 101, 120, 310, 314, 374, 431, 451, 453, 473, 556, 570; on Emerson, 529–531; on Emerson and John Brown, 498; and free verse, 477; on optimism, 537–538; sends Emerson *Leaves of Grass,* 527
Whittier, John Greenleaf, 399; "Ichabod," 477
Wilde, Richard Henry, 168
Wilkins, Charles, 636
Wilkinson, J. J. Garth, 444, 451
Williams College, 173
Willich, August, 472
Willis, Nathaniel Parker, 485
Wilson, John (Christopher North), 443
Winchester School, 466
Wirt, William, 278
Wogan, William, 21
Wolf, F. A., 13, 49
Wollstonecraft, Mary, 24
Woodall, Guy R., 618
Woodbury, Charles, 173, 180, 202
Woolf, Virginia, 94, 342
Wordsworth, Dorothy, 149
Wordsworth, William, 16, 81, 115, 149, 376, 378, 443, 520, 543, 556
Wright, Elizur, 413
Wright, Frances, 247, 302
Wright, Henry, 381, 385, 387
Wyman, William, 386

Xenophanes, 216

Young, Brigham, 565
Young, Edward, 24, 168

Zahn, Wilhelm, 487
Zarathustra, 351
Zeno, 216, 233
Zoroaster, 346, 379
Zoroastrianism, 122, 184, 351

Designer: Barry Moser
Compositor: Braun-Brumfield, Inc.
Text and Display: Garamond
Printer: Haddon Craftsmen, Inc.
Binder: Haddon Craftsmen, Inc.